FOR A WORKING-CLASS CULTURE IN CANADA

A SELECTION OF COLIN MCKAY'S WRITINGS ON SOCIOLOGY AND POLITICAL ECONOMY, 1897-1939

FOR A WORKING-CLASS CULTURE IN CANADA

A SELECTION OF COLIN McKAY'S WRITINGS ON SOCIOLOGY AND POLITICAL ECONOMY, 1897-1939

EDITED AND ANNOTATED BY IAN McKAY
RESEARCHED AND INTRODUCED BY LEWIS JACKSON AND IAN McKAY

Canadian Committee on Labour History
Department of History
Memorial University of Newfoundland
St. John's, NF A1C 5S7
CANADA

ISBN 0-9695835-6-7

Typography by New Maritimes

Printed and bound in Canada

This book has been published with the help of a grant from the Humanities and Social Sciences Federation of Canada, using funds provided by the Social Sciences and Humanities Research Council of Canada.

Canadian Cataloguing in Publication Data

McKay, Colin, 1876 - 1939

    For a working-class culture in Canada

    Researched and introduced by Lewis Jackson and Ian McKay.
    Includes bibliographical references and index.
    ISBN 0-9695835-6-7

1. Working class — Canada — History.
2. Industrial relations — Canada — History.
3. Canada — Social conditions.
   I. McKay, Ian, 1953 -
   II. Canadian Committee on Labour History.
   III. Title.

HD8106.M34 1996   305.5'62'0971   C96-950082-3

PREFACE

Colin McKay was a seafarer, labour activist, poet, short story writer, sociologist, political economist, and journalist. Above all, he was a socialist. He identified wholeheartedly with the ideal of an egalitarian society, characterized by production for use and not for profit, in which human beings do not dominate one another. In the closing years of the twentieth century, and the opening years of the twenty-first, as Canadian socialists begin a new cycle of renewal, reclaiming the legacy of Colin McKay may be a useful first step towards a rethinking of the past and future of their movement. Canadian sociologists, hitherto woefully ignorant of their past, may find much here that surprises them; and Canadian labour historians may well find they emerge from McKay's works with a more complex and interesting vision of the Canadian working-class movement in both its trade-union and political aspects. But my deepest hope is that this book may inspire some of the Colin McKays of the future, who will need every bit of his will power and conviction if the next century is to prove more hopeful for the great ideals of the Canadian socialist movement than the present one has been.

As a man who was active in the left for an unusually long time -- from the 1890s to the 1930s -- McKay left posterity a massive body of writings. Our research in the labour and mainstream press of the day has uncovered 952 of his articles. Only 134 of these are repesented here, some in radically abridged form: and this is still a very long book! There can be no doubt that further research will uncover many other articles, probably not just in Canada, but in the various ports McKay visited in the course of his long seafaring career. Our own efforts have concentrated on the *Montreal Herald, Shelburne Budget, American Federationist, Halifax Herald, Eastern Labor News, Industrial Banner, Canadian Fisherman, Saint John Standard, Le Monde Ouvrier/Labor World, Canadian Railway Employees Monthly, One Big Union Bulletin, Canadian Labor Advocate, Canadian Unionist, Canadian Forum, Saturday Night, New Commonwealth, Citizen and Country, Dalhousie Review, Labor Leader,* the Shelburne *Coast Guard,* the *Shelburne Gazette,* the *Toronto Globe,* and the *Yarmouth Times.* There are likely more treasures to be found, although I doubt if scholars will ever be able to say, with certainty, that they have located them all.

In selecting these writings for this publication, I have sought to retain the gist of McKay's arguments while removing material that has lost its interest over the years. I also attempted to give a sense of the overall pattern of McKay's intellectual development, and hence writings that appeared in print before the Depression stand a much greater chance of being included than the more numerous articles published during it. This strategy has at least given us a reasonable selection of his writings from each of the five decades in which he was active. In some cases, I have edited McKay with a strict hand. On questions of culture and political economy, I have been more apt to let him have some room. I have

generally removed the subheadings within articles, and have re-titled
many articles to better convey a sense of their contents to a modern
readership.

Generally, I have tried to impose a consistent editorial standard without
interfering too much with the original texts. I have placed in square
brackets [ ] changes to the text which are obviously called for because of
typographical or grammatical errors, and also words I had difficulty
reading. Where there is some doubt, I have left the original word, which is
then followed by my suggested change in square brackets. The titles of
books have been placed in italics, in conformity with contemporary
Canadian usage. One of the minor oddities of Canadian cultural history is
that our spelling has become more British as our economy and popular
culture have become more American: turn-of-the-century Canadians had
few reservations about replacing "our" with "or" wherever it seemed
convenient. I have generally "Canadianized" these words in accordance
with contemporary usage. Obviously, the biggest problem throughout has
been "labour," which McKay generally spelled as "labor," and often gave
a capital letter -- perhaps to indicate how important he thought Labour
was in the making of a better world. I have preserved his idiosyncratic and
inconsistent capitalization of "Labour" but Canadianized his spelling of
the word (except when it is included in the official titles of organizations
and publications). Other minor changes: "employes" has been changed
throughout to "employees," "in so far" to "insofar," "business man" to
"businessman," and "St.John" to "Saint John" (to distinguish the city in
New Brunswick in which McKay lived from the capital of Newfoundland). I
have changed the placement of quotation marks to accord with modern
Canadian usage; in general, this has meant the replacement of single
quotation marks with double quotation marks. I have also changed the text
to make the verb agree with the subject, where McKay's error was
obviously unintentional.

To enhance the scholarly value of this book, I have tried to provide exact
references for McKay's direct quotations. This intricate mission in itself
proved to be an education in the world of early twentieth-century
socialism. Those who wish to cite the quotations will want to check the
footnotes, in case some small slips are found in McKay's transcription.
Using biographical footnotes, for which Russell Johnston's research
assistance has been invaluable, I have tried to identify all the authorities
and personalities who may be obscure to general readers in late twentieth-
century Canada, and have done the same for some prominent Canadian
names that may not be familar to those who read this book outside the
country. Finally, each section opens with an introductory essay that seeks
to place the selected McKay articles in the overall context of his life and
work. The references in these introductory essays should serve as a
convenient avenue to further exploration of aspects of McKay's work
which are not fully represented in this collection.

This book has been a very long time in the making, and in that long time I have had the help of many librarians, archivists and fellow researchers. A wholly fortuitous conversation with Lewis Jackson helped both of us gradually piece together most of the story of the elusive Colin McKay. Lewis uncovered scores of articles in the *Canadian Fisherman*, the *Canadian Unionist, the Canadian Railway Employees Monthly*, the *Montreal Herald*, the Shelburne *Coast-Guard*, and other publications. He could also draw on his ties to Shelburne and to the McKay family for invaluable insights. Although responsibility for selecting the articles and placing them in context rests with me, Lewis made many of the discoveries in the libraries and archives without which this book could not have been produced. He has also been a discerning reader and critic of the manuscript.

Some research expenses were underwritten by the Principal's Development Fund and the Advisory Research Council, Queen's University. I should also like to thank the Boag Foundation for funding the preparation of the indispensible Index. This book has been published with the help of a grant from the Humanities and Social Sciences Federation of Canada, using funds provided by the Social Sciences and Humanities Research Council of Canada.

Many others helped as well. Peter Campbell has generously shared his many insights into the Canadian socialist movement; and he uncovered the articles in the *One Big Union Bulletin, Le Monde Ouvrie/Labor World,* and other labour papers; most important, however, were his detailed, page-by-page comments on the first and second drafts of the manuscript. Russell Johnston worked intensively on the biographical research that is reflected in the footnotes, and also on tracing many of McKay's quotations; he also pursued McKay in the American Federation of Labor and Gompers papers. Other research was undertaken by my son David McKay. Greg Kealey has been a supportive and enthusiastic presence within the Canadian Committee on Labour History, and David Frank's constructive critique provided much-needed encouragement and perspective. I should like to pay special tribute to the anonymous reviewers for the Aid to Scholarly Publications Program, who were perceptive and tough. Bob Babcock, Gerald Friesen, Andrew Nurse, Bryan Palmer, the late George Rawlyk (who stoutly defended the CCF-NDP tradition he loved so deeply), Marlene Shore, Allen Seager, and Mariana Valverde all supplied useful commentaries on particular themes of this work. It has been a pleasure to have the final text typeset, the pages laid out, and other final work undertaken by Michael Boudreau and Scott Milsom of *New Maritimes*. Finally, my deepest thanks go to Gary Burrill of Upper Musquodoboit, N.S., for his support during the Winter and Spring of 1994. I.M.

TABLE OF CONTENTS

INTRODUCTION
by Lewis Jackson and Ian McKay

WRITINGS OF COLIN MCKAY
Part I:
**If Christ Came to Montreal: A Liberal Christian Progressive Looks
at Society, 1897-1906**

Part II:
**Evolutionary Sociology and Applied Ethics: The Struggle for a
"Working-Class Culture," 1907-1914**

i. Capitalism As A System

ii. The Need for Sociology

Colin Campbell McKay of Nova Scotia

by Lewis Jackson and Ian McKay

On 15 December 1896 The *Montreal Herald* carried a short story profiling "Two Men." One of the men is the head of a prosperous concern, surrounded by "every evidence of wealth." He is raging because he has just been outwitted in a business speculation. The other man is a poor sailor, standing on the crowded street:

He was alone, with the awful solitude of a vast, strange city. He had just come off a long and wearisome voyage, and his weather-beaten face yet bore the marks of privation and hardship. Around him were wealth, beauty, happiness; but in these he had no part. The people flitted past, but there were none to give him hand-clasp, or welcome. A well-dressed blood brushed against him ... ; a policeman hustled him along, a lady clad in the silks and shimmering stuffs he and his ilk had risked life and limb to bring from far, far lands, cast a contemptuous glance his way, gathered up her skirts and took the other side of the walk.

But there were $200 in his pocket. He touched it -- it burnt him and he swore. It was money, and money alone, [that] was the cause of his utter desolation. It was this that forbade the true man to give him a hand; it was this that made the true woman gather up her skirts and hurry past. He curses it. He looks at the bright, happy faces around, and there is a wistful longing in his gaze. But in the world's happiness he has no part! A sigh wells from the great loneliness of his heart. He draws his hand across his brow, as if to shut out the sight, and turns... in the glittering saloon over the way. There, at least, would he find welcome, so long as he had money. He takes a last, lingering look at the beautiful world around; he curses his fate; and then he wends his way to forgetfulness....[1]

---

[1]*Montreal Herald*, 15 December 1896. The story is unsigned and there can be no guarantee that it is McKay's. But it sounds a great deal like him, especially in its use of dialogue. It also appears in the newspaper in which his work was soon to become prominent.

That, in all likelihood, is the first example we have of the Montreal writings of Colin McKay. Although not entirely autobiographical -- McKay was an enthusiastic pipe-smoker but not a committed drinker -- it still probably captures some of his first impressions of Montreal, when he arrived in the city as a young sailor from Nova Scotia. Like his protagonist, McKay never felt at home in the class-divided, status-obsessed, hypocritical and cruel world of capitalist modernity, as he experienced it in Montreal and throughout much of the world. Capitalism, one might say, never lost its strangeness for him. From this faltering first attempt at "progressive fiction" to his last analytical articles in the Marxist tradition, he can be described as someone who was trying to master this strangeness, and to help others understand just how uncanny and disordered the world around them truly was.

Colin Campbell McKay (1876-1939) was a Christian *and* a Marxist, a storyteller *and* a scholarly sociologist, a rank-and-file worker *and* a library-addicted intellectual. He looked at Montreal, he looked at everything, with a mind that was cued both to "objective data" and "ethical meaning." He refused the tidy categories and hierarchical distinctions that help late twentieth-century people put the people of the past -- and the people of the present -- "in their place." The only label he would have accepted, for much of his life, was "socialist." It was as a believer in socialism that he organized unions, wrote his muckraking pieces in the newspapers, and explored the intricacies of history, sociology, and economics. Socialism was the meaning of his life.

He looked at the world with a seafarer's eye. Like so many Nova Scotians, and unlike so many other Canadians, McKay could never forget the international context of Canadian life. He had worked and lived in the "North Atlantic Triangle" which defined so much of Canada's economic, political and cultural life. Although in one sense a "Provincial" -- the common name for Maritimers who sought to earn a livelihood outside their native region -- McKay was, like many Maritimers, less "provincial" in his attitudes than conventional regional stereotypes might lead one to suspect. By his mid-thirties he had travelled to scores of North Atlantic ports and had probably ventured as far afield as the Pacific Coast of South America. He captured much of this world-travelling experience in sea stories and poems that brilliantly blended social criticism with yarns of male adventure on the high seas.[2] One biographical dictionary of 1912 -- Henry James Morgan's The *Canadian Men and Women of the Time: A Hand-book of Canadian Biography of Living Characters* -- quoted an authority who praised his "tremendous ability in writing of the sea" and

---

[2]See Lewis Jackson and Ian McKay, eds., *Windjammers and Bluenose Sailors: Stories of the Sea by Colin McKay* (Lockeport, N.S.: Roseway Publishing, 1993).

reported another's opinion that McKay was a second Joseph Conrad.[3] He was by no means a second Conrad -- the "Canadian Jack London" might have been a more accurate label -- but by insisting on reporting labour's side of the so-called Golden Age of Sail he certainly charted a unique course among the Canadian wind-and-water romantics. At least one knowledgeable critic of the *genre* believes McKay wrote one of the best sea stories ever written in the Maritimes.[4]

His attachment to the sea was not surprising. The McKays of Shelburne, Nova Scotia were the heirs of a famous shipbuilding tradition.[5] McKay's grandfather, who was also called Colin Campbell McKay, was born in Shelburne in 1823. He was a master shipbuilder of great distinction. When Colin McKay Sr. died in 1862, his son Winslow was a lad of 12. Devoid of property or a trade, young Winslow McKay was taken under the protection of master craftsmen in the community, and went on to become a respectable shipbuilder in his own right.

When, in 1876, Winslow named his first-born son Colin Campbell McKay, he honoured both his father and the shipbuilding tradition he represented. This second Colin Campbell McKay was always deeply fascinated by the shipbuilding legacy. We know little about his early years, but later he wrote often (and quite romantically) about the joys of self-sufficiency in a rural setting, the pleasures of hunting, and the sights and sounds of the Nova Scotia coastline. Although his formal education did not extend past mid-adolescence, it must have been a sound one: McKay's command of the English language could not have emerged out of thin air. One of the most significant formative influences on McKay was the Anglican church. McKay attended "plain neat well-constructed" Christ Church, to use the words of Bishop Charles Inglis, who consecrated the church in 1790.[6] Although we can only surmise what Colin learned from

[3]Henry James Morgan, ed., *The Canadian Men and Women of the Time: A Hand-book of Canadian Biography of Living Characters* (Toronto: William Briggs, 1912):773.

[4]John Bell, Review of Colin McKay, *Windjammers and Bluenose Sailors*, in *The Northern Mariner*, 4, 2 (April 1994): 48-49. There is no truth to the implication in this review, however, that Colin McKay was directly related to Donald McKay, the famous Nova Scotia-born and Boston-based builder of clipper ships. Nor, for that matter, is the present author connected to Colin McKay (unless the matter is pursued back into the distant Highlands).

[5]The most famous of all the North Atlantic shipbuilders, Donald McKay, was also from the Shelburne area, but he was not closely related to Colin McKay's family.

[6]For Christ Church, Shelburne, see Marion Robertson, *King's Bounty: A History of Early Shelburne, Nova Scotia* (Halifax: Nova Scotia Museum, 1983): 177-180. On the South Shore, affiliation with the Church of England did not imply the same elite status it did in some other parts of Canada. In the late nineteenth century, the denomination was very much taken up with "Social Gospel" issues, such as the abolition of the truck system in the coalfields.

Sunday School and Anglican church services, his later writings (even those sharply critical of organized religion) assume the reader's ready familiarity with scripture and with religious imagery, and (perhaps unconsciously) imply a distinctly Protestant "common sense" (one distrustful of ritual and authority, yet also respecting the radical message of a Christ one could know directly and personally).

Like so many teenagers on the South Shore -- roughly, the Atlantic coastline of Nova Scotia from Halifax to Yarmouth -- McKay achieved independence from his family by following the sea.[7] In the summer of 1891, he won a seaman's position on the *Agnes Macdonald*, a cutter of the federal Fisheries Protection Service, and for the next five years found berths on other sailing vessels plying the coastal, West Indies, and international trades. McKay then made the transition from sail to steam. Between 1896 and 1905 McKay apparently worked for the Elder Dempster line, which had vessels plying between Montreal, Boston, Saint John, Halifax, Portland, Liverpool, London and Bristol. Between 1906 and 1912 , at various times, he served not only on the Elder Dempster line but also on the Pickford and Black line of steamers which ran between Maritime ports and the West Indies. By the age of 39, McKay had visited ports throughout the Atlantic and Caribbean worlds.

Wandering, treating cities like temporary winter posts rather than permanent homes, never developing a firm and lasting context: McKay's lifestyle must have carried some high personal costs. Yet we should also note its advantages. One reason why he always seemed to be ahead of most Canadian socialists in his thinking, particularly during the 1920s and 1930s, was because he was a world-traveller who had been exposed to a wider range of thought and experience than many Canadians. And the ability to go to sea must have given McKay a certain independence from land-based employers, with their often narrow views of political decorum and deference. By his own admission, seafaring suited his temperament. Colin McKay was a restless man. By his fifties (when he finally settled down in Ottawa) McKay had lived for periods of his life in Montreal, Saint John, Toronto, Glasgow, London, Paris, and Halifax. Many of these cities were selected for their convenience as ports between voyages.

"I served my time in sail," McKay reflected in 1913, in a very rare moment of personal reminiscence, "but being rather restless did not

---

[7]He thus stands out from the pattern noted for other socialist intellectuals in Canada, of origins in the "labour aristocracy", often in Britain. See J. Peter Campbell, "'Stalwarts of the Struggle': Canadian Marxists of the Third Way, 1879-1939." PhD Thesis, Queen's University, 1991, 15. McKay's own position at sea would have initially been that of an unskilled worker, although he worked his way up to the position of second mate. He retained much of a working seaman's attitude to life in his subsequent journalistic career.

follow the sea steadily, and never got beyond mate of a sailing vessel or second mate of a passenger liner. Between times I have worked as a reporter in various cities, and done other odd jobs.... I don't know that I have had any first-class adventures. I have been shipwrecked, with a fire at sea; in prison; through an able-bodied hurricane; hungry, thirsty, frostbitten, and through the ordinary vicissitudes of the life of a sailor and rover."[8] In 1901, McKay recalled other experiences as a seaman, serving on American vessels on which "the scuppers ran red" and men had been killed; he also recalled other incidents in which men were "on the verge of cannibalism."[9] He apparently never wrote a more detailed account of his seafaring life. Family tradition and his sea stories suggest an active part in the campaign for sailors' rights.[10]

McKay was a private man; he rarely spoke of his personal life. Into this silence, and into his wandering life, it is tempting to read a rift with his family. However, the evidence suggests that McKay never felt estranged from his background, and maintained close contacts with home. He often returned to the South Shore.[11] Leaving home at 15 and gradually becoming a Marxian socialist did not mean shaking the dust of Nova Scotia from his feet. It meant seeing his home in a new light.

---

[8]*Adventure*, 6, 2 (June 1913), 216-217.

[9]*Montreal Herald*, 2 February 1901. [See §.13., "What Workingmen Expect of the Church: A Rebuttal by Colin McKay," in this volume]. Here and throughout, references to materials which can be found in selections in the book are placed in square brackets with the number and title of the section.

[10]The *Canadian Railway Employees Monthly*, March 1939, reported that as a second officer on passenger and fruit boats in the Mexican and South American trade, McKay wrote "articles and letters to editors, keeping up an agitation for the organization of seamen, and for better conditions in the Merchant Marine." It sounds entirely plausible. We have no direct evidence.

[11]His visits home were often recorded in the local papers. See *Shelburne Gazette and Coast Guard*, 22 March 1919; 16 September 1920; 3 August 1922; 23 August 1928; 5 September 1935; *Coast Guard*, 6 August 1936. The local press also proudly hailed his achievements as a writer. See Yarmouth *Telegram*, 31 December 1903; Shelburne *Gazette and Coast Guard*, 23 April 1914. According to Edgar B. McKay, his first cousin, Colin's imprisonment in Quebec was talked about with pride by his brother and sister, even though they were Conservatives and not normally supportive of labour unions. Prof. Edgar B. McKay to Ian McKay, personal communication, 3 December 1987. It is interesting to note that the McKay family in Shelburne kept close track of McKay's exploits in a scrapbook, and carefully preserved a clipping from *Citizen and Country* detailing McKay's trial and imprisonment in 1899 and 1900. Undated family scrapbook, in the possession of Dr. Colin MacKay, who notwithstanding the extra "a" in his name is indeed the grand-nephew of Colin McKay. Our thanks to Dr. MacKay for permission to look at this source.

On the other hand, one might well imagine that a certain psychological distance emerged between the shipbuilding family back home in Nova Scotia and their fiery world-wandering son. Colin certainly did not fit the Conservative family mould. The family adhered to the mainstream of the Church of England; McKay in his 20s demanded a radical "Social Gospel" that would link Christianity directly to the struggles of the poor and the workers, and in his 30s he was calling for a secular "Science of Society" to bring about a socialist order. The family was Conservative; McKay became more and more radical. He turned first to Wilfrid Laurier's Liberal Party, which he (like many other workers in turn-of-the-century Canada) hoped would live up to William Gladstone's ideal of helping the masses against the classes; then, as the Liberals disappointed him more and more after coming to power in 1896, he gravitated towards socialism, which he gradually came to see as a project not of piecemeal moral reform but of total social transformation. Even had McKay not become a socialist, there were other things that might have distanced him from his home community. The South Shore of Nova Scotia has never been famous for its love of trade unionism; in his life-time McKay identified with (and at times worked for) the American Federation of Labor and, subsequently, its industrial nemesis, the All-Canadian Congress of Labour. And his intellectual enthusiasms must have sometimes set him apart: McKay loved to explore economic history and to expound the labour theory of value, enthusiasms unlikely to have been shared by many fishers and shipbuilders in the area.

McKay himself would have found any suggestion of a necessary split between intellectual work and life as it was lived on the South Shore wholly unacceptable. In the labour theory of value, and especially in Marx's descriptions of the expropriation of the peasantry, he would have said, working people, on the South Shore as anywhere else, could read the story of their own difficult attempts to survive in a fast-changing capitalist world. There was no "world of theory" over and above the "world of experience," but one real world, and understanding that world required both theory and experience. He came to believe that the social history of his birthplace and his family could be understood only in light of Marx's work on the concentration and centralization of capital.

McKay grew up knowing a way of life that was quite different than industrial capitalism. In his youth, self-employed artisans had enjoyed a greater measure of self-sufficiency and independence than was enjoyed by industrial workers. And he had watched this qualified independence change as the world of capitalism changed. The McKays, and Shelburne, had experienced directly the impact of the great capitalist transformation of the nineteenth century. Because his grandfather had died when his father was a mere lad of 12, Colin's family had faced serious economic hardships throughout his youth. In his early years, his father did not own a shipyard but instead supervised the construction of vessels for affluent merchant yard owners all along Nova Scotia's South Shore, even venturing all the way to the Bay of Islands in Newfoundland to find work. When McKay later argued -- in various Marxist articles in 1911 and 1912 -- that the small businessmen and primary producers of the Maritimes were menaced by poverty, insecurity and outright elimination under the ruthless pressures of an expanding capitalism, he was speaking from first-hand experience. Some of the facts in his writings on the precarious position of small businessmen in the region are drawn directly from his father's shipyard in Shelburne. Although he firmly identified with the working class (and was, for most of his life, a wage worker, albeit in his later years an "unproductive" one in the orthodox Marxist sense), McKay always kept in mind the other subaltern classes of the liberal capitalist order.[12]

Over and over again, the small businessman, the inshore fisherman, and the boatbuilder figure in McKay's analyses: and they probably do so because McKay could see, in Marx's descriptions of the dispossession of the peasantry and of the Clearances of the Highlands, elements of his own personal biography, and of the biographies of thousands of his fellow Nova Scotians. When Marx spoke of the proletariat, McKay could think of the brutally exploited merchant seamen; when Marx spoke of proletarianization, McKay could think of the legacy of his family and so many others along the South Shore. Because industrial capital was, in a

---

[12]For a provocative analysis of the early intellectuals in the Socialist Party of Canada that argues that socialism reflected the interests of a section of the middle class rather than the working class, see Mark Leier, "Workers and Intellectuals: The Theory of the New Class and Early Canadian Socialism," *Journal of History and Politics*, 10 (1992): 87-108. Certain of McKay's writings, and his position as a "brainworker" at the Saint John *Standard* and other newspapers, might be seen as confirmation of Leier's thesis. But there is also much to be said against it: McKay's long spells as a workingman at sea, his particular identification with *certain* elements of the petit bourgeoisie far more than others (such as fishers and shipbuilders), and his whole-hearted support of labour campaigns from the 1890s to the 1930s all tell against simply numbering him among the "petit bourgeoisie." Thus he was *both* a "labourist," who supported union label campaigns, craft unionism, and the restriction of hours; and a "socialist," who wanted workers to build a completely new form of society. Leier argues that his analysis illustrates why socialist intellectuals of the day would have refused the slogan, 'All power to the workers,' but this was surely the burden of many of McKay's political analyses [see, for example, §.125, "The Necessity of a Labour Party," among many others]. Finally, it is problematical to lump farmers and other primary producers into an umbrella "middle class" category, for such people were economically pressured (and productive) in a way that white-collar intellectuals were not. (Moreover, in the Maritimes, with its widespread traditions of occupational pluralism, many people were workers in one season and farmers, fishers, or seafarers in another: as indeed was often the case with McKay). Leier's article is a stimulating first step, nonetheless, to piecing together the socio-economic context of early Canadian socialism.

sense, a new form, and because McKay never lost a sense of the staggering moral and social implications of a life centred on the exploitation of one class by another, his writings, down to the 1930s, strove to "defamiliarize" the face of capitalism -- to make the conventional and the accepted daily life of capitalism seem foreign, unusual -- even monstrous. This sometimes gave the writings of this sometimes hard-nosed Marxist a distinctly romantic tinge: McKay's vision of a day when the Canadian yeomen was "free to take up virgin land, to build a log cabin, to stock the family larder with wild game, fish, berries, maple sugar, etc.," a time now ended by the invasion of the frontier by private interests, was pure Jefferson, although it was also, of course, in keeping with the Marxist account of the plight of the artisan and the primary producer under capitalism [§.134, "Economic Democracy Must Come!"].

When McKay arrived in Montreal in the 1890s, seafaring had already transformed him into a critic -- albeit a radical liberal critic -- of the capitalist social order. He quickly became a leading figure on the city's labour scene. From the mid-1890s to c.1900, he seems to have functioned as "labour's spokesman," one of the men English-language newspapers called upon to explain the workers' perspective. (This status was somewhat curious, in that for at least some of this time McKay was simply wintering in Montreal between voyages.)[13] He was involved in the editing of the *Saturday Times* (1894-1895), a prominent labour reform publication with a dominion-wide profile.[14] He was also directly involved in the Federated Trades and Labor Council of Montreal, and threw himself into the vibrant world of Montreal daily newspapers: by any measure, he was one of the major figures in Anglophone working-class politics in Montreal.[15]

---

[13] As suggested in Morgan, ed., *The Canadian Men and Women of the Time*: 773.

[14] For a brief description of labour journalism in Montreal, see Ron Verzuh, *Radical Rag: The Pioneer Labour Press in Canada* (Ottawa: Steel Rail, 1988): 83-90. The *Saturday Times* was the successor to the muck-raking *Echo*. For a brief introduction to Quebec trade unionism, see Bernard Dionne, *Le Syndicalisme au Québec* (Montréal: Boréal, 1991), ch.1. Interesting parallels might be drawn between the labour journalism of the *Herald* and the contemporaneous efforts of *La Presse*.

[15] The Anglophone working class and socialist movement in Montreal -- one of the largest and most significant in Canada -- remains curiously understudied by scholars: perhaps it has fallen between the stools of Francophone Québec labour historiography and an Anglophone labour historiography that takes "English Canada" as its context. For an important study illuminating one aspect of McKay's social milieu in this period, see Ralph F.H. Hoskins, "An Analysis of the Payrolls of the Point St. Charles Shops of the Grand Trunk Railway," *Cahiers de Géographie du Québec*, 33, 90 (décembre 1989): 323-344. This shows, among other things, that from 1902 to 1917, Anglophones were greatly in the majority among the skilled, metal-working tradesmen in these important shops, with however a significant rise in Francophone carpenters in the car department and on the painter crew. It is reasonable to suppose that the Point St. Charles railway shops were an important element in the lives of many of those who patronized the

The daily press was a key arena for struggle, and the *Montreal Herald* was the key English-language paper.[16] Here was a Liberal daily trying to respond to two challenges. One was building circulation, and in the age of yellow journalism and muckraking progressivism, this required a new sensitivity to social issues. The second challenge was to overcome a well-deserved reputation for being anti-labour, the result of a major strike at the paper in 1890.

Under the leadership of James Samuel Brierley, the *Herald* rapidly became one of the most interesting muckraking newspapers in the country.[17] Brierley brought a high moral tone to his conception of the journalist's calling:

> The reporter must, in the first place, be in earnest. It is business, not pleasure, on which he is bent. He must be active, courteous and of good address. He should have the faculty of telling his story clearly, in plain, matter-of-fact English, that he who runs may read. He should prove all things, and hold fast to that which is true. "Faking," or forgery of news, he should avoid as he would the plague. He should keep faith with the men from whom he obtains

---

socialist organizations of that vibrant neighbourhood at the turn of the century and supported the AFL organizing drive in which McKay was involved (and, as well, the Socialist Party of Canada). For invaluable insights into the world of work in Montreal, see Peter Bischoff, "La formation des traditions syndicales chez les mouleurs de Montréal, Hamilton et Toronto, 1850-1893," *Bulletin*, Regroupement des chercheurs-chercheures en histoire des travailleurs et travailleuses du Québec, 16, 1 (hiver 1990): 19-61, a prospectus for his thesis on the same subject. Jean De Bonville, *Jean-Baptiste Gagnepetit: Les Travailleurs Montréalais à la fin du XIXe siècle* (Montréal: Les Éditions de l'Aurore, 1975), and Paul-André Linteau, *Histoire de Montréal depuis la Confédération* (Montréal: Boréal, 1992), both convey much useful information. An interesting discussion of turn-of-the-century labour politics can be found in Alfred Charpentier, "Le Mouvement Politique Ouvrier de Montréal (1883-1929)," in Fernand Harvey, ed., *Aspects historiques du mouvement ouvrier au Québec* (Montréal: Les Editions du Boréal Express, 1973), 147-167, which however largely ignores the pre-1904 socialist movement. There is room for much more work on labour thought, utopian socialism, and trade-union struggle in turn-of-the-century Montreal.

[16]See Russell Hann, "Brainworkers and the Knights of Labor: E.E.Sheppard, Phillips Thompson, and the *Toronto News*, 1883-1887," in Gregory S. Kealey and Peter Warrian, eds., *Essays in Canadian Working Class History* (Toronto: McClelland and Stewart, 1976): 35-57, for a discussion of the important role of a Toronto daily in working-class journalism in the previous decade.

[17]On Brierley, see Morgan, ed., *Canadian Men and Women of the Time* 140. The *Herald* had earlier been sympathetic to the Knights of Labor: see Noel Belanger et al., *Les Travailleurs Québécois 1851-1896* (Montreal: Les Presses de l'Université du Québec, 1973), Chapter 4.

news, betraying the confidence of none, and living scrupulously to
the spirit, as well as the letter, of any promise he makes.[18]

The young McKay and the muckraking newspaper seemed made for each
other. Between 1897 and 1906 no fewer than 97 articles signed by McKay
appeared in the *Herald*. He undoubtedly also contributed many other
unsigned items to the paper's labour columns, which represent a major
source for historians of the city's labour movement.

Brierley may have been initially enthusiastic about hiring McKay; he lived
to regret his decision. McKay was a whirlwind. He promoted the use of
union labels to combat the sweating system, pointed out defects in the
Quebec factory Act, and attempted to encourage the development of
producers' co-operatives. He went so far as to attack Cecil Rhodes in South
Africa and the Klondike Gold Rush: Rhodes was a warmonger and the
goldseekers simply gamblers, he argued. His advocacy journalism
included publishing detailed suggestions for the reform of the Quebec
Factory Act and for the rewriting of the laws regulating foodstuffs. He
participated in the *Herald*'s Civic Reform Petition in 1899, publicly took a
swing at McGill University for not hiring professors of economics or
sociology, and baited the clergy into responding to the charge that they
were alienated from the working class [§.11, "Why Workingmen Distrust
Churches"].

Although none of these initiatives was alarming in itself, cumulatively they
probably meant that McKay was pulling the *Herald* further and faster than
it wanted to go down the path of engaged radical journalism. By 1900, in a
note to Mackenzie King, Brierley sounded rather exhausted by the young
reporter on his staff.[19] McKay, whose priority was social change and not
journalism, must have sometimes been a trial. In November 1898, *Herald*
articles, subsequently attributed to McKay, accused Col. George A. Hughes,
superintendent of police, of misappropriation of funds. The articles led to
a suit for defamatory libel. Although the *Herald* won this action before
Mr. Justice Wurtele under the banner of "Liberty of the Press" in the
spring of 1899, there was the additional complication of further charges
for publishing an article that some suspected was written to influence the
jury.[20]

---

[18]James S. Brierley, "The Making of Newspapers an Interesting Pursuit," *Montreal
Herald*, 4 March 1905.
[19]James Brierley to Mackenzie King, Mackenzie King Papers, Vol.1, Reel C-1902, 17
September 1900, National Archives of Canada.
[20]Montreal *Herald*, 10, 11 April 1899; *Le Canard*, 29 avril 1899 has a diverting cartoon
on the case. Subsequent muck-raking by the *Herald* in civic politics is detailed in the
Montreal Herald, 30 December 1899.

But that was not the extent of McKay's pushing of the limits. For McKay, the municipal corruption story, however interesting, was no match for an investigation into the conditions of labour in Montreal. An unsigned 1897 article titled "The Sweating Evil. Its Prevalence in the City of Montreal. Overcrowded Tenements. Where People Work for Eighty Hours a Week," sounded the tocsin for a new labour crusade. McKay's opening shot was an example of his gift for blending moral critique with empirical detail:

> Of all the evils of the present industrial system which baffle the efforts of humanitarians and reformers, the sweating system as applied to garment making, is perhaps the worst and the most general. Much has been written about the miseries which this system entails to thousands of unfortunate beings in such large cities as London and New York; but perhaps few Montrealers are aware that the system is proportionately as great in Montreal, and that it is fast spreading. In fact, the sweating system has been heretofore an inseparable adjunct of the ready made clothing business. To save themselves the trouble of having suitable shops and work rooms, the large dealers give out the work to families or to contractors, who bid for the work at the lowest possible price and depend upon their ability to "sweat" poor women and children to make their profit....
>
> Occupied as they are from early morning until night, they have little time, even if they had the inclination, to give a thought to the sanitary condition of their surroundings, which are often simply vile. The combination living room and workshop offers one of the saddest spectacles which can be sought by any humanely disposed person, who seeks light on the subject of human misery.
>
> The president of the factory inspectors, Mr. Lessard, asserts that the ordinary week's work of these people is from 75 to 80 hours. Men and women who work out, bring work home to do it on Sunday. They go though the employer and offer to work two or three hours extra, if given a chance to work, thus subjecting themselves to a condition of slavery. There is in fact no limit to the hours of labour, but that of physical endurance, and the pay is kept down to the starvation point. Trousers are made in Montreal for from 8 to 10 cents a pair. It is not surprising that destitution, suffering, intellectual and moral depression should be the normal condition among the unfortunate victims of this permissious [pernicious] system.[21]

---

[21] *Montreal Herald*, 3 February 1897. It seems relatively safe to attribute this unsigned article to McKay: it is written in his style, it cites British precedence, and it is echoed, albeit not directly, by his later writings on the question. For response to the *Herald's*

More and more people -- including young Mackenzie King, the future Prime Minister of Canada -- were drawn into this *Herald* crusade against sweating [See §.3, "The Abolition of the Sweating System: A Call For Action"].

In February, 1899, McKay extended the campaign to include the cigar factory of one J.M. Fortier. This is a case that deserves to be much more widely known and intensively explored. Historians might make much greater use of it to explore a number of themes, such as French/English relations in working-class Montreal, the limits of freedom of expression in Canada, and the use of the law to enforce certain notions of property and propriety.[22]

In retrospect, the McKay/Fortier confrontation was virtually foreordained. As Jacques Rouillard has noted, as early as the 1860s, and (in reorganized form) with greater force in the 1880s, the cigarmakers' union had played a key role in the Montreal working-class movement; a massive strike in 1883, a founding role in the city's first labour day commemorations in 1886, and a position among those forces demanding a royal commission into the relations of capital and labour all suggest the organization's dynamism.[23] This trial also pitted the city's foremost muckraking anglophone journalist of the late 1890s against Montreal's most notorious exploiter of child labour. By the 1890s, Fortier had established a dominion-wide reputation for the horrible conditions in his factory : his defence (before the Royal Commission on the Relations of Capital and Labour) of such measures as hitting workers over the head with heavy metal implements and punishing children by isolating them in the "black

---

expose of sweating, see *Montreal Herald*, 6, 13 February 1897. For Mackenzie King's later pieces on the "Sweating System in Montreal," see *Montreal Herald*, 16, 23 April 1898. McKay subsequently prepared a draft act, drawn from a study of American and European legislation, as a guide to provincial legislators: see "An Act to Regulate Conditions of Garment Trade," *Montreal Herald*, 2 December 1899. It should be noted that both King and McKay were preceded in this field by A.W.Wright's *Report upon the Sweating System in Canada* (Canada, *Sessional Papers*, 1896, Vol.11, Sessional Paper No.61), which took a rather more sanguine view of the situation: Wright wrote more as if the problem were something which might happen in the future, rather than a pressing issue of the present.

[22]So far as I can make out, the present discussion is the first published account of the case. Forsey, *Trade Unions in Canada 1812-1902* (Toronto: University of Toronto Press, 235), mentions the strike against Fortier, but not the court case. The standard sources on Québec labour history do not seem to devote attention to the struggle. It may well have been overshadowed by the very large cigarmakers' strike which followed in 1901.

[23]See Jacques Rouillard, *Histoire du Syndicalisme Québécois* (Montréal: Boréal, 1989), 50-53.

hole" has become deservedly famous among labour historians.[24] Fortier was also one of Canada's most fiercely anti-union employers. And he had a reputation for litigiousness. Just three years earlier he had sued the American Tobacco Company on a charge of conspiracy.[25] It was inevitable that Fortier would fight a pro-labour, muckraking journalist without mercy. When in December 1898 Fortier unceremoniously "let go" of 39 unionized workers, the incident was certain to be challenged by McKay and Montreal's labour community.[26] A significant battle in the the long war between capital and labour in Canada was set to begin.

---

[24]For the details, see G.S.Kealey, ed., *Canada Investigates Industrialism: The Royal Commission on the Relations of Labor and Capital, 1889 (Abridged)* (Toronto: University of Toronto Press, 1973): 213-229; Fernand Harvey, *Révolution industrielle et travailleurs* (Montreeal: Boréal Express, 1978). For the original, see *Report of the Royal Commission on the Relations of Capital and Lahor in Canada*, Evidence--Quebec, Part I (Ottwa, 1889): 32-135. Fortier's testimony is found on pages 123-134. It is curious that so little was made of the "black hole" in the subsequent labour agitation, but this perhaps suggests the gap between the skilled male workers and others in the trade. For descriptive material on living and working conditions in Montreal, see Jean De Bonville, *Jean-Baptiste Gagnepetit: Les Travailleurs Montréalais à la fin du XIXe siècle*. Montréal: Les Éditions de l'Aurore, 1975, although he does not cover this specific case. For a fascinating and moving study of a francophone working-class intellectual and socialist in Montreal, who apparently did not intersect with McKay, see Claude Larivière, *Albert Saint-Martin, militant d'avant-garde (1865-1947)* (Laval, 1979).

[25]*Montreal Herald*, 10 December 1896; 4 January 1897.

[26]*Montreal Herald*, 23 December 1898. Fortier initially denied that there was any strike or lock-out on his premises: he simply claimed that a number of workmen, discharged some weeks earlier, had come back to apply for work and were turned down. The affected employees, on the other hand, argued that "for many years Mr. J.M. Fortier has refused to concede to his employes the right to organize to protect their wages and provide for hard times and those of sickness. All that time Mr. J.M. Fortier has been paying fifty cents to three dollars less per thousand cigars than other shops. Eight months ago Mr. Fortier, through his foreman, notified the men that each of them had to furnish him with a note certifying that they did not belong to the union, and those that could not furnish same, their job was up. On that occasion all the men left the shop, and a committee from the union interviewed Mr. Fortier and the difficulty was adjusted for the time being. Four of the men were discharged after the affair because they were known to have worked towards organizing the others. On the 19th of November last all the men were laid off for the alleged reason that there was no work, and a few days afterwards the non union men were at work and Mr. Fortier was advertising in the daily press for boys and girls. As there was a few days pay coming to the men, they were told to come some time the following week to draw their money, and when they did they were offered work at reduced wages. In our efforts to settle the difficulty we wrote to Mr. Fortier asking him if he had any objection to meeting a committee, but he did not think it worth his while to answer. Recently he has endeavored to again secure many of his former workmen at reduced wages, but now that the fight is on and the matter is in

This time, possibly because the editor at the *Herald* was growing weary of his radicalism, McKay pursued his crusade outside the columns of the conventional daily press. With the "financial and moral support" of the Federated Trades and Labor Council of Montreal, McKay launched *Canada's Democracy*, published in the interests of labour but with a specific initial focus on this case.[27] *Canada's Democracy* pressed the case against Fortier with an unrestrained muckraking enthusiasm. Echoing the American Populist Henry Demarest Lloyd, McKay accused Fortier of "growing rich off the flesh and blood of his employees," and of being a "moral dynamiter" and an "industrial copperhead." Especially wounding, apparently, were the words McKay put into print on the subject of Fortier's Christmas turkeys. *Canada's Democracy* alleged that, when the accompanying wage reduction was taken into account, the turkeys Fortier had paternalistically given his employees the previous Christmas had actually cost each one of them between $50 to $100 apiece. Fortier's workers were urged to start their own co-operative cigar factory and thus undermine Fortier in the marketplace.[28] Although *Canada's Democracy* lasted for only two numbers, quite enough had been said to persuade

---

the hands of the union, the men are determined to remain out until Mr. Fortier agrees to the scale of prices as paid in other shops...." *Montreal Herald*, 29 December 1898. This detailed account is more persuasive than that put forward by Fortier. However, it is a moot point whether, technically, this dispute was actually either a strike *or* a lockout. It is interesting that cigarmakers figure so largely in narratives about turn-of-the-century Montréal activism: undoubtedly such cigarmakers as Adolphe Gariépy, Ben Drolet, and George Warren, all later significant in radical labour politics, brought an added intensity to this struggle.

[27]See *Montreal Herald*, 2 December 1898. McKay was also likely responsible for a resolution in support of the Fortier cigarmakers at the annual meeting of the Canadian Trades and Labor Congress in Montreal during September, 1899. On that occasion it was proposed that Alderman Martineau of St. Denis Ward should be defeated at the next civic election as he was engaged as counsel for the plaintiff in the Fortier libel action. Discussion on the issue was only brought to a halt when the Congress adopted a resolution of sympathy for the cigarmakers union. *Montreal Herald*, 22 September 1899.

[28]*Citizen and Country*, 25 March 1899. The "ungrateful" employees argued "that while Mr. Fortier had for years been paying 50 cents to $4 per 1,000 less than other cigar makers, he had shortly before Christmas cut the already low rates from $1 to $1.50 per 1,000 cigars, which meant a reduction of $1 to $2 per week to each employee. Each turkey, according to the computation made, therefore cost each employe from $50 to $100, as the 'pdesentation' ["presentation"] was made only annually. This was regarded as a pretty heavy burden to bear, but in January further action was taken when the shop was temporarily closed 'for lack of work.' Then Mr. Fortier offered to resume work if his employes would agree to a further reduction of wages. This they refused to do, but the shop was started with some non-union men and a few boys and girls, who were persuaded to accepted the wages offered. The union men asked for an arbitration, but that was refused." There followed a list of the cigars manufactured by Fortier -- Chamberlain, La Fayette, La Coronet, Creme de la Creme, Rosedale, Noisy Boys,

Fortier to take the publication, and some cigarmakers, to court on a charge of defamatory libel.[29]

The week-long Fortier-McKay trial which opened on 15 September 1899 in the Court of Queen's Bench was a classic illustration of labour's precarious legal position in the late nineteenth century. It came to be seen as a test case, pitting the strength of the Cigarmakers' Union against that of Fortier. Many of Fortier's employees confirmed McKay's description of the controversy; some did not. Great attention was focussed on the issue of the Christmas turkeys, obviously a sore point. On 16 November 1899, the venerable Mr. Justice Jonathan Saxton Campbell Wurtele summed up the case for the jury. As befit the old seigneur of River David,[30] his one-sided summation was a masterful expression of contempt for the rights of labour and for the rights of the labour press.

Defamatory libel, Wurtele explained, consisted of a statement published without justification or excuse, and "of such a nature to injure someone by exposing him to the hatred or ridicule of the public. Thus it was that the peace of the land was endangered by such publications, as men's passions were thereby aroused and crimes were committed." Wurtele conceded that if a statement were true and of public interest, justification might be pleaded. "For instance," he explained (no doubt with the *Herald*'s earlier muckraking crusade against the City of Montreal in mind) "a paper might criticize the government of the land, with moderation when, if true, it might be of interest. The same rule held good of a large corporation like the city of Montreal, when if an act of dishonesty was referred to without exaggeration, and if it were established, the court then could instruct the jury it was of public interest." But "public interest should not be confounded with the interest of a few, or a small body of citizens, forming a class. The whole people or society was intended." Workers now doubtless enjoyed the right to combine for better wages, hours, or

---

Clock Cigars, Pets Special, Richard L. Our Governor, La Espanola, La Carlina, El Caga, Canvas Back, Minerva, Fin de Siecle, Florida Queen, Princess Teck, Mi Rosa, La Manaca, Alexander III., Washington Irving, Vanderbilt, Walter Scott, La Valrosa -- with the obvious (if unstated) implication that union supporters should not buy them.

[29]Charges against the cigarmakers were quietly dropped. See *Montreal Herald*, 15, 20 October; 9, 16 November, 1900. They had been pending for over a year. For the general context of Canadian journalism and libel law in the late nineteenth century, and on the Montreal *Herald* as a target for libel actions, see Paul Rutherford, *A Victorian Authority: The Daily Press in Late Nineteenth-Century Canada* (Toronto: University of Toronto Press, 1982) 190-194. Rutherford does not specifically mention the McKay case, which arguably does not fit a model of a class-unified "Fourth Estate".

[30]Wurtele (1820-1904) was descended, on both his mother's and father's side, from old United Empire Loyalist stock. Son of Jonathan Wurtele, he had succeeded at an early age to the seigneurial estates of his father at River David.

conditions, but "personal liberty should not be lost sight of." Employees might refuse work, but they had no right to prevent others from working. "If workingmen had the right to protect themselves, they had no right to attack capitalists. Neither could any union hinder a man not of their society from working. That would be a great abuse of personal liberty. Nor could they prevent the manufacturer from hiring such men. It was all a question of co-ordination. No union could force a manufacturer to accept their scale of wages. All they could do would be to use persuasion."

Having laid out these tidy, classically liberal anachronisms, Wurtele then informed the jurors that only if the defence could demonstrate the truth of all its allegations, *and prove that they had been made in the public interest,* would justification be established. It thus became a trial that turned on the question of whether McKay, in calling Fortier a "moral dynamiter," a person who had grown rich on the flesh and blood of his workers, an "industrial copperhead," and someone who had profited from giving his employees their Christmas turkeys, had been writing *both* truthfully -- in this context, it seemed "truthfully" meant "literally" -- *and* in "the public interest" -- meaning not just in the *particular* interests of the working class, but in the *general* interests of everybody. The jury was asked to bear in mind that *Canada's Democracy* had been published only twice, and that "not having met with approval, the accused ordered 5,000 copies extra to be distributed in town." Thus the jury was asked to weigh what the intention of the accused was "in forcing upon the public a paper they would not patronise."[31] With these narrow market criteria of what constituted the public interest ringing in their ears, the jury took only ten minutes to find McKay guilty. He was quickly sentenced to three months in jail.

McKay and much of the labour movement in Montreal considered the verdict an outrage. Wurtele's pedantic insistence on the literal meaning of phrases such as "dynamiter" demonstrated a "superb ignorance of the English language, or [an] audacious indifference to every principle thereof," McKay argued. The judge had not understood, apparently, that the phrase "moral dynamiter" referred to an employer whose exploitive zeal undermined society. Instead he had disingenuously asked: "Is Mr. Fortier a dynamiter? Does he go around blowing up buildings and killing people right and left?" A moral dynamiter was a destroyer of good will and harmony; the judge, however, had implied (in French) that a "dynamiter" was the equivalent of an "assassin." In his five-hour review of the evidence, the judge had reviewed the evidence from only one side of

---

[31]*Montreal Gazette*, 20 November 1899. See also *Montreal Herald*, 20 November 1899; *La Presse,* 20 novembre 1899 [18 novembre publié par erreur dans le journal]. The learned judge was no doubt aware that the extra copies of the newspaper had been used as strike propaganda.

the case [§.5. Of The Social State, Freedom of Speech, and J.M. Fortier: The Case for the Defence].

On 7 December 1899, the Montreal Federated Trades and Labor Council unanimously resolved that "Mr. Colin McKay's health is in such a precarious condition that it would be dangerous for him if he was to serve that sentence; therefore be it resolved that a petition for his immediate release be circulated among the taxpayers of the city, and that the same be forwarded to the Minister of Justice."[32] McKay apparently travelled home to Nova Scotia to restore his health, returning to Montreal in the spring to serve his three-month sentence. When he wrote to the socialist magazine *Citizen and Country* in May, 1900, he was described as writing "from the confines of a martyr's cell." McKay was in jail, argued *Citizen and Country*, for having "called a spade a spade."[33]

The trial and subsequent imprisonment probably harmed McKay's health, but they did nothing to hurt his reputation in turn-of-the-century Canadian labour and socialist circles. In the midst of the battle against Fortier, McKay was playing a key role in the foundation of Canada's first national formation of socialists, the Canadian Socialist League (CSL) which started in Montreal and Toronto during the summer of 1899. McKay seems to have been immersed in the dynamic progressive community of turn-of-the-century Montreal, and especially in the bustling hive of utopian and ethical socialists in Pointe St. Charles. The *Herald* frequently reported on happenings at the semi-socialist Pleasant Sunday Afternoon Society[34] and on the Sunday afternoon lectures at Fraternity Hall, which (the *Herald* approvingly noted) were not "declamations of destructive socialism" but "essentially educative," often presented by

---

[32]*Montreal Herald*, 8 December 1899. It is not clear in what sense McKay's health was in danger.

[33]*Citizen and Country*, 4 May 1900. The case seems to have done the Cigarmakers' Union no harm: shortly thereafter the union reported that it was nearing complete organization of the trade (including its women workers). *Montreal Herald*, 19 November 1900.

[34]..."The Sunday afternoon lectures at Fraternity Hall, under the auspices of the Pleasant Sunday Afternoon society, are productive of much good. The management has been fortunate in securing some of the most prominent city speakers for these occasions, and the subjects chosen have generally been of vital importance to the workingmen....These meetings are characterized by a free and friendly spirit of discussion. The speaker is apt to have all the weak points in his argument exposed by the keen intellects present, but everything is taken in good part. The lecturer is asked to come and teach, but not infrequently he learns a lesson himself before he leaves the hall. A good number of men and women have learned to take advantage of these meetings to become familiar with the socialism advocated by the members of the Pleasant Sunday Afternoon Society." *Montreal Herald*, 26 February 1897.

"reformers of the noblest character."[35] McKay was probably the *Herald* reporter at the lecture of Mr. Roswell Fisher at the Philosophical Society of Canada, in which socialism was seen as a doctrine that had evolved from the most ancient religions and reformers, found a niche in the ethics of Christ, and received fresh impetus from Voltaire, Rousseau, St. Simon, Owen, Lasalle, Marx, and many others.[36] This same lecturer developed the theme of "A Socialist Utopia." in the following year, again before the Philosophical Society at its hall on St. Catherine Street.[37] The Reverend Herbert N. Casson, M.A., a well-known socialist, spoke to the group in 1897; it was remembered then that he had spoken the previous winter, and had won large numbers to the cause of Christian Socialism. The *Herald* -- again, judging from the sympathetic but slightly sardonic style, its reporter was *probably* McKay -- felt that Casson had shown conclusively that "man was but a fraction of the great union of humanity; that there was the strictest interdependence between all men in all ages...."[38] The Pleasant Sunday Afternoon Society , under the guidance of William Darlington, seemed to continue many of the labour reform traditions of the Knights of Labor, in which Darlington had played a leading role. Certainly Montreal was buzzing with new ideas, many of them "socialist" in the highly elastic, late-Victorian sense of that ambiguous word.

This turn-of-the-century socialism was, McKay would later argue, long on sentiment and short on specifics. He might have cited his own strange poem, "The Socialist Policy," as evidence of both sentimentality and vagueness:

> To guide the shuttles flashing through the loom
> Of Canada's imperious destiny
> To give each force, each effort, righteous room,
> Stern justice and most gracious liberty.
>
> To aid her growth -- direct development --
> To check, to change destructive tendencies,
> To ease the travail of fore-born events
> And drain from circumstances the dregs and lees.
>
> To reconcile the jarring elements,
> Remove the causes of industrial strife
> Establish peace within the hostile tents,
> And lend an uplift to the larger life.

---

[35]*Montreal Herald*, 8 March 1897.
[36]*Montreal Herald*, 19 December 1896.
[37]*Montreal Herald*, 1, 2 March 1897.
[38]*Montreal Herald*, 17 March 1897.

> *To watch lest overgrown monopolies*
> *Should usurp unjust power with forceful hand*
> *And, trampling on the people's liberties*
> *Bringing reck revolution on our land.*
>
> *To guard the people's rights -- whate'er may come --*
> *To stand between them and their enemies --*
> *To lift the weary hosts of labordom*
> *To nobler lives and larger liberties.*[39]

Surely no one, socialist, liberal, tory or otherwise, could have disagreed with such a genial, commonsense, well-mannered "Socialist Policy" as that? Revolution appears as a menace, to be averted by a far-seeing government of labour reform capable of balancing social forces and reconciling jarring elements. A militant rhetoric of Labour Rights coexists with a much milder, liberal sense of a balanced social order.

McKay played an important role in the organization of the CSL. He was instrumental in the 1899 foundation of the Montreal Branch No.1, and quickly became a local leader of the Socialists. The League adopted a moderately democratic platform, calling for abolition of the Senate; adult suffrage and proportional representation; public ownership of all franchises; land nationalization; a national currency and government banking system; public ownership of all monopolies; abolition of patent laws; and government remuneration for all inventors, with the aim of facilitating the shortening of the work-day through labour-saving machinery. It was a platform that had something for the disciples of Henry George (land nationalization), for the Populist currency reformers who were then in vogue, and for slightly impatient liberals. The "recommended books list" of the CSL included Marx's *Capital*, Robert Blatchford's *Merrie England*, Bellamy's *Equality*, the *Fabian Essays in Socialism*, and a large number of publications emphasizing the links between Christian teachings and socialism, broadly defined.[40] In an examination of the Toronto case, Gene Homel has convincingly argued that "...the CSL represented little ideological rupture with the radical movement that had led up to it. The League held the allegiance of many liberals-in-a-hurry; its platform and personnel were drawn from pre-socialist radicalism."[41] After 1898, almost 6,000 subscribers were brought

---

[39]Unidentified clipping, McKay family scrapbook. The likely location is the *Montreal Herald* and the probable date 1899-1900.

[40]*Citizen and Country*, October 1900. Alfred Charpentier, "Le Mouvement Politique Ouvrier," 151, remembers his father receiving two socialist visitors in 1904 (one of whom was Dick Kerrigan, who was the next year to attend the founding convention of the IWW); they bore with them a French translation of *Merrie England*.

[41]Gene Homel, "James Simpson and the Origins of Canadian Social Democracy," PhD Thesis, University of Toronto, 1978: 93.

this eclectic socialist message through the CSL's publication *Citizen and Country.*[42]

McKay's status among the Montreal socialists was suggested by his role as their delegate to the CSL's founding national convention in 1901 in Toronto. The convention itself, attended by 70 delegates from 18 Socialist leagues across the country, provided further evidence of his rising star. McKay was chosen, along with John Spargo, a famous British socialist and special lecturer of the Fellowship Society of Chicago, to be an *ex-officio* member of all committees formed at the convention.[43] He thus clearly played an important role in this significant moment in the history of Canadian Socialism: the foundation of the first dominion-wide homegrown socialist party.

McKay probably helped shape the platform of the CSL, and he certainly endorsed its moderation and idealism. Advancing towards the CSL really required a troubled but persisting Liberal to take but a few easy steps. A left Spencerian -- and by this point McKay was significantly influenced by Herbert Spencer's philosophy of social evolution -- would have identified warmly with both the limited nature of the CSL's economic program and with the goal of land nationalization, as presaged by Spencer's own critique of private land ownership in *Social Statics*, published almost five decades earlier. And although it was true that the CSL included the public ownership of certain means of production among its objectives, much weight could be placed on the word "eventual" that qualified this seemingly radical suggestion.

In gravitating to the CSL, McKay was not only choosing its combination of Christian idealism and mild reformist socialism, but also actively rejecting the leading left-wing Marxian alternative, the Socialist Labor Party (SLP). McKay was not impressed by the SLP. A *Herald* reporter -- McKay, we can be quite sure, judging by the style of the piece -- dropped in on a Montreal meeting of the SLP in 1899 at St. Joseph's Hall on St. Catherine Street. He described a tiny but chaotically divisive group of

---

[42]*The Canadian Newspaper Directory*, 3rd edition (Montreal: A. McKim and Co.,1901): 105. The circulation figure given there is 5,963.

[43]With the benefit of hindsight, McKay would later say of Spargo's address to the Toronto socialist convention that it was "merely the Utopian or sentimental Socialism of a century or more ago," and remembered sitting beside "a reporter of one of the Toronto papers, a Scotsman, who anticipated nearly every paragraph of Spargo. When I asked him where he'd heard Spargo before he answered: 'Nowhere. But my old man had a collection of books and pamphlets published in Robert Owen's time and I can usually guess what a sentimental Socialist is going to say.'" Colin McKay, "The 1901 Socialist Convention," letter to *New Commonwealth*, 5 June 1937. Spargo later reconsidered his commitment to the cause of socialism, and McKay remarked: "I was not greatly surprised by Spargo's defection. It was partly immanent in his sentimentalism."

eccentrics, whose preoccupation seemed, oddly, to be military strategy. Chairing the group was Richard Kerrigan, whose attempts to wed the SLP and the Central Trades and Labor Council forced many fierce debates in the latter body, which had (the reporter remarked acidly) "not waxed the stronger for it." McKay saw the SLP as a divided, unrealistic, and dogmatic body,[44] hampered by its lack of Canadian roots, and more significantly by its underlying philosophy of materialism, which was truly a "repudiation of the only tenable basis for a socialistic system of society," an "abolition of the basis of morality" without which socialism could not be justified [§.11, "Why Workingmen Distrust Churches," originally published as "Why Workingmen Distrust Churches. The Herald Secures an Expression of Opinion From a Prominent Labor Writer on the Reasons for Indifference"].

A further difficulty with the SLP was that it did not agree with the young McKay's sense of what a left *praxis* should entail. A leftist should be *useful to* (but never attempt to *dominate*) the labour movement, and a leftist should develop a day-to-day contact with workers, without which no socialist movement worthy of the name would develop. The new unionism of the turn of the century -- the drive to organize many of the unorganized workers launched by the American Federation of Labor, coinciding with a fresh wave of energy in progressive circles -- impressed him far more as a strategy for effecting social change than what he saw as the rhetorical fireworks and flamboyant gestures of the SLP. An article in the *Herald* in September, 1900 -- unsigned, but either written by, or reflecting the views of, labour editor McKay -- conveyed excitement at the dramatic rise of the AFL unions in Montreal :

> In Montreal during the past three or four years the labor movement has made the most remarkable progress. The great interest that International trades union officials have recently manifested in matters here is a striking testimony to the development and possibilities of the movement in Montreal. In the past the independent union has been a favorite form of organization here, but the last four years has shown the inefficiency of the isolated society, and as a consequence nearly all these bodies have been merged into the international unions of different trades.

> All recent developments tend to show that the workers of this city have come to the conclusion that their best course lies in allying

---

[44][Colin McKay], "Our Socialists. An Insight Into Their Aims and Strength. Theories of War. Comrade Rodier Gives British Generals a Lesson. A Meeting Which Affords Many Opinions for its Size," *Montreal Herald*, 30 November 1899. Kerrigan went on to a distinguished career in the Socialist Party of Canada.

themselves with the movement inspired and directed by the American Federation of Labor.

The Knights of Labor, once a great force in the Montreal labour movement, had admittedly also made some gains over the past few years in Montreal, but, according to the *Herald*, they had only done so by copying the AFL method of organizing along trade-union lines, with each assembly restricting its membership to a particular trade.[45] McKay supported the AFL both by praising it in the *Herald* and in a contribution to the federation's journal, the *American Federationist*; John Flett, AFL organizer in Canada, reciprocated by boosting the opinions of McKay.[46] McKay's involvement went far beyond such gestures, to include dispensing detailed technical advice to particular unions. In 1899 he questioned Garment Workers' Union No. 140 regarding its response to a demand for an enquiry into sweatshops, and was asked if he himself would take the matter in hand.[47] He explained the intricacies of enforcing the union label to the local Wholesale Cutters, and called upon the Federated Trades and Labor Council to boost the union label.[48]

Like many AFL supporters, and even many "socialists" in the CSL, the young McKay saw no contradiction between supporting "Socialism" and "Labour" on the one hand, and the federal Liberal Party on the other.[49] At the turn of the century, the ruling Liberals were seen as sincere allies of the working class, as enemies of monopoly and privilege. Through the

---

[45]*Montreal Herald*, 22 March 1902.

[46]*Montreal Herald*, 16 February 1901. There are two letters in the Samuel Gompers letterbooks to Colin McKay. On 18 December, 1902, Gompers -- writing to McKay at 633 Dorchester Street, Montreal -- acknowledged receipt of a manuscript entitled "The Labor Movement in Montreal" sent "some time since" for publication in the *American Federationist*. McKay was urged to revise it to date, for publication in the following February or March issue of the magazine. On 27 February, 1903, R. Lee Guard, secretary to Gompers, wrote to Colin McKay at Shelburne, acknowledging receipt of McKay's "The Right to Work," and suggesting that Gompers would most likely be pleased to publish it in the *American Federationist*. University of North Carolina, Davis Library, Microfilm Collection 1-41, Samuel Gompers Letterbooks, 1888-1924; the William Green Letterbooks, 1924," Reel 63; Reel 65. It seems rather surprising that there should not have been more correspondence on the subject of McKay's trial and imprisonment on a question of trade-union rights in a city the AFL was determined to organize.

[47]*Montreal Herald*, 7 March 1899.

[48]*Montreal Herald*, 11 October 1899, 21 November 1900.

[49] In 1912, after he had written off both the traditional parties in Canada, McKay would remark that he had never voted for either of the old parties in Canada. The comment obscured the depth of his early loyalty to the Liberal Party. Colin McKay, "President Johnston a Socialist," *Eastern Labor News*, 5 October 1912.

election of 1900, McKay even wrote poems hailing the Liberal cause and the leadership of Prime Minister Wilfrid Laurier.

> *Wide, wide her gates the regal city flings*
> *To welcome him, the great and gracious Knight;*
> *Loud, loud, with burgher cheers the welkin rings,*
> *To honour him, Fate's dearest favorite.*
>
> *No armed band across the wide veldt swings,*
> *No haughty herald thunders at the gates,*
> *Yet -- poor your triumphs seem, ye warrior kings! --*
> *The mighty town in haste capitulates.*
>
> *No sullen mayor irks to yield his keys,*
> *No tearful townsmen mutter in the marts,--*
> *Our chieftain comes to nobler victories,--*
> *The conquest of a grateful people's hearts.*[50]

While the noble Liberal Sir Wilfrid captured the hearts and souls of Montrealers, the Conservative Charles Hibbert Tupper was depicted as poisoning the entire country:

> *From Yukon's icy mountains,*
> *From Dawson's golden sand,*
> *Where Hibbert's fabled fountains*
> *Corrupt the virtuous land,*
> *With dudgeon and with dander,*
> *Ere soon he comes again,*
> *To bark, and snarl and slander*
> *Like the coyote of the plain....*[51]

In his eleven violently partisan poems about the election in the *Herald*, McKay certainly added to his reputation as a Liberal partisan, if not to his reputation as a socialist or as a poet.[52] Describing himself as a "poet-Laurier'ate for the grits," McKay sent copies of four of the poems to Wilfrid Laurier, with a covering note addressed to "Wilfrid, the

---

[50]"C.M.," "The Conqueror Comes," *Montreal Herald*, 20 September 1900.

[51]"C.M.", "From Yukon's Icy Mountains." *Montreal Herald*, 12 June 1900.

[52]An unidentified clipping in the family scrapbook contains this vicious remark about McKay's poems: "The 'only' Colin McKay quotes me as saying verse-making indicates softening of the brain. My reference only applied to 'mature minds.' Anybody who reads McKay will know that as yet he is quite young. There can be no softening of the brain in his case."

Conqueror."[53] The poems suggest a young man who had absorbed many ideals of manly chivalry and honour from the world around him; they also suggest that, like so many working-class men, he had fallen to some extent under the sway of a Kiplingesque romance of empire, not excluding its overtly racist elements. His disparaging comments on Asiatic immigration and the "pigtail pest" stand out (in the context of all his lifetime of work) as rare departures from his humanitarianism. Oppression not directly related to class scarcely existed for McKay. (For most early-twentieth-century Canadian Marxists, "survival of the fittest" pertained primarily to class conflict, other questions being strictly secondary). The person who read McKay as an authoritative guide to what was going on in twentieth-century Canada would never guess that waves of immigrants were reaching the country's shores, that Native peoples were beginning to challenge state domination, or that women were creating strong movements. The ethnic essentialism evident in McKay's poems makes them rather painful reading today; it in no way minimizes McKay's departure from both Christian and Marxian universalism in these pieces to observe that a later McKay would explicitly renounce this form of argument, to the point of critiquing western capitalist civilization in the light of (an imagined) non-European experience. What the Prime Minister made of these effusions is unknown.

McKay may have sent the poems to Laurier because he was angling for a job with the federal Department of Labour. Brierley of the *Herald* wrote a letter of recommendation on his behalf to Mackenzie King, the new deputy minister, on 17 September 1900. Since he qualified his favourable impression of McKay ("a remarkable and decent young man whose contacts with labor organizations might make him a very valuable assistant") with a suggestion of instability and fanaticism ("one so devoted to the labor class that on occasion he is something of a crank") it is not surprising that McKay did not win a position with the Department.[54] Had he done so, he would have joined a number of other

---

[53]Colin McKay to Wilfrid Laurier, Laurier Papers, MG 26, G, Vol. 173, pp. 49673-49672, National Archives of Canada.   As late as 1905, McKay's attachment to Liberalism was clear. His coverage of the Ontario election for the *Herald* was brazenly partisan as well as being quite wrong in predicting an increased Liberal majority in the election. See Colin McKay, "Ross to Win," *Montreal Daily Herald*, 12 Jan. 1905.

[54]James Brierley to Mackenzie King, Mackenzie King Papers, Vol.1, Reel C-1902, 17 September 1900, National Archives of Canada. He also remarked that McKay was "not a man that we can make much use of on a paper like the Herald. He might be able to do indoor work very well however." By this he possibly meant that McKay was unsuited (perhaps because of his socialist convictions) to represent the Herald on the beat, but was acceptable as an editor and a rewrite man.

turn-of-the-century labour figures and radicals in gravitating towards the Department of Labour in these years.[55]

The years following this unsuccessful attempt to secure a federal position were devoted to economic research, seafaring, and writing. Although the exact steps McKay took to acquire competence in economic reasoning are not clear, it is obvious that he underwent an extensive process of self-education in 1901-1904. His contemporaries in Montreal valued his credentials as a "radical political economist" enough to elect him president of the local Economic Association., and the *Herald* turned to McKay in 1904 when it sought a correspondent who could spend two months in Great Britain "looking into the various phases of the fiscal question."[56] The available evidence also suggests a growing attachment to the Nova Scotia Fishermen's Union in Nova Scotia, the producers' association headed by Moses Nickerson, a prominent Liberal politician, journalist and editor: in its campaign for an effective fisheries instructor, the Union -- prompted, one might guess, by Nickerson -- came to focus on McKay as its preferred candidate for the position.[57] For his part, McKay wrote a polemic in which Christ's message to the fishermen was construed as "socialism," and the Union's critics, who had insinuated that mere fishermen could not understand the complex issues facing the industry, were likened to Pharisees: this presumably did not help him in the ultimately unsuccessful attempt to secure this position from mainstream Liberal Party politicians.[58] McKay was nothing if not wide-ranging in his writings and in his travels: Montrealers could read McKay's impressions of Toronto's progressive schemes for industrial training, European left-wing movements, and British labourism. He was back in Shelburne in the winter of 1902-3; in Bristol and Glasgow in the Fall of 1904; in Toronto in January 1905; in Nova Scotia in Summer 1905; and back in Montreal later that November. The following year he could be found in Cape Breton. The articles he published in the Montreal *Herald* show that technical education, housing, and port redevelopment had become his major issues. He remained very cautiously progressive on most of them.[59] In 1905 he signed on with the Pickford & Black line of passenger and freight steamers which ran between Halifax and the West Indies. McKay served as an officer on the steamer *Sokoto* between Halifax and Montreal between 1907 and 1909, and filed at least one newspaper story on the markets for

[55]For example, T. Phillips Thompson, labour reformer and future organizer for the Ontario Socialist League, was correspondent for the Department of Labour from 1900 to 1911. See Jay Atherton, "Introduction," to T. Phillips Thompson, *The Politics of Labor* [1887] (Toronto and Buffalo: University of Toronto Press, 1975): xiv.
[56]*Shelburne Gazette*, 18 August 1904.
[57]*Coast Guard*, 6 May 1909.
[58]*Yarmouth Times*, 3 April 1908.
[59]*Montreal Herald*, 3,6, 12 November 1904 (Glasgow), 27 November (London); 14 January 1905 (Toronto); 5 June 1905 (Halifax); 24 September 1906 (Cape Breton).

fish in Mexico.[60] South American experiences, although rarely mentioned in his analytical works, would figure largely in the sea fiction he published. From 1903 to 1913, McKay published a series of sea stories in such magazines as *Adventure, McClure's* and *Ainslee's*.[61] On 20 December 1909 McKay sat for his second mate's papers.[62] It is very probable that it was while serving on the *Sokoto* that McKay became a Marxist and an apostle of "sociology."

Then in September, 1910, came a period of land-based stability. McKay settled in Saint John, New Brunswick, where he lived until 1914. Here he worked as a journalist with the Saint John *Standard*. McKay arrived in Saint John at a time when its labour and socialist circles were no less vibrant than those of Montreal ten years before. Saint John was a labour hotbed, with more strikes in the period 1901-1914 than any other Maritime city.[63] At the same time, Single Taxers, Fabians, and members of the Socialist Party of Canada (SPC) created a vigorous left outside of the mainstream parties. And the *Eastern Labor News* with its small but significant following, was close by in Moncton.[64]

McKay was also heavily involved, at the insistence of P.M.Draper of the TLC, in restarting the local Trades and Labour Council in Saint John. At the local TLC's first meetings, McKay was struck by the flamboyant interventions of local members of the SPC, one of whom once had a narrow escape from a violent attack because of his snide criticisms of trade unionism at a public meeting. Just as in his days in Montreal, McKay was unimpressed by this ultra-radical style. Of one Socialist who had provoked trade unionists, but then devoted himself to organizing the longshoremen, McKay remarked in 1913: "My own impression is that he has done more to make converts to Socialism by his connection with the trade union movement than by any of his speeches in the Socialist Hall" [§.71, "The Difficulties Faced By Socialists in the Maritimes"]. To be a Marxist intellectual meant something more than repeating the correct Marxist formulae and flamboyantly maintaining a position of sectarian purity: McKay would always be impatient with socialists who attached "more importance to Marxian phrases than to the Marxian method," and

---

[60]*Yarmouth Times*, 20 March 1908. It unfortunately appears to be impossible, because of a gap in the back files of the *Coast Guard*, to consult the original of this article.
[61]See Jackson and McKay, eds., *Windjammers and Bluenose Sailors*.
[62]Board of Trade Records, National Archives of Canada, B-4049, 28, Vol.7, p.44, #2875, McKay, Colin. He has apparently left no trace in the crew lists housed at the Maritime History Archives at Memorial University.
[63]See Ian McKay, "Strikes in the Maritimes, 1901-1914," in David J. Bercuson, ed., *Canadian Labour History: Selected Readings* (Toronto: Copp Clark, 1994): 128-130.
[64]According to *The Canadian Newspaper Directory* (Montreal: A. McKim and Co., 1911), the circulation of the paper was 750. However, it was widely quoted in the mainstream media. And this figure comes from early in the paper's history.

who failed to recognize the importance of trade unions [§.47, "The Importance of Trade Unions for Socialism," first published as "The Workers are Waking Up"]. "The pure-and-simple socialist who believes in nothing but political action," he wrote, aiming a clear shot at "impossibilists" who derided trade unionism, "is as bad as the pure and simple trade unionists. Labor must use all weapons possible" [§.47, "The Importance of Trade Unions for Socialism," first published as "The Workers are Waking Up"].

Rather surprisingly, given his earlier rejection of the SLP, and his continuing interest in working with the AFL in its bid to organize local workers, McKay gravitated towards the very SPC he had criticized for its ultra-leftist approach to the trade-union question. By March, 1913, he was the Secretary of the Saint John local of the SPC.[65] His decision to join the SPC can only be taken as evidence of his deepening radicalism, although we have no reflections from McKay's pen explaining why the political answers that had seemed satisfactory to him in 1900 -- utopian socialism linked to Liberalism -- no longer sufficed in 1913. Two general explanations can nonetheless be tentatively suggested to explain his rapid and thoroughgoing shift to the left.

First, along with many other workers of the day, McKay was disappointed with the Liberal Party as an instrument of labour reform and more generally of social progress As early as 1907, McKay was shouting his discontent. He saw the hand of corruption in Liberal monetary policy, and condemned W.S.Fielding, the Minister of Finance in the federal Liberal government, for currency legislation that gave the banks a present of $24,000,000.[66] The Tories were no better. By the time of the Reciprocity Election of 1911, McKay was convinced that the entire debate between the Liberals and the Conservatives over free trade was misconceived. (He would later make delighted use of Marx's aphorism "that free trade was of as much interest to the worker as the manner of its dressing was to a roast goose.")[67] Workers who allowed themselves to be distracted by the debate over tariff policy were deceiving themselves. For all that they blustered against protectionism and monopolies, Liberals had themselves long since rejected the fundamental principles of liberal political economy in practice. They were no longer, in any sense, really "radicals." The Laurier government took pains to assure manufacturers that "it has no intention of interfering with their privileges."[68] The federal Liberals (the very politicians McKay had eulogized in 1900) had become "the same old

---

[65]*Western Clarion*, 1 March 1913.

[66]Colin McKay, "What Chance Have the Plain People?" Letter to the *Halifax Herald*, 31 March 1908; see also Colin McKay, "Favored Finance: Methods of Money-Makers to Bunco the Multitude," *Yarmouth Times*, 5 March 1907.

[67]C.M., "Pearls from the Supposed Wise," *O.B.U.Bulletin*, 15 November 1932.

[68]Letter from Colin McKay, *Coast-Guard*, 3 August 1911.

group of grafters who have been handing the country over to the corporations."[69] On the provincial level, New Brunswick Liberals were equally hypocritical in championing "the economic sophistries which are the [logical] outgrowths of our high tariff doctrines." Whereas an older generation of protectionists had been disarmingly frank in admitting that the immediate purpose of protective tariffs was simply to help the capitalist (with workers reaping secondary benefits), the new "liberal protectionists" made hypocritical claims about direct benefits to workers and even primary producers. "Nowadays the principal argument for high tariffs is that by protecting the manufacturer we benefit the workingmen," he noted, even though the kind of capitalist development accelerated by protection simply further undermined the producers' independence and intensified the relative poverty of the workers [§.24, "The Master Magicians"]. Moreover Liberals, for all they had claimed to represent "the people" against "the interests," were no less corrupt than the Tories. In New Brunswick, there were constituencies where party leaders who had shouted against graft on the hustings, shortly afterwards sought to control companies engaged on public contracts.[70] One had only to look to Britain to see how workers organized in an effective labour party could do much more than the Liberals for the cause of justice.

Arguments for or against Reciprocity exposed not just the hypocrisy of the Liberals, but the outmoded philosophy of individualism to which they still appealed. In this limited sense, the Conservatives at least seemed dimly aware that something had changed in the body politic.

> The reciprocity arguments used by the liberals, being as they are based upon the old philosophy of individualism, appeal to the farmers who historically speaking have not advanced beyond the stage of individual production, who still use the individual tool and are consequently still possessed with the spirit of individualism. The anti-reciprocity arguments used by conservatives, being imbued with a perception -- hardly an adequate conception -- of the great part played by the principle of co-operation in modern progress, appeal with more or less force to the fruit growers, who have learned the advantage of co-operative effort over individual effort and are seized with the modern spirit; to the city workers who have long since abandoned the ideas of individualism which went with the use of the individual tool and have learned to adapt their ideas to the new industrial methods which associate the labour of many persons in the production of a single commodity; to the business men whose realization of the need of depending upon the cooperation of

---

[69]Colin McKay, Letter from Colin McKay, *Coast-Guard.* 31 August 1911.
[70]Colin McKay, "Time for a Labor Party is Now," letter to the *Eastern Labor News*, 11 November 1911.

many increases the extent and number of his business enterprises.[71]

But in fact , despite this interesting attempt at a Spencerian explanation of the political landscape of 1911, McKay was unable to see much of interest in the public profiles of the two parties. Neither Conservatives nor Liberals were able to respond creatively to the new age of capital.

McKay's writings could be misconstrued as being somewhat sympathetic to the Conservative side. They were not. He was sickened by both of the old parties. Perhaps mistakenly perceiving in his cynical comments on reciprocity and the Liberal Party a leaning towards Toryism, some Shelburne County Conservatives evidently toyed with the idea of running McKay as their candidate in 1911. McKay responded to them with a statement of his utter disillusionment with party politics in Canada. Young people were tired of "electing representatives whose only real business is to look after the distribution of local patronage." Parliaments in Canada suffered from paralysis, because the people were content to elect straight party representatives, whose function was merely to echo what their leaders said. Party organizations were controlled from above, and from without, never by the rank and file. Both parties were also dependent upon contributions from the big corporations, and so were careful not to offend their patrons by exposing the methods "by which the corporations rob the people." The same corporations contributed to both parties' campaign funds and paid out thousands of dollars "to maintain newspapers that call one another liars." They obviously knew that it was in their interest to keep politicians and newspapers busy, to allow the corporations "to pursue unmolested their manifold schemes for plundering the people." Canadian politics was a stale and puerile game of party politics, in which the dice were always loaded.[72] And it was idle "to blink the fact that protection is in some cases merely a form of graft."[73] Robert Borden's Finance Minister would be selected by the Bankers' Association just as Laurier's Finance Minister had been, and would be no less subservient "to the big bankers and financial grafters."[74]

Since 1900, in short, McKay -- in company with many trade-union leaders and rank-and-file workers -- had become disillusioned with the Liberal Party and no less unenthusiastic about the Conservatives. In his opinion, whatever encouraging political signs there were in 1911 could be found outside the brain-dead traditional parties. They could be found in a resurgent farmers' movement in the west, marching in large numbers on

---

[71]Colin McKay, "Reciprocity," *Coast-Guard*, 27 July 1911.

[72]Colin McKay, untitled letter, *Coast Guard*, 8 September 1910.

[73]Letter from Colin McKay, *Coast-Guard*, 3 August 1911.

[74]Colin McKay, "Time for a Labor Party is Now," letter to the *Eastern Labor News*, 11 November 1911.

Ottawa, and effecting and implicitly breaking with individualist liberalism in the very act of demanding that the Liberals live up to their principles; above all, they could be found in the idea of independent labour parties -- whether on the model Keir Hardie had made famous in Britain and which he had recently popularized during a tour through the region, or on the more modest scale of the labour parties shooting up across the Dominion, especially in Saint John and Halifax.[75] These new forces were at least challenging the dead hand of an individualist liberalism that had yielded control over the lives of Canadians to corporate interests.

A second general explanation for McKay's radicalization in the years from 1906 to 1910 was his exposure to a wide range of new books, many of which he no doubt read at sea. This self-education in socialist classics made him impatient with ideologies that emphasized individual moral renewal rather than systematic change. His socialism in 1900 had been Christian in tone (although, one must say, rather vague in theological terms: an Arminian belief in the goodness of human nature and Christ's love for humanity was not placed in the context of doctrines concerning salvation, grace, and so on). His socialism in 1910 was more secular, collectivist, and professedly revolutionary. He had done a lot of reading. His grasp of Herbert Spencer became more critical and more wide-ranging; he read extensively in American and European sociology; and he explored the many Socialist works published by the remarkable Charles H. Kerr Company of Chicago, from whose catalogue a generation of North American radicals acquired their understanding of evolution and economics.

Most important, McKay read Marx. Just when he started to think of himself as a Marxist is unclear, but it is certain that by the time he started writing for the *Eastern Labor News* in Saint John, McKay had read a good deal of Marx and Engels, certainly the first volume of *Capital*, the *Communist Manifesto*, and perhaps a few other titles. (Of course, many of what are now considered to be the most interesting and important writings of Marx -- such as the *Grundrisse* and the *Economic and Philosophic Manuscripts* were not then accessible: some existed only in manuscript form, and others had not be translated). After this point, his social and economic writings refer to Marx as a respected authority on the patterns of evolution of a capitalist order. McKay seems to have followed a consistent path away from the Christian idealistic socialism of the turn of the century towards a social-evolutionary understanding of the world. He had also delved deeply into the anthropological writings of Morgan, the evolutionary theories of Huxley, the sociological theories of Small, Ward and Spencer, the political economy of J.A.Hobson, and the historically-based theological writings underpinning the Social Gospel. By 1911, McKay had clearly evolved into a very different kind of socialist than he

---

[75]Colin McKay, "The Dignity of Labor," *Coast-Guard*, 5 January 1911.

had been in 1900. The man who had once mocked the Socialist Labor Party now sensed no contradiction in holding office in a party whose leadership outrivalled that of the SLP in its claims to doctrinal purity.

Yet the puzzle of McKay's gravitating to the SPC may be more apparent than real, for the SPC was a more complicated and dispersed body than one that can be easily summed up with words like "impossibilist" and "chiliasm." The SPC seems to have had room for rebels of many stripes; it may also have varied markedly from centre to centre. The SPC in Saint John diverged radically from the conventional image of the SPC as a sect of theory-crazed fanatics, indifferent to trade unionism and content to pursue a goal of unqualified political purity (Campbell's recent work has called this characterization sharply into question).[76] Perhaps thanks to grounded working-class intellectuals like McKay, Roscoe Fillmore, Seaman Terris, and scores of coal miners, the SPC in the Maritimes was not often sidetracked into abstract and unproductive discussions over the ultimate value of trade unionism, and was more inclined to consolidate links with the wider working-class and progressive movement. The SPC in the region certainly seemed to find a greater possibility for subtlety and originality in its labour politics than is alleged to have been the case in the West.[77] In Saint John, the SPC local was not particularly distant from the labour movement; one prominent socialist, Fred Hyatt, had played a key role in the formation of a longshore union affiliated with the International Longshoremen's Association in 1911,[78] and McKay himself was involved in the reconstitution of the Saint John Trades and Labor Council in the same period. McKay's reports as Secretary of the local SPC suggest a lively social network of comrades, with regular propaganda meetings, New Year's parties that broke up at 1 a.m. after ample servings of turkey, and the holding of fairs to pay the rent of the local's hall.[79] Notwithstanding the early provocations documented by McKay, the SPC in Saint John did not separate itself from the city's trade unions; nor, evidently, did it lavish time on the correct line of interpretation with regard to Marx.

So McKay, who lacked an inner will to dogmatism, seems to have been quite at home in the local SPC, which -- like other elements of the party -- did not live up to the party's perhaps rather exaggerated sectarian image.

---

[76]See Peter Campbell, "'Stalwarts of the Struggle': Canadian Marxists of the Third Way, 1879-1939." PhD Thesis, Queen's University, 1991

[77]Note David Frank and Nolan Reilly, "The Emergence of the Socialist Movement in the Maritimes, 1899-1916," *Labour/Le Travailleur*, 4 (1979): 85-113. The major published work that developed the image of SPC impossibilism in the West is A. Ross McCormack, *Reformers, Rebels, and Revolutionaries: The Western Canadian Radical Movement, 1899-1919* (Toronto: University of Toronto Press, 1977).

[78]See Robert Babcock, "Saint John Longshoremen During the Rise of Canada's Winter Port, 1895-1922," *Labour/Le Travail* 25 (Spring 1990): 32.

[79]*Western Clarion*, 1 March 1913.

It appears that, for once, he even had a circle of close friends and associates. The pre-war years in Saint John were perhaps the happiest and most productive of his life. He enjoyed his full-time job at the Saint John *Standard;* he was able to help sustain both the *Eastern Labor News* (writing no fewer than 119 signed articles over four years) and the local Socialist Party; and he served as a correspondent for the *Western Clarion* and *B.C.Federationist* in British Columbia and the *Industrial Banner* in Ontario. In these years he wrote some of his most interesting essays on working-class culture and socialist politics.

Then why leave it all for service in the Great War, on behalf of the distant British Empire? Certainly others in the Saint John left protested against the war; at least one was arrested for anti-recruiting speeches. McKay followed the path taken by many male socialists in Europe and North America. He apparently never attempted to justify this decision, but one may surmise that it had much to do with his complete identification with Britain. To an extent late-twentieth century Canadians find difficult to imagine, the Empire was not distant for a man like McKay: he was more a citizen of the British Empire than he was of the Dominion, and "Greater Britain" was the imagined community to which he belonged. British authors, British politicians, British place names: all of these figure easily in his writing, as aspects of his imagined "home" which he assumes do not need to be explained to the reader. (Such sentiments were particularly strong in the Maritimes, where seafarers and traders had long seen themselves as part of a British imperium.) Only a few Socialists took an overtly anti-British stance in the early years of the war. Even the most radical miners -- many of whom were to form the core of the Communist movement in the 1920s -- did not condemn the war effort. Although imperial nationalism had never been a predominant theme of his early writing, in 1909 McKay, in the context of a polemic on the Canadian Navy Question, had questioned the view that fishermen would automatically submit themselves in times of peace to service in the Canadian navy, and had called for a more "patriotic standpoint" from the Canadian government along lines already developed in France and the United States.[80] Apart from this, we have very little to go on in understanding McKay's decision to join the war effort. It was entirely in line with that taken by most members of socialist parties affiliated with the Socialist International.

In May, 1915, McKay -- who had polemicized against war as a capitalist plot not a year before -- offered his services to the Empire in its struggle against Germany. He signed up as 3rd officer on the S.S. *St. George.*

---

[80]*Yarmouth Times*, 30 July 1909; Colin McKay, "The Crews for A Canadian Navy," *The Globe* (Toronto), 24 July 1909. In this *Globe* polemic, McKay went so far as to refer to Canada's indifference to foreign involvement in coastal shipping as a "sorry reflection upon our Imperialism"!

Previously on the Saint John-Digby route, the C.P.R. steamer had been requisitioned by the British Admiralty and was slated to serve as a hospital ship on the channel run between France and England as part of the "Butterfly Fleet." a term coined by naval transport authorities to describe boats carrying troops across the English Channel. This fleet carried over ten million passengers during the course of the war. It was dangerous work, with the constant threat of attacks from U-boats and enemy aircraft.[81] McKay signed up for it after completing a series of articles (remarkably frank given the context) on the state of the British war effort, which were published in the Saint John *Standard.*

On the H.M.S. *St. George*, McKay served as second officer and settled into the routine of delivering wounded soldiers from Rouen to Southampton. On September 18, 1915, McKay jumped overboard from the vessel to rescue a wounded and deranged soldier who had attempted to commit suicide by drowning. Fellow officers of the H.M.S. *St. George* were lavish in their praise of McKay's heroism and forwarded a detailed account of his actions back home for publication in the *Standard*. Apart from this incident, he seems to have had a relatively uneventful war.[82] He returned to Saint John, N.B. aboard the troop carrier H.M.S. *Metagama* in February 1919 and resumed his post as a journalist in Saint John.

The reticent McKay seems never to have explained why he went to war, nor what inner meaning the experience later held for him. Patriotic attachment to the Empire was certainly part of his earlier writings, which are suffused with a sense of imperial culture typical of Anglo-Canadians of his day. And like many Canadians, the Great War was a turning point for him in how he saw the world: the ultimate consequence of the war was to impress him with the irrationality of the capitalist system and to concentrate his attention more closely on Canadian problems and Canadian interests. Even as early as 1917, a critical tone had entered a letter he sent to his mother in Shelburne: "Well the war is still going on, and lots of people are making money out of it."[83]

However, McKay's views were not immediately radicalized by the War. His politics in the immediate postwar period avoided issues of class conflict -- at the time of the Winnipeg General Strike and the labour wars in Cape Breton -- and spoke comfortably of the interests of "the community." (In avoiding radicalization in the early 1920s, McKay was not typical of his generation of workers and socialists). He approved, for example, of the emergence of more institutionalized procedures for negotiations between capital and labour. It seems McKay believed sincerely in the promises of

---

[81] See McKay's description of the operations in *Shelburne Gazette and Coast Guard*, 27 March 1919.

[82] See the Saint John *Standard*, 30 October 1915.

[83] *Shelburne Gazette and Coast Guard*, 22 February 1917.

social reform made in the course of the Great War, and particularly in the promise -- ratified at Versailles, so it was often thought -- of a new deal for labour.

These promises were not kept. In the wake of the war came a serious economic slump, felt particularly in Britain, but with international repercussions. The "heroes" of the Great War, promised decent homes and a new world order, received lay-offs and wage reductions instead. In 1922, a disillusioned McKay published a vicious parody of "Flanders Fields" (it must have seemed shocking to do this so soon after the conflict) that summed up his sense of broken promises.

> *In London streets ex-soldiers go,*
> *Unkempt, ill-fed and wan with woe,*
> *Seeking a job, or with the cry:*
> *"For God's sake, buy some shoe-strings; my*
> *Missus is sick, my kiddies cold."*
>
> *Heroes they were short days agone,*
> *Marching through hell in the thundering dawn,*
> *Smashing the power of a haughty foe,*
> *Saving the world for a shilling or so,*
> > *In Flander's mud.*
>
> *The quarrel is done -- the victory vain --*
> *The torch is out and the faith forgot --*
> *And broken men in the murk and rain*
> > *Stand mazed in London gutters.*
>
> *Their country does not need them now.*
> *To the gods of gold their masters bow,*
> *And cynically smile at the tommyrot*
> *They bravely talked when the terror stalked*
> > *Thro' Flanders' fields...*
>
> *On Flanders' fields the poppies droop,*
> *And dead men rising, troop on troop,*
> > *Go stumbling thro' the dismal rain;*
> *Grim, mangled horrors, mad with pain*
> *And anger that they cannot sleep,*
> > *In Flanders' fields.*[84]

---

[84]McK., "In London Streets," *Canadian Railroad Employees' Monthly*, Vol.8, No. 12 (February 1923), 209. The attribution of this poem to McKay seems reasonably safe on the grounds of style, not to mention his frequent use of this *nom de plume*.

There was McKay's verdict on the "Great War." His writings would, from this point on, no longer take for granted a "common sense" of British patriotism. He identified himself strictly with Canada and with the Canadian working class: his frequent analyses of the world situation would now be written from a Canada-centred perspective. He became a Canadian labour nationalist, deeply convinced that Canadian workers must follow their own independent path: like so many Canadians, perhaps, his disillusionment with the war affected his perceptions of the Empire for which it had been fought.

He resumed his old ways, wandering from city to city, boarding house to boarding house.[85] With no immediate family, geographically and perhaps spiritually somewhat distant from his family of origin, and few close associates, labour journalism became his vital connection to the wider world. McKay was in fact living the life of rootless modernity that he had critiqued so eloquently in some of his early Montreal writings. One great unifying thread in this wayward life was a connection to labour journalism and the labour movement. A second was his continuing attachment to Nova Scotia, which seems to have served as a kind of symbolic anchor for him. For all his advanced reading in sociology and his questioning of religious and social certainties, McKay always had a home to come back to: he was securely rooted in his family, his community, and in the landscape of the Maritimes. When he went looking for illustrations of "The Evolution of Property" in 1931, he naturally brought up the perfidious Duchess of Sutherland, whose evictions in the far north of Scotland had particular bearing on the history of the McKay clan during the Highland Clearances (§.42, "The Evolution of Property"). He was proud of the legacy of Donald McKay, the legendary Nova Scotian shipbuilder to whom a memorial was erected in 1925.[86] Although in a sense an "exile" by virtue of his long periods of life in Montreal, Ottawa, Britain, and France, McKay also spent many years in Saint John as a journalist with the *Standard* and some time in Halifax, where he was the day officer for the Canadian Press. More than most of his contemporaries, he sought out the realities of the Maritimes first-hand. He went out on the trawlers and the schooners, and visited the shipyards; sometimes the source of his insights into the sentiments of small businessmen in the Maritimes seems to have been his own father [See, for example, §.61, "The Knockabout Schooner"]. He would return, again and again, to Nova Scotia for renewal.

After a short stint at the Saint John *Standard* after the war, McKay worked in Halifax as editor of the Maritime Day Service of the Canadian Press. It

---

[85]His final address in Ottawa was 37 York Street, near the Bytown Market, a boarding house owned by Wilfrid and Gracia Tasse. This boarding house no longer stands. *The Ottawa City Directory*, 1938 (Ottawa: Might Directories, 1938): 374.

[86]Colin McKay, "The Donald McKay Memorial," *Canadian Fisherman*, July 1925, 221.

was as a Canadian Press correspondent that McKay launched, in the columns of the Halifax *Herald* and on the pages of the *Canadian Fisherman*, a campaign for an international schooner race. According to fellow journalist Andrew Merkel, McKay "sold Dennis [the publisher of the *Herald*] the idea it would be a good thing to promote a series of races among the Nova Scotia fishermen, at the close of their Summer season on the Banks, as the preliminary to an international contest, between the fleetest fishing schooners of the United States and Canada."[87] On 11 August 1920 Colin McKay published in the *Herald* an article entitled "Why Not A Fishermen's Race For Canada and The States?" which appears to have been the first public airing of the idea of the race.[88] McKay could link his advocacy of the race with his socialist principles: for a Marxist, the progressive improvement of the "social forces of production" -- in this case, the fishing fleet -- was something which would hasten the coming of a more rational economic system. (The races would then be something like laboratory tests). If the races became annual events, he predicted, their effect would be to give "a stimulus to the improvement of the build and design of fishing vessels," provided organizers rigidly adhered to the principle that entries should be limited to vessels which were equipped as they would be if they were strictly fishing vessels.[89] It is a piquant fact that the *Bluenose*, that durable figment of the Maritimes tourism industry and the icon of conservative neo-nationalism in Nova Scotia, can claim at least one Marxist grandparent.

In the Fall of 1922, McKay travelled back to Europe as a Canadian Press correspondent reporting on post-war reconstruction, and then was subsequently employed as a night editor for a newspaper in Paris. He returned home to join the editorial staff of both the Saint John *Standard* and then the Quebec *Chronicle*. His final journalistic resting place was in Ottawa, where he laboured as the parliamentary correspondent of the Montreal *Standard*.

Through the 1920s, McKay's labour writings became more radical and more sophisticated, as he read intensively and widely in the field of economics. There was a new confidence, a new acuteness, to his work. He ranged across various theories of political economy to back up his arguments. And these theories were interwoven with an astute selection of data. Many of the facts cited by McKay were acquired as he worked at his day job in the mainstream press; at night, they were then presented in the far different light of radical political economy. He came to have an impressive grasp of the history of economic thought. As the editor of one journal remarked, "In addition to his regular job as a press reporter, he

---

[87] Andrew Merkel, "Racing Fishermen," Draft Manuscript, Merkel Papers, MS.2 326, C.9, Dalhousie University Archives.
[88] *Herald*, 11 August 1920.
[89] *Herald*, 30 October 1920.

toiled late into the night to explain to the workers the occurrences and tendencies of the times, and to suggest how the useful section of the community might best protect its interests. Always he related the present to the past in pointing to the future. The works of the classical philosophers and economists were at his elbow and their teachings were familiar in his mouth as household words. He wrote with authority, challenging authority...."[90] Another writer remembered him as "a Socialist. More than that, he was a Socialist who had read his Marx, who had read as well the classical economists. He could speak as familiarly (though he would despise the thought of parading his knowledge) of Mill and Spencer and Bentham and Adam Smith as he could of contemporary leaders."[91]

By the 1930s, McKay had achieved a reputation, at least among trade unionists, as Canada's premier labour economist. As a staff correspondent on the International Labor News Service, and contributor to a half dozen labour and socialist publications he reached a wide public. His publication record was impressive: he was a frequent writer in the *One Big Union Bulletin* (162 contributions), the *Canadian Unionist* (83), *Labour World/Le Monde Ouvrier* (274) and the *Canadian Railway Employees Monthly* (64). Of the 951 pieces of McKay's writing we have located, no fewer than 545 were written in the 1930s. His work covers an extraordinary range of subjects. We find commentaries on philosophy, labour organization, theories of evolution, economic theory, the One Big Union, the Communist Party, the Co-operative Commonwealth Federation, the causes of the Depression, and the imminence of Fascism. More impressive, perhaps, is the intensity of McKay's drive to analyze the underlying causes of events and his mastery of left-wing economic theory.

On returning from Europe, McKay resumed the practical work with trade unions that had marked his periods in Montreal and Saint John. He advised the Canadian Brotherhood of Railway Employees on various railway amalgamation schemes, and became something of a labour expert on the intricacies of the Canadian railway system.[92] (A number of the unsigned editorials in the *Canadian Railway Employees Monthly* were written by him.) Within the All-Canadian Congress of Labour, his views acquired particular status. McKay 's was one of the more influential voices pressing for the establishment of the new Congress, and he apparently even helped the new centre come up with its name.[93] From his extensive participation in *Le Monde Ouvrier/The Labor World*, one can sense that McKay had a continuing sense of connection with Montreal and its labour movement, although it would be an exaggeration to claim that he was a key figure in that newspaper's columns, in the labour movement in

---

[90]*Labor Review*, 3 (February 1939): 29.

[91]*Ottawa Journal*, 14 February 1939.

[92]*Canadian Railway Employees' Monthly*, March 1939.

[93]*Canadian Unionist*, February 1939.

Montreal, or even in editor Gustave Francq's network.[94] In these Ottawa years, McKay more than ever was a "specific intellectual," providing insights for (but never seeking to dominate) the workers' movement. As one of the ACCL's most important writers and thinkers, he obviously felt responsible for undertaking specific acts of economic analysis, and to that end integrated a wide range of theories. On the other hand, he never relinquished his intellectual independence as a free-thinking Marxist. At a time when A.R.Mosher was seeking an alliance between labour and the CCF, for example, McKay brought out his tough-minded critique of the party.

What sort of man was Colin McKay? No collection of private papers, and only a few letters, are available to us. McKay seemingly preferred the company of books over that of most other human beings. He was a lifelong bachelor, and (one infers from his virtually all-male short stories and the tone of distant chivalry of his polemics on women's rights) was such by choice. One imagines McKay lived most vividly when he was at sea and when he was writing. Perhaps writing was his way of keeping the world at bay -- of both distancing himself from humanity at the same time as he sought to connect with it. Irony, satire, and self-deprecating humour were characteristic of a good McKay article. Even the most serious of personal reversals -- imprisonment in Montreal, exposure to mass death in the Great War -- could provide materials for deadpan irony. The same weapons of irony could be trained with telling effect on pompous prime ministers, the local business class, and self-proclaimed "economists". He often deflated the pretensions of the present by pointing out just how much "modern" thinkers were merely rehashing the views of long-dead prophets and mystics. There was a substantial streak of cynicism in his

---

[94]On Francq 's ideology, see Geoffrey Ewen, "The Ideas of Gustave Francq on Trade Unionism and Social Reform as Expressed in *Le Monde Ouvrier/The Labor World*, 1916-1921," M.A. Thesis, University of Ottawa, 1982, and André E. Leblanc, "Le Monde Ouvrier/The Labor World (1916-1926): an Analysis of Thought and a Detailed Index," D.E.S. Thesis (History), University of Montreal, 1971. It is difficult to say whether McKay's attachment to *Le Monde Ouvrier/The Labor World* was a product of a personal connection with Francq, or arose from a more general sense of political obligation. A continuing Marxist and critic of the AFL such as McKay would have had grave difficulties with the tone of the newspaper in the late 1930s, when the conservative Bernard Rose figured as one of its key writers. ("We are against all subversive movement [sic] as a menace to organized labor, and the democratically organized society in which capitalism can function," the newspaper proclaimed on 12 August 1939. "We are proudly and defiantly Canadian!") It seems telling that, having published at least 274 pieces by McKay in the 1920s and 1930s, *Le Monde Ouvrier/The Labor World* did not see fit to give him an obituary. But on 3 June 1939, there *was* room -- on the front page -- for a fulsome tribute to the visiting Royal Family, and the entire issue was "respectfully dedicated to Their Gracious Majesties with the loyal homage and respects of the Editor and Staff."

writings -- it seems he found real joy in writing debunking, satirical attacks on revered authorities and traditions. McKay did not expect life to be easy, and did not waste time detailing his sufferings nor those of the working class in general. He had a modest sense of what one person could do and of his own role in the labour movement. He was a stoic and a realist.

At the same time, there was a strain of wistful romanticism in him. He celebrated the simple pleasures of growing up in rural Nova Scotia, the ties of community in fishing communities, the glories of the "Age of Sail." He had a firm sense, never explicitly articulated, of right and wrong. His polemics were always governed by an underlying sense of restraint: the typical McKay polemic was more an exercise in irony than in malice, and lacked the bloodthirstiness of so much contemporaneous writing on the left. (Even in writing of the enemy in war, McKay seemed to lack any real hatred). McKay had seen a great deal of the world, and this perhaps made him less likely to judge individuals harshly. What he did judge harshly was the logic of the capitalist system. Stoically accepting the capitalist revolution as a fact, *the* fact of modern life, McKay reserved the right to dissent from its values. After his day job was done, alone in his study, he would set to work destabilizing the solemn truths of his time, and developing a more human and progressive framework of understanding. As he got older, McKay withdrew more and more into his favourite books. Whether or not he found his quasi-monastic existence satisfying or painful is impossible to say.

All those who described McKay in his later years characterized him as reserved, quiet, and unassuming. "Colin McKay had no intimates," reflected the *Labor Review* at the time of his death. "A sturdy, lonely figure, inordinately modest, he never spoke about his personal affairs, but his reticence was relieved by a cynical humour."[95] The *Canadian Unionist* said of McKay, "One of the most reticent of men, he had no intimates, and much of his career must remain unknown."[96] The editor of the *Canadian Fisherman* remembered a man who was "reserved and unassuming, though possessed of a quiet sense of humour which enlivened his apparently serious and reticent manner."[97] "He was not a man to make a display of affection," added the *Canadian Railway Employees Monthly*, "but he had a deep love for his fellow-workers, a sympathetic understanding of their problems, a keen interest in their welfare. He was of an exceptionally quiet and retiring disposition, utterly unselfish, asking

---

[95] *Labour Review*, Vol.3, No.2 (February 1939): 29. On the other hand, the Halifax *Herald*, 14 February 1939, commented: "Now he has gone from us at a comparatively early age... and he will be missed by the many with whom he had formed genuine and enduring friendships." But this has the insincere sound of a formula obituary.
[96] *Canadian Unionist*, February 1939.
[97] *Canadian Fisherman*, March 1939.

understanding of their problems, a keen interest in their welfare. He was of an exceptionally quiet and retiring disposition, utterly unselfish, asking only for an opportunity to serve in the way for which he was best fitted."[98] The *Shelburne Coast-Guard* simply observed that McKay had "a quiet unassuming disposition and was never known to tell about his success in the profession in which he was engaged."[99] His friend Moses H. Nickerson thought that McKay's unassuming disposition had cost him a high public position.[100] In the hands of the *Ottawa Journal*, the image of the unassuming McKay attained truly romantic proportions:

> A lone wolf, he lived on his own spiritual and intellectual resources, content with his own company and the companionship of his books. He had, one thought, no intimates, and he never spoke of friends. When he died in Ottawa on Saturday, only a few paragraphs in the newspapers chronicled the fact. It was what he would have liked.

> Humanity is compounded of strange human beings. Colin McKay was one of the strangest. In many ways, and certainly in sheer characterful independence, he was one of the greatest.[101]

"He was alone, with the awful solitude of a vast, strange city.... Around him were wealth, beauty, happiness, but in these he had no part." What McKay had written about the sailor ashore in Montreal in 1896 might have had a wider resonance in his own wandering life.[102] He often seemed alone in the vast, strange cities of capitalism. His life seems to have found its centre and meaning in the attempt to map their streets. In the lonely hours of the early morning, McKay would repair the awful solitude of modern life by connecting again with a broader working-class humanity, as he found it in his books and as he knew it in the unions. The books became his real intimates, and he knew them very well, so well that he could paraphrase long passages and distill entire arguments in a few of his own words. He had deeply internalized his books, and the quest for a socialist future that they embodied. And in that way, one would like to think, he did find the inner wealth and happiness that the capitalist order had otherwise denied him. McKay's compassion for others, his wry sense of humour, his unselfishness, his passionate enjoyment of the language of the Bible and Shakespeare, his deep love of learning, and (above all) his fierce, 40-year loyalty to the cause of working-class emancipation -- all these are to be found in the writings and the life themselves. The sources,

---

[98] *Canadian Railway Employees Monthly,* March 1939.
[99] *Shelburne Coast Guard,* 10 February 1939.
[100] *Shelburne Coast-Guard,* 2 March 1939.
[101] *Ottawa Journal,* 14 February 1939.
[102] *Montreal Herald,* 15 December 1896. Assuming, of course, the 1896 writer was McKay.

Colin McKay died in Ottawa from heart failure on February 10, 1939, at the age of 63. The mainstream obituaries were respectful, if undiscerning. Back home in Shelburne, the *Coast-Guard* singled out his "clever sea stories" and (of all things) a minor piece of promotional writing boosting New Brunswick in the book *Commercial Canada*; his reputation as an able writer on economics, his socialism, his imprisonment, and his commitment to the labour movement went unrecorded.[103] The Halifax *Herald* referred to his radicalism, but in a patronizing and off-hand manner: "If in the pre-war years he was regarded as 'a bit radical' it was because he had moved on a little in advance of most of the rest of us. He was an able writer, and his 'radicalism' was sound because he believed in facts and had an unusual store of knowledge in a well-ordered mind."[104]

The labour obituaries were more insightful. The *Labor Review* observed, "He was a worker in the workers' cause, intent on contributing the last ounce of his energy, through an intellect burnished to brilliancy in life's battle, for the alleviation of the lot of his fellows, and it is as such that he would want to be remembered."[105] For the *Canadian Unionist,* writing from the vantage point of national industrial unionism, McKay's greatest single contribution was seen to be his critical analysis of labour questions. "No writer in this country has defended more ably the rise of National unionism, or discussed with greater insight the desirability of independence for Canadian workers," the *Unionist* observed. "While those of us who are closely associated with the National movement must be grateful for the invaluable assistance he gave to it... It is no small part of Colin McKay's service to the movement... that he was instrumental in promoting the idea of an "All-Canadian" Congress. It may be added that no one associated with it took greater pride in its progress and achievements than he did."[106]

The *Canadian Railway Employees Monthly* struck perhaps the most fitting note. It called upon McKay's admirers to remember the cause to which he was so devoted. It then chose for McKay's requiem the lines of Robert Louis Stevenson, who too had wandered the earth :

Under the wide and starry sky,
Dig the grave and let me lie.
Glad did I live and gladly die,
And I laid me down with a will.

[103]*Shelburne Coast-Guard*, 16 February 1939.
[104]Halifax *Herald*, 14 February 1939. There was evidently no editorial comment in the Halifax *Chronicle*.
[105]*Labour Review*, Vol.3, No.2 (February 1939): 29
[106]*Canadian Unionist* February 1939

This be the verse you grave for me:
Her he lies where he longed to be,
Home is the sailor, home from the sea,
And the hunter, home from the hill.[107]

Colin McKay is buried in Shelburne, Nova Scotia, within sight and sound of the sea.

---

[107] *Canadian Railway Employees Monthly,* March 1939.

PART I

If Christ Came To Montreal:

A Liberal Christian Progressive Looks at Society, 1897-1906

In this section are gathered nineteen articles by Colin McKay from his "liberal" period. They document the depth of McKay's belief in the tenets of liberalism, his interest in linking liberalism and labour, and his later enthusiasm for a number of progressive reforms consistent with a liberal order. They also suggest the extent to which turn-of-the-century liberals were scrambling to find coherent approaches to a world whose economic and social realities made their individualist premises seem increasingly dated.

1. The World of a Turn-of-the-Century Working-Class Liberal

McKay looked at Montreal -- and urban capitalism in general -- through eyes unaccustomed to its ways and values. He measured Montreal, in part, against the standards of his Nova Scotia upbringing. Throughout the entire forty years, from the 1890s to the 1930s, that McKay was to spend analyzing the mysteries of capitalism, he would often return to the stark contrast he first developed in his writings on Montreal, between the self-sufficiency and individualism of small-town Nova Scotia and the instability and wage-dependence of the urban proletariat. In the 1930s, he would recall the natural resources which sustained a sense of independence in the Nova Scotia of his childhood:

> When I was a youngster, in the way of sport, before or after school, it was an easy matter to supply the family larder with game and fish. One shot rabbits, partridge and woodchuck with a bow and arrow, and caught lobsters and salmon with a fish spear. With hook and line one caught all kinds of sea and river fish within a mile radius; with a fowling piece one shot plenty of wild duck and geese, and with a rifle deer and moose. But capitalist enterprise has wiped out the forests, dried up the river, destroyed the natural plenty, created artificial scarcity.[1]

---

[1]Colin McKay, untitled letter, *Labor World/Le Monde Ouvrier*, 17 March 1934.

There was often a certain element of romanticism in McKay's evocations of a recent time of pioneer self-sufficiency, starkly contrasted to the present day of dependence and poverty under capitalism. Actually, as was suggested in the introduction, McKay's upbringing had represented a complex blend of independence and insecurity. McKay knew, at first hand, both the qualified independence of life in rural Nova Scotia and the precariousness of the master artisan's circumstances at a time of rapid change. The figures of the embattled "labour aristocrat" and "small businessman," the theme of the struggling fishing and farming communities, were never very far from his conception of the world, and his sociological writings return to them repeatedly. Gathering from the way he cited Marx's *Capital,* the passages in Marx that spoke to him most powerfully were those explaining how once-independent producers had been forced off the land.

For the young McKay, there was something new, overpowering, and strange about the capitalist system. Whether measured against the ideal of a "propertied independence"[2] based on the resources of land and sea, or against that of the "craft independence" of the master shipbuilder or skilled worker in a merchant economy, capitalism entailed drastic change. It destabilized and destroyed old values -- particularly the Christian values McKay had internalized in the evangelical Anglican home of his youth. Capitalism, he would often say, rode like a juggernaut over living beings. He had a sharp sense, sharper than most of his contemporaries, that capitalism's social arrangements were novel, that its "laws" were not those of eternity. McKay experienced capitalism in a defamiliarized manner: it always, even in the 1930s, seemed a shocking way to live. He spent his entire life as a working-class intellectual trying to map the labyrinth of capitalism and escape the monster at its core. Metaphors suggesting the "unnatural" and the "uncanny" -- of monstrosity and insanity -- were never far away from a McKay description of modern capitalism, much as he also always tried to capture the processes of capitalism as natural processes occurring in a rational world.

Yet McKay in Montreal was no awestruck provincial on his first visit to the big city. Like many Nova Scotians of his day, he was well-connected to the wider North Atlantic world of social movements and ideas: he in no way was isolated from the currents of his time. As a merchant seaman he knew the streets of Boston, Saint John, Halifax, Portland, Liverpool, London, and Bristol; in the first decade of the twentieth century, he would frequently compare Montreal unfavourably to the planned, progressive cities of Europe. His seafaring experiences gave him something more than a broader international vision than many of his contemporaries:

---

[2]For a remarkable exploration of this ideal in one Maritime context, see Rusty Bittermann, "Escheat!: Rural Protest on Prince Edward Island, 1832-1842," Ph.D. Thesis, University of New Brunswick, 1991.

they also gave him a perspective from which to view danger and crisis on land. A man who (as we have seen) could blithely report having experienced shipwreck, fire at sea, imprisonment, hurricanes, hunger, frostbite and the other perils of the life of a "sailor and rover,"[3] who had witnessed men on the verge of committing cannibalism [§.13, "What Workingmen Expect of the Church: A Rebuttal by Colin McKay"], and who had been in Puerto Rico during the Spanish-American War and in Cuba during the second American occupation of that island,[4] was unlikely to quake in terror before a judge in a Montreal courtroom. Nor was he likely to be overawed by the pious respectability of the middle class, whose comforts and sense of security rested on the sweated labour of men in the stokeholds of steamers and of women in the city's tenements. There was personal experience as well as moral exhortation in the labour poem he wrote in 1899:

> Oh, come, my toiling brother, yielding body, soul and brain,
> An awful sacrifice unto the master's greed of gain,
> --And come, my gentle sister, weaving in the woof of wealth,
> The happiness and womanhood, thy beauty and thy health.
> [§.10, "Fight for the Cause, Ye Workingmen."]

His activism was based not on an abstract moral objection to capitalism, but on the hard-won practical knowledge of a merchant seaman: throughout his life, McKay would be impatient with abstractions and ideals that did not connect with the realities of exploitation and work as he knew them first-hand. Although fired with the most intense idealism, he had little use for utopian political romances that were unlikely to be of practical assistance in changing the world.

One has the image of a proud, self-taught, fearless and perhaps rather arrogant young man, who loved the cut-and-thrust of debate, and who took up with enthusiasm (and a certain degree of showmanship) the rôle of one of the leading labour lights of turn-of-the-century Montreal. A habitué of the Fraser Library, McKay loved books, especially those brought out by Charles H. Kerr & Company, which he devoured. His articles of this time radiate with the enthusiasm, the love of learning, the drive of a young self-taught thinker, who took delight in standing up to the rich and their stuffy intellectual apologists and showing their ideas to be superficial, confused, short-sighted, and impractical. (With the benefit of mature, and chastened, hindsight, he would look back and find his own positions of this time equally confused and "sentimental.") McKay was never deferential to those whose book-learning and social position had given them official qualifications as society's intellectuals. He was loftily

---

[3]*Adventure*, 6, 2 (June 1913): 216-217.
[4]Colin McKay, "The Socialist View of War," *Eastern Labor News*, 8 March 1913.

indifferent to status, wealth, and position. Although he became sharply critical of individualism as an approach to society, he was nonetheless very much his own man. The ideal of the free individual's pursuit of knowledge and the right to speak truth to power were always to be bedrock values for him.

During his first years in Montreal, McKay was a radical working-class liberal, who took inspiration from the promise of equality implied by liberal doctrine. Many workers and primary producers in nineteenth-century Canada viewed liberalism from this perspective, as a politico-ethical creed centred on human freedom -- freedom of expression, freedom of association, freedom of trade -- and permanently opposed to the "vested interests," monopolies, class privileges and corrupt practices of the world around them.[5] In 1899, when McKay came to found his own short-lived newspaper, he fittingly called it *Canada's Democracy.*[6]

Rank held no intellectual privileges in this framework. In a polemic with the eminent liberal professor Goldwin Smith, on the issue of unemployment, McKay noted that years earlier the learned Smith -- the former Regius professor of history at Oxford -- had argued that thrift and increased facilities for saving would contribute to the alleviation of inequality. Workers, on the other hand, had taken a very different view -- and they had proved the professor wrong. No wonder they had developed

---

[5]There are significant parallels here with British working-class liberalism, and (less obviously) with Italy. Gramsci, for example, before 1913, was a regionalist (Sardinian) critic of Italian protectionism, who initially abandoned Italian liberalism because it had turned its back on free trade. Dante Germino, *Antonio Gramsci: Architect of a New Politics.* (Baton Rouge and London: Louisiana State University Press, 1990): 21, 76. For a fine study of Canadian workers and turn-of-the-century liberalism -- although I think one that also may tend to overemphasize the extent to which we can speak of labourism as a distinct ideological current on the Canadian left -- see Craig Heron, "Labourism and the Canadian Working Class," *Labour/Le Travail* 13 (Spring 1984): 45-76. If McKay is anything to go by, one could simultaneously be a utopian socialist, a labourite, and a supporter of the federal Liberal Party. In my view, it is important to see the liberalism-in-transition animating all three stances.

[6]I find it difficult to agree with David Spencer's view that, at the end of the 19th century, "labour journalism became divided into two distinct and uncompromising ideological camps of reformism and socialism." See David Spencer, "An Alternate Vision: Main Themes in Moral Education in Canada's English-Language Working-Class Press 1870-1910," Ph.D. Thesis, University of Toronto, 1990: 5. On the contrary, my sense is that even within the "socialist" camp one finds many who were in essence "reformers" or "liberals." McKay's history is difficult to fit within these categories. But so too is the recurrent liberalism of W.U.Cotton of *Cotton's Weekly.* The turn-of-the-century ideological terrain seems far more complicated than dichotomous categorizations suggest.

a "fine contempt" for educated opinions![7] Liberalism of McKay's radical stripe entailed a democracy of the intellect: arguments should be defended on their own merits, and in light of the evidence, not sustained through appeals to tradition or shored up by the social prestige of those who made them.

The young McKay shared with many Liberals a distrust of the state and, at times, held the view that private enterprise should be preferred over state enterprise. On the question of whether the government should assist in improving the steamship service between Canada and the Caribbean, for example, McKay produced a traditional liberal position on the inadvisability of a direct subsidy: government subsidies seemed to represent an attempt to "force trade rather than merely to assist it, something which is hardly within the province of governments."[8] He also advanced the traditional liberal critique of high tariffs, which he viewed as injurious both to capital and labour. "If protection really benefitted industry it would be only logical, in order to get the utmost possible benefit of the system, to prohibit all imports," he argued. "But protection will not stand the test of progression, which is the touchstone of principles. Under protection one industry is developed at the expense of another, and the resultant violence to the natural development of industry reacts injuriously on both capital and labor." This was a liberal position -- but not just that of employers and farmers. It was also that taken by the Trades and Labor Congress of Canada at its Berlin Convention in 1902.[9]

Underpinning and allied with his liberalism was a Protestant ethic. McKay's earliest polemics on the sweating system, the labour question, and unemployment are passionately Christian in their mode of argument and their social vision. They appeal directly to an underlying grid of Christian values to provide certain guidance on difficult questions, especially when rights were in conflict. They also suggest that the resolution of the labour question, held to be feasible within a liberal order, would entail a mutual recognition of capital and labour, and the restoration of a lost harmony and balance in society. Liberal individuals

---

[7]"C.C.M.," "Labour and Its Interests, *Montreal Herald*, 30 October 1897. McKay was being simplistic in his assessment of Smith. As Gene Homel has argued, Smith had, over the years, "sustained cordial if argumentative relations with a number of socialists and union leaders. He spoke on occasion to labour audiences and was accorded a polite, even warm, reception." Homel, "James Simpson and the Origins of Canadian Social Democracy," Ph.D.Thesis, University of Toronto, 1978: 239. Smith actually spoke at the opening ceremonies for the Labour Temple in Toronto (209). And he accepted at least some of the planks of the "progressivism," such as city planning and rational government.

[8]Colin McKay, "The West Indian Steamer Service," *Montreal Herald*, 29 June 1905.

[9]Colin McKay, "Labor Views on High Tariffs,"*Montreal Herald*, 29 October 1902.

might learn to live in the "social state," as parts of a wider whole, if they interpreted the realities around them in the light of Christ's message. Here McKay (although using the language of Herbert Spencer) was well within the mainstream of a labour reform tradition that went back several decades.[10]

"Labor's Thanksgiving," an 1898 essay, took the form of a sermon. It was true that labour did not receive its rightful share of the beneficent blessings of God and that many men were unemployed; it was true that unemployment was rife. But the solution of these problems was also at hand: thanks to the work of the democratic labour movement, individual hearts and minds were being moved to a more elevated and idealistic sense of the role of individuals in society. It was because "men are learning that brotherhood is the law of God and nature and reason, and that unless they stand together they cannot endure life" that labour should give thanks; and because more and more people were coming to the realization that industry needed "democratizing and Christianizing" [§.9, "Labour's Thanksgiving"]. This was, admittedly, a *radical* statement of Christian liberalism, that extended the democratic ideal to industry and the critique of autocracy to the very principles of society. (In that sense, it can be understood in the context of the theories of "new liberalism" that replaced *laissez-faire* with organicism in the late nineteenth century).[11] Still, it was, in its vision of "reform aspirations" leavening "all classes of society," and bringing about "the spirit of brotherhood" fundamentally consistent with the evangelical liberalism of a William Gladstone or a Richard Cobden.

The same might be said of McKay's long critique of the sweating system in Montreal, which assumed that "no man or woman with a brain and heart" could be complacent in the face of "the awful sacrifices of human life, health and happiness required by the gods of competitive industry." Such sacrifices were "foreign to the spirit of Christian civilization," and would no longer be overlooked at a time when "our industrial system is being called to the bar of Christian conscience, and is being pronounced guilty of many sins." When "Christian hearts and minds" learned to direct evolution along its proper path, the car of progress would "not crush, but will carry men." Christians cried out for a "Moses" to release them from this "industrial Egypt" [§. 1, "This Industrial Egypt."] Ultimately, according to both McKay and John Flett (the highly active organizer for the American Federation of Labor in Canada) the labour movement was the truest contemporary exponent of Christianity. Christ

---

[10]Note T. Phillips Thompson, *The Politics of Labor* [1887] (Toronto and Buffalo: University of Toronto Press, 1975): 172-174.

[11]See L.T. Hobhouse, *Liberalism* (New York: Oxford University Press, 1964 [1911]) for the best short contemporary statement on the "new liberalism."

was seen as the first union organizer.[12] A Protestant vision of Christ and a liberal vision of labour could be effectively associated with each other.

2. The Economic Crisis of Turn-of-the-Century Liberalism

Yet this sense of firm Christian and liberal principles coexisted in McKay's writings with a mass of conflicting sentiments and intuitions. The same turn-of-the-century mind that embraced so many maxims of liberalism was also engaged in a radical questioning of its epistemological core. All around McKay there seemed to be evidence of far-reaching economic changes: the rise of trusts and monopolies, the related decline of small business, mass unemployment, the uncontrolled growth of large cities. Many liberals found themselves incorporating, incrementally and slowly, non-liberal elements into their social thought; meanwhile, some workers (many of them in such strategically significant spheres as coal mining and transportation) questioned the very tenets of liberalism.

The most fundamental economic change liberals confronted was the transformation of capitalism from a system of many small competitive producers to one dominated by trusts and monopolies. How could one retain a liberal political economy predicated on the individual, when the key economic forces in society were massive corporations?

In an 1897 analysis of trusts, McKay indicated how far he had, as a liberal, already travelled from classical liberal political economy. McKay initially adopted the standard, cynical stance of many Socialists: in removing competition and centralizing the forces of production, trusts were simply carrying out the mission of social evolution: "Messrs. Rockefeller & Co. are fulfilling Karl Marx's prophecies." Trusts were not "strangling industry" but performing a great service for society. As "products of the time, and evidence of evolution," trusts were abolishing competition and introducing a system of co-operation; they were bound to become larger and larger. In essence, the capitalists were building the economic framework of the co-operative commonwealth: "They are building the economic and industrial house, and when the house is finished men will get their eyes open and walk in at the front door and makes themselves at home."[13]

The other side of the rise of the trusts was the decline of small business. One of McKay's many objections to Goldwin Smith was that he had assumed, on the grounds of classical political economy, that "Thrift,

---

[12]Colin McKay, "Church and Labor: Organizer Flett on his Campaign in Quebec," *Montreal Herald*, 16 February 1901.

[13]C.McK., "Trusts," letter to the Montreal *Herald*, 6 November 1897. This whole train of reasoning was highly reminiscent of Bellamy's *Looking Backward*.

increased facilities for saving and for the employment of small capitals will promote equality of distribution." But this was exactly what was *not* happening: despite the great man's predictions, fortunes were accumulating in single hands, economic opportunities were being monopolized, the employment of small capitals was being squeezed out, and there was no sign that equality of distribution was at hand.[14] Although there were a few fields left for small capitalists, they subsisted on the insecure margins of the economy. With the plight of the small master artisan and the harried grocery-store proprietor, McKay felt a tremendous sympathy. For example, his analysis of the sweating system in the Montreal garment trades was unusually sympathetic towards the small "sweating" employer who had little choice but to put himself and his workers under extraordinary pressure to meet the demands of larger capitalists. Sweated labour was a symptom of a much larger structural problem, not a morality tale in which a bloated middleman sacrificed workers to his heartless greed. Paradoxically, however, McKay's reform program for the sweated industries would nonetheless have involved the "euthanasia of the small master," by so increasing the costs of entry to such trades that small capitalists would be unable to enter them [§. 1, "This Industrial Egypt"]. This was a form of indirect regulation whose implications were inimical to the classical liberal ideal of free competition.

If classical liberalism seemed unable to help workers in their struggle to transform sweating, it also seemed hopeless as a guide to the problem of mass unemployment -- a great Canadian issue in the 1890s. Orthodox [i.e., liberal and bourgeois] economists, McKay argued, had put their faith in the "iron law of wages," which enabled them to disregard the problem of unemployment. Under capitalism, insofar as labour was concerned, supply did not create its own demand; nor could this "equilibrium" ever actually exist over the long term in a capitalist economy, for the functional reason that capitalists required a "reserve army of labour" -- McKay borrowed Marx's phrase, although not at this point much of Marx's theory -- in order to allow for rapid expansion in certain spheres. Production followed a movement of alternate expansion and contraction, seemingly a necessary accompaniment of modern industry, and was obviously a process outside the control of any individual [§.7, "The Right to Work"]. Drawing on the iron law of wages, Goldwin Smith's classically liberal response to the suicide of a young unemployed man was that "society" could not provide work, if work did not exist. McKay regarded his jaundiced response as incredible, given the vast range of unmet economic needs among working people.

In confronting Smith -- albeit a somewhat oversimplified version of him -- McKay came face to face with the densely interwoven assumptions about

---

[14]"C.C.M., "Labour and Its Interests," *Montreal Herald*, 30 October 1897.

humanity, freedom, and social purpose at the nucleus of the liberal view of humanity. Some might say, he argued, that restricting the hours of labour and permitting no man to work more than a certain number of hours a day would be to restrict liberty. But what, in fact, was liberty? Why shouldn't the government restrict a workingman from taking the job away from another, when that was tantamount to murder? [§.6, "The Scourge of Unemployment"]. Fundamental liberal assumptions were obviously under siege, even in the mind of an ardent Liberal worker who wrote poems in praise of Wilfrid Laurier.

What of the principle that many nineteenth-century observers would have placed at the heart of the liberal tradition: Free Trade? McKay, who had scorned protection from a "labour point of view" in 1902, turned his attention to Free Trade in the context of England in 1904. Here he found that Joseph Chamberlain had radically affected the cherished traditional [i.e. liberal Free Trade] theories of his countrymen: he had "shattered beyond repair the silken web of illusions in which for the past generation or two they have canopied their careless souls." Outside the "inner sanctuary" of official liberalism, where the "bald dogmas of Free Trade" were still worshipped, the illusions of liberal political economy were, according to McKay, fast dissolving. Even the disciples of Richard Cobden, the mid-Victorian prophet of Free Trade, had cause to be disappointed: Free Trade had not ushered in a new moral world, it had not drawn nations and races together, it had not united humanity in eternal peace. After more than fifty years of Free Trade, poverty dominated the English cities. But protectionism was no panacea either, for problems that originated ultimately in the way British industry was organized [§.18, "England's Industrial Problem."] Writing from Glasgow, McKay reported in detail, and with obvious sympathy, Labour opinions (especially those of Philip Snowden) which viewed Chamberlain's schemes of imperial tariff protection as unrealistic and reactionary.[15]

Even if Free Trade had guaranteed industrial growth, McKay was keenly conscious of the alienation and confusion that such growth entailed under capitalism. Montreal was a particularly good example of the social logic of capitalism, with its tendency to class-segregation, abysmal infant mortality rates, and an accelerating division of labour.[16] Within a liberal

---

[15]Colin McKay, "Trade Unionists are Suspicious. British Workmen Think Protectionist Campaign the Prelude to a Fresh Attack Upon Their Organizations," *Montreal Herald*, 10 October 1904. See also Colin McKay, "Mr. Chamberlain, As Seen by the British Workingman," *Montreal Daily Herald*, November 24, 1904.

[16]Note the fascinating discussion of Robert Lewis, "The Segregated City: Class Residential Patterns and the Development of Industrial Districts in Montreal, 1861 and 1901," *Journal of Urban History*, 17, 2 (February 1991): 123-152. An interesting feature of this piece is a theme radically underplayed in McKay's work: the ethnic complexity of the Montreal working class: "In Saint-Jacques, to be working class was to be French,

order, Canadian cities had expanded to become swollen, unplanned, dangerous and alienating: "freedom" had a very different meaning in this radically new context. Echoing John Gray and anticipating Walter Benjamin,[17] McKay described the archetypal modern experience: wandering the city streets in all their crowded anonymity. He wrote pointedly of one Montrealer, the "Un-Prominent Citizen," caught without car fare in the heart of the city, who was required to walk the gauntlet of its thoroughfares, passing side streets and alleys uncleaned since the memory of man, "whence issued foul and sickening odors of decaying things," attempting to evade blinding storms of dust and filth, a water shower from the hose of a bar-tender "busily washing the gaudy face of a gin-palace," wildly driven hacks, and aggressive fruit-vendors.[18] McKay's experience in a Montreal jail brought home to the readers of the *Herald* the underside of the city's freedom, the existence of a class of confirmed young criminals, and the alienating irrationality of a system of law which, rather than acting as a "social doctor" and treating "social disease scientifically," simply punished the effects of social disorder.[19] Both on the sidewalks and in jail one encountered the shock of the new, the amazing impersonality and inner coldness of life in a capitalist civilization. The sweating system McKay exposed in the Montreal garment trades of the city was a prime example, not just of the economic logic of capitalism, but of the cold, inhuman aspects of capitalist culture: and unlike many of his contemporaries, McKay (who had himself a sense of being an immigrant to a metropolis) was not inclined to blame the Jews, Italians, or East Europeans who crowded Montreal's streets and factories, but the capitalist system itself. Here was a city in which people were so morally indifferent to one another that they simply ignored the deaths and diseases of the sweated labourers in their midst.

The article on the "sweating system" was in many respects the best -- and certainly the most radical -- thing McKay wrote in this period. It can be used as a way into the complexities of liberal faith in late-Victorian Canada, especially when it is set beside the contemporaneous study of the

---

a shoemaker or a cigar maker; in Sainte-Anne it was to be English or Irish, a machinist or a carter" (144). For another invaluable perspective on capitalism in turn-of-the-century Montreal, see Gregory J. Levine, "Class, ethnicity and property transfers in Montreal, 1907-1909," *Journal of Historical Geography* 14, 4 (1988): 360-380.

[17]See Walter Benjamin, "On Some Motifs in Baudelaire," in Hannah Arendt, ed., *Illuminations* (New York: Schocken Books, 1969), 155-200.

[18]C.M., "The Un-Prominent Citizen," *Montreal Herald*, October 19, 1906.

[19]For McKay's impressions of jail life in Montreal, see Colin McKay, "Experience in Montreal Jail. A Man Who Spent Some Days Within Prison Walls Writes About Them. Didn't Like 'Skouse.'" *Montreal Herald*, 17 June 1899. It would seem McKay went to jail for refusing to post bail when first charged for having libelled Fortier, but this is not altogether clear from the article, a decidedly whimsical view of imprisonment in which the absence of literature (other than religious tracts) emerges as one of the gravest hardships of the imprisoned.

same problem by that other turn-of-the-century liberal, William Lyon Mackenzie King, the future Prime Minister of Canada. (King published in 1898, and McKay in 1899, but McKay -- as the anonymous author of a series of articles in the *Montreal Herald* in 1897 -- had almost certainly been ahead of King in raising the issue in Montreal).[20]

In his analysis of the problem, Mackenzie King rather primly defined sweating as "a condition of labor under which a maximum amount of work is exacted from a human being at a minimum wage, the said work usually being continued for long hours day by day and amid surroundings which are not infrequently unhealthy." The "condition" was begotten of "competition in its keenest form," and reared upon "the ignorance, weakness, or indifference of those who are its victims." Commonly accompanied by sub-contracting, sweated labour drew upon workers "obliged, through the necessities of the hour to take advantage of any opportunities of slight remunerative work which may be had."[21] King regarded the question of wages in sweating as "only one phase," and perhaps, "having regard to the physical and moral welfare of the worker," not even the most important aspect of the question. More detrimental in the long run than the "scantiness of earnings" received, were the surroundings in which the work was performed: small, badly-ventilated rooms, overcrowded with a dozen or more persons of both sexes and a variety of ages, pervaded by "odors of the most obnoxious sort," and located in garrets, basements, and other out-of-the-way places. No effort was made in such places to confine the garments to one area: "They are scattered often about the house, members of the family pass in and out, and in cases by no means rare the workroom serves by day as kitchen and dining room as well, or sleeping room at night." The "moral effect" of such conditions was "distressing to contemplate," and even worse for King was the "utter ruination of the home" when part of it was converted into a shop. If that were the whole story, continued King, "the ever-indifferent public might be expected to stand aloof, and while expressing compassion for the poor wretches whom it allows to suffer, draw its own skirts aside and pass by on the other side." But the garments emerging from the sweatshops were in fact probably *dangerous* to the health of the middle-class public: "The question arises, is there no possibility of contagion from garments which have been made in homes subject to no supervision or inspection of any kind, in quarters of the city where disease is likely to find its easiest way, or even in country homes where the people may be of an undesirable sort, filthy in their habits and modes of living?"

---

[20]"The Sweating Evil. Its Prevalence in the City of Montreal. Overcrowded Tenements. Where people Work for Eighty Hours a Week," *Montreal Herald*, 3 February 1897. The government asked Mackenzie King to investigate government clothing contracts in a letter dated 21 September 1897.

[21]William Lyon Mackenzie King, "Sweating System in Montreal." *Montreal Herald*, 16 April 1898.

No examples of such contagion could be documented from Montreal, but King recounted evidence of a smallpox epidemic in Chicago, and even retailed a story of the daughters of Sir Robert Peel, who were said to have contracted a fatal disease through contact with a riding habit.[22]

McKay's analysis of sweating in Montreal diverged in interesting ways from Mackenzie King's, suggesting deep (if still quite inchoate) differences between two kinds of liberal social vision. King's analysis was preoccupied with the empirical pattern, and, with the masterful evasiveness characteristic of him, avoided any clear causal statements. McKay's analysis, on the other hand, was preoccupied with the underlying *conditions of possibility* for the existence of something like sweating. (One might almost say that whereas King was satisfied with a merely empirical description, McKay was attempting a structural analysis of the sweating system). King's supplied more detail, but McKay's went much further in trying to explain why sweating had emerged in the first place. To a much greater extent for McKay than for King, sweating was no isolated occurrence: it summed up "the economic or industrial aspects of the problem of city poverty," and could be found in the "lower branches of all trades," even including those of the "clerks, shopmen, and the lower class of brain workers." Across this occupational spectrum, similar causes were at work. While both men were liberal Protestants looking at the same problem, one rested his case on a wide range of empirical evidence of markedly uneven quality, while the other tried to probe the underlying logic of the phenomenon. Although McKay did focus specifically on some of the "minor causes of sweating" in the garment industry, such as the buying habits of the public and the strategies of wholesalers, he insisted that the root causes of sweating were the unemployment and low wages characteristic of capitalism. The underlying cause of all sweating was "the presence of a large number of unemployed and unskilled working men and women. So long as there is a large surplus of labour, the sweating system will continue in large cities." Placing the burden of blame on small masters, wholesalers, or even the general public was misleading: in sweating one saw a crystallization of the logic of labour's exploitation under capitalism.

This emphasis on the underlying economic logic of sweating -- what a later generation would call a "structural analysis"[23] -- did not commit

---

[22]William Lyon Mackenzie King, "Sweating System in Montreal City."*Montreal Herald*, 23 April 1898. Some of these picturesque details were omitted from the official report published in 1898 and reprinted in 1899: see *Report to the Honourable the Postmaster General of the Methods Adopted in Canada in the Carrying Out of Government Clothing Contracts* (Ottawa: Government Printing Bureau, 1899).

[23]Later structural analysis would, of course, argue that in light of the evidence of sweating, McKay's emphasis on the inevitable concentration and centralization of capital was misplaced. As one historian argues in a study of the London sweated trades,

McKay to a strategy of passively waiting for the structure to change. Far more than King, McKay wrote as an engaged reformer. He was willing to support the palliative of a better system of sanitary and industrial inspection, and in fact prepared a draft bill along these lines for the Montreal labour movement, on the basis of an intensive study of American and European legislation. He fully supported tightening up the Quebec Factory Act to remove the loophole that allowed domestic manufactures to slip through its provisions for inspection. "A better system of registration, an extension of the act so as to make it applicable to domestic workshops, and an increase in the power of the inspectors, would lead to the abatement of some of the worst evils of the sweating system in Montreal," he argued. "Laws should also be introduced tending to increase the legal responsibility of the employer, and to eliminate the small master and crush the small workshop by imposing irksome and expensive conditions." But McKay did not believe such reforms could ever permanently uproot the sweating system: they would at best reform its worst evils, and teach workers some new things about the system as a whole.[24]

One of the benefits of such legislative reform would be an intensified public debate: like King, McKay felt it would be valuable to turn "the wholesome light of publicity upon the evils of sweating." Once again, however, the similarity between the two liberals is misleading. McKay's strategy for generating such wholesome publicity was very different from King's. The latter's approach was both state-centric and individualistic: the

---

"...the experience of the workers in the London clothing trades points to a well-known but often neglected fact about economic and social change: the movement of labor and industry toward the factory system and the concomitant fusion of the working class was not inexorable. Industry, in the case of the clothing trades, was transformed not by centralization, but by decentralization": James A. Schmiechen, *Sweated Industries and Sweated Labor: The London Clothing Trades, 1860-1914* (Urbana and Chicago: University of Illinois Press, 1984), 192. For a related study, arguing that the characteristics of sweating were not confined to unregulated workplaces but were a feature of both larger and smaller production units, see Jenny Morris, "The Characteristics of Sweating: The Late Nineteenth-Century London and Leeds Tailoring Trade," in Angela V. John, *Unequal Opportunities: Women's Employment in England 1800-1918* (Oxford, 1986): 95-121. The best general source for the topic in Canada is Robert McIntosh, "Sweated Labour: Female Needleworkers in Industrializing Canada," *Labour/Le Travail* 32 (Fall 1993): 105-138.

[24]Colin McKay, "An Act to Regulate Conditions of Garment Trade," *Montreal Herald*, 2 December 1899. For a good overview of protective labour legislation in Quebec, see John A. Dickinson, "La Législation et les travailleurs québécois 1894-1914," *Relations Industrielles* 41, 2 (1986): 357-381. With reference to McKay's campaign on behalf of the Federation of Labour, Dickinson notes that faced with evidence from workers and the inspectors charged with the application of the factory law, the state did in fact make a number of modifications. Nonetheless, despite such improvements, aimed at limiting the sweating of women and children, more than half Québec workers were left unprotected by legislation as of 1914.

state would undertake neutral and scientific enquiries, and the consumer, although perhaps normally indifferent to working-class issues, would respond on the basis of his or her *individual* personal concerns. His analysis implicitly invited one to identify with the hapless middle-class consumers (such as the poor daughters of Robert Peel) affected by disease-ridden garments, made by people who might well be "of an undesirable sort."

Conversely, McKay's approach was in essence   collectivist in spirit and class-based in strategy. The publicity he called for was a campaign that would undermine the anonymity of the modern city and its coldly respectable streets. Publicity would melt away the bogus middle-class proprieties that allowed the wholesaler, "in the shadow of the so-called respectability of his house," to force contract prices down "until the small master has to sweat his employees and himself half to death in order to make a livelihood." The sweating sub-contractor was a "screen to the employing firm." Public opinion would turn on a business house that drove labour in so savage a manner, but which "the secrecy of the sweater's place" allowed him to operate with impunity.

Contrary to King, educating public opinion meant much more than issuing gruesome official reports: it meant the day-to-day struggle for the union label, trade unionism, and factory legislation. Ultimately, these measures would transform the economic framework within which individuals made their decisions. Unlike King's state-centred strategy of official documentation, McKay placed much greater reliance on the union label as an educational tool. He also saw a legal crackdown, especially laws against rural outwork, as offering potential benefits for workers. Responding to the challenge of unregulated competition from rural outworkers, who were likely always to be outside the range of effective inspection, McKay argued that urban workers, entirely dependent on the work for their livelihood, had a claim to protection from rural labour, and supported such forms of regulation as a ban on the export of clothing work outside the city, and some form of tax on clothing made outside Montreal. (Revealingly, his "good liberalism" required him to add the contradictory rider that although he personally regarded "such methods of regulating trade as wrong in principle," he felt they were justified in this particular instance) [§. 1, "This Industrial Egypt"and §.2, "The Secret of Poverty"].

Ultimately the two texts on sweating were also very different in their implied audience. While King had written of unclean workers of an "undesirable sort," McKay's analysis invited his readers to identify with these very workers, whose feelings of gloom, anger and illness stemmed from the poor conditions under which they worked. And he invited readers to consider the only effective response to sweating as lying within working-class *praxis* : the struggle for trade unions, for the union label, and ultimately for a new political economy in which low wages and unemployment would be removed.

McKay could be seen throughout 1898 and 1899 carrying out his own prescription: encouraging both Garment Workers Union No. 140 and the Federated Trades and Labor Council of Montreal[25] in a general anti-sweating crusade[§. 3, "The Abolition of the Sweating System: A Call for Action," originally published as "To Abolish The Sweating System. The Federated Trades Council Takes the Initiative of an Active Campaign"], and also mobilizing the male craft workers' arguments of chivalry and familialism to extend the scope of the anti-sweating struggle to the Local Council of Women [§.4, "Women in the Sweating System"]. Within the unions, McKay came to be an expert on the question of the union label, intervening, for example, to settle a dispute between garment workers who were paid by the piece and those paid by the week.[26] He had a special affinity for the cigarmakers, who had found the strategy of the union label particularly successful; by 1900, the trade was thought to be almost completely organized, with a number of women "enrolled... under the banner of the union."[27] His most dramatic intervention against overwork and low wages came in *Canada's Democracy* when he denounced J.M.Fortier's treatment of his tobacco workers. It was a mark of his stature in the labour movement that the labour council petitioned the minister of justice on his behalf, and it was an indication of the intensifying contradictions of a liberal order that a journalist should go to jail for describing the conditions of sweated labour in Montreal.[28]

The significance of McKay's many activities as an "engaged labour intellectual" in winning acceptance and a more informed response to the rapidly rising labour movement in Montreal should probably not be understated. He was probably instrumental in igniting concern over sweating (and hence indirectly useful indeed to the young Mackenzie King), pivotal in advising unions, and important in providing what was still seen as a new and somewhat illegitimate movement with an eloquent voice. As late as 1897, the legal status of trade unionism itself had been challenged in the city, when, on appeal, the Stonecutters' Union's right to exist and conduct a strike was acknowledged in a majority report (the minority report holding -- still -- that trade unions were illegal

---

[25][C.M.], "The Wage-Earners' Budget,"*Montreal Herald*, 21 November 1900. The turn-of-the-century Montreal labour movement was divided between the Montreal Central Trades and Labor Council and the Montreal Federated Trades and Labor Council. The latter body was made up of international unionists who had split from the former in 1897, alleging that the Knights of Labor exercised an undue influence over it. Until 1902, both councils were recognized by the Trades and Labor Congress of Canada.

[26]"Labor Notes," *Montreal Herald*, 11 October 1899.

[27]*Montreal Herald*, 19 November 1900.

[28]*Montreal Herald*, 8 December 1899.

combinations in restraint of trade).[29] McKay constantly publicized the activities of unions in the daily press and sought to link trade union struggles to the concerns of the wider public. He became an eloquent defender of international trade unionism against various "national" alternatives, on the grounds that through international unionism, Canadian workers would have access to the resources, expertise, and political realism of the American Federation of Labor [§.8, "In Defence of International Trade Unionism," originally published as "No Separate Union for the Dominion"]. Far more than any other movement or reform, trade unionism (connected with but not subordinated to labour politics) came to be regarded as the best source of answers to the crisis of a liberal capitalist order.

In this emphasis on class politics, McKay was completely opposed to Mackenzie King -- "Liberals" and "liberals" though they both were. In the juxtaposition of their two analyses of sweating we have an intriguing snapshot of two very different strands of an emergent new liberalism.

3. The Philosophical Crisis of Turn-of-the-Century Liberalism

The problem of sweatshops could not be raised, let alone solved, using a conventional liberal analysis of the individual and the individual's interests. It no longer seemed very realistic to assume that "the individual" or his actions could be usefully separated, even at the level of abstract analysis, from society. (For classical liberalism, which was only slowly changing in this period, only the male property-holding person was a true individual). When a classical liberal political economist looked at the entrepreneur pursuing his interests by investing in new machinery, he saw the vital core of the expansive market economy: an individual, by maximizing his own wealth, was unintentionally enriching the entire social order. To interfere with the individual, in this or other senses, was warranted only when the pursuit of his interests interfered with those of one or more other individuals also pursuing their own interests. When, however, many turn-of-the-century liberals and radicals looked at the same individual entrepreneur with his machine, they saw something quite different. They saw both the entrepreneur and the machine as complex social phenomena They saw a person whose profits were entirely dependent on the social order within which he operated, and they saw the machines from which he profited as the outcome of past generations of invention and labour.[30]

---

[29]*Montreal Herald*, 24 February 1897.

[30]The importance given to this issue of capitalists deriving the benefits from past inventions explains the salience of patent legislation in the founding program of the Canadian Socialist League. McKay would later find in the writings of American sociologists (such as Ward) powerful analyses of this problem.

Like so many radical thinkers of the day, McKay developed this challenge to individualism by focusing on the controversial figure of Andrew Carnegie. Although the whole community had developed the steamer and the railroad, Carnegie as an individual reaped the profits: where was the justice in that?[31] This radical questioning of individualism could draw upon a number of quite distinct theoretical traditions, which turn-of-the-century liberals often ran together indiscriminately. Evolutionary theory could place Carnegie in the context of the vast sweep of natural forces; Marxian analysis would focus on his economic function and on the "dead labour" incorporated in his machine, whose very existence depended on the expropriation of surplus value from the living labour of Carnegie's workers. For his part, the young McKay turned more readily to the communitarian implications of the Christian notion of "stewardship." Could a man like Carnegie make restitution to the community? he wondered. If you began with the assumption that "a man may do what he pleases with his wealth," then Carnegie was perfectly justified in "assuming a sovereign function and treating the people as if they were paupers" by deciding how to invest the wealth generated by the community. But if one applied a Christian standard of stewardship, the entrepreneur was not in fact morally free to do with his money as he wished: he was "morally bound to employ his wealth in productive enterprises." From this perspective, if Carnegie in fact burned his money, or if the investors in Montreal utilities burned their stock certificates, they would be releasing the community from a lien upon its wealth, and perhaps liberating it to utilize that wealth to greater advantage [§.17, "Should Rich Men Burn Their Money?"]. McKay was echoing, perhaps, the message he may well have already heard from Rev. H.N.Casson who had informed his audience in Point St. Charles that, under the present economic and social conditions, such a thing as the "private individual" was no longer possible.[32]

Just as a classical liberal political economy premised on the free individual seemed more and more mistaken to McKay, so did those forms of Christian social analysis that began and ended with individual salvation. Of the three principal defects of the (Protestant) church that were alienating workingmen -- dogmatism, autocracy, and an individualistic gospel -- McKay in 1900 gave most weight to the latter. The church's "individualistic gospel" had "little sanction in the utterances of Christ, and none whatever, from the teachings of modern social scientists." It did not act on, and perhaps did not recognize, the principle

[31]Colin McKay, "Socialism and the Single Tax," *Montreal Daily Herald*, 19 December 1900. The context of the remarks is a debate with Reverend Robert Hopkins, Secretary of the Montreal Ministerial Association, who had recently read a paper entitled "Poverty: Its Causes and Cures."
[32]*Montreal Herald*, 17 March 1897. I am assuming here that the unidentified *Herald* reporter filing the story was McKay.

that "improvement in the the individual can only proceed *pari passu* with the improvement in society." Imprisoned by *laissez-faire* doctrines, it ignored the effects of the environment on the individual, and violated its own ideal of human brotherhood. The Church hypocritically applied a double standard, forgiving evils in social institutions that it denounced at the level of the individual. Christians (along with Socialists) were mistaken in favouring the individualist utilitarianism implicit in the liberalism of John Stuart Mill (and which, McKay might have noted, underwrote so much political discussion in Canada), for both "The ethics of Christianity and of Socialism require an authority of more consistency and finality than utilitarianism affords." Given the church's inability to define its own position with any conceptual clarity, it was small wonder that workers, seized as never before "with the force of a new revelation," found little of value in the church. Unless the church divorced itself from traditional liberal political economy, it ran the risk of workers turning to atheism and materialism, as was the case in Europe. And, for the young McKay, this would be a tragedy, because both Christianity and socialism placed social duties ahead of individual rights; both required the individual to make sacrifices that could not be strictly justified on the basis of individualism; and both built on similar assumptions, such as eternal justice, transcendental moral law, and the immortality of the soul. If such a divorce between Christianity and the working class was bound to be disastrous for the church, it would be equally damaging for the socialist cause. For socialism required Christianity as an ethical foundation: no doctrine of equal rights and no doctrine of duties could ever be deduced from Darwinism, and no "ought" could be derived from a world of natural law [§.11, "Why Workingmen Distrust Churches"].

This important essay suggested the extent to which McKay's position on religion was in flux: he -- in company with his sparring partner Goldwin Smith, ironically enough[33] -- seemed to be searching for a *terra firma* on which ethical decisions could be firmly grounded. In this first phase of his socialist writing, the debate with individualist Protestantism loomed very large for him. Whereas secular socialists somehow tried to base their ethics on utilitarianism, natural science, and the material world, he argued, Protestant social reformers often erred in grounding their ethics on transcendental ideals, otherworldly sentiments, and unrealistic expectations. They idealistically assumed that uplifting the poor first entailed making them "moral, thrifty, temperate, etc.," and unless this moral reformation were first accomplished, unless moral and intellectual improvement preceded social reconstruction, all the labours of the trade unions and socialists would be in vain. Far better than this "comfortable view," McKay argued, was one which stressed that economic diseases such as poverty were caused by the "vicious operation of our present system of

---

[33]See especially Goldwin Smith, "Genesis and the Outlook of Religion," *The Contemporary Review*, 78 (July-December 1900): 898-908.

industry." Pharisees taunted the poor with their vices and inefficiency, whereas true Christians were applying themselves to the basic principles of economics [§.2, "The Secret of Poverty"].

McKay was therefore impatient with the temperance crusade, which for many Protestants was *the* major social reform movement of the period. Temperance confused a symptom with an underlying cause: in ways which were typical of the Protestant tradition, it refused to acknowledge the economic genesis of social disorders, preferring instead to place the emphasis on the moral failings of the individual. In 1904, McKay attacked temperance with a Nova Scotian insouciance. Might it not be better to begin at the beginning and reform the weather? Or do something about the awful standards of Canadian cooking? The Temperance Alliance should ask for legislation against salt and fried meats, not to mention "the pies our mothers used to make." A cookery inspector would be more useful than a liquor inspector![34] As for sabbatarianism, McKay jokingly came out against a proposed by-law legalizing Sunday athletics, because he felt that athletics was a "sort of national craze, distracting attention from grave political and social evils," which had turned young men into "mono-maniacs," and turned their attention away from "political, social, ethical problems, or good literature." At least the "better class of workmen" preferred to spend Sunday improving their minds. Instead of a Lord's Day Alliance, why not organize a movement to suppress newspapers that devoted a page every day to sporting news, and only a column once a week to literary topics -- "and no space at all to the labor movement and sociology"?[35] One notes from this whimsical commentary that McKay did not fundamentally object to standard Christian definitions of what constituted moral conduct nor diverge very much from the Victorian notion of the "better class of workingmen." His early "constructive" and "ethical" socialism was sharply distinguished from the materialism of the Marxists. Even in 1910, after much in McKay's intellectual universe had changed, he would write unhesitatingly of "the vital truths of Christianity" [§.14, "The Political Gag"]. Although he later came to embrace a "materialist" view of the universe, McKay's sense of right and wrong, and (arguably) his sense of progress and purpose never lost their Christian overtones.

4. The Political Turmoil of Liberalism

Between 1904 and 1906, towards the end of his first period of working-class activism, McKay developed a more secular approach to politics, and closely identified with a number of practical causes often seen as aspects of "progressivism," defined as a strategy of safeguarding the liberal order through the application of "neutral" and "rational" principles of science

---

[34]Colin McKay, "Begin at the Beginning," Halifax *Morning Chronicle*, 11 April 1904.
[35]*Montreal Herald*, 2 October 1900.

and of planning. (There were obvious links here with the Fabians in Britain). When progressives looked at their society, they saw its deep divisions and social problems, but held these to be corrigible by expert planning, often under the auspices of a somewhat enlarged state and a more responsible capitalist class.[36]

Viewed from the standpoint of 1899-1900, McKay's articles of 1904-1906 are surprising in content and tone. The Christian radical of 1900 seems to have been transformed into a mild-mannered Fabian by 1905, shifting his emphasis from class conflict to social cohesion. In content, the articles of the later period focused less upon the negative side of capitalism -- the sweating system, the jails, the civic corruption -- and more on the positive achievement of certain important limited reforms: technical education, urban planning, and corporate welfare. It is difficult in these years to hear even the echoes of the anti-utilitarian in search of ethical standards in a corrupt and changing world.

Technical education was, for McKay and other reformers, one of the crucial reforms needed to bring about a more progressive order.[37] In

---

[36]The distinction between "progressivism" and "new liberalism" is not very clearly argued in the historiography: Americans speak more readily of the first, and the British of the second. Yet perhaps there is a further way of usefully distinguishing between these terms. "New liberals" by definition were those who sought to preserve liberal freedoms and a measure of possessive individualism by bringing liberal doctrine into line with the evolutionary insight that society functioned and evolved as an "organic whole," in which each part of the organism was deeply and irremediably affected by whatever happened to the other parts and by the greater entity. There was no necessary logical link between this "organic conception" and advocating the usefulness of a scientific, value-free, efficient approach to the social order. Similarly, "progressives" were those who sought to remedy the defects of a capitalist liberal order by perfecting efficient and scientific techniques in industry, government, and social reform movements. There was no necessary logical link to an organic view of the world. However, in both cases, links were made: new liberals found support for organicism in arguments based on science and efficiency, and progressives found support for the scientific reform of society in arguments based on organicism. Canadians like J.S. Woodsworth seem to have combined the two discourses of social reform; and others could find in eugenics a movement which smoothly combined them both.

[37]See Gene Homel, "James Simpson," 164-165 on the enthusiasm for technical education in Toronto labour circles. "Labour... regarded technical education with a proprietary interest. It represented the potential for upward mobility, self-improvement, and some measure of control over the workplace and the labour supply" (182). In Winnipeg, such radicals as Dick Johns and Bob Russell had also promoted technical education. Writing in 1913 on his earlier passion for technical education in 1904-1906, McKay noted that his enthusiasm for this educational reform in 1904-1906 had been based on the assumption that technical education would benefit the working class by enhancing the efficiency of the workers. ("At that time I called myself a Socialist," he observed, "but I still had the individualistic view point.") Although he had distanced himself from his earlier enthusiasm, McKay still praised aspects of technical

1904, the argument he advanced for technical education was that it would make workers more efficient and enhance the industrial status of Montreal. He made his appeal, at least in part, to the city's Manufacturers' Association, and advanced the classic progressive argument that the manufacturers and the government should consolidate and rationalize the existing industrial schools, so that they could perform at a much higher level. Having maintained trade and technical schools in Montreal, the provincial government had done good work; in conjunction with the Council of Arts and Manufactures, a committee appointed by the government, and the Manufacturers' Association, this system could be greatly extended.[38] A government system of technical education would be more efficient than a single private institution, for it could present different methods of technical education, rather than just one narrowly-focused approach.[39] He even pitched his case for technical education in the time-honoured rhetoric of competitive boosterism: Montreal was being overtaken by Toronto![40] The appeal of technical education was summed up in the headline for one story from 1905, entitled "Employers Want Men Who Know."[41] These were eminently progressive writings, in that they began with the apparent assumption that all of Montreal had an interest in the triumph of technical education, which would make the city more competitive and its industries more rational. The "socialism," individualistic or otherwise, in these calls for the reform of technical education is not readily apparent.

One can find *some* connections between the argument for technical education and a socialist perspective. Most orthodox socialists of the day would have held that any progress in the organization of the forces and relations of production, especially one which enhanced their interdependence and efficiency, was also bound to hasten the day of the socialist revolution. Moreover, McKay, along with many others, may well have thought that technical education, by raising the intellectual level of the workers, would make them more powerful proponents of far-reaching social changes. He did explicitly present the case that technical education could potentially offer opportunities to workers who, because they had

education: he lauded it especially because it would tend to cultivate the power and the "habit of reasoning among the working class." Colin McKay, "Mr. Hatheway and Technical Education," *Eastern Labor News*, 18 January 1913.

[38]Colin McKay, "The Nucleus of a Technical School," *Montreal Herald*, 20 December 1904, *Montreal Herald*, 20 December 1904.

[39]Colin McKay, "Various Kinds of Technical Education," *Montreal Herald*, 30 December 1904.

[40]Colin McKay, "Beating Us. Toronto's Provision for Technical Education Long Way Ahead of Montreal's," *Montreal Herald*, 14 January 1905; Colin McKay, "Something Montreal Should Have," *Montreal Herald*, Jan. 21, 1905;

[41]Colin McKay, "Employers Want Men Who Know," *Montreal Herald*, 23 January 1905.

entered the factory as child labourers, had been denied an adequate education. The technical school offered a way of training skilled workers and foremen, and "a remedy for the injustices the factory system imposed upon young workpeople...."[42]

This "working-class perspective" was, however, promptly balanced by the point that employers would derive as great a benefit from technical education as the workers, because they would be able to select competent foremen from the rank and file. Because the ordinary worker's knowledge of the whole process of production was necessarily limited, training foremen required an additional process of training over and above that received on the job. And capitalists would also benefit from the designers turned out by technical schools, and from the higher grade of workers generally. In an age when capitalism had wiped out so many skills and traditions of apprenticeship, technical schools would also provide skilled workers for those remaining processes which still required manual skills. The "socialist agenda" of such arguments -- if there was one -- was so well concealed that most readers would surely have missed it. McKay's coolly neutral arguments for technical education were far removed from the impassioned polemics he had directed against the capitalist system in 1899, and which he would repeat in 1912.

Much the same pattern of "progressivism" can be found in McKay's advocacy of urban reform in Montreal, although in this instance the connections to the reform socialism of the Fabians are more easily identified. In 1905, McKay noted the significance of the local Trades and Labor Council's decision to support the labour party as a "purely independent movement" in the forthcoming civic election. It was, he argued, a clear warning to a city that did "nothing for your ignorant and boss-led voters." The city government should make sure a street railway company did not "take a tithe" from a factory girl's earnings and make her stand in a cold and crowded car; that utilities did not gouge the working-class public; that tenements were fit and sanitary; that children were transported to and from school. Only if it provided such real services would the city government have any claim to the hearts of the poorest voters.[43]

Here was a program of "civic idealism" designed to inject an "ethical impulse into civic politics." A new progressive view of the city enabled its citizens to distinguish between "industries which have a public, and those which have a private character," and to demand that the city operate public utilities. "A public corporation," wrote McKay, paraphrasing the view of labour but also developing his own view, "is more responsible to

[42]Colin McKay, "Beating Us. Toronto's Provision for Technical Education Long Way Ahead of Montreal's," *Daily Herald*, 14 January 1905.
[43]Colin McKay, "Labor and City Politics," *Montreal Herald*, 4 November 1905.

the demands of morals than a private corporation can be, and is bound to make the most of the social aspects of public utility services while private corporations must naturally ignore them, since they cannot be translated into dividends."[44] Such civic idealism, with its modest extension of public enterprise into municipal utilities, was to be found in the programs of progressives across North America.

When McKay looked about to find a working model of such civic idealism, he focused on Britain. Here he found Glasgow, the second city of the United Kingdom and the model of municipal socialism: "Its civic government is unquestionably the most perfect in existence; its enterprise has excited the admiration and the wonder of the world. No city has more successfully grappled with the problems of urban life; no city has done, or, is doing, more for the comfort and well-being of its citizens." Everything about Glasgow had been transformed under the beneficent hand of planning and civil idealism. Where once had clustered "a multitude of narrow streets, dismal lanes, and filthy closes, where disease and death held high carnival, and vice and crime lifted up their heads unabashed," the light and air of heaven now rested upon "broad and cheerful streets." Civic planning had reduced the death rate, increased the area of public parks from 370 to 1,000 acres, and developed twenty-odd children's playgrounds. Once the duties of the municipality had been confined to police administration and supplying water and gas. Now it owned and operated the tramway and telephone systems, provided electric lighting and water for hydraulic power, and maintained "markets, public parks, museums, picture galleries, public halls, baths and wash-houses, lodging-houses and model dwellings for the working classes and a nursing home." The Improvement Trust Committee was "continually engaged tearing down unsanitary localities and making proper provision for the housing of the poorer classes." But the strongest evidence that here was the progressive city of the future could be found in the "most perfect sewage purification system in the world." On the unlikely subject of the sewage water of Glasgow, McKay waxed positively lyrical: the filthy waters of the Clyde had been transformed, in wonderful sewage establishments, into sparkling water, "not unpalatable and quite harmless," that had been extracted from the sewage of the great metropolis.[45] (One imagines readers of the *Herald*, reading their newspapers at the dining-room table, were aghast at the clear insinuation that McKay had actually consumed the impeccably treated sewage!) The Clyde epitomized the bright promise of progressivism. Municipal socialism could bring purity out of danger. It brought sunlight and fresh

---

[44]*Ibid.*

[45]Colin McKay, "Glasgow Enterprise" *Montreal Herald*, 3 November 1904. See also, for a discussion more specifically focused on municipal socialism in Glasgow and housing, Colin McKay, "The Housing Problem," *Montreal Daily Herald*, 12 November 1904.

air into congested Glasgow neighbourhoods, and clarity and cleanliness out of the Clyde. Science and efficiency brought hope to the hopeless.

In this stage of his life, McKay evidently placed great hope in the progressive planning of the environment as a way of restoring a sense of community and purpose among workers. Whether accomplished by municipal socialism, as in Glasgow, or as part of an ambitious scheme of corporate welfare, as at Port Sunlight [§.16, "A Vision of Benevolent Capitalism"], the scientific planning of a community could end the strangeness, disorder, and danger of the city. So much had the "garden cities" of Britain done to restore a sense of belonging, McKay reported in 1911, that in these co-operatively planned communities, "the outdoor festivals and sports on the green of merrie England have been revived -- spontaneously apparently."[46]

McKay as a progressive reformer looked persistently to Britain -- to Glasgow's municipal socialism, to Port Sunlight's corporate welfare, to the Garden Cities' co-operativism -- for models of a better and more humane capitalist modernity. His historical imagination fed far more avidly on   British than on Canadian narratives: Robert Blatchford's romantic description of a pre-capitalist England, "a merrie England, the home of a vigorous race of beef-fed men," made a particularly deep impression on him.[47] In this phase of his life, he looked to the British Labour Party as an example of a party which had successfully combined pragmatism with socialist principle. He recommended that Montreal workers, whose labour leaders had made the "hasty decision" to contest Montreal divisions at the coming election, look to Britain for insight into how such electoral campaigns should really be fought. In Montreal, the labour leaders seemed to view politics as a pastime, and one merely needed a few "elocutionary exercises of an evening or two" to prepare for it.   British Labour seemed to take a much more professional attitude towards politics. "Having made up his mind that he needs labor representation," McKay remarked admiringly, "the British worker is going about securing it in a thorough workmanlike way."[48] So often and so adamantly did McKay refer his readers to British precedents and models, that one might mistake his turn-of-the-century "Montreal" for any other city of the Empire: we often seem to be reading of some Glasgow on the St. Lawrence. Certainly from the perspective of the late twentieth century, McKay's Montreal seems remarkably de-ethnicized and simply "urban": one is forcibly reminded of the "universal functionalism" of the Chicago

---

[46]Colin McKay, "Garden Cities," *Coast-Guard*, 12 January 1911.

[47]Colin McKay, "Does Canada Need a Leisured Class?", *Eastern Labor News*, 5 November 1910.

[48]Colin McKay, "The British Labor Party," *Montreal Daily Herald*, 15 November 1904.

School sociologists who, two decades later, would take Montreal as a "case study" of the "North American city."[49]

At the same time, McKay was probably somewhat more sensitive to Montreal's status as the centre of French-Canadian culture than many of his anglophone contemporaries in the labour movement. Going from his critique of the Judge's translation at his trial, it seems likely that he was at least partially bilingual in 1900; his later journalism suggests he subsequently read widely in French. His 1903 article "The French Canadian as a Trade Unionist" [§.15] stands as an interesting document, hitherto apparently unknown, in which an anglophone socialist and AFL sympathizer attempted to come to an understanding of the specificity of the French-Canadian situation. One imagines that this important piece of evidence could be cited by either side of the emergent debate over the place of international unions in the history of turn-of-the-century Québec. From the standpoint of Robert Babcock (at least in his classic *Gompers in Canada*) and Jacques Rouillard,[50] this fascinating article in the AFL's official publication could be interpreted as confirmation of the AFL's (and McKay's) patronizing attitude and of a tendency to exoticize the "French Canadian," a being evidently living in utter isolation from something called the "American spirit" and in utter ignorance of the international proletarian movement.[51] (McKay's belief that certain *ethnies* had certain unalterable behavioural characteristics will surface again when he comes to speak of the Eastern Europeans in Cape Breton [§.72, "The Awakening of Labour in the Maritime Provinces"].) Moreover, McKay in this article seems to be quite unaware of the depth and tenacity of religious faith as a force in its own right within the working class. On the other hand, from the standpoint of those like Bernard Dionne, who has forcefully underlined the extent to which the AFL did in fact manage to become a strong force in Montreal and to achieve a substantial francophone base before 1940, the appearance of this article in the *American Federationist* (which saw the light of day with the approval of Sam Gompers himself) could be cited as evidence that the AFL's indifference toward, and ignorance of, French-Canadian workers has been

---

[49]Marlene Shore, *The Science of Social Redemption: McGill, the Chicago School, and the Origins of Social Research in Canada* (Toronto: University of Toronto Press, 1987), Ch.4.

[50]Jacques Rouillard, *Histoire du Syndicalisme Québécois* (Montréal: Boréal, 1989), Ch.2; Robert Babcock, *Gompers in Canada: A Study in American Continentalism Before the First World War* (Toronto: University of Toronto Press, 1974), 124-133. Babcock (whose account remains a landmark of Canadian labour historiography) remarked that the "French factor in Quebec" was among those distinctive elements of Canada that were "filtered out or warped by a bureaucratic structure and system of values which had arisen from the experience of Gompers and the AFL solely in the United States." (viii)

[51]Gustave Francq, fraternal delegate to the AFL in 1913, would make similar points himself when he spoke of "a peculiarity of the Latin race": Babcock, *Gompers in Canada*, 131.

overestimated.[52] After all, for all the ethnic essentialism characteristic of the time, McKay's main point is clear: he is suggesting that French-Canadian Montrealers make better trade unionists than their anglophone counterparts, are remarkably tolerant on questions regarding the language of trade union affairs, and (because of the sensitivity of their position on the continent) are also quick to resent "gratuitous interference with the conduct of their affairs" [§.15, "The French Canadian as a Trade Unionist"]. The AFL is thus put on notice that it should respect the abilities and the self-government of French-Canadian trade unionists.

A non-specialist hesitates to enter this important debate in Québec labour history, which holds such important consequences for the ways in which class, ethnicity, and religion are conceptualized in Montréal.   However, one who has studied McKay's writings intensively *does* feel entitled to comment on the unusual level of incoherence and contradiction in McKay's article on this question. The "racial" characteristics adduced in the first section of the article would seem to be utterly confounded by the "organizational" achievements described in the second: the attribution of solidity and conservatism with which the article begins, is then seemingly utterly contradicted by evidence that French Canadians, in numbers larger than those of anglophone Montrealers, have thronged to the AFL (which McKay would have identified at this time as an unqualified "force of progress.") The highly contradictory quality of this article stems from the difficulty turn-of-the-century liberals experienced when confronted with the question of nationality (a difficulty that was to be inherited by many Marxists). McKay was undoubtedly unusual in the lengths to which he went to build bridges across the French/English divide in Montreal and his sympathy and active engagement with French-Canadian workers.[53] Both in the struggle against Fortier and later in his work with *Le Monde Ouvrier/Labor World*, McKay seems to have been genuinely concerned to bridge the gulf of ethnicity and language. At the same time, he seems to have had a shallow grasp of "national questions" in Canada, and specifically never indicated that he had an understanding of the depth and tenacity of French-Canadian nationalism.[54] On such vital questions as

---

[52]Bernard Dionne, "Les 'Unions Internationales' et le Conseil des Métiers et du Travail de Montréal, de 1938 à 1958," Ph.D. Thesis, Université du Québec à Montréal, 1990, ch.2. Dionne's evidence of the widespread and durable implanting of AFL craft unionism in Montreal suggests that Babcock's position was susceptible to further development and refinement.

[53]He was far ahead of W.U.Cotton in this regard: see Edward M. Penton, "The Ideas of William Cotton: A Marxist View of Canadian Society (1908-1914)." M.A.Thesis, University of Ottawa, 1978, 123.

[54]In the many articles he sent to *Le Monde Ouvrier/The Labor World* in the 1920s and 1930s evidently only two make specific and sustained reference to events in Québec: one critiques Montreal mayor Camilien Houde for his advocacy of a "back-to-the-land" scheme for the unemployed (C. McKay, "Mayor Evades Issue," *Labor World/Le Monde Ouvrier*, 15 June 1935); the other criticizes Maurice Duplessis as disruptive to

Catholic unionism, the Church's continuing role in education, the rise of the Union Nationale, the influx of French Canadians into Montreal and the rise of a French-Canadian proletariat, McKay evidently had little or nothing to say. Québec's cultural specificity was largely invisible to him. He preferred to devote his space in *Le Monde Ouvrier/Labor World* to the analysis of economic issues that were common to labour across Canada and throughout much of the world. Perhaps his halting and partial efforts to come to terms with cultural difference, whether we choose to judge them harshly or kindly, are most interesting as examples of a pervasive difficulty of both liberal and early-Marxist thought: that of understanding forms of belonging that cannot be straightforwardly read out of class position.

5. The Eclecticism and Contradictions of McKay's Liberal Thought

The articles of Colin McKay from 1897 to 1906 suggest, in all these ways, an intellectual struggling to find coherence in the world around him, and moving with the liberal currents of his day without finding his own clear sense of direction. Moulded by a Christian tradition he never explicitly renounced, and just as profoundly by a liberal individualism which would continue to exert a quiet, profound influence on him, long after he became a Marxist, McKay was at sea (he would have appreciated this figure of speech) in a world that had seemingly displaced the Christian and liberal truths that he both accepted and questioned. How often did this troubled liberal turn to irony as a way of handling his world! Yet the sardonic thrusts at utopians, SLPers, and temperance advocates could not conceal the radical cast of his mind and the democratic goals he harboured (even when these took the strange form of utopian fantasies about the spontaneous revival of folk dancing in British garden cities!) McKay was torn, between celebrating modernity as "progress" and condemning it as "degeneration"; and he was also divided between thinking in the individualist way of the traditional liberal, and the newer collectivist doctrines of the socialist movement.

His reading at this time was extremely wide: of the many renowned authors referred to, Herbert Spencer, Karl Marx, and J.A. Hobson predominate. Yet the writing based on this reading seemed to lack integration, and the strategy of quotation suggests a rather superficial grasp of diverse and often contradictory arguments. His reading of Marx, for example, does not suggest at this point a real comprehension of Marx's theory of history, and his dialogue with Spencer engaged not the fundamentals of Spencerian theory but only its controversially individualist political implications. In this, McKay was perhaps like many neophyte intellectuals, reading as many people as quickly as possible,

---

"Canadian unity" (C.M., "Nation Wide Interest in Trépanier's Fight," *Le Monde Ouvrier/Labor World* 29 October 1938).

without a clear sense of how such reading would fit into a wider coherence. His articles of this period are consequently mainly interesting as documents from a liberal in transition, searching for a pattern in the confusion and noise of a fast-changing world.

McKay would retain for later use many aspects of the democratic liberalism he espoused in his early years.Spencer's emphasis on a universal, integrating process of social evolution would leave a permanent impression on him. The value-idea of freedom transcended the crass and inhuman uses to which it had been put in liberal theory, and McKay never abandoned it, although he would later find that to be consistently devoted to the value-idea of freedom meant transcending the liberal order, and attaining a new form of democracy based on the full socialization of the economy. In 1907, McKay's analysis of the "Methods of Money-Makers to Bunco the Multitude" was transitional: McKay's populist attack on big corporations and "frenzied finance" was coupled with a call for a "renaissance of citizenship -- some such interest in public matters as prevailed in Nova Scotia when Joseph Howe was fighting battles of the press."[55] "One of the tenets of the old liberal philosophy," noted McKay with approval, "was that men ought to think for themselves" [S.24, "The Master Magicians"]. A 1908 article in the Shelburne *Coast Guard* -- "A Modern Prophet's Opinion of Fishermen, Or Why Did Christ Choose Fishermen as Apostles?" -- provides a fascinating example of McKay's liberalism in transition. On the one hand, McKay was concerned to defend the *Coast Guard* and the Fishermen's Union against the charge of "socialism" brought by its critics, and on the other hand he was intent on proving that socialism was nothing other than the message of Christ, and its opponents nothing more than present-day Pharisees:

> Christ was crucified for preaching socialism to fishermen. But that Christ should assume that fishermen were intelligent hardly justifies the editor of the Coast Guard in assuming the same thing. At any rate Canadian Pharisees don't think so, and wisdom was born with them and apparently died in infancy.
>
> For what is socialism. The fishermen, who undertook to propagate the Gospel of Christ, believed in it, and followed it; but then we know -- we have Mr. Whitman's word for it -- that fishermen are not intelligent. Hence it would be folly for us to accept the gospel of socialism.

For all the "socialism" of this position, however, McKay's depiction of capitalists was still tinged with a liberal critique of hereditary rights and with a defence of individualism:

---

[55]Colin McKay, "Favored Finance: Methods of Money-Makers to Bunco the Multitude," *Yarmouth Times*, 5 March 1907.

...we are told that socialism and human liberty are incompatible --
that socialism would reduce us all to a dead level of uniformity.
On the contrary, socialism, by establishing an equal start, by
suppressing the hereditary privileges, which assure industrial,
social and political leadership to so many mediocrities and
incompetents -- by rescuing from ignorance and poverty
thousands of noble intellects which need but a little light and well
being to realize their possibilities, by developing, through
systematic organization, the general and technical capacity of all
workers, would enable everybody to make the most of their
abilities, and carry to a maximum human knowledge, the power of
man over nature, and consequently liberty in its fullest sense. "All
men," says Grant Allen, "are created free and unequal." The aim
of socialism is to maintain this natural inequality, and draw the
greatest possible benefit from it.[56]

McKay admired the liberal tradition , even after he had grown beyond it,
for its defence of important freedoms. He could bring himself to write
warmly of the antiquely ultra-liberal Saint John *Globe*   ("always
independent and fearless") when it defended, on classically liberal
grounds, the right of socialists to hold open-air meetings.[57] A McKay
argument generally probed the merits of the opponent's arguments, and
conceded the limits on its own claim to truth.   There were certainly
important elements of the liberal tradition in McKay's later vision of a
radical economic democracy, a political order in which each person
would shape society and be shaped by it in turn, when each person would
be deeply connected by the deepest bonds of belonging to all, and when
each person would receive according to his or her needs, and give
according to his or her abilities. One might even say that his mature
socialism emerged as the   temporary resolution of many of the
contradictions of his youthful liberalism.

---

[56]Colin McKay, "A Modern Prophet's Opinion of Fishermen, Or Why Did Christ
Choose Fishermen as Apostles?" *Yarmouth Times,* 3 April 1908 [reprinting the original
article in the *Coast Guard*].
[57]Colin McKay, "No Public Forum for St. John Citizens," *Eastern Labor News*, 6 July
1912.

1. This Industrial Egypt: A Christian Looks at the "Sweating System" in Montreal[58]

Sweating, as an industrial term, was first applied to the practice of overwork under sub-contractors in the lower branches of the tailoring trade. Its meaning, however, has gradually expanded until now it has become a term to express the condition of all over-worked, ill-paid, badly-housed workers in large cities. It sums up the economic or industrial aspects of the problem of city poverty. In the lower branches of all trades there is always more or less of sweating -- a portion of the people who are miserably oppressed. This is true, not only of tailors and unskilled laborers, but of clerks, shop men, and the lower class of brain workers. In nearly every case the same pitiable conditions obtain; and, in nearly every case, the causes are much the same.

In this paper we will confine our remarks on sweating to the condition of the garment-workers in Montreal; not, however, because the nature of the industrial disease is different from that in other trades, but because the malady is at present more aggravated and touches more directly the primary conditions of life.

The custom tailors of Montreal have their work done by highly-skilled and well-paid workmen. In the ready-made clothing trade, however, the bulk of the work is done by sweaters. As a rule these sweaters are skilled tailors, who superintend the work of unskilled hands, and work themselves. In the larger workshops the worst symptoms of sweating are usually absent, though wages are poor enough. In the small workshops, which are increasing in Montreal, the common evils of the sweating system assert themselves -- overcrowding, bad sanitation, and long hours of labor. These shops are generally run by Jews. When the Jew has become an expert tailor he has a penchant for starting business on his own hook. He opens a room in his place of abode generally, puts in several machines and hires four or five girls and men. Then he takes contracts for making up clothing from the big wholesale houses, and starts to work. He sweats himself as well as his employees. Often he makes less on his contracts than he would in wages as a worker in the large shops. But he likes to be his own master, to be independent, and he is content to make less for a time. He works long hours, and expects his employees to do the same. In these shops bad sanitary conditions prevail. In summer the atmosphere is stifling, and makes the inmates feel gloomy, angry and sick, and unfits them for work. In winter the shops are overheated or cold, dismal and dark. As a rule there are no conveniences in such houses, and the workers,

---

[58]Originally published as "Sacrifices of Gods of Industry. A Chapter Out of the History of the Sweating System as it is Being Written in Montreal.(First Paper)," *Montreal Herald*, 7 January 1899.

male and female, have to leave an overheated room and go out of doors on the coldest winter's day.

The industrial and sanitary inspectors seldom attempt to remedy the conditions prevailing in these shops. In the first place the law, as it stands, is not calculated to cope with the sweating system in this form. A man may open a tailor shop and carry on business without the inspectors being aware of its existence. The law requires that a master shall notify the inspector within 30 days from the opening of a new establishment. The sweater may or may not comply with the act. He may go on for years without the inspectors discovering his business. If discovered he may claim that he is running a "domestic workshop," and as shops wherein only members of a family are employed do not come under the provisions of the act governing industrial establishments, the inspector is powerless. A sweater's contention that he is running a domestic workshop may be false, but the inspectors will hardly take the trouble to prove it so. As a garment worker said to me, the inspectors are quite willing to believe that all the Jews in Montreal belong to one family.

The inspectors could no doubt do a great deal of good -- much more than they do now -- if they tried to enforce the present regulations in a more energetic way. But, nevertheless, a revision of the law is necessary. In Pennsylvania, before a small master can take a contract from a large wholesale clothing establishment, he must show a license from the inspector, certifying that his shop is in a sanitary condition and suited to the purpose of making clothes. Such a provision throws the responsibility on the wholesale house, and effectually prevents the evasion of the law. In Montreal at present the wholesale men do not inquire or care whether the clothing is made up under sanitary conditions or not. Their only concern is to get the work done as cheaply as possible. In the shadow of the so-called respectability of his house the wholesaler can take advantage of the competition for work among the small shop men, and force contract prices down until the small master has to sweat his employees and himself half to death in order to make a livelihood.

In the popular mind, the sweater has been pictured as an idle, bloated middleman, who drank champagne and smoked cigars, while he watched the sallow faces and cowering forms of the wretched creatures, whose happiness, health and very life were being sacrificed to his heartless greed. This human spider is not to be found in the Montreal tailoring trade. In many of the worst sweating dens the master sweater does not on an average make a larger income than the better paid of his operatives. Most of the sweaters work along with their employees, and work just as hard. Some people have represented the sweater as one who thrusts himself between the proper employer and the working man in order to make a gain for himself without performing any service. In the government work this species of middleman has been common enough until recently. But in the general trade, the sweater, even when he does not occupy himself in detailed manual labour, performs the useful work of [superintendency] and management. The sweater can get more work at a cheaper rate out of the poorer workmen than the manager of a large firm. In his capacity he is a convenience. He acts as a screen to the employing firm. A business house would not be permitted by public opinion to employ workers directly under its own roof upon the terms which the secrecy of the sweater's place enables them to pay.

In the second view of the system the responsibility is shifted upon the wholesale houses. The small master, it is seen, sweats others, because he is sweated in the low terms of the contract he makes with the employer. Some employers are responsible for the hardship and degradation inflicted upon the workers in these dens. But many are not. In many firms the rate of profit is at the minimum of subsistence; that is to say, if higher wages were paid to employees, the rate of profit would become so low that capital could no longer be obtained for investment in such a trade. The individual employer, under ordinary circumstances, is no more to blame for low wages, long hours, etc., than the middleman. He could not greatly improve the condition of his employees, however much he might wish to do so.

A third view, which is a little longer-sighted than the others, casts the blame on the purchasing public. It is argued that wages must be low, because the purchaser insists on low prices. The rage for cheapness, for bargains, is the real cause according to this line of thought. A few years ago the customer willingly paid a fair price for a fair suit of clothes. The tradesman could thus pay a price which would enable the manufacturer to pay decent wages, and in return insisted upon good work. But modern competition has changed things. Advertising has taken the place of regular customs, the shopkeeper seeks to sell the largest quantity of goods, and the consumer to pay the lowest price. A deterioration in the quality of goods is the result. The ready sale of clothing of bad workmanship is no doubt directly responsible for many phases of sweating.

If the public insisted on buying good articles, and paid the price necessary for their production, sweating might disappear. But we must remember that the payment of a higher price would be no guarantee that the workers would not be sweated. If a white list of firms which paid good wages [and] dealt only with manufacturers who paid good wages, were formed, purchasers who desired to discourage sweating might feel sure that their efforts were not altogether futile. If the public insisted upon the Garment Workers' Union label appearing on the clothing, much good might also result. In Montreal no firm uses the label. Garment workers say that no firm in its working conditions conforms to the requirements necessary to obtain the use of the label; that no ready-made clothing is manufactured under union conditions -- good sanitation, fair wages, and fair hours. Obviously the garment workers' trade in this city is in a bad state of affairs.

The conditions in the trade in Montreal have been greatly aggravated by a practice recently adopted by the big firms. Some years ago several of the wholesale houses began sending their work out of town to farmers' families. As the farmers' wives and daughters do not take in such work through necessity, but only in order to get money, to buy finery and luxuries for themselves, they can afford to do it for very little in their leisure time during the winter. At present a large amount of work is being done by outsiders, who have no particular need of it, while our city workers are vainly seeking for work. As a consequence there is much poverty among the garment workers, especially in the winter, and this poverty results sooner or lated [later] in imposing burdens of various kinds upon the city. In the interests of the citizens, as well as the workers directly concerned, it would be advisable to prohibit the practice of sending clothes to the country to be manufactured into garments by farmers' families. The more work that is done outside, the worse [become] the evils of the sweating system, and the greater its menace to the public health. If all the work that is now done in the country were given to the city garment workers, there would be employment for nearly all the latter, and the chief cause of sweating, a surplus of labour, being removed, the worst evils in this trade would disappear for a time. The garment workers of the city claim that they ought to be protected by imposing a tax in some form upon clothing made outside. The farmers who sell farm and garden produce in the city are required to pay a tax in the form of a license. Why? Because they compete with grocers and those who contribute to the civic revenues. Then why should not those who compete with the garment workers be required to pay a tax? Probably because the garment workers are not in a position to secure legislation in their interests, like other classes. While personally regarding such methods of regulating trade as wrong in principle, I believe that the condition of the garment workers in Montreal would justify legislation of this character for the present at any rate.

In this paper we have only dealt with a few of the minor causes of sweating -- those most susceptible to legislative remedy. While the removal of these branch causes would no doubt better the conditions of the garment workers, it should be remembered that the sweating will continue in one form or other so long as the root evil of the system remains. That root -- the underlying cause of all sweating -- is the presence of a large number of unemployed and unskilled working men and women. So long as there is a large surplus of labour, the sweating system will continue in large cities. Legislation on the lines we have suggested may produce good results, but it can never permanently uproot the sweating system, unless it deals first and foremost with the problem of the unemployed. Philosophic economists tell us that the movements of modern industry require a large surplus of labour. But this explanation gives little satisfaction. No man or woman with a brain and heart can contemplate with complacency the awful sacrifices of human life, health and happiness required by the gods of competitive industry. Such sacrifices are foreign to the spirit of Christian civilization. In all parts of the world our industrial system is being called to the bar of Christian conscience, and is being pronounced guilty of many sins. Will men escape from this industrial Egypt? The Moses has not yet appeared. But let us have hope. Political economists hitherto have only succeeded in pointing out the difficulties in the path of progress. They have only dealt with man as a machine. But man is more -- much more. Hitherto progress has been a car of Juggernaut -- all advance has required awful sacrifices. But when Christian hearts and minds learn to direct evolution along its proper path, the car of progress will not crush, but will carry men.

2. The Secret of Poverty[59]

In a former paper we pointed out the need of a revision of the act respecting industrial establishments in order to cope with the sweating system as it exists in Montreal.

As there is no effectual system of registration, there is great difficulty in discovering and exercising the necessary supervision over the smaller workshop. As the power of the inspectors and sanitary physicians "to enter at all reasonable times, by day or by night," industrial establishments, is not applicable in the case of dwelling rooms used for workshops, many sweat shops can exist in defiance of the law. In many places where sweating exists in its worst forms, the inspector must obtain the consent of the occupant before he can enter, and the time which elapses before such consent is given will generally suffice to enable the sweater to remove all evidence of infringement of the law.

A better system of registration, an extension of the act so as to make it applicable to domestic workshops, and an increase in the power of the inspectors, would lead to the abatement of some of the worst evils of the sweating system in Montreal. Laws should also be introduced tending to increase the legal responsibility of the employer, and to eliminate the small master and crush the small workshop by imposing irksome and expensive conditions.

While legislation of this character may abate many of the symptoms of sweating, it can not touch the centre of the malady -- low wages. It may secure good sanitary conditions for the workers, but it [is] not calculated

---

[59]Originally published as "The Secret of Poverty. Mr. C. McKay Discusses the Millstones Around the Necks of the Poor and Declares They Are Economic Rather Than Moral," *Montreal Herald*, 14 January 1899.

to secure good wages, food or clothes for them. It may, however, by turning the wholesome light of publicity upon the evils of sweating, be of indirect assistance in preventing the payment of wages which public opinion would condemn as insufficient for a decent livelihood.

Sweating, as an industrial disease, is primarily of economic origin. The industrial degradation of the sweated workers arises from the presence of a large number of unemployed. As long as there is a surplus of labour, the wages of low skilled workers can never be materially raised, at least under our present system of industry.

Orthodox economists, putting their faith with philosophic resignation in what Lassalle[60] called the iron law of wages, have never bothered about the problem of the unemployed. In their theories there never was such a problem. If wages decreased through any cause the workers would rear fewer children, and in process of time the decrease in population, or supply of labour, would, through the increased demand for labour by the capitalists, tend to raise wages. If, on the other hand, wages increased, the number of labourers would increase, and the over-supply of labour would in time operate to bring wages down again. This beautiful iron law of the economists -- this splendid see-saw business -- which inevitably readjusted things in the normal style, however much they might vary this way or that -- which always operated to abolish by the gentle process of lingering starvation, an oversupply of labourers, or vice-versa, increase an undersupply -- which thus solved the problem of the unemployed, or produced it, according as there was need -- this so-called law has made men almost despair of ever bettering the condition of the low-skilled labourers as a class. The economists' habit of treating as an absolute law what is only a conditional phenomenon, has made the science of political economy a sad and dismal farce. No two economists agree on any two points, yet each lays down his theories as absolute immutable, infallible laws. The writers on "evolution" are no more diverse in views, no more absolute.

Political economists have no solutions to offer for the problems of sociology. They grope in the darkness of terms, and inhuman vocabularies, and will not see the light. As Mrs. Stetson[61] says:--

---

[60]Ferdinand Lassalle (1825-1864) was one of the most important leaders in the socialist movement in Germany. He had recourse to "the iron law of wages" to explain the persistence of subsistence levels of income despite general prosperity. His conciliatory approach to the state and his non-revolutionary social philosophy distanced him from Marx and Engels. Contrary to McKay's suggestion in this article, his views on wages were not in fact espoused by most orthodox economists at the turn of the century.

[61]The American writer Charlotte Perkins Gilman, who wrote under the name of "Stetson" until her marriage to Houghton Gilman in 1900, was an avid Spencerian,

"They shut their eyes and call it night;
They grope and fall in seas of light."[62]

Many intelligent people who have had their minds darkened by the dismal science of political economy despair of solving the problem of poverty.

Another class of good citizens who hold that the most important factors in such problems are moral, say that legislation, or industrial reconstruction, will never remedy such evils as sweating, etc. Philanthropists of moral and religious temperaments, who interest themselves in the miserable condition of the poor, see so much of the moral symptoms of the disease of poverty that they mistake them for prime causes. Men or women of this character scarcely perceive the economic aspects of poverty and never dream of the applications of economic remedies. Mr. Arnold White[63] expresses a common view when he says: "It is a fact apparent to every thoughtful man that the larger portion of the misery that constitutes our social question arises from idleness, gluttony, drink, waste, indulgence, profligacy, betting and dissipation." Are these vices the private property of the poor? No! The poor, for the most part, are incapable of practising some of them. These vices are more common to the rich. The social question is the outcome of idleness, gluttony, drink, waste, profligacy, indulgence, etc., among the rich more than the poor. Now, we don't mean to say that these vices do not exist among the poor. As a matter of fact some of them are common enough among the poor. The people of the slums have no desire, no time to be moral, intellectual or even clean. What they want is better food, and more of it, warmer clothes, better shelter, and greater security of permanent employment or decent wages. Unless these lower desires are gratified, the people of the slums will never awaken to the higher moral and intellectual desires. Help these people out of the body-dwarfing,

---

socialist and feminist. Her works include *Women and Economics* (1898), and the novel *Herland,* serialized in 1915. Mariana Valverde has remarked on the extent to which Canadian feminist circles cited Gilman (along with Elizabeth Blackwell and Frances Willard): see "'When the Mother of the Race is Free': Race, Reproduction, and Sexuality in First-Wave Feminism," in Franca Iacovetta and Mariana Valverde, eds., *Gender Conflicts: New Essays in Women's History* (Toronto: University of Toronto Press, 1992): 4.

[62]McKay is quoting Charlotte Perkins Stetson, *In This Our World* (Boston: Small, Maynard and Company, 1893): v.

[63]Arnold Henry White was an English writer and politician. He was a key proponent of militarism and played a significant role in developing the "naval scare" in Britain in 1901. He also argued for eugenics. Among his writings are *The Problems of a Great City* (1886), *Efficiency and Empire* (1901), *When War Breaks Out* (1898), and *The Navy: Its Place in British History* (1912), revised as *Our Sure Shield The Navy* (1917).

mind-blighting, soul-scarring hell of poverty, and they will become more and more intellectual of their own accord.

No: that is the wrong way of tackling the question, say the religious and social reformers. If you would uplift the people of the slums you must first make them moral, thrifty, temperate, etc. If you were to place these poor people in good economic conditions, their vices would soon bring them to their former state. If you do not first bring about a change in their nature it will be useless to change their economic conditions. No radical improvement of industrial organization, no work of social reconstruction can be of any avail unless it is preceded by the moral and intellectual improvement in the condition of the mass necessary to make the new machinery effective to its higher ends. This "moral" view has much to recommend it on first sight. The vices of the poor are visibly responsible for the misery and degradation of the vicious and their families.

As this view of poverty represents the condition of the poor to be chiefly their own fault, it lessens the sense of responsibility on the part of the well-to-do. It also flatters the pride of the rich man by representing poverty as an evidence of incompetency, salves his conscience when stirred by the contrasts of misery and luxury around him, and enables him to secure his material interests by adopting an attitude of repression towards industrial or political agitations in the interests of labourers. It is comfortable, too, no doubt, to feel that you are reaping the reward of a higher moral life. It also justifies you in exploiting labourers, in order to endow churches and moral reform agencies, inasmuch as the poor must first be made moral before it will be wise to trust them with the material blessings of earth.

But is this "moral" view correct? Is poverty a disease of a moral or economic nature? Aristotle said: "It is needful first to have a maintenance, and then to practice virtue."[64] How can moral or intellectual education improve human beings whose whole energies are absorbed in the effort to secure bare physical support[?]

In accordance with nature, material growth precedes moral. Reformers must understand that material reform comes first, and unless proper

---

[64]McKay is perhaps paraphrasing the following passage from Aristotle: "But happiness also appears to require external goods, as we have mentioned: for it is impossible or not easy to act nobly if one is not furnished with external goods. For many actions are done through friends or wealth or political power, as by means or instruments....What goes by the name of 'self-sufficiency,' too, would apply to theoretical activity most of all; for although wise men and just men and all the rest have need of the necessities of life, when they are all sufficiently provided with then, a just man needs others towards whom and with whom he will *act* justly...." Aristotle, *Selected Works*, trans. H.G. Apostle and L.P.Gerson (Grinnell, Iowa: Peripatetic, 1982): 1099a30 - 1099b5; 1177a25-1177a30.

precedence be yielded to it, we can never attain the higher ends of humanity. It is impossible to effectually apply moral or intellectual influences to the poor unless we have first placed them on a sound basis of physical existence.

Often we hear men and women who are incapable of earning the money they spend say that the inefficiency of the poor is the cause of poverty. The poor, as a class, are very inefficient workers. A child of the slums, ill-fed in body and mind, brought up amid the industrial degradation of low city life, without a chance to learn a trade or acquire the habits of steady industry, will hardly become a good workman. It is the bitterest portion of the lot of the poor that they have no opportunities of learning to work well. It is pharisacal [pharisaical] insolence to taunt them with inefficiency. As a class, the poor in cities have no more chance under present conditions of attaining efficiency in work than of acquiring a refined, artistic taste or literary culture or holiness.

If you consider personal vices, like intemperance, unthrift, etc., in reference to poverty, you will be driven to the conclusion that they are merely symptoms and not causes of poverty. Approach the problem from whatever point of view you will, it is evident... that poverty is a disease of an economic nature -- that its chief cause is the vicious operation of our present system of industry.

The only real remedy for civic poverty must be one which will deal with its economic aspect. Our economists must find the remedy, and our legislators must apply it. Our economists are not trying to find an economical solution for the problem of poverty. Nobody is. It wouldn't pay. Instead of seeking to obtain a knowledge of the basic principles of Christian economics and apply them to industry, our men of brains are delving in a hundred sciences and arts. A man who really understood the science of economics might serve society, but, you know, a man who understands the practical sciences, is more able to serve his own ends.

McGill men are trained in the sciences which will enable them to serve themselves. But they are not trained in the sciences which will fit them to serve society and cope with the great social problems of the day. While McGill has dozens of professors of sciences and arts, it has not one of economics or sociology.

"Is it well that while we range with science, glorying in the time,
City children soak and blacken soul and sense in city slime?
There among the glooming alleys Progress halts on palsied feet.
Crime and hunger cast our maidens by the thousand on the street.
There the master scrimps his haggard seamstress of her daily bread,
There a single sordid attic holds the living and the dead."

3. The Abolition of the Sweating System: A Call for Action[65]

The Federated Trades and Labor Council has undertaken an active crusade against the sweating system, which, admittedly, prevails to a great extent in Montreal. The factory inspectors themselves have repeatedly admitted the fact, only to say, as it has often been said elsewhere, that they are powerless -- mainly owing to the fact that many of the small establishments where the worse conditions prevail, cannot be considered as factories under the law.

The Council's first step will therefore be to seek an amendment to the present factory law. But realizing that it takes time to move legislators and that all law, to be effective, must be backed by public opinion, the Council has resolved to press the union label upon the attention of the public, as a remedial instrument which attests that the garment sold has been made under sanitary conditions. The Council will shortly issue thousands of circulars setting forth its views on the subject. One of these circulars, from the pen of Mr. C. McKay, says:--

"In Montreal the clothing industry is carried on almost entirely on the sweating system. Members of the Garment Workers' Union say the general conditions of the trade are lower here than in New York and London. If this be so -- and the opinion of these workers is based on experience in the three cities -- the conditions call for attention and earnest effort in the direction of... reform. An analysis of the situation inclines us to the opinion that the responsibility for the working conditions rests largely with the purchasing public. As long as the public are content to wear sweatshop products, the manufacturers are not likely to improve their methods of making up clothing.

The problem then is to arouse the purchasing public into a sense of responsibility. If the public realized their guilt they would refuse to buy the product of the sweating system, and thus force the manufacturers to adopt improved methods. In general the Montreal public and large manufacturers themselves have no idea of the misery and horror attending the sweating system.

In most industries improved building methods, sanitation and factory legislation have improved the working conditions. The clothing industry constitutes the chief exception to the rule. The centralization of industry, the introduction of the large and well equipped factory, the elimination of small masters, which have been the marks of industrial progress during the last generation or so, have not extended their operations to the clothing trade. In the midst of modern manufacturing methods, the great

---

[65]Originally published as "To Abolish The Sweating System. The Federated Trades Council Takes the Initiative of an Active Campaign," *Montreal Herald*, 3 July 1899.

factory and direct employment system, the clothing industry still clings to the domestic workshop and the petty contract system. And why? It is said that manufacturers have found that it costs more to manufacture clothing in large establishments, under improved conditions, than by giving the work to small contractors, because a garment can be made more cheaply in a small shop, where the services of the family can be used and where there is no particular limit as to the length of the work day. According to this contention, the alchemy of centralization which has revolutionized so many industries, fails in application to the clothing trade. Many intelligent and observing garment workers however, claim that centralization in the clothing industry would enable manufacturers to have their garments made up as cheaply as under the small-shop regime. The real reason that the clothing industry remains almost the only exception to the general tendency is that the establishment of large and properly equipped factories would involve, besides the worry incidental to management and the responsibility for the working conditions, an immediate outlay of a large amount of capital. As the simplicity of methods at present employed enable many men to become manufacturers, the competition is intense and the clothing industry has never appeared a promising field for the investment of capital. It is not certain, however, that its nature renders it unsusceptible to the economizing influences of operations on a large scale. In fact, the clothing industry is only an evidence of the sociological law that bad conditions brought about by the short-sighted methods of irresponsible individual greed tend to conserve themselves. The clothing manufacturer, finding that present methods not only enable him to evade all responsibility, but enable him to realize large and immediate profits on little outlay, is not likely to invest capital in improving the methods, even though in the end he might be able to reap larger results.

If the public will shoulder their responsibility and grapple with the sweating problem, a reform instrument, independent of factory legislation, is ready to their hand. It is the Union Label. If the public could be induced to only purchase clothing bearing the Union Label the sweating evil would disappear. The label is designed to fulfil all the functions of factory legislation -- and much more -- without any expense to the State. No legislation, however radical and however rigorously enforced, could guarantee to a purchaser that any particular piece of clothing was manufactured on sanitary premises by competent workers, receiving fair wages and working decent hours.

The Union Label, however, can guarantee this...."

4. Women and the Sweating System: Why Women are Women's Foes in Labour's Sphere[66]

The Local Council of Women,... have interested themselves in the sweating problem. The question is more of a woman's question than a man's, and therefore demands their attention. Apply the four chief heads in the sweating disease -- low wages, long hours, irregular employment and unsanitary conditions -- to women's work, and it will be found that the pressure in each case is very much heavier on the weaker sex.

In a report upon textile industries it is shown that where women work at piecework along with men, they get as high wages as men for the same quantity of work. This is sometimes true in other trades, but in the majority of instances it is not the case. As a rule, women workers do not receive the same wages as men for equal work. It is said to be due to a male prejudice or sentimental bias, but such a contention is hardly tenable. If women workers, possessing the same skill as male workers, were as strongly organized, they would be able to command the same rate of wages in any trade.

The general condition of women workers has many elements of industrial weakness unknown to men, and these keep down wages. Apart from the fact that a free woman is able to keep herself in a working condition on a lower scale of expenditure than a man, there are several economic causes which bring down women's wages. Many women workers are not dependent for their full livelihood upon the wages they get. Married women, in order to procure special comforts for themselves, or increase the family income, work at wages they would not be willing to accept if they were working for full maintenance. Many unmarried women live at home, more cheaply than they could by themselves. Young women, being largely supported at the expense of the family, are willing to toil long hours for a small sum to spend on superfluities. Again, there is the competition of women assisted by charity. The whole effect of this "uncommercial" competition falls on that miserable minority of their sisters who have no extra source of income, and who have to make the lower wages fund clothes and shelter for themselves, and perhaps a family of children. These bounty-fed women, being able and willing to take work at anything, keep the wages of women in sweating trades incredibly low. It is this and not male prejudice that makes women's wages lower than men's; women are the real enemies of women.

Women suffer more from irregularity of employment than men. One reason is that the season determines the condition of many women's

---

[66]Originally published as "Women are Women's Foes in Labor's Sphere. Sweating System Has More Interest for Women Than Men -- Its Abolition Should be a Woman's Fight." *Montreal Herald*, 11 November 1899.

trades, such as fur-sewing, confectionery, laundry work, match-making. Another is that the changes in fashion affect many women's trades. These fluctuations favour two important factors in the sweating problem, sub-contract and irregular homework.

The Factory Act is supposed to limit the hours of labour for women workers, but it only regulates a few trades, and in these special dispensations may be granted. The most important women's trades do not come under the operation of the act at all. Women, being largely employed in small workshops or their own often overcrowded homes, unsanitary conditions of work affect them more than men. In such places, where the Factory Act is not in force, they work longer hours, and hence poor ventilation or drainage, etc., injure their health more than men.

In addition to these considerations, there are special burdens incidental to women -- domestic work, care of children, etc.

In a civilized society we would probably have effective legislation regulating the employment of women in all trades, but unfortunately our civilization is more concerned with making provision for the employment of dum-dum bullets. If that great artist in blood and thunder was to take up the white women's burden, he would find a task worthy of his genius.[67]

Large employers of labour nowadays show a tendency to regard their men less as men than merely as so much producing power. Women workers are even less considered as personalities. Once in a while, on election days, the employer of male labour has to consider that these masses of producing power are resolved into votes. No employer, however, has to analyze the political force of women. This is probably one of the chief reasons why the industrial grievances of women are worse than those of men. To withhold political rights from women workers is the greatest crime of the century. Here is a state of affairs worse than in the Transvaal; here is taxation without representation, or any possibility of representation. It would have been more to the credit of their mothers' boys to stay right here in Canada and fight for the franchise for their mothers and daughters. But this new-fangled knight-errantry does not recognize the suzerainty of the fair sex. It may be chivalrous to help the lion kill the goat with the golden legs for the benefit of the fox, but we think another contingent might be organized to redress the more grievous wrongs at home. "The Empire is in danger" -- not from Oom Paul,[68] but

[67]McKay refers to Rudyard Kipling, "The White Man's Burden," perhaps the most popular expression of late-Victorian imperialism. He was by no means unusual among left-wingers of his time in treating Kipling's poems as a rhetorical resource; even Antonio Gramsci cited Kipling.
[68]McKay refers to Stephanus Johannes Paulus Kruger (1825-1904), vice-president of the South Africa Republic (Transvaal), 1877-1882, four times elected president 1882-

from the industrial system that trades in the liberties, rights and maternity of women workers....

[Women's] being factory workers first and mothers afterwards, is probably the chief cause of the high death rate among the children of the poorer classes. Roseher [Roscher] the German economist,[69] attributes the comparatively low death rate among Jewish children the world over to the fact that Jewish mothers seldom or never work outside their home. Legislation calculated to safeguard the rights of the unborn, is badly needed.

5. Of The Social State, Freedom of Speech, and J.M. Fortier: The Case for the Defence[70]

[McKay's struggle alongside the cigarmakers union against J.M.Fortier was a classic case involving labour's rights against capital, and his conviction led to a petition campaign . However, after an eight-day trial, McKay was found guilty of criminal libel, and did eventually serve his sentence. The following presents McKay's side of the events:]

According to the address of the judge, the case was a test of strength to some extent between labour and capital. The verdict, which was merely a reflection of the Judge's charge to the jury, cannot be any more satisfactory to Mr. Fortier than to the defendants. "The greater the truth the greater the libel," unless the articles complained of are in the public interest.

As the learned judge charged the jury to the effect that public interest was not an admissible plea in the case before them, the verdict cannot be said to have been given on the merits of the case. Indeed, the learned judge as good as admitted that the allegations complained of had been proven, but that was not enough. Was their publication for the public benefit? In charging the jury to the effect that their publication was not in the public interest, Judge Wurtele practically overruled Judge Ouimet's decision on the plea of justification by public interest last term.

1902, and leader of the republic during its war with Great Britain, 1899-1902. "Oom" in Afrikaans roughly translates as "uncle," and the nickname was applied generally in South Africa and eventually abroad.

[69]McKay refers to Wilhelm Roscher (1817-1894), professor of political economy at Göttingen (1840-1848) and later Leipsig (1848-1894). He was one of the founders of the German historical school of economics. In English, his most accessible work at this time was *Principles of Political Economy*, trans. by J.L. Lalor , 2 vols. (1878) For a discussion, see Jacob Oser, *The Evolution of Economic Thought*, 2nd. ed. (New York: Harcourt, Brace and World, 1970): 189-191.

[70]Originally published as "Fortier Vs. McKay. Suit of a Montreal Manufacturer Against a Publisher Who Criticized His Treatment of Employees -- Arbitration Refused -- The Defendant Convicted -- The Trial Reviewed." *Citizen and Country*, 4 December 1899.

Under the circumstances, the verdict only means that the jury thought the accused had published articles likely to arouse the ire of the plaintiff, and create a breach of the peace. According to the judge, when the truth was told about a man's fault, he was more apt to get mad than when lies were told about him.

Judge Wurtele, in his charge to the jury, said Canada was a Christian country. The defendant laboured under a similar impression when he wrote the articles complained of. But now he probably knows that there is a good deal of the leaven of paganism in society, especially in the law. As expounded by the learned judge, the law of the land does not agree with the law of Christ. In the first book, 18th chapter, verses 15-18 of the law of Christ[71], it is writ:

"If thy brother shall trespass against thee, go and tell him his fault between thee and him alone; if he shall hear thee thou hast gained thy brother.

"But if he will not hear thee, then take with thee one or two more, that in the mouth of two or three witnesses every word may be established.

"And if he shall neglect to hear them, tell it unto the church; but if he neglect to hear the church, let him be unto thee as a heathen and a publican."

In regard to Brother Fortier, not only the spirit but the letter of the law was fulfilled.

When Mr. Fortier discharged the cigarmakers at the beginning of winter, in order to reduce wages, the union men offered to arbitrate the matter privately, but he would not hear them. Then they called in the Federated Trades Council, as witnesses, and that body made representations to Mr. Fortier, but he would not hear them. And then, through the defendant they told it unto the trade unions of Montreal which being based in the great principle of brotherhood proclaimed by Christ, are essentially a church in the sense Christ employed the words.

And though merely fulfilling the law of Christ, we are tried under a law based on the old mean conception that every man is naturally bad and liable to make trouble, if told the truth about himself. In a Christian country, the dispensation of regeneration would prevail, and every person would be glad to have his faults pointed out, in order that he might see in what respects he might become a better man. The chief reason then Christianity has not influenced men more is that its ministers have never

[71]i.e., *Matthew* 18: 15-18.

told men of their faults in the manner Christ did. Witness how Christ, speaking to certain rich men in Jerusalem, called them whited sepulchers, vipers, etc. [72]

The learned judge charged the jury to the effect that the plea of justification on account of public interest did not hold as law in the present case; that public interest should not be confounded with the interests of the few, or a small body of citizens forming a class. That which affected a portion of the public did not affect the public at large. Well, that may be law, but it is contrary to the established opinions of social science and Christianity.

Herbert Spencer says: "The well-ordering of human affairs in remotest communities is beneficial to all men, the ill-ordering is injurious to all men. And though the citizens may be slightly acted upon by each particular good or evil influence at work within his own society; and still more slightly by each of those at work within other societies; yet it is on the cumulative effect of myriads of these infinitesimal influences that his happiness or misery depends....The interdependence which the social state necessitates makes all men's business his business in an indirect way....While men continue as social units, they cannot transgress the life principle of society without disastrous consequences somehow or other coming back upon them....A nation is a living organism analogous to the human body."[73]

And Christ, the wisest of all philosophers, said, "We are members of one body,"[74] and he expressly and implicitly laid it down that what affects one member affects each and every member of that body.

The learned judge admitted that the statements in the main article complained of were true, though, if it was not a matter of public interest, that did not justify them. The allegations that aroused the ire of the learned judge were certain quotations from well-known writers on ethics and economics, which were applied to the complainant. Thus there was a quotation .... stating that men, like the complainant, who refused to arbitrate with their employes, were "moral dynamiters."

---

[72]See *Matthew* 23: 27-29. A modern translation of "whited sepulcher" would be "white-washed tomb." These comments were not in fact addressed to "certain rich men," but more specifically to the scribes and Pharisees.

[73]McKay is drawing upon Herbert Spencer, *Social Statics; Or, The Conditions Essential to Human Happiness Specified, and the First of Them Developed* (New York: D. Appleton and Company, 1875): 484.

[74]This was in fact said by Paul, in *Ephesians* 4:25: "...for we are members one of another."

Another question [quotation] from an economic writer, Henry Lloyd,[75] alleged that the complainant was getting rich out of the flesh and blood of his employees.

The complainant stated under oath that he did not know the meaning of such phrases or terms, and his lawyers, although they grossly misinterpreted the sense, did not lay much stress on them.

The learned judge, however, not only refused the counsel for the defendant the right to show the jury the sense in which such phrases are employed by standard writers on ethics and economics, but, in his charge to the jury, interpreted their meaning in a manner which showed a superb ignorance of the English language, or audacious indifference to every principle thereof. For instance the statement that the complainant was growing rich out of the flesh and blood of boys and girls. That is a mere physical and economic fact. All wealth is the product of human labour, and all labour, all human exertion, necessitates the expenditure of muscle, sinew and brain -- that is, flesh and blood. In the strictest treatises of political economists employers are often charged with growing rich upon the flesh and blood of their employees. And yet the learned judge said: "Has the complainant lived by eating the flesh and drinking the blood of boys and girls? If not, the prisoner at the bar is guilty."

Was that a fair representation from the premises? Or was the English language outraged? The cigar makers examined were of poor physique, and in bad health. Why? From childhood they had been rolling their flesh and blood into cigars, in order to make their employer rich, and have never had time to grow, or develop properly. And when the strictly scientific statement complained of was translated into French its English meaning was unrecognizable.

The quotation from a book by Rev. Dr. Brown[76] was treated in the same way. Mr. St. Pierre wanted to produce the book, but was overruled. [The captains] of industry who [refuse] to arbitrate with [their] employees, who [stand] on [their] divine rights and [refuse] to recognize the interests or rights of those who invest their stock in trade, their labour, in [their businesses], are dangerous obstructionists, and moral dynamiters. They create dissension, excite passion, and misrepresent the attitudes of the generality of employers. But the judge exclaimed: "Is Mr. Fortier a

---

[75]McKay refers to Henry Demarest Lloyd (1847-1903), 1894 congressional candidate for the Populist Party, supporter of the utopian socialist Edward Bellamy, and author of *Wealth Against Commonwealth* (1894). This book was the probable source of the offending phrase.

[76]The reference is very likely to the writings of Rev. William Thurston Brown, a Social Gospel advocate who wrote *The Real Religion of Today* , *The Relation of Religion to Social Ethics*, and *After Capitalism, What?*, all of them published by Charles H. Kerr.

dynamiter? Does he go around blowing up buildings and killing people right and left?" In French he called it assassin -- a representation which the English significance does not warrant. The learned judge took no account of the qualification, "moral." A derivation of dynamics, dynamiter cannot be confounded with assassin, and a "moral dynamiter" cannot mean anything worse than a destroyer of good-will and harmony in society or a section thereof, if the English language means anything. The learned judge spoke for five hours, though he said he only intended to speak for fifteen minutes. But he only reviewed the evidence of one side of the case.

It is not to be expected that organized workingmen will grin and bear a knock-down like this from any judge. As we know where we stand, the law should be made to understand that a difficulty between an employer and his men is a matter of public interest, and that unless legal provision is made for arbitration, workingmen will demand their right to criticize an employer, especially when, as was proved in the Fortier case, that employer uses the public press to insult workingmen, to misrepresent their actions, and thus provoke criticism on their part. Mark the inconsistency of the law. An employer who discharges 76 men, out of whose labour he has grown rich, at the beginning of winter, and deprives them of the opportunity to earn a livelihood, certainly commits an act likely to arouse passion, and drive men to crime in order to live. But no matter whether men are driven by disgrace to crime or suicide, the employer is legally all right. But public comment on such employer's action is not in the public interest, and is a criminal offence, forsooth.

Workingmen, what do you think? It is for you, in your labour halls, and in the public press, to continue this trial before the bar of public opinion, reason and common sense. The defendant was allowed out on bail, pending sentence, which the judge said would be light, as he only wished the principle involved to be condemned. The idea of a judge wishing a principle -- a principle, mind -- to be condemned!

6. The Scourge of Unemployment: A Critique of Goldwin Smith[77]

Editor of the Herald:
Sir,-- An article written by Prof. Goldwin Smith[78] appears in your paper last night. "A young man," says the professor, "committed suicide because

---

[77]Originally published as a letter signed "C.McK." and titled "Socialism Round The Corner. A Correspondent Replies to Prof. Goldwin Smith Regarding the Labor Problem and Its Solution." *Montreal Herald*, 6 November 1897.

[78]Goldwin Smith (1823-1910) was one of the most well-known liberal intellectuals of Victorian Canada. He was Regius Professor of Modern History at Oxford 1858-1866, a founder member of faculty at Cornell University, Ithaca, New York, and, after 1871, a leading intellectual of Toronto, where he helped form the Canada First Movement. His

he could not get work to support himself and his relatives. There followed an angry call upon society to provide work. But how can society provide that which does not exist. If hands were wanted, they would be employed; if, unhappily, they are not, how is employment to be created?"

Does Prof. Smith mean to tell us that there is not enough useful work for these unemployed men? Surely, he cannot. Cast a glance at these men themselves; they need better clothes, food and shelter. Millions of workingmen need better dwellings, furniture and garments. The country needs more schools, better roads and improvements everywhere.

Why could not these unemployed be set to work to meet these demands?

"What is to be done if hands continue to multiply and machinery and other industrial and commercial economies continues to diminish.the demand for them?" asks the professor. That such a question should be asked by one who sets himself up as a philosopher, must make the angels weep.

The answer is, reduce the hours of labour.

The majority of the toilers, in spite of the constant want of employment, work 10, 12, 14, 16, yea 18 hours a day. Is it not plain then, that if there is not enough work for all to be employed 18, 14, 12 or 10 hours a day, the hours of those who work so long must be reduced? Why should some work from 10 to 16 hours a day and not enjoy life, while others are starving?

Are such conditions natural? Surely not! God never ordained that some men should work themselves to death, while others die from the lack of work. These conditions are only the results of the folly and ignorance of man, and hence man has the power to change them. One step out of this "social dilemma" is to reduce the hours of labour.

If all of the workingmen who are now unemployed and who necessarily consume but a small portion of the products of industry, were given work, there would at once be a demand for commodities of all sorts, and not only these men would be benefitted, but businessmen in general would benefit by the increased demands for commodities. This is self-evident. When a businessman gives a workingman employment he increases the consuming power of the community, and directly or indirectly the increased demand for commodities benefits himself. When a

---

books included *Canada and the Canadian Question* (1891), *My Memory of Gladstone* (1904), and *Labour and Capital* (1907). Smith was frequently involved in polemics against labour reformers and leftists, although he was by no means strictly a hidebound, *laissez-faire* liberal.

businessman discharges a workingman he harms not only the workingman, but himself also.

A general reduction of the hours of labour is a vital factor in the solution of the problem of the unemployed. The Government should reduce the hours of labour and allow no man to work more than a certain number of hours a day. Some will say that this would be trespassing on the "liberty" of the labourer to work as long as he pleases What is liberty? As well say that the Government should not trespass upon the liberty of one man to kill another man. The workingman who does his own work and then steps in and takes the work for which another is starving, is simply murdering his fellow, and it would be just as well to argue that a government has no more right to interfere with a man's liberty to kill his fellow man, as to argue that a government should not interfere with a man's liberty to do another man out of his means of earning a livelihood.

One reduction of the working hours, however, would not be a solution of the problem of the employed, except for a time.

Production would be increased in cost, and consequently there would be a great stimulus to invention. Machinery to supplant human labour would be perfected, and the old army of unemployed would soon appear again. Then it would be necessary to further reduce the working hours, and to keep on doing so. This if kept up indefinitely would be a solution of the problem of the unemployment, but it wouldn't be a solution of the Labour Question at all. The condition of the great wage-earning class would remain practically unchanged. Men would still live from hand to mouth, and in the midst of an over-abundance of the requirements of life they would remain as now, ill-fed, ill-clad and ill-housed.

The reduction of the working hours, as I have said, would solve the problem of the unemployed, but it wouldn't solve the labour question. Only a radical change in our social and economic system can do this. And a change is at hand. The labour question can and will be solved once and for all. "A way," says Prof. Smith, "will probably be found out of the social dilemma, as a way has been found out of other social dilemmas, apparently desperate, before." Prof. Smith is right. And what is the way? There is only one remedy for our social ills; there is only one adequate solution of the labour question. And that is the nationalization of the means of production and distribution. Prof. Smith informed us some years ago that the people's hopes of taking over (nationalizing) the industries of the country and operating them in their own interests were "false hopes." He would hardly volunteer such information to-day. If the signs of the times are to be trusted the people's hopes in this respect are in a fair way of being realized. New Zealand has solved the problem of the unemployed entirely, and is now solving the labour question at a great rate. The Government of that country has taken over its railways and many other industries, and the experiments have been so successful that it is expected that the country in a few years will nationalize all its industries. The Trades and Labor Congress of England have declared for the nationalization of everything. Influential men in every country are advocating the Government ownership of railways, telegraphs, etc. Many cities are taking over their franchises, and are making experiments in municipal socialism with good results. These things teach us that before many years the people will take over the means of production and distribution, and operate them in the interest of all. The way out of our present social lunatic asylum is into socialism. And socialism, as Grant Allen[79] says, is only "round the corner."

7. The Right to Work[80]

When a strike is in progress some capitalists are always greatly exercised about the non-union labourer's right to work. They very frequently invoke the courts to protect the poor fellow in his alleged rights. In the plutocratic view, however, the right to work merely consists in encouraging non-union men to take the place of strikers. If every man had a right to work and was fully protected in that right, employers would not be able to find idle men ready and willing to take the places of men struggling to improve their condition of life.

In fact, many employers believe that we should have a relatively redundant population of labourers -- that is, men who ordinarily have no right to work, no opportunity to work. These great masses of men must be at hand so that they can be thrown suddenly on decisive points without injury to the scale of production in other spheres.

The characteristic course of modern industry -- namely, a cycle of average activity, production at high pressure, crisis and stagnation -- depends on the constant formation and the greater or less absorption and reformation of this industrial reserve army, or surplus population.

The expansion by fits and starts of the scale of production is the preliminary to its equally sudden contraction. The latter again evokes the former, but the former is impossible without disposable human material, without an increase in the number of labourers independently of the absolute growth of population -- an increase effected by immigration and by improved machinery "setting free" a part of the labourers.

---

[79]McKay refers to the prolific author Grant Allen (1848-1899), born in Kingston, Ontario, but resident for much of his life in England, who wrote many books on natural science as well as novels. *The Woman Who Did* (1895) focused on a woman's decision to live common law; *Individualism and Socialism* (1889), contains some of his political ideas.

[80]*American Federationist*, April 1903, 258-259.

As the heavenly bodies, once thrown into a certain definite motion, tend to repeat this, so it is with production as soon as it is once thrown into this movement of alternate expansion and contraction. Effects in their turn become causes. Even political economy then sees that the production of a relative surplus population is a necessary accompaniment of modern industry.

Suppose, says H. Merivale,[81] formerly professor of Political Economy at Oxford, suppose that on the occasion of some of these industrial crises the nation were to rouse itself to the effort of getting rid by emigration of some hundreds of thousands of superfluous men, what would be the consequence? On the first returning demand for labour there would be a deficiency. However rapid reproduction may be, it takes, at all events, the space of a generation to replace the loss of adult labour. Now, the profits of our manufacturers depend mainly on the power of making use of the prosperous moment when demand is brisk, and thus compensating themselves for the interval during which it is slack. This power is secured to them only by the command of machinery and manual labour. They must have hands ready by them, they must be able to increase the activity of their operations when required, and to slacken it again, according to the state of the market, or they can not possibly maintain that pre-eminence in the race of competition on which the wealth of the country is founded.

Capital increases its supply of labour more quickly than its demand for labourers. The overwork of the employed part of the working class swells the ranks of the reserve part; while, conversely, the greater pressure that the latter by its competition exerts on the former forces them to submit to overwork and subjugation under the dictates of the employers. Thus the inter-action of the over-employed and the unemployed becomes the means of enriching individual capitalists, and at the same time accelerates the production of an industrial reserve army in an ever-increasing degree.

If the capitalist methods of industry at once produce and require as a condition of continued exploitation an army of unemployed labourers -- what hypocrisy is it to prate of the "right to work!"

In the foregoing cursory analysis of the form of the movement of modern industry the modifying influence of trade-unionism has not been taken into account. Against modern capitalistic methods -- over-exploiting the

---

[81]McKay refers to Herman Merivale (1806-1874), professor of political economy at Oxford from 1837-1842, later permanent under-secretary of state for the colonies, 1848-1859. He wrote *Introductory Lecture upon Political Economy* (1837), and *Lectures on Colonization and the Colonies* (1841).

labour power of one part of the population, depriving the other part of the opportunity to work, and playing off one part against the other -- trade-unionism opposes the only effective and rational resistance. When employers tell of the labourers' right to work, they mean their own alleged divine right to pit one worker against another -- to assure for themselves more profit. When they condemn trade-unionism, which is the embodied desire and effort of the worker to secure for himself and his fellows the right to work, they give expression to their real views regarding the right of anybody to work.

Not the employer with his solicitude for the non-unionist, but the trade-unionist with his contempt for that species, is the one who is endeavouring to realize and guarantee the right to work. As trade unions advance wages they develop a greater capacity for consumption, and hence a greater demand for labour to produce necessary commodities. As they shorten the hours of labour they increase their consuming power in another way and by a two-fold process.

Thus trade-unionism, by increasing opportunities of employment and preventing overwork of the employee, tends to realize, not only for its adherents, but for the non-unionist as well, the right to work.

8. In Defence of International Trade Unionism[82]

The parties who are advocating the trade unionists of this country to withdraw from the American Federation of Labor and form a Canadian federation, are not regarded in Montreal as the friends of workingmen. Although many references to this alleged movement have been published in the newspapers, the name of any responsible labour leader has never been connected with it, nor, in fact, the name of any person or *bona fide* labour organization. Apparently these reports have been inspired by parties outside of labour unions, with the design of creating disturbances in labour circles and retarding the progress of the labour movement in Canada.

The veiled prophets who are trying to create the impression that "the labour organizations of Canada are paying more -- far more -- into the treasuries of United States labour unions than they are ever likely to receive by way of return" cannot be intelligent union men or they would exhibit a little more knowledge of the facts.

The Cigar-makers' Union of Montreal has probably expended $100,000 during the present strike, and of this amount 95 per cent. has come from their fellow-workers in the United States. In the next hundred years the

---

[82]Originally published as "No Separate Union for the Dominion," *Montreal Herald*, 14 December 1901.

cigar-makers of Montreal will not pay into the International treasury the equivalent of what they have received in eight months.

Again, the iron moulders, during their difficulty not long ago, received more money from their International than they will pay back in the next generation, and besides, effected advances in wages of from 30 to 50 cents per day -- only because they had the United States unions behind them.

And these are not exceptional cases. An international officer recently in the city offered to wager $100 that there wasn't a Canadian labour union connected with the American Federation that had not received twice the equivalent of the money paid into the International treasury, either in strike pay, sick and death benefits, or in the shape of an advance in wages or a reduction of hours. Nobody has yet accepted the wager.

Anyone who knows anything of the condition of the members of an international union as compared with that of the members of independent unions, know that it would be folly for Canadian labour unions to sever their connection with the American Federation of Labor. A Canadian federation for purely political purposes would be of great service, but such an organization would be more socialist in character than trade unionist. It could not fill the place of trade unions, or carry on the operations in the economic domain which are now conducted by the regular trade unions, and which under present conditions of industry and education are absolutely necessary.

The report that the labour unions of Canada will revolt from the American Federation at the beginning of the year may be regarded as an iridescent dream of the enemies of the working classes. Even when labour unions have developed into a socialist labour party, there will always be the closest relations between the workers of the continent.

9. Labour's Thanksgiving[83]

Labour in Canada lifts up horny hands in thanksgiving to the Most High. Though the workers of other parts of the world may have felt the heavy after effects of industrial depression, the toilers of the Dominion have enjoyed a year of comparative prosperity. True, over 300,000 able bodied men lack employment, and thence the means of sustenance, in our country today; true, labour does not receive its rightful share of the beneficent blessings of God; but true, nevertheless, it is that Labour in Canada has many causes to return thanks. And Labour, therefore, gives thanks that God has so abundantly blessed the work of its hands.

---

[83]*Montreal Herald*, 28 November 1898. The same text was published in the *Amherst Daily News*, 5 December 1898.

But not alone for material blessings received does Labour give thanks. In the fruition of the work of its mind and heart, Labour has far greater cause to return thanks. It gives thanks that the Labour Movement -- "the effort of men to live the lives of men" -- is progressing so well. It gives thanks that its democratic ideals are becoming the inspiration of some of the greatest minds of our time. It gives thanks that a spirit of social compunction, or a realization of the duties and responsibilities of the "social man," is spreading among all classes. It gives thanks that men are realizing that rivalry and distrust, competition and covetousness, are not the natural, but the unnatural condition of human society; that social separation is disruption, damnation and death. It gives thanks that men are learning that brotherhood is the law of God and nature and reason, and that unless they stand together they cannot endure life. It gives thanks that the great gulf which has so long separated the educated from the ignorant, the rich from the poor, and which has made money the root of all evil, is being bridged over. It gives thanks that the pagan religion of self-interest and competition is yielding place to the Christian religion of mutual service and co-operation. It gives thanks that the sorrow and darkness of the civilization of making money is passing away before the light and gladness of the civilization of making men.

Yes, Labour has cause to return thanks. The Labour question is receiving the attention of the noblest minds of the day, and all men pray for light to solve it. Why are men, able and willing to work, compelled to pass their time in idleness? is the question all men with hearts and brains are asking. Some men say there is no work to do, but that is untrue. Look at the majority of the workingmen. They need better food, clothes, houses, education, etc. Look at the employers, too. They are harassed, driven to death, with lessened enjoyment in life. Why cannot the idle men be employed in providing the many needed things? Why cannot life be made better, easier, happier, for both employers and workingmen?

And thoughtful men are beginning to realize that the reason is this -- society is based on unrighteous principles. Our industrial system is wrong in too many respects. Its operative principle is profits; its gods, self-interests and big per cents; its religion, competition and "do" your fellow-men.

Industry has been largely aristocratic in its motives and purposes, and pagan in its methods and operation. It needs democratizing and Christianizing. If we can have democracy in political affairs, why cannot we have democracy in industrial affairs? If political democracy can ensure all men opportunity to vote for Government and the rights of citizenship, why cannot industrial democracy ensure all men opportunity to work for society and the rights of livelihood?

As for the Christianization of the methods of industry, that is going on every day. The central precept of Christianity is "agapao," [agape] which rightly construed in English means "service" or active love....

Most men go into business not to serve their fellows, but themselves. They believe in the stupid idea of those political economists who say that each man best serves his fellow men's interest by seeking his own. Competition, they say, is the law of progress.

But co-operation is the law of progress, according to the spirit of industry. McAndrew's engines are singing for joy that they are made. They know their lesson, yours and mine, that combination is the watchword of progress in modern industry. Commerce is the profoundest expression of the law of mutual helpfulness.

Men are beginning to realize that they must cease their selfish strife, and seek to serve their fellow men, and thus make life happier and nobler for each and all. And because men are turning longingly to the ideals of democracy, because the spirit of brotherhood is becoming more and more manifest, because social reform aspirations are leavening all classes of society -- because of these things Labour returns thanks.

10. Fight for the Cause, Ye Workingmen[84]

Oh, workingmen of Montreal come join ye in the fight,
And bear the labour movement on with irresistless might;
Stand up like men, assert your rights, your honour, and your worth,
And claim thine ancient heritage, a free-hold in God's earth.

Oh, toilers, break the fetters of the wizardy of wrong,
The superstition-slavery ye have endured so long,
And muster all your forces in the ranks of truth and right,
And boldly, proudly bear the brunt of Freedom's holy fight.

Oh, come, my toiling brother, yielding body, soul and brain,
An awful sacrifice unto the master's greed of gain,--
And come, my gentle sister, weaving in the woof of wealth,
Thy happiness and womanhood, thy beauty and thy health.

Come all ye who are weary of industrial slavery,
Come band your ranks together and fight, fight for liberty,
Come help the gallant workers who are battling in the van,

---

[84]*Montreal Herald*, 21 January 1899. On such labour song-poems in general, see Clark D. Halker, *For Democracy, Workers, and God: Labor Song-Poems and Labor Protest, 1865-95* (Urbana and Chicago: University of Illinois Press, 1991). McKay's poem is rather reminiscent of the sea chanteys sung on the South Shore of Nova Scotia.

And speed the glorious dawning of the Brotherhood of Man.

11. Why Workingmen Distrust Churches[85]

(The constant repetition of the statement that workingmen have no
interest in the churches of to-day prompted The Herald to ask an
explanation from Mr. Colin McKay, one of the leaders in labour circles in
this city. Mr. McKay, taking the standpoint of the workingman, as he sees
it, discusses the matter as follows):

In some countries, especially in Germany, and, in a lesser degree in
France and England, the majority of workingmen openly adopt an
antagonistic attitude towards the church. In Canada, workingmen at
present are merely indifferent, but the tendency is towards hostility. If the
church desires to check this tendency and regain its lost prestige, it must
make a fundamental change in its attitude to the social and economical
problems of the day.

The reception that workingmen may be accorded at church doors has
little to do with the question; they do not go to see whether the rich man
or his ushers are there to extend him a welcome, or look askance at him.
It is not superficial reasons, but fundamental causes that keep workingmen
away from the church.

To many workingmen it seems that in the first place, the church is more
concerned with dogmas than principles. In the second, though
democratic in form, it is out of touch with the democratic spirit of the
age. In the third, its individualistic gospel has little sanction in the
utterances of Christ, and none whatever, from the teachings of modern
social scientists. It does not recognize the fact that improvement in the
individual can only proceed *pari* [*passu*] with the improvement in society
-- at least it does not adequately seek to act on this principle. Its *laissez
faire* doctrines in regard to defective social, economic and political
institutions, the ignoring of the effects of environment on the individual,
do not conform to the doctrine of human brotherhood.

The church tells the community that bad social institutions are necessary
evils, that we should be content in the conditions to which it has pleased
God to call us, and yet a minister would be shocked at the idea of telling
an individual that his bad habits are necessary evils, and that he should
be patient and long-suffering with them.

---

[85]Originally published as "Why Workingmen Distrust Churches. The Herald Secures an
Expression of Opinion From a Prominent Labor Writer on the Reasons for Indifference,"
Montreal Herald, 24 November 1900.

As a class clergymen appear to have little sympathy with the labour movement, the principle and ideals of which are seizing hold of the workingmen with the force of a new revelation, and, in consequence, the impression prevails among workingmen that the church is controlled by the money power. In European countries, labour workers work on this prejudice, not only to attack the church, but to undermine the religious faith of the masses. According to German labour leaders, the church has always joined hands with despotism to exercise oppression over the masses. Religion, says their manifesto, is the bane of humanity. It teaches men that the more they suffer during this short life, the greater will be their happiness throughout eternity -- on which principle a man would be an idiot to seek present welfare. In order, therefore, to induce the workers to assert their rights and seek happiness in this life, we must uproot religion, dethrone the church and inaugurate an era of atheistic culture, they say.

In Canada, such a form of propaganda would not meet with any sympathy. In materialism, rationalism -- those caricatures of so-called science, which give authority and ideals to the German labour movement and exercise a lasting and fatal influence on social and political tendencies, as well as on the intellectual and ethical character of the working classes -- Canadian labour leaders see nothing that appeals to them. The Socialist Labor Party, which on this continent corresponds with the Social Democracy of Germany, has made few recruits among Canadian workingmen. In a few cities branches have been established, but the promoters have usually been foreigners -- expatriated Germans or Jews. Our Labour leaders doubt the desirability of an economic and political system founded upon an anti-Christian, materialistic conception of the universe. In our opinion the propaganda of the German Socialists not only manifests ignorance of the real character, province and operations of Christianity (as distinct from Churchianity),[86] but constitutes a repudiation of the only tenable basis for a socialistic system of society. What the Germans call the annihilation of the superstructure of superstition, we look upon as the abolition of the basis of morality. Instead of wanting to eradicate religion and reduce society to a material basis, we desire a reinstatement of the fundamental principles of Christianity, regarding the brotherhood of man, and the universality and practicability of the golden rule; and the establishment of society upon a basis of Christian ethics.

---

[86]McKay borrowed this phrase from contemporary labour discussions of Christianity. It was extensively used in polemics in the *Industrial Banner*. For an interesting discussion, and commentary in particular on the phrase "churchianity" as opposed to "Christianity," see James Frederick Stein, "The Religious Roots of the Canadian Labour Movement: The Canadian Labour Press from 1873 to 1900," M.A.Thesis, University of Winnipeg/University of Manitoba, 1986: 69-70.

In atheism, materialism, there is absolutely no foundation for socialism. How German labour leaders can reject religion, that is, philosophy in its highest sense, and adopt the teachings of Darwin, is more than we can understand. It appears impossible to reconcile the principles of socialism with the doctrines of Darwinism. Application of the doctrine of naturalism to social relations issues inevitably in the impeachment of the practicability or desirability of any system of socialism. It is impossible to deduce the socialistic doctrine of equal rights from naturalism or materialism. According to the law of natural selection, the strongest survive -- therefore might is the only right that nature recognizes.

The distinctive character of socialism, as of Christianity, is that it defines and places duties before rights. From each according to his abilities, to each according to his needs. If we cannot deduce any doctrine of equal rights from Darwinism, still less can we devise any doctrine of duties. As Kant says, you cannot get the word ought out of a universe of natural law.[87]

In cutting away from science the knowledge of divine things, that is, of first causes, you reduce men to relegate the sentiments of right and duty to mere expediency. Thus Morley[88] says it is idle to talk of the natural rights of man, all rights being merely the creation of positive law; and British publicists in general glory in the separation of politics from ethics.

Socialism can not find adequate sanction in materialism, or any other strictly scientific conception of things. It is based on moral intuitions, rather than natural principles. Its primary doctrines are based on assumptions -- assumptions which are like fundamental axioms of Christianity, namely, the current conceptions of eternal justice, absolute, transcendental moral law, and the immortality of the soul.

Its ethics are identical with the ethics of Christianity, and require the same authority. "In the Golden Rule of Jesus of Nazareth," says Mill, "we read the complete spirit of the ethics of utility." And yet, in the same essay, he claims that utilitarianism justifies and authorizes retaliation, the infliction of injury for injury received -- a direct repudiation of the Golden rule, and likewise of Socrates' conception of justice. The ethics of Christianity and

---

[87]McKay somewhat loosely paraphrases a conclusion arrived at by Kant in *Foundations of the Metaphysics of Morals*. See Immanuel Kant, *Foundations of the Metaphysics of Morals*, trans. L.W. Beck (New York: Macmillan, 1969): 93-94. See also Immanuel Kant, *Grounding for the Metaphysics of Morals*, trans. James W. Ellington (Indianapolis: Hackett, 1981): 61-62.

[88]McKay refers to John Morley (1838-1923), prominent Liberal intellectual and disciple of John Stuart Mill, and a key popularizer of important French thinkers in the *Fortnightly Review*, which he edited from 1866 to 1881. He served as first secretary of the India Office from 1905 to 1910, and achieved some renown as a Victorian positivist.

of Socialism require an authority of more consistency and finality than utilitarianism affords.

Again: "Some Communists consider it unjust that the produce of the labour of the community should be shared on any other principle than that of exact equality; others think it just that those should receive most whose needs are greatest; while others hold that those who work harder, or produce more, or whose services are more valuable to the community, may justly claim a larger quota in the division of produce. And the sense of natural justice may be plausibly appealed to in behalf of every one of these opinions."[89]

In the parable of the labourers and the vineyards, Christ settles that point according to Bellamy's ideal. In other utterances, too, he spoke authoritatively on the greated [greater] obligations of superior natural abilities and opportunities. In the conceptions of Christianity, alone, can socialists find authority for their stand on this important point.

In order to inaugurate and maintain a system of socialism, individuals would have to make sacrifices of self -- sacrifices which Spencer's ethical system would not sanction, sacrifices which would be insanity in the materialistic view.

As we understand, socialism is more of an ethical system than an economic one -- the labour movement an effort to rehabilitate Christian ethics in political and social systems.

It is some such considerations as these that induce Canadian labour leaders to preach what they call Christian socialism. They have no quarrel with religion, like their compeers across the sea, but they are of the opinion that the church is a rather poor exponent of Christianity. If the clergy would give less attention to the celestial aspects of Christianity, and deal with its earthly aspects -- if they would knock off dogmatizing over questions we are not concerned with till we are dead, and fearlessly apply Christian ethics to human affairs, then workingmen would probably go to church.

---

[89]McKay quotes directly and with no changes from John Stuart Mill, *Utilitarianism* (1863). For these quotations in a recent edition, see J.S.Mill, *Utilitarianism. On Liberty, and Considerations on Representative Government* (London: Everyman's Library, 1984):17.

12. The Response to McKay's Challenge[90]

[The preceding article -- i.e., §.11 -- was brought to the attention of a number of prominent Canadian religious figures, a number of whom responded to it on the pages of the *Montreal Herald* .]

George Grant, Principal of Queen's:
1. I, too, am of opinion "that the church is a rather poor exponent of Christianity." How could it be otherwise?
2. A poor exponent is better than none at all.
3. The church, poor as it is, has almost always taken the side of justice.
4. I hope the church will continue to do all that poor human nature aided by the Divine Spirit can do, whether all working men go to church or not.
5. Workingmen who attend church help on the good cause. Those who stay at home do not. This applies to others as well as workingmen.

George H. Graham, Rector of Trinity Church, Montreal:
The statement of Mr. Colin McKay, upon which you invite criticism, is based upon a postulate which needs ... proof before it can be accepted., viz., that the workingman does not go to church.

This is a very serious charge both against the workingman and against the church. Is it true? I should like to have better proof of it than the mere bald statement. I should like to hear what percentage of trades unionists are non-churchgoers and whether that percentage is larger than that in other classes.

My limited experience leads me to believe rather that the very strongest and most dependable element in our churches is the class of workers, which class I take to include all who have to work hard to earn their livelihood. And certainly some of the strongest and most progressive churches in Montreal are those whose congregations are drawn substantially from the artisan class, witness especially Grace Church, Point St. Charles, and Taylor Presbyterian Church.

Mr. McKay also says that the church is a rather poor exponent of Christianity. The church is the only exponent of Christianity, and the history of the church, which tells of an ever-widening horizon and a constantly growing and admittedly beneficial influence over the hearts and lives of men, proves Mr. McKay's estimate of her to be superficial and mistaken.

The Bishop of Nova Scotia:
....If there is one thing more prominent than another in the preaching of the present day -- not in one denomination, or church, alone, but in all --

it is the endeavor of the clergy to apply the principles of Christianity to the solution of the problems of human life, in politics, in municipal government, in commerce, and in the disputes which are continually arising between employer and employed -- or capital and labour. And therefore it sounds curious when one reads, "If the clergy would give less attention to the celestial aspects of Christianity and deal with its earthly aspects -- if they would knock off dogmatizing over questions we are not concerned with till we are dead, and fearlessly apply Christian ethics to human affairs, then workingmen would probably go to church." It may be that here and there a clergyman may be found whose sermons are a careful statement of what he believes and asserts to be church doctrine, which he thereupon demands belief in at the risk of perdition if it be rejected, and without showing its practical application to the daily life of the Christian; but, without the possibility of contradiction, this is not true of what may be called the ordinary run of sermons, which have little or no dogma in them and treat of everyday topics. Indeed the complaint of many is that there is a total absence of doctrine in present day preaching.

T.G.Williams, St. James Methodist Church:
...I take it by "Christian Socialism" he means the theories advocated by Kingsley[91], [Maurice][92], and others, which propose that "Christianity should be directly applied to the ordinary business of life and that in view of this, the present system of competition should give place to cooperative associations, both productive and distributive, where all might work together as brothers." They held that this condition could only be made possible by a change of the labourer's life brought about by education and elevation of character especially through Christianity. This indicates the course which the Christian church should pursue. Now the Gospels teach that for man to reach his highest level, or that nearest Christ's level, he "must be born again." This dogma then must have a first place in the Christian pulpit, and it must not be banished as one of the questions, "we are not concerned with till we are dead." Whatever may be laid to the charge of past years it will be generally conceded that this teaching has a prominent place in every evangelical pulpit at the present day, and certainly Mr. McKay would not exclude it. The next duty of the church is to press for the practical application of the life into which one is thus brought, by what the apostles named "conversion," in the intercourse of society. This is not and cannot be done by the Church as a mass, or multitude, acting as a unit, but must be carried out by the

---

[91]Williams refers to Charles Kingsley (1819-1875), minister of the Church of England, and author of *Alton Locke*, *Tailor and Poet*, and *The Water Babies*. He argued that the exploitation of labour by capital went against Christ's teachings, and promoted the formation of workingmen's associations.

[92]Williams refers to Frederick Denison Maurice (1805-1872), who, with Kingsley, was a leader of the Christian Socialists in Victorian Britain. He was the founder and principal of Workingmen's College, London. Most of his writings were theological.

individuals claiming to be followers of Christ. The best Christians are the men and women who most perfectly reproduce in life, the new life they obtained through Christ in conversion, and the best church is the church which has the largest proportion of such followers of Jesus Christ....

13. What Workingmen Expect of the Church: A Rebuttal by Colin McKay[93]

As a discussion of the relationship of the church to the people may not be unfruitful, I gladly comply with your request for a few remarks, more or less by way of answer to your recent symposium.

Those ecclesiastical lights who do not perceive the breaking up of the church as a dogmatic organization, or the tendency not only of workingmen but of all classes to indifference and then hostility to churchianity, should read Goldwin Smith's article in a recent number of the *Contemporary Review,* wherein he points out the growing disposition to question the authority of Christianity itself.[94]

As I pointed out in a previous article, many of those who take an active part in the Canadian labour movement, realize the perfection of Christ's ethical system, the soundness of His economic doctrines, and the splendour of His democratic ideals, and, believing that His teachings admit of practical application to the wordly relations of men, accept Him as the prophet of the Kingdom of God, on earth, and His teachings as a revelation of the purest sort of reason and commonsense, or the supreme intelligence behind the phenomena -- whichever you like.

---

[93]*Montreal Herald*, 2 February 1901.

[94]McKay refers to Goldwin Smith, "Genesis and Outlook of Religion," *Contemporary Review*, 78 (December 1900): 898-908. The most pertinent paragraphs read: "The churches, as dogmatic organizations, both in Europe and America, are apparently breaking up. Active-minded ministers in all of them are in rebellion against dogmatic creeds; in all repression, at once scandalous and futile, in the shape of heresy trials, is going on. Even the body of the clergy in their preachings are sensibly receding from dogma, and not from dogma only but from the supernatural generally, and from the ascetic or spiritual disregard of the present world. There is a falling back upon the ethical parts of Christianity, and there is a tendency to dwell less upon a future and more upon the present state....Among the quick-witted artisans in all countries, not scepticism only, but atheism, is making way. In France they have come to a comic Life of Christ. Socialism, which seems to be fast spreading, is generally atheistic or sceptical; it derives its strength, in part, from the determination of the working man, as he no longer believes in another world, to secure his full share of this, while attempts to capture it by Catholic priests or Christian philanthropists such as Maurice or Kingsley, have come to naught" (899). Smith presents no empirical evidence of a growing tendency to question the authority of Christianity pertinent to a Canadian discussion.

With what the church calls the supernatural side of Christianity, they appear to be very little concerned. As taught by Christ, Christianity is merely supernatural, in the sense that reason is a supernatural or divine attribute.

Christ told the people little of "heavenly things." Some of his very few alleged utterances dealing with heavenly things are at variance with his character, and are as likely as not the interpolations of some of the early potentates of the church.

Indeed, none of the great religions of mankind, are so purely humanitarian in character as that derived from the teachings of Jesus of Nazareth. Christ enunciated ever pregnant principles of economic and social reform. He did not seek to found a church with ritualism and formalism; He merely established a brotherhood for the practice of His philosophy of life.[95]

After His death His followers inoculated [infected?] his teachings with a lot of pagan superstitions, and exalting Him to a pagan deity, bade the world bow down to Him, and accept their version of His teachings on pain of eternal damnation. It seems to me impossible to imagine the humble and lowly carpenter of Nazareth, commanding mankind to bow the knee to Him. Certainly, one who loved men so much as He, would not threaten them with destruction, if they did not or could not, appreciate His teachings. When Paul and a few other politicians had finished putting the new wine of Christianity into the old bottles of paganism, Christ the meek, the loving, would not have recognized Himself, or His religion either.

If, as the Rev. Osborne Troop and another correspondent, try to make out, belief in, or worship of, Christ Himself is more important than conformity to Christ's ethical system, "however beautiful," then God would appear to be a sort of oriental despot.

---

[95]McKay suggests here that he had been closely following the new Biblical criticism. Much contemporary writing on Jesus bears out McKay's point, and focuses especially on the contrast between the divine person presented in the Gospel of John and the historical figure of the synoptic gospels. See Marcus J. Borg, *Meeting Jesus Again for the First Time: The Historical Jesus and the Heart of Contemporary Faith* (San Francisco: Harper, 1994), for an interesting discussion. For a key Canadian discussion of historical criticism and its challenge to Christian belief, see Michael Gauvreau, *The Evangelical Century: College and Creed in English Canada from the Great Revival to the Great Depression* (Montreal and Kingston: McGill-Queen's University Press, 1991). This discussion, and many other comments in the labour press, suggest that the debate over such religious questions extended far beyond the theological colleges and church synods that have to date largely preoccupied Canada's religious historians.

According to the platitude of Paul, which Mr. Troop quotes, a man's eternal salvation hinges on the mere accident of birth; "God loves the world," says Paul, and yet his declaration implies that the myriads of the human race, who never heard of Christ, may have no hope of eternal life. Such a statement is at once inconsistent in itself, and cruel, which was not a characteristic of Christ or His gospel.

When the rich young man asked what he should do that he might have eternal life, Christ did not bid him believe in Jesus of Nazareth. Christ even rebuked the young man for calling Him good master - which shows that Christ did not care about or want the worship or homage of man. He merely wanted the young man to regulate his conduct according to His ethics. "If you wilt be perfect," said Christ, "go and sell all that thou hast and give it to the poor."[96]

The majority of your clerical correspondents admit that the "church is a rather poor exponent of Christianity," but they claim that it is the only exponent. Rev. G.G. Huxtable, however, says that "There is nothing nobler under heaven than Christian Socialism." Unless the church is over heaven, Christian socialism is nobler than churchism. In that view I most heartily concur. The labour movement is a better exponent of Christianity than the church.

The Bishop of Nova Scotia offers us compensation hereafter, for suffering here. As I pointed out previously it was this very doctrine that aroused the ire of European labour leaders against the church. It induces content, and keeps the people from demanding their rights. Church catechisms bid us be content in that condition of life to which it has pleased God to call us. Could anything be more unnatural or opposed to Christ's teachings -- to the building of the Kingdom of God on earth.

Organizer Flett[97] goes up and down the land preaching what he calls "the gospel of divine discontent." He does not promise us mansions in the skies, but points out the way to obtain better conditions of life. He does not, like Archbishop Ireland and many ministers, blame the Creator for conditions which entail poverty and other evils on a portion of the race. He knows that such a view, in face of their own declarations that God loves the world, is the grossest blasphemy; he knows that a little exercise of reason and the spirit of Christ would so adjust things that crushing poverty would not be necessary.

---

[96]*Matthew* 9: 21.

[97]McKay refers to John A. Flett, appointed in February 1900 by Samuel Gompers to serve as the American Federation of Labor's general organizer for Canada. See Robert Babcock, *Gompers in Canada: a study in American continentalism before the First World War* (Toronto: University of Toronto Press, 1974), Chapter 4.

Rev. T.G. Williams says that Maurice and Kingsley held that socialism could only be made possible by a change of the labourer's life brought about by "education and elevation of character especially through Christianity." It is not necessary that everybody should be angels in order to bring about a change in society, or a heaven on earth. Once I sailed in a Yankee ship with a woman aboard, and the whole trip was like a Sunday school. When, however, I tried another trip in the same ship, [without] an angel aboard, the scuppers ran red. The afterguard[98] killed a couple of men, and fixed up the rest of the crew for the hospital.

If we had half a dozen Christians in Canada, they would constitute sufficient leaven, to raise up a Christian system of society -- in other words bring about socialism.

The church has been often the exponent of paganism. "The church and clergy of late," says Goldwin Smith, "have, perhaps been giving the believer in righteousness and humanity reason for grieving less at their departure; flag worship and the gospel of form, may be propagated as well without them."[99]

In what respects do the clergy preach the gospel, or follow in the footsteps of Christ? Christ rebuked the oppressors of the poor and weak. Where is [are] the ministers of Canada who would dare to rebuke the robber barons of this age, as Christ rebuked the exploiters of the people in His day. Christ called them vipers, serpents, white sepulchres. Was it any wonder he was crucified? A workingman a short time ago asked a prominent Montreal clergyman why he didn't preach common sense sermons on the rights of the people. The minister said he didn't want to lose his job.

And that is the manner of men the majority of the ministers are. They haven't the spirit of Christ in them -- the capacity to sacrifice themselves to the good of humanity. In my opinion the skeptical labour leaders of Germany will stand higher in the estimation of Christ than the clergy of this country. The German labour leaders do not fear the sacrifice; in the last twenty years they have served a couple of centuries in prison for their principles and the uplifting of humanity.

Christ preached self-sacrifice -- not ascetic or spiritual self-denial, but sacrifice of self-interest for a purpose, the promotion of the welfare of

---

[98]The officers of the vessel.

[99]McKay is evidently quoting from memory; the actual passage from Goldwin Smith reads, "The churches and the clergy of late have, perhaps, been giving the believer in righteousness and humanity reason for grieving less at their departure; flag worship and the gospel of force can be as well propagated without them...." Goldwin Smith, "Genesis and the Outlook of Religion," *Contemporary Review*, 78 (December 1900): 899.

humanity. And His life illuminated His teachings. In how far do the clergy follow His example?

Do they rebuke the senseless luxury of the well-to-do classes? In order to minister to the selfish arrogance and desire of display among the rich, thousands have to toil night and day, wearing out their bodies and stifling their souls. Many of the clergymen and their fine patrons may believe... that the prodigality of the rich is the providence of the poor, but if they would consider the matter a moment they would see the fallacy of such a view. Herbert Spencer and other wise men, have exposed the fallacy of the idea that all employment is beneficial, but still belief therein is widely current.[100]

This doctrine is largely responsible for the oppression of the people and, yet, though Christ exposed it both in his teaching and his conduct, how often is it discussed from the pulpits of to-day.

The clergy inveigh, halfheartedly against the liquor traffic. They ought to see that it is a necessary concomitant of the profit-mongering system, which will continue just as long as the motive principle of industry is private profit, because it affords an easy method of amassing wealth. Under the system of socialism, where industry was carried on for public welfare, not individual aggrandizement, the liquor traffic would disappear, because nobody would have any interest in prosecuting it. For the same reason, a hundred other promiscuous employments which under present conditions direct labour from the vital and necessary employments, thereby increasing the amount of human toil unnecessarily, would disappear too.

Prof. Herron[101] and Tolstoi say the church is the greatest propagator of immorality known to history. If so, it should be abolished, but these present day prophets appear to be little popes on their own hook, and we may not feel called to see eye to eye with them. A good many workingmen in this country would like to see the church abolished but there are many who would be content with a reformation in the church. Some of your correspondents seem to insinuate that as the rich pay to

---

[100]McKay is generally paraphrasing *The Study of Sociology*, in which Spencer does develop an argument for subordinating work to life. For a good discussion of Spencer's critique of industrial capitalism, see J.D.Y.Peel, *Herbert Spencer: The Evolution of a Sociologist* (New York: Basic Books, 1971): 214-218.

[101]McKay is probably referring to George D. Herron (1862-1925). A Congregational Minister, Herron occupied the Chair of Applied Christianity, Iowa College (now Grinnell); in 1901, he followed Eugene Debs in splitting the Socialist Labor Party, to become a founding and influential member of the newly formed Socialist Party of America. His books include *The New Redemption* (1893); *The Christian State* (New York, 1895); and *Between Caesar and Jesus* (1899). McKay was most likely to have encountered his *Why I Am A Socialist* which was accessible via Charles H. Kerr.

keep up the church, the workers have no right to look for preaching pleasing to them. But the workers do have such a right, because they will ultimately have to bear the burden of keeping up the church. The toilers have to labour so much harder to keep up a non-producing class like the ministers. While we are groping for the light, it may be well to employ philosophers and guides, but I hold that the church at present does not render adequate service to the community for the heavy burden it entails upon the working classes. It may be wrong to judge the church by commercial standards, but seeing that the spirit of commerce or mammon has enthroned itself in the hearts of men unrebuked by the church, it must accept the consequences. The clergy must concern themselves with the affairs of men. It must realize that individual righteousness is impossible amid social and economic unrighteousness -- that it is idle to talk about being born again in the midst of an unregenerated society, they must knock off palliating the results of evil conditions, and apply the pregnant principles of Christianity to causes. They need not be so hard on high and mighty wrongdoers as Christ was, and yet do their duty to humanity. They need not go on a political platform, yet [let them] purify politics. Let them [educate their] pupils to apply Christian ethics to systems, not to men. Our political system is bad; that is the reason that a politician is regarded as a synonym for dishonesty. Our system of jurisprudence is a product of paganism; that is why we have so many criminals, and why we are wont to put lawyers in the same category. Our industrial system is paganistic in its motives, and barbarous in its operations -- that is the reason of the perpetual war between labour and capital.

All of us high or low, rich or poor, are victims of vicious systems, but those who profess to be followers of Christ should not only condemn these systems but point out to the people that it is possible to reorganize society on different and better principles. Looked at in the light of Christianity many of our so-called benefactors and philanthropists are no better than the Pharisees of old, but as the clergy have never preached Christianity to them and as they have never considered the subject themselves it would not be just to judge them.

Mr. Williams has a poor opinion of human nature apparently, but, though I have seen men on the verge of cannibalism, I have a high opinion of human nature and its possibilities. Men are not bad by inclination, except in a few cases, where criminal tendencies are hereditary....

In Canada, at least, the character of the people is sufficiently elevated to inaugurate socialism, which... is applied Christianity. All that is needed is reason and knowledge, and we look to the church to throw the light of reason of Christianity on the conditions of life.

14. The Political Gag[102]

A revolution has been in progress in the minds of men as noticeable in
its way as the revolutions in the methods of production. Faith and
obedience were the watch words of the past; reason will be the guide of
the future. In the good old time it was a crime to doubt or to question; in
the future it will be a moral duty to criticize and test the truth of all the
phenomena of life.

Men no longer accept the doctrine of the Divine Right of Kings. We no
longer regard disease as a visitation of providence punishing personal
sins. We are assured that, though disease is the result of social or
communal sins, it is not always the direct result of personal sins.
Epidemics of typhoid can usually be traced to some neglect of the
sanitary laws of life; but it strikes down innocent children as well as the
old. And as we realize that it is impossible for the human body to remain
healthy in an anti-hygienic environment so we are coming to feel that
moral health is an impossibility in [a] system of society whose institutions
are built on the essentially immoral principle of class exploitation of the
necessities of the masses, and impregnated with the miasmas of the
competitive struggle for existence. The leaders of the old political parties
bulk large on our imaginations, though it is a patent fact that their
leadership consists largely in arousing passions over petty issues, and
balking or side-tracking the efforts of the people to establish industrial
democracy; also in using all their powers to send into retirement any
politician who presumes to think for himself. Indeed, in politics,
opposition to freedom of thought and expression is more pronounced
than in other departments of life, mainly, perhaps, because the political
state is the ally and bulwark of the industrial autocracy. The clergymen
today do not, as a rule, seek to oppose the spread of knowledge; they know
that while science may shatter some church dogmas, it only increases the
understanding of, and reverence for, the vital truths of Christianity.

15. The French Canadian as a Trade Unionist[103]

In French-speaking Canada the labour movement, as represented by the
American Federation of Labor, has had to contend with conditions of a
peculiar character, conditions offering obstacles to its progress not met
with in other parts. In the first place, the French Canadian, with his pride
in the traditions of his race, is very conservative. He possesses, no doubt,
the characteristics of the typical Frenchman, but with modifications and
in a lesser degree. He is less emotional, less impulsive, and consequently
not easily enthused with new ideals and new principles.

---

[102]*Eastern Labor News*, 24 December 1910.

[103]Originally published as "The Labour Movement in Montreal," *American
Federationist*, October 1903, 1034-1035.

His loyalty to his language isolates him. He does not appreciate the American spirit, and because the radical literature of old France does not reach him he knows little or nothing of the proletariat movement of the Old World. Naturally, his passionate fondness for his traditions and his comparative isolation makes him slow to respond to movements involving a radical readjustment of his ideas and manner of life.

In the second place, the climate in its effect on industry produces economic conditions decidedly unfavorable to the efficient organization of workingmen. A labor organization here is usually only effective in the spring, and consequently unions have had a habit of springing up like mushrooms at that time of year and passing out of existence as soon as they effected their object or failed to effect it.

In face of these difficulties the labor movement in Quebec has, nevertheless, made considerable progress. In Montreal, the metropolis of Canada, its progress during the past four years has been really remarkable.

After proving the futility of the isolated method of organization, the French Canadian workingmen have come to realize that their chief hope of salvation lies in identifying themselves with the movement allied with the American Federation of Labor. In Montreal practically all the trade organizations, formed during the independent regime, have affiliated with the internationals of their respective trades, and all new unions recently organized have taken out charters from an international brotherhood.

The organization of the Federated Trades and Labor Council, four years ago, marked the beginning of a new era in the labor movement of Montreal. At its inception this council was composed of delegates from four unions; at present it represents more than 50 bona-fide trade unions and a membership of over 25,000.

The movement to consolidate the labour forces of Montreal under the federated council was attended with considerable difficulty. Its amazing progress sufficiently indicates the strength of the appeal the American Federation of Labor makes to French Canadians.

The importance the labour movement has assumed in Montreal may be judged from the fact that several French and English papers employ labour correspondents and daily devote considerable space to the doings of local unions.

The reflex action of this publicity on the movement in general is very beneficial.

While the French Canadian workingmen have, for the reasons referred to, been slow to organize, they very frequently develop, under proper discipline, into the best possible union men. Among well-established organizations the esprit de corps is remarkable.

The French-speaking workingmen are not only numerically, but relatively, much better organized than their English speaking confreres. While there are about three French to one English speaking person in Montreal, the proportion of French trade unionists to English is probably six to one. Various causes are responsible for this, chief among them being the dual educational systems. Two semi-public school systems, which are in themselves manifestations of race and religious prejudices, are not conducive to the promotion of relations of intimacy between the races. While the education of the people is left in the hands of diverse and opposing influences, the Premier's ideal of a united people, who are Canadians first and foremost and French and English only incidentally, is unattainable. Under present circumstances the French and English never come to fully understand one another, and consequently there is little inclination to unity of effort in matters of mutual interest.

As the French-speaking element are generally the majority in any trade, the English feel that their influence can not count for much, and this deters them from taking much interest in the movement. Many unions are composed entirely of French; in others they are both French and English; but in only two trades, those of the printers and machinists, have there been locals for English-speaking men only. The presiding officer of a mixed union must understand both languages, and is therefore usually a Frenchman. With characteristic courtesy, some unions where the French are greatly in the majority transact their business wholly in English for the benefit of two or three English members.

In dealing with French-Canadian workingmen international officers would do well to remember that they are more susceptible in their present stage of development to the influence of a forceful personality rather than to a new principle, however pregnant with possibility; and that their peculiar position on this continent makes them very sensitive and very prone to resent gratuitous interference with their conduct of their affairs.

16. A Vision of Benevolent Capitalism: Port Sunlight[104]

In the past dozen years or so many employers have come to realize that there is an intimate relation between the industrial efficiency of their workmen and the social conditions surrounding their lives. In Great Britain, more especially, enterprising employers have developed a lively and intelligent interest in the welfare of their workpeople, and various movements aiming at the promotion of the physical, intellectual and social well being of the workers have been set on foot. The employer who provides comfortable homes for his work people may seem to be prompted by philanthropic motives, but he is in reality less of a philanthropist than a far-seeing businessman. The employer is as much interested in promoting the comfort and welfare of his employees as in providing suitable accommodation for his machinery, in establishing cordial relations with his employees as in the harmonious arrangement of the various parts of his plant.

The most important movement in this direction is undoubtedly that in progress at Port Sunlight, in England. Considered both as a business undertaking and as a social experiment, the works and village of Port Sunlight rank among the most noteworthy achievements of the time. Where sixteen years ago cattle grazed in vacant fields, there stand to-day enormous and well-planned factories, employing directly 3,000 people, and a garden city, peopled by workmen and their families, and provided with more institutions, more facilities, for the advancement of the religious, educational, and social well-being of its inhabitants than many large cities can boast of: a workingman's paradise which has attracted the attention and the wonder of the world. At all seasons of the year visitors from every corner of the globe avail themselves of the privilege freely granted, of inspecting the famous works and village. Oriental princes, captains of industry from America and Australia, famous statesmen and savants from Europe, labour delegations, members of mothers' meetings, jack-tars -- all classes are proudly shown through the works, and afforded a chance to admire the unique social surroundings of the village. The number of strangers inspecting the works and village frequently exceeds 5,000 a month.

The factory -- an enormous single-story structure -- covers ninety-three acres of ground, and as the aim has been to make the works as self-contained and comprehensive as possible, upwards of sixty different trades are carried on under its roof. The main employees work forty-eight

---

[104]Originally published as "Prosperity Sharing," in *Montreal Daily Herald*, 6, 12, 17, and 31, December 1904. For a contemporary vision of Port Sunlight, see E.W.Beeson, *Port Sunlight: The Model Village of England* (New York: The Architectural Book Publishing Company, 1911). See also Lever Brothers, Port Sunlight, Limited, *The Story of Port Sunlight* (London, 1953).

hours a week; girls forty-five. The village accommodates six hundred families at a nominal rent of three or five shillings a week, according to the plan of the house; while the employees who live in Birkenhead and other plants are conveyed to and from their homes in special trains at the company's expense. A large dining room, managed by the company, provides the girls with an excellent mid-day meal at the cost of the food. It seats 1,500 girls at once, and in it a girl may obtain for six cents a dinner as good as you would get in Montreal for twenty-five cents. The company has also erected a large dining room for the use of the men, and has turned the management over to the men themselves.

The promoters of Port Sunlight, however, emphasize the fact that the prosperity-sharing system, which provides the workers with healthy homes and pleasant surroundings, is but a form of philanthropy. They hold that the extraordinary development of their business is in no small degree due to the increased efficiency and definite interest in the company's welfare on the part of the employees, resulting from the adoption of the system of prosperity-sharing.

The village of Port Sunlight, consisting as it does entirely of workpeople's dwellings, together with a most complete system of religious, educational and social institutions, is admittedly the finest community of its class in the world. Everything that is required for health and comfort has been provided. Some idea of the size of the village may be gathered from the fact that there are upwards of 680 dwelling houses, and four miles of roadways, widening out at each junction into open spaces.

In its westward aspects the village as a whole is architecturally as superior to Westmount as Westmount is to Griffintown. The creation of Port Sunlight -- a colony of villas which present to the eye the charming picture of a village artistically conceived and admirably carried out -- is undoubtedly one of the artistic triumphs of English architecture. The beautiful and substantially built brown stone cottages, festooned with ivy, clematis and climbing rose, and well trimmed lawns and flower gardens fronting them, the wide clean-swept streets, tree-bordered like so many avenues, the shrubbery dotted parks and park-grounds -- all these blend happily into a symmetrical artistic effect which appeals to one like [a] symphony. In Port Sunlight you see no monstrous and depressing rows of brick and stone, none of the hard distressing regularity, which give to modern cities their brooding and sinister aspect -- their impression of some gigantic and troubled monster imprisoned in brick and stone. The pretty, dainty-looking cottages, in that early English style of architecture which appeals so strongly to that pronounced national characteristic, love of home, are built mostly in irregular blocks ranging from two to seven house in a block, and every block exhibits some new feature of the artistic fancy. No two blocks are alike. There is no overcrowding here. You are told that Mr. Lever will not permit the erection of more than seven houses to an area, because he believes any more would be unhealthy. Each cottage is provided with every modern sanitary convenience, and each has a bath, a privilege which inmates of many a house of three times the rents sigh for in vain. In addition to the lawn and flower gardens in front, each has a back garden which gives the villagers an opportunity to indulge their taste for the cultivation of flowers and vegetables to the full. Moreover, each cottage has the privilege of cultivating allotments of land on the outskirts of the village....

And this garden city is peopled by factory workers -- men who pay three and five shillings a week rent. And in summer you can stand at the very door of the factory and listen to the thrush, blackbird, lark and linnet trilling their joys over the village; an eloquent testimony to the happy environment of the workers.

Port Sunlight is not only a revelation in regard to the possibilities which surround the important problem of the housing of the working classes; it is also an impressive object lesson in regard to the possibilities of commercial life. This village, with its population of about 3,000 souls, is provided with every facility, every convenience, necessary to the rounding out of the social, intellectual and moral life of its inhabitants. Of course, being primarily an industrial community, it has its Technical Institute, one of the best equipped for its special purposes in that part of the kingdom. Not only employees and villagers of Port Sunlight, but non-residents as well are permitted to avail themselves of its educational facilities. The class rooms are lofty, well-lighted and fitted up in the most modern style. There are classes for both sexes and instruction is given in a wide variety of subjects -- from French, German, etc., to mathematics and chemistry, building and machine construction and electrical engineering. The children's schools are as interesting in their way as the other institutions of the village. Both the Park Road and Church Drive schools are situated in open spaces, with lawns and playgrounds on every side, and architecturally, whether viewed from within or without, are very pretty and picturesque. Indeed, these buildings, clad with ivy and clematis, look more like cathedrals built for fairies than ordinary day schools. They are fitted with the latest apparatus, with every convenience and appliance for the sound education, comfort and happiness of the young folk. Both in the senior and junior standards hand and eye-training is inculcated, and manual instruction in wood-work is given to the boys....

All these institutions have been provided at the company's expense, but most of them are managed by committees elected by the employees. The company offers prizes to encourage interest in the work of the various institutions and also in healthy sports. In order to develop a love of music, for instance, three scholarships for singing are offered annually by Mr. Lever for competition among the girl employes, who must also be connected with one of the musical organizations of the village. But, having provided the necessary buildings, the company makes it a condition of their use that the employee shall carry on the work of the various institutions at their own expense.....

17. Should Rich Men Burn Their Money?[105]

When Mr. Carnegie declared that it was a disgrace to die rich he no doubt had in mind the law of Moses that every Jubilee year a man should make restitution to the community of the property he had acquired in the interval [106]-- an interval corresponding to the working life of the average patriarch. Mr. Carnegie, however, would follow the spirit rather than the letter of the old Mosaic law, and make restitution during his life time.

It is a fair question whether the methods by which men like Mr. Carnegie or Rockefeller seek to dispose of their wealth, really constitute a restitution to the community -- whether they are the best that might be employed? Endowments of colleges only benefit a very limited class, a class too, which for the most part has no need of charity. Gifts of libraries, too, only benefit a limited and sometimes idle class.

When wealthy men present a cheque to build libraries or colleges, they give the trustees a lien on a certain amount of the capital and labour of the community. In many cases the net effect may be to divert capital and labour from productive to unproductive enterprises, thus from an economic standpoint, injuring rather than benefiting the community. If we accept the Christian principle of stewardship, a rich man is morally bound to employ his wealth in productive enterprises. Whether the nation or Mr. Rockefeller builds a college, the economic effects so far as the people are concerned, only differ in degree, not in kind, but it is the Government's -- the people's -- privilege, to say if they want or need colleges, libraries, etc. Of course if we accept the view that a man may do what he pleases with his wealth, this argument falls to the ground; a man is perfectly justified in assuming a sovereign function and treating the people as if they were paupers.

But if it is a disgrace to die rich -- Mr. Carnegie's aphorism embodies an absurdity, since a man by the act of death renounces all his wordly possessions -- if a man is morally bound to restore wealth for which he has no use, he might find better ways to do it than by building colleges to train up frenzied financiers. Mr. Hays asked the other day: "What would you have Mr. Carnegie do with his money. Would you have him burn it?" If Mr. Carnegie burnt some of his money, and thus destroyed the lien on the wealth of the community it represents, the community would in all

---

[105]*Montreal Herald*, 8 November 1905.
[106]McKay refers to the Mosaic laws concerning property outlined in *Leviticus* 25: 8-55.

probability utilize that wealth to more advantage than Mr. Carnegie does. A rich man might become a great public benefactor if he burnt his stocks and bonds.

If our gas magnates, for instance, wanted to make an endowment to the Montreal public, the fairest way they could go about it would be to burn their stock certificates, and permit the managers of the plant to utilize the profits now employed to pay dividends in improving the service and reducing rates. If all the shareholders would go and do likewise the Montreal public would be presented with a gift in trust of a gas plant, and would be able to procure gas at cost price. Even if the company only burnt its watered stock, and relieved us of the necessity of paying dividends upon it, its action would be commendable.

In this connection, it may be noted that some years ago a company of public-spirited citizens in Indianapolis began an experiment in social philanthropy, on a modification of the principle outlined above. The experiment is working out successfully, and saving the people $1,000,000 a year in gas charges. The company is organized on much the same lines as our big universities.

It is provided that when the stockholders have received in dividends the amount of their investment, they will then renounce their claims to further dividends, and permit the trustees to furnish gas at cost. Thus, the public-spirited company will, by means of a temporary loan without interest, be able to present the people a gift in trust of a gas plant before many years. The company raised the necessary capital by popular subscription, the shares being fixed at $25 in order that as many citizens as possible might be directly interested in its success. By the terms of incorporation the shareholders assign their shares to a self-perpetuating Board of Trustees, who have irrevocable power to vote the same for the directors. If a majority of the shares fell into the hands of one person he would have no control over the company. The trustees serve without compensation and fill vacancies in their own body. The concern is therefore not under the control of the stockholders, though it can be controlled by legal processes, if there is evidence of corruption or mismanagement. The immediate management of the plan is in the hands of directors chosen by the Board of Trustees, and all books, accounts, etc., are open to public inspection.

This plan seems to embody the best features of public control over public utility industries. As the trustees can derive no pecuniary advantage, they must serve from the social motive and may be expected to administer their trust with due regard to the public interest. Interference of politicians with the management is debarred, though the management will ultimately be amenable to the control of public opinion in much the same way as the big educational institutions are. The plan secures the complete

socialization of the value of civil franchises after the original investment
has been returned, and yet does not throw the strain of frequent oversight
of complex institutions upon the public conscience -- something
eminently desirable, since therein lies the main difficulty of successful
municipal operation of public services. If these functions were controlled
by a board deriving their power from the political authorities, they would
be subject to all the fitful changes of political life and all the dangers and
inconveniences resulting from administrative instability and
incompetence; that is unless the Board should become an intolerable
bureaucracy. But this plan of having these undertakings administered by a
trust of business men, while assuring the most highly developed business
methods, provides for a management whose policy cannot be
revolutionized by a spasm of popular prejudice, yet which would be
gradually readjusted to meet social needs by the pressure of public
opinion at important crises -- for a management and policy under legal
rather than political control.

18. England's Industrial Problem[107]

In the days of the Diamond Jubilee, the Englishman was quite satisfied
that his tight little island was the hub of the universe, and his countrymen
the crowning achievement, the glory of the ages. But the glamour created
by that triumphant pageant has departed; the mood has changed since
1897. John Bull is not so sure of his supremacy either politically or
commercially. Mr. Chamberlain[108] has rudely challenged the great
traditional theories of his countrymen, and shattered beyond repair the
silken web of illusions in which for the past generation or two they have
canopied their careless souls. The old spirit of confident and arrogant
superiority has given place to a feeling of uneasiness.

In all quarters, except perhaps in the inner sanctuary of official liberalism
where the high priests still bow down, in blind fetish worship, to the bald
dogmas of Free Trade -- there is a questioning of gods, a searching of
souls. Mr. Chamberlain's crusade is after all only one of the signs of the
times of the new uneasiness. The great protagonist of Imperialism has
asked his countrymen "to learn to think Imperially." The Englishmen are
not yet thinking Imperially, but they are thinking. They are taking stock of

---

[107]*The Argus,* Vol.1 No. 7 (19 November 1904).

[108]McKay is referring to Joseph Chamberlain (1836-1914), Liberal MP for Birmingham
from 1876 to the 1890s, and a Unionist thereafter to 1906. Chamberlain championed
municipal control of gas and water utilities, and adhered to a high-tariff position which
in 1903 had the effect of splitting the Unionists. He formed the Tariff Reform League in
1903, backed by manufacturers. An ardent imperialist, Chamberlain resigned in 1905 to
proselytize for the cause of Imperial tariff preference. Among his works, see *Patriotism*
(1897), and *Foreign and Colonial Speeches* (1897).

their position, they are considering the conditions and guarantees of their commercial security.

.... In reviewing their position even the disciples of Cobden[109] can hardly find much cause to be enamoured of Free Trade. Certainly the sanguine expectations of its great prophet have never been realized. Cobden, fired by the idea that his policy would act on the moral world as the principle of gravitation on the physical universe, drawing nations together, thrusting aside the antagonisms of race, creed and language, and uniting men in the bonds of eternal peace, had brilliant visions of the nations of the world entering into a Free Trade paradise. This splendid optimism prompted him to predict great and far-reaching results from the adoption of his policy by England, but unfortunately, the world has not lived up to his high opinion of it, and none of his glowing prophecies have been fulfilled. The adoption of the system of free imports by Britain was not followed in five years by the abolition of every tariff in Europe. ... It has not brought international peace. It has not settled industry, or improved agriculture. It has not provided such ample margins of profit that improvements in industrial methods can readily be made; it has not increased wages so substantially that old age pensions are unnecessary; it has increased rather than diminished the aggregate rent and the dividends on dead capital which the producing classes have to bear. It has not absorbed the unemployed, or brought pauperism within compassible limits. Fifty years after England opened its ports, Mr. Charles Booth[110] published his studies of industrial London, showing that over 35 per cent. of the population lived below the poverty line, and that 78 per cent earned, when in work, under 30 shillings per week. Ten years later still, Mr. Rowntree[111] wrote of York, that over 51 per cent of the population were earning, when in work, less than 21 shillings a week. Sir Henry Campbell-Bannerman estimates that 12,000,000 persons in the United Kingdom are always underfed, and perpetually on the verge of starvation. The Committee on Physical Degeneration reports that the population is becoming stunted in growth, while its general condition of life is such that its morale is being undermined, and its spiritual state shows even more threatening signs of collapse than its physical.

---

[109]McKay refers to Richard Cobden (1804-1865), Member of Parliament and the most famous advocate of Free Trade. In 1838 he joined the Anti-Corn Law League, which in 1846 triumphed when laws protecting agriculture in Great Britain were repealed.

[110]McKay refers to Charles Booth (1840-1916), pioneer social investigator and founder of the Salvation Army. After making his fortune as a shipowner, Booth focussed on the social problems of London; his *Life and Labour of the People of London* (1889-1891) was a classic of social investigation.

[111]McKay refers to Benjamin Seebohm Rowntree (1871-1954) who in 1901 published *Poverty: A Study of Town Life*. Rowntree did for York what Booth had done for London. He became an ardent advocate of corporate welfare schemes, and a founding member of the Industrial Welfare Society (1918).

But while recognizing that the present position of British industry calls for an impartial reconsideration of the basis upon which the last century left it, while admitting the foreign menace, John Bull shows little disposition to take Mr. Chamberlain's protectionist panacea on trust. Now that industrial and economic issues have been forced to the forefront John Bull is considering them with characteristic thoroughness -- with more thoroughness perhaps than Mr. Chamberlain desires. At any rate, though accepting Mr. Chamberlain's premises, he seems disposed to arrive at other conclusions. Under Free Trade Great Britain has become the pivot of commerce and finance. The National Income has increased from £600,000,000 to £1,750,000,000 per annum, and, if the great increase in national wealth has not been fairly shared in by the working classes, still their position has been vastly improved. The industrial fabric of the country has grown up, the population has multiplied in dependence on cheap supplies of raw material and food. Under the circumstances the country cannot adopt protection without seriously dislocating its whole industrial and commercial fabric, and imposing great hardships upon the masses of the people.

As the examination of the industrial outlook proceeds it is seen that, though the mere free trade position may command but a limited view of the future, still there is no hope of salvation in a return to the inefficiency and timorousness of protection. If free trade has not solved industrial and social problems, neither has protection solved them. In protectionist Germany industrial depressions are more severe than in England, and the working classes labour fourteen hours a day and live on horse flesh and black bread. And even in the United States, in spite of, or rather because of, protection, industrial and social problems of a very grave character are rapidly maturing for solution.

The Englishman, therefore, while admitting the growth of new conditions which bear with them pressing problems for the British statesman, manufacturer and workman, is disposed to conclude that neither protection nor the newly discovered.... zollverein has any direct bearing upon them. Great Britain does not need protection against foreign competition, but her producing classes do need relief from those remnants of antiquated feudalism which now hang as millstones around the neck of industry. The producing classes are handicapped, not only by the burdens they have to carry of excessive taxation for municipal and imperial purposes, but indirectly also for the maintenance of a leisured class. The British landlords exact from the producing classes an annual tribute of 250,000,000 pounds; an antiquated railway system imposes charges from two to four times higher than the rates in Europe or America, while English mining rents and royalties as compared with those obtaining in other countries impose a similar handicap upon the productive forces of the nation.

Then Britain's business organization and industrial equipment [need] to be improved. The country must appropriate the German secret of success, efficient education, and it must also learn the American secret, efficient co-ordination and organization of industry.

19. Dominion Coal Treat Their Men Well[112]

A short time ago the Halifax Herald published a series of rather remarkable articles upon labour conditions in the coal mining regions of Cape Breton, alleging that as a result of the grievous or petty oppressions of the coal companies the miners were notoriously discontented and ready to give their dissatisfaction expression in any desperate enterprise -- even to the launching of a new political party. Of course, the Halifax journal undertook to prove, for the benefit of the miners, that there was no room for a third party in Nova Scotia, and that the only way the men could secure redress for their multifarious grievances was to help to overthrow the Government that had given the Dominion Coal Company opportunity to apply efficient mining methods to the exploitation of valuable coal areas.

As the Provincial Workmen's Association[113] has, like the miners' organizations in Great Britain, often made use of its political influence -- usually supporting Liberal candidates, in return for legislation in the miner's interest -- the report that it was about to abandon the old tactics and organize an independent party, seemed, if true, to be of more than passing interest and seemed, indeed, if inspired by any general or specific grievances of the miners, to call into question the wisdom of the Provincial Government in creating the Dominion Coal Company. So when my wanderings recently brought me to Cape Breton I was at some pains to discover how much truth there was in the Halifax journal's representations in regard to matters in the mining regions. When I visited the collieries of the Dominion Coal Company and sought to discover the causes of the dissatisfaction and discontent alleged to be so rampant among the miners, the union officials received my queries with some amusement, and assured me that anybody who gave credence to

---

[112]*Montreal Herald*, September 24 1906.

[113]Established in 1879, the Provincial Workmen's Association was not affiliated with any federation of labour at this time. Although commonly regarded by labour historians as backward-looking and conservative, it was in fact highly militant and contained many socialists who sought to change the union's Liberal proclivities. Ultimately frustrated in their efforts to reform the PWA, such socialists organized a Nova Scotia district of the United Mine Workers of America. The split between the two unions was key to a bitter and violent strike in the coalfields (1909-1911). Ultimately the UMW replaced the PWA in the course of the Great War. In this article, McKay shows no awareness of the first serious stirrings of independent labour politics in Cape Breton in 1904. It is telling that he did not even get the name of the union consistently right.

everything appearing in Halifax papers was -- well, something of a curiosity in that part of the world. If the miners had any general or particular grievance, they knew nothing about it. Naturally, the company and the men not infrequently had disputes, but the questions which arose from time to time were always adjusted amicably. Since the organization of the Dominion Coal Company, there had not been a strike of any magnitude on the part of the employees.

The management has never stood on its dignity when dealing with the union's representatives, and when circumstances permitted, has given favorable consideration to the demands of its employees. Since 1900 the rates paid miners have been advanced from 22 to 25 per cent., and that by no means constitutes the sum of their gains. The Company's enterprise has assured the men steady work, and made possible the abolition of the [banking] rates -- that is, the reduced rates formerly prevailing in the winter months, when, owing to the difficulty of shipping, the operators [banked] their winter output near the pits. Then too, the introduction of the most improved methods in all branches of the industry, the employment of air locomotives and mining machines, has rendered the labour of the men less arduous and less dangerous.

As intimated above, the management appears to be imbued with the democratic spirit -- to be in some respects almost patriarchial in its attitude towards the employees. Officials of big corporations are often disposed to be arbitrary and arrogant, and employees of such concerns are often so overawed by the power of capital that they are almost afraid to call their souls, much less their tongues, their own. But the Dominion Coal Company might almost have a soul, so frank and friendly is the feeling the men entertain towards it. To me this achievement of the Company, the winning of the good will of the men, seemed even more impressive than the ponderous paraphernalia of that colossal colliery, Dominion No. 2, the biggest and best equipped colliery in the world; and to the miners from the Old Country it seemed also a particularly noticeable and somewhat surprising thing.

A canny Scotch miner, red haired, and with a whimsical way of expressing himself, referred to it enthusiastically in the course of a conversation I had with him. To the query whether he found conditions in this country very much of an improvement on the old, his reply was characteristic. He had only been a month out here, and hadn't learned everything there was to learn about this country yet. Men worked longer hours here, and made more money. But then you must remember that in the Old Country you could buy a pennyworth of lots of things, while here you couldn't get anything for less than five cents. At home you could get a bottle of pop, or a bottle of beer for a penny; here pop costs five cents and beer twenty cents bottle. Another thing, there [weren't] many amusements. For the men there was little to do except to work and sleep; and for the women, it seemed a rather dreary life.

"But then meat and such things are cheaper than in the Old Country, and house accommodation too -- when you could get a decent house at all. The Company owns a lot of houses round here, and is building new ones all the time; not very pretty houses, but substantial and comfortable; and the rent is very reasonable -- from $4 to $6 per month; mighty reasonable when you consider that any miner worth his salt can make $2.50 a day, while lots of them are making $5, $6, $7, and even more a day. Some of the farmers round here have built cottages which they rent to newcomers -- and ramshackle structures they are, some of them. When I first landed I rented such a house -- the only one I could get just then. When it rained we had to move the bed to the middle of the floor, and even then I thought the wife and I would float away sometimes."

"Now, however, I've got one of the Company's cottages, and intend to buy it. The Company encourages miners to purchase a home of their own; gives them much better terms, I understand, than you could get from any building or loan society. You pay so much a month; very little more than you would pay for rent; and in a few years you would have a home of your own. My wife is going to take in boarders and that will help along. At home she wouldn't do that. Women there like to tog themselves out and show themselves to their neighbours. But here it's different. Nobody is too proud to work, and the wife -- maybe because she has not made many acquaintances as yet -- wants to do something to keep her busy."

"But what I like most," he continued, after a pause, "what I like most about this country is the opportunities it offers, the sense of freedom a man enjoys. Why there are boys hardly sixteen years old, in yon mine earning $2 a day. At home they would count themselves lucky if they were getting a shilling and three pence. And then you can go to work when you please and knock off when you please; neither the company nor the union attempts to dictate the length of the working day, or the amount of work you shall do. You get your wages every fortnight and you can deal at the Company's store or the men's co-operative stores, or wherever you please. Freedom. A man is as free as the air he breathes.

"At home the relations of the masters and men are seldom more cordial than those of an armed truce, and even in the most powerful union one is conscious of a sense of oppression; a sense too, of impotence and futility, as if the imperialism of concentrated wealth had reached such a pitch that it not only made future efforts on the part of the men to better their conditions of little avail, but constantly menaced the position they had already achieved -- as if the very structure of society rendered it folly for the great mass of workers to hope for more than a living wage. But here there is no such feeling -- no such brooding hopelessness. One is conscious of a different atmosphere altogether -- a buoyant optimism that sees in capital an ally rather than an enemy. The Company seems to be regarded as a sort of special providence dispensing prosperity -- a providence from which the men if they are only sufficiently alert may feel certain of securing a fair share of its bounties. The native born miners have no conception of a state of affairs where a big company literally holds a man's life and self-respect in the hollow of its hands, where by simply depriving him of a job, it may force him and his family into pauperism and all that it stands for. Apparently -- and perhaps rightly so -- they reason that the Company has more need of their services than they have of the Company's money. Most of them come from farms, many still own farms in the back country and they could go back to their farms if necessary, and not feel that they were making much of a sacrifice. In this fact, the facility with which men may pass from one employment to another, one gets the secret of the free and independent spirit, the sense of power, characteristic of the native born. It struck me as rather curious when I first came here that the union did not care whether the new comers joined their ranks or not."

As I listened to the random observations of this Old Country miner, I became curious to know what effect men of his type had had upon the local labour movement -- whether the labour spirit of the old world transplanted into the more favourable conditions of the new had in any way influenced the outlook or aspirations of the native born? As about thirty per cent. of the miners employed by the Dominion Company come from the old world -- principally from the United Kingdom, though Germans and Austrians are coming over in increasing numbers -- the question seemed of some importance, and it was evidently so regarded by the union leaders to whom I put it.

"After twenty years in this country," said another Scotchman, a prominent leader of the Workingmen's Provincial Association [Provincial Workmen's Association], "I am satisfied that the Canadian, whether capitalist or workingman, is a better man than his Old Country prototype; but I am not quite convinced that he is the better citizen -- not at any rate in the present stage of our political and industrial evolution. The Canadian is an individualist -- a practical opportunist, more concerned to seize an opportunity to get up in the world than to uplift his fellows, or even to do justice to them. On the other hand, the Old Country men who come over here are imbued with socialistic doctrines -- the idea of the solidarity of labour and the [interdependence] of human interests -- so much so, that many, I verily believe, would sooner seize an opportunity to uplift their class than an opportunity to make a fortune at the expense of their class. The class-conscious spirit may not in some of its manifestations be a very attractive thing; but it seems to me to mark the beginning, the birth, of a social conscience.

"You have probably heard something of the formation of an independent labour party here. As yet no definite steps have been taken in this direction, but the question is being canvassed with more or less enthusiasm. Our men have not been unimpressed by the rise of the labour party in the Old Land, but left to themselves, it would be a long time before they undertook to form a new party. Our organization has not been loath to make use of its political influence, and as between the parties we have easily held the balance of power in several constituencies, the Government at Halifax has usually given respectful attention to our demands for legislation. Our local men would be satisfied to proceed along these lines for years, but the influx of the Old Country element introduces a new factor -- the desire, so long realized by the miners of the Old Country, of having typical labour representation in Parliament. The labour spirit of the old world is making itself felt here, giving to the miners new and larger ideals, a broader outlook, and a clearer conception of economic movements and social values. To my mind it is destined to play an important part, to fulfil a useful and necessary function, in the future development of Canada.

"Up to the present capital has received a great deal of encouragement from the Government, and while one may admit that in a new country capital needs and deserves such encouragement, looking around he sees that the capitalist appetite for public support is becoming somewhat insatiable. Capital should now be able to take care of itself. At any rate the big corporations now hold most of the advantages in any conflict with labour, and beyond question labour may claim more consideration at the hands of Government than it now receives, without prejudice to the rights of capital. In the contemplation of our marvellous industrial progress, the Government, like the rest of us, is apt to forget that the increase of wealth is not the main object of a nation, and that an even more important part of its duty than the encouragement of capital is the protection of labour, the source of all wealth."

"It will be seen, then, that the movement looking to the formation of an independent labour party here, as in other parts of Canada, is mainly the result of the old world labour spirit working upon the increasing consciousness of labour that under the new industrial forms and forces called into being by capitalist enterprise, the power of Government needs to be constantly invoked to promote the well-being of the millions who toil, and is not therefore the result of any specific grievance of the miners. You will hear miners complaining because they only make $45 or $50 in a fortnight; but grievances like that hardly call for drastic measures. Of course, all the Company's employees do not do as well as the miners; though even men doing common labourers' work earn anywhere from $1.35 to $2.00 a day."

PART II

Evolutionary Sociology and Applied Ethics:

The Struggle For a "Working-Class Culture," 1907-1914

This section brings together 40 of McKay's articles on evolutionary sociology and working-class struggle, most of them written between 1907 and 1914 (but some appearing as late as the 1930s). These document a transition from the rather inchoate organicism of his new liberal period to a much more systematic and coherent approach -- an approach founded on doctrines of materialism, social evolution, and class struggle. Rather than seeking to reform society by confronting it with stark evidence of its inability to live up to Christian principles (the line he had taken from the late 1890s to c.1902), or vesting his hopes in a planned and progressive scientific capitalism (the dominant position from 1903 to 1907 or so), he now argued that only a revolutionary response to the contradictions of capitalism made sense. He sought a synthesis of sociological knowledge and revolutionary practice. It was possible, using the conceptual tools of both Spencer and Marx (notably those of social evolution, the labour theory of value, and the class struggle) to base strategies for working-class struggle on an objective understanding of the laws of motion of the capitalist system. This objective understanding could be decisively important in shaping a new politics of labour, aiming towards a post-capitalist co-operative commonwealth; failing to have such an understanding, conversely, would condemn labour and the socialist movement to defeats. Such a theoretical breakthrough required the emergence of a new working-class culture, constructed by workers with the help of the socialist intellectuals closely allied with them. Undergirding this approach to class and politics was a unified framework of theories that explained everything from the evolution of the cell to the ultimate destiny of the capitalist system: a vision of socialism as part of the massive patterns of the entire cosmos. Putting it in a nutshell: McKay had discovered *evolutionary sociology* and *revolutionary socialism*: for him (as we shall see), the theory of *social evolution* sustained a vision of *politico-cultural revolution*.

1. The New Age of Capital

Although McKay's turn-of-the-century writings had been preoccupied with the emergence of monopoly capitalism as the central fact of social and economic life, they did not attempt to explain this phenomenon rigorously in terms of long-term trends in the system. McKay's transition to a more "sociological" framework of analysis may well have been prompted by the intensification of the consolidation and centralization of capital. In 1897, McKay had seen "trusts" as somewhat constructive forces, whose rationalization and consolidation of industry was paving the way for full socialization. As a self-described revolutionary, however, he saw them very differently, as elements of a massive capitalist Leviathan bearing down upon small producers and workers. The process of the consolidation and centralization of capital could no longer be viewed in the same way.[1]

Capitalism, McKay now insisted, was based on the expropriation of the surplus value generated by primary producers and workers: as he explained to the readers of the Shelburne *Coast-Guard*, under capitalism, industrial workers and other subordinate classes received only the "commodity value of their labour -- that is, they get enough to keep themselves and reproduce their kind, and procure sufficient education to fit them for certain employments."[2] The surplus over and above this minimum was expropriated by capitalists, who could use it to accumulate yet more capital.

This was, of course, in simplified form, a version of Marx's labour theory of value, applicable to all phases of capitalist development (for McKay never would have accepted that monopoly capitalism was an entirely distinct phase of economic development; because it was a form of capitalism, monopoly capitalism was by definition "a system of competitive anarchy" [§.30, "Socialism as the Science of Social Evolution," originally published as "Socialism"]). What made monopoly capitalism so much more exploitive than earlier forms of capitalism, however, were the hidden taxes applied to the working class through watered stock (that is, stock issued for speculative purposes far in excess of the actual value of the capital of a company) and the hypertrophic expansion of corporate parasitism. Noting that, according to the 1911 census, the capital in stocks and bonds outstanding against Canadian

---

[1]One reason, of course, was the greatly accelerated pace of economic concentration and centralization. According to McKay's estimate, there had been 41 industrial amalgamations in Canada, which had absorbed 196 individual companies, in 1911 alone. Colin McKay, "What The Trusts Are Doing," *Eastern Labor News*, 17 February 1912. His sense of a widespread merger movement (if not his precise statistics) is generally supported by the literature.

[2]Colin McKay, "Letter from Colin McKay," *Coast-Guard*, 3 August 1911.

industries totalled over $1,000,000,000, McKay predicted -- accurately, it turned out -- that over-capitalization would prove to be eminently suited to keeping workers' wages down and prices up. Companies would simply create fictitious capital and require people to pay interest on it; if challenged, they would always be able to demonstrate that their enterprises were not paying fair dividends, and that workers were asking for too much.[3] To this condemnation of the parasitism of stock-watering McKay added a general evolutionary critique of all those who drew dividends but did no actual work. Evolutionary theory dictated that such functionless parasites would eventually vanish, because it was "an inexorable law of nature that useless organs must disappear.... our economic development has outgrown our social organization, and in accordance with the fundamental biological law a social organism out of adjustment with its economical environment must perish as unfit."[4] Clearly a language of fitness, parasitism, and function could operate on both a moral and a "social scientific" level. Perhaps most effective were those passages which pushed the argument on both levels simultaneously: "In order that we may deliver wealth to a class which for the most part have ceased to perform any useful economic function, we submit to conditions, robbing us of our independence, and the bulk of the fruits of labour. Worse still the planless system of modern production, the duplication of plants, the enormous crowd of parasites, obliges the productive workers to labour many more hours than would be necessary under a rational system of things."[5] Clearly, the parasite and the monopoly capitalist were burdens, and their existence could not be justified. They imposed hardships on workers and producers, without performing socially useful work themselves.

Workers, who had once been accustomed to having large families, now could no longer support them: in Saint John, McKay noted, the birthrate barely exceeded the death rate, "and the great increase in the number of women and children at work is incontestable evidence that the average worker today is not able to support a large family."[6] It was absurd: a vast increase in the productivity of labour and the output of industry had generated almost no benefits for workers. Drawing on the researches of American statistician Carroll D. Wright, McKay noted that the "food-and-

---

[3]Colin McKay, "The Result of Over-Capitalization," *Eastern Labor News*, 9 November 1912.

[4]Colin McKay, "Urges the Workers to Strike at the Ballot Box for Redress," letter to *Halifax Herald*, 1 October 1910. This captured, in Spencerian biological metaphors, the clash between forces and relations of production that was (and is) central to the productivist interpretation of Marx's thought.

[5]Colin McKay, "Time for a Labor Party is Now," letter to the *Eastern Labor News*, 11 November 1911.

[6]Colin McKay, "Urges the Workers to Strike at the Ballot Box for Redress," letter to *Halifax Herald*, 1 October 1910.

shelter-getting efficiency of man" had increased at least 10 times over 25 years; drawing on the analysis of an Austrian economist, he remarked that mechanization now made it conceivable for five million people to supply a population of 20,000,000, on the basis of a working day of one and a half hours. Yet under the rule of capitalists and politicians -- those "predatory classes" -- most people were not better off than they had been a generation before.[7] The census did not support any of the Liberal government's claims of a rising standard of living, remarked McKay in 1908.[8] "Progress may mean prosperity for the big capitalists, and it may mean more business at a less rate of profit for the little capitalist," he argued, and added (starkly reversing his earlier optimistic appraisal of progress under capitalism): "But for the worker it usually only means increased exploitation". In industry after industry, efficiency had been increased, even a hundred-fold: it had once required 200 hours to place 100 tons of ore on railway cars, but now it took only two. But had workers benefited from this 100-fold increase in efficiency? If not, why not? Where were the benefits going? [§.22, "Industrial Corporations and the People"].

To his indictment of capitalism on the grounds of its unfairness and irrationality, Colin McKay added the charge of manslaughter. Reverting to the vivid imagery he had used in his polemics against sweating, in 1910 he attacked "those modern juggernauts, the railways and the industrial establishments," for killing over 2,000 and wounding over 6,000 people a year in North America.[9] That monopoly capitalism had degraded the position of the worker was also brought home by the horrific Canadian coal-mine fatality statistics. McKay did not hesitate to drive home the lesson that a coupon-clipping absentee capitalist class had brutally degraded the labour process, and killed workers, in its crass pursuit of profits [§.21, "Capitalistic Development and Its Cost"]. Here was evidence of the profound radicalization of the writer who, not so very much earlier, had written that uplifting sermon, "Dominion Coal Treats Its Workers Well" [§.19].

McKay also changed in his stance toward the state. An implicit assumption of his "new liberal writings" was that the state could act, in Glasgow and elsewhere, as a neutral regulator, imposing rationality and purpose on the disordered social landscape of capitalism. He now conceptualized the state very differently: as an active force in the transfer of surplus value from the workers to their exploiters. Without himself endorsing their viewpoint, McKay noted that even "men of large and progressive minds" had come to accept as a fundamental truth the political doctrine that "the best way to take care of the many is to help the few, that to give the corporations special privileges is all that is necessary

---

[7]Colin McKay, untitled letter, *Coast Guard*, 8 September 1910.

[8]Colin McKay, untitled letter to the *Halifax Herald*, 27 April 1908.

[9]Colin McKay, untitled letter, *Halifax Herald*, 21 May 1910.

to secure the well-being of the workingmen" [§.22, "Industrial Corporations and the People"]. This relatively new form of the state was actively committed to monopolization, he argued. Almost all the combines and mergers of the day, McKay noted in 1911, operated under federal charters, which were granted without the state taking the precaution that the new corporate giants would not exercise their powers to gouge the public. Ever since Confederation, and operating at the "behest of capital," Canadian governments had been occupied in "making it easy for corporations to absorb all the advantages flowing from the progress of science, and the introduction of machinery."[10] Although the process was not as far advanced as in the United States, the Canadian merger movement had nonetheless involved capitalists and politicians in schemes that verged on fraud and public pillage: "Companies may be wrecked, shareholders robbed, the people plundered -- and ... our laws offer no redress [§.22, "Industrial Corporations and the People"]. The responsibility for this state of affairs rested with the state, which was, at least in theory, capable of regulating the merger movement.[11]

The protective tariff had undoubtedly been significant in facilitating the merger movement, but for McKay it was not the decisive factor. Protection taxed consumers and rewarded certain capitalists. McKay drew on the industrial census in 1906 to argue that Canadians had paid more than $5,500,000 to protect the cotton industry; $3,500,000 of that represented a direct bonus to the manufacturers. Had Canadians bought their cotton on the open markets of the world, they would have been able to pay cotton workers their wages to do nothing, and still have been $2,000,000 dollars to the good.[12] Monopoly capitalism in the case of the state-subsidized steel industry (most recently the Dominion Iron and Steel Company) had profited speculators but bankrupted the incautious "mechanics" who had taken "their savings from the banks and bought up the stock." In the age of the "buccaneering exploits of some of our railway and similar corporations," working-class Canadians had to rethink the fundamentals of political economy.[13] The classic liberal prescription -- undermine monopoly by bringing down the tariff walls behind which it had grown -- was simplistic. It underestimated the strength of the new corporations, allied as they were "with the banks and railways," and it flew in the face of analogous problems in Britain, the home of free trade. ("It is a patent fact that the game of exploiting the people proceeds as industriously in free trade England as in protectionist Canada.") Protection enabled "some businessmen to capture a share of this surplus value; free trade enables another set of men to capture a share." There

---

[10]Colin McKay, "Letter from Colin McKay," *Coast-Guard*, 3 August 1911.

[11]*Ibid.*.

[12]*Ibid.*

[13]Colin McKay, "Favored Finance: Methods of Money-Makers to Bunco the Multitude," *Yarmouth Times*, 5 March 1907.

consequently was no good reason to believe "that the total obliteration of the tariff wall" would undermine the power of the monopolists. The Liberals who argued for this panacea needed to explain why the anti-combine clauses in the present Liberal tariff had failed to operate, and why after 1905, under a Liberal government, "we have been developing combines faster than they were ever raised in the States." "Neither protection nor free trade will solve the problem of enabling the common people to reap the full fruits of their labour," McKay remarked. His sense of the great Reciprocity Debate of 1911 was that it was largely beside the point.[14]

The implications of the new corporate capitalism for economic theory were profound. The emergence of the combines destroyed "the validity of the arguments which were formerly urged in support of the policy of protection by the conservatives and accepted by the liberals after they attained to responsibilities of office," and yet also demolished the arguments for free trade. They also destroyed McKay's earlier belief in the progressive rôle of trusts in creating the preconditions of a socialist economy. Given the tendency of the combines to restrict production and close down factory after factory, their record of expanding the forces of production was not commendable. But the revolutionary theoretical impact of the new economy went even further, completely making a myth out of Ricardo's law of diminishing returns and even of the law of supply and demand. The imposing theories, laws and predictions of the "older economists" had been reduced to nothing.[15]

Yet this did not mean that most people had succeeded in renovating their conceptual frameworks in order to take account of the new reality. Although twentieth-century capitalism clearly demanded completely different methods of analysis, participants in the Reciprocity Debate of 1911 remained stuck in a Victorian time warp: liberal chieftains drew their arguments from J.S. Mill's *Principles of Political Economy*, and their protectionist critics from the works of Friedrich List. Older categories could no longer grasp the interdependence and complexity of the modern world. McKay would wonder if even Marxism, although far more valid than the older economics, had adequately registered the novelty of the new age. Had it taken sufficient account of the extent to which capitalist property was overthrowing the institution of private property, as it had traditionally been defined? In its typical form, capitalist property

---

[14]*Ibid.* There are interesting parallels here with the development of Gramsci's views away from free-trade liberalism and towards radical socialism. See Germino, *Antonio Gramsci*: 84. I owe to Peter Campbell the very plausible suggestion that the more proximate influence on McKay was likely Bellamy's discussion of the issue of protection in *Equality*, which we know McKay had consulted [see §.88, "Monetary or Credit Reform Schemes Illusory."]

[15]Colin McKay, "Reciprocity," *Coast-Guard*, 27 July 1911.

now presented itself as a "a piece of paper, which confers upon its holder an impersonal right. No stockholder of the C.P.R. has any personal property rights in any locomotive, car or station of that railway." Citing the work of the Austrian economist Anton Menger, McKay underlined the revolutionary significance of this massive depersonalization of capitalist property, which effectively separated speculative greed from all connection with the actual labour of the property-holder [§.23, "The Small Businessman"].[16]

This vital distinction between "capitalistic property" (the result of the labours of many men working with machines) and individual private property, "which was the result of the labour of the proprietor and perhaps an apprentice or two," remained fundamentally important to McKay for the remainder of his life. It required nothing short of a new "conception of freedom, different from that of a simpler day...." This new concept of freedom would be based on the fundamental insight that "freedom is relative" -- meaning, particularly, relative to the economic resources available to the person exercising the freedom [§.134, "Economic Democracy Must Come!"]. By refining their understanding of property, socialists could begin to think rationally about the position of all subaltern classes and groups in capitalist society. For perhaps the most vivid indication of the new age of monopoly was the acute crisis confronting farmers, fishermen, master artisans, small businessmen, and even some professionals. These "plain people" were caught between the capitalists and the working class. The *petite bourgeoisie* -- to use a collective term McKay himself did not use -- were members of the "uneasy class" [§.23, "The Small Businessman"], caught in a highly unenviable position of dependence on a capitalist order they could scarcely influence or even understand, and whose development seemed to require their rapid and painful destruction.

By the end of the first decade of the twentieth century, Canadian farmers were perhaps the uneasiest members of the "uneasy class," having launched the first of many massive protest movements which were ultimately to shake the Canadian political order. It was a crude misconception, argued McKay, to see farmers simply as "capitalists on the land," and hence as people logically and inevitably opposed to the interests of the proletariat. In looking at an average farm, it was important to draw a distinction between legal ownership and economic ownership. (Modern day rural sociology might make much the same point in drawing a distinction between "formal ownership" and "real ownership.")The real

---

[16]McKay's analysis thus anticipated in some respects the analysis of Adolph A. Berle and Gardner Means, *The Modern Corporation and Private Property* (New York: Macmillan and Company, 1932), which is often interpreted as a decisive text in shifting perceptions of North American capitalism. To my knowledge, he never cited Berle and Means.

owners of the average farm were "the men who control the agencies by which farm produce is placed in the hands of the consumer." Ordinarily farmers and fishermen were not paid the value of their products, but merely the commodity value of their labour: and the price for their labour (or their "wage") never varied much above what sufficed to support them and reproduce their kind, according to prevailing standards of living.[17]

In essence, farmers were caught in the same position as workers: exploiters extracted the surplus over and above that required to keep them alive. Although, like workers, farmers had effected massive improvements in efficiency, their economic position was little better. They were as "helplessly in the grip of the iron laws of capitalism as the city wage-earners." Superficial improvements in living standards (such as that of moving up from wool and homespun to cotton and shoddy) were juxtaposed to the farmers' acute insecurity and *relative* poverty. The farmer had once stood in a "personal relation to his market," and had received, "practically speaking, "the use-value of the products of his labour;" social harmony, reflected by such co-operative events as harvest bees, had once pervaded rural economic life. However, those days of rural self-sufficiency were gone: a "rural revolution" had transformed the Canadian countryside. The rural craft producers who had once lived in the countryside had been undercut by urban manufacturing, and had left for the city to become wage earners. Many functions "once performed by the farmer or his family on the farm or in the home have been incorporated in the factory system." Such functions as "butter making, spinning, weaving, sugar making, etc.," had been taken over by capitalist industry. Agricultural tasks themselves had changed: "Technically the farmer has become more or less of a specialist, leaving to others the task of working up some forms of his raw material into finished products, leaving to others all the work of delivering his products to the consumer. He no longer products [produces] for a communal market. He sells practically all his product in an indefinite, impersonal general market, governed by forces of which he has little knowledge, and over which he has no control. He sells through commission merchants and middle men whom he may never have seen, and whose honesty he very often has good reason to doubt...." And enhanced transportation facilities meant the farmers of a given locality had to compete with farmers of the whole Dominion [§.66, "The New Brunswick Farmer"].

Fishermen, too, were caught in the same contradiction of formal independence and real dependence. The enlarged markets promised by a reciprocity agreement with the United States would not benefit the fishermen "except in so far as they control the marketing of their products." Those fishermen who had clearly benefited from freer trade

---

[17]Colin McKay, "Reciprocity and Co-operation," *Coast-Guard*, 30 March 1911.

with the United States were those who, like the lobster fishermen of south
western Nova Scotia, had been able to become their own merchants.
Under ordinary circumstances, "the fishermen are not paid the value of
their products, but simply the commodity price of their labour. If
reciprocity brings the producer into closer relations with the consumer, if
as it were it establishes reciprocity between the two, then the fishermen
will stand to gain something more than a slight increase of wages due to
extra labour. But the only way for them to be sure of making any
important or permanent gains is to establish co-operative societies to
market their products on their own account, and eliminate in so far as
possible the middlemen." Even so, there were limitations: fishermen
under capitalism could not hope to obtain the full value of their products,
because they had "to pay tribute to the transportation companies, banks
and various commercial organizations which they would be obliged to
deal with even if they all worked under some co-operative arrangement
embracing the whole province, and with selling agencies in the States."[18]

The heavily qualified independence of the fishermen was analogous to the
position of the master artisans of the city. Although "capitalists" in the
strict sense that they often employed other people, many small employers
were being so tightly squeezed by the system that they genuinely could not
afford to pay higher wages to their workers. "Many small employers,"
reported McKay, "do not make as much in a year as their employees do.
They are merely vassals of the larger capitalism." Even in a trade like
painting, little affected by machinery, a condition of hyper-competition
and the high prices exacted by suppliers brought the small master down
to the economic position of the worker [§.69, "The Fear of Progress"]. The
older generation of master artisans had not claimed to be engaged in
business to benefit the people, but "were probably honest enough to
admit that they were not in business for the purpose of giving
employment to labour, but for the purpose of making profits for
themselves, by obliging the workers to create products worth considerably
more than their wages." But modern railway promoters and manufacturers
worked in a far different world, and were sustained in part by generous
concessions on the part of the state, not to mention exorbitant protective
tariffs [§.24, "The Master Magicians"]. Small shopkeepers were in an even
more difficult position, required to work longer hours for less pay than
most skilled workers. Small businessmen of this type were menaced by the
competition of the big department stores and mail order concerns on the
one hand, and by the "combines of manufacturers and wholesalers bent
on reducing them to a condition of economic vassalage," on the other.
How much had they really progressed, when they felt obliged to fight the
"early closing movement" tooth and nail to defend their right to work
eighteen-hour days? A most eloquent testimony to their plight was the
annual record of failures in the small business world -- "a pitiable record

[18]*Ibid.*

of blighted ambitions and ruined hopes" [§.23, "The Small Businessman"]. Or as McKay put it on another occasion, the small employer was "often a greater slave to present conditions than the man who works for wages," partly because of the ever-present menace of business failure.[19] Even some professionals might be sufficiently "uneasy" to listen to the socialist message.[20]

All these members of the "uneasy class" shared a problem of separating the ideal of property-holding from the actual realities of corporate property in a modern capitalist economy. They thought of themselves as "capitalists" or "businessmen" by virtue of proprietorship in their business. This idea of property carried with it a sense of dignity and independence. What they actually possessed, however, was merely self-earned "private property," not real "capitalist property." The proprietorship of an individual enterprise did not make the individual who owned it into a capitalist. The new monopoly capitalism had completely transformed the economic character of private property. Property acquired by personal labour had been supplanted by capitalist private property based on the labour of others. "The capitalist mode of production and accumulation and therefore capitalist private property have for their fundamental condition the annihilation of self-earned private property," McKay argued, and cited as evidence the fact that farmers who owned their own farms received "only a meagre wage for their labour." Even when the proprietor of a small business employed help, he became a capitalist only in the sense that he exploited the labour of others, not in the sense of being able to convert his private property into capitalist property and obtain a capitalistic return from it. The type of "private property" owned by the small businessman was in fact rapidly being subverted by capitalism itself [§.23, "The Small Businessman"].

It was obvious that workers and the "uneasy class" had many common problems and common interests. McKay drew the strategic conclusion that they should also build a common movement, with workers in a position of leadership, but articulating their program to the interests of members of the "uneasy classes." He arrived, in almost all but name, at

---

[19]Colin McKay, "Time for a Labor Party is Now," letter to the *Eastern Labor News*, 11 November 1911.

[20]Colin McKay, "Organize the School Teachers," *Eastern Labor News*, 15 November 1913. But the line had to be drawn somewhere. As for lawyers, McKay seems to have recommended that they simply reflect long and hard on their parasitism. See Colin McKay, "The Lawyer and the Boy," *Eastern Labor News*, 15 June 1912. In this improbable story, a boy manages to shame a lawyer into the realization of his objectively parasitical existence, whereupon he becomes an ardent reader of socialist literature! There may well have been here an echo of the old Knights of Labor hostility to lawyers as a group. McKay never considered professionals to be an important element in the struggle against capitalism.

Gramsci's theory of hegemony as a key to working-class emancipation.[21] There was one thing, for example, that farmers could do about their position of dependence within capitalism: they could join together to form co-operatives, and then ally themselves with the workers to construct the Co-operative Commonwealth [§.66, "The New Brunswick Farmer"]. In other words, responding effectively to the new capitalism required the "subaltern classes" to unite in a new kind of alliance, one based on a transcendence of their immediate economic-corporative interests in order to transform the social order and win political power. A political party *"embodying the ideals of labour* must represent the general interests of humanity *of all classes except the big capitalists."* McKay's formula was subtle and precise. Workers, small businessmen, *some* professionals, farmers, and fishermen, among others, would come together on the basis of a shared understanding of the workings of the capitalist system and of their common interests in creating a different political and social order.[22] But this was *not* populism: the interests and ideals of the working class, and not those of other classes, would be those at the nucleus of a new political formation in which the interests and ideas of other subaltern classes were also to be respected and considered.[23]

---

[21]Gramsci argues, especially in "Some Aspects of the Southern Question," that the proletariat can become a hegemonic class, only if it transcends its immediate economic interests and wins the support of other exploited classes, such as the poor peasantry. Hegemony is defined "by an expansion beyond immediate economic class interest into the sphere of political direction through a system of class alliances" (See D. Forgacs, ed., *An Antonio Gramsci Reader: Selected Writings 1916-1935* (New York: Schocken Books, 1988): 422-423. Hegemony is therefore always rooted in one of the fundamental classes of a social order, but it must provide non-fundamental classes and groups with leadership genuinely attuned to their values and interests. Hegemony was never in Gramsci's thought exclusively cultural, but it did have the connotation of combining political, cultural and moral leadership. The argument in Canada would be that the working class could not aspire to become a hegemonic class unless it articulated to its own program the views of other, subaltern groups. This was not, however, to be the pattern of "left-alliance-building" in Canada before the Second World War. It should be noted that Gramsci's thought was not available in Canada when McKay was considering the problem. He more likely was influenced by the thinking of Karl Kautsky's *The Social Revolution*, although he does not seem to have cited it. To the best of my knowledge, Gramsci's Canadian career started on 24 March 1958, with a review of *The Modern Prince* in the *Canadian Tribune*.

[22]Colin McKay, "Time for a Labor Party is Now," letter to the *Eastern Labor News*, 11 November 1911. Emphasis added.

[23]It would be tempting to claim that McKay was unique in Canada in formulating the critical issue of class alliances in this subtle -- almost Gramscian -- manner, but the issue has yet to receive sustained attention. He does appear to have taken a very different position than the Marxist journalist W.U.Cotton, writing at the same time and influenced as strongly by the writings of Karl Kautsky. According to Edward M. Penton, Cotton "welcomed the growth of trusts and dismissed the small merchants and businessmen as necessary victims of historical development": see "The Ideas of William Cotton: A Marxist View of Canadian Society (1908-1914)," M.A.Thesis,

McKay was thus arguing the urgent need to construct what Gramsci would later call a "historic bloc" of the subaltern classes -- farmers, fishermen, small businessmen and workers -- on the clear basis of the ideals of labour (what he would elsewhere call a "working-class culture") and on the foundation of a solid theoretical understanding of how the capitalist system worked. McKay spent much of the period 1910-1913 crafting a discourse which would speak powerfully both to the workers and to the "uneasy classes," and develop their sense of a common interest. This would remain a preoccupation of his into the 1930s.[24]

Workers needed a strong voice in order to build effective alliances, under their unifying leadership, with other subaltern classes and groups. Unless members of the "uneasy class" were won to labour's side, the struggle for socialism could not be won, because the working class (strictly defined) was -- and was likely long to remain -- in a minority. McKay suggested the new labour party in Saint John gather information about the methods of propaganda employed by labour parties elsewhere, and "carry on an extensive campaign of education, not only in regard to the immediate demands of labour but for the purpose of making the workers generally realize their position and understand their historic mission in the world." A labour party had to represent firm principles; hoping for support merely on the basis that a workingman was running for office was futile, and it was more important that the Labour party "plant its principles in the minds of the working class than to elect its candidates."[25] In the New Brunswick context, with the Liberal Party in acute disarray, the working class should organize to win the support of the farmers for the labour party.[26] Beyond this base, the labour party should appeal to small businessmen, to the "professional classes," to the unemployed, and to primary producers. Such people should be appealed to on the basis of their common interest in opposing a system that robbed them of their independence, and which was dominated by a class that had ceased to perform any useful economic function. All the subaltern classes and groups could appreciate the injustice of bourgeois control of political power, and the extravagant hand-outs to large industry. But this party was not to be a populist grab-bag. The new political party was to embody the ideals of labour and represent the general interests of humanity of all

---

University of Ottawa, 1978: 175. McKay had once argued in this manner, but he had gone past this position by 1913.

[24]See, for example, "British Columbia's New Deal," *Canadian Unionist*, Vol.8, No.8 (January 1935): 196-199.

[25]Colin McKay, "How To Make a Live Labour Party," letter to the *Eastern Labor News*, 4 May 1912.

[26]Colin McKay, "The Labor Party's Opportunity," letter to *Eastern Labor News*, 29 June 1912.

classes except the big capitalists.[27] Socialists could not in fact consistently support any candidate who did not "take his stand on the grounds of the class struggle and declare for the overthrow of capitalism and the abolition of the wage system." The key point of electoral politics was to educate workers and all other subaltern groups and classes on the revolutionary possibilities of a co-operative commonwealth. Winning reforms from the system was an incidental consideration [§.54, "Industrial Unionism and Labour Politics"].

McKay's seemingly "populist" use of phrases like the "plain people" or just "the people" was in fact a subtle aspect of this democratic bloc-building strategy. "The people", for example, had a strong interest in preserving the jury system, especially at a time when "the tendency to government by injunctions" was so strong: jurors were more apt to be influenced by considerations of justice than by legal technicalities.[28] In drawing up his indictment of industrial corporations, which had expanded industrial efficiency ten- or twenty-fold, McKay put the case in terms of the "plain people": "Are the plain people, the small merchants, and workingmen, ten or twenty times better off than they were a generation or so ago? Or have the hours of labour been reduced ten or twenty times?" [§.22, "Industrial Corporations and the People"].

McKay did not underestimate the difficulties of building such a historic bloc of workers, farmers, fishers, and the *petite bourgeoisie*. Many Canadian-born workers who owned their own homes or property of some sort, were "intellectually... hardly differentiated from the small businessman." Such a "man with a small property" was not partial to strikes, because they endangered what little property he held, whereas the "propertyless worker," bound neither to his community nor to his employer, had nothing to lose. It was natural for the small businessman to regard a strike "as an unmitigated disaster," for he lost trade, and might well have to assume the debts of defaulting customers. On the other hand, the "uneasy classes" needed to remember that they maintained their precarious positions only because workers had struggled to keep up wages, and only because workers had not been compelled to develop their own co-operative societies [§.57, "The Labour Question Explained to Businessmen"].

In a sense, this was a veiled threat, a negative vision of the threatened reduction of the *petite bourgeoisie* (and a reminder that the working class was to exercise hegemony within the projected alliance). McKay would elsewhere see the problem more dialectically. The development of a bloc of "plain people" on the basis of a working-class outlook required not just

---

[27]Colin McKay, "Time for a Labor Party is Now," letter to the *Eastern Labor News*, 11 November 1911.
[28]Colin McKay, "Judges and Juries," *Coast-Guard*, 28 July 1910.

a "negative" view of the capitalist forces reducing the independence of the *petite bourgeoisie* but a "positive" view of a socialist order in which small property-holders would have a place. McKay insisted that the socialist order meant the transformation of capitalist property into collective property, but not the expropriation of the small property of workers and the *petite bourgeoisie*. Removing the power of exploitation which resided in capitalist property and vesting it in the people as a whole would "leave the small trader in possession of his business, *if it is socially necessary*, and allow him to get something more than a mere subsistence wage" [§.23, "The Small Businessman," emphasis added]. Drawing on the analysis of Karl Kautsky, McKay urged that a socialist order would not mean just one structure of property-holding, but rather a complexity of arrangements. (Kautsky had urged, "The most manifold forms of property in the means of production -- national, municipal, co-operative and private -- can exist beside each other in a socialist society.") Initially, at any rate, socialists meant to socialize the great industries which had already become monopolies, or which were rapidly tending to become monopolies. McKay quoted with approval Kautsky's view that in agriculture, for example, those plants which had already become capitalist industries would collapse with the general fall of the wage system, and be transformed into "national, municipal, or co-operative business." But "the proletarian governmental power" would have no inclination to take over the property and business of the small farmer. Small agricultural industries would probably be aided, not undermined, by a socialist regime [§.56, "Saint John and the Single Tax"].

These were important moves away from crude Bellamyite images of a future dominated by a monolithic industrial army, towards a much more sophisticated and complex sense of a socialist order. And they were by no means outright capitulations to the world view of small property-holders. McKay continued to insist that the core ideals of the new party would be those of the working class. And he also retained -- and indeed viewed as one of the greatest arguments for socialism -- a belief in the abolition of "the vast number of socially unnecessary employments," and the concentration of human energies on the "really useful" activities. Those of the "uneasy class" who were truly not performing socially useful work (most lawyers and professors, for example) would be required to find new productive roles for themselves in the new society. All of the subaltern classes, and workers especially, would benefit (through shorter hours and higher wages) from the removal of the burden such parasites had imposed upon them.[29]

---

[29]Colin McKay, "Time for a Labor Party is Now," letter to the *Eastern Labor News*, 11 November 1911.

2. Disenchantment with Liberalism and with the Institutions of Christianity

There were obvious similarities between this political vision of a historic bloc and the liberal cross-class alliance McKay called for in the 1890s against sweating, but there was also a profound difference. In his earlier, liberal period, McKay had visualized such an alliance as one that focused on a specific issue, and not as a permanent working-class transcendence of narrow economic interests for the purpose of achieving a new society. The starting-point was still, in his earlier liberal phase, the individual. In most of his writings from 1910 to 1939, McKay rejected the individual as the foundation of theoretical analysis or political work. Class analysis became the vital nucleus of his mature thought.

Although McKay would retain many of the values of free expression and debate that had once been historically associated with liberalism, his break with classical liberal social and economic thought was complete: henceforth McKay was a rigorous critic of economic liberalism in its various manifestations, whether classical, Fascist or corporatist. Liberal individualism was a kind of ideological illusion with real material effects, McKay would argue in the 1930s. Promising "freedom," it delivered "but the illusion of freedom." And it was "but the illusion of freedom which makes the purblind individualist refuse to recognize the obvious necessities of a rational organization of society based on economic planning." Real freedom could not result from a philosophy or politics of individualism: "In actuality, we can only attain real freedom by understanding natural and social laws and applying them to our ends."[30] The preservation of a "democratic polity" meant that "current notions of freedom may have to be revised", McKay wrote (softening the blow a little, perhaps because he was writing for the middle-class readers of *Saturday Night*). "True freedom is only realized by adaptation to the laws of nature and of economics."[31]

As McKay came to see liberal doctrines as simply those of capitalism, and liberalism as a vindication of the free market, his opposition to them became more and more total.[32] An earlier questioning of liberal individualism had hardened into an outright rejection of it. Those systems of ethics which, according to McKay, were founded on individualism should be rejected. Kantian ethics, for example -- a woolly version of which he had earlier defended -- was now seen as the apotheosis of a bourgeois conception of individual freedom: "Rising capitalism required

---

[30]Colin McKay, "British Columbia's New Deal," *Canadian Unionist*, Vol.8, No.8 (January 1935), 196-199.

[31]*Saturday Night*, 4 February 1939.

[32]Colin McKay, "British Columbia's New Deal," *Canadian Unionist*, Vol.8, No.8 (January 1935), 196-199.

freedom for the producers of commodities, freedom of competition, freedom of exploitation: incidentally, it required a free labour market, a mass of workers free to labour on dictated terms or starve. Thus 'freedom' became the slogan of the young bourgeoisie in its struggle for political power; the French added the slogans 'equality' and 'fraternity.' Kant's ethical theory had attempted to reconcile individual interests and social welfare, but all he arrived at was "an ambiguous excuse for the inability of the bourgeoisie to live up to its moral codes," by placing the moral law outside of time and space [§.135, "The Shadows Fade"]. However mistaken many Kantian socialists would find this as an evaluation of their moral theory, this critique was a dramatic indication of the extent to which McKay had rejected the individual as the starting-point of political analysis.

This rejection of individualism fuelled a furious denunciation of institutionalized Protestantism. From 1910 to 1914 McKay elaborated a multi-faceted (although many might say also rather simplistic) critique of the Protestant church, which paralleled in many instances his critique of classical liberalism. Like classical liberalism, much of Christianity -- insofar as it still was a faith -- found itself hopelessly outdated by the intellectual revolution of the twentieth century. McKay often even implied that the Age of Faith had simply been one of superstition, repression and fear. "Faith and obedience were the watch words of the past; reason will be the guide of the future," McKay proclaimed in 1910. "In the good old time it was a crime to doubt or to question; in the future it will be a moral duty to criticize and test the truth of all the phenomena of life" [§.14, "The Political Gag"]. No longer would faith (or credulity) be regarded as merits. Rather than believing "any absurdity," as had been the case under the feudal system, workers had a responsibility to develop an all-questioning stance toward the social world, as part of the "new philosophy of life" or "new culture" of the working class. McKay's venom was not reserved for the (Catholic) middle ages; he took care to single out Luther and Knox, in particular, as anti-human primitives, and reminded his readers that the Puritans had burned "countless numbers of women at the stake" [§.49, "Working-Class Culture"].

Inspired largely by certain somewhat fugitive and episodic passages in Marx, McKay saw Protestantism, no less than liberalism, as the vehicle of an outmoded individualism, inappropriate in the new age. The rise of the middle class and the development of new forms and forces of production had meant the erosion of the old feudal system, with its complex systems of vassalage, and the disappearance of a Catholic culture and religion that had "made faith its cornerstone, and prohibited freedom of thought." This process entailed a new "spirit of individualism" which supplied ideas for the reformation, exalted the Bible over the church, and developed a culture that was both more individual and narrower than the culture it had overthrown [§.49, "Working-Class Culture"]. Puritanism allowed the bourgeoisie to emphasize its revolutionary character "by the sharpness of the contrasts between its social and moral codes and those prevalent under feudalism" [§.31, "Bourgeois Morality"].

Champions of only those forms of liberty that suited their needs, the Puritans allowed little liberty of thought or action to the working class [§.49, "Working-Class Culture"]. And now the twentieth-century descendants of the Puritans were caught in a fast-changing society, for which their outlook was pathetically inadequate: "Inept and futile Puritanism faces the modern world, aghast at the struggle of contending classes which it does not understand, forgetful that it was once the expression as well as the inspiration of a revolutionary movement, unable to offer a world eager for a new dispensation anything better than the pitiful banalities of individual propriety "[§.31, "Bourgeois Morality"]. Inept and futile! His words came lashing out, in what seems to have been a settling of accounts with the religious beliefs of his childhood (but one which historians might find inherently puzzling, given the centrality of North American Protestantism to the creation of modernity). McKay was impressed by the extent to which the bourgeois mind was "fatalistic," "prone to superstition and a mystical belief in chance." The notion of a special providence could help businessmen handle the instability of capitalism and soothe any consciences troubled by the "glaring injustices of the social order" [§.52, "The Worker Must Learn to Think"]. The Protestant Work Ethic -- the very one we are entitled to imagine he must have grown up with in Shelburne -- had always served the purpose of stimulating accumulation under capitalism; under socialism, on the other hand, the "right to be lazy" and the ideal of enjoying life to the utmost would be important social principles.[33]

McKay was outraged at the individualist bias of the Church. Sunday Schools miseducated children. Immature Christians were even taught to admire Joseph from the Old Testament -- the acquisitive individual thrown out of his tribe "because his fawning disposition and acquisitive propensities menaced the communistic social arrangements of his tribe." (McKay did not consider whether Sunday Schools might not be holding up other aspects of Joseph's story for admiration). Better to admire this reprobate, it seemed, than the revolutionary Jesus [§.51, "The Mis-Education of the Young"].

---

[33]Colin McKay, "Time for a Labor Party is Now," letter to the *Eastern Labor News*, 11 November 1911. The "right to be lazy" was drawn from Paul Lafargue's book of the same name. It is interesting to note that McKay's working-class Marxism drew -- from such seemingly unlikely traditions as Spencerian Sociology and Historical Materialism -- arguments that sustained a vision of life in which relaxation and enjoyment were central and available to all. Although he himself must have worked extremely hard, he never saw "hard work" and "self-denial" as fundamental socialist values. Perhaps

Those Church members who thought that the gulf between their practical conduct and their religious beliefs were of no consequence were in essence distorting the message of the Bible. "Religion is not solely a matter of the relations of the individual to a personal God," McKay insisted (unconsciously echoing the views of many Christians of his day). "Christ laid particular emphasis upon its bearings upon man's relations to his fellows -- the code of ethics that should govern our daily conduct. Christian theology should throw an august and abiding light upon the political problems of the day -- should offer us a guiding clue out of the labyrinth of the maladjustments of our social system which issue in so much wretchedness and evil." Clergymen who answered demands for radical social change with the pat response, "First you must change human nature," were twisting the Bible's message. In the Book of Genesis itself, "God gave man dominion over the earth and the beasts thereof, but He did not give man dominion over his fellows."[34] Equally myopic were those Christians who focussed narrowly on such issues as temperance[35] and sabbatarianism, which McKay mocked as a class-biased and hypocritical attempt to control the workers' time [§.31, "Bourgeois Morality"]. The bourgeois Christian might be sincerely sickened by capitalist civilization. But all he could come up with were pitifully sentimental schemes that failed to address the underlying issues. Everywhere, McKay wrote in 1913, the bourgeoisie could be found "busily discussing housing problems, social evils and what not, exhibiting a sentimental and generally fruitless interest in reform. That merely means that they are dissatisfied and more or less disgusted with the civilization which their class has created" [§.26, "Capitalism -- The Modern Frankenstein"].

Christian Socialists who spun out utopian fantasies about ideal societies, and who had not attempted to grasp the economic logic of the system, were generally unable to make any real difference. "Adventures in idealism are always interesting," McKay noted , "but their practical value is problematical. Is the labour movement any stronger today, or the working class any nearer their emancipation from the wage system, because Bellamy painted an ideal state of society in "Equality," or Charles Sheldon wrote "What Would Jesus Do?" [§.88, "Monetary or Credit Reform Schemes Illusory"]. McKay was somewhat more favourably disposed toward the Social Gospel, although even here his verdict was somewhat mixed. In a review of Walter Rauchenbusch's *Christianity and the Social Crisis*, he criticized the author for overemphasizing the religious element of history, and accurately noted that he probably did

---

revolutionary asceticism appealed more deeply to   socialism's middle-class recruits than to its rank-and-file workers?

[34]Colin McKay, "Preaching and Practice," *Coast Guard*, 22 December 1910.

[35]Colin McKay, "Begin at the Beginning," letter to the Halifax *Morning Chronicle*, 11 April 1904.

not accept "the materialistic conception of history as stated by Marx, and developed by Kautsky and other Socialist writers." Although the "scientific value" of the book was not enhanced by Rauchenbusch's efforts to show "that the social message of Jesus if consistently heeded, would work a revolution in industry as complete as that desired by the socialist," and although history did not afford much hope "that socialist clergymen will be able to make the official church recognize and seek earnestly and intelligently to realize the social message of Christ," it would still be useful for the revolutionary working class "to have the blessing of the church."[36] One senses immediately the difference a decade had made: whatever impact the Church might make, was now seen as marginal.

But the extent to which McKay became a wholly secular thinker might nonetheless be overstated. It is crucial to pay attention to his important distinction between "churchianity" and "Christianity." He had not in fact burned all his bridges to Christian social thought. He wrote in 1910 of "the vital truths of Christianity," which could in fact be harmonized with the truths of science [§. 14, "The Political Gag"]. In criticizing the belief that "moral laws are absolute, that they have a supernatural sanction and remain the same under all conditions," McKay nonetheless held out the prospect of a more-or-less universal morality, inspired by Christ's ideals, once the workers had abolished class society. If the glory of the early Christians, those followers of "Christ,...the first world-conscious workingman," had been "their desire to make the observance of tribal morality a universal condition," realizing such a goal would have to wait for the completion of a "long and painful historic development," until the day when "sectional and class interests would be swallowed up by the greater interests of humanity as a whole, or the most useful part of it, the working class" [§.48, "A Working Class Morality"].

Even on the eve of the Great War, we read of McKay's faith: "Christ's words are forever true. The money power, and through it the unscrupulous exploitation of the people is the root of all evil" [§. 43, "Moloch and Mammon"]. He emphasized the profound tension between Christian teaching and capitalism which, perhaps, transcended the momentary interpretations that Puritans and others had made of their religion. Christians had to understand that capitalism had made the serious and sustained practice of their religious faith intensely difficult. Under capitalism, it was almost impossible to practise the Golden Rule: "Under our present system of society it is almost impossible to obey the command to love our neighbours as ourselves. Where things are more or less of a gamble, where there is [are] a hundred applicants for one job,

[36]Colin McKay, "Christianity and the Social Crisis," letter to *The Eastern Labor News*, 1 February 1913. See also Colin McKay, "The Church and the Working Class," *Eastern Labor News*, 1 February 1913.

where a big fish catch on one part of the coast may mean bad prices and hard times on another, envy and uncharitableness must abide."[37]

Even in the interwar period, as McKay's writings grew more and more focused on political economy, they still hinted at possible connections between radical socialism and radical Christianity. He referred in 1932 to genuine "economic planning" based on social interests as a "spiritual revolution in man's attitude to his work and to his fellowmen" [§.96, "Rationing Investment"]. His 1938 discussion of "Economic Planning Under Capitalism," which drew heavily on the R.H.Tawney's discussion of the "functional society," suggested the enduring impact on McKay of a form of Christian idealism [§.108, "Economic Planning Under Capitalism"]. He returned to the pre-war emphasis on Christ as the first visionary of that world-consciousness which, two thousand years later, was transforming the world through the socialist movement and evolutionary theory: and the "same historic law which inspires the conviction that the workers will attain world-consciousness and conquer the world" also supported the idea that "the evolution of the human mind, freed from the necessity of giving any more thought to the struggle for existence than the lillies of the field, will develop organs of intelligence capable of using cosmic forces, now uncontrollable or unknown, in the service of humanity, by means as miraculous in their way as any of the stories of the great deeds of the Miracle Worker, known as the Carpenter of Nazareth."[38] In passages such as these, evolutionary theory and historical materialism created an almost millennarian vision of the proletariat as a sort of Collective Christ.

3. The Discovery of Sociology as a New Way of Seeing

A central part of the historical process of proletarian world consciousness was the science of sociology. Colin McKay believed that the new discipline represented a breakthrough in human understanding. Taking his definitional cues from Herbert Spencer, Albion Small and Lester Ward, McKay noted that sociology dealt with human society, and sought "to generalize the whole range of human activities and formulate the laws of social evolution." Although sociologists and socialists were not necessarily of one mind, McKay believed that the results of the "new science" were in fact highly favourable to the left and that Marxists could "conscript" the findings of non-Marxist sociologists. Both the socialists and the sociologists accepted "the principle of historical materialism as the pass key to social phenomena." They generally agreed that to understand political movements was to seek the causes of which they were "but a manifestation" [§.29, "The Message of Sociology"]. McKay credited "the sociologists" with having completely renovated the arsenal of the modern

---

[37]Colin McKay, "Preaching and Practice," *Coast Guard*, 22 December 1910.
[38]Letter from Colin McKay, *Shelburne Gazette and Coast Guard*, 2 October 1913.

critical thinker; in 1911, he remarked *à propos* of the Reciprocity Debate, that rather than "attempting to employ the machine guns in the arsenal of the sociologist, the leaders on both sides of the controversy have apparently determined to fight it out with the old blunderbusses of the old orthodox economists."[39]

From c. 1908 to his death in 1939, Colin McKay consistently argued that political and economic practice should be informed by a science of society based on an understanding of evolutionary theory. His understanding of what this science entailed emerged from a reading of Herbert Spencer, Alfred Wallace, Enrico Ferri, Albion Small, and Lester Ward, all of whom were brought into relation with the traditions of historical materialism.

Sociology -- especially that of Herbert Spencer, notwithstanding the philosopher's own political beliefs -- presented itself as a heaven-sent weapon against that individualist liberal political economy McKay was sworn to oppose. Sociology undermined the validity of liberal economic categories, and suggested that "the present economic system is a transitory phase of a process of evolution, and that it is destined to be succeeded by another system wherein men, by the collective planning of production to supply the wants of all the people, will become the conscious masters of economic forces instead of being their victims" [§.116, "The Future of Industrial Unionism"]. Just as natural science had "stripped the veil of mystery from the natural forces which once filled our ancestors with fear" and "made possible the subordination of natural forces to the human will," so could social science penetrate the "dark mystery" that still surrounded such phenomena as "business depressions, unemployment, and poverty in the midst of plenty." Just as people had once regarded diseases as visitations of an angry Providence, so too did many contemporaries regard economic phenomena as inevitable consequences of the operation of the law of supply and demand, and felt as "helpless as primitive man did in the presence of natural forces he did not understand."[40] Workers would find in modern science a most important message: that of their potential emancipation from wage slavery. Small wonder that the school, the press, even the pulpit drowned out the revolutionary message of sociology in a sea of triviality [§.28, "Science and the Working Man"]. Indeed, any college professor who attempted to apply to the study of society "the fruitful scientific methods which have transformed physics, biology, etc.," would quickly be told that his business was not to explore the truth, "but concoct excuses for the existence of a parasitic class."[41]

[39]Colin McKay, "Reciprocity," *Coast-Guard*, 27 July 1911.
[40]Colin McKay, War and the Economic System," *Canadian Railway Employees' Monthly*, Vol. 18, No.4 (April 1932): 80-81.
[41]C.McKay, Untitled Letter, *Labor World/Le Monde Ouvrier*, 13 January 1938.

In creative Marxist hands, evolutionary theory could also be drawn upon to explain the emergence of working-class consciousness. "Evolution imposes the necessity of the working class developing a method of thinking different from that of the bourgeoisie," wrote McKay in 1923 [§.52, "The Worker Must Learn To Think"]. This formula seemed more fatalistic than in fact it was. To carry out this task set by "evolution," the workers needed to master "evolution" theoretically: which was why the privileged classes attempted to prevent the spread of the knowledge of social sciences and to belittle or distort them, and also why the ways of thinking and feeling of so many people in the developed world were "more tainted with the cruder doctrines which the ruling class read into Darwinism" than was the case elsewhere.[42]

Evolutionary theory was *revolutionary*. Acceptance of *evolution* as a general theory and of *evolutionary political processes* was perfectly congruent with acknowledgement of *social revolution* as politico-ethical imperative and of *revolutionary political processes* as means of realizing it. The evolution/revolution dichotomy, subsequently hypostatized in the period of the Cold War, and complicated by the red herring of Edouard Bernstein's neo-Kantian "evolutionary socialism," obscured the point that almost the entire Second International, Lenin included, endorsed "evolutionary theory" *and* "revolutionary theory." (The clearest evidence is the continuing importance of Kautsky, deeply admired by Lenin, supported by the majority of the German Social Democratic Party, and a consistent upholder of both "historical materialism" and "working-class revolution" as imperishable tenets of Marxism). In theory, and to a large degree in practice in North America, evolutionary socialism did *not* prescribe a narrowly electoralist parliamentary outlook; the transition to this more contemporary notion of "social democracy" took place in stages after the First World War.

In McKay's hands, the language of evolutionary theory was immensely flexible. With it, for example, one could situate the need for vigorous internal debate within unions: "For any natural organism, activity, struggle of some sort are conditions of its survival and growth; if it falls into a state of passivity it atrophies, and soon perishes. What is true of a natural organization may not always be true of a social organization. Dissension in the Labour movement may be a symptom of decadence and disintegration; on the other hand, internal conflict of opinion, agitation for this or that principle, may well be a sign of vitality and progress."[43] From this evolutionary perspective, the struggle for a true science of society was an integral part of the struggle for socialism. Two modern

---

[42]Colin McKay, "The Task of Social Reconstruction," *Canadian Railway Employees' Monthly*, July 1938: n.p.
[43]Colin McKay, "Industrial Unionism Challenges A.F. of L.," *Canadian Unionist*, October 1936, 120-121;124.

sciences in particular -- first, the materialist science of cognition, an understanding of the nature of human consciousness, and second, the "science of society, an understanding of social evolution" -- made it possible for human beings "to become masters of their fate and consciously to build a new form of civilization when the old one fails them."[44]

McKay evolved many of these positions through an intense and passionate relationship with the works of Herbert Spencer. That Herbert Spencer should have so influenced McKay may seem surprising, given the former's extreme *laissez-faire* views, but as McKay correctly discerned, Spencer's political conclusions did not necessarily follow from his evolutionist premises. (McKay was, and is, in good company on this question).[45] McKay had in 1899 explicitly polemicized against Spencer's *The Man Versus The State* and *Social Statics*. In the course of that polemic, McKay had underlined this passage from Spencer's *The Man Versus The State*: "And yet, strange to say, now that this truth is recognized by most cultivated people, now that the beneficent working of the survival of the fittest has been so impressed on them that much more than people in past times, they might be expected to hesitate before neutralizing its action -- now more than ever before in the history of the world are they doing all they can to further the survival of the unfittest." From *Social Statics* -- a book he deeply admired -- McKay had objected particularly to Spencer's claim that "Those shoulderings aside of the weak by the strong which leave so many in shallows and in miseries" represented in fact the working out of this natural law [§.27, "The Duty of the Rich to the Poverty-Laden"].

In response, the young McKay began by conceding that there was "a great deal of truth in the principle of evolution," but proceeded to question whether this principle followed the same lines in human society as in animal and plant life. Spencer's philosophy, he charged, was excessively totalizing: he had not proved his theory of evolution was applicable to all departments of life, "whether of plant, animal, human, mental or moral." It was a basic error to attempt to analyze human beings as if they were merely parts of the natural world. Many of Spencer's theories had been falsified "by man's ingenuity in escaping the rigid operation of laws which the lower forms of life are unable to evade." The law of selection among animals differed from the law of selection in human society, because whereas animals struggled for survival "on the individualistic principle," humans, in general, combined with each other. (McKay was implicitly

[44]Colin McKay, "The Task of Social Reconstruction," *Canadian Railway Employees' Monthly*, July 1938: n.p.

[45]Perhaps the most perceptive discussion of the gap between Spencerian evolutionism and Spencerian politics is David Wiltshire, *The Social and Political Thought of Herbert Spencer* (Oxford: Oxford University Press, 1978).

appealing to the Aristotelian definition of human nature here.) "Animals are the slaves of nature; they are powerless before nature's forces. Men are the masters of nature; they harness nature's forces -- bridle them to their will." There were "no striking evidence[s] of the operation of such a law" of natural selection in human society: it did not appear, *pace* Spencer, that the strong were in fact becoming more numerous [§.27, "The Duty of the Rich to the Poverty-Laden"].

Spencer had denounced the idea of patterning governments or societies on the basis of the "law of sympathy" found in families, but his vision of the survival of the fittest assumed, unrealistically, a society based on perfect individualism. But the notion of a perfect individualism, besides constituting an unattractive denial of the value of "civilization," was wholly out of keeping with the realities of the modern world. In the modern world there was in fact little individualism: modern civilization was the result of the "application of co-operation." Ultimately the critique of Spencer came to rest on a Christian ethical commonsense: surely no one would deny the justice of the winners in the struggle for existence compensating those losers whose lives had been made more difficult? Indeed, this ethical lesson could be extrapolated from a key (and significantly misquoted) passage from *Social Statics* itself: "All classes of society mutually affect one another, and their moral states are much alike. Thus the alleged homogeneity of national character is abundantly exemplified. And so long as the assimilating influences productive of it continue to work, it is folly to suppose any one grade of a community can be morally different from the rest. In whichever rank you see corruption be assured it pervades all ranks -- be assured it is the symptom of a bad social diathesis. Whilst the veins of depravity exist in one part of the body politic, no other part can remain healthy." It was therefore in the interest of the rich and strong to uplift the poor and weak, if all parts of the body politic were in fact so interconnected. "All these considerations go to show that it is unwise to trust to the grim gods of evolution to work out the salvation of society," McKay concluded. "They are pagan gods -- they require awful human sacrifices" [§.27, "The Duty of the Rich to the Poverty-Laden"]. Yet this did not mean that one could simply discard Spencer. From *Social Statics* especially -- a book that advocated self-determination, freedom of opinion, the emancipation of women, the rights of children, and the socialization of land, as well as an early, highly teleological form of evolutionary theory -- McKay felt that much of political value could be learned.

McKay's interpretation of Spencer was revised after 1908. McKay maintained his skepticism about too pronounced a tendency to draw parallels between natural and social evolution, but he now tended to support Spencer in emphasizing a continuum between biology and human affairs, as brought out by the theory of evolution. Socialism came to be defined as "a science of social evolution," although with the distinctly non-Spencerian twist that the recent discoveries of Weismann in heredity and De Vries in evolutionary theory meant that "evolution instead of being a steady movement, is an oscillatory process, changes taking place by sudden leaps." Socialists could therefore be quite justified, on biological grounds, in "predicting a speedy change in the organization of society" -- i.e., revolution could be seen as part of evolution. Spencerian biologizing thus led to distinctly non-Spencerian conclusions [§.30, "Socialism as the Science of Social Evolution," originally published as "Socialism".] A Spencerian-Socialist language (e.g., "inoculating" the workers with scientific socialism, so that socialist ideas would "germinate") is everywhere in his political analyses of 1910-1914 [see, for example, §.71, "The Difficulties Faced by Socialists in the Maritimes," originally published as "The Maritime"]. The influence on McKay of a thorough immersion in the Charles H. Kerr evolutionary curriculum was obvious, but perhaps the underlying reason why a "tougher Spencerianism" now appealed to McKay was his growing separation from liberal individualism and a more vivid appreciation of the extent to which life under capitalism really did resemble in important respects the brutal, uncompromising struggle of the fittest to survive that Spencer had discerned in nature.

It is clear that much of the "evolutionism" so evident in the writings of 1908-1913 was heavily influenced by Spencer, particularly in its assumption of a law of social evolution which paralleled (although it could not be strictly reduced to) the law of natural selection discovered by Darwin. And McKay continued to quote approvingly from Spencer into the 1930s. Interestingly, however, he started to single out those passages in Spencer that stressed that the law of evolution often entailed a law of "devolution," the inevitable decay of an organism (or a whole society) that had failed to adapt to its environment. "After evolution, what?" asked McKay à propos of the growth of working-class freedoms under capitalism. "According to Herbert Spencer, devolution, decline, decay. In this phase, capitalism turns a harsh and brutal face to the workers. The Gladstone tradition goes by the board."[46] And Herbert Spencer, appropriated yet again for left-wing purposes he would not have approved, turned over once more in his much-turned grave.

Spencer's impact on McKay was profound. As late as 1924 (when the philosopher's influence was mainly confined, ironically enough, to the ranks of working-class autodidacts) McKay hailed Spencer as "one of the great English philosophers of the Victorian era," whose writings on the subject of warfare were still useful.[47] As late as 1938, in trying to understand the British ruling class, McKay invoked Spencer's law of devolution: "'When a society has evolved to the limit of its type, a

---

[46]C.M., untitled letter, *Labor World/Le Monde Ouvrier*, 13 July 1935
[47]Colin McKay, "War, A Product of Internal Injustice," *Canadian Railroad Employees' Monthly*, June 1924, 67-68.

progressive dissolution begins,' said the philosopher Herbert Spencer. If the society has a class structure, as all 'civilized' societies have had, the top layer, or ruling class, bestirs itself to buttress its position. But as the process of disintegration is general throughout society, the greater the agitation of the top layer the deeper it sinks into difficulties."[48]

Similarly, labour organizations were very much like natural organisms and subject to Spencer's laws of evolution or devolution: "The changes in their structure may be so slow as to be imperceptible to the ordinary observer, nevertheless changes take place under the impulse of forces engendered by changes in their external environment, and the influence of ideas."[49] The Canadian middle class in the thirties, with its stubborn adherence to partial explanations of the Depression in terms of particular causes, had not grasped "the import of the Spencerian theory that within a system evolution proceeds till it reaches a climax and that then a period of devolution follows has not come home to them" [§.103. The Middle Class and a National Government]. There is reason to suppose, on the basis of this evidence, that Spencer strongly influenced McKay throughout his adult life.

There was however nothing passive in McKay's relationship with the Spencerian canon: he borrowed what he found to be useful and jettisoned the rest. He was well aware by the 1920s that Spencer had dated, and that many of his *laissez-faire* opinions were outlandish by any modern standard.[50] He borrowed many Spencerian ideas about evolution, but transformed them all by placing them within an interpretive grid that

[48]C.M., "Suicidal Policies of Britain's Ruling Class," *Labour World/Le Monde Ouvrier*, 15 October 1938.

[49]Colin McKay, "The Broad Scope of Industrial Unionism," *Canadian Railway Employees' Monthly*, March 1939, 66-67; 70.

[50]Colin McKay, untitled letter, *Labor World/Le Monde Ouvrier*, 20 April 1929: "I do not understand that Spencer passes for a philosopher today. In the practical exposition of his theories he was a reactionary of the first water. He opposed factory legislation, the plimsall [Plimsoll] mark on ships, fixing the number of life boats, free compulsory education and public schools, public libraries, limitation of child labour, protection of dangerous machines, everything that interfered with individualism. Everything the working class has been fighting for during the last generation." One notes in passing that McKay singled out those positions of Spencer that were most meaningful for him as a seafarer. Yet McKay may not have been entirely fair to Spencer about this. In Spencer's *The Study of Sociology* (New York: D. Appleton and Company, 1875): 352, we find this passage: "Though, in our solicitude for Negroes, we have been spending £50,000 a year to stop the East-African slave-trade, and failing to do it, yet only now are we providing protection for our own sailors against unscrupulous shipowners -- only now have sailors, betrayed into bad ships, got something more than the option of risking death by drowning or going to prison for breach of contract! Shall we not call that, also, a *laissez-faire* that is almost wicked in its indifference?" Does this not suggest Spencer *supported* some protective legislation for seamen?

held that, in some sense, the human mind could rise above the laws of nature. Far from being the slave of evolution, humanity could be its master. Bringing the process of evolution under human control was the only way to avoid catastrophe, and it would involve a conscious transformation of human institutions far beyond the worst nightmares of Spencer. In time, humanity would become the conscious director of its own social evolution, but not in the near future: "The collective intelligence, will and moral courage necessary to promote progress in an orderly manner is lacking. In existing society, the anarchy of production, which is the source of so much misery, is at the same time the great cause of progress. To have progress without anarchy, it would be necessary to substitute social control for private control of the means of production; and such a transition would require a complete abandonment of some existing institutions and drastic modifications of other institutions" [§.35, "The Conservatism of the Mind"]. The social relations of the new capitalism, and the growth of social science, gave human intelligence "the privilege of taking conscious control of the evolution of economic affairs, and of so ordering them that the forces of production will be the servants and not the masters of men."[51]

McKay was able to extract this positive message from Spencer partly because he could place the philosopher's doctrine of social evolution in the context of other socialist evolutionary writings. Although there is little evidence of a direct, prolonged exposure to the works of Darwin, McKay did draw on the writings of the socialist Alfred Wallace, regarded as the co-discoverer of the principle of natural selection. The same British society Spencer had seen as coddling the unfit, Wallace diagnosed as troubled by organic social ailments: McKay was struck in particular by a passage from Wallace's *Social Environment and Moral Progress* : "Taking account of these various groups of undoubted facts, many of which are so gross that they cannot be overstated, it is not too much to say that our whole system of society is rotten from top to bottom, and the social environment as a whole, in relation to our possibilities, is the worst that the world has ever seen...." When a scientist of Dr. Wallace's stature found "socialism" to be the "only hope for human advancement," workers should begin "to study their position in society" from numerous publications "dealing with every phase of the evolution of human society from the view point of the working class."[52]

McKay was also influenced by the work of Enrico Ferri, one of the founders of Italian criminology. This influence made some sense given Ferri's interest in working out the implications of combining Spencerian and Marxist theory. Here the key work seems to have been Ferri's

---

[51] *Canadian Fisherman*, June 1935, 9-10.
[52] Colin McKay, "Social Environment and Moral Progress," *Eastern Labor News*, 23 August 1913.

Socialism and Modern Science (which McKay likely read because it was promoted by the SPC). Passages from this book relating to the class struggle particularly impressed McKay, who quoted them *in extenso*. "It is doubtful if in the whole range of socialist literature there is a more graphic interpretation of the class struggle than Ferri gives. He writes with the authority of a profound student of both natural science and sociology," McKay enthused. When Ferri argued that the "class struggle in the Darwinian sense renews in the history of man the magnificent drama of the struggle for life between species, instead of degrading us to the savage and meaningless brute strife of individual with individual," McKay noted that he had recognized that the struggle for life was not the sole, sovereign law of nature: there was as well "the law of solidarity or co-operation between living being....even in animal societies" [§.36, "The Struggle for Existence"]. McKay could also draw on Ferri to portray the indifference of the ruling class to the poverty in its midst as a type of "moral suicide," indicative of a fatalism that suggested the bourgeoisie was losing its own struggle for existence.[53]

He also kept a watchful eye on developments in more professional sociological circles. The American sociologists Albion Small and Lester Ward were both accorded lengthy treatment in the *Eastern Labor News*. McKay believed Small when he claimed, in *General Sociology,* that sociology would "serve as a pass key to all the theoretical difficulties about society that each of us may encounter." He noted in particular the passages in the book which explored the parasitism of capital and the limitations it imposed on personal development [§.29, "The Message of Sociology"]. But of all the American sociologists, Lester Ward exercised the most enduring influence: first cited in 1911, Ward's work was still being cited extensively in McKay's writings in 1928. For McKay, Ward was "the greatest of the American sociologists" [§.28, "Science and the Working Man"], and Ward's *Applied Sociology* and *Pure Sociology* were two of the most mind-changing books he had ever read. McKay seems to have been attracted by the combination of deep historicism and moral critique in Ward's analysis of the private appropriation of human achievements, and by his thorough critique of those who put forward Darwinism as "a justification of the competitive system in industry." He enthusiastically underlined Ward's argument that mankind wanted "no elementary schemes, no private or state benefactions, no fatherly oversight of the privileged classes nor any other form of patronizing hypocrisy. They only want power -- the power which is their right, and which lies within their grasp. They have only to reach out and take it" [§.29, "The Message of Sociology"]. Here was the revolutionary, inspirational message of American sociology! A sharp sense of the unfairness of a system that allowed a tiny minority to profit from the social achievements of countless past human beings was henceforth woven into McKay's moral

---

[53]C.M., "Our Masters Are Dead from Stomachs Up," *O.B.U.Bulletin,* 10 May 1934.

critique of capitalism, often in words which directly echoed Ward's work, even when they did not mention him by name. "Marconi owes to society a million times more than society owes to him, because without the social achievements of the ages Marconi would have only been an ignorant root- or rat-eating savage," McKay would argue in 1913. [54] This was pure Ward. And it was an argument that must have seemed particularly powerful to working-class socialists, who every day encountered inventions that had emerged from centuries of social evolution (not to mention working-class ingenuity), only to be commandeered by a small group of short-sighted and self-centred capitalists.

And Ward also provided McKay with precious ammunition against the right-wing appropriation of the principle of natural selection (so-called "Social Darwinism"[55]), and against left-wing economic reductionism. Interestingly, McKay noted passages from Ward that warned against the excesses of scientism, particularly attempts to build arguments about society on the basis of "natural law." Any such attempt to reckon without the "the intellectual or rational factor" would simply lead to errors: "this factor is so stupendous that there is no room for astonishment in contemplating the magnitude of the error which its omission has caused." Crucial for Ward was the sum total of human "achievement," meaning permanent additions to the sum of human knowledge. McKay was particularly enthusiastic about a passage in Ward's *Applied Sociology* which declared that the purpose of applied society was to "harmonize achievement with improvement. If all this achievement which constitutes civilization has really been wrought without producing any improvement in the condition of the human race, it is time that the reason for this was investigated. Applied sociology includes among its main purposes the investigation of this question. The difficulty lies in the fact that achievement is not socialized. The problem, therefore, is that of the socialization of achievement" [§.34, "Property and Progress"].

---

[54]Colin McKay, "Teach Them to Measure Value," *Eastern Labor News*, 1 April 1912. The same critique of the "appropriation of invention" can be discerned in the program of the Canadian Socialist League. It seems a fascinating measure of the extent to which the innovations of industrial capitalism were still registered as novelties by turn-of-the-century socialist thought.

[55]So far as I am aware, this phrase never comes up in McKay's work. In his experience, it probably would have been more associated with the *left* rather than with the *right* : Ferri would claim to be developing a "social" Darwinism, i.e., a Darwinism fully cognizant of, and under the control of, "society" as a whole. (The phrase "social control" also started out on the left, to denote *social* control -- today we might say "communitarian control" -- over economic and social development). For a discussion of right-wing "Social Darwinism" that sees it mainly as the bogey of leftists and progressives, see Robert C. Bannister, *Social Darwinism: Science and Myth in Anglo-American Social Thought* (Philadelphia: Temple University Press, 1979).

How could the socialist movement appropriate the work of such sociologists without falling into the trap of inconsistency and eclecticism? For McKay, it was important to have a firm underlying grid of theory. He was not a careless and indiscriminate reader of the social sciences of his day. He was careful to select those quotations, and those writers, in accordance with the "historical materialist perspective" to which he had been converted c.1908. McKay conceived this materialism as an integral, comprehensive world view, with its own epistemology, methodology, and a large body of well-founded scientific theories.

The fundamental ontological issues had been settled for McKay by Josef Dietzgen, widely regarded in the early twentieth century as the principal "proletarian philosopher." (Dietzgen's materialism was praised by both Marx and Lenin, although in both cases not without reservations). Dietzgen's *Positive Outcome of Philosophy* had, according to McKay, established that "thinking is a physical process which cannot exist or produce anything without materials any more than any other process of labour." Reason -- the faculty of thought -- was not a mystical object producing individual thoughts. No: "individual thoughts are the products of perceptions gained in contact with certain objects, and... these, in connection with certain brain processes, produce the concept of reason." Philosophy (as normally defined) had been completed, Dietzgen argued, and could be replaced by the natural science of the human mind. However, because traditional philosophy had proved so indispensable for the ruling class, and because that class was wedded to the "mystery" of the mind, the holy sanctuary of its dualistic conception of mind and matter had survived in bourgeois ideology. Incapable of a "dialectical understanding of the cosmos," bourgeois materialism differed fundamentally from the Marxian materialism expounded by Dietzgen.[56] McKay went so far as to argue that, even more than an emphasis on the class struggle, this materialist conception of thought was Marxism's greatest contribution to human knowledge: "The Socialist theory of cognition is the completion of the quest of philosophy which now has only a historical interest as the record of attempts of man to understand himself and his relations to the universe," he would proclaim. "Now its place is taken by science of the mind as a branch of natural sciences" [§.37, "The Faculty of Thought"].

This view of knowledge and the universe -- a form of dialectical materialism -- was monist but not static, energized as it was by the Hegelian dialectic (interpreted -- or misinterpreted -- as applying to matter as well as to thought). As the researches of scientists had tended to show that all matter was made up of positive and negative charges of electricity in constant motion, one could draw the conclusion that "conflict, struggle, collision, eternal change, are fundamental principles of

---

[56]Colin McKay, "Why War Is Possible," *Labor Leader* (Winnipeg), 18 April 1935.

matter and of life, conditioning them and making their existence possible." As it was in the natural world, so it was in the sphere of human relations: "the same universal law holds sway, for all progress, all civilization, all advance depend upon conflict of opinion, upon argument and discussion, in the endeavour to find better ways of doing things, of solving problems, of making life richer and fuller." The socialist society of the future would not be one in which struggle had ceased, but rather one in which the focus of struggle had changed: "Whatever the particular form of the next order of society may be, it will provide primarily for conscious human co-operation in the struggle against nature; it will inaugurate a new cycle, a higher phase in which human beings will consciously seek to control the process of evolution. That is the mission of the working class; that is what differentiates the working class from the capitalist class, for the latter seems to stand in awe of the blind economic forces which its system of production has called into being, and regards them as uncontrollable."[57]

In trade unions, and in society as a whole, struggle was necessary for a positive life. It seems characteristic of McKay that, even in the face of something as deterministic and restrictive as the full-blown dialectics of matter as developed by Dietzgen he found elements to support a view of human life and creativity.

The Hegelian dialectic dovetailed with the evolutionist framework, providing it with a principle of forward movement. Human society was a "natural, living organism in which the only thing constant is change," and it would evolve in ways not fully anticipated by logical theories, for no "blueprint" would be able to capture what was a dynamic process, not a static "edifice" [§.116, "The Future of Industrial Unionism"]. Hegel's contribution to evolutionary theory had been immense, McKay wrote, even if in his attempt to explain the evolution of human society he had wandered off "into the metaphysical realms of absolute mind." By critically revising Hegel's *Philosophy of Law*, Marx had discovered that the legal relations and forms of the state could only be understood if they were rooted in the material conditions of life. Nonetheless, the Hegelian dialectic had paved the way for the advanced evolutionary theory of the twentieth century.[58]

Guided by knowledge of the dialectic, a theorist would expect the unexpected from "a social system crowded with contradictions." For example, a "strictly logical" analysis of the predicament of the Canadian labour movement in the Depression would lead to the most pessimistic conclusion that the working-class movement faced a period of

---

[57]Colin McKay, "Struggle -- The Way of Progress," *Canadian Railroad Employees' Monthly*, July 1927.
[58]C.M., "The Last Straw," *O.B.U.Bulletin*, 29 December 1932.

"disintegration, feebleness and frustration." However, a dialectical approach would produce an awareness of the need to grasp the contradictions and their potentially surprising outcomes. For example, it was remarkable that the bourgeois press, although hostile to the CIO unions, had nonetheless given them invaluable publicity and thus had unintentionally helped change the social system. Or one could look at the apparent disarray and internal feuding that characterized the Canadian trade unions of the 1930s: Was this a sign of internal crisis? It all depended on the nature of the internal struggle, McKay answered. If that struggle was merely about "preserving this or that tradition, this or that inherited form," the result might be disintegration. But "if the struggle revolves around the question of what principles and forms will best serve the movement in its efforts both to realize its immediate external objectives and to accomplish its future mission, then it is fairly certain that the outcome will be, sooner or later, a reconstructed and re-energized movement; a stronger movement, more adaptable to changing conditions, and more resourceful, because the educative force of internal conflict of opinion and debate will have forged new knowledge, which is power."[59]

Dialectical analysis for McKay does not seem to have entailed a consistent emphasis on a view that something called "the dialectic" was at work throughout the universe, both in nature and society; "dialectic" more often entailed looking at the many-sidedness and historical context of a given politico-ethical problem. Dialectical analysis allowed one to understand that "the truth" was itself a dialectical outcome of historical processes. After all, McKay argued, "Nothing is constant in this world. Truth, as a principle, may always be true; but truth looks different to different generations, viewing it from different material conditions."[60] For example, in the struggle between industrial unionism and craft unionism (McKay in later years became an ardent partisan of the former, having championed the latter in his youth), he aimed at a "dialectical view," which would recognize "that the struggle is the outcome of evolutionary processes which it is useless to oppose" (which was not the same as saying that the outcome of the struggle was completely predetermined) [§.116, "The Future of Industrial Unionism"]. This dialectical view enabled one to appreciate both the achievements and limitations of the craft union form. Similarly, a mechanical and unsubtle analysis of the American New Deal might simply condemn its contradictions and the insincerity of some of the plutocrats who had made a deathbed conversion to economic planning. A dialectical analysis, on the other hand, would understand what might be fruitful about some of Roosevelt's contradictions. His program

---

[59]Colin McKay, "Industrial Unionism Challenges A.F. of L.," *Canadian Unionist*, October 1936: 120-121;124.
[60]Colin McKay, "Labour-Farmer Co-operation: Winnipeg's Contribution," *Canadian Unionist*, March 1933: 173-175.

was full of contradictory policies, "but action begets a kind of [dialectical] understanding capable of resolving contradictions in a higher synthesis." Having embarked on a "great adventure in state capitalism," Roosevelt could hardly try to stop the process "without disaster to his reputation, and disillusionment and degradation for the people" [§. 107, "The New Deal as a Social Experiment"].

The methodological implications of this dialectical reasoning were clear to McKay. Although natural and social evolution were not to be confused, they could both be studied using the scientific method. (The exact nature of this scientific method was never really established in McKay's writings, although one may infer that he meant a method that combined observation/induction and logic/deduction, and that formulated hypotheses which could be tested against rigorously gathered evidence). It was undialectical to forget the profound interconnectedness of the economics, culture and politics of the capitalist world. Part of the extraordinary appeal of the idea of evolution was the sense it offered of grasping an immense complex whole in all its extraordinary , dynamic systematicity.[61]

Applying the concept of dialectical evolution to the social order generated a dynamic and coherent image of a system whose vital, determinant nucleus of capital evolved in response to its environment and its own internal contradictions. Capital in turn shaped capitalism, a whole ethico-political context shaping thoughts, feelings, and nature itself. Understanding the core meant understanding at least something about the whole. To grasp the evolution of capital, for example, was to discover something about the nature of the law in society. "The masters" no longer had to pass laws allowing them to capture workers and brand them in order to retain their services; now all they required was the force of hunger. Nonetheless, the position which enabled the employers to pose as the benefactor of the worker was "no less a tribute to the power of law. The master class have always recognized the power of law, and have always made it a point to keep control of the political power...."[62]

Hence "dialectical evolution" -- or "economic determinism" -- did not imply fatalism. In fact, one reason why workers needed to understand

---

[61]As early as 1903, McKay had already been struggling to capture the dynamics of the business cycle in imagery which suggested the complexity and interdependence of a system: "As the heavenly bodies, once thrown into a certain definite motion, tend to repeat this, so it is with production as soon as it is once thrown into this movement of alternate expansion and contraction. Effects in their turn become causes. Even political economy then sees that the production of a relative surplus population is a necessary accompaniment of modern industry" [§.7, "The Right to Work."]

[62]Colin McKay, "The Capitalist Class and the Law-Making Power," letter to the *Eastern Labor News,* 17 May 1913.

evolution and the historical background of capitalism was precisely in order to combat the fatalism inherent in bourgeois ways of thinking, especially those about the supposed universality of supply and demand. Even though the bourgeois mind had years earlier accepted evolution in nature, it balked at the idea of evolution in society. Everyone could see that industrial capitalism was not the same as "primitive tribal communism," but the bourgeoisie needed to believe that the process of evolution had stopped, and that "capitalism will continue world without end." Lacking any sense of history, many workers developed a purely fatalistic attitude toward the world. "Men see little change in society in their time, and the relation of master and men under the wage system seems destined to endure for all time," McKay observed. "Hence the inertia which is the bane of trade unionism."[63] Only if they were taught how to look at things from a more critical and longer-term perspective would the workers' fatalism be overthrown.

Rather than leading to a sense of helplessness, a grasp of evolution and social history would reveal the transitory nature of capitalism and open up the possibilities for radical change. In this regard, McKay's frequent recourse to anthropology -- Morgan figuring almost monotonously as *the* authority -- was connected, not so much with his interest in developing a working-class culture, as with his efforts to make the capitalist world seem strange and new for his readers, and thereby enhance a sense of their own possibilities.

Much of McKay's Marxism came through in his intervention against an anti-Marxist article printed by the *Canadian Forum* in 1932 [§.74, "Marxism and Fatalism"]. Drawn, like so many of his contemporaries, to Marx's famous 1859 *Preface to a Critique of Political Economy* ("In the social production which men carry on they enter into definite relations that are indispensable and independent of their will....") -- a passage that provided so many interpreters with exactly the "deterministic" Marx they were looking for -- McKay, just like Antonio Gramsci, emphasized instead the more "voluntaristic" implications of Marx's belief that there was an important distinction between "the material transformation of the economic conditions of production" and the "legal, political, religious, aesthetic or philosophic--in short, ideological forms" in which people became conscious of conflicts inherent in such transformations and fought them out.[64] Rather than the metaphor of "base/superstructure," McKay -- once again, like Gramsci -- often conveyed the significance of economic relations in a very different (and rather Spencerian) language: "Politics and economics are but different aspects of the material basis of

[63]Colin McKay, "Evolution Cannot be Discredited," *Canadian Railroad Employees' Monthly*, January 1924: 185-186.
[64]C.M., "The Last Straw," *O.B.U.Bulletin*, 29 December 1932.

the life process of society."[65] His various outline histories of the development of capitalism did not emphasize the *forces* of production so much as the *social relations* of production. In some cases, in fact, the social forces of production were presented as the dependent variables: in his concrete analysis of Saint John's declining industries, for example, McKay urged that up-to-date plants would *result* from the workers demanding higher wages and compelling their employers to find another way besides low wages to maintain their competitiveness.[66] There was little that was "fatalistic" about this conception of the relationship between the forces and relations of production.

McKay even implied that Marx's analysis of economic determination was itself an ethico-political critique of an order in which material things had mastery over people. "The stand-patters of the old parties are the true believers in historical materialism," he wrote provocatively -- almost anticipating Gramsci's call for a "revolution against *Capital*" -- "the Marxian theory that material conditions shape human thought and action. They are the true believers because they wish to perpetuate a state of society in which material things have the mastery over men instead of being controlled by them."[67] What McKay called the "socialist's touch-stone of economic determinism"[68] was, in no small part, an ethical critique as well as a methodological principle. The key to the integration of politics and ethics within the framework of "economic determinism" was value.

From the evidence presently available, McKay appears to have acquired his grasp of the labour theory of value in 1911 or 1912, but the full integration of value theory into his perspective did not occur until at least a decade later. His letter on reciprocity in 1911 put the argument that "neither protection nor free trade will solve the problem of enabling the common people to reap the full fruits of their labour; the industrial workers, the farmers, fishermen and small businessmen under the competitive system of industry operated for profit only get the commodity value of their labour -- that is, they get enough to keep themselves and reproduce their kind, and procure sufficient education to fit them for certain employments.... Their joint labour creates what the economists call surplus value, and it is over the division of this surplus value taken from the people by legal processes that the financiers,

---

[65]C.M., "Nation Wide Interest in Trépanier's Fight," *Labour World/Le Monde Ouvrier*, 29 October 1938

[66]Colin McKay, "Saint John Workers Waking Up," *Eastern Labor News*, 5 April 1913.

[67]Colin McKay, "They Prefer Disorder," *Canadian Unionist*, Vol.7, No.6 (November 1933), 90-91.

[68]Colin McKay, "Workers Should Protest Against Further Military Expenditure," *Eastern Labor News*, 28 September 1912

corporations and their henchmen the politicians quarrel."[69] The most involved enunciation of value theory was presented in the *Eastern Labor News* in 1912. "Labour is a commodity, subject to the same laws as other commodities," he argued. "The value of any commodity is determined by the average social labour necessary to reproduce it. In the same way the value of labour is determined by the average cost of production. On the average the worker gets just enough to feed, clothe, shelter, and educate himself for his particular calling, and also to take a wife and bring up children to take his place when he is sent to the scrap heap." Closely following the analysis of the first volume of *Capital*, McKay continued: "...the capitalist when he buys labour power buys something different from a pair of shoes or any other commodity -- he buys a creative force. He puts the labourer to work. Probably on the average the real productive worker creates by working two hours or two hours and a half, commodities equal to the wages or commodity value of his labour, but he continue[s] to work six or eight hours longer. *In those six or eight hours he creates what economists of the socialist school call surplus value, and all he creates in those hours is absorbed by others.*"[70]

McKay attempted an interesting socialist defence of the importance of trade unionism in 1913 on the basis of the labour theory of value (now identified as "the socialist method of reasoning"): his version of the law held "that the value of a commodity is the cost of reproducing it, and that on the average price corresponds [to] the value," which suggested his reading of Marx's *Capital* had not advanced much beyond Volume One [§.47, "The Importance of Trade Unions for Socialism," first published as "The Workers are Waking Up"].

The concrete application of these theories of dialectical and historical materialism was always McKay's primary objective. For someone who had sought to merge the insights of Spencer and Marx, the tropes of "organicism" were highly significant: they were meant to be something more than illustrative figures of speech. The functions of useful organs in a capitalist society would grow; conversely, useless organs would atrophy and eventually disappear. If one defined "usefulness" narrowly in terms of the labour theory of value, this entailed the withering away of the *rentier* and most of the large capitalists, an evolutionary process which workers through their revolutionary politics might do much to accelerate.

Writing in 1910 in a highly Spencerian vein (and equating natural and social laws in a manner he would later criticize), McKay argued that it was an "inexorable law of nature that useless organs must disappear," and since the absentee, dividend-drawing class had long since delegated the

---

[69]Letter from Colin McKay, *Coast-Guard*, 3 August 1911.
[70]Colin McKay, "Teach Them to Measure Value," *Eastern Labor News*, 1 April 1912. Emphasis in original.

useful functions of management to salaried employees, their disappearance was to be expected. "Thus our economic development has outgrown our social organization, and in accordance with the fundamental biological law a social organism out of adjustment with its economical environment must perish as unfit."[71] McKay would later be more cautious in his use of "the fundamental biological law," but one can argue that he never fundamentally abandoned his sense of social evolution as a process following natural laws and closely linked to the processes of evolution analyzed by Darwin and other evolutionary theorists.[72] "As with any living organism, the prime requisite of a Labour union is ability to adapt itself to changing conditions," he wrote (under the subheading: "Adaptation -- A Law of Life") in one of his last works, published after his death [§.121, A Philosophy for Labour Organization"]. Clearly, after c. 1908, he never abandoned evolutionism.

Some of the enduring Spencerianism in McKay's Marxism can be seen in his discussion of "parasitism" as a distinguishing feature of capitalism. In 1928, McKay cited Paul Lafargue's argument in *The Evolution of Property* : "The parasitical nature of the role of the modern capitalist is recognized and proclaimed by the creation of anonymous companies whose shares and obligations -- the bourgeois titles to property -- pass from hand to hand, without exerting any influence upon production, and, on the Stock Exchange, change hands a dozen times a day....The Rothschilds, Goulds, and other financiers of that stamp practically demonstrate to the capitalists that they are useless, by cheating them out of their shares and bonds by Stock Exchange swindling and financial hanky-panky, and by accumulating in their strong boxes the profits derived from the great organisms of production." McKay observed that Lafargue's analysis was quite apt in the context of the typical industry of his time, in which the capitalist was no longer "an appendage of his property. Great enterprises are now mostly directed by salaried executives, who may or may not be capitalists in their own right, but do not necessarily hold their positions by virtue of that fact. A capitalist may draw profits from shares in an investment he has never seen, and knows nothing of beyond the information he gleans from the annual reports." Therefore, the capitalistic organization of industry had made a parasite of the capitalist *per se*. The

---

[71]Colin McKay, "Urges the Workers to Strike at the Ballot Box for Redress," letter to the *Halifax Herald*, 1 October 1910.

[72]At least some of McKay's writings took the analysis of the interdependence of the "two environments" shaping humanity -- i.e., the natural and the social -- in directions that anticipated, to a certain extent, modern environmental thought. As early as 1913 he was applying his holistic Spencerian vision to the troubled state of the environment in Shelburne County, admittedly within a conventional perspective which still held that the function of the natural world was to provide "resources" for society. Colin McKay, "The Two Social Factors," *The Coast-Guard,* 20 October 1910; Colin McKay, "Reforestation. An Interesting Letter from Colin McKay on this Question," *Shelburne Gazette and Coast Guard,* 18 September 1913.

proprietors of the modern impersonal corporations did not necessarily contribute any intelligence or energy to the direction of their enterprises. Although such property-owners relied to an ever-increasing extent on administrators, the "bourgeois economists" continued to ring the changes on the arguments that management "so overtops in importance all other factors in industry that it is entitled to dispose of all profits in excess of a living wage for labour, even though it disposes of such excess by handing it to shareholders who have made no personal contribution to the success of such management" [§.34, "Property and Progress"]. Deployed in this manner, "parasitism" was a powerfully integrating trope. It effectively linked the Marxian labour theory of value, Spencerian organicism, and the Christian condemnation of injustice.

McKay was well aware both of the limitations and strengths of such biological parallels. He carefully critiqued a speech by Angus MacInnis, the Labour member for Vancouver South, and probably the one M.P. whose outlook was closest to his own. MacInnis had drawn the parallel between cancer in the human body, caused by one of the cells of the body ceasing to co-operate with the other cells and becoming predatory in character, and the behaviour of individuals and corporations in society, which, thinking only of their own interests, ignored their responsibilities to society. They thus became (said MacInnis) "cancers in the social body." McKay remarked: "A biological principle does not necessarily have an analogy in social phenomena, but there are certainly many analogies, and the above one seems specially impressive. You may say that whatever produces a cancer in the human body is unconscious of what it is about. And you may say that in human society the individuals and corporations are conscious of what they are doing; that consciousness implies a sense of responsibility."[73]

Some limit had to be placed on the free range of biological metaphors, because it was crucial -- for McKay, and for the entire left -- to challenge arguments for capitalism based on "human nature" as the unchanging premise of individualism. The dominant capitalist class used its control over "the agencies of public education and public opinion" to convince people that "capitalism is the highest possible stage of evolution, destined to continue forever," and that the socialist alternative, premised as it was on some fundamental alteration in human nature, could be considered only in the far distant future.[74] Such arguments for capitalism on the biological grounds of human nature and the fundamentally individualistic struggle for survival could be countered by arguments founded on more social instincts, such as that of reproduction: "Nearly all animals except the beasts of prey are gregarious; they have social instincts, they have learned that by going in herds, that is by adopting the principle of co-

[73]C.McK., untitled letter, *Labor World/Le Monde Ouvrier*, 29 June 1935.
[74]Colin McKay, "Stand Pattism," *Eastern Labor News*, 19 October 1912,

operation, they are safer," wrote McKay, echoing the words of Prince Kropotkin.[75] The class struggle, in turn, could be founded, at an even more elemental level, in the pattern of conflict, collision, and eternal change in nature, as evidenced by positive and negative charges of electricity.[76] The development of socialism as a force in the modern world could be viewed as a "natural product which must pass through the phases of infancy and youth in order to attain a mature development. This is a necessary law of the evolution of anything in the natural or social world" [§.130, "The Conceits of the Communists"]. The pace of social evolution might be hastened somewhat, particularly by improvements in the means of production, but even at a faster pace, this law of evolution would hold. And the direction of social evolution -- towards a more and more co-operative, planned society -- could be ascertained with certainty [§.80, "Can the Capitalist System Be Stabilized?"]. Progress -- "the substitution of organization for unrelated units, of order for chaos"[77] -- was both necessary and possible, although "devolution" could occur should workers fail to become fully conscious of their mission in the modern world.

If socialism was the science of evolution, socialists were those who tried to apply this science in the daily world. The political implications of evolutionism were many, but two obvious ones stood out. One was a rejection of a "labour party" or a "labour interest" that lacked any comprehensive vision of its place in an evolving world or of the future possibilities inherent in it. A pragmatic, bread-and-butter labourism, for all its apparent "practicality," was in fact dangerous, because it would rob workers of their potential to build a society in which they were truly emancipated. The workingmen elected to office through trade-union support had been "of little use because they did not represent a propaganda or a policy. They were good enough fellows in their way, but it was a very small way. They had capitalistic minds, and from the standpoint of the interests of the worker they were quite as dangerous as the direct representatives of capital." Comprehending neither modern industry nor "the laws of social evolution," they generally looked at all economic questions from a narrow economistic point of view.[78] Insofar as the Co-operative Commonwealth Federation in its initial years was a loose alliance of discordant groups, many of whom were tempted by capitalistic and utopian schemes, McKay's critique of labourism applied even more powerfully to it, since the C.C.F. threatened to blur the class lines separating the middle class and labour.

---

[75]Colin McKay, "Ruling Class Morality Restricts Operations of Social Instincts," *Eastern Labor News*, 27 September 1913.

[76]§.33,"Struggle -- The Way of Progress."

[77]Colin McKay, "Agriculture Needs Planning," *Canadian Unionist* (September 1934): 107-108.

[78]Colin McKay, "How To Make a Live Labour Party," letter to the *Eastern Labor News*, 4 May 1912.

The second implication was a rejection of the Stalinist strategy of socialist transformation, exemplified in Canada by the Communist Party. Although (as we have seen) McKay had drawn on Weismann and De Vries as natural scientists who had shown that evolution could be conceptualized as an oscillatory process, with some changes taking place in sudden leaps [§.30, "Socialism as the Science of Social Evolution," originally published as "Socialism"], he expressed serious doubts about the applicability of this biological model to the ideas of the Communist Party. Identifying the "normal processes of social transformation" as "evolution and revolution," McKay thought it by no means certain that human society, as "a natural living organism," would undergo sudden transformations. He agreed that societies might undergo "explosions" similar to those associated with certain species of plants, but added, intriguingly, that "analogies between natural and social phenomena should be accepted only with caution "[§.130, "The Conceits of the Communists"]. The Communists' central "conceit" according to McKay, was to pretend to have a profound insight into a body of abstract theory they scarcely understood. Their threat to others lay in an adventurism rooted in their neglect of a realistic consideration of the underlying patterns of the social order. This ignorance of social evolution was especially manifest in their arrogant elitism. The Communists were unable to form effective or long-term bonds with workers because they did not approach them with the requisite degree of insight and understanding [§.130, "The Conceits of the Communists"].

Communists, McKay argued, had replaced scientific knowledge and practical understanding with fetishism and magic, theory with dogmatism. This turn of mind was influenced by the Communists' misunderstanding of the Soviet Union as the sole fount of Marxist truth, when in fact the Soviets were constructing not socialism but a variant of state capitalism. State capitalism in the Soviet Union had achieved impressive things, McKay wrote, especially in the context of the Great Depression, but even the immense willpower of the Soviet regime could have only a limited impact on the course of historic development: the Communists were speeding up evolution, not changing its course. The processes of development in the Soviet Union were still essentially capitalistic, and "the organs of a Socialist society appear to be in process of development though they are weak and insignificant as compared with organs of State capitalism."[79] On this reading, the so-called "revolution" had signally failed to change, or even to understand, the processes of social evolution it had set out to transform.

The true student of sociology would thus view the reformist schemes of social democracy and the Communist experiment in the Soviet Union as

---

[79]C.McK., untitled letter, *Labor World/Le Monde Ouvrier*, 26 November 1932

small steps along a much longer road to a new social order. McKay's evolutionary Marxist theory did not contend that this process would necessarily be smooth, nor that whole societies might not "devolve" and depart from the road altogether. Massive war, for example, could easily plunge societies into chaos, and since war was "mainly an extension of internal injustices into international relations," it remained a strong possibility so long as society was divided into mutually antagonistic classes. Nations would only be just in their external relations "in proportion as they learn to suppress within their own borders the fundamental injustice which springs from the unintelligent control of the forces of production, and the irrational distribution of wealth."[80]

A Spencerian Marxist argued that human society was "a natural, living organism in which the only thing constant is change"; consequently, the project of socialist construction entailed a holistic strategy that was not confined to the workplace, but comprehended a wide diversity of social relations. McKay argued that relations between men and women had been decisively changed by the advent of industrial capitalism and defended the enfranchisement of women as an aspect of social evolution; he traced a narrative from the burning of "millions of women" as witches to the two-career marriage of the twentieth century [§.44., "Votes for Women"; §45., "Women's Suffrage"].[81] And because of the pervasiveness of change, attempts to predict the future in detail were futile. Yet, an evolutionary Marxist like McKay would still insist, a *direction* could be assumed, towards ever greater planning, discipline, and order, towards a society in which the interests of the individual were subordinate to the welfare of the public. All signs pointed to the socialization of economic life, and the elimination of capitalism's gross irrationalities [§.116, "The Future of Industrial Unionism"]. If he was generally somewhat vague about the precise dialectical process through which capitalism was to be eliminated -- the tendency of the rate of profit to fall was less frequently invoked in his writing than a contradiction between the rational interests of workers and the irrationality of the capitalist order -- there can be no question about his ultimate certainty that capitalism was a system of crises.

---

[80]Colin McKay, "War, A Product of Internal Injustice," *Canadian Railroad Employees' Monthly* (June 1924): 67-68.

[81]For a discussion of socialism and women's enfranchisement, see Janice Newton, *The Feminist Challenge to the Canadian Left, 1900-1918* (Montreal and Kingston: McGill-Queen's University Press, 1995), Ch.7. It would seem essential in all discussions of this issue not to overgeneralize: in McKay's case, he takes it for granted that there is *general support* among socialists and trade unionists for "equal rights," but is concerned to critique the *specific form* of the case made by the Women's Suffrage Association, with its explicit reference to the rights of property. Many Saint John socialists of the day would have made much the same argument.

This has the sound of faith more than Marxian political economy, but faith in humanity was an indispensable element of McKay's social vision. He maintained, in the face of the horrific chaos of a capitalist system in crisis, that a course of evolutionary development could be discerned in history tending toward a society in which material life was organized in a co-operative and planned manner, and in which the injustices and irrationality of life in a class society would be abolished. This optimism of the will shaped his entire sense of the past and future of the Canadian socialist movement.

4. Sociology and Working-Class Culture

Socialists and the working class could not exist without each other: the future of the Canadian socialist movement would be determined primarily by the working class, the class which had a direct interest in the abolition of class society. Hence it was a matter of urgent importance to influence the ideas of workers, since the socialist project would wax or wane according to the workers' stance towards it.

The working class needed to develop its own philosophy, economics, politics, literature: in a (problematical) word, its own culture. This cultural transformation would be assisted by socialist intellectuals, organically linked to the working class and understanding its lived experiences, but also connecting the workers' interests to the more abstract theories that could help them understand their experiences in a class society. To be a real socialist meant developing practical and effective ties with the working-class movement as well as having a sound grasp of the Marxian theory of social evolution. It did not mean treating socialism as a new secular religion, impervious to the critiques of non-socialists[82] (here McKay discerned one of the conceits of the Communists) or luxuriating in an "impossibilist" revolutionary rhetoric whose only outcome would be to alienate the very people who needed to be reached (here was one of the conceits of certain SPCers) or in weakening the distinctiveness of socialist ideology (here McKay found the pragmatic conceits of the CCFers). These were all false trails branching off the road of a socialism based on scientific and practical reason.

McKay was not an armchair theorist, spinning out his notion of working-class *praxis* in his library. Until the end of the Great War, McKay had retained his connection to seafaring, and never lost a merchant seaman's vivid sense of being a disposable worker, unprotected from the direct power of capital. In addition to formative experiences at sea, McKay developed strong, practical connections with the labour movement. At

---

[82]See Colin McKay, "The Common Cause," *Eastern Labor News*, 3 May 1913, for his reflections on the benefits derived from reading an anti-socialist magazine which helped clarify his own socialist ideas.

various times in his life -- especially 1897-1904, 1910-1914, and 1929-1939 -- McKay threw himself into the cause of workers' education, writing hundreds of columns in the labour press. He was actively engaged in fighting exploitive conditions and in helping to establish labour organizations. McKay's analyses were almost always focused on a specific incident or problem from the labour world, which he sought to connect to some wider pattern. (Even the somewhat more abstract explorations of economic theory in the 1930s were clearly written with the economic crisis in mind). At times McKay struck a note of irritated impatience in writing about his fellow workers. More commonly he wrote of the strange combination of their intelligence and their susceptibility to bourgeois propaganda. Workers often expressed socialist sentiments. "It is a matter of observation that not a few workers who never saw a socialist publication are thinking socialist thoughts. I have met such men on the banks of Newfoundland, in the hinterlands of Quebec, in obscure hamlets in Spanish America -- most unlikely places in various parts of the world," he remarked in 1911.[83] From this it followed that a primary task for socialists was then literally one of "education" -- of drawing out of workers the knowledge they already possessed, and then expressing it in such clear, logical terms that workers could perceive the revolutionary implications of their own everyday intuitions.

McKay was under no illusions that labour organizations by themselves would transform capitalism. Still, he held them to be invaluable for workers in their struggle to wrest back some of the surplus value expropriated by capital and as training-grounds for political organization.[84] He particularly emphasized the worth of labour councils, which would help workers transcend the sectional and "petty" issues that sometimes preoccupied them.[85] McKay thought that Saint John was the "most bourgeois city in the world," and was mystified by the hold its governing classes held over the workers. It seemed the party spirit permeated every aspect of life.[86] And it was the puzzle of this ideological

---

[83]Colin McKay, "What Socialism Aims To Do," *Eastern Labor News*, 25 November 1911.

[84]Peter Campbell has convincingly dispelled the illusion that Socialist Party of Canada intellectuals were monolithically hostile to trade unions. "Leading SPCers such as Bill Pritchard... dismissed as preposterous any attempt to attack the trade unions themselves. They also recognized the essentially economistic nature of the trade union, and argued that the unions had to get beyond concerns with wages and working conditions. They also had to get rid of the 'parasitic' leaders who were duping the workers...." Campbell, "Stalwarts," 38. An instructive parallel might be drawn between McKay and William Pritchard, who was similarly "of, and yet significantly apart from, the mass of skilled and unskilled workers in the industrial working class" ("Stalwarts," 158). Such people were likely to appreciate the necessity of trade unionism.

[85]Colin McKay, "Saint John T. and L. Council," Letter to the *Eastern Labor News*, 17 September 1910.

[86]Colin McKay, "Brains Beguiled," *Coast-Guard*, 3 November 1910.

hold of the bourgeoisie over the workers in Saint John that prompted what was perhaps McKay's most original and penetrating work: his articles on the need for a working-class culture and the ways such a culture could be generalized through society. "Unfortunately the views of the ruling classes determine the mental operations of the uneducated workers...." [§.44, "Votes for Women"]: the workers of Saint John seemed to be under the spell of what Gramscian theorists would later diagnose as bourgeois hegemony, and McKay proposed some prescriptions for the problem not far removed from those suggested by Gramsci.

First, workers needed to develop their own culture, morality, and sense of history. This call for a "working-class culture" differed in fundamental respects from two later usages of this term. Unlike certain calls for a "Proletarian" or "Workers' Culture" in the Soviet Union in the 1920s, McKay's vision did not call for the suppression of non-working-class cultural forms, nor did it discount the value of all non-Marxist works. McKay's commitment to the value-idea of freedom, to free discussion and scientific reason, would have inoculated him from the temptations of "Proletarian Science" as it developed under Stalin and the Communist Party of the Soviet Union. At the same time, McKay's sense of what a "working-class culture" would entail also bore little resemblance to the meaning this term has acquired since 1960 in academic history in Britain and in North America, where it seems to function as a way of categorizing historical or contemporary cultural phenomena according to whether the phenomena in question is expressive of a pre-given class essence or concept. (Thus, for example, although workers in the past may not have understood their leisure activities in this way, historians have retrospectively categorized such phenomena as baseball, fraternal orders (less often churches or political parties), taverns (less often temperance crusades) and other phenomena as elements of a "working-class culture." In such treatments, culture becomes an "implicit essence" within discrete activities, none of which may have been conceptualized in this manner by people in the past, but all of which can be grasped in this manner retrospectively by a scholar through the exercise of a kind of retrospective ethnography.) Whatever the scholarly justifications may be for this mode of historical anthropology,[87] it is important to see that it bears little resemblance to the "Working-Class Culture" McKay was advocating in the early twentieth century. McKay thought of working-class culture *not* as something that *already existed* -- in taverns and on baseball fields and so

---

[87]Of the many Canadian constructions of "working-class culture" in this sense that one might cite from the historical literature, perhaps the most attractive and compelling is Peter de Lottinville, "Joe Beef of Montreal: Working Class Culture and the Tavern, 1869-1889," *Labour/Le Travail*, 8/9 (1981-82): 9-40. Bryan D. Palmer, *A Culture in Conflict: Skilled Workers and Industrial Capitalism in Hamilton, Ontario, 1860-1914* (Montreal: McGill-Queen's University Press, 1979) is historiographically significant as a moment in this anthropological conceptualization of working-class culture.

on -- but as a potential force rank-and-file workers and socialist intellectuals could together *bring into being in the future*. "The working class must develop a *new* philosophy of life, a *new* culture" [§.49, "Working Class Culture", emphasis added]. Working-class culture did not yet exist; workers did not as yet have their own culture, but were under the influence of the bourgeoisie. Working-class culture had to be created, and its creation would entail the conscious efforts of workers and the intellectuals who were connected to them. Moreover, this working-class culture was far less the unselfconscious reflection in leisure activities of an "essential" class identity already in existence (which is an implication of much subsequent historiography) and more the active construction of a new body of knowledge and expertise, a multifaceted *proletarian discipline* capable of undermining and replacing the bourgeois commonsense of a liberal capitalist order. On this reading, a radically oppositional "culture" would likely not emerge spontaneously from workers' leisure or even workplace activities: such a new knowledge could only emerge through conscious political and intellectual *praxis*. One might encapsulate the project with the phrase, "a working-class Enlightenment".

McKay thought the obstacles in the path of this cultural experiment were formidable. Workers tended to be overawed and mystified by the bourgeois culture around them. Although capitalism was visibly rotting, "it need not follow, however, that capitalists are rotten in the eyes of the people. The over-ripe apple is generally the finest looking apple in the orchard. The capitalists, those who do no useful work, but draw handsome dividends, are generally the most refined product of modern civilization" [§.26, "Capitalism -- The Modern Frankenstein"]. McKay was especially taken aback by the respect workers showed for the "smooth front and glib tongue," and the extent to which they were persuaded that they lacked the ability to understand or change the world around them. Yet these same workers were the ones who carried out all the useful work of the world, who built and operated railways, and carried out all the complicated processes of modern production. For Socialists to make any impact, they had to convince workers of their own inner strength.[88] "...What strikes one most forcibly is the lack of self-confidence on the part of the worker -- or perhaps more properly a lack of respect for his class," McKay said of the workers of the Maritimes.[89]

The workers' sense of powerlessness and deference could be attributed, on a general level, to the omnipresent influence of individualism, perpetuated by mainstream liberalism in politics, conventional Christianity in religion, and bourgeois commonsense views of human

---

[88]Colin McKay, "Time for a Labor Party is Now," letter to the *Eastern Labor News*, 11 November 1911.

[89]Colin McKay, "What Socialism Aims To Do," *Eastern Labor News*, 25 November 1911.

nature in daily life. But this ideological success was also dependent on the functioning of specific practices and institutions. One of the most important -- and one often neglected in much post-1980 "cultural analysis" on the left -- was work itself. Workers were exhausted after the long day at work: chronic overwork had an important cultural dimension. "Physical exhaustion usually means mental inertia and that means apathy and hopelessness. A worker who has not studied history from the view point of the working class is bound to be a pessimist" [§.68, "The Awakening of Labour in Eastern Canada"].[90] Another significant cultural force was direct political repression and state violence. In Saint John, even had workers wanted to vote socialist, they were denied the chance in 1911 through a manipulation of the electoral rule-book.[91] At the local library -- funded, appropriately enough, by the blood-money Andrew Carnegie had gouged from his workers -- the authorities declined to take labour papers.[92] The civic authorities even tried to prevent Socialists from meeting in public squares.

Beyond such overtly coercive measures was the vast, complex realm of bourgeois common sense, sustained by an immense institutional matrix: "The schools, the pulpits, the press, every agency of public education, and public opinion, inculcate ideas favourable to the maintenance of the capitalist system, and the workers unconsciously absorb capitalistic ideas" [§.68, "The Awakening of Labour in Eastern Canada"]. The two institutions McKay considered most essential for this inculcation of capitalist ideas were the churches and the schools. In the case of the church, Sunday Schools allegedly offered children models of servility and deference by systematically twisting the message of the Bible. (It is by no means clear that McKay had recently been to such a Sunday School). In the case of the schools, one had to remember the interests of the State, the guardian of class interest, whose instruction was designed "to train the workers for a position of docile servitude,... to teach the children to be docile slaves of a class state."[93] One of the key elements in this "chloroforming effect" -- McKay's rhetoric at this point is vintage Socialist Party of Canada -- was

---

[90]He made a similar point in another article: "The lawyer, with his legal subtleties, the politician with his arts, are generally able to humbug and fool the people. But it is a foolish thing to assume that the workers are ignoramuses. The men who build ships and sail them, who build and operate railways, who construct all kinds of machinery and carry on the complicated processes of modern production, are not deficient in intelligence. The only trouble is that they have been too busy to think about social economics." Colin McKay, "The Evolution of Society," letter to the *Coast-Guard*, 9 November 1911.

[91]Colin McKay, "What Socialism Aims To Do," *Eastern Labor News*, 25 November 1911.

[92]Colin McKay, "Double Morality in Saint John," *Eastern Labor News*, 28 June 1913.

[93]Colin McKay, "Mr. Hatheway and Technical Education," *Eastern Labor News*, 18 January 1913.

the bourgeois abuse of history: Children were taught history in a particularly ideological way. "Every thing of importance is represented as the work of some great man, or a special providence, but the mass movements of the working classes are generally described as insurrections or rebellions of the lowest of the low without any definite or decent motive," McKay argued [§.51, "The Mis-Education of the Young"]. Another contribution bourgeois education made to society was to foster "the emotional woof and web of snobbery" [§.35, "The Conservatism of the Mind"].[94] Against critics of socialism who charged that it would reduce everything to a dull uniformity, McKay held up the example of the bourgeois educational system:

> Our people are frightened by the idea that the state would cut all garments by one pattern. Yet they consider it quite natural that the state should attend to the intellectual shaping of their children, and force their young brains into a rigid mould. Happily, socialism no more contemplates compelling the people to wear the same uniform or eat the same dish than it would think of continuing the present stupid system of so-called education which, by trying to trim children's mind's to one pattern, usually has the effect of dwarfing their faculties. My own idea is that, under socialism, parents would attend to the education of their children -- something they cannot do at present, as they have neither the time or opportunity to educate themselves. The capitalist state merely teaches children the three "R's" -- which do not constitute education at all, for very few of the ancient Greeks, the most cultured people of any age, could read or write -- because the capitalists need people acquainted with the three R's in their business.[95]

These criticisms of mindless conformity, so divergent from the stereotype of the "Socialism of the Second International," could have as easily been

---

[94]One observes many parallels between McKay's writings in Saint John and the agitations of the labour movement around educational questions in Winnipeg: see Bill Maciejko, "The Working Mind: The Radical Workers' Response to Public Education, Winnipeg, 1912-1921," M.A.Thesis, University of Manitoba, 1985., and the same author's "Public Schools and the Workers' Struggle: Winnipeg, 1914-1921," in Nancy M. Sheehan, J. Donald Wilson and David C. Jones, eds., *Schools in the West: Essays in Canadian Educational History* (Calgary 1986): 213-37. For an excellent discussion of the issue of workers and the educational system in the Vancouver context, see Jean Barman, "'Knowledge is essential for Universal Progress but Fatal to Class Privilege': Working People and the Schools in Vancouver During the 1920s." *Labour/Le Travail* 22 (Fall 1988): 9-66.
[95]Colin McKay, "A Modern Prophet's Opinion of Fishermen Or Why Did Christ Choose Fishermen as Apostles?" *Yarmouth Times,* 3 April 1908 [reprinting the Shelburne *Coast-Guard*].

drawn directly from the equally non-conformist work of Herbert Spencer, who was also a harsh critic of the dreariness of the educational system.

These institutions, targetting above all the children of workers, did their job well. (Were he writing today, McKay would surely also focus on television and "mass culture.")[96] Workers did internalize capitalist ways of thinking and make them their own. To awaken the ability of workers to think for themselves consequently involved a complex and painful process of questioning and rejecting old certainties. When the worker began to think for himself, it would be discovered "that he will have to put behind him most of his cherished beliefs and opinions ground into him by his capitalistic environment, and he will find the process of mental emancipation a rather painful one. For thought is always revolutionary and disturbing."[97]

Three strategic implications for socialists followed from this line of cultural analysis. One was that socialists who approached workers with an all-knowing, dogmatic superiority, based on their supposed grasp of the internal necessities of capitalist development, and who hence dismissed workers' efforts to organize themselves into strong trade unions, did more harm than good. Another was that many (thought not all) workers, because their opinions had been moulded in bourgeois institutions, could not "spontaneously" produce a socialist analysis of their situation: their analytical categories, and their underlying mental attitude of subservience, had been too well planted. So, and third, if Socialists (including socialist workers) really wanted to change the categories through which most workers apprehended reality -- and it was on such a change that all their hopes and dreams depended -- they needed to mount a patient, careful but unrelenting campaign to explore the contradictions in bourgeois civilization and demonstrate how these contradictions could be better explained within an alternative framework. Cultural struggles were not "peripheral" to socialists; without them, in fact, nothing would change. Not even the most massive strike could be revolutionary if, to some extent at least, it was not perceived as such. Herein lay the logic of McKay's focus

---

[96]He largely ignored questions of "mass culture," so far as one can judge from the available evidence: there appears to have been no attempt to understand the significance of radio, for example. He did call attention in 1937 to the noxious effect of violent pulp magazines, which he held were preparing the population for war (Colin McKay, Untitled letter, *Labor World/Le Monde Ouvrier*, 6 March 1937). One might also mention his discussion of tourism (§.67), and his ruminations on the power of advertising (§.46), as well as his disparagement of the cult of sporting activities in Montreal: thin pickings, which is not surprising from a working-class intellectual who generally remained, in his philosophical allegiances and literary tastes, a man of the pre-1914 world.

[97]Colin McKay, "The Awakening of Labour in Eastern Canada," *Eastern Labor News*, 12 October 1912.

on cultural issues in 1910-1914 and, more generally, the rationale for an adult lifetime devoted to workers' education and labour journalism.

McKay's emphasis on the success of the bourgeoisie in presenting its world-view as "common sense" led him not to fatalism but to an optimistic sense of the number of fronts on which socialist workers could wage a meaningful struggle for their own vision of reality. He urged workers to try to get hold of school boards, for example, to make sure "that their children were taught history and everything else from the view point of their class, were made to realize the position of their class under capitalism, and to understand the methods by which they are exploited out of the bulk of the product of their labour."[98] Motivated perhaps by McKay's article, the Saint John Trades and Labor Council did request a representative on the School Board. McKay argued that even in their defeat, they could learn a positive lesson. The reverse might "induce some workers to reflect on their position in capitalist society; if they do that they will doubtless come to the conclusion that the people who do the work in this world don't really count for much. And then they may ask themselves, 'Why shouldn't the workers have something to say about the education of their children?'" [§.46, "Labour's Will and Labour's Methods"].

The School Board issue, the demand that labour have representation within the new structure of civic government in Saint John, the applause workers showered on speakers who voiced socialist sentiments: all these were impressive harbingers of change. Workers were starting to speak out. In Saint John, a scant two and a half years earlier they had remained silent when addressed by "representatives of the property interests"; in 1913, they showed that they could present better arguments than the manufacturers.[99] Clearly there were signs of profound change everywhere one looked. So what should socialists do to help shape an emergent working-class consciousness?

One important measure was to conduct a non-stop, powerful propaganda offensive. Whenever a union met, McKay wrote in 1938, it had a responsibility to demand "economic reconstruction and social change" from all three levels of government. Workers should bombard the politicians with correspondence and articles explaining the need for radical change. This would help break the deadly hold of fatalism, and encourage workers to see themselves as active participants in the cause of labour and humanity. Even a few unions might provoke quite a widespread

---

[98]Colin McKay, "Mr. Hatheway and Technical Education," *Eastern Labor News*, 18 January 1913.
[99]Colin McKay, "Saint John Workers Waking Up," *Eastern Labor News*, 5 April 1913.

sense of upheaval.[100] The labour movement should also develop its own working-class experts: every trade union should have its own statistician to refute insidious propaganda for low wages. It was a weakness on the part of the Canadian labour movement that it gave so little attention to "the propaganda of the economic realties on which it is based. It gives indifferent and inadequate support to its own papers. It seldom makes a protest against patent economic fallacies promulgated by the daily press."[101] From McKay's perspective, to neglect such matters was to betray the socialists' duty to undertake cultural struggle.

In order to construct a new culture, socialists had to destroy the assumptions of the old. The bourgeoisie and its legacy of individualism had to be discredited wherever possible, in propaganda that appealed to the emotions and the senses as well as to logic. McKay's description of the elite St. George's Society banquet in Saint John illustrates his own way of "defamiliarizing" the culture of the bourgeoisie: having listened to the Bishop of Fredericton and the American consul at Saint John both deliver speeches warning of growing social turmoil, the good burghers of Saint John returned to their dinners: "the warnings of the Bishop and the Consul made little impression upon the gathering, gorged to repletion and mellowed by champagne. Subsequent speakers did not rise above the balderdash, dear to the heart of the infatuated bourgeoisie. The death-head at the feast did not worry the ancient Egyptians. Eat, drink and be merry, etc. Whom the gods would destroy they first make mad or blind..." [§.26, "Capitalism -- The Modern Frankenstein"].

His polemic against the bourgeoisie was subsequently pushed further to encompass a condemnation of the ethical double standard that made such hypocrisy possible. McKay unrelentingly reminded his readers of way of the bourgeois world, wherein there was one standard "for precept and especially for the edification of the workers," and the other standard "for practice if possible." The bourgeois mind was puzzled by contradiction between the ideals of justice, honesty and morality and the everyday business practice, but this "dualism" could hardly be overcome while his life was ruled by economic forces that were apparently "indifferent to his efforts to guide the economic machine" [§.52, The Worker Must Learn to Think"]. College professors -- Stephen Leacock was a favourite target -- who proved too complacent to question the perpetual reign of the bourgeoisie were denounced for their lack of integrity. Professors of political economy who went beyond merely collecting statistics and turning "their science into comedy," would lose their salaried chairs if they actually started to explore the workings of the

---

[100]Colin McKay, "The Task of Social Reconstruction," *Canadian Railway Employees' Monthly*, July 1938.
[101]Colin McKay, "The Crime of Low Wages," *Labor World/Le Monde Ouvrier*, 18 April 1925.

system. They were just capitalism's ideological hired hands.[102] Those who worked in the business heart of the system, or on its academic periphery, stood little chance of preserving their integrity.

Working-class propaganda required the building of powerful working-class institutions capable of withstanding the immense economic and cultural pressures of the capitalist order. In addition to trade unions and labour parties, the labour press was of fundamental importance. McKay complained in 1913 that workers did not lend enough support to the labour press, without which they could not aspire to wage a constant struggle for their ideals.[103] One of the key tactics of the *Eastern Labor News* should be to win the teachers to socialism and labour organization. McKay attached more importance to achieving long-term cultural change. He encouraged the *Eastern Labor News* to issue a special "teachers' number," to persuade teachers of their interest in the common cause. Labour organizations had everything to gain from having teachers, who shaped the minds of the next generation, study (and presumably absorb) the philosophy of the labour movement.[104]

What was this philosophy? If the organizational form of the new culture was to be a politico-cultural alliance under the hegemonic leadership of the working class, the practical philosophy of the new culture was to be one of co-operation. Within the emergent working-class culture, a new and almost universal morality could be articulated, in anticipation of the transition to socialism. As McKay explained, in a class-ruled state the virtues that were most carefully inculcated were respect for authority, obedience, contentment, and a credulous attitude toward life. Such characteristics helped keep workers submissive. In a socialist society, however, "new ideals, more splendidly human than those of any other class, take possession of the worker's mind, and rules of conduct tending toward the realization of these ideals become the moral standards of his class. And because, as in the case of other class[es], solidarity is essential to the accomplishment of working-class possibilities, it is becoming so that a worker who becomes a scab is regarded by his class as a traitor...." [§.48, "A Working Class Morality"].

Elements of a new socialist order could thus be brought into being within working-class culture, even before the final crisis of capitalism. McKay still held this vision of an anticipatory socialism -- the emergence of a new way of life within the ruins of the old -- two decades later: "The sun begins to shed light before it rises above the horizon; and just so, a new, impending system of production sheds its light upon the minds of men,

---

[102] C.McKay, untitled letter, *Labor World/Le Monde Ouvrier*, 13 January 1938.

[103]Colin McKay, "Organize the School Teachers," *Eastern Labor News*, 15 November 1913.

[104]*Eastern Labor News*, 15 November 1913.

before it has "fully materialized" [§.135, "The Shadows Fade"]. Unless the socialist movement succeeded in bringing such anticipatory forms of socialism into being, there could be no transition to socialism. Just as the principle of solidarity could be expanded, under the hegemony of the working class, to incorporate other social groups, so could it transcend national boundaries in recognition of a common humanity. "The ruling classes have taught the workers to fight among themselves," McKay remarked, on the eve of the Great War. "But when the workers learn to fight for themselves, there won't be much further need of fighting."[105] His sense of the working-class mission to save civilization would become even more urgent in the interwar period, when he saw the rise of state capitalism in its various forms as both an opportunity and a terrible menace for the working-class movement. By then the choice was an elemental one: either an ever-worsening world crisis, with capitalism, the mad master of the modern world, sweeping civilization to oblivion, or a socialist order, in which "the interests of the individual will no longer be at war with the welfare of society" [§.135, "The Shadows Fade"].

---

[105]Colin McKay, "Ruling Class Morality Restricts Operations of Social Instincts," *Eastern Labor News*, 27 September 1913

i. Capitalism As A System

20. The Wise Men. A Fable for the Otherwise[106]

The Three Wise Men of Gotham who went to sea in a bowl, sailed on and
on till they came to the uncharted Isle, and there they landed and sitting
them down in the shade of a cocoanut palm spake thankfully among
themselves. And while they thus pow-wowed, the population of that Isle
blew out of the bush and forming in a circle round about kow-towed
genially.

"What, and who, why, and whence?" quoth the natives. Quickly the Wise
Men took stock of the population. And when they perceived that it
consisted of a bare baker's dozen of simple folks wearing garments that
were not loud and smiles that were friendly, they put on their most
pompous air and made proclamation that they were the emissaries of
civilizations come to bring its blessings to that Isle. "It sounds good to us,"
quoth the simple folk. "Show us, we're from Missouri." So the Wise Men
arose and proceeded to organize the forms and shower the blessings of
civilization upon the people of that Isle. And when they had explained
that civilization could only be constructed in the form of a pyramid,
balanced upon its apex, and resting upon a basis of gold, they set a
portion of the population to work digging for gold. And at this the simple
folk marvelled somewhat and one of them, a crank, an impossible fellow,
full of idle curiosity, went about muttering:

"Now wherefore all this digging of holes in the ground -- of shifting sand
in the riverlets? What good does it do us? Is it not [our] labour wasted?
Would not these argonauts be better employed planting yams? It is
funny."

But the Wise Men heard not these sayings of the crank, and the simple
folk heeded him not. For were they not being civilized? Has not the wise
man who had made himself governor, been busy making laws for them?
Was not the wise man who represented the learned professions busy
looking after their souls, their morals and their brains? And would not the
banker, when he discovered gold, work wonders for them?

And so while the Wise Men wrought mysteriously and talked learnedly, the
simple folk laboured harder and longer than they had ever done to

---

[106]Originally published as "The Wise Men. A Fable for the Otherwise. Wherein is
Related how the Wise Men Established Civilization on the Isle of the Simple Folks,"
Eastern Labor News, 25 May and 1 June, 1912. For the significance of fantasies,
allegories, and science fiction in the imagination of turn-of-the-century socialists, see
Mark Pittenger, *American Socialists and Evolutionary Thought, 1870-1920* (Madison,
Wis.: University of Wisconsin Press, 1993), Ch.4.

keeping the pot a-boiling -- and civilization grew apace. And at last there came a day of rejoicing -- the banker and his men had discovered gold.

And after the celebration the Wise Men set some of the simple folk to build a great strong house, and when it was finished they placed the gold therein and locked it in vaults of triple steel. And at this the simple folk marvelled a little, and the crank said:

"Now wherefore do ye this? What good does it do us -- this gold locked up in dark places? Or is it a god that we build it a better house than we build ourselves? Or is it a devil eager to do us evil, that we gaol it so carefully? Verily, it is funny."

Now, when they heard these things the Wise Men were much astonished and exceeding[ly] wrath[ful]. And they spake strongly to the people of the gold standard and sound money and such things -- and of how, now that they had gold in their vaults, they would issue bank notes based upon it and so furnish the people with a public representative of value.

"But why didn't ye issue your representative of value in the first place?" queried the crank. "Why not have your circulating medium based on real wealth or useful labour? Would we not be richer in real wealth if the goldseekers had been performing useful labour instead of digging holes and shifting sand? And why should these bank notes based on gold, these paper representatives of the holes in the ground, possess certain special and extraordinary powers of absorbing the products and commanding the services of useful labour? Does not this round-about process of creating a medium of exchange invoke an unnecessary increase in the labour of all of us, and make possible the perpetration of grievous wrongs? If this be so, and it seems to be so, then I begin to understand the legend of the Golden Fleece."

At this the Wise Men lifted up their voices, saying, "It is not the part of wisdom to answer a fool according to his folly." And therewith they proceeded to explain how difficult it was to explain the wonderous workings of the system of finance. And they talked so loud and so long, so earnestly and learnedly, they invested the whole business with such mystery and wove around it such an intricate network of theories and speculations, that the simple folk were mightily mystified and highly edified -- so much so that they set upon the crank and silenced him.

Thereafter the Wise Men proceeded rapidly with the work of civilizing that Isle. They reorganized the industry of the land, and after explaining the law of supply and demand, put the simple folk to work at $1.50 a day. Also they elected themselves to parliament, and voted themselves right and title to the land. And when they sent around their bills for rent, and the people murmured thereat, they explained they were only following the precedent set by the mother of parliaments, and how private ownership was the foundation stone of, and incentive to, progress. And they explained so many other things and spoke with such authority, that the simple folk were astonished at their own presumptions, and hastily presented the wherewithall to pay the rent.

And so civilization progressed in that Isle. The Wise Men worked in mysterious ways their wonders to perform, and the simple folk laboured long and hard, and producers multiplied in the land. And the Wise Men, seeing how their larders filled up with good things, said, 'The county is prosperous", and straightway they put up rents and prices. Also they picked out the stoutest of the simple folk and made a policeman of him, and they took others and made servants and secretaries of them.

Thereafter, the Wise Men took their ease and fared sumptuously every day. But the simple folk who tilled the fields, and tended the flocks and did other useful chores, being now fewer in number, found they had to labour harder and longer than ever before. And they found, too, that because of the higher rents and prices, their wages got them less of the good things of life than before. And so they began to murmur among themselves, and at last they did make demand for more wages. Now when the Wise Men heard this demand they did take stock of things, and seeing quickly that their larders were full to bursting, they fell straightway into a panic, and, hastily [calling] the people together, they said [unto] them:

"Behold, a crisis is upon us! Over-production is here. Our larders are full to bursting, and we have no market for our surplus." And at this the crank lifted up his voice, saying, "Why not, then, give us more wages, that we may buy more goods of you? Would not your markets be enlarged thereby?"

But the Wise Men shook their heads [pityingly] at these foolish sayings, and they said unto the people:

"What music is there in the bay of an ass? How can we give you more money if we do not first get more money ourselves, and how can we get more money ourselves if we do not first sell our surplus products? 'Tis plain the country is too prosperous. We have been living beyond our means and we must go slow for a time. We must limit output, and reduce working hours and wages. Also we must give the most of you a holiday."

When now the Wise Men had thus made their wisdom manifest, the simple folk were exceedingly mystified; and they went back to their homes, pondering upon the blessings of civilization. And presently they found that having no work to do, they drew no wages, and drawing no wages they could buy no food, and so they grew hungry. And to add to their troubles the Wise Men sent word by the policemen that if they didn't pay their rents they would have to get off the land.

But now the Wise Men's words failed to please the simple folk, for they were very hungry, and they listened to the riddles propounded by the crank, and murmured loudly among themselves. Also they looked with greedy eyes upon the bursting larders of the Wise Men, and when the policeman would have run them off the land they took him and put him under the pump.

And the Wise Men heard and saw these things and were mightily astonished, and grievously troubled. "Society is in peril," they said, "and unless we take steps, revolution and anarchy will be upon us." So they took counsel among themselves, and called the people together and said to them:

"Our hearts are contracted at your ingratitude for all we have done for you -- and so is our credit. But nevertheless we will take steps to set the wheels of progress together again. We cannot get you to work creating those things whereof we have now a superabundance -- that would accentuate the present evils. But we will borrow capital, and set you to work building railways, establishing new industries, and developing our resources generally. Then will everything boom again like a bell."

So the Wise Men sent forth the banker to a foreign country and when he returned he was waving a piece of parchment above his head.

"Eureka!" he cried. "Behold it -- the capital. Now will the wheels of progress roll on again."

"And what? Do you call that capital?" exclaimed the crank. "Will it clothe and feed and house us while we are building new railways and starting new industries? Verily your bit of parchment must have strange magic to it."

But the Wise Men lifted up their voices and spake loud and learnedly, explaining how difficult it was to explain the mechanism of exchange. And when they had shown how the piece of parchment was a lien on foreign capital which like some wizard's wand would enable them to utilize the capital stored in their own bursting larders, the simple folk were much comforted, and petitioned that they be put to work at once so they might eat.

So the Wise Men put them to work building railways and constructing machines and such things, and they gave them $1.50 a day and sold them as many things as they could buy with their wages. Also the Wise Men rose up in parliament and spake loudly of the marvellous developments going

140   *For a Working Class Culture in Canada*

on in the land; and the people were duly edified and thankful for the return of prosperity.

Now when some time had passed the Wise Men ladened a ship with good things from the larders, and sent her away; and the simple folk marvelled greatly thereat. But when the Wise Men explained how interest must be paid on the borrowed capital, they were content -- all save the crank who still went about muttering his foolish riddles.

"Now wouldn't that jar you?" he would query in his foolish fashion. "Is it not so that we use up the good things created by our labour aforetime, when we build these railways? And if so, how comes it that we must pay foreign capitalists for the privilege of using our own capital? Does it not work out that to build the railway by means of this foreign loan, we must not only provide the capital to build the railway, but must also send to these foreign money lenders, money sufficient to build another railway -- nay, since the interest will equal the amount of the loan itself by the time we have paid it off, two railways? Would it not have been cheaper if our government had issued the magic parchment? Would we then have been obliged to provide the capital to build three railways?"

Meantime, civilization progressed. But its course was like that of true love -- it couldn't run smooth any length of time. When the Wise Men again took stock of their larders they saw that while there was much going out there was little coming in, for now that the people were employed in the higher industries there were none to produce the essential things. And forthwith the Wise Men fell into a great state of consternation, and put up prices so high that the simple folk found their wages would scarce compass a diet of potatoes. But even so the Wise Men saw that they were only putting off a little while the coming of the evil day when they would have nought themselves. And they saw too, that the simple folk saw that though they laboured harder than ever before, yet they continued to grow hungrier and ever hungrier.

So the Wise Men were grievously troubled and did hastily consult the moon and the stars. And presently they saw signs and wonders in the heavens and when they had interpreted them they learned that the country needed immigration. And so they sent forth and brought in half a dozen simple folk from another Isle, and they set them to work in the fields and sweatshops.

And again civilization progressed, and prosperity prospered. But ere long the Wise Men saw that though they sold more good things in the home market than before and sent many away to satisfy the claims of the foreign capitalist, yet did their larders fill up apace, for the simple folk were now assisted in their labours by machinery and railways and produced good things at a great rate. And the simple folk saw these things, too, and they said, "Give us more wages, O Wise Men, that we may buy more of the good things flowing in to your larders so rapidly. Or else over-production will be upon us again." But the Wise Men liked not this demand and made answer saying: "If we give you more wages you'll only waste it on drink and other forms of dissipation and thus will your efficiency be reduced. Our concern for your welfare will not permit us to put temptation within your reach. We must find another remedy for the evils that threaten us." So they consulted the heavens and learned that the country needed foreign markets. And they ladened many ships with good things and sent them away.

So it fell out that for a time there was a great stir in that Isle. The Wise Men had to spend all the day and half the night counting up their gains, and the simple folk had to labour from sunrise to sunset, yea till long after sunset, to supply the foreign markets. And yet, for all [that] so many good things were shipped away, it so happened that the Wise Men's larders began to fill up again and at last they were full to bursting.

So again the Wise Men called the people together and said to them:

"Behold the country is again too prosperous. Another cycle of over-production has rolled round. You must quit work for a time." But now the Wise Men's words fell not as balm upon the troubled feelings of the simple folk, and they began to murmur sullenly among themselves. "This civilization -- is it not a funny business? Once one laboured little, and yet we lived in clover, and moreover we had leisure to commune with nature and with one another. But since the Wise Men came among us we have laboured harder and ever harder, longer and ever longer, and what is our reward? We have built many fine temples to house the gold of the Wise Men, and the parchments whereon is written the tale of their wealth -- yet we live in hovels that are nigh to tumbling about our ears. We have created many good things to fill the larders of the Wise Men, and send away to foreign capitalists and foreign markets -- yet how few good things do we enjoy ourselves? And now at the end of all our labour we are told that there is no work and therefore no food for us, and presently, because we have not the wherewithal to pay the rent, we will be ordered off the earth. Verily civilization has brought us strange blessings. Yea, verily, it is a riddle too hard for simple folk to read."

Now when the Wise Men heard these sayings they were greatly grieved and shocked that so much wickedness and foolishness should dwell in the hearts of the simple folk after all they had done to teach and train them for a civilized life -- and for a while they could not trust themselves to speak. But when their emotions had subsided they took council with the wisdom and goodness of their hearts and lifted up their voices and gravely and sadly rebuked the people.

"Is it the part of wisdom to bother itself with riddles? Is not the wise man he who knows how little he can know? Is not existence a riddle? And must not civilization, which is but an extension of existence, be an ever greater riddle? Why then seek you to unriddle everything that comes to pass? This phenomenon of over-production -- who shall account for it? The moon and the stars offer no light, and though some say the spots on the sun will explain it,[107] yet what do we know? Do you want roses without thorns? Why then do you expect progress without poverty? Has not the thorn its function, and has not poverty its value? How could you appreciate good times if ye knew not hard times? Does not civilization, like Providence, move in mysterious ways its wonders to perform? How then should you hope to understand the ways of civilization? Go home simple people, and puzzle not your woolly minds."

When the Wise Men had thus spoken, the simple folk were greatly abashed in that they could not understand wherein lay the wisdom of these sayings, and having no answer ready they went home and pondered long upon the marvels of civilization. And in the morning they rose up early, and seeing that their cupboards were bare, they went out and spake earnestly among themselves. "Verily," they said, "the Wise Men's wisdom is too much for us. And verily, too, their civilization moves in mysterious ways its blunders to perform upon us. Behold whither it has brought us! After making us labour long and greatly, now that it has no present use for our services, [it would compel] us to fade away because of lack of subsistence or be driven off the earth because of the lack of the wherewithal to pay the rent. Even at its best the Wise Man's civilization is hardly worth the cost, and now that it shows it has no use for us it is high time we showed that we have no use for it. Let us have done with it, let us return to a state of nature. Then we shall at least achieve those things whereof civilization has robbed us: independence and security of livelihood."

And so it befell that while the Wise Men were sitting in parliament busy voting money to open soup-kitchens, the simple folk rushed in and drove them out, and began to turn civilization topsy-turvy, and of course the Wise Men waxed mightily indignant thereat and summoned their policemen, their servants and secretaries and bade them take up their weapons and exterminate the enemies of society. But their command did not seem good to their retainers. "They're too many for us," said the policemen. "Let us take to the tall timber."

And so the simple folk proceeded unmolested with the work of overturning society, and when the destruction was fully accomplished they

---

[107]McKay is making fun of W.S.Jevons, who theorized that sun-spots had caused bad harvests and consequently economic depressions in the nineteenth century. See T.W.Hutchison, *A Review of Economic Doctrines 1870-1929* (London: Oxford University Press, 1953) 39.

came out and saw the Wise Men, their policemen and servants, roosting in a tall tree, trembling and in fear of their lives.

"Take all our possessions, but spare our lives," the Wise Men pleaded tearfully.

Whereat the simple folk were mightily amused -- so much so that they could scarce contain themselves with laughter.

"Behold!" they said. "Once the Wise Men made donkeys of us, but now they make monkeys of themselves. Verily it is a reversion to type." But when they saw that the Wise Men were like to really turn into gibbering apes for very fear, they called unto them:

"Come down ye jackanapes. What want we of silly lives? Ye would have had your retainers slay us, but we follow not in your wise and loving ways. We have other use for you than to slay you. Come down and we put you to work."

Thereupon the simple folk made proclamation that the commonwealth of simpletons was now fully established; and they set every man, wise and simple, to work at some useful labour, and unto each they gave a meal ticket, so that none might go hungry in that Isle. Also they turned the temples of finance into places of abode, and the gold in the vaults they beat into vessels for their tables. And now, because everybody laboured, they found that a few hours work each day sufficed to produce all the necessities and most of the luxuries that [were] good for them, so that they had many hours to spend playing with their children in the sunshine and teaching them many things or prying into the secrets of nature and the wonders of the heavens, or in whatsoever manner seemed good to them. Also the Wise Men that had been fat and unwieldy, grew lean and agile and strong of of wind and limb, and the simple folk, that had been lean and sallow, grew robust and of a fine and ruddy colour. And, moreover, because of plenty and health and leisure, they all knew much contentment, and there was much sport and great merry-making, and large increase in knowledge and love of nature and of humanity. And behold all the people were greatly astonished at the change that had been wrought in them, and in everything about them, and none more so than the Wise Men themselves.

"Verily, it is marvellous," they said one to the other. "Once we were fat and our fatness was a sore trouble for us, because of it we suffered with hardness of heart and indigestion and slept ill of nights. Once, too, we had great possessions and they also were a sore trouble to us, because of them we sat all day in stuffy offices making endless hyrogliphics on endless reams of parchment and always we worried greatly less robbers should despoil us. And moreover, because our sole ambition and desire was to do our fellows, we looked with distrust and suspicion upon all men, and our hearts were full of guile, and avarice, and every and all uncharitableness. But now, behold we are no longer cumbered with grossness of flesh, but are strong of mind and limb, and skip about in the sunshine like young roebuck rejoicing to run a race. And now, too, we look about with frank eyes, and lo, it is as though scales had fallen from them, for we see new beauties and new wonders in nature and in our fellow men. And moreover,we greet the simple folk like brothers, and rejoice to shake our hearts to them and in turn they shake out their hearts to us -- and wonder of wonders -- they are full of great and unsuspected treasures. Verily our wisdom is not to be compared with the simplicity of the simple folk."

But it came to pass that civilization heard how matters were going on the Isle of the simple folk, and how that the people did eat the victuals out of golden vessels and did leave stacks of the precious metal lying carelessly in their backyards; and naturally it was indignant, that the riches of the earth should be put to such barbaric and foolish uses. And so civilization did make proclamation that it had a mission to civilize that Isle, and it sent out a gun boat and blew the simple folk into the tall timber, and planted a colony there. And thus civilization was established in that Isle.

21. Capitalistic development and its cost[108]

That the development of capitalism in Nova Scotia has degraded the position of the workers is emphasized by Mr. McLachlan's[109] letter in the *Labor News* of August 24. It may be of interest to direct attention to another phase of the degradation of the working class. In the earlier stages of industrial development when the industrial capitalist is the dominant factor, some respect is shown for human life and limb. Some years ago the number of men killed or injured in the mines of Canada was very small. But since the financial capitalists have seized control of the mining industry of Canada, a brutal disregard of human life and limb has become apparent. The financial capitalists as a class have absolutely no conscience and no consideration for the working class; they have converted the coal mines of Canada into death traps. According to a report of the Canadian Conservation Commission for 1911, the number of coal miners killed in Canada is proportionately greater than in any other country. The report shows that, for the ten years from 1898 to 1908, the rate of fatal accidents per year for each thousand employes in various combines was as follows:

---

[108]*Eastern Labor News*, 31 August 1912 [letter to the editor].
[109]J.B.McLachlan (1869-1937), secretary-treasurer of the Nova Scotia district of the United Mine Workers of America, would subsequently become the most famous labour leader and radical politician in the history of the province.

Canada.......................5.00
United States...........3.50
Great Britain...........1.30
Belgium.....................1.03
France........................1.65
Prussia........................2.13

The report states that the death rate from coal mine accidents in Canada has been steadily on the increase for a number of years. In the west the death rate is considerably higher than in Nova Scotia, though the rate in the latter province is about twice as high as in Great Britain.

Capitalism develops a morality that supersedes the ten commandments. It controls all the organs of society; it has even hypnotized the working class. As against the interests of capital, human life has no sanctity; if capital is thereby consecrated, it is entirely right to kill the workers either in war or industry. And the capitalist view of the matter seems to be quite agreeable to the majority of the working class. No special opprobrium attaches to the capitalists who, to save a few dollars, maintain working conditions which inevitably cause loss of life and limb to members of the working class. Trade unions seek to help the victims of industrial accidents, but generally speaking have given little attention to the problem of preventing the maintenance of conditions conducive to accidents. Can you off-hand cite an instance of a trade union striking because working conditions were dangerous to life and limb?

22. Industrial Corporations and the People[110]

While in Canada gigantic conspiracies against the common weal such as the United States has been busy unearthing, are not in evidence as yet, it is unfortunately true that we do not lack manifestations of the evils of machine politics and frenzied finance. Our political bosses, our magnates of finance, and our captains of industry, have not yet grown sufficiently drunk with power to treat the rights of the people with cynical contempt; but at the same time it becomes more and more apparent that corporate rapacity -- working through various economical and political agencies, is insidiously undermining the public welfare. Corporations engineer schemes and carry on practices that the private individual would not dream of undertaking -- schemes and practises that often involve a violation of the rights of the people even though they be in strict accordance with the laws of the lands. Companies may be wrecked, shareholders robbed, the people plundered -- and our laws offer no redress.

---

[110]*Halifax Herald*, 5 August 1910 [letter to the editor].

The fact is not without an alarming significance. Government must establish rigid control over the corporations in the interest of the people, or a confederation of corporations will usurp the sovereign functions of government, and exercising them for their sole use and benefit, reduce the people to a galling state of dependence. Already our governments seem altogether too amenable to the control of the corporations; a big percentage of the legislative measures adopted by our parliaments are especially designed to assist corporations of some sort in the accomplishment of their purposes. And our legislators, while thus lending themselves to the service of aggregations of capital too often turn an unfriendly eye upon the plain people. That something is radically wrong, is shown by the fact that the corporations have absorbed practically all the advantages arising from the advancement of science and the progress of invention. The introduction of machinery, and the specialization of labour, have increased the productive capacity of men many times. As will be seen, by the following figures showing the hours of labour required to produce certain products by hand and by machinery, our good-getting efficiency has in many instances been multiplied over 20 times.

	Machine hours	Hand hours
Barley (100 bushels)	9	211
Oats (160 bushels)	28	265
Wheat (150 bushels)	7	160

Again where formerly it required [120] hours of hand labour to produce a plough, three hours of labour, aided by machinery, suffices for the same work, that is to say, the productivity of labour in this instance has been increased forty times. Where formerly it required 200 hours to place 100 tons of ore on railway cars, 2 hours is now sufficient; in this case efficiency has been multiplied 100 times, and so it goes through a hundred industries.

But have the people as a whole, reaped any adequate advantages from this amazing increase in efficiency? Are the plain people, the small merchants, and workingmen, ten or twenty times better off than they were a generation or so ago? Or have the hours of labour been reduced ten or twenty times? It is said that Canada's remarkable industrial development in recent years has greatly benefitted the workingman -- that he enjoys more comfort, more conveniences and luxuries. But it may be said, too, that what he has gained in these respects had been more than discounted by his loss of independence and security. When industry was carried on by individuals, the workingman was more independent and more secure of employment, because there was not only a relatively larger number of employers competing for his services, but [also because] it was then a comparatively easy matter for him to take up some craft or business on his own account. But now that industry is concentrated in big establishments controlled by corporations, the many are dependent upon the few for the opportunity to earn a livelihood -- at any rate this is the case in cities. Able men may still rise from the ranks; but they rise by assisting the growth of the corporations -- not by establishing independent industries. And as the position of the corporations is strengthened, that of the mass of the workers becomes more helpless, absolutely dependent upon the corporations for the opportunity to live; the city worker hardly dares call his soul his own, and he lives in constant fear that some new invention, or change in the managerial policy, will throw him out of his job.

The white man's civilization is, indeed, a curious thing; the more we advance, the greater the poverty and distress in our big cities. In England, the richest and in some respects the most progressive country in the world, the bulk of the working classes are, according to Professor Thorold Rogers[111], thirteen times worse off than they were in the fourteenth century; and Froude[112], the historian, was of a very similar opinion. And unhappily the conditions established in England seem to be in process of evolution in the new world. Clearly, then, the great increase in the efficiency of labour, due to the progress of science and invention and the organization of production on a large scale, has brought no corresponding advantages to the working classes. Nor has it brought many benefits to the small merchants and businessmen. Indeed, the position of this class, both in cities and towns, is in some respects less secure than that of the workingman. Struggling against the competition of big departmental stores or mail order concerns, they are often hard put to it to keep out of bankruptcy.

The present situation is not at all flattering to our intelligence or self-respect. A confederation of corporations has usurped about all the benefits flowing from the progress of civilization, and the tendency of things in Canada as in other countries is to divide society into two classes; the few who own and manage everything and the [many] who [grow] more and more dependent upon the few for the opportunity to earn a meager living. That government policies, to a great extent, evoke and aggravate this evil cannot be seriously denied. Note the subjects and course of

---

111McKay is referring to James E. Thorold Rogers (1823-1890), an English economist and historian. He taught at King's College, London, and also served as an M.P. His books include *History of Agriculture and Prices in England, 1259-1793* (1866-1902), 7 vols.; *Six Centuries of Work and Wages* (1884); *The Relations of Economic Science to Social and Political Action* (1888). Rogers's historical approach provided significant inspiration to those eager to challenge classical economics.

112McKay is referring to James Anthony Froude (1818-1894), historian and imperialist propagandist, who took up the editorship of *Frazer's Magazine* following a tempestuous involvement with the Oxford Movement. His works included *History of England from the Fall of Wolsey to the Death of Elizabeth* (1871); *English Seamen* (1895).

legislation, study the spirit of the laws, and you cannot fail to perceive that more and more the idea of the "transfer" of the surplus products of industry, and the creation of facilities for it, available to the cunning and quick as against the dull and slow, has come to pervade the whole fabric of that which we call government. Even men of large and progressive minds have come to accept as a fundamental truth in political doctrine the idea that the best way to take care of the many is to help the few, that to give the corporations special privileges is all that is necessary to secure the well-being of the workingmen.

23. The Small Businessman[113]

Small businessmen do not occupy a very enviable position. Many of them cannot earn as much as the skilled mechanic, most of them are obliged to put in more hours of service than the mechanic. On the one hand they are menaced by the competition of the big departmental stores and mail order concerns, on the other by the combines of manufacturers and wholesalers bent on reducing them to a condition of economic vassalage. And their position is much more precarious than that of the skilled workingman, who has a certain measure of security and livelihood. Witness the great number of failures in the small business world every year -- a pitiable record of blighted ambitions and ruined hopes. Note too the hostility of the small trader to the early closing movement. The marvellous progress and prosperity we read so much about can not have brought in any advantages to this class, when they deem it necessary to be at their counters 16 or 18 hours a day....

Sometimes the small businessmen are referred to as members of the uneasy class. And certainly they have some cause for uneasiness. Every day some of them are being crowded off their precarious perch into the ranks of the wage workers or unemployed. And even those who manage to maintain a foothold are losing all semblance of independence.

Many small traders think they are made of finer clay and occupy a better position than the workingmen. Many of them have a proprietorship in their business, and the idea of property carries with it an idea of dignity and independence. But the fact is the proprietorship of an individual enterprise does not make a capitalist of the individual who owns and operates the enterprise or business. The development of the larger capitalism in the form of the impersonal corporation has... transformed the economic character of private property. Capitalist private property based on the exploitation of the labour of others, has supplanted private property acquired by personal labour and based on the union of the

---

[113]Originally published as "The Small Business Man. How the Capitalist System Annihilates Self-earned Private Property and Reduces the Small Business Man to the Economic Category of the Worker," *Eastern Labor News*, 8 June 1912.

individual, independent and isolated, with the conditions of his particular work, says Marx in effect.[114] Great capital in its record phase of development attacks the small capitalist. The capitalist mode of production and accumulation and therefore capitalist private property have for their fundamental condition the annihilation of self-earned private property.

Here is an important point. A man does not become a capitalist by virtue of his possession of self-earned private property. The farmer working his own piece of land without help, the small trader running his own store, get no returns upon their capital investment, they only get a meagre wage for their labour. The carpenter has to invest a good deal of money in tools, but we do not find the all-round carpenter in a small town with an extensive kit of tools making as much money as the specialist carpenter in a larger city with comparatively few tools, as we might expect to do if property in tools was a form of capital. Capitalistic property in the means of production begins with -- or at least implies the possibility of -- the exploitation of the labour of others.

...The development of capitalism, while leaving the small traders, the farmers and other classes in legal possession of their means of existence, nevertheless appropriates most of the fruits of their labour and ingenuity. Yet there is little doubt that the small trader is exploited quite as effectively as the farmer and the industrial worker. If the proprietor of a business carried on by himself without help owns his shop or store, he may get a return that corresponds to rent, provided there are a sufficient number of his competitors occupying rented premises to make it customary to incorporate the item of rent in the prices charged consumers. If, however, all or a considerable majority of his competitors own their premises he has as little chance of receiving interest on his store capital as on his stock in trade.

When the proprietor of a small business employs help he becomes a capitalist in the sense that he becomes an exploiter of the labour of other[s], but it does not follow that he is thereby able to convert his private property into capitalist property, and obtain capitalistic returns. The Saint John *Globe* the other day declared that few daily papers in Eastern Canada could be considered as capitalistic journals, because the

---

[114]See Marx and Engels, *The Communist Manifesto*, trans. Samuel Moore (Chicago: Gateway, 1954), 41-42: "We Communists have been reproached with the desire of abolishing the right of personally acquiring property as the fruit of a man's own labor, which property is alleged to be the groundwork of all his personal freedom, activity and independence....Hard-won, self-acquired, self-earned property! Do you mean the property of the petty artisan and of the small peasant, a form of property that preceded the bourgeois form? There is no need to abolish that; the development of industry has to a great extent already destroyed it, and is still destroying it daily."

best of them hardly provided a livelihood for their proprietors. Many other businesses representing a considerable capital investment and employing as many people as a daily newspaper do not yield their proprietors much more than wages of superintendence. Newspaper enterprises, being carried on for political or other purposes, are not typical of this class of business, though they have the same characteristic of not readily lending themselves to centralization and of being dependent upon local conditions or serving special needs. The larger capitalism does not crush out these enterprises, but when it ... controls essential factors in the carrying on of such enterprises it can easily absorb the lion's share of the profits. There is little danger of the big paper companies, the telegraph companies, and the press associations, allowing the proprietors of small daily papers to die rich. And now that we have for instance, a Canadian boot and shoe manufacturers' combine, there is not much danger that it will allow the proprietors of the smaller shoe stores to achieve fortunes that will make it difficult for them to enter the Kingdom of Heaven.

Capitalist property is rapidly overthrowing the institution of private property, or robbing it of any virtue. In its typical form it presents itself as a piece of paper, which confers upon its holder an impersonal right. No stockholder of the C.P.R. has any personal property rights in any locomotive, car or station of that railway. In this depersonalization of capitalist property, [this separation of] greed from all connection with the actual labour of the possessor, the economist, A. Menger[115], sees an important factor in the process of transforming capitalist property into collective or public property: "The more the disproportion between legal title and real power," he says, "the more complete the change from moderate to small property to large property and from the latter into the mere possession of titles, the weaker grows the inner structure of the whole system of private titles. In this increasing separation between legal title and physical power, which is certainly one of the characteristic traits of our epoch, I see the most important factor which is pushing our system of private titles into socialism. This juridical fact is more important than the economic concentration of the means of production into a smaller number of hands upon which Marx and other socialists principally insist."

When the small traders realize that the business they carry on cannot be generally regarded as their personal property, when they perceive that the institution of private property is no longer the basis of civilization, they will recognize the necessity of hastening the process of evolution and transforming capitalist property into collective property, that is to take out

[115]McKay is referring to Anton Menger (1841-1906), who was professor of civil procedure at the University of Vienna from 1877. He was noted for studying the juridical theory of socialism rather than its strictly economic aspects. His works include *The Right to the Whole Produce of Labour* (1886); *Neue Staatslehre* (1903).

of the hands of the few and vest in the public the power of exploitation which resides in capitalist property -- a consummation which will leave the small trader in possession of his business, if it is socially necessary, and allow him to get something more than a mere subsistence wage. The larger capitalism has reduced the small businessmen, as it has the farmers, to the same economic classification as the piece-worker in industry, and since their interests are identical with the workers, they must, as they are doing in Germany, join with the workers in a political movement to capture the government, the executive committee of the capitalist class and use their political power to overthrow capitalism and establish the co-operative commonwealth.

24. The Master Magicians[116]

The Saint John Globe the other day remarked that it was surprising that an editor of fifty years ago did not boast about the benefits of the shipbuilding industry in the way of giving employment to workingmen. The reference seemed to be made in a satiric vein. The Globe is one of the few newspapers in Canada that have remained loyal to the political philosophy of liberalism, and I suppose it was taking a sly dig at one of the shibboleths with which the modern capitalist has hypnotized the public mind. Its remark at any rate was very significant, in that it throws a side light upon the present predicament of the Liberal Party in the province.

The old shipbuilders evidently did not waste much time boasting about how their industry benefitted the people. The[y] probably took the view that they were building ships primarily for their own benefit; they were probably honest enough to admit that they were not in business for the purpose of giving employment to labour, but for the purpose of making profits for themselves, by obliging the workers to create products worth considerably more than their wages. They paid their taxes and do not seem to have expected many favours from the public. Railway promoters had not trained the people to provide corporations with money and credit to construct railways, to be operated for the benefit of the corporations. Manufacturers had not educated the people into an almost unshakeable belief in the doctrine of protection.

One of the tenets of the old liberal philosophy was that men ought to think for themselves. That involves effort. So we have allowed the seekers of privileges of various kinds to think for us. We have been persuaded that every corporation is in business mainly for the benefit of the public. Our governments act on the idea that the best way to take care of the many is

---

[116]Originally published as "The Master Magicians: How the Seekers of Privilege have Hypnotized the Public Mind, and Incidentally Destroyed the Liberal Party," *Eastern Labor News*, 6 July 1912.

to begin by helping the few. We have swallowed a curious array of arguments in support of protection; we accept without question a whole system of sophistries built upon them. So thorough is our education that we are eager to grant tax exemptions, free water, free sites, bonuses and subventions to anybody who proposes to start a new enterprise which will employ perhaps a few women and boys....

Considering how completely we have been hypnotized by ideas which embody the desires of the capitalist or landlord for public plunder, it is no wonder the so-called Liberal Party has suffered such severe reverses. So far as New Brunswick is concerned there is a measure of poetic justice in the rout of the so-called Liberals. Mr. Pugsley's organs have been ardent champions of the economic sophistries which are the [logical] outgrowths of our high tariff doctrines. Note that I say our high tariff doctrines -- that is, the arguments now advanced in support of the protective policy. When protection was just mooted in the United States there were certain fairly good arguments advanced in support of it, but those arguments are not often used now. Alexander Hamilton, the father of protection in the United States, frankly stated that protective tariffs were intended to help the capitalist. He made no pretense whatever of benefitting the workingman; his whole argument was that the American workingmen were getting such high wages that the American manufacturer could not compete with his foreign rival unless he had special privileges in his home market. Nowadays the principal argument for high tariffs is that by protecting the manufacturer we benefit the workingmen, a rather plausible argument, but none the less misleading and mischievous. The development of our protective industries has increased the number of workers, but it is hard to see how it has benefitted the workers as a class. Certainly they are less independent, less secure of a livelihood than their fathers were, and relatively they are worse off than the workers of any age, because they get a much smaller proportion of the values they produce than the workers of any previous era.

This idea that capitalistic development spells prosperity for the workers has been industriously fostered by the capitalists, landlords, and other beneficiaries till it has come to pervade all our thoughts. Yet it is not an idea that workingmen would have much faith in if they studied history or looked around them. In Pittsburgh and Sydney we find capitalistic development in its most typical forms, and it is precisely in those great industrial centres, blessed by high protection, tax exemptions, and bonuses that we find the more deplorable conditions of labour.

In the 18th century the Venetian Monk Orter [Ortes][117], a writer on economics, said: "The wealth of a nation corresponds with its population,

---

[117]Giamaria Ortes (1713-1790) was an Italian economist who anticipated Malthus in noting the tendency of population to increase in a 'geometrical ratio' while food tended

and its misery corresponds with its wealth."[118] About the same time, Townsend,[119] an English parson, glorified misery as a necessary condition of wealth, arguing that everything from the view point of the rich, depended upon making hunger or the fear of it, a permanent condition among the working class.

And deTracy[120] blurted out brutally: "In poor nations, the people are comfortable; in rich nations they are generally poor."[121]

Our governments, federal, provincial, civic, have been according all kinds of public support to capitalists, without, as a condition of these special favours, placing any restrictions calculated to protect the workers or the general public. Tory and Liberal governments alike have protected the manufacturer's product from competition, while spending millions of the people's money to bring in immigrants to compete with the workers for jobs -- certainly a great injustice. If we had not been hypnotized by capitalistic ideas, we would surely have tried to organize a labour party, or in some way to compel our governments to impose upon capitalists enjoying special privileges, the obligations of sharing some of the fruits of progress with the working class.

But we are shallow thinkers -- so shallow that we do not see that governments always act in the interests of big business. Here in Saint John

---

to increase merely in an 'arithmetical ratio.' He also paralleled the work of contemporaneous English mercantilists. His main works include *Reflessioni sulla popolzione* (1790) and *Economia nazionale* (1744).

[118]McKay is borrowing this quotation (from G. Ortes, *Della economia nazionale libri sie*) directly from Marx, *Capital: A Critique of Political Economy,* Vol. I (New York: Modern Library, n.d.), 709-10.

[119]Joseph Townsend (1739-1816), an English clergyman who wrote on the subject of poor laws, population growth, and travel in Europe. McKay is borrowing directly from Marx, *Capital: A Critique of Political Economy*. See Marx, *Capital: A Critique of Political Economy,* Vol.I (New York: International Publishers, 1967), 800. Among Townsend's works are *Observations on Various Plans for the Relief of the Poor* (1788) and *Free Thoughts on Despotic and Free Governments* (1781).

[120]Count Antoine-Louis-Claude Destutt de Tracy (1754-1836) was a *philosophe*, army officer and politician. Committed to the principles of the French Revolution, in 1789 he renounced his titles and privileges and voted for the rights of man; he was imprisoned in 1792 at the height of the Terror. He initiated the concept of "ideology" and wrote an important commentary on Montesquieu. His ideas concerning the measurement of value were subsequently of significance for Ricardo. His works include *Quels sont les moyens de fonder la morale chez un peuple?* (Paris, 1798); *Commentaire sur l'Esprit des lois* (Paris, 1828); *Eléments d'idéologie* (Paris, 1801).

[121]McKay is borrowing this quotation (from de Tracy's *Traité de la Volonté et de ses Effets,* 1815) directly from Karl Marx. See Marx, *Capital: A Critique of Political Economy,* I (New York: International Publishers, 1967), 648. He has even retained Marx's polemical tone.

we are continually told that if it hadn't been for Pugsley there would never have been any great developments at Courtenay Bay. Were we to consider the matter for a moment we would recognize that the development of Courtenay Bay was a foregone conclusion before Pugsley entered federal politics. When certain railway magnates persuaded the government to build them a new transcontinental, they also laid plans to get the government to provide a winter terminal at the people's expense. They played their cards well by running the road to Moncton, started a rivalry between Halifax and Saint John, and induced both cities to demand that the government provide the terminals -- something that the railway magnates ought to do at their own expense. And naturally the most natural location for the winter terminals was selected. Of course part of the game was to allow Mr. Pugsley and other politicians to make a parade of their own importance, and talk as if they were something more than mere puppets.

25. Mr. Hatheway and Technical Education[122]

Mr. W.F. Hatheway[123] has written many articles and made not a few speeches on the subject of technical education. Probably his efforts have not been altogether in vain, but a man with new or rather modern ideas, is generally regarded as a disturber of the peace in Eastern Canada. Sometime ago an Americanized Frenchman paid a visit here and put his impressions in a book saying the people of this province shut their minds against the revelations of science and clinging to the ideas of their grandfathers, fell asleep and snored. So far as the working class is concerned this criticism appears to be correct; they sleep so soundly and snore so loudly that they do not know what is going on in the world....

Nevertheless I sympathize with Mr. Hatheway's ideas. Some years ago I was an enthusiast about technical education. I wrote many articles on the subject for the Montreal Herald and the Montreal Standard. At that time I called myself a Socialist, but I still had the individualistic view point. I thought that the increased efficiency of the workers was the chief benefit to be derived from technical education.

---

[122]*Eastern Labor News*, 18 January 1913.

[123]Warren Franklin Hatheway (1850-1923) was one of the most prominent social reformers in New Brunswick in the early twentieth century. He actively fought for workers' compensation, housing reform, and women's suffrage, while also functioning as a businessman. He ran unsuccessfully as a Conservative candidate in Saint John in 1903, and won a seat in the Legislative Assembly of New Brunswick in 1908. Among his books are *God and the Doubter* (n.d.); *Poorhouse and Palace: A Plea for a Better Distribution of Wealth* (n.d.); *Canadian Nationality: The Cry of Labour* (1906); *Why France Lost Canada, and other Essays and Poems* (1915).

Today I am not so sure of that. Today I realize that while technical education may advance the interests of certain members of the working class it does not follow that it will improve the condition of the working class as a whole. Nothing is more certain than that with the increase in the productivity of labour the position of the labourer has become more precarious....

Technical education is desirable for the reason that it will tend to cultivate the power and habit of reasoning among the working class. Our public school and Sunday School education is not calculated to make us reasonable beings; they teach us to believe things that are contrary to reason. Even the pedagogues themselves admit that public school education has proved a failure. Usually it is true, the pedagogues' point of view is not of any importance; they think they have failed because everybody does not become millionaires. But they are right in one respect -- our public and Sunday School instruction is unscientific and unreasonable. Most of us have gone through the mill, and most of us are credulous, bigoted humbugs, swayed by silly prejudices, easily led by the nose by crooks of all sorts, with the gift of gab.

Often you hear it said: The State's greatest asset is an educated citizenship. But at present the State is merely the guardian of class interest, and State instruction is merely designed to train the workers for a position of docile servitude. Nothing could be more absurd than for the workers to commit the education of their children to immature girls in public schools or Sunday schools, paid by a class state, to teach the children to be docile slaves of a class state. If the workers were awake they would try to get control of the school boards and see that their children were taught history and everything else from the view point of their class, were made to realize the position of their class under capitalism, and to understand the methods by which they are exploited out of the bulk of the product of their labour.

26. Capitalism--The Modern Frankenstein[124]

Capitalism is getting over-ripe and rotten. It need not follow, however, that capitalists are rotten in the eyes of the people. The over-ripe apple is generally the finest looking apple in the orchard. The capitalists, those who do no useful work, but draw handsome dividends, are generally the most refined product of modern civilization....

....At the St. George's Society banquet in Saint John the other day the Bishop of Fredericton declared that unless the men who controlled the sources of the world's wealth gave a better account of their stewardship, there would be an overthrow of the existing order by the oppressed

---

[124]*Eastern Labor News*, 3 May 1913.

masses. Mr. Culver, the United States Consul at Saint John, spoke in a similar strain, deploring the oppression of the masses in his own country, and expressing grave fears that unless the public authorities rose to the emergency and curbed the power of the octopus there would be a great revolution, a general overthrow of the cherished institutions of capitalism.

Such speeches, delivered on such an occasion, are significant. A banquet of St. George's Society is one of the most typical of bourgeois functions. But the warnings of the Bishop and the Consul made little impression upon the gathering, gorged to repletion and mellowed by champagne. Subsequent speakers did not rise above the balderdash, dear to the heart of the infatuated bourgeoisie. The death-head at the feast did not worry the ancient Egyptians. Eat, drink and be merry, etc. Whom the gods would destroy they first make mad or blind....

Anybody who reads the papers with a discerning eye must be struck by the decadence of capitalist society. Scarcely a day passes without the papers reporting some event which indicates that the bourgeoisie are arrant hypocrites or merely mad. Everywhere, even in Saint John, we see them busily discussing housing problems, social evils and what not, exhibiting a sentimental and generally fruitless interest in reform. That merely means that they are dissatisfied and more or less disgusted with the civilization which their class has created.

But there is no reason to suppose the bourgeoisie can put a new spirit into their Frankenstein creation. Capitalism is beyond repair. The bourgeois nations, unable to trust one another, are irresistably carried toward bankruptcy. Even so-called statesmen admit that the race for armaments is sheer madness. But every bourgeois nation is spurred on to more frantic efforts to hold its place in the mad race; the more they talk of peace the more strenuous becomes the race. Where will it end? It must end in bankruptcy. No nation can indefinitely keep on building battleships, or increasing its military forces; and a war between England and Germany would not settle anything -- it would only lead to the more speedy bankruptcy of both nations.

The bourgeoisie, because they have no faith in God or man, are running headlong into a cul de sac. They cannot carry civilization any farther forward. Their rule must be broken, the capitalist system must be overthrown, the working class must take charge of affairs in the interests of humanity.

ii. The Need for Sociology

27. The Duty of the Rich to the Poverty-Laden[125]

"And yet, strange to say, now that this truth is recognized by most cultivated people, now that the beneficent working of the survival of the fittest has been so impressed on them that much more than people in past times, they might be expected to hesitate before neutralizing its action -- now more than ever before in the history of the world are they doing all they can to further the survival of the unfittest." -- Herbert Spencer, in *The Man vs. The State.*[126]

And therefore, the rich, and the strong should not seek to uplift the poor and the weak. It is reprehensible to interfere with the operation of the law of natural selection -- the law of Spencer, of nature, of God. The rich and the strong are not only justified in leaving the poor and weak in their miserable condition, but would be justified in aggravating those conditions, in order to crush out, to eliminate, the poor, the weak, the unfit. As Spencer shows the operation of the principle of natural selection, or survival of the fittest is always beneficial -- there might is always and inevitably right. "Those shoulderings aside of the weak by the strong which leave so many in shallows and in miseries" (*Social Statics*)[127] are God's chosen means of improving society under the working of this natural law. Thus, in a natural, just and righteous state of society the perfect rule is -- every man for himself and the devil take the hindmost.

While there is no doubt a great deal of truth in the principle of evolution, it is doubtful whether its operation in human society follows the same lines that it does in animal and plant life. Anyway it is highly improbable, as Goldwin Smith remarks, that the history of evolution as propounded by Spencer or Darwin will satisfactorily explain everything in heaven and on earth. Spencer's philosophy may explain things which were not dreamed of in Horatio's philosophy, but it does not cover the universe.

If Spencer had not been so intent on proving his theory of evolution applicable to all departments of life, whether of plant, animal, human, mental or moral, he should have perceived that the operation of the principle of evolution as exemplified in human society, differs from its operation in the lower forms of life. In man, there is a reasoning

---

[125]Originally published as "Duty of the Rich to the Poverty-Laden. The Philosophy of Charity, Showing it to be to the Interest of the Rich and Strong to Help the Weak," *Montreal Herald*, 21 January 1899.

[126]McKay is citing Herbert Spencer, *The Man Versus The State* (London: Watts & Co., 1909), 59.

[127]McKay is citing Herbert Spencer, *Social Statics: Or, The Conditions Essential to Human Happiness Specified, and the First of Them Developed* (New York, 1875): 354.

intelligence, which, as it develops, enables him to rise superior to the laws of nature. Of this factor Spencer has taken little account. As a consequence, many of his theories in regard to the operation of evolution in human society are falsified by man's ingenuity in escaping the rigid operation of laws which the lower forms of life are unable to evade.

A little consideration will convince anyone that the law of selection among animals differs from the law of selection in human society. In the animal world competition is perfect; the struggle for survival rages on the individualistic principle. In human society competition, except among the most primitive peoples, has never been perfect; the selfish and unjust have combined against the sympathetic and generous, the strong against the weak. Animals are the slaves of nature; they are powerless before nature's forces. Men are the masters of nature; they harness nature's forces -- bridle them to their will. In human societies where men have not yet learned the mastery of nature, where some have not learned to combine against others, the operation of the law of selection might produce good results. But in the present system of society it is apparent that the survival of the fittest has degenerated into the survival of the slickest. ...

In one of his works Spencer protests against the law of sympathy in families being made the law of guidance in government or societies.[128] The law of survival of the fittest precludes not only help, but sympathy, to the unfit. If society was based on perfect individualism, no one would need help or sympathy, for perfect individualism implies not only perfect equality of opportunity, but equality in all respects. Individualism means the ignoring of all social relations, the repudiation of the brotherhood of man. If we had perfect individualism we would have no civilization. As protection in its ultimate application would prohibit each family from trading with every other family, so individualism precludes the individual from enjoying the benefits of industrial or social intercourse with other individuals. In the world to-day there is little individualism. Our civilization is the result of the application of cooperation. As men combine to carry on industry, or for any purpose, we get further and further from the primitive individualism. A combination of men destroys equality of opportunity and makes the struggle for existence harder for those who do not combine. As a consequence, those for whom the struggle for survival has been made more difficult, become, by the extra tax on their energies, weaker than their more fortunate fellows. In this manner inequality was born into the world, and becomes more marked with the better organization of industry and the increasing complexity of society.

Now, will anyone contend that those who, by combining, destroyed equality, increased the difficulties of existence and thus made many

---

[128]McKay is paraphrasing Spencer, *Social Statics:* 348-352.

weaker and less fitted for the struggle, do not owe some compensation to the men who suffered in order that they (the combiners) might make the struggle easier for themselves? It seems to us that the rich and strong are responsible to a large extent for the pitiable condition of the poor and weak, and that therefore they are in duty bound to help their less fortunate fellows. In fact, it is to their interest to do so. A greater philosopher than Spencer has said, "We are members of one another"[129]; and consequently if one member suffers all members must suffer with it. Spencer himself admits this. As Baalam of old,[130] Spencer saddles his ass of "evolution" and seeks to go with the princes of Moab. But often the ass of a theory turns aside out of the way. And when Spencer would go down to curse the poor children of Israel, the ass of evolution opens its mouth and says:

"All classes of society mutually affect one another, and their moral states are much alike. Thus the alleged homogeneity of national character is abundantly exemplified. And so long as the assimilating influences productive of it continue to work, it is folly to suppose any one grade of a community can be morally different from the rest. In whichever rank you see corruption be assured it pervades all ranks -- be assured it is the symptom of a bad social diathesis. Whilst the veins of depravity exist in one part of the body politic, no other part can remain healthy." -- *Social Statics.*[131]

---

[129]McKay is citing Paul's Letter to the *Ephesians* 4:25, which in the King James version reads: "Wherefore putting away lying, speak everyman truth with his neighbour: for we are members one of another."

[130]McKay -- assuming, as did most writers of his time, that his readers would have a thorough knowledge of the Bible -- is citing the *Book of Numbers*, 22:1-24:25. Balaam, a man who could speak with God, and beseech His intervention in human affairs, learned from God that the Israelites were His chosen people; he nonetheless persisted in consorting with the princes of Moab. On the road to Moab, an angel of the Lord appeared to Balaam's ass, at which the ass refused to go forward. After Balaam had struck the ass three times, God spoke through the ass's mouth, repeating his command that Balaam not go to Moab. The implication: by stubbornly persisting on a course he knew to be wrong, Balaam was led astray; in the end, the Truth was revealed. Spencer, in his attempt to ride the ass of evolutionary theory to reactionary ends, would find that the evolutionary theory he had developed would subvert his intentions. Many contemporary Spencer scholars are in complete agreement with McKay's critique.

[131]McKay is citing, with significant modifications, Herbert Spencer, *Social Statics:* 256. In the original, Spencer remarks, "...a reference to the sporting papers will show that the lingering instincts of the savage are at this moment exhibited by about an equal percentage of all classes," and, in the next paragraph, writes: "Thus the alleged homogeneity of national character is abundantly exemplified. And so long as the assimilating influences productive of it continue at work, it is folly to suppose any one grade of a community can be morally different from the rest. In whichever rank you see corruption, be assured it equally pervades all ranks -- be assured it is the symptom of a bad social diathesis. Whilst the virus of depravity exists in one part of the body politic, no other part can remain healthy." It would seem clear, from his "bending" of Spencer's text, that McKay is reading into Spencer a doctrine of the permanent mutuality of

If, as Spencer shows, all suffer together, reason prompts us to prevent the degradation and suffering of the lower strata in society. If the rich and strong suffer with the poor and weak, then it is to the interest of the rich and strong to help to uplift the poor and the weak out of their misery. Such a course is the logical conclusion from Spencer's premises in this case. If it cannot be reconciled with the policy of laissez faire -- the non-interference with the "beneficent operation of the survival of the fittest" -- it only shows Spencer's inconsistency and the necessity of making reservations in the theory of natural selection as an operative principle in human society.

It is a fact that the working of natural selection tends to eliminate the unfit and weak, and increase the fit and strong. In human society there are no striking evidence[s] of the operation of such a law. Take a fact of everyday observation in connection with this survival business. Are the strong and the fit increasing in numbers? Are the poor and weak going to the wall and becoming extinct? It does not appear so. The strong, the rich, the fit, the managers and captains of industry, are not very [busily] engaged in peopling the world with their kind. They have few children. On the other hand, the poor, the unfit, bear children at a reckless rate. As the old proverb says, "The workingmen for babies." The lower down in the scale the greater the number of the unfit that are born into the world. Abject poverty induces a recklessness and indifference and the poor propagate their kind without thought or care how they are to provide for them. It may be mentioned, too, as a well known biological fact, that badly nourished people are generally more prolific than those in better circumstances. In New Zealand, the number of births has decreased with the betterment of the circumstances of the working class. Of course, this result should not be wholly attributed to the lower fecundity of better nourishment, but also to the higher notions of comfort, and the desire of the workingmen to prevent his children from descending in the scale.

All these considerations go to show that it is unwise to trust to the grim gods of evolution to work out the salvation of society. They are pagan gods -- they require awful human sacrifices.

The rich and strong owe a duty to the poor and unfit, and many are beginning to realize and accept the responsibility. In obedience to the imperative impulse of the spirit of Christianity the "social conscience" is awakening among men. Out of the ashes of Aristocracy, Phoenix-like, the new Democracy arises. In the acknowledgement of the Fatherhood of God, men accept the law of the brotherhood of man. As the best men rise to the conception of the brotherhood of man, they realize that their moneys

---

classes not to be found in the original. And structural interconnections via "veins" are far more enduring and substantial than interconnection via a virus, which may be of short duration.

or talents are stewardships to be used not to subserve mere personal ends, but to minister to the welfare of their fellow-men.

In Canada, the social conscience is beginning to find noble expression in all departments of life. The great universities and churches are becoming the seats of social unrest -- the leaders in social reform. The clergy realize that the question of wages is more of a religious question than the question of the trinity, the problem of the unemployed than the problem of Jonah and the whale. The professors realize that social problems of England today are of more vital interest than those of Greece and Rome. And they accept the social responsibilities shouldered upon them by the awakening of the social conscience of the new democracy. They know that it is wrong that men should vainly seek work -- that thousands should want in the midst of luxury -- that girls should be driven by hundreds of thousands to the streets -- that unjust social relations should make a mockery of life. And they feel that it is the duty of the strong and the rich to right these wrongs -- to help men to live the lives of men.

28. Science and the Working Man[132]

Modern science is for the most part an unexplored world to those for whom science has the most pregnant message -- the workingmen. Our minds are stuffed with the metaphysical garbage of the middle ages. In the school, the press, even in the pulpit, ideas are gravely presented as serious and important truths which to say the least have no positive relations to the facts or conditions of modern life. And a large number of time-serving intellectual lackeys are engaged in distorting the truths of science which tend to set the working men thinking, and make them realize the possibility of emancipating their class from the unsatisfactory conditions obtaining today, with the result that a large number of working men have become suspicious of science itself.

Darwinism is put forward by some as a justification of the competitive system of industry. But Darwin himself would have been the first to repudiate such an idea.[133] Evolution in the natural world does not operate in quite the same way as evolution in human society. The mental environment is the dominant influence in the life of a plant or an animal, but the economic environment, which man creates for himself, may be a more important influence than his natural environment. As Ward,[134] the

---

[132]*Eastern Labor News*, 18 November 1911.

[133]That this may have been wishful thinking on McKay's part emerges forcefully from Adrian Desmond and James Moore, *Darwin* (New York: Warner Books, 1991).

[134]Lester Frank Ward (1841-1913) turned to sociology after a stint in the American treasury department and a career as a geologist and botanist; he began writing *Dynamic Sociology* with the explicit purpose of refuting Spencer. He occupied the chair in sociology at Brown University from 1906 to 1913, and was the first president of the

greatest of the American sociologists, says, "the environment transforms the animal, but man transforms his environment." [135]

Civilization is a development beyond the animal stage. Its chief factor is psychic -- the application of reason to the problems of life. Nature is largely irrational -- insanely wasteful of life. Society is increasingly rational -- it uses its power to conserve life. Nature is largely competitive; society is increasingly co-operative.

Society's wealth consists of human achievements -- inventions or improved processes of production. According to those who rigidly apply the principles of biology to human affairs, all the fruits and achievements should be appropriated by inventors, those who make achievement possible. Cunning and intelligence is said to be the reason why some persons occupy higher and others lower positions in the strata of society, just as physical strength formerly determined one's position. This, it is said, is the natural state and as it should be. It is moreover affirmed that being natural there is no possibility of altering it.

But as Ward in his *Applied Sociology* points out, the whole history of the world shows that "those who have achieved have received no reward."[136] It is a common saying that inventors usually die in beggary. Edison is the conspicuous exception which proves the rule. Great thinkers have been as unfortunate as the inventors.

And there is no possibility of all the fruits of achievement going to those who made them possible, and no reason either. The inventor [himself drew] upon the sum of human knowledge, developed by the co-operation of many minds, most of them dead for thousands of years. A modern locomotive represents 22,000 inventions.

There is only one rational way to deal with the inventions, the improved processes, which have so greatly increased the productivity of labour. They should be utilized for the benefit of all -- not for the benefit of a class who by the accident of its position, and its control of the political power, is able to absorb all the advantages of civilization.

American Sociological Society. His books include *Dynamic Sociology* (1883), *Psychic Factors of Civilization* (1906); *Pure Sociology* (1903); and *Applied Sociology* (1906).

[135]McKay is citing (and slightly changing) Lester F. Ward, *Pure Sociology: A Treatise on the Origin and Spontaneous Development of Society* (New York: Macmillan, 1925), 16: "The formula that expresses this distinction [between organic and social evolution] most clearly is that *the environment transforms the animal, while man transforms the environment*."

[136]McKay is citing Lester F. Ward, *Applied Sociology: A Treatise on the Conscious Improvement of Society By Society* (Boston: Ginn & Company, 1906), 22: "The whole history of the world shows that those who have achieved have received no reward."

29. The Message of Sociology[137]

Sociology is a comparatively new study. Its exponents call it the crown of all the sciences. It deals with human society, and seeks to generalize the whole range of human activities and formulate the laws of social evolution.

One of the best known sociologists in America is Professor Albion Small.[138] He does not call himself a Socialist. But both Socialists and trade unions may find in his *General Sociology* many observations which support their view of the mission of the working class.

Prof. Small claims that sociology will "serve as a pass key to all the theoretical difficulties about society that each of us may encounter." And he arrives at the socialist position by showing that the sociologist, like the socialist, accepts the principle of historical materialism as the pass key to social phenomena. Popular histories are mainly concerned with the political aspects of human progress and to that extent are superficial. To understand political movements we must seek the causes of which they are but a manifestation; we must use the key of economic determinism. Small says, "Indeed, we have come to realize that politics at bottom is very largely a manoeuvering to control the means of controlling wealth."[139]

Small is no respecter of capitalistic property or capitalistic ethics. "In the first place," he says, "capital itself produces nothing. It earns nothing. This is contrary to general economic presumption." And again, "Civilization involves an approach to a situation in which each person shall be a person not a commodity to other persons, in which also each person shall be equally free with every other person to develop the personality latent in his natural endowment, not the sort of personality to which he would be limited by arbitrary division of opportunity."[140]

137*Eastern Labor News*, 14 September 1912.

138Albion Woodbury Small (1854-1926) graduated in divinity from Colby College in 1876, studied history in Berlin and Leipzig from 1879 to 1881, and took up the teaching of sociology while president of Colby College. In 1892, he was invited to initiate the department of sociology at the newly-established University of Chicago. He founded the *American Journal of Sociology*, which he edited from 1895 to 1925. Among his books are *General Sociology* (Chicago: University of Chicago Press, 1905); *Adam Smith and Modern Sociology: A Study in the Methodology of the Social Sciences* (Chicago: University of Chicago Press, 1907); *The Cameralists: The Pioneers of German Social Polity* (Chicago: University of Chicago Press, 1909); and *The Meaning of Social Science* (Chicago: University of Chicago Press, 1910).

139McKay is citing Albion Small, *General Sociology: An Exposition of the Main Development in Sociological Theory From Spencer to Ratzenhofer* (Chicago: University of Chicago Press, 1905), 29; 300.

140McKay is citing Small, *General Sociology* 268; 349.

The distinctive features of the capitalist system are that it makes labour a commodity, enforces arbitrary division of opportunities, leaves the worker little freedom except to starve, little leisure to develop his personality. Small, then, ... foresees that with the advance of civilization, capitalism must give way to a new order, and the wage system must be abolished.

Lester Ward, another famous American Sociologist, has pointed out that the socialization of achievements is the aim of sociology. "Mankind", he writes, "wants no elementary schemes, no private or state benefactions, no fatherly oversight of the privileged classes nor any other form of patronizing hypocrisy. They only want power -- the power which is their right, and which lies within their grasp. They have only to reach out and take it. The victims of privative ethics are in the immense majority. They constitute society. They are the heirs of all the ages. They have only to rouse and enter upon their patrimony that the genius of all lands and of all times has generously bequeathed to them."[141]

Now there is only one way to socialize achievement and enable all to share in the fruits of progress. We must take the control of the wonderful forms and forces of modern production out of the hands of the few, we must institute collective ownership of the means of production, we must abolish the ... chaos, and the waste of the capitalist system, and establish a co-operative commonwealth, wherein the progress of society, the welfare of all, will be in conformity with the full and free development of the individual. And to this the workers must organize, educate and agitate, both on the industrial field, and in the sphere of politics.

30. Socialism as the Science of Social Evolution[142]

Socialism is a science of social evolution.[143] Since Marx and Lassalle it has drawn rich blood from all the sciences and there is scarcely a sociologist of repute among men of science who is not a Socialist. Since

---

[141]McKay is citing, with some changes, Ward, *Applied Sociology*, 326: "Mankind want no fatherly oversight of the privileged classes, nor any other form of patronizing hypocrisy. They only want power -- the power that is theirs of right and which lies within their grasp. They have only to reach out and take it. The victims of privative ethics are in the immense majority. They constitute society. They are the heirs of the ages. They have only to rouse and enter upon their patrimony that the genius of all lands and of all time has generously bequeathed them."

[142]Originally published as "Socialism" in *Eastern Labor News*, 14 September 1912.

[143]McKay is probably paraphrasing Arthur M. Lewis, *Evolution Social and Organic*, Sixth Edition (Chicago: Charles M. Kerr and Company, n.d. [1910]): "Socialism may be defined as the application of the theory of evolution to the phenomena of society. This is precisely what Marx and Engels accomplished...." (58) This entire article could be seen as a *précis* of Lewis's book.

the great German biologist Weismann[144], put forward his theory of heredity, sociology has been practically [rewritten] on socialistic lines, and since De Vries[145] revolutionized the theory of evolution by showing that evolution instead of being a steady movement, is an oscillatory process, changes taking place by sudden leaps, Socialists have felt justified in predicting a speedy change in the organization of society. The industrial revolution is almost complete now, it must be followed by a social revolution. And anybody who watches current events will be inclined to think that the time is nearly ripe for the accumulated social tendencies set in motion by the industrial revolution to express themselves in an "explosion", analogous to that which De Vries has shown marks the birth of a new species in the biological world. Whether the "explosion" which will result in the birth of a new form of society is marked by violence and bloodshed or not, depends on whether the trade unions and the Socialists have succeeded in completing an organization strong enough to control the situation.

---

[144]August Frederich Leopold Weismann (1834-1914) was a German biologist whose major work was carried out at the University of Freiberg. He developed an early genetic theory to explain the facts presented by Darwin, arguing that all heritable characteristics were carried in a special hereditary substance, in the sperm and the egg, which Weismann called "germ-plasm". The position was intensively debated. (Modern biologists would now refer to "germ plasm" as DNA, chromosomes, and genes). In political terms, Weismann's concept of the germ plasm could be interpreted as a blow to socialism, suggesting that the material of heredity was impervious to all environmental influences. McKay's contrary assessment, however, follows the line of interpretation developed by Arthur M. Lewis, *Evolution Social and Organic* (1908). Lewis observed that abandoning the argument of the inheritance of acquired traits strengthened rather than weakened the environmentalist position, by removing arguments that linked the presence of intelligence in one generation to the accomplishments of the former generation: in essence, Weismann's position could allow for a greater degree of unpredictability and flux in matching the cultural achievements of individuals to their class situation. Among socialists, McKay and Lewis were distinctly in the minority on this. See A. Weismann, *The Evolution Theory*, trans. J.A. Thomson and M.R. Thomson (London, 1904), 2 vols.

[145]Hugo De Vries (1848-1935) was a Dutch biologist, and professor of plant physiology at the University of Amsterdam. He developed a theory of genetic mutation from his close observations of the Evening Primrose. He postulated that abrupt mutations sometimes punctuate the gradual evolutionary process with great effect. (It is now thought that minute changes take place in individual specimens with cumulative effect). His lasting contribution is his focus on the importance of mutation to evolution. Socialists of a revolutionary disposition could cite De Vries as evidence of the "naturalness" of political revolutions and other far-reaching, drastic changes in society. See H. De Vries, *Intracellular Pangenesis*, trans. C.S. Gager [1889] (Chicago, 1910); *The Mutation Theory*, trans. J.B. Famert and A.D. Derbyshire [1900] (London: 1910) 2 vols.; *Species and Varieties: Their Origin by Mutation*, 2nd. ed., trans. D.T. MacDougal (Chicago: 1910).

The capitalist system is doomed because it is a system of competitive anarchy, in which even the average businessman is liable to become bankrupt at a day's notice and see his children reduced to poverty. The capitalists as managers have been a much greater failure than the feudal lords, because with the splendid opportunity opened up to them by the increase in the efficiency of labour due to science and invention they have not only not improved the condition of the masses but have not even made their position secure.

31. Bourgeois Morality[146]

Although Sunday labour in the interests of the big corporations generally seems to be permissable, the Lord's Day Alliance has managed to suppress Sunday band concerts on King Square. Many good churchmen go up the river on Sunday in their motor boats, others take a jaunt in their motor cars. We needn't blame them. We are told that the rich will have a hard task to get into Heaven, so they should take their pleasures while they may. But now that the International Society of Bible Students has by a majority vote abolished hell, and it is no longer certain that our portions in the new world will be the inverse ratios of our lot in this world, it is about time the working classes who cannot get out of the city in autocars or motor boats should be allowed some harmless pleasures on Sunday.

We are told Saint John is a progressive modern city. But the spirit of progress is evidently not very powerful here; at any rate the old spirit of Puritanism was able to exert an easy domination in the matter of Sunday band concerts. For generations, Puritanism was the... expression of the principle of progress. When the middle class arose within the body of the feudal world, it developed a new industrial system, new social forms, and new moral conceptions. In its fierce struggle against feudalism and the Roman church, the commercial or trading class, the bourgeoisie necessarily emphasized its revolutionary character by the sharpness of the contrasts between its social and moral codes and those prevalent under feudalism. In the fight against a corrupt extravagant and licentious nobility, who however chivalrous towards members of their own class, were brutes in their relations to the working class, the rising middle class found the preaching and practice of continence, temperance, thrift, industry, frugality, all the tenets of Puritanism, powerful aids in winning the support of the working class. Moreover, the historic mission of the bourgeoisie being the accumulation of capital, the economic virtues which expressed its class interests equally embodied that... interest when applied to the wage workers.

In accordance with their necessities and purposes, the Puritans gave to the Sabbath a character which would no doubt have amazed the Israelites.

---

[146]Colin McKay, untitled letter to the editor, *Eastern Labor News*, 21 September 1912

Being relatively poor, and bent on accumulation, they naturally made it a drab and sober affair; naturally too they presented a marked contrast to the festive licence of the feudal Sunday. But chiefly for the bourgeoisie, Sunday became a day of exhortation, counsel and admonition, a day consecrated to the solidifying of class interest and sanctification for the struggle against feudalism and its bulwark the medieval church.

But Puritanism has about fulfilled its historic mission. It offers no solution of the vital problems of today. The large capitalism has uprooted its economic base. Inept and futile Puritanism faces the modern world, aghast at the struggle of contending classes which it does not understand, forgetful that it was once the expression as well as the inspiration of a revolutionary movement, unable to offer a world eager for a new dispensation anything better than the pitiful banalities of individual propriety.

32. Evolution Cannot Be Discredited[147]

A wave of revolt against the theory of evolution has recently swept over the United States. It had its genesis in an allegation attributed to a leading British scientist, that modern science was not satisfied with the theory of evolution. The scientist in question denies he ever made such a statement. What he said was that science was not satisfied with its knowledge of the process of evolution. Modern scientists recognize the evolutionary process; but the why and wherefore of that process is still a mystery.

It is significant that an attempt to discredit the theory of evolution should be made during a period when trade unionism in the United States had apparently lapsed into a period of timidity. Anything that discredits the theory of evolution must discredit the labour movement. If there is no evolution, the hopes of labour are vain dreams. If the advocates of reaction can dethrone evolution, they can justify the present social system, and show that the efforts of trade unionism to improve the condition of the working class are unnatural and unreasonable.

The bourgeois mind years ago readily recognized the operation of the principle of evolution in the natural world; but it has balked at the idea of evolution in society. Of course it has admitted that the social order has changed in the past; that there has been an evolution from primitive tribal communism through chattel slavery and feudalism to the modern form of society, known as capitalism. But the bourgeoisie want to believe that the evolution of society is complete, that capitalism will continue world without end. They want to believe that they are the finished product of creation, the final as well as the noblest work of God. The old feudal

---

[147]Originally published under this title in *Canadian Railroad Employees Monthly*, January 1924, 185-186.

lords had the same notion; they could not conceive the possibility of an order of society ruled by capitalists.

The overlordship of the few, the domination of the many, has been a necessary evil for ages, and will no doubt continue to be so for some time yet. But humanity makes progress towards freedom, and those who now hold dominion over the many by virtue of property or other circumstances will pass to their reward. Leaders there will doubtless be; but not masters in the sense that the capitalists now control the jobs and therefore the lives and fortunes of the workers. Leaders are essential to trade unions, for instance, and such leaders may at times exercise arbitrary powers; but they cannot continue to dominate the membership against its will. The leaders of the industrial democracy of the future will be analogous to the leaders of trade unions; they may at times usurp arbitrary powers; but in the long run their authority will rest upon their accomplishments in the way of helping the workers to a fuller and better life.

A great many people have no sense of history. They are unable to think backwards or look ahead. Their knowledge of the world is largely limited to their own recollections or those of their relatives. A man may retain some remembrances of what he studied in his school histories; but these are of little use or no help to enable him to understand the historical evolution of society as a connected process. School histories too often only present an unrelated series of pictures of the doings of kings and high personages; the common people only appear when they revolt against tyranny; and the reason of the revolt is usually glossed over and the reader is left with the impression that the common people were graceless vagabonds, too stupid to know what was good for them.

This lack of a sense of history is largely responsible for the fatalistic attitude many workers take to the world and the affairs of their class. Men see little change in society in their time, and the relation of master and men under the wage system seems destined to endure for all time. Hence the inertia which is the bane of trade unionism.

But evolution proceeds. Science, invention, new technical forms, are preparing the way for great changes in the structure of society. Not so long ago nearly every industry was owned by an individual or a family; enterprises were small. The joint-stock company came in with steam-moved machinery, which made great enterprises, employing many persons, possible. And these great enterprises have made it impossible for great bodies of workers to indulge the hope of owning a business of their own, as every enterprising worker might hope to do when industry was primitive. And for such workers now their hopes of betterment lie in the improvement of their class position through trade unions and political action.

33. Struggle - the Way of Progress[148]

The researches of scientists tend to show that all matter is made up of positive and negative charges of electricity in constant motion.[149] Conflict, struggle, collision, eternal change, are fundamental principles of matter and of life, conditioning them and making their existence possible. In the sphere of human relations, the same universal law holds sway, for all progress, all civilization, all advance depend upon conflict of opinion, upon argument and discussion, in the endeavour to find better ways of doing things, of solving problems, of making life richer and fuller.

Without struggle the trade unions cannot gain anything worth having, any more than one can gain a prize in athletics without strenuous physical exercise. Even when the working class is sufficiently organized to reconstruct society on a more equitable basis, struggle will still be the law of existence. Whatever the particular form of the next order of society may be, it will provide primarily for conscious human co-operation in the struggle against nature; it will inaugurate a new cycle, a higher phase in which human beings will consciously seek to control the process of evolution. That is the mission of the working class; that is what differentiates the working class from the capitalist class, for the latter seems to stand in awe of the blind economic forces which its system of production has called into being, and regards them as uncontrollable. The trusts and combines in which the capitalists seek to imprison the blind forces of production make the life of the workers increasingly precarious and intolerable, and let loose a new social demon -- the specter of chronic unemployment. The period which has witnessed the greatest technical triumphs of capitalism has seen also the greatest accumulation of economic problems, and the most rapid aggravation of social evils. What governments are doing in the political sphere, capitalists are doing in the economic domain -- piling problems on the shelf.

On the other hand, labour profits by the logic of events, faces its problems and seeks solutions, with an increasing understanding of its part in the world-process of evolution. Labour is driven to solidify its ranks, as much by the attitude of the capitalists, as by the growing social consciousness of the workers. In the classic period of its development, capitalism created a large middle class, and showed a more or less

---

[148]Originally published under this title in *Canadian Railroad Employees Monthly*, July 1927, 103.

[149]McKay is evidently attempting to capture some of the spirit of modern post-classical micro-physics, in which it is "in principle impossible to measure or predict the position and momentum of a micro-particle with complete exactness at one and the same instant": see Gustav A. Wetter, *Dialectical Materialism: A History and Systematic Survey of Philosophy in the Soviet Union* (New York: Praeger, 1958): 407.

friendly countenance to the "aristocracy of labour." But the newer capitalism is something of a steam roller, something of a leveller of whatever comes in its way. In England, the skilled trades which were once the chief aids of English capitalism in drawing to itself the wealth of the world are now hardly better paid than common labour. But the skilled or highly organized trades are finding it increasingly difficult to secure concessions progressively raising them above the status of labour in the mass. The railway companies, for instance, are now resisting the efforts of the more highly paid men to secure wage increases as much as the demands to the lower rated men, though in event of a show-down, the former have more chance of winning than the latter, for the reason that, as has been stated, they are better organized, and the railways are often willing to grant a considerable increase to the comparatively few men involved, because the amount required is less than would be necessary to pay even a slight increase to a more numerous body of employees.

On the other hand, the more highly organized capitalism becomes, the more difficult it is for one class of workers to raise their status above other classes. A point is reached above which the higher-paid men cannot raise their wages until the lower-rated men have secured wage scales more or less appropriate to the relative degrees of skill or other qualities required by their respective services. This inevitably creates a new sense of democracy, a new feeling of the interdependence of interests of all workers. It should ultimately lead to co-operation, federation, and the helping of the weak by the strong. A strong union may find co-operation with a weak union a source of strength to both; but it is no business of a strong union to fight the battles of a union so supine that it sits on the side-lines. No union can have any positive life without struggle, nor make any worthwhile advance unless that is a dominant factor in its policy.

34. Property and Progress[150]

The ownership of capital, the form of property at present predominant, is a means of power and profit, of obliging workers, divorced from any form of property except their personal belongings, to contribute to the production of goods or services an amount of labour whose social value is in excess of the wages paid them. The protection of property is a main concern, a chief function, of the modern state, which itself is founded on territory and property. In any legislative body, the raising of a question of the "rights of property" rivets the attention of the representatives of the "people" in a way that a question of the rights of mere people to a full, free and happy life never does. And the courts, agents of the power of the State, are more generous in their interpretation of the privileges of property than of the "rights" of persons.

---

[150]*Canadian Railroad Employees Monthly*, November 1928, 206-207; 214.

In the era of small property and petty industry, the proprietor's relation to his property was direct and intimate; an enterprise depended upon the personal character of the proprietor, his intelligence, activity and thrift; just as the perfection of the work of an artificer of the period depended upon the skill with which he handled his tools. The proprietor fulfilled a social function.

But in typical industry to-day, the capitalist is no longer an appendage of his property. Great enterprises are now mostly directed by salaried executives, who may or may not be capitalists in their own right, but do not necessarily hold their positions by virtue of that fact. A capitalist may draw profits from shares in an investment he has never seen, and knows nothing of beyond the information he gleans from the annual reports.

The capitalistic organization of industry has made a parasite of the capitalist *per se* : the same organization, by making possible the rapid expansion of mechanical production, has had a complementary development in the fact that the artisan's technical skill, once a form of personal property, has largely lost its value, and the wage earner has been turned into a servant of the machine.

"The parasitical nature of the role of the modern capitalist is recognized and proclaimed by the creation of anonymous companies whose shares and obligations -- the bourgeois titles to property -- pass from hand to hand, without exerting any influence upon production, and, on the Stock Exchange, change hands a dozen times a day," writes Paul Lafargue[151] in *The Evolution of Property*. "The Rothschilds, Goulds, and other financiers of that stamp practically demonstrate to the capitalists that they are useless, by cheating them out of their shares and bonds by Stock Exchange swindling and financial hanky-panky, and by accumulating in their strong boxes the profits derived from the great organisms of production."[152]

---

[151]Paul Lafargue (1842-1911) was one of the key figures in the history of French Marxism, as well as being Karl Marx's son-in-law. With Guesde, he founded the first French collectivist party, the Fédération du Parti des Travailleurs Socialistes de France (1880), but was unable to guide the party in a Marxist direction. He was the chief theoretician and propagandist for French Marxism for three decades after 1880. He pioneered the application of Marxist concepts in anthropology, aesthetics and literary criticism, and may even be seen as an anticipator -- although only to a modest extent -- of the fundamental theoretical breakthroughs of Antonio Gramsci. Among his books are *La Droit à la Paresse, réfutation du 'Droit au Travail' de 1848* (1883); *La Religion du Capital* (1887); *Pie IX au Paradis* (1890). Most North American socialists would have been exposed only to the first of these, translated as *The Right to Be Lazy, and Other Studies*, and published by Charles H. Kerr.

[152]McKay is citing, with a few minor modifications, Paul Lafargue, *The Evolution of Property From Savagery to Civilization* (New York: Charles Scribner, 1905), 171: "...the capitalistic organisation of industry has made a parasite of the capitalist. The

It must be admitted that the proprietors themselves, when their relations to their property were direct and personal, brought a good deal of intelligence and enterprise to the task of developing their industries, and to the business of accumulation. If their enterprises yielded high profits, they felt they were only receiving the legitimate reward of superior intelligence and ability. The proprietors of the modern impersonal corporations do not necessarily contribute any intelligence or energy to the direction of their enterprises; they can go out in the market-place and hire administrators with keen minds and trained executive ability. But still the bourgeois economists ring the changes on the arguments that management so overtops in importance all other factors in industry that it is entitled to dispose of all profits in excess of a living wage for labour, even though it disposes of such excess by handing it to shareholders who have made no personal contribution to the success of such management....

"The emancipation of the working classes requires that they lay hold of the science of the century," wrote Joseph Dietzgen,[153] German tanner, and the first great philosopher of the working class movement, who resolved the controversy concerning mind and matter, and relegated to... limbo the intellectual [bogeys] with which the bourgeois lackeys have been wont to scare the workers. "Philosophy is a subject which closely concerns the working class," Dietzgen added. "This, of course, does not imply that every workman should try to become acquainted with philosophy and study the relation of between [sic] the idea and matter. From the fact that we all eat bread, it does not follow that we must all understand milling and baking. But just as we need millers and bakers, so does the working class stand in

---

parasitical nature of his *role* is recognized and proclaimed by the creation of anonymous companies whose shares and obligations -- the bourgeois' titles of property -- pass from hand to hand, without exerting any influence on production, and on the Stock Exchange change hands a dozen times a day. The Rothschilds, Grants, Goulds, and other financiers of that stamp, practically demonstrate to the capitalists that they are useless, by cheating them out of their shares and bonds by Stock Exchange swindling, and other financial hanky-panky, and by accumulating in their strong boxes the profits derived from the great organisms of production."

[153]Josef Dietzgen (1828-1888) was the epitome of the self-taught working-class socialist philosopher. A tanner by trade, he became an associate of Karl Marx, was involved in the First International, and eventually became active in the Socialist Labor Party in the United States, serving as editor of *Der Sozialist* in New York and later of the *Chicagoer Arbeiterzeitung*. His philosophy starts from a reverence for science and an abhorrence of all dualisms; *The Nature of Human Brain-Work, presented by a Workingman* (1869) argued that the task of philosophy was to apply scientific methods, even to such concepts as "soul" and "thought." In *The Positive Outcome of Philosophy* trans. by W.W. Craik ([1906] 1928) Dietzgen claimed that thought in general involves mental representations of an objective material reality entirely independent of it. This was a position that influenced Lenin in his philosophical writings. His works were very popular in certain working-class radical circles down to the 1930s.

need of keen scholars, who can follow up the tortuous tricks of the false teachers and lay bare the inanity of their ideas."[154]

The bourgeoisie know how to use scientists for their own purposes, and even bourgeois science is an arsenal of weapons which the working-class might wield to advantage for the particular purposes. It is true that the intellectual hangers-on of capitalism habitually distort science in order to oppose obstacles to every working-class aspiration and to justify the appropriation by capital of the lion's share of the wealth produced by labour; and, unfortunately, too many workers have little or no acquaintance with science beyond the bunkum which passes for science in the popular press. A perhaps natural, but, lamentable consequence, is that some workers are suspicious of all science.

Too many workers assume that the evolution of human society proceeds from some inherent force and follows rigid natural laws, and that the process of evolution cannot be quickened or retarded, or its course varied, by the actions of men; a comfortable view, absolving men as it does from any positive effort to improve the world in which they find themselves, and justifying the complacent philosophy of fatalistic acceptance of things as they are.

But this assumption that the rational faculty of man is not a factor of any importance in shaping the course of evolution of human affairs is not entertained only by some simple-minded socialists. The errors [to] which it has given rise forms the subject of an important work by Lester Ward, a leading American sociologist, with a great international reputation. Ward points out that while "the indispensable foundation of all social and economic science is the fact that all human activities and social phenomena are subject to natural law," the very adoption of this "altogether sound abstract principle led to the greatest and most fundamental of all economic errors, an error which has found its way into the heart of modern scientific philosophy, widely influencing public opinion and offering a stubborn resistance to all efforts to dislodge it."

---

[154]McKay is citing, with a few minor modifications, Josef Dietzgen, "The Religion of Social Democracy": "Philosophy is therefore a subject which closely concerns the working class. This, of course, does by no means imply that every working man should try to become acquainted with philosophy and study the relation between idea and matter. From the fact that we all eat bread does not follow that we must understand milling or baking. But just as we need millers and bakers so does the working class stand in need of keen scholars who can follow up the tortuous ways of the false priests and lay bare the inanity of their tricks." Josef Dietzgen, *Some of the Philosophical Essays on Socialism and Science, Religion, Ethics, Critique-of-Reason and the World-at-large* (Chicago: Charles H. Kerr and Company, 1917): 131. Possibly McKay was relying on yet another version of this noteworthy *aperçu* of Dietzgen, which can be found in Arthur Lewis, *Evolution Social and Organic* 171.

"This error," Ward continues, "consists in practically ignoring the existence of a rational faculty in man, which, while it does not render his actions any less subject to natural laws, so enormously complicates them that they can no longer be brought within the simple formulas that sufficed in the calculus of mere animal motives. This element creeps stealthily in between the child and the adult, and all unnoticed puts the best-laid schemes of economists and philosophers altogether agley. A great psychic factor has been left out of the account, the intellectual or rational factor, and this factor is so stupendous that there is no room for astonishment in contemplating the magnitude of the error which its omission has caused."

Ward dwells on the vast difference between the ways of Nature, with its blind forces and appalling waste of potential life, and the economy of human society with its mental arrangement of means to ends -- an adjustment of means to ends pretty effective insofar as the ends are the interests of the dominant classes. "No one will object," says Ward, "to having Nature's methods fully exposed and explained, and thoroughly taught as a great truth of science. It is only when Nature is held up as a model to be followed by man and all are forbidden to 'meddle' with its operations that it becomes necessary to protest....I shall endeavor to show more fully that Nature's method is wholly at variance with anything that a rational being would ever conceive of, and that if a being, supposed to be rational, were to adopt it, he would be looked upon as insane."

Ward elaborates the familiar truth that the difference between an animal living in a state of nature and man living in human society is that man uses tools, and points out that the development and use of tools are due to that application of reason called the inventive faculty, which no animal possesses. The immense advantage which the use of tools gives man over the [animals] has been overlooked by the strictly biological sociologists, he opines. But this advantage makes an immense difference; "the environment transforms the animal, while man transforms the environment."

Another thing which differentiates rational society from irrational nature, Ward points out, is that nature is competitive, while society is increasingly co-operative. This co-operation he attributes to the development of the psychic factor, or capacity for reasoning from cause to effect. In the development of civilization, the psychic factor, the application of mind to the problems of life, has been of first importance, in Ward's view. Civilization and "human achievement" are synonymous terms with him. "Achievement does not consist in wealth. Wealth is fleeting and ephemeral. Achievement is permanent and eternal." Achievement means, in effect, the knowledge of inventions and processes of production, technique and skill, rather than perishable products or the perishable machines that produce them. The vital thing is the knowledge of the process of production, for if all the implements of production were spirited from earth, man could reproduce them. This, of course, is the socialist contention: that, since the knowledge of the process of production is the result of human achievement through the ages, the means of production should be socially owned and operated for the good of humanity generally.

Unlike most professors, Ward makes no attempt to avoid the socialistic conclusions which follow logically from his premises and argument. Turning from human achievement, the subject-matter of *Pure Sociology*, to *Applied Sociology*, he writes: "The purpose of applied sociology is to harmonize achievement with improvement. If all this achievement which constitutes civilization has really been wrought without producing any improvement in the condition of the human race, it is time that the reason for this was investigated. Applied sociology includes among its main purposes the investigation of this question. The difficulty lies in the fact that achievement is not socialized. The problem, therefore, is that of the socialization of achievement."

"We are told that no scheme for the equalization of men can succeed; that at first it was physical strength that determined the inequalities; that this at length gave way to the power of cunning, and that still later it became intelligence in general that determined the place of individuals in society. This last, it is maintained, is now, in the long run, in the most civilized races and the most enlightened communities, the true reason why some occupy lower and others higher positions in the natural strata of society. This, it is said, is the natural state and as it should be. It is, moreover, affirmed that, being natural, there is no possibility of altering it."

"Of course, all this falls to the ground on the least analysis. For example, starting from the standpoint of achievement, it would naturally be held that there would be a great injustice in robbing those who by their superior wisdom had achieved the results upon which civilization rests, and distributing the natural rewards among inferior persons who had achieved nothing. All would assent to this. And yet this is, in fact, practically what has been done. The whole history of the world shows that those who have achieved have achieved no reward. The rewards for their achievement have fallen to persons who have achieved nothing. They have simply for the most part profited by some accident of position in a complex, badly-organized society, whereby they have been permitted to claim and appropriate the fruits of the achievements of others. But not [no] one would insist that these fruits should all go to those who made them possible. The fruits of achievement are incalculable in amount and endure forever. Their authors are few in number and soon pass away. They would be the last to claim an undue share. They work for all mankind and for all time, and all they ask is that all mankind shall forever benefit by their work."[155]

35. The Conservatism of the Mind[156]

The human mind is essentially conservative. And this conservatism, being due to sheer mental inertia or mere stupidity, is responsible for terrible social cataclysms. It leads the average man to take institutions for granted, to regard them as fixed for time and eternity. But nothing is constant except change. And all human institutions must change or become impediments to progress. In times when the modes by which men get their living change rapidly, that is in times of rapid technical development of the forces of production, institutions that may have served the needs of former times very well, become rapidly outmoded. And if they are not adaptable to the new conditions, they must finally disappear. But the process of getting rid of outgrown institutions has in the past been exceedingly painful. And such is the mental inertia of the masses, the flabbiness of the social will, and the dullness of the social conscience, that getting rid of even such an absurd institution as poverty in the midst of plenty may be a very painful process. Man has so far been the unconscious object of evolution; in time he will probably become the conscious director of social evolution, as he is now, in important respects, master of nature. But the time is hardly yet. The collective intelligence, will and moral courage necessary to promote progress in an orderly manner is lacking. In existing society, the anarchy of production, which is the source of so much misery, is at the same time the great cause of progress. To have progress without anarchy, it would be necessary to substitute social control for private control of the means of production; and such a transition would require a complete abandonment of some existing institutions and drastic modifications of other institutions.]

It might be supposed that men would have a sufficient sense of social responsibility to their children to abandon outgrown institutions before the conditions surrounding them became intolerable. But that has not been the case so far. The great revolutions of history have begun as protests against conditions which have become intolerable. The institution of the monarchy in France was not openly questioned when the great bread riots broke out in Paris....

---

[155]McKay is citing Lester F. Ward, *Applied Sociology* 21-22.
[156]Originally published as an untitled letter, *Labor World/Le Monde Ouvrier*, 1 July 1933.

36. The Struggle For Existence[157]

Tanks and armoured cars may be the great teachers for which the working class has waited. An object lesson of the existence of the class struggle they seem to have impressed the workers of Stratford, Ont., enough to induce them to elect a mayor and six out of ten councillors. That is better than workers merely overawed by militia with rifles and bayonets have done. It is possible to put over the pretext that the militia was called out in the interest of law and order; but the mask is off when tanks and armoured cars take sides in the struggle of capital and labour.[158]

"The expression 'class struggle,' so repugnant when first heard or seen (and I confess that it produced that impression on me when I had not yet grasped the scientific import of the Marxian theory) furnishes us, if it be correctly understood, the primary law of human history, and, therefore, it alone can give us the certain index of the advent of the new phase of evolution which socialism foresees and which it strives to hasten."

That is a quotation from *Socialism and Modern Science* by Enrico Ferri,[159] who collaborated with Lombroso in founding the scientific school of criminology. Ferri was a product of a more liberal Italy. His works, along with those of Prof. Labriola of the University of Rome, did much to spread socialistic ideas in Latin Europe and Latin America.

It is doubtful if in the whole range of socialist literature there is a more graphic interpretation of the class struggle than Ferri gives. He writes with

---

[157]*O.B.U. Bulletin*, 14 December 1933.

[158]These are reflections on one of the most famous Canadian upheavals of the Depression, a violent confrontation at Stratford, Ontario. About 700 furniture workers, organized by the Communist-led Workers' Unity League, went on strike for higher wages, shorter hours and union recognition. The mayor of Stratford called in military aid, including four machine-gun carriers and 120 soldiers. After the furniture workers gained their objectives, women chicken-pluckers went on strike. In the next municipal election, one of the strike leaders was elected mayor and the six successful labour candidates dominated a council of ten. See Desmond Morton, "Aid to the Civil Power: The Stratford Strike of 1933," in Irving Abella, ed., *On Strike: Key Labour Struggles in Canada, 1919-1949* (Toronto: McClelland and Stewart, 1974).

[159]Enrico Ferri (1856-1929) was a pioneering criminologist, who applied positivist theories to the classical criminology he studied at the University of Bologna and the University of Pisa. He was a lecturer in 1879 at the University of Turin, a professor of criminal law at the University of Bologna, and a professor at the University of Pisa, a position he lost because of his enthusiasm for socialism. He was editor of the journal *La Scuola Positiva* and in 1912 founded the School of Applied Criminal Law and Procedure. *The Positive School of Criminology* (1913) and *Socialism and Modern Science (Darwin-Spencer-Marx)* (1909), would have been the two Ferri books that affected McKay; he explicitly cites only the latter. Perhaps the best critique of Ferri can be found in the great *Prison Notebooks* of Antonio Gramsci.

the authority of a profound student of both natural science and sociology. Ferri says:

"The only scientific explanation of the history of animal life is to be found in the Darwinian law of the struggle for existence; it alone enables us to determine the natural causes of the appearance, development and disappearance of vegetable and animal species from palentological times to our day. In the same way the only explanation of the history of human life is to be found in the Marxian law of the struggle between classes; thanks to it the annals of primitive, barbarian and civilized humanity cease to be a capricious and superficial kaleidoscopic arrangement of individual episodes and becomes a great drama, determined -- whether the actors realize it or not, in its smallest internal details as well as in its catastrophes -- by the economic conditions, which form the indispensable, physical basis of life and by the struggle between the classes to obtain and keep control of the economic forces, upon which all the others -- political, juridical and moral -- necessarily depend...."

"Now, the great importance of the Marxian law -- the struggle between the classes -- consists principally in the fact that it indicates with great exactness just what is in truth the vital point of the social question and by what method its solution may be reached."

"As long as no one had shown on positive evidence the economic basis of the political, juridical and moral life, the aspirations of the great majority for the amelioration of social conditions aimed vaguely at the demand and partial conquest of some accessory instrumentality, such as freedom of worship, political suffrage, political education, etc. And, certainly, I have no desire to deny the great utility of these conquests."

"But the *sancta sanctorum*[160] always remained impenetrable to the eyes of the masses, and as economic power continued to be the privilege of the few, all the conquests and concessions had no real basis, separated, as they were, from the solid and fecund foundation which alone can give life and abiding power."

"Now that Socialism has shown -- even before Marx, but never before with so much scientific precision -- that individual ownership, private property in land and the means of production, is the vital point of the question -- the problem is formulated in exact terms in the consciousness of contemporaneous humanity....

---

[160]The holy of holies: a place in a house of worship proscribed for all but high priests, or, in a private dwelling, a room that is off limits to everyone but the master or the mistress of the establishment.

"To assert the existence of the class struggle is equivalent to saying that human society....is not merely...the sum of a greater or smaller number of individuals; it is....a living organism which is made up of diverse parts, and this differentiation constantly increases in direct ratio to the degree of social evolution attained....

"This theory not only gives us the secret motive-power and the only scientific explanation of the history of mankind; it also furnishes the ideal and rigid standard of discipline for political Socialism and thus enables it to avoid all the elastic, vaporous, inconclusive uncertainties of sentimental socialism."[161]

Unfortunately, political socialism has failed to live up to that standard, but it still remains the standard for the judgment of political movements.

Ferri, writing in 1894, emphasized that the conquest of economic power could not be achieved by mere political decrees, but would require class conscious organization in the economic and political spheres....

37. The Faculty of Thought[162]

Marx showed that the progress of mankind since the dawn of civilization could be explained by class struggles. In the gentile order before it became corrupt, there was no room for classes with privileges and powers based on property and office, though struggle with environment and the struggle of tribes was the law of progress.

In primitive societies the relations of men with their fellows were clear and simple, and hence there were no social mysteries. Men then, however, were troubled by the mysteries of their relations with nature. Civilized man is not much troubled today by natural mysteries, but he is still plagued by social mysteries arising out of his economic relations with his fellows. The chief merit of Marxism is that it gives the key to an understanding of these social phenomena which appear to many to be produced by mysterious and irrational powers beyond human control.

---

[161]McKay is citing from Enrico Ferri, *Socialism and Modern Science* (Chicago: Charles H. Kerr & Company, 1909), 74-79. He has significantly reordered the paragraphs to make the condemnation of utopian ("sentimental") socialism emerge as the conclusion of the analysis.

[162]Originally published as "The Glow Worm," Halifax *Herald*, 15 September 1936 [letter to the editor].

What is the merit of orthodox economics? Prof. Stephen Leacock,[163] after 40 years teaching it, said: "For our social problems today orthodox economics has as much light as a glow-worm."

The recognition of the obvious existence of class struggles is not the chief contribution of Marxian Socialism to human knowledge. More important was the recognition that what philosophy has been seeking is an understanding of the nature of human brain-work, of how the faculty of thought functions. The Socialist theory of cognition is the completion of the quest of philosophy which now has only a historical interest as the record of attempts of man to understand himself and his relations to the universe. Now its place is taken by science of the mind as a branch of natural sciences.

iii. Economic Determinism and Trade Unionism

38. Labour Politics[164]

Seers, prophets, poets, from time immemorial have been drawing pictures of ideal states of society. But ideals and visions have not played a very important part in the march of mankind. In the mass men learn by experience, the only sure motive force is the urge of economic interest. It is idle to hope that the workers of the Maritime Provinces will learn much from the experience of the militant working-class movement in Germany or any other country; they will only profit by their own experience. In every community the working-class movement follows practically the same processes of evolution. Labour parties have appeared in Saint John and Halifax and disappeared, because they did not have any definite purpose beyond the election of workingmen and the adoption of reforms. No doubt they accomplished something in the way of breaking down the old party spirit, no doubt too they will appear again, and achieve permanence and follow similar lines of evolution to the labour party of Toronto which recently declared for the overthrow of capitalism....

---

[163]Stephen Leacock (1869-1944) was Canada's best-loved humorist, whose light-hearted books -- e.g., *Sunshine Sketches of a Little Town* (1931) -- won him a large audience throughout the British Empire. He was also professor of political economy at McGill University in Montreal from 1901 to 1935, and as such a favoured target for McKay's barbs. His academic publications include *Elements of Political Science* (1906); *The Unsolved Riddle of Social Justice: The Social Criticism of Stephen Leacock* ([1920] 1973); *Economic Prosperity in the British Empire* (1930), as well as numerous books of history.

[164]*Eastern Labor News*, 5 July 1913.

39. The Evolution of Trade Unionism[165]

The trade union movement seems to be undergoing a process of transformation, and more or less consciously adapting itself to the new government which the rise of trusts and combines is creating. Up to a few years ago a feature of the labour movement on this continent was the rapid increase of membership of the union owing allegiance to the A.F. of L. [American Federation of Labor]. Laterly the increase in membership has not been so marked, but nevertheless great and significant developments have been in progress.

The spirit of unionism has been manifesting itself in new ways. The labour movement is not losing any of its vigour; what has been lost in the rate of expansion has been fully offset by the greater integration of the movement -- the welding of the various elements into a more effective weapon for fighting purposes.

Some years ago the A.F. of L. was much occupied with judicial functions. It was a sort of umpire between the unions; at the annual conventions there were long wrangles over questions of craft jurisdiction. Unions of allied crafts wasted a lot of time and energy fighting one another. The average worker regarded his craft skill as his capital, a form of property, and he was mainly interested in protecting what he considered his property rights in his craft. No doubt he took a sentimental and altruistic interest in the struggles of other craft unions, but he did not have a very clear conception of the independence [interdependence] of all crafts, the common interest of the working class. He looked at the labour problem from the point of view of his craft group, rather than from the standpoint of his class. His attitude was a reflex of that of the capitalist, or rather the small trader; he had something to sell, his skill and labour power, and he considered the mission of his union was to get him "A fair day's pay for a fair day's work." Generally he had a secret hope that some fluke of fortune would enable him to rise into the employing class. Old ideas and instincts, survivals of the handicrafts era, made him individualistic in his aspirations and outlook, and he had little class consciousness, and no conception of, or interest in, the historic mission of the working class as a whole.

But in recent years a new spirit has taken possession of the labour movement, and is working mighty changes in its aspirations, its methods, and tactics. In Europe and more recently in England, some of its manifestations have been rather extreme. The new spirit is militant, but its logical expression is not necessarily sabotage and other forms of violence such as have characterized the [syndicalist] movement of France, and which is perhaps only a passing phase. The principle of industrial

---

[165]*Eastern Labor News*, 31 August 1912.

unionism, the idea of co-operation between the trades for the general uplift, is more and more permeating the ranks of labour. Even the Trades and Labor Congress of Canada has endorsed the principle of industrial unionism. It is not necessarily bound up with the idea of a general strike. In fact, the new idea of the solidarity of labour might be better expressed by the term political unionism. It is on the political rather than the industrial sphere that its more notable manifestations may be expected.

40. Land, Labour and Capital[166]

Land, labour and capital unite to produce, but when it comes to a division of the products of industrial co-operation each factor falls a different way.[167] In this struggle the landlord and the capitalist have obvious advantages over the individual labourer. Hence the rise of the trade union which is an embodiment of the claim that labour does not obtain the share that it is entitled to.

When our forefathers came to Canada they had scarcely more than their bare hands. They worked hard for a living but every one had enough and to spare. If there were no rich, there were no poor people. Since then workingmen have been massed together in cities; in order to increase the efficiency of labour, steam, machinery and wonderful inventions have multiplied a hundred fold the productiveness of labour; the development of the railroad, the steamship and the telegraph have made it possible to carry the abundance to those who want it with the least waste of its substance. When we consider the amazing increase of productiveness arising from machinery and associated labour, we might reasonably expect that everybody in this country is much better off than its founders. Undoubtedly the bulk of the population is better off, that is, they enjoy more of the conveniences of life, but at the same time the lot of the city toiler is not an exceptionally happy one. Capital and land have absorbed the largest share of the benefits arising from our increased industrial efficiency. Millionaires are common enough. A resolution has been effected in the relative relations of employee and workman. Capital has been organized under the form of the impersonal corporation; labour has of necessity been organized in the trade union.

It is often urged against trade unions that they are combinations seeking to defeat the operations of economic laws, that they cannot deal satisfactorily with the wage question because the rate of wages is

---

[166]*Eastern Labor News*, 27 July 1912.

[167]This discussion echoes Chapter 48 of Karl Marx, *Capital*, Vol. 3. See Karl Marx, *Capital: A Critique of Political Economy*, trans. David Fernbach (New York: Vintage Books, 1981). McKay was unusual among SPCers in stressing this part of Marx's work; the party generally and adamantly adhered to the more basic argument of Vol.1. (My thanks to Peter Campbell for this point).

determined by the inexorable laws of supply and demand, or with the hours of labour, because these are determined by industrial necessity. Of course, these propositions which some economists and newspaper writers are fond of hurling at our heads, are expressions of the old wage-fund theory. The fallacy that at any time there was a fixed quantity of capital to be expended in wages and that consequently the number of labourers competing for a share in that fixed quantity would inevitably determine the rate of wages. If the capital functioning in the form of wages is a fixed quantity, why do we need the elaborate modern system of credit? One of Henry George's[168] contributions to political economy was to show that money wages represented to a certain extent a mortgage upon the product of labour -- that the workers created the products which paid them their wages as they went along. Like many other ruling-class [theories], the wage fund idea was promulgated to make the workers think that their condition was inevitable and that it was useless to struggle for more comfort and well being in this life.

41.What is Capitalism? A Survey of Economic History[169]

According to Henry George, the savage who, finding a fruit tree, exchanged some of the fruit with other savages for other desirable things became a merchant capitalist. If he planted seed and raised another fruit tree, he engaged in a capitalist enterprise.[170]

According to W. Roscher,[171] a once-famous economist, the primitive fisherman, who, being able to catch each day three fish, left in pools by the receding tide, prudently reduced his consumption to two fishes per day for 100 days, and then used his stored up supply of 100 fish to devote his whole labour-power for 50 days to the making of a boat and fishing nets, was the original capitalist. By abstinence he acquired capital -- boat

---

[168]Henry George (1839-1897) was probably the most influential political economist of the late nineteenth century; his *Progress and Poverty* (1879) sold over two million copies in several languages. George's focus on the injustice of unearned wealth derived from land speculation -- which some held to be *the* key to social injustice -- was doubtless influenced by his experiences in San Francisco during the land speculation craze pending arrival of the first transcontinental railway. Single Taxers, inspired by George, could be found in every major Canadian and American city. The impact of Georgeite ideas on the radical editor of the Halifax *Critic* is noted by Judith Fingard, "The 1880s: Paradoxes of Progress," in E.R. Forbes and D.A. Muise, eds., *The Atlantic Provinces in Confederation* (Toronto: University of Toronto Press and Fredericton: Acadiensis Press, 115).It is thus quite possible that McKay first encountered Georgeite views in Nova Scotia.

[169]*Canadian Railway Employees' Monthly*, November 1931, 246.

[170]The reference is to an argument by Henry George in *The Science of Political Economy* (London: Kegan Paul, Trench, Trubner & Co., 1898): 294-295. This book was completed by George's son after his father's death.

[171]See Ch.1, note 69.

and fishing net -- by which he was able to increase his production to 30 fishes per day.

A savage subsisting on fish caught by his bare hands would hardly know how to cure fish so as to preserve them for 150 days. He would not build a boat until he had invented stone axes and learned how to produce fire. Nor could he make a fishing net until he learned something of weaving. Primitive man did not develop such arts overnight. Between the savage catching fish with his bare hands, in tidal pools, and the savage capable of constructing a boat or net there must have been a vast interval of time.

The savage who became a capitalist through abstinence is a legendary figure.

Moreover, primitive societies, long after men had learned the use of tools, and acquired an extensive culture, had no place for capitalists. Members of a gens, clan or tribe, considered themselves blood-relatives. The means of production were common property, not private capital. Game, fish, maize, domesticated animals, were not commodities for sale, but articles for consumption. In a social organization, based on the bonds of blood, fraternity and equality were realized in economic relations; that some members of a clan should want while any food was available was inconceivable. Such a social organization permitted division of labour -- first, the natural division based on sex -- but production continued to be for use, or direct exchange for other articles. So long as the producers exchanged their products directly with one another, the exchange value of an article was synonymous with its use-value. Nobody made a "profit" or accumulated "capital."

With the increasing productivity of labour, communities began to produce a surplus they did not need. The trader appeared, first bartering the surplus products of one community for the surpluses of different kinds of products of other communities. Money then [appeared] as a medium of exchange, and a means of converting the "profits" made by the traders into capital. Merchants' capital was realized in the form of precious metals.

Under feudalism, production continued to be mostly for direct use. The obligations of the tenant to the feudal lord, were measured by so many days of labour, or so many bushels of wheat; money did not figure in their relations. Within, or alongside of, the feudal order, free towns arose, but the medieval handicraft guilds, which governed these towns, imposed rules that checked the accumulation of capital. Master craftsmen were permitted to employ only a small number of journeymen and apprentices, and could not become wealthy.

The merchants were accumulating capital in the form of precious metals; but they could not employ their capital in production. They could not build shops and hire craftsmen to work in them so long as the guilds were able to enforce their rules, and while the merchants could not buy the labour power of dependent men they could not become industrialist [industrial] capitalists.

But eventually, in the holy name of freedom, the merchants accomplished their great revolution, and achieved freedom from the fetters of feudalism and the restrictions of handicraft guilds -- freedom to buy and sell labour power and land, as well as commodities. Then merchant capital was transformed into industrial capital by the erection of large shops, employing increasing numbers of hired workers. Feudal property was transformed into private land; common lands were appropriated; people were driven from their little farms to make room for sheep and furnish a labour supply for the new manufacturing shops. And, much later, power machinery was invented and industrial capital entered upon the development that has made it the mad master of the modern world.

42. The Evolution of Property[172]

The men who wield power today are men of property. The "rights" of property are paramount. The struggles of the workers for a fuller, securer life bring them up against the "rights" of property. Private ownership of the major means of production and exchange means power to exploit labour, to take the lion's share of created wealth. An understanding of the institution of private property is necessary to an understanding of the social problem. In the final analysis the badly-used power of private property is responsible for poverty in the midst of abundance, for "over-production" in the midst of under-consumption, unemployment and other disorderly phenomena of business.

The political state is based upon private property. Laws are mostly definitions of the rights of property; the main business of governments, courts, policemen, is the protection of the interests of property owners.

The law makes suicide a crime, but it does not admit that a propertyless man has the right to live. It may acknowledge a claim to charity, but not a right to live. A man down-and-out in order to command the right of protection from the law has to commit an offence against the law. He cannot, by legal right, sleep in a police station except as a legal offender.

Our public school education is designed to convey the impression that the institution of private property has always existed in its present form. But the most powerful form of property is a very modern invention.

---

[172]*Canadian Unionist*, March 1931, 239-241.

Capitalist property now rules the roost; it carries the power of exploiting labour. It is a very different form of property from the ownership of the house in which a man lives.

The very word capital is modern. It has no equivalent in the ancient Greek or Latin languages: proof that capitalist property was non-existent in ancient times, at least as a means of exploiting the masses. Yet it is true that the term capital is a derivative from the rich Latin tongue.

It was only in the 18th century that capitalist property arrived at the stage of a social and economic phenomenon. The growth of capitalist property led to the French Revolution, though it took some time for the French people to discover that the revolution accomplished in the names of liberty, equality, and fraternity was really a process of exalting the rights of bourgeois property. In 1802, nearly a generation after the Revolution, Sebastien Mercier,[173] publishing a *Dictionnaire de Mots Nouveaux* in Paris, deemed it necessary to insert the word "capitaliste" and to append the following interesting definition:--

"Capitaliste: This word is well nigh unknown in Paris. It designates a monster of wealth, a man who has a heart of iron and no affections save metallic ones. Talk to him of the land tax -- and he laughs at you; he does not own an inch of land, how should you tax him? Like the Arabs of the desert who have plundered a caravan, and who bury their gold out of fear of other brigands, the capitalists have hidden away our money."[174]

Evidently there was no great respect for capitalists in France in 1802 -- only 128 years ago. French capitalists have become more important today. The Bank of France is being blamed by jazz economists for all the world's trouble; hoarding of gold in France is said to be responsible for the depression. The United States Federal Reserve Bank is also held partly

---

[173]Louis-Sébastien Mercier (1740-1814) was a French *philosophe* and politician. After a career as a playwright and politician, serving as a member of the Assembly (and imprisoned during the Terror), he established himself as a professional gadfly, attacking the famous and the pompous. Among his books are *Portraits des rois de France* (1785), and *Néologie, ou Vocabulaire de mots nouveaux, à renouveler ou pris dans des acceptions nouvelles* (1801), 3 vols.

[174]McKay is quoting from L.-S.Mercier, *Néologie, Ou Vocabulaire De Mots Nouveaux, A Renouveler, Ou Pris Dans Des Acceptions Nouvelles*, t. 1 (Paris: 1801), 98-99: "Capitaliste. Ce mot n'est guère connu qu'à Paris. Il designe un monstre de fortune, un homme au coeur d'airain, qui n'a que des affections métalliques. Parle-t-on de l'impôt territorial? il s'en moque: il ne possède pas un pouce de terre; comment le taxera-t-on? Ainsi que des Arabes du desert qui viennent de piller une caravane, enterrent leur or, de peur que d'autres brigands ne surviennent, c'est ainsi que nos Capitalistes ont enfoui notre argent." Given Mercier's particular position, it may well have been somewhat incautious of McKay to assume that his cynical definition of capital represented general opinion in early nineteenth-century Paris.

responsible. But curiously the depression held off until the French capitalists began to "hoard" gold. The jazz economists have a hit-or-miss method of reasoning.

It is important to trace the evolution of the idea of property rights, in order to understand the present exploiting power of property. In primitive society, there was no conception of property rights, as sanctioned and sanctified by law today. The notion of ownership did not extend beyond objects of personal use -- weapons and ornaments.

In the ancient, gentile order of society, property could not be a means of exploitation. Primitive man, though more self-sufficing than civilized man, in the sense of being able to gain a living, had no sense of his individuality as distinct from the groups, gens, or tribe in which he lived.

All civilized races have passed through similar stages of evolution. When the white men came to this continent, Red Indian society was about in the same stage as the British had reached in the time of Boadicea, or the Greeks just before the Homeric age.

Among the Indians the idea of special property rights had not yet developed. "If a man entered an Iroquois house," said Morgan,[175] "it was the duty of the women to set food before him......A guest was held sacred, even though an enemy...."[176]

Julius Caesar and Tacitus observed similar customs among the Saxons, Germans and other northern European races....

The classic example of the expropriation of people from the land was afforded by the "clearing" of the Highlands of Scotland. From time immemorial the Highland clans had owned the land they lived on. The clan chiefs were only the titular owners of the land, just as the king of England is the titular owner of all the national soil. The Highland chiefs transformed their nominal right into a right of private property, induced the British parliament to recognize the transformation, and employed soldiers to drive the clansmen from the land. "A king of England might as

---

[175]Lewis Henry Morgan (1818-1881), after a career as a lawyer in Rochester and a senator in the New York state legislature, achieved his lasting fame with his pioneering work as an anthropologist and a theorist of cultural evolution. Morgan initially focused on the Iroquois, but gradually expanded his range of inquiry. He was credited by Engels (in *The Origin of the Family, Private Property and the State*) with having independently discovered the principle of historical materialism. For socialists of McKay's time, the pivotal work of Morgan was *Ancient Society* (1877).

[176]See Lewis H. Morgan, *League of the Ho-De-No-Sau-Nee, or Iroquois* (Rochester, N.Y.: Sage & Brother, 1851), 327-328, for similar comments on hospitality, although not this exact quotation.

well claim the right to drive his subjects into the sea," said Professor Newman. In a few years the Duchess of Sutherland, a mistress of William of Orange, drove out 15,000 men, women, and children from "her estates"....[177]

Thus the institution of private property in land, as a means of levying tribute, arose as a result of violation of time-honoured obligations and of sheer robbery. With the development of modern industry property in the machinery of production became a more effective means of exploitation than even the ownership of land. This form of property which corresponds to the term capital has had a prodigious development, but it is a form of ownership that contains the seeds of its own destruction. Absentee capitalist ownership is no more tolerable than absentee landlordism. The modern capitalist may own stock and lands in enterprises he has never seen; he has no personal interest in the human beings whose labour provides him interest and dividends.

Not only does impersonal property replace the older personal properties, but there is a return to collective property on a higher plane than in primitive society. Civilization, progress, more and more becomes a process of replacing private ownership and individual functions with public ownership and social functions. So far from private property being eternal, it is a mere incident in human history.

iv. Working-Class Culture

43. Moloch and Mammon[178]

Considered in the light of the economic determinism of history, the new imperialism is a fearful and wonderful thing. Unwillingly, perhaps, Hon. Leslie Shaw[179], while secretary of the United States Treasury, revealed the real meaning of this movement.

"Our factories," he said, "are multiplying faster than our trade, and we will shortly have a huge surplus, with no one abroad to buy and no one at

---

[177]McKay is here closely following Karl Marx, *Capital: A Critique of Political Economy*, Vol.I; Marx in turn was citing from F.W. Newman, *Lectures on Political Economy* (London 1851). See Marx, *Capital*, Vol.1 (New York: International Publishers, 1967): 723, 728-729.

[178]*Eastern Labor News*, 7 January 1911.

[179]McKay refers to Leslie Mortimer Shaw (1848-1932), American banker and politician. Shaw was a governor of Iowa, and subsequently Secretary of the Treasury Department under Theodore Roosevelt from 1902 to 1907. Among his works were *Current Issues* (1908) and *Vanishing Landmarks: The Trend Towards Bolshevism* (1919).

home to absorb it, because the labourer has not been paid enough to buy back what he created.

"What will happen then? Why men will be turned out of the factories -- hundreds of thousands of them. Then will they become a greater danger to the country, for they will be hard to deal with."

Then Mr. Shaw shows how these idle men are to be provided with employment -- how the capitalist nations will attempt to dispose of their surplus products.

"The last century was the worst in the world's history for wars," he said. "I look to this century to bring out the greatest conflicts ever waged in the world. It will be a war for markets, and all the nations of the world will be in the fight, for they are all after the same thing -- markets for the surplus products of their factories."

Consider the awful significance of these words addressed by an American statesman (?) to the students of Rockefeller's University. Capitalism destines the rising generation to slaughter. The organic culmination, the logical projection, of present tendencies is universal carnage. Soon the nations, with fully developed individualities, and fully developed productive machinery, will stand face to face, each producing much more than its people can consume -- each confronted with the necessity of finding a market for its surplus products. What then? If history has any lessons for us it is that before economic necessity, ideals, sentiments, beliefs, principles go down like chaff before a gale. In a time rapidly approaching, the people must take over the machinery of production, and institute production for use instead of for profits, or they must fight for new markets -- and as the exploiting interests control the state and the organs of opinion, it is likely they will set to work fighting first.

All the big nations are feverishly preparing for war. Perhaps this preparation is not the conscious expression of the will of the money powers, for the money powers of a nation are blindly unaware of what they are doing most of the time. Our stupid politicians assure us that war between Britain and German is only a question of time; and it will be if the people do not wake up, and cease their blind worship of the blind Juggernaut of the money power. Christ's words are forever true. The money power, and through it the unscrupulous exploitation of the people is the root of all evil.[180]

---

[180]*Timothy* 18:10, "The love of money is the root of all evil."

44. Votes for Women[181]

Sometime ago I heard a workingman ask, "If women were given votes wouldn't chivalry disappear?"

This chap, I take it, believed that men are so generous and chivalrous in their relations to women that it would be unfortunate for women that their rights were acknowledged by the law of the land. The intellectual retainers of the ruling class frequently lament the decay of chivalry, but that does not prevent them opposing womanhood suffrage on the ground that it would cause chivalry to disappear. And unfortunately the views of the ruling classes determine the mental operations of the uneducated workers. There is a popular impression among English speaking people that chivalry blossomed the brightest when knighthood was in flower. And no doubt there is a historical reason for this impression. Chivalry was a product of the feudal system. But it was merely a class relationship, the expression of class interest. As the art of agriculture was developed, the habits of the hunters were abandoned, and tribes acquired fixed abodes. Tribal chiefs gradually acquired over lordship of the lands, and thus became able to transmit property rights or privileges to their offspring. With the development of the power of transmitting property, the loose marriage relations which characterized the age of barbarism assumed a sinister aspect at least for the master class. The overlords naturally wanted to be sure that their rights and privileges were transmitted to their offspring. So the marriage relation assumed a new importance; monogamy became essential; chastity on the part of the women of the proprietary class became the cardinal virtue. And in order to emphasize the importance of this virtue, the feudal lords assumed a protective and chivalrous attitude towards women of their own class. But the feudal morality was essentially a class affair, dictated by economic class interests. The feudal lords showed no courtesy or chivalry to women of the working class. Even down to the time of the French revolution the French nobles claimed and exercised the rights of the first night with women on their estates. The English overlords were not so brutal; being usually foreigners their economic interests counselled restraint. Roans, Danes, Saxons, Normans, all were naturally disinclined to actions calculated to goad the natives to desperation and after feudalism was fully established the barons were busy fighting among themselves and anxious to command the good will and support of their vassals; but for all that the English nobility have been licentious enough in their attitude to the women of the working class. Even today the gentleman's son considers the serving maid fair game.

Clergymen frequently put forward the claim that the church was responsible for the development of chivalry towards women. To weigh the worth of this claim we have only to remember that the feudal lords

---

[181]*Eastern Labor News*, 12 October 1912.

treated working class women with contemptuous brutality. Certainly the medieval church used its power in the interests of the ruling class; it was a strong supporter of monogamy. Only the Pope could dissolve a feudal marriage, and he would not because [of] the interests of the feudal lords as a class. The exigencies of feudal inheritance were bound up with monogamy. But there is certainly no evidence that the church was at all concerned to elevate the women of the common people. Many of the clerical princes, then lords of great [feudal estates], made a generous use of the right of the first night. In the eleventh century the church under Pope Gregory VII showed its contempt for women by ordering its clergy to refrain from marriage. This order merely expressed the economic interest of the church; the clergy had been appropriating so much of the church property to bequeath to their sons that the hierarchy had become annoyed. After the reformation, when the church was robbed of its property by the nobles and bourgeoisie, the Protestant clergy were permitted to marry because there was no particular economic reason why they should continue in celibacy. One thing the Reformation and the rise of the trading class, bringing with it a new form of property, did for women was to liberate love, and give a sanction to love marriages, a kind of union which among the ruling classes in the feudal era was as unusual as love marriages among royalty today. But even after the reformation the clergy were wrangling over the questions whether women had souls, and millions of women were burned as witches.

Owing to the fact that in the reigns of Charles II, James II, and William of Orange, the feudal aristocracy and the trading classes amalgamated their interest, the virtues of both classes have been unduly emphasized and we have been given false or hypocritical ideas of English history. If you don't believe me, read ... the Roman Tactitus' account of the customs of our ancestors, the ancient Saxons, Teutons and Celts, wherein he shows that women occupied a position she has never since held in any of the so-called Christian nations.[182]

45. Women's Suffrage[183]

It may be doubted whether the Women's Suffrage Association of Saint John have done their cause much service by asking the Provincial Government to extend the provincial franchise to women holding property and entitled to vote in civic elections. It is true they have also demanded the suffrage for all women, but the fact that they have made a

---

[182]See Tacitus, *Dialogus Agricola and Germania* (Oxford: Clarendon, 1908), 94: "...the Germans fear far more anxiously for the women's sake than for their own, and the strongest hold upon the loyalty of these tribes is got by demanding as hostages girls of noble family. Indeed they believe that there is in women some divine spark of foreknowledge, and they do not despise their advice or neglect their answers."

[183]*Eastern Labor News*, 22 February 1913.

special appeal for women holding property does not argue a very intelligent appreciation of the conditions which make it advisable that women should have the suffrage. At any rate it is not an appeal that can be very well supported by socialists and trade unionists, who, on general principles, believe in equal rights for women....

Often you hear clergymen, politicians and other sorts of people, who do not realize how the bourgeois regime is overthrowing its own cherished institutions, saying that the family, the home, are the bulwarks of the nation, an antiquated sentiment conveniently forgotten when questions of business or trade arise. Once upon a time economic conditions made marriage the logical step for man and woman. When a man took a wife, he got not only a cook, but a real help mate, a woman to weave, spin, sew and carry on many other industrial arts. Then there was rhyme and reason for the bourgeois sentiment that the woman's place is in the home. There were no factories, no other place in which she could work and earn her livelihood.

But the industrial revolution has changed all this. A man who takes a wife only gets a cook, and often a poor one at that. A survival of a sentiment developed in the old condition makes him think it a disgrace to allow his wife to work outside of the home, a sentiment which no doubt has some justification in the fact that conditions of labour in factories which have taken over the old home industries are usually about as disgraceful as they can be. Hence a demoralization of the married women of the masses as well as of the classes.

Under all the older orders [the woman was always a great worker], not only as a cook, but as a manufacturer of household and family necessities. The only reason why a modern man should consider it a disgrace for his wife to work in a modern factory is that the conditions of labour are not what they ought to be. And this is one of the main points that justifies -- though that is hardly the word -- the women's movement for the suffrage. Everybody recognizes today that the political authority can and does exercise a powerful influence upon the conditions of labour, and it is important that the political power should be used, not only to improve labour conditions for the unmarried women who work in a factory, but also to improve them to the end that no man should consider it a disgrace to have his wife working in a factory and doing her share in the world's work. The fact that such a condition is only attainable by the abolition of capitalistic property in the means of wealth production is -- well, matter for another article, as well as a straight contradiction of the policy of asking for votes for women on the ground that they are property holders.

46. Labour's Will and Labour's Methods[184]

Scant consideration was given to the request of the Saint John Trades and Labor Council that a representative of labour be appointed to the Board of School Trustees. That was to be expected. In some rural communities, or small towns, workers do serve as school trustees, but in such communities class lines are not closely drawn, and the worker hasn't any working-class ideas anyway. In the larger city things are different; the bourgeoisie hedge themselves in with a certain divinity, and don't want a labour man to appear on the stage, unless indeed they are sure they can use him for their own purposes. It would be a dangerous precedent to admit a representative of organized labour to the school board, because organized labour stands for revolutionary ideas. There are men on the school board who might call themselves workers, but no one could consider them as representatives of labour.

But the refusal of the request of the Trades Council may do some good. It may induce some workers to reflect on their position in capitalist society; if they do that they will doubtless come to the conclusion that the people who do the work in this world don't really count for much. And then they may ask themselves, "Why shouldn't the workers have something to say about the education of their children?" When they begin to ask such questions they won't be long in coming to the conclusion that there is something in the socialists' arguments, and that it may be worthwhile to study socialism.

Of course it was to be expected that the request for labour representation on the School Board would be turned down, but that is no reason why the request should not be repeated. Many will say, what is the good of demanding something we know we won't get, or asking for an office already filled? But that is the mark of a servile mind. The bourgeois representatives bank on that very attitude of mind. They know they can afford to deny the workers what they demand, because the workers do not usually have gumption enough to continue demanding what they want, because they have abundant evidence that at election times the workers are fool enough to forget their own interests.

Of late the Trades Council of Saint John has shown a disposition to make demands, and they should continue this policy. Every time they make a demand upon the City Council, the provincial council or any other body, whether the demand is refused or not, it is bound to do some good in the way of educating the working class. There is no sense, for instance, in waiting for another vacancy on the School Board before demanding representation there. At every meeting of the Trades Council, at every

[184]Originally published as "Keep Up the Fight! Lack of Will Power is Labor's Greatest Handicap," *Eastern Labor News*, 2 August 1913.

meeting of a trade union, a resolution on the matter should be passed and forwarded to the City Council. If this policy were pursued, it would provoke discussion in the City Council, and among the people. And it would give organized labour a reputation for determination that would make the politicians sit up and take notice.

Every trades council and trades union should have printed forms setting forth what they want this or that public body to do, and at every meeting the resolutions on such printed forms should be read and passed, filled in with the names of the president and secretary and mailed to the public bodies in question. If trade unions and socialists had an elementary knowledge of [psychology] they would make greater progress than they do. The importance of advertisement cannot be over-estimated. The fortune of Post, the manufacturer of breakfast foods, and one of the greatest enemies of labour, has been built up of advertisement. Organized labour has unlimited opportunities for advertising itself, its needs and its demands; and generally it neglects them. This is a great mistake. Any businessman knows that one or two advertisements [are] of little or no value; he knows that if he wants results he must keep on advertising. You know as well as I do that if you see an advertisement of something new for the first time it makes little impression; but you know that if that advertisement confronts you from a number of different sources, or for number of times, you become interested. Personally I have more faith in the power of suggestion than in the power of argument. If a man believes in a certain thing it is generally useless to try by argument to win him to another belief, because while you are arguing with him all his ideas are stationed about his beliefs, and even though your arguments are the more logical you can't move him. The advertiser who has studied psychology does not make the mistake of trying to argue anything; he merely suggests. The advantage of his method is that he catches you off your guard; at any rate you are not aggressively armed against him. And everybody knows the cumulative power of suggestion.

Take an illustration. The Typographical Union sometimes sends a letter to the City Council, asking that the city printing bear the union label. The newspapers refer to the request. The members of the City Council ask one another: "What do they mean by the union label?" That is not always a pose. Many members of City Council never heard of the union label until the City Clerk read a casual communication from the printers' union. Naturally they paid no particular attention to such communication, and usually by the time another letter was sent in, another set of city councillors were in charge of affairs.

That has been the way with the demand that the city of Saint John have its printing done in a union shop. But if the same demand had been made at every meeting, something would have resulted and the general public would very likely have been moved by the insistence of organized labour to enquire what the union label stood for. When the businessmen want anything from public organizations they keep on demanding it till they get it.

47. The Importance of Trade Unions for Socialism[185]

....Some socialists attach more importance to Marxian phrases than to the Marxian method. Hence they do not recognize as socialists like Kautsky[186] do [the] importance of trade unions. By the socialist method of reasoning it is easy to show the value of trade union effort. It is said that the value of a commodity is the cost of reproducing it, and that on the average price corresponds [to] the value. Suppose a worker in a shoe factory does work equivalent to the production of five pairs of shoes a day. His wage is $2, the shoes are sold at $2 a pair, or $10. Leaving out of the question costs of raw material and overhead charges, the worker gets one-fifth of the product of his labour.

Now suppose through his trade union he puts up his wage to $4. Assuming that the value of shoes is determined by the cost of production and prices on the average correspond with values, the manufacturer will add the $2 a day extra for wages to the price of the five pair of shoes, and they will sell for $12 instead of $10. That is the worker will be getting one-third of his product.

Certainly a trade union must have accomplished something if it enables a worker to increase his share of the product from one-fifth to one-third.

The pure-and-simple socialist who believes in nothing but political action is as bad as the pure-and-simple trade unionists. Labour must use all weapons possible.

---

[185]Originally published as "The Workers are Waking Up," *Eastern Labor News*, 23 August 1913.

[186]Karl Kautsky (1854-1938) was the most influential German social democratic theorist of the early twentieth century. Prior to 1914, his writings were highly esteemed by most socialists, including Lenin and Engels; however, his support for the War distanced him from many former comrades. He was noted for his opposition to attempts (associated with Eduard Bernstein) to "revise" the basic Marxist orientation of the German Social Democratic Party. He was the founder and editor of the important organ *Die Neue Zeit* (1883-1917). His writings include *The Economic Doctrines of Karl Marx* (1887), *The Class Struggle* (1892), and *The Road to Power* (1909). McKay would probably have read Kautsky in the Charles Kerr translations, which included, by 1913, *Ethics and the Materialistic Conception of History*, *Life of Frederick Engels*, and *The Social Revolution*.

48. A Working-Class Morality[187]

One of the things we are supposed to believe is that moral laws are absolute, that they have a supernatural sanction and remain the same under all conditions. But morality after all has its roots in the social relations of men, and changes with alterations in material conditions. Men very early discovered that in order to live together in peace and security, certain rules of conduct would have to be adhered to, and if necessary enforced by the will of the majority. In the tribal period such rules were only binding as between members of the tribe or gens. Take the Mosaic laws. Even the ten commandments were not supposed to be observed universally. The same God who is supposed to have engraved on a tablet of stone the commandment "Thou shalt not kill", frequently commanded the Jews to slay men, women and children of other tribes....

As nations were developed through federations enforced or voluntary of various tribes, the rules of conduct essential to social life became of wider, but still limited application....

The glory of the early Christians was their desire to make the observance of tribal morality a universal condition. But their splendid hopes were not destined to be realized immediately because men who only learn from experience had to go through a long and painful historic development, before they arrived at the stage where sectional and class interests would be swallowed up by the greater interests of humanity as a whole, or the most useful part of it, the working class.

Christ was, I think, the first world-conscious workingman, and the fact that he addressed his message to the workers is of the greatest significance from the historical point of view. Unlike Buddha, who was a king's son, the Nazarene carpenter apparently saw that the lowly of all lands had common interests, and that only the workers could develop a universal morality. But Christ's ideals were not capable of realization, because material conditions and the state of culture made the organization of a world wide working-class movement impossible. And after the ruling classes under Constantine captured the movement of the early Christian proletariat,[188] they put an interpretation upon the gospels calculated to keep the workers quiet and submissive by transferring the hope of a

---

[187]*Eastern Labor News*, 20 September 1913.

[188]McKay refers to Constantine I, Emperor of Rome, whose victory at the Battle of the Milvian Bridge in 312 A.D. represented the moment when he set himself up as the protector of his Christian subjects. Few contemporary scholars of the Early Church would share McKay's conviction that its history can be related so neatly to class interests. For an accessible discussion, see Henry Chadwick, *The Early Church* (Harmondsworth: Penguin, 1967), Chapter Eight.

Kingdom of Heaven on earth to an abode of bliss beyond the skies. Besides, the workers were not a distinct class in the sense they are today.

Only recently have the conditions making possible a morality of more or less general application begun to appear. Capitalists moved by no higher inspiration than the lust of lucre, are creating conditions which compel the workers to unite in ever-enlarging organizations. The rise of international trade unions and the growth of a world-wide socialist movement, are accompanied by the evolution of a distinctive working-class morality. In a class-ruled state the virtues most carefully inculcated are respect for authority, obedience, contentment, and a credulous and uncritical attitude towards life generally; everything is good which tends to keep the workers quiet and submissive. But the morality which is specially designed to protect and promote ruling class interests, is losing its hold upon the working class. The militant proletarians are declining to accept the view at the basis of ruling class morality that everything is ordered by a divine Providence for the best. Investigation and a little independent thinking show that things are ordered not according to a divine plan, but according to the interests of a comparatively small class. And the worker begins to realize that it is possible to have affairs conducted in a manner more conducive to the general interest. New ideals, more splendidly human than those of any other class, take possession of the worker's mind, and rules of conduct tending toward the realization of these ideals become the moral standards of his class. And because, as in the case of other class[es], solidarity is essential to the accomplishment of working-class possibilities, it is becoming so that a worker who becomes a scab is regarded by his class as a traitor, and though the workers do not hang and quarter a traitor to them as the greatest and worst of criminals as other classes have done, they treat him with contumely.

49. Working-Class Culture[189]

The working class must develop a new philosophy of life, a new culture. Authority and tradition ruled the past; for the worker to doubt what he was told by the ruling classes was a crime. Faith or rather credulity was the principal virtue; the masses of the people were expected to believe any absurdity. Anybody who exhibited a critical spirit was regarded as an infidel and visited with various forms of master class displeasure.

No doubt under the feudal system faith was an appropriate virtue. This power of the lord and the security of the vassal depended on mutual fidelity. In the heyday of feudalism the baron was more interested in making his retainers contented and loyal than in making money. The great baron regarded himself as a being superior to the common clay, but he had to have the same virtues of courage, fidelity and hardihood that he

---

[189]*Eastern Labor News*, 8 November 1913.

expected in his retainers. There was something noble and fine about the old ceremony of swearing homage -- something not found in relations of master and man under capitalism. When the old baron took the hand of his retainer, he swore to protect his life and rights, before the retainer swore fealty. There was a personal, even spiritual quality in the bargain between the old baron and his vassal -- something not found in the bargain between a modern capitalist and his wage-slave. The philosophy of the feudal system may have been false, but it was not hypocritical. Socially the feudal system was based on faith between man and man, master and vassal; and quite naturally as it developed it produced a culture and a religion that made faith its cornerstone, and prohibited freedom of thought.

When men began to develop new forms and forces of production, when different communities or districts began to specialize in the production of certain commodities, and there appeared a class which undertook to establish trade on an extensive scale between the different specializing communities, the feudal system, with its customs and culture, had to undergo drastic changes. Under feudalism the idea of personal freedom was non-existent, serf, yeoman, esquire, knight, little baron and great baron, everybody was a vassal of somebody higher in rank and the overlord of all was in turn a vassal of the Deity.

When production began to lose its individualistic character, when it was no longer feasible for the producer to market his product, a distinctive trading class appeared, a class whose interests demanded freedom of trade. The feudal lords had by that time begun to appreciate the value of portable wealth and had formed a habit of levying tribute upon the caravans of traders. The heads of the feudal system developed this practice in various ways; we are told that one of the principal grievances that led to the rebellion against Charles I of England was the levy of ship money. Previous to the reign of Charles I the trading class had begun to assess itself, and its need of freedom of trade had given birth to the idea of personal freedom. So we find a new spirit of individualism coming into the world, a spirit which supplied the moral fervor of the so-called reformation, cut off the head of Charles I with its feudal ideas, exalted the bible over the church, and developed a culture more individual and in some respects more narrow than the culture which it had overthrown. Luther exhibited contempt and hostility towards the working class. John Knox's philosophy was based on a profound contempt for the great mass of humanity. Some superstitions appropriate to feudalism were overthrown, but the business classes had their own superstitions. The Puritans were believers in witchcraft, and burnt countless numbers of women at the stake. They were fierce champions of such forms of liberty as suited the needs of the bourgeois but allowed scant liberty of thought or action to the working class.

50. Labour's Message and the Teachers[190]

Labour organizations should always be working towards their ideals. Those organizations which merely mark time, stagnate. Agitation and education must be continuous, if, as they say, a sucker is born every minute. Socially the working class must be placed in the category of suckers. Certainly they allow themselves to be flim-flammed and fooled to the limit. They carry the work of the world, create great wealth, slaughter their fellows by wholesale, and never get more than a meagre livelihood.

In England, Germany, France and other countries the workers have arrived at a sufficiently advanced stage of intellectual development to realize the value of labour papers. They have not in this country. The amount of money which labour organizations pay over to capitalist papers for advertising regular meetings -- not very useful advertising -- would go a long way to help make the labour press a really effective fighting force.

Let me indicate one way labour organizations can help labour papers and the labour movement. The school teachers have little knowledge of the operation of economic and social forces. They have to be taught that their interests are bound up with the interests of the whole wage earning class. They have also to be taught the need and value of organization on trade and class lines.

At the present time it would be a thing for the *[Eastern] Labor News* to issue a teachers' number, containing articles indicating the need of the teachers joining in the general labour movement, and for the labour organizations in different cities to arrange for the distribution of such a number among the school teachers. Even in Saint John it would only require a few dollars to send a copy to the hundred odd school teachers in the district. Their names and addresses can be easily secured. And labour organizations have much to gain by getting the teachers to study the philosophy of the labour movement. They shape the minds of the rising generations.

---

[190]Originally published as "Organize the School Teachers," *Eastern Labor News*, 15 November 1913.

51. The Mis-Education of the Young[191]

The ruling class at present control the system of education. Up till recently the public school courses of instruction were arranged mainly with a view to preparing the pupil for a college course. More recently in obedience to the demands of the new industrial conditions, there has been a cry for some form of technical instruction to take the place of the training master was obliged to give his apprentice in other days. In Germany, England and other advanced countries, extensive systems of technical education have been established and here in Canada the matter is receiving some attention. But like the old, the new form of education is perhaps more in the interests of the masters than the workers, though no doubt it is more advantageous to the workers to receive a technical education. One thing it will do will be to train the workers to scientific methods of thought, and when the workers begin to think along scientific lines there will be some danger to capitalist society.

So far the capitalist class has seen to it that the kind of instruction given the masses had a more or less chloroforming effect. School histories are written from the point of view of the dominant class, and give a very peculiar version of the course of human affairs. Everything of importance is represented as the work of some great man, or a special providence; but the mass movements of the working classes are generally described as insurrections or rebellions of the lowest of the low without any definite or decent motive.

Even in the Sunday schools much of the instruction is of a kind to encourage servility among the masses. Looking over some Sunday school lessons recently I noticed Joseph was held up as a hero to the children. In one lesson Joseph was described as a figure, or a sort of forerunner of Christ; in another children were advised that if they imitated Joseph they, too, might be great men. Now from the working class view point Joseph prefigured Christ about as much as Joseph Chamberlain represents Karl Marx. Joseph was thrown out of his tribe because his fawning disposition and acquisitive propensities menaced the communistic social arrangements of his tribe. The rising autocracy of Egypt found in him a useful tool; with the help of his peculiar abilities and by the connivance with the Egyptian priesthood then also reaching out for new powers, the Pharaohs were able to reduce the Egyptian peasantry to a condition of slavery. More than this, they reduced Joseph's brethren, the Israelites, to slavery. Joseph was the original monopolist, the organizer of the first corner in grain. Note that the peasantry had to give their lands and then sell themselves into bondage to the Pharaohs in order to get grain. Why did their crops fail at the critical time? It is well known that the ancient

[191]Originally published as "Mental Dopesters," *B.C.Federationist*, 12 December 1913. Another version of the same article appears in *Eastern Labor News*, 16 August 1913.

priesthood controlled the irrigation system of Egypt. It was not a difficult matter when the time was ripe to carry out the designs of Pharaoh and Joseph upon the freedom of the people, for the priesthood to cause a failure of the crops.

Christ was in character, purpose and achievements the direct antithesis of Joseph, yet in Sunday schools where the Carpenter's views are supposed to be taught, Joseph is held [up] as an example to young people.

52. The Worker Must Learn To Think[192]

A reformer once brought to the attention of Gladstone a scheme to improve the lot of the working class, so the story runs:

The statesman told him to lay his scheme before the workers and then come back and tell him what they thought about it. Years later the statesman met the would-be reformer.

"Well, what did the workers think of your famous scheme?" he asked.

"To tell you the truth, sir, they don't think," was the reply.

The story unfortunately contains more truth than poetry. The workers do little thinking about matters that really concern them. Not that they are deficient in brains; most of the important technical knowledge of the world is held in the brains of the working class. But the day's work absorbs a large share of the mental energy of brain and manual workers, and hence their minds find it difficult to think positively about the world in which they live. Their minds are the minds of tired people, submissive, uncritical. They are content to accept the ideas of the possessing class, ideas that find expression in the press, in politics, courts, pulpits; ideas that reflect property interests. Thus there is a good foundation for the saying: "The ruling ideas of any age are the ideas of the ruling class."[193]

But conditions are more and more rendering it necessary that the working class develop a mind of its own. Evolution imposes the necessity of the working class developing a method of thinking different from that of the bourgeoisie. Many members of the working class already think along real "labour" lines; but their influence is little because the great majority of the

---

[192]*Canadian Railroad Employees' Monthly*, March 1923, 5-7.

[193]McKay refers to Marx and Engels. *The German Ideology*: "The ideas of the ruling class are in every epoch the ruling ideas: i.e., the class which is the ruling *material* force of society is at the same time its ruling *intellectual* force." Karl Marx, Frederick Engels, *Collected Works*, Vol.5, *Marx and Engels: 1845-1847* (New York: International Publishers, 1975), 59.

workers still have passive minds and no real understanding of working class logic.

The businessman thinks largely in terms of commodities. Hence his ideal of low wages and long hours of labour. But he can't help himself. Even quite important trade union officials who have done good service to their fellows think in terms of commodities. As trade union officials, they are merchants of labour power. They repudiate the suggestion that labour is a commodity; but they know very well that if the union controls the available supply of labour power it fixes the price or wage at a comparatively high rate, just in the same way a merchant does if he controls the commodities in sight. The merchant cares nothing about what becomes of a commodity after he [sells] it; the labour leader is concerned about the conditions in which labour works, but not in the results of the application of labour power. But it is precisely in this result that labour is vastly concerned, and ought to be interested.

In primitive conditions the producer controls the product. He produces for the family or community use, or for direct sale to a neighboring community. The satisfaction of needs is the first consideration; people do not waste effort piling up a surplus of commodities which they will not use and cannot sell or exchange.

But with the development of commodity production, and the division of labour in various forms, the producers no longer control their products. On the contrary, the products often control the producer; at any rate the more products pile up the sooner a crisis arrives, and large bodies of producers plunge into unemployment, penury and misery.

The capitalists control the means of production and distribution. They may not own a farm, which is a means of production. But they do control the strategic positions in production and distribution. And because they have the direction of the production and distribution of products they are necessarily concerned with the causes which govern them. The worker as a mere labour unit, has no direct concern in the productive process; he contributes his labour power and passive obedience and receives a wage -- that is the measure of his direct interest. Indirectly, he is of course concerned about the continuance of the productive process, on which depends his work and wages.

But while the capitalists direct production and distribution they no longer control these processes. The application of steam and electricity [has] made the productive forces so powerful that control of them is impossible even for the gigantic combinations of capital which seek to monopolize their benefits. The inability of capitalists to control production is shown by the periodic business depressions, and is manifest continually in the vagaries of the stock exchange, and fluctuations of prices of commodities.

A good many unthinking workers blame the capitalists for these recurring phases of our anarchistic system of production; they do not always see that the system is responsible, but are vexed with the employers when work is slack, or not available at all.

If the bourgeoisie were able to control the forces of production, there would be no depressions, for these phenomena strike terror to the heart of businessmen as well as workers. They ruin capitalists by the thousands. That is the proof that while the capitalists direct the productive processes they do not control them. They do not even understand why they cannot control them. They cannot admit that their system is at fault, or that they are incompetent. They cannot throw the responsibility on spots in the sun, as they did at one time,[194] so they attribute the perturbations of production to what they call economic laws, mysterious agencies which distribute rewards and punishments like heathen deities. Hence the bourgeois mind believes the economic world is regulated by an unknowable force, or mysterious spook, just as the savage thought the natural world was the plaything of pagan gods. And because the bourgeoisie neither comprehend or control economic forces they regard them as sacrosanct mysteries not to be questioned by the vulgar, things as uncontrollable as the causes of the weather. When these forces throw prosperity into the lap of business they accept it gratefully as [rewards] of virtue; when these forces spread ruin and despair the bourgeoisie endure them with what stoicism they possess, and counsel the workers to exhibit patience.

To-day the causes of the weather are uncontrollable. To the uneducated man they are mysterious; violent storms were to the savage mind a terrifying manifestation of the wrath of irresponsible deities or demons. But to the meteorologist there is nothing mysterious about the weather; his predictions are more reliable than the predictions of businessmen about economic movements. If he disposed of sufficient energy, man could learn to control the weather.

Natural causes [affect] the play of economic forces. A drought means a poor harvest, and a poor harvest affects business. But a greater portion of the productive process is mechanical. Manufacturing is largely independent of weather. Economic forces are the resultant of human activities; and this law therefore should be largely subject to human control. The intelligence that harnesses a great natural force like the Niagara should not be daunted by the forces which human activities set in motion. Science has harnessed to human service many natural forces that terrified and bewildered the savage. Even our haphazard economic order is capable of discounting the effects of a disaster due to nature, such as a

---

[194]McKay is exaggerating how widely Jevons's speculations about sun-spots were generally accepted by anybody. See Note 107.

crop failure. Irrigation defeats dry weather. In any case, transportation improvements have made the world so small that a crop failure here and there need not spell disaster; it is possible to draw supplies from the ends of the earth. And the peculiar thing is that the farmers usually find a short crop an advantage. In 1921 when Quebec suffered from drought the farm crops of that province had a much higher value than they did in 1922 when the quantity [of] production was much greater. Again the present business depression in Canada and the United States began while agricultural production on this continent was at its peak. So the troubles of our economic order cannot be wholly ascribed to nature or her laws.

The capitalist system has extraordinary powers of production, but private direction of them is no longer adequate. Some form of collective control has become essential; but for society to operate these marvellous productive forces for the satisfaction of society's needs requires a new method of thinking, and a new conception of property. The next advance society makes will not be easy; but it has to be made if we are to escape from the present recurring evils of depression and hard times. Conscious control, by intelligent organs of society, of the means of production and distribution are necessary if we are to escape from the present haphazard economic order, an anarchical regime which foster[s] social inequalities, portions wealth to parasites and a bare existence to workers, and engenders wars and economic upheavals which our wise men can only attribute to chance and mysterious causes.

The capitalist world is topsy turvy. It is a puzzling play of economic forces, distributing good fortune and bad fortune, without obvious rhyme or reason. It is full of strange idols, the principal being the Golden Calf. Its temple is the stock exchange, the altar of chance. Its success and failures are often inexplicable, dependent upon unforeseen events. Here, a man inaugurates a carefully conceived enterprise, and labours skilfully and industriously; a crisis, and the enterprise collapses; a dry goods merchant may be ruined by an unforeseen change in fashion, a grocer by the change in the location of a factory. There a man launches an enterprise lightly, in a happy-go-lucky fashion, and perhaps makes a great success of it, to his own and others' amazement.

The typical bourgeois mind is fatalistic. It is prone to superstition and a mystical belief in chance. Troubled by the unknowable of the social order it seeks within itself an explanation of the ups and downs, the come and go, of business. Hence a belief in a special providence, awarding success or failure in an arbitrary manner, not always with regard to justice or deserts. The bourgeois mind, however, believes that this special providence is not altogether indifferent to the glaring injustices of the social order. Hence the belief that the special providence will repay the victims of its blunders in this world by special consideration in the hereafter. It is a comforting belief for the bourgeois who is unable to account for his failures in this world; and [as] it appears to the bourgeoisie as a whole it is a convenient doctrine wherewith to quiet their consciences when the injustices of their world cry for redress. It would be presumptuous for bourgeois society to show an interest in the making of laws designed to punish big pilferers in high places when a special providence will attend to the task in the hereafter. It would also be presumptuous for the bourgeoisie to tackle the problem of making life richer, fuller and happier for the workers, when the more misery they endure during their temporary sojourn here, the greater will be their happiness throughout the ever lasting hereafter. Besides, for the bourgeois it is highly convenient to offer the labourers a blank cheque on the hereafter when they ask for more wages in this world.

But the capitalists as a class are more eager to lay hold of the gold and dross of this world than to increase their claims upon the bank of the hereafter, and they will not, when economic forces carry them forward on the flood tide of [prosperity], share their good fortune with the workers, unless the workers are organized strong enough to cause trouble; and then what they share with one hand they often contrive to take back with the other. They do not consider themselves bound by their own precepts. Hence the bourgeois world has two codes of conduct -- one for precept and especially for the edification of the workers, the other for practice if possible. The contradiction between current ideas of justice, honesty and morality and the common practice puzzles the bourgeois; but it cannot force him to efforts to establish a regime of justice. This mental bewilderment, which does not prevent him acting in what he considers to be his interest, is the reflection of the confusion which exists in the economic order. And he cannot get rid of the dualism of his mind while his life is ruled by economic laws which apparently are indifferent to his efforts to guide the economic machine.

v. Trade Unionism and Labour Politics

53. Reform or Revolution[195]

The more I have studied the social problem, the stronger my conviction that mere reform is futile. Not that I have any objection to reforms; according to my way of thinking the faster reforms are tried out, the better. Some people cry out against reforms because they imagine reforms will prolong the life of the capitalist system. My own opinion is that reforms merely hasten the evolution of the capitalist system, disillusion the workers, and bring nearer the revolution that will inaugurate the co-operative commonwealth. Germany has marched farthest along the road of reform and in Germany we find the strongest Socialist movement.

---

[195]*Eastern Labor News*, 12 April 1913.

Every system of class rule after having attained a certain stage of development begins to destroy itself. Capitalism in advanced countries has already attained that stage. More and more governments excite the derision and antagonism of intelligent workers; parliaments make themselves the objects of ridicule. Big capitalists not only oppress the workers, they arouse the hatred of the small capitalists. For some years American magazines have been exposing the corruption and general cussedness of the big businessmen, and now it is dawning on intelligent people that business, big or little, is corrupt to its marrow, that the interests of business [are] always and everywhere opposed to the welfare of the people....

....Even if we could place a government composed of socialists, class conscious workers, in power at Ottawa tomorrow they could do little or nothing to help the workers. If they tried to establish the co-operative commonwealth, the capitalist governments of Great Britain, the United States, and any other country whose people have investments here would send soldiers to show us the need of submitting to the rule of capitalism. The overthrow of feudalism and the rise of the businessmen to political power took place at different times in different countries, but the overthrow of capitalism and the rise of the working class must be an international event; at least it must synchronize in the more powerful nations. Therein lies the great significance, the real reason, of international trade unionism.

54. Industrial unionism and labour politics[196]

At the public meeting in the Court House, Saint John, some time ago a union bricklayer, illustrating the effects of progress and prosperity, said:

"Six or seven years ago I could save a little money; today I cannot save anything, and I certainly have no extravagant habits." Possibly the speaker's family had grown a little and that added to his expenses. Nevertheless his statement points a moral. The Bricklayers and Masons' Union is the strongest organization in Saint John, or on the continent. With steady work, its members should be fairly comfortable. However they probably have as steady work now as they did some years ago, that phase of the problem does not affect the complaint of the bricklayer who considers he is not as well off now as he used to be. Other classes of workers are finding it increasingly difficult to make ends meet. Many workmen in Saint John a generation ago used to own their homes. Very few workers of the young generation own their homes, or expect to. Mr. Hatheway's scheme to have workers build homes on city land has not attracted a great deal of attention, mainly because few workers are in a position to build homes of their own. The Simms Company made

---

[196]*Eastern Labor News*, 26 April 1913.

enquiries among their employees, and found that practically none had money to put up a house.

If it were not for the trade unions the workers would be much worse off than they are. But it is idle to blink the fact that trade unionism is not achieving the results we ought to expect. Comparatively few unions have been able to put up wages faster than the cost of living has been increased. The railway unions and organizations which have conducted energetic label crusades have secured improvements in the position of their members, but when all is said the benefits obtained have not been great. Many trades have barely held their own, and that through costly strikes and great sacrifices....

Industrial development creates new conditions and compels a readjustment of ideas and methods. Not that industrial unionism is going to jump the workers into the promised land. They will plod along much the same as now on the economic field, hard put to keep wages a notch ahead of the cost of living. What mainly we have to expect from the emergence of the principle of industrial union [unionism], is the organization of a real labour party, standing in [on] a class conscious platform. With the recognition of the need of close co-operation between the unions in one industry, grows also the recognition of the interdependence of all unions, and the common interests of all members of the working class. So long as the worker's interest is centered in his craft union, he cannot be expected to have any definite conception of the way the interests of his craft [are] bound up with the interests of the working class as a whole; and lacking such a conception he does not see the need of political action on the part of the class conscious working class. When he realizes the need of co-operating with other crafts on the economic field, it is only a step for him to realize the need of adding a new weapon to his arsenal, and using his political power.

The workers in this country have been indifferent to labour politics. Probably they were wiser than they knew. To vote for a candidate simply because he is a member of the working class is neither here nor there. It is not only the socialists who refuse to follow a mere reform party calling itself a labour party; the workers in all countries, except Australia, have refused to take much stock in such a party. In Germany, France, England and other countries we find the labour party attracting adherents just in proportion as it becomes revolutionary; just in proportion as it takes its stand on a class conscious platform. In Toronto at the last civic elections, a labour party, composed of socialists and trade unions, declaring its aim to be the overthrow of the wage system, polled a very good vote. In previous elections labour candidates in Toronto received little support even from trade unions.

Socialists cannot consistently support any candidate who does not take his stand on the grounds of the class struggle and declare for the overthrow of capitalism and the abolition of the wage system. And there is no particular reason why they should support candidates outside the socialist party, as they did in Toronto, because if a man recognizes the necessity of the abolition of the wage system he ought to be in the socialist party. It is not at present important that we should elect class conscious workers to parliament; the one thing important is to educate the workers to a knowledge of the class structure of society. An election campaign from the standpoint of the revolutionary proletariat is simply a matter of utilizing opportunities of education. The main value of the socialist party in Germany or the revolutionary Independent Labour Party in England is the ability to use parliamentary position to educate the workers. The part they play in effecting reforms is of no great moment. Reforms may improve the social position of the workers, but often they enable the capitalists to intensify the economic exploitation of the workers. No countries have adopted more reform legislation than Germany and England, but the economic position of the workers in those countries is even worse than in Canada or the United States. English and German workers have made but one outstanding gain -- through education and political organization they are nearer the capture of the citadels of political power, and therefore nearer the revolution that will overthrow capitalism and usher in the co-operative commonwealth.

55. Reply to Jack Plane of the Truro *Citizen*[197]

A Socialist writer having remarked that Borden and Laurier ought to give a practical exhibition of their military spirit, Jack Plane of the Truro *Citizen* observes,

"Just so, and why does not this socialist writer get into overalls and put his theory about working conditions into practice. There is a fearful lot of people preaching idealism who never attempt to practise it. The pen is lighter than the hammer or trowel, therefore they choose the pen in preference to the more heavy instruments of practical work."

Certainly there are many writers who are socialists, but they are socialists because they have intelligence -- not because it is in their interests. Nobody ever made a fortune writing for socialist or labour papers; those able to pay for contributions are few and far between. And generally the writer who is a socialist has sacrificed chances of advancement either because of the time he has devoted to writing things for which he gets nothing, or because the fact that he was known to be socialist has prejudiced powerful people against him.

---

[197]*Eastern Labor News*, 2 August 1913.

A certain old gentleman in Saint John believes that Samuel Gompers gets $25,000 a year, and that the workers would be happy if they did not hand over their money to boated union officials. I have shown the *American Federationist* to him, but its report of the salary paid to Gompers makes no more impression than water on a duck's back. Nothing can shake his belief.

Similarly there seems to be a belief that socialist writers and agitators are paid princely salaries. In Canada at any rate, socialist agitators are not making a fortune; even the men who are sent out as organizers rarely get more than their expenses. The editor of the *Western Clarion* is paid $10 a week for his work, and certainly none of the writers to that paper ever received a cent for their contributions. *Cotton's Weekly* has always been in debt and has only been kept in existence because the editor's father was willing to give him money.

Our friend Jack is no doubt well-meaning. But he has not lived in the 20th century. His mind is a chaos of capitalist ideas; he hasn't any real knowledge of the working class movement. He is charmed at the idea that the king issued instructions that Prince Albert was not to receive any more attentions than the ordinary midshipman, and thinks if the leaders of the four hundred showed similar good sense there would be less social unrest. But so long as class rule obtains, so long as capitalism flourishes, there is bound to be social unrest; the Royal example cannot do anything to allay it. If all the leaders of the four hundred arrayed themselves in sackcloth and ashes, and still continued to exploit labour, the discontent would grow for the social unrest springs from the growing knowledge of the workers that they are a subject class....

56. Saint John and the Single Tax[198]

What has become of the Single Tax agitation in Saint John? The organs of the movement for the commission form of government were formerly strong supporters of the agitation for remodelling the assessment system and placing the burden of taxation on land values. The civic commission had done nothing in this direction of any moment and it has shown no inclination to do so. The organs of the commission movement have not shown any special eagerness to promote the land tax since the commission was established. Ex.-Ald. Potts, while in the Council, was a consistent advocate of the land tax but since he was turned down by the people who were carried away by the commission movement, he has kept quiet. You can hardly blame him for that. But Potts has not forgotten his old love. "There's no money for me in civic politics," he said to me the other day. "But if the commissioners don't show some interest in the land tax, I may be a candidate next election."

---

[198]*Eastern Labor News*, 9 August 1913.

Probably there is a considerable difference between Henry George's single tax ideas and the views of the land taxers in Saint John, ex-Ald. Potts included. It is a good many years since I read *Progess and Poverty*, and my impression is that Henry George contemplated the diversion to public purposes of all the unearned increment in land values.[199] Moreover his system contemplated the public ownership and operation of all public utilities, and if I remember right, all industries that lent themselves to monopoly. In many respects Henry George's system in its entirety was practically the same as the socialist system, at the outset at any rate. So far as I know socialist authorities only contemplate socializing, in the beginning at any rate, the great machine industries, those which have already become monopolies, or rapidly tend to monopoly. "It is not to be expected that all small private industries will disappear," says [Kautsky], one of the greatest authorities on socialism. "This will be specially true in agriculture. To be sure those agricultural plants which have become capitalist industries would fall with the wage system and be transformed into national, municipal, or co-operative business." But "the proletarian governmental power would have absolutely no inclination to take over the properties and businesses of the small farmer. Indeed it is highly probable that these small agricultural industries would receive considerable strengthening through the socialist regime. It would bring an abolition of militarism, of burdens of taxation, bring self-government and the nationalization of schools and road taxes, and the abolition of poor relief and perhaps a lowering of mortgage burdens, and many other advantages...." And [Kautsky] adds: "The most manifold forms of property in the means of production -- national, municipal, co-operative and private -- can exist beside each other in a socialist society."[200]

But while the Henry George system in its entirety is incipient socialism with a strong tendency to full socialism, I don't think the land tax as it has been advocated in Saint John is the same thing by any means, though if the city was to take a referendum on the land tax I would certainly vote for it. Very few bourgeois advocates of the land tax would justify a tax that virtually amounted to the taking over by the public of the whole increased increment in land values. And under existing conditions taxation of land values to the limit, while it would certainly benefit the industrial capitalist,

---

[199]McKay is perhaps referring to Henry George, *Progress and Poverty: An Inquiry into the Cause of Industrial Depressions and of Increase in Want with Increase of Wealth. The Remedy* (New York, 1906), 326: "To extirpate poverty, to make wages what justice commands they should be, the full earnings of the laborer, we must...substitute for the individual ownership of land a common ownership. Nothing else will go to the cause of the evil -- in nothing else is there the slightest hope."
[200]McKay is citing Karl Kautsky, *The Social Revolution* (Chicago: Charles H. Kerr and Company, 1908): 159-166. The concluding quotation has been slightly modified: "The most manifold forms of property in the means of production -- national, municipal, co-operatives of consumption and production, and private can coexist beside each other in a socialist society...." (166).

would have little or no effect upon the position of the worker. An essential part of the Henry George philosophy is the socialization of industries of a monopolistic character. So long as private parties control the public utility and monopolistic industries, they can absorb any benefits arising from the single tax. Still in the interests of social progress taxation of land values is a thing to be desired. To a certain extent it means the elimination of the landlord and the remnants of feudalism. It tends to make more clear the lines between capital in its most modern and powerful form and the working class; it tends to clarify the real issue.

57. The Labour Question Explained to Businessmen[201]

Many businessmen and wage-workers are too busy to study the world in which they live. They are often [ideologists], immune to the import of facts. Their historical studies have not gone much beyond those insane treatises used in the public schools, in which the drama of history appears for the most part as a succession of unrelated scenes, inspired by the whim of a king, the wrath of a warrior, or the caprice of a courtesan. In our archaic school histories the state appears not only as the creation of society, but its creator and support. Gods, demi-gods or heroes were the founders of the state in the child-like legends of most peoples....

Hence the naive belief that labour agitators are the principal factors in the labour movement; that they exercise a wonderful influence over the masses of work people.

Here and there an agitator appears as an important personage; but even Larkin[202] is a mere creature of circumstances; he merely typifies the spirit of a general reaction against conditions in Dublin. He did not cause the strike any more than Laurier or Borden caused the recent industrial depression; the strike was caused by conditions surrounding the Irish workers....

The labour agitator does not pluck ideas from heaven or the other place, set the world on fire with them, and then induce masses of men to take

[201]Originally published as "The Other Side of the Labour Question," *Busy East*, February 1914, 11-12.
[202]McKay is referring to James Larkin (1876-1947), union organizer and socialist in Ireland. Larkin was a stalwart of the Independent Labour Party and the National Union of Dock Labourers, and subsequently the Irish Transport and General Workers Union, formed in 1908. Through his writings in the *Irish Worker* and his militant activities, Larkin came to be identified with the tendencies of "new unionism" and direct action that agitated the British Isles before the Great War. He later moved to the United States, where he became involved with the Industrial Workers of the World and the Communists. By "the strike" McKay is referring to the massive confrontation in 1913 between the Irish Transport and General Workers Union and the Dublin Employers Federation.

collective action without regard to their material interests. The boss, familiar as he is in politics, is rare in trade union circles; and even in politics the boss rules not because of his own personal powers, but because he is the agent of big business interests behind the scenes. Whatever may be its faults the labour union is the most democratic organization yet developed.

Some businessmen believe that the big international labour unions maintain paid agitators who come to these provinces for the special purposes of stirring up trouble. And every labour organizer is called a foreigner and American. On the other hand local trade unions are continually complaining that their general offices do not send organizers down east frequently enough. Very seldom do the general offices send an organizer this way unless trouble is brewing or has developed and generally speaking the organizer is sent with the hope of smoothing over matters.

It is a well known fact that in highly organized crafts strikes are rare, while there is usually trouble somewhere in the ill-organized trades. If businessmen took the trouble to investigate the organization of international unions and their methods of procedure they would realize the absurdity of the frequent statements that paid agitators are sent here to stir up trouble. When the members of a Saint John union, for instance, want better conditions they on their own initiative draw up a series of demands, and present them to their employers. At the same time they may vote to strike if the demands are refused, and authorize their executive officers to call a strike at their discretion. But usually the employer's answer is submitted to the union membership before a vote is taken on the question of declaring a strike. While negotiations with the employers are in progress the International headquarters may at the request of the local union send an experienced official to assist in presenting their claims. Today this official is in a great majority of cases one of the Canadian vice presidents, a man who has had experience in dealing with employers and negotiating wages schedules in Toronto, Montreal or other Canadian city. When the Saint John Longshoremen moved for higher wages last fall, their International was represented by a Saint John man J.E. Tighe, third vice president of the International Union.

If the negotiations fall through the local union may strike on its own initiative, but in order to get strike pay it must first have the sanction of the International officers. Having to provide strike funds the international general officers are an influence for peace; they do not sanction a strike unless their experienced representative on the spot advises that a strike is opportune; very often they oblige the local union to moderate its demands and reopen negotiations with the employers.

International trade union officers whether they be Canadian or American citizens, do not go about interfering with local matters unless invited to do so. The United Mine Workers did not enter the field in Cape Breton until they had been requested to do so by a large percentage of the miners there. Nor did they create the trouble. Conditions had developed which the Provincial Workmen's Association, because of its archaic form of organization, was not fitted to deal with in a satisfactory manner. The United Mine Workers appeared on the scene because the miners wanted a new form of organization, a more effective weapon of defence.

To-day the so-called labour leader does not lead. He is more conservative than the mass of organized workers. Witness the recent great strikes in England and South Africa, undertaken by the men themselves in defiance of the advice of their leaders.

In the Maritime Provinces organized labour has not been militant to any extent. A large percentage of native workers own their homes or property of some sort; their ideas run along property lines. Intellectually they are hardly differentiated from the small businessman. But with the development of great capitalistic enterprises, which necessitate also the development of a proletariat, a mass of propertyless workers, the labour movement, certainly in the industrial centers, will enter upon a militant stage. The man with a small property is not partial to strikes; he may get in debt and lose his property. But the propertyless [worker], being gathered in our industrial centres, has nothing definite to lose, a strike often presents itself to him as a holiday. He is not bound to any locality; he cares little about the progress of the community in which he resides, and he favors an aggressive policy on the part of his union.

The small businessman, the grocer, butcher, and merchant, look upon a strike as an unmitigated disaster, and so it is in large measure to him. He loses trade. His customers run up bills, and depart. At the same time a large number of small businessmen on this continent maintain their positions by the grace of the fact that the workers have struggled to keep up wages. If the Canadian or American working classes had to be as careful of the pennies as they have to be in Great Britain and European countries, they would form co-operative societies, and many a small businessman would be crowded to the wall. Already in Canada since the high cost of living has begun to worry the workers we have the railway employees and others starting to organize co-operative societies, a movement that will doubtless be encouraged by the great corporations, since it is a frequent complaint that when a great corporation increases wages the merchants within its sphere of employment usually raise prices and force the men to move for another increase in pay. The small businessman can well afford to make a sympathetic study of the labour movement, since there are not a few forces combining to drive him off his precarious perch into the ranks of the proletariat.

PART III

Capitalism in the Maritimes

1900-1935

In this section are gathered fifteen pieces reflecting on the Maritime Provinces of Canada. Although McKay is a forgotten figure in the region, he has some claim to be regarded as one of its earliest and most perceptive radical sociologists. Many writers on such issues as working-class formation and the position of primary producers have unknowingly reproduced arguments first developed in the early twentieth century by him.

1. Colin McKay as a Maritimer

Colin McKay was a Maritimer, a fact of some significance in the general interpretation of his thought and in any appreciation of his impact. Even though he left his native Nova Scotia in the summer of 1891, going to sea did not mean severing his ties with the region and, in a real sense, he never left the Maritimes. His sea stories often evoked the Nova Scotia tradition, and his writings in the Montreal press frequently turned to Maritime subjects. Although McKay came from a family of hard-shell Conservatives (his father was the Mayor of Shelburne for a time) whose livelihood had come from a Shelburne shipyard, and which might have been expected to reject a socialist son who had turned to journalism in the big city, there is little evidence of a deep rift. Had Colin been a truly outcast "black sheep," it is doubtful that we would read of his comings-and-goings to and from Shelburne as often as we do in the Shelburne *Gazette and Coast Guard* from 1914 to 1935, as he was reported to be visiting his father, W.C. McKay.[1] It is also unlikely that his extended family would remember the story of his trial in Montreal, albeit in somewhat

---

[1] For McKay's visits home, see Shelburne *Gazette and Coast Guard*, 23 April 1914; Shelburne *Gazette and Coast Guard*, 22 March 1919; Shelburne *Gazette and Coast Guard*, 16 September 1920; Shelburne *Gazette and Coast Guard*, 23 August 1928; Shelburne *Gazette and Coast Guard*, 5 September 1935; Shelburne *Coast Guard*, 6 August 1936.

altered form.[2] The modest success of "the young Canadian" as a writer of sea stories, publicized in the *Yarmouth Telegram*,[3] and the local fame he earned through his distinguished service in the war may well have eased the family past the difficulties they must have had with his political radicalism.

His Nova Scotian background thus had affected him deeply, but he was never a "regionalist" in a contemporary sense. So far as one can tell, he never sympathized with separatism (which had waxed strong enough, particularly in places like his native South Shore, to return the Liberals to power on a secessionist platform when he was a boy in Shelburne), or even with Maritime Rights. Colin McKay never argued that the "centre" exploited the "periphery," or that "Upper Canada" exploited "Nova Scotia": his work always returned to the underlying framework of the capitalist system. There was room in his analysis for the damaging effects of Confederation -- the abolition of customs tariffs between the provinces left British capital free to prefer Central Canada to the Maritimes -- but even here, he disagreed with any interpretation that argued that Confederation had simply been a bad bargain. The region's problems stemmed from the exploitation of workers in the capitalist system. His underlying pattern of explanation was straightforwardly economic. Insofar as "region" can be said to have become a major category of analysis in McKay's work, it was in the context of arguments that blamed low wages and productivity on hostility to unions and fragmentation in the labour movement.[4]

But this is not the same as denying that, in a more subtle sense, McKay was extremely attached to the Maritimes, and valued the region more than any other place on earth (which did not mean, of course, that he was any the less intense in his defence of more general Canadian interests). Rather than turning him against an imagined Canadian "Other," McKay's intense allegiance to his Maritime background intensified his sense of the strangeness and inhumanity of capitalist modernity everywhere. Like Gramsci, who never ceased to be a Sardinian after he became an

---

[2]Professor Edgar B. McKay [first cousin of Colin], Letter to Ian McKay, 3 December 1987: "I do know that when Uncle Winslow and Jean talked about Colin's jail term, they were proud of his stand even though they were Tories and not usually supporters of labor unions, etc." In the family story, M. Fortier's cigar factory had become a cotton mill.

[3]*Yarmouth Telegram*, 31 December 1903: "Colin McKay, a Shelburne boy, is making a hit in sea tales. A prominent Canadian journal printed and illustrated on Saturday last a tale "Out of Herring Cove," by the young Shelburne writer, and also gave a photo of the latter, describing him as Colin McKay, the young Canadian whose sea tales have been among the most successful of this season's short stories."

[4]See Colin McKay, "Lessons of Higher Wages and Friendly Relations," *Canadian Congress Journal*, 3, 4 (April 1924): 21.

internationalist revolutionary, McKay never lost his sense of home for all the years he spent far away in Montreal and Ottawa. (Perhaps many of the most creative socialists are those who, as emigrés from "provincial" or marginalized regions, are required to internalize the tension between the old and the new ways within their very being). McKay's Maritime writings may be among his richest and most imaginative because they compelled him to face up to his acutely divided loyalties, and added a measure of historical depth to what was sometimes a rather unreflecting enthusiasm for progress. As a Spencerian, a Marxist, and an intellectual in Edwardian Canada, McKay was passionately committed to progress, science, and the march of a socialist modernity. He was also deeply attached to his home, whose attractions did not dim with the years he spent away from it. So, when he wrote of the "trawler question" in the 1920s, he wrote with ardent sympathies on either side of the debate: limiting the incursions of the trawlers was in one sense a reactionary attempt to stop progress, yet allowing the trawlers to revolutionize the fishery threatened the very existence of the coastal communities and the older generation within them [§.63, "The Machine Age and the Fisheries" and §.64, "The Machine Age with its Trawler and Its Relation to Our Shore Fishermen"]. These were among the finest analyses of the famous "trawler question" ever written, precisely because their author had so deeply internalized both sides of the issue. One can only regret that he did not live to write on the not dissimilar issue of the forced resettlement of the Newfoundland fishing communities in the 1960s.

There was a more intangible sense in which a "Maritime feel" permeates McKay's writing: the abstractions almost always connect with some down-to-earth, practical problem in the world. McKay had no use for theory-for-its-own-sake. He wrote many articles on how best to navigate vessels at sea. At times, his blunt anti-romanticism can be almost comic: an article on "What Youths with Sea Passion Should Know," for example, was not (as an unsuspecting reader might have guessed) about romantic sunsets, adventures in wild storms, and the glowing stars of the Southern Cross but ... the importance of getting a good eye examination: "All boys and girls who desire to follow the sea as a career should at the outset have their eyes tested for colour blindness and distance vision.... If this precaution is not taken the youngster may, after four years at sea, discover that he is not eligible for an officer's position, and that so far as a career is concerned, he has wasted the best years of his life...."[5] This down-to-earth practicality led McKay to visualize the International Fishermen's Races as practical exercises in the refinement of schooner design;[6] what he would have

---

[5]Colin McKay, "What Youths with Sea Passion Should Know," *Canadian Fisherman*, August 1924, 237.

[6]Colin McKay, "Fishermen's Vessel Race: Interest Awakening in Scheme - Sold Old Wind Jammer Records," *Canadian Fisherman*, September 1920, 195-196.

made of the massive media spectacular that the *Bluenose* subsequently became can only be imagined.

Many of McKay's Maritimes-focused articles were published in the mainstream or business press, and he adjusted his tone accordingly. Sometimes this "double vision" led to some rather odd contrasts between McKay-the-mainstream-writer and McKay-the-Marxian-sociologist. For example, readers of his chapter on "The Province of New Brunswick" in a 1913 book on Canada's commerce were presented with a portrait of a progressive province abounding with opportunity: here was a land making "remarkable progress," infected with a strong spirit of optimism, "bright with promise," and bound to be known in Britain as a land of "happy and contented people," not to mention "great and flourishing industries."[7] Could this possibly be the same place that McKay described in his labour journalism as rife with serious social conflicts, and that he depicted in his socialist pamphlet on agriculture as populated with downtrodden farmers, barely clinging to existence under the weight of monopoly capitalism? [§.66, "The New Brunswick Farmer"] Or could the happy, independent, enterprising and prosperous coastal fishermen of Nova Scotia, recently released from tbe bondage of the truck system and making excellent returns from the lobster fishery -- all this from a 1909 article in the Toronto *Globe* -- be squared with McKay's socialist (and admittedly somewhat later) denunciation of the exploitation of these primary producers?[8]

McKay, in his enthusiasm for signs of modernity in the Maritimes, could sometimes look past the most glaring evidence of its harsher side. Some of his writing would have not been out of place by the local Chambers of Commerce and Boards of Trade. The rosy-cheeked inhabitants of Grand Manan, for example, became walking advertisements for the wonderful qualities of dulse (indeed, McKay affirmed that "Many girls prefer dulse to bonbons"), progressive schooling, and the local fisheries -- which one must imagine, somehow, as being completely separate from the problems McKay diagnosed so acutely in other contexts![9] In this context, his portrait of that fair and just employer, the Dominion Coal Company, written in the waning days of his liberalism (and Liberalism) must stand as one of the most rose-coloured evaluations of industrial Cape Breton ever written [§.18, "Dominion Coal Treat Their Men Well"].

McKay's adoption of a Marxist perspective between 1906 and 1910 obviously affected his interpretation of the region. For example, when in

---

[7]Colin McKay, "The Province of New Brunswick," in Fred Cook, ed., *Commercial Canada: Its Progress and Opportunities* (Leeds: Redman Book Co., Ltd., 1913): 145.

[8]Colin McKay, "The Crews for A Canadian Navy," *The Globe* (Toronto), 24 July 1909.

[9]Colin McKay, "Grand Manan and its Fisheries," *Canadian Fisherman*, June 1914, 177-178.

1912, McKay returned to the subject of the transformation of Cape Breton, he quite adroitly cited much the same evidence he had earlier generated, but put it in a critical context.[10] One might say that McKay went from one extreme to another in his writings on the region: sometimes arguing in a very upbeat way that the Maritimes was advancing steadily along the path of progress, and sometimes arguing the classic "miserabilist" interpretation, in which economic problems were getting worse and worse. Often this miserabilist interpretation cast a golden glow over the good old days (or the isolated little present-day pockets) of economic self-sufficiency and cultural independence. It seemed difficult for McKay, in writing of the capitalist transformation of the Maritimes, to maintain a critical balance between boosting industrial development -- and hence the forces of production -- on the one hand, and damning development's socially disruptive effects on the other. This radical oscillation is true even of his commentaries in the *Eastern Labor News*, which are among the most thoughtful contemporary analyses of social and economic change in the Maritimes.

McKay was a Maritimer fascinated by his region, but there was little room for regionalism (as we understand it today) in his world-view. Social evolution set certain tasks for progressive workers around the world, and deviations from its universal mandate (the "international pattern") were ill-advised. Political movements could be evaluated by international and objective criteria. A tone of impatience enters into some of McKay's polemics aimed at Maritime workers: they were constantly being held up to the higher socialist standards of workers in Other Places. In a somewhat pessimistic piece explaining his native region to the readers of the *Western Clarion*, McKay (who rather understated the geographical range of socialist activity in the region) underlined the impact of "religious feeling and race -- or rather sectional -- prejudice," which was almost certainly a reference not to "race" in the modern sense, but conflicts between Anglophones and Francophones [§.71, "The Difficulties Faced by Socialists in the Maritimes"]. At times in McKay's polemics against the plight of Maritime workers, it seemed that they themselves were wholly to blame for their predicament: he cited J.W.Longley's claim that the Maritime Provinces supplied the rest of Canada with brains, then acidly observed that the region evidently did not have enough brains left over "to realize that its intellectual atmosphere is so charged with the idea of capitalism that the machinery by which the privileged and predatory classes retain control of the minds of the people works almost automatically."[11]

---

[10]Colin McKay, "Do Capitalists Help or Exploit the Workers?" *Eastern Labor News*, 22 Jun 1912.
[11]Colin McKay, "Brains Beguiled," *Coast-Guard*, 3 November 1910.

Yet McKay's analysis often went beyond this somewhat superficial condemnation of regional "working-class conservatism" to a more thoughtful analysis of the origins of the region's apparent peculiarities. In an otherwise conventional analysis of the region's workers, written for a western labour paper, McKay speculated that "the habits of thinking and feeling of the Maritime workers are those peculiar to small-scale industry," and also argued that increasing exploitation did not necessarily lead to the germination of Socialist ideas: "Among the fishermen of Nova Scotia I have been surprised at the tendency to Socialist modes of thought and that in the districts where they are today more independent and prosperous than they have ever been. Probably the fact that the fishermen have long worked under a form of co-operation enables them to more readily grasp the possibilities of co-operation generally" [§.71, "The Difficulties Faced by Socialists in the Maritimes," originally published as "The Maritime"]. In a related, more theoretical observation, McKay -- like many sociologists since -- was impressed by the specific regional importance of Marx's emphasis on proletarianization, and his view of the genesis of the capitalist system as lying in the divorce of the mass of the population from the means of livelihood.[12] Farmers in New Brunswick had not been able to adopt in its entirety the "characteristic mode of capitalist production, and that for the simple reason that the primary condition, a mass of agricultural labour divorced from and unable to obtain access to the land, has been wanting."[13]

2. McKay's General Analysis of Capitalist Transformation in the Maritimes

Despite such evidence of an incomplete transformation of the Maritimes countryside, many of McKay's writings on the pre-1914 Maritimes stressed the scope and rapidity of socio-economic change. These analyses are coloured very much by McKay's location at the city desk of the Saint John *Standard,* in a city enjoying a boom and a massive strike wave from 1910 to 1913. The city described by McKay was certainly undergoing a rapid transformation. The booming economy was fed, in part, by the federal redevelopment of the port. Many of McKay's articles in the *Eastern Labor News* focused on how workers should respond to such uncontrolled and rapid growth. Here was a city of high rents, slum housing, low wages, runaway capitalist speculation: most of the urban realities that progressive muckrakers across North America were exploring. McKay clearly found it fascinating.

---

[12]For the most recent scholarship of "rural capitalism" in the Maritimes, see Daniel Samson, ed., *Contested Countryside: Rural Workers and Modern Society in Atlantic Canada, 1800-1850* (Fredericton: Acadiensis Press, 1994).

[13]Colin McKay, "Regarding Immigration," a letter to the *Eastern Labor News,* 6 January 1912.

His attitude toward such growth was complicated. In one article on the boom and the working class, McKay argued that Saint John's advantages as a site for manufacturing were offset by very high prices for power. Some form of state regulation of power rates, the argument implied, would make local industry more competitive, and thereby aid the working class. Yet at other times McKay painted a bleaker picture. At "a gathering of Saint John workingmen", participants debated the question "Does speculation and the investment of capital in new industries benefit the working class?" The answer was in the affirmative, but McKay was inclined to doubt it, and cited the development of the winter port at Saint John: "Are the longshoremen as a class better off than they used to be?" he asked. "Years ago they used to work 8 or 9 hours a day and they got $5 a day and over at a time when the dollar was almost as good as two dollars are now. More men get work on the winter port but the workers' position is worse than it was before." His conclusion was that "capitalist speculation and investment" might bring temporary benefits to workers in a given locality, "but when new enterprises are started new workers soon flock in and in the end the condition of the class shows no improvement."[14] Statistics on wages and the cost of living tended to confirm, in McKay's view, the miserabilist vision of working-class urban life.[15] Because working-class problems were systemic, McKay had little use for the reformist socialists (well-represented indeed in Saint John) who rallied to such causes as W.F.Hatheway's philanthropic housing schemes. Not only would most of the homes be beyond the financial reach of workers, but the development would have negative cultural consequences: it would encourage workers to adopt a private property orientation.[16]

In general, politics in Saint John had not kept pace with the rapid pace of economic and social change. Civic politicians seemed perversely indifferent to the working-class interest: they would vote $2,000 "to a more or less ornamental official, and turn down a recommendation of the chief of the fire department to raise the pay of the probationary drivers from $35 to $40 a month." Property qualifications kept workers off the council, and a municipal law prohibiting those who had not paid their taxes punished workers in an extra-legal manner by removing their right to vote -- a clear case of taxation without representation. Taxation itself was onerous for workers. In 1910, the worker paid at least four different taxes (the manufacturers' tax, embodied in high prices, the merchants', hidden in the same way, the landlords', embodied in high rents, and direct civic taxes); even improvements to houses were taxed. McKay drew attention to comments in a Calgary paper, which had discussed the tax system of Saint

[14]Colin McKay, "Do Capitalists Help or Exploit The Workers?" *Eastern Labor News*, 22 June 1912

[15]Colin McKay, "Wages and the Cost of Living," *Eastern Labor News*, 14 June 1913; and "Progress and Poverty," *Eastern Labor News*, 29 June 1912

[16]Colin McKay, "The Housing Problem," *Eastern Labor News*, 22 March 1913

John under the caption "The Amazing East." "Gentle reader," it had said, "this wonderful system of taxation is in force, not in China, but in the pretentious winter port of Canada. It is bolstered up by arguments that would make a western horse laugh," or words to that effect.[17] The Chief of Police and the "Safety Board" had even denied Socialists the right to hold meetings "on some street or square where they would not interfere with anybody; a very reasonable request, a right enjoyed by the people of nearly every British city." One ignorant alderman had added his opinion that Socialists were "a lot of ragamuffins."[18] It was all part of the stagnation of life and thought in what McKay guessed might be "the most bourgeois city in the world," where petty partisanship, an all-pervasive party spirit, and prejudice took the place of the serious, constructive analysis of the issues of modern life.[19]

McKay's anti-Saint John jeremiads need to be taken with several grains of salt. As he knew full well, the city was also to become the first in Canada to adopt the most radical form of commission government, and workers in the city were in the midst of a major labour rebellion. And there is the obvious fact that McKay, the other Socialists, the Fabians, and the Hatheway pro-labour faction of the Conservative Party were all jockeying for influence with workers looking for alternatives in a time of radical change. After all, in the dynamic twentieth century the "most bourgeois city in the world" was unlikely to be a place of stagnation!

3. The Resource Industries

Of all McKay's writing on the transformation of the Maritime region, those which focused on resource industries, especially fishing, were the best-researched and the most subtly analytical. He brought to the analysis of fishing a first-hand experience of work in the region's ship-yards and shipping industry; and he could draw on his first-hand experiences as a seafarer in describing the treacherous working conditions and the suddenness of death in the offshore fishery.[20] He supplemented this personal knowledge with a catholic reading of books and articles on the fisheries in both French and English, and many visits to the coastal communities of the Maritimes. Much of his writing on fisheries issues appeared in the *Canadian Fisherman,* a business publication; but he also explored the contradictions of the North Atlantic fishery on the pages of the radical *Eastern Labor News* and in the columns of the right-wing *Saturday Night.*

[17]Colin McKay, "St.John Notes," *Eastern Labor News*, 17 September 1910.

[18]Colin McKay, "Against Freedom of Speech," *Eastern Labor News*, 2 March 1912.

[19]Colin McKay, "Brains Beguiled," *Coast-Guard*, 3 November 1910.

[20]Colin McKay, "On a Grand Banker Out of Lunenburg," *Shelburne Gazette*, 2 February 1905;

His analysis of the fishing industry emphasized, as one might expect, the development of capitalism. In 1909, McKay described a Nova Scotia fishing economy that had emerged from the long years of "a patriarchal order " characterized by the truck system to enjoy higher standards of living, the greater flexibility and independence brought about by the adoption of new and faster small craft powered by gasoline engines, and the lucrative lobsters markets of New England. In brief, a producers' "revolution" had overthrown the older patriarchal system. McKay credited the fishermen themselves, as well as the competitive pressures exerted by the higher wages and better conditions in the United States and the impersonal evolution of market forces, for effecting this change.[21] However, he would subsequently add, this revolution had merely laid the basis for a further development of capitalist social relations: the independence thus won was also being eroded. As capitalism evolved within the fishing industry, he argued in 1913, it would follow the course taken in other industries: "In time the workers in the fishing industry will find themselves in the same position as the workers in all capitalistic industries. The laws of expanding capitalism operate to reduce practically all classes of workers to the same status." At the same time, McKay was alert to what Marxists would later call the law of uneven and combined development.[22] Capitalism in the Nova Scotia fishing industry entailed a strange combination of extremely advanced and archaic forms: moreover, these seemed to be linked in a symbiotic relationship: "Here we have a phase of full fledged capitalism, cheek by jowl with the old methods of carrying on the fish business and at once the old methods become mere tributaries to the stream of profits of the characteristically capitalist method." Even in his rather short first analysis of capitalism in the fishing industry, McKay complicated the standard narrative of the rise of capitalism with the suggestion that, if fishermen could mobilize quickly to organize co-operatives, they might in fact alter the eventual shape of capitalist development in the industry [§.59, "The Application of Capitalistic Methods to the Fishing Industry"]. The direct interest of nation-states in securing access to the fisheries, and their salience in Canadian diplomacy, further complicated the picture. State policies are rarely present as major elements in their own right in McKay's pre-1930s writings; but they could not be avoided in any discussion of fisheries.[23] McKay placed increasing emphasis on the ability and willingness of the Canadian state to plan the fisheries, and its backwardness when contrasted

---

[21]Colin McKay, "The Crews for A Canadian Navy," *The Globe* (Toronto), 24 July 1909.

[22]For an account which lays particular stress on Trotsky's contribution, see Michael Löwy, *The Politics of Combined and Uneven Development: The Theory of Permanent Revolution* (London: Verso, 1981).

[23]C.McK., "Newfoundland Fisheries Question. May Develop Features Fraught With Menace -- Present Conditions in the Dominion of Canada," *Standard* (Montreal), 29 December 1906.

with Europe, where far-sighted states had remodelled fisheries ports, secured the fishermen's livelihood through market regulation, and poured money into technical development.[24] By comparison, and for all the diplomatic attention they had received, the fisheries were the orphans of Canadian policy-making, lacking prestige in the bureaucracy, and subject to patronage, uncontrolled experimentation, and top-down indifference to the fishing communities.[25] Even where there was a closer connection between the state and the fishing industry, and a strong and active movement of reform, as in the Dominion of Newfoundland at the time of W.F.Coaker's Fishermen's Union, traditional merchants would myopically oppose any state regulation of the shipment and sale of the country's fish.[26] They seemed unable to advance beyond a competitive, anarchic and self-destructive form of capitalism.

By the 1920s, McKay was giving publicity to the view that the fisheries question was, in the long run, one of whether Canada was going to take advantage of its proximity to the greatest fishing grounds in the world to develop a "great industry," or cede this opportunity to the Americans.[27] He drew attention to the startling fact in 1923 that, "although 69,550 square miles of the best fishing grounds in the world are within easy reach of her ports, Nova Scotia's annual fish harvest is not, in point of quantity, much greater than it was forty years ago." The reasons for this stagnation were many. The little brigantines that had once carried fish and lumber to the West Indies started to find it difficult to secure profitable return cargoes. The European fish-producing countries had become strong competitors.

---

[24]Colin McKay, "Water Temperatures for Cod Fishing," *Canadian Fisherman*, March 1934, 11. See also Colin McKay, "Icy Water--Abundance of Cod," *Canadian Fisherman*, June 1934, 9-10; "Preserving Fish in Snow," *Canadian Fisherman*, May 1916, 189."Artificial Drying of Fish," *Canadian Fisherman*, June, 1916, 204; Colin McKay, "Easy Term Loans to Fishermen: How It is Done in France and Elsewhere"*Coast Guard* (Shelburne), 27 September 1934.; "The Question of Fishery Credits," *Canadian Fisherman*, June 1925, 159-160; 193; "European Fishing Ports: How the British, Dutch and Germans Build Fishing Ports and Administer Them," *Canadian Fisherman*, October 1918, 1054-1056; "How Europe Serves the Fishing Industry," *Canadian Fisherman*, September 1925, 281-282; "France to Spend $40,000,000 on Fisheries," *Canadian Fisherman*, July 1920, 158.

[25]Colin McKay, "Maritime People," *Halifax Herald*, 15 April 1920; "Increasing Production for British Markets: Utilize the Bounty to Assist Fishermen with Motor Engines," *Canadian Fisherman*, March 1917, 89; "A Practical Minister -- When?", *Canadian Fisherman*, October 1926, 316; "Union of Departments of Marine and Railways Advocated: Separate Fisheries and Make it a Portfolio by Itself," *Canadian Fisherman*, September 1926, 271-272.

[26]Colin McKay, "The 'Crerar' of Newfoundland: History of Fishermen's Union story of achievement closely intertwined with career of Hon. W.F. Coaker," *Canadian Fisherman*, August 1922, 176.

[27]Colin McKay, "Maritime Fisheries at Cross Roads," *Canadian Fisherman*, July 1928, 33-34; 43.

Nova Scotia had hesitated before developing the fresh fish trade and the market in Central Canada. Now that the province finally was doing something, the fisheries of British Columbia and Ontario were offering strong competition.[28] Despite dramatic changes in technology, advances in research, above all the arrival of the trawler -- all developments in the forces of production hailed by McKay -- the situation by the 1920s was grim: a vast expansion in capital had been accompanied by a marked reduction in employment [§.62, "The Employment Question in the Fishing Industry"]. As early as 1904, McKay had described the outmigration of Nova Scotian fishermen to the North Pacific and the South Seas in search of better financial returns in pelagic sealing than they could find locally in fishing.[29] By 1938, the indirect incentives to forced outmigration included the depletion of fishing grounds, the disappearance of shipping jobs as supplements to fishing, the monopolization by large companies of cold storage plants, the increasing costs of transportation, unfavourable tariffs, and even the destruction of local wild-life [§. 65, "Too Many Fishermen"]. Underlying all such factors was the chaotic expansion of capitalism and the Canadian state's unwillingness to undertake comprehensive planning.

McKay's analysis was prophetic. It was unfortunately overlooked by the many reports covering the on-going crisis of the capitalist fisheries in the decades following his death, perhaps because it did not accord with the modernization theory that was to provide federal fisheries planners with their key ideological framework.

A consistent demand McKay made was for greater and more systematic state involvement and regulation of the industry. He actively campaigned for technical education for fishermen, and won significant support for his cause from the mainstream press. He called upon Ottawa to build a Fisheries College where research as well as teaching could advance.[30] He urged the need for tough government inspection to make Canadian fish competitive with the European product. Why were there experimental farms for agriculture, he wondered, but no experimental facilities for fishermen?[31] A Fisheries Information Bureau which could bring fishermen

[28]Colin McKay, "Atlantic Industry Has Slow Progress. Industry must look to interior markets and co-operate to guarantee regular and permanent supply," *Canadian Fisherman*, January 1923.

[29]Colin McKay, "Bluenose Sealers," *Montreal Daily Herald*, 8 December 1904.

[30]Colin McKay, "A Governor's Good Sense," *Coast Guard*, 15 September 1910; "Standardization and Inspection of Fish Products Calls for Technical Education," *Canadian Fisherman*, September 1920, 200; "Need for a Fisheries College," letter to the *Halifax Herald*, 1 May 1920. A McKay letter on the need for a fisheries college sparked an editorial on this question in the *Halifax Herald*, 21 April 1920.

[31]Colin McKay,"The Application of Science to the Fishing Business," letter to *Coast-Guard*, 23 November 1911.

a "greater knowledge "of the general conditions governing the migrations and habits of fish as well as the more specific conditions bearing upon the problem of capturing them, would be an important aid in promoting the development of the fisheries on systematic lines," following the approach already pursued by the United States, Great Britain and other countries. Granted, such a pooling of knowledge might not appeal to all fishermen, who would need to be persuaded that "the promotion of the interests of the industry as a whole will be the best interest of all engaged in it." Nonetheless, in the fisheries no less than elsewhere, competition had to give way to co-operation. Businessmen who had once made a fetish out of competition were now being converted to the gospel of co-operation. The fishing industry, traditionally associated with the most rugged individualism, now exemplified the opposite, because individual businessmen had come to realize that the reputation of all hinged on the reliability of each producer. [32]

Although the businessmen who subscribed to the *Canadian Fisherman* would have had to read between the lines of McKay's analyses to find the socialist message, he was more candid elsewhere. The problem of the fisheries could not be separated from the general problems of Canadian capitalism, with its lack of balance between consumption and production, and its inability to plan beyond the next dip in the business cycle.[33] In the absence of effective state control and planning, it was up to producers themselves to fight to reshape the fisheries. McKay, a friend of M.H.Nickerson, the leader of the Nova Scotia Fishermen's Union, gave the "union" publicity and support, all the while recognizing that it was an organization of "men who for the most part usually own their boats and gear, and who are thus small capitalists as well as workers" [§.58, "The Nova Scotia Fishermen's Unions"]. He also saw merit in fishing co-operatives, in both Quebec and Nova Scotia.[34] Like many observers of the day, he also took inspiration in 1914 from the "co-operative" example of Lunenburg, although he was more realistic than most in acknowledging that model's limitations: although the system whereby fishermen bought shares in the profits of the vessel had potential, much of that promise had been squandered because there was no co-operative marketing and because no state agency had attempted to develop the fresh fish trade. Perhaps because he was writing in the *Canadian Fisherman*, McKay did not underline the unequal economic rewards, dangerous working

---

[32]Colin McKay, "A Fisheries Information Bureau," *Canadian Fisherman*, June 1914, 208-209.

[33]Colin C. McKay, Letter to the Editor, *Coast Guard*, 4 October 1934.

[34]Colin McKay, "Fishermen's Co-operatives in Quebec," *Canadian Fisherman*, December 1928, 17; 47.

conditions, or low living standards that also went along with the Lunenburg model.[35]

Long before the Antigonish Movement, an interwar movement for credit unions and co-operatives led by certain Catholic priests in eastern Nova Scotia, McKay was arguing that the best reform within capitalism for the region's primary producers would be co-operatives as they had been organized in Denmark, where producers were "profiting because they have applied co-operation on an extensive scale. In the first place they have co-operated on the political field and have obtained a certain measure of control over the government and through the government of the railways and steamship lines which carry their products. They own cold storage plants, packing establishments, and practically every agency between the producer and consumer." Such co-operatives, McKay would have been quick to add, could in no sense be construed as providing a "third path" between capitalism and socialism, because though the Danish farmers had eliminated the middlemen and other agencies of direct exploitation, they still did not get the full social value of the product of their labour, because they had to sell their produce to working-class consumers unable to pay the social value of the products they consumed because they themselves were exploited by capitalism [§.66, "The New Brunswick Farmer"]. In 1922, McKay also argued that the 605 "factories" of the lobster industry of the Maritimes and Quebec -- then the only canned lobster industry of any importance in the world -- were long overdue for a similar movement of "co-operation."[36]

As in agriculture and fishing, so in forestry: the "scientific direction of the communal consciousness" had become crucial to primary producers and to society as a whole. The forest fires that devastated hundreds of square miles of forest in early twentieth-century Nova Scotia were nothing but graphic illustrations of the high costs of the separation of private and public in a liberal capitalist order: They made "glaringly manifest the dangers of trying to divorce public and private interests," McKay wrote. There had been many advocates of forest conservation, but because knowledge was only "potential power," there was no guarantee that such far-sighted voices would be attended to. The government had, to be sure, appointed forest ranger and commissioned a survey; but it had done nothing to oblige the owners of woodlands to consider the general interests of the public and the long-term need for fire safety, reforestation, and sound environmental management.[37] Even in such phenomena as the disappearance of salmon and alewives in Nova Scotia's Roseway River,

---

[35]Colin McKay, "Co-operation in the Fishing Industry," *Canadian Fisherman*, March 1914, 77.

[36]Colin McKay, "Co-operation in Lobster Industry," *Canadian Fisherman*, August 1922, 162-163.

[37]Letter from Colin McKay, *Shelburne Gazette and Coast Guard*, 2 October 1913.

one could trace the ecological consequences of the liberal capitalist order, which had allowed private individuals to reap the benefits of the forests without taking steps either to protect or replant them. In burning over the watersheds of the rivers, the short-sighted capitalists had destroyed of the habitats of such species.[38]

4. Progressive Movements in the Maritimes

How could any of these deep-seated patterns of capitalist development in the region be changed? After c.1908, McKay was certain that no useful answers would be coming from the conventional political parties. In an age when Liberals had *de facto* accepted the protectionism of the National Policy, and Conservatives had accepted political liberalism, there were few substantive differences between the two parties. In espousing protection, both parties were simply aiding the capitalist, no matter how much they tried to disguise the fact. Protection had increased the number of workers, but it had not benefitted workers as a class, who were less independent, less secure of a livelihood, and indeed relatively worse off (because they received a much smaller proportion of the values they produced) than the workers of any previous era [§. 24, "The Master Magicians," originally published as "The Master Magicians: How the Seekers of Privilege have Hypnotized the Public Mind, and Incidently Destroyed the Liberal Party"]. Tariff reform was a red herring for workers.[39] So were most of the issues raised in the run-of-the-mill election.

The mystery was that Maritimers, both working-class and bourgeois, nonetheless seemed firmly traditional in their adherence to the old parties, even though such parties offered no coherent programs. McKay's writings sometimes provide comfort to those who champion the conventional view of the unchanging, conservative Maritimes. On occasion he wrote of Maritime conservatism almost as if it were an incurable condition. Reviewing Edgar Dupuis' *Eastern Canada and the People Therein*, McKay underlined a passage that argued that "intellectual progress of the broad and modern type finds little favor with most New Brunswickers. They persist in looking at the world through the wrong end of a telescope and shrink in a fright before a new idea. Well satisfied with what they are, they wrap themselves in their littleness, fall asleep and snore....Newspapers, surprisingly good, are doing all in their power to awake the people from their chronic lethargy and again it avails but little." McKay thought perhaps the author had exaggerated, but in essence he agreed that New Brunswickers were "very conservative in their habit of mind. New ideas do not meet with a ready reception." Wage earners in

---

[38]"Fire Prevention. Another Interesting Letter from Colin McKay," *Shelburne Gazette and Coast Guard*, 4 September 1913.

[39]Colin McKay, "The Red Herring of Tariff Reform," letter to *Eastern Labor News*, 14 June 1913.

particular were "intellectually behind the times," indeed "intellectually slothful."[40] The readers of the *Western Clarion* were also informed that "the main streams of modern thought" seemed to have passed the Maritimes by, "or at any rate have not disturbed to any extent the placid somnolence of their intellectual life." Socialists would find it tough to organize in a region in which the small-town communities were "often very democratic, employer and employee mingling freely in fraternal societies and social organizations of various kinds. Again there is a good deal of religious feeling and race -- or rather sectional -- prejudice" [§.71, "The Difficulties Faced by Socialists in the Maritimes"].

Some of McKay's writings clearly support, at least on a superficial reading, the most conventional interpretations of the past and present of the Maritimes in terms of an immemorial conservatism and stasis (stereotypical impressions that have been influential among leftists and progressives). Yet in fact, McKay's analysis of the region was always double-edged. The overstated diagnoses of conservatism were matched by no less dramatic descriptions of dramatic cultural change. In Saint John, McKay found the change in the workers' outlook remarkable. In 1913, he remarked that two and a half years earlier, the Trades and Labor Council in Saint John had held a public meeting; the "representatives of the property interests" had given the speeches, and the workers had not had a word to say. "The other evening a public meeting was held in the court house with the Mayor in the chair, and the workers showed they could put up better arguments than the manufacturers. It shows that something has been moving here. The workers are developing self-confidence. They are becoming class conscious and showing a spirit of revolt."[41] That the Saint John working class had been fragmented along the lines of religion and occupation was obvious; that McKay's polemics against this legacy of fragmentation and pettiness occurred in the context of his successful campaign in 1910 to reorganize the Saint John Trades and Labor Council might be overlooked.[42] Many of his condemnations of regional conservatism were made in the full knowledge that they would be received by readers of a radical labour press, who, it was hoped, would respond to them.

McKay's pre-1914 writings actually also sustain a reading completely opposed to the thesis of regional conservatism. For example, his somewhat exaggerated sense of the dense intimacy of small-town life needs to be set beside his own evaluation of co-operatives in fishing communities challenging the hold of the corporate interests also active within them [§.59, "The Application of Capitalistic Methods to the Fishing

---

[40]Colin McKay, "The Conservatism of New Brunswickers," *Eastern Labor News*, 3 August 1912.

[41]Colin McKay, "Saint John Workers Waking Up," *Eastern Labor News*, 5 April 1913.

[42]Colin McKay, "Saint John Notes," *Eastern Labor News*, 29 October 1910.

Industry"]. As part of a general revival of progressive energy in the
Maritimes, he wrote in 1912, workers in the Maritimes were shaking off
their lethargy [§.68, "The Awakening of Labour in Eastern Canada"]. An
article entitled "The Fear of Progress" launches what had become the
standard McKay polemic against the dead hand of custom in the region,
but also includes an interview with one master painter who argued that the
only salvation for the small employer and businessman was Socialism
[§.69, "The Fear of Progress"]. "Short-Sighted Workers," published in the
Eastern Labor News in 1913, powerfully described the insularity and
narrowness of the Saint John labour aristocracy, combined with a
condemnation of the docility and gullibility of the workers: it also noted
the strategic intelligence and unity of the longshoremen and coal
handlers [§.70, "The Aristocracy of Labour and the Short-Sighted
Workers"]. An article on the "Apathy of the Workers" reached a more
balanced conclusion than its title implied: the local workers were not
mired in conservatism so much as they were "in a state of transition from
one stage of intellectual development to another." Some had even
"attained the viewpoint of the militant proletariat," but even the minds of
those who clung to their petit-bourgeois ways of thinking were "in
ferment."[43] This aspect of McKay's writing is most valuable, perhaps, not
for its polemics against immemorial conservatism but as compelling
evidence of a changing region, at a time when both "conservatism" and
"radicalism" could be discerned within it.

5. The Maritimes in the 1930s

McKay left his native region in 1915 to fight the Great War; and although
he returned to his job at the Saint John *Standard,* and took up a Canadian
Press appointment in Halifax, he never again felt as closely tied to the
Maritimes as he had felt in the years 1910-1913. After he left for Europe in
1922, the next 17 years of his life were spent "away." His later writings on
the region lack the immediacy and polemical fire of his Saint John days,
when it had seemed that everything and everyone was in transition, and
the great questions were being decided. He found it difficult to interpret
the very different realities of the interwar Maritimes.

Some of the old polemics still worked. He wrote effectively on the pivotal
election of 1933 in Nova Scotia as the search for a "Political Moses." At a
time when the fisheries were in deep crisis -- fish prices had collapsed
more drastically than wheat prices in the Depression, with prices for cod
declining from $2 to $3 per hundredweight to between 30 and 70 cents --
the two main parties insulted the Nova Scotia electorate with mild talk of
reform. The Nova Scotians remained wedded to "peanut politics,"
mesmerized by the "mass feeling of a political meeting," even though
they might privately indicate that they had little faith in the ability of

---

[43]Colin McKay, "Apathy of the Workers," *Industrial Banner,* 15 May 1914.

either of the mainstream parties to respond to the economic disorder. Yet for all Nova Scotians talked of a need for change, "of the brutality of a 'system' that engenders poverty in the midst of plenty," they were mostly very vague about the changes they wanted: they seemed to be hoping that Liberals or Conservatives would produce a message "answering the general disillusionment and bewilderment." But never had such hopes in the old parties been more futile. The welfare measures promised by the government were inadequate and even below what the Russians were providing -- mere palliatives "designed to deal with the effects of a disorderly economic system." Politics in Nova Scotia were lamentably superficial, at exactly the time when people were looking for profound analyses.[44] McKay's analysis was interesting, but it also suggested his distance from his native province: there was no sense here of the originality and distinctiveness of Angus L. Macdonald as a striking new liberal presence on the political scene.

Perhaps the most telling sign of the distance both McKay and the region had travelled since the heady days of 1913 was his remarkable 1933 article on tourism: "The Maritimes: Playground of a Happier Canada." Because he bridged the worlds of daily journalism and Marxist commentary, McKay was often in the position of writing about new social phenomena that escaped the attention of more narrowly focused labour journalists. Probably alerted by the contemporaneous Senate hearings on the subject, he wrote what may have been the first Canadian socialist analysis of the rise of tourism as a moment of a new culture of consumption. He glimpsed a future in which workers would have the ability to design their leisure time, and a society in which the state would underwrite their standards of living. In such a society, there would be a demand "for small yachts, co-operatively owned by several people, and for small boats for sport, pleasure, and amateur fishing. To meet this demand the Maritimes have a surplus of skilled workers trained in wooden-shipbuilding yards, whose occupation has practically vanished during the present depression" [§.67, "The Maritimes: Playground of a Happier Canada"]. In this generous and original vision of "social tourism," the Maritimes was to function as kind of therapeutic space for the Dominion. McKay loyally struggled to invest the region's destiny as a mere "playground" with the glory and excitement of the Age of Sail, and uneasily confronted the regionalist argument that the unfair arrangements of Confederation had worsened the region's plight with the argument that capitalism was universally to blame for economic imbalances. It was not a very regionally-specific argument, and in consequence perhaps not a very convincing one.

The all-encompassing tragedy of his native region is most palpably presented to us in McKay's writings on the trawler question. It was a classic

[44]C.M., "Nova Scotia Looking For Political Moses," *Labor World/Le Monde Ouvrier*, 10 August 1933.

issue which seemed to pit the forces of progress and capitalist modernity against the forces of "traditionalism", and one might have expected McKay to take the line of least resistance and support the transformation of the forces of production that trawler technology represented. And this was indeed McKay's first line of attack. Drawing on the European precedents he knew so well, he offered a qualified defence of the steam trawlers: the ecological argument against them had not been proven. Perhaps because the steam trawler could work at great depth and range far afield, and still land its catches in a fresh condition, this meant that "under proper regulations extensive fishing may serve to mitigate, if not entirely overcome, the evils of intensive fishing [§.60, "Steam Trawling and its Effect on the Fisheries"]. But a darker tone gradually enters his writing on this question. By 1926, he was reflecting on the stark, irremediable tragedy of those who were to be displaced by this new technology -- which must have included many of his friends and relatives on the South Shore. What would become of them? The new machines, the use of motor craft and steam trawler, railways and refrigerator cars, all transformed old routines and traditions; the "mentality of the fisherman" was forced to change, some communities were ruined, the fishing industry became more concentrated in a few large ports: in short, there was a high price to be paid for "development" [§.63, "The Machine Age and the Fisheries"]. For the business readers of the *Canadian Fisherman*, McKay maintained an air of studied neutrality on this issue: his commentary on the MacLean Commission, that seminal investigation into the interwar fisheries of Nova Scotia, was a model of "journalistic balance." Yet under the ostensible "balance" the undercurrents of a more radical (and even, for an orthodox Marxist, "unorthodox") questioning of capitalist "progress" were swirling. The depopulation of some of the fishing villages, menaced by the steam trawler and its advanced technology, had been foreshadowed by a similar pattern in Europe after the advent of steam vessels. Whatever its advantages in efficiency and offshore safety, the trawler posed a life-or-death challenge to many in the fishing villages: "Even though the fishing communities are populated by a hardy breed, there are people everywhere, especially old folks, who just hang on to existence, and a little shock such as may arise from a realization of an upset of their traditional environment, may shake them from the tree of life like ripe fruit. This is one of the tragedies of progress" [§.64, "The Machine Age with Its Trawler and Its Relation to Our Shore Fishermen"]. McKay in this moving passage, based one suspects on personal knowledge, was right on the knife edge of the dilemma: hailing capitalist progress and efficiency, as a good Marxian economist was obliged to do; and yet unable to avert his gaze from some of its deadly and inhuman consequences.

Should life really come down to this? The death of whole ways of life, the death of actual people, simply to meet an insatiable process of capitalist accumulation? Wasn't there a subversive sense, in this restrained but moving polemic against the trawler, that there were things that were more

important than progress? McKay saw the trawler question as both tragedy
and triumph. The tragedy was the elimination of communities and the
core logic of capitalism itself. The triumph was the power of popular
resistance. By resisting the steam trawler, the inshore fishermen had
shown the way forward to intelligent planning in a co-operative
commonwealth [§.96, "Rationing Investment: A Critique of Donald
Marvin's Explanation of the Depression"]. That McKay would have cited
the resistance of the producers of the Maritimes as a shining example for
all Canadian workers provides an arresting counterbalance to his many
denunciations of regional conservatism.

i. Economic Consolidation and the Resource Industries

58. The Nova Scotia Fishermen's Unions[45]

At the last session of the Nova Scotia Legislature, an Act was passed, making provisions for the organization of fishermen's unions, and already a number of locals have been formed in various parts of the province.[46] The movement owes its inception mainly to M.H. Nickerson[47], M.P.P., of Cape Island, and has attained the greatest strength among the lobster fishermen of that locality. So far the efforts of the organizers have been confined to the shore fishermen the men who for the most part usually own their boats and gear, and who are thus small capitalists as well as workers.

Various circumstances led to the launching of the movement. The time is one of consolidation and organization of trade agreements, and collective bargaining, and the fishermen have, like other classes, caught the contagion and begun to realize that in union there is strength. In the last few years certain species of fish have almost ceased to make their appearance upon the coast and the movements of others have been somewhat erratic, phenomena which have directed attention to the need of better fishery protection regulations and their more efficient enforcement; in other words, the need of concerted action on the part of the fishermen to protect their industry. Again, the efforts of the New England fish trust to secure control of the markets, have somewhat exercised the fishermen of the western section of the province, most of whom market their fish in the United States.

Perhaps the latter circumstances had most to do with bringing the fishermen together. At any rate, the principal object of the union is to protect its members against the encroachments of the trust, which aims to monopolize the American market, and thus achieve a position enabling it to compel our fishermen to accept any price for their products it may

---

[45]*Montreal Herald*, 31 August 1905.

[46]The Fishermen's Union of Nova Scotia was a "union" only in a very specific sense. It was oriented mainly to self-employed inshore fishers, and hence was not a "union" as this is conventionally understood in modern industrial relations. For background, see L. Gene Barrett, "Underdevelopment and Social Movements in the Nova Scotia Fishing Industry to 1938," in Robert Brym and R. James Sacouman, eds., *Underdevelopment and Social Movements in Atlantic Canada* (Toronto: New Hogtown, 1979), 127-60.

[47]Moses Hardy Nickerson (1846-1943) was a public school teacher, journalist and politician in McKay's home county of Shelburne. He was the owner and editor of *The Coast Guard* from 1897 to 1911 and Liberal M.L.A. for Shelburne from 1902 to 1912. Known as the "Fisherman's Apostle," he was a founder and spokesperson for the Fishermen's Union of Nova Scotia, and in his day was considered the Dominion's leading authority on the fishing industry. He was also a long-time friend and correspondent of McKay's. See *Carols of the Coast* (1892), for his poetry.

choose to offer. The trust is continually extending the area of its operations, and without organization the provincial fishermen would probably soon be at its mercy, and the lobster fishermen especially would suffer seriously. In view of this possibility, the fishermen have decided to unite their forces for mutual protection, and propose, should it become necessary, to apply the co-operative principle to the disposal of their products -- to adopt the plan which has been worked out so successfully by the Danish farmers, who when a produce trust was formed in London, opened co-operative agencies in that city, and secured to themselves the profits which formerly went to the commission merchants.

Although the Nova Scotia fisheries have been steadily increasing in value, employing an increasing number of men, and yielding larger average returns, some fishermen consider the future prospects far from optimistic. "A cloud has arisen in the west," said Mr. Nickerson, the other day, "that seems likely to spread and overshadow the prosperity of the men engaged in the Atlantic coast fisheries. I refer to the growing importance of the Pacific coast fisheries. The coastal waters of British Columbia and California teem with cod and halibut of an excellent quality, as well as with salmon and other food fishes. Up to a short time ago little or no effort was made to exploit the cod and halibut fisheries, owing perhaps to the fact that the people were for the most part fully occupied in other enterprises, but now the New England Fish Company has a fine fleet of halibut fishermen operating from British Columbia. And the company's enterprise in this direction has proven so successful that perhaps the bulk of the halibut sold in Canada and even in New England comes from the Pacific over the C.P.R. The Pacific fishermen have very obvious advantages over our people; they operate near the coast while the halibuters of the Atlantic frequently have to dare the dangers of the deep even as far as Labrador and Greenland; then they have much more favorable weather conditions than our people who prosecute their calling in one of the stormiest regions of the world. The number of vessels and men, to say nothing of the value of the gear, annually lost in the north Atlantic fisheries is often appalling. So great are the advantages that the New England Company can sell Pacific halibut in Boston cheaper than the Gloucester vessels can."

In the past, perhaps, the development of the cod fisheries of the Pacific was hindered by the fact that the climate was not favorable to the old methods of curing fish. But now that the big companies have entered the business with new methods of curing fish, climatic conditions are no hindrance. If cod are as plentiful on the Pacific coast as they are reported to be, we may expect great developments in the near future, and since the Pacific fisheries can be prosecuted more cheaply than on this side of the continent their competition is bound to react unfavorably upon the Atlantic fisheries. Already many of the smartest Gloucester and Boston fishing shippers, have abandoned the Grand Bank fisheries, and betaken themselves with their vessels and crews to the Pacific coast.

59. The Application of Capitalistic Methods to the Fishing Industry[48]

The evolution of capitalism in the fishing industry of Nova Scotia throws into relief some features of the capitalist system not generally understood by workers. Here we have a phase of full fledged capitalism, cheek by jowl with the old methods of carrying on the fish business and at once the old methods become mere tributaries to the stream of profits of the characteristically capitalist method.

Cold storage companies buy the fishermen's product at prices ranging from 50 cents to $1.50 per hundred pounds, and after putting it through various processes, sell for $8 or $10. Occasionally, but not often, they compete for fish, and their prices to the fishermen may go up to $4.00 or $4.50. Of course the original cost of a cold storage plant is considerable but even taking in account overhead charges and the cost of manufacturing processes, there is a goodly margin of profit. And anyway the cold storage companies are heavily subsidized by the government, and usually enjoy other privileges, such as exemption from municipal taxation, free water, and in some cases free sites.

Some years ago, writing in the *Coast Guard,* I predicted that unless the fishermen organized an extensive system of co-operative societies, typically capitalistic methods would be applied to the fishing industry, and that eventually the fishermen would find themselves in much the same position of dependence as the city workers. Many of the characteristics of advanced capitalism have appeared in the fishing industry. Where the fisherman formerly caught, cured and often took his fish to market, the industry has been decomposed into distinct branches, and specialization and sub-division of labour proceed apace. That this process of evolution is a good thing cannot be denied; it tends to increase production and put the fish before the consumer in a more palatable condition. Unfortunately the fishermen, curers, packers and other workers in the industry are not likely to reap the advantages arising from the improvements in methods.

In the next ten or twenty years quite a number of cold storage companies will appear on the Nova Scotia coast. For a time there will be competition between them, and the fishermen will get good prices for their catches, so much better prices than they have been accustomed to, that they will not feel the need of co-operative effort. Unless they are very much wiser than

[48]*Eastern Labor News*, 13 September 1913.

other workers, I would not be surprised if the present fishermen's unions, which correspond to the agricultural societies of the farmers, disappear.

But more quickly than in other industries the big companies, by agreement, will cut out competition, and prices paid the fishermen will be reduced to what will only yield a living wage. By that time the big companies will have secured control of all the marketing facilities and the fishermen will have to submit. Then, their independence gone, they will be ripe for organization. They will form militant unions, and organize strikes. But they will find themselves opposed to a combination of forces so compact and strong that their union will not be of much value except from the socialist standpoint.

If the fishermen had organized a big co-operative society, and undertaken the establishment of cold storage plants and the organization of marketing facilities, they might have absorbed all the advantages of improved methods. That they can regain lost ground, and develop cold storage and marketing facilities in face of the competition of the big companies already in the field may be seriously doubted. Only a very big co-operative society could successfully fight the big companies backed by millions of capital, and a big co-operative society could only arise as a result of a combination of operations of small local societies. And the big companies can easily overcome the small isolated local societies, unless the members have rare powers of self-sacrifice. In order to break up such a society the big companies would offer its members a great deal higher prices for their catches than the society could afford to pay. If the fishermen yielded to the temptation of high prices, the co-operative society would disappear, because it could not keep its trade. Even if the fishermen stood by their society, the big companies could still beat the small co-operative society by invading the markets and underselling it. And as soon as the co-operative society was driven from the field the big companies would make the fishermen pay the expense of putting their society out of business.

So there is every reason to expect that the evolution of capitalism within the fishing industry will follow the course it has taken in other industries. In time the workers in the fishing industry will find themselves in the same position as the workers in all capitalistic industries. The laws of expanding capitalism operate to reduce practically all classes of workers to the same status. Capitalism itself develops class conscious workers, and creates conditions from which the only way of escape is by the overthrow of the rule of the capitalists and the establishment of the co-operative commonwealth. And as Marx points out, the very mechanism of the capitalist mode of production, educates, organizes and disciplines the workers for the work of conquering the world in the interests of humanity.[49]

60. Steam Trawling and its Effect on Fisheries[50]

The question whether the use of the otter and beam trawl depletes the fisheries -- and if so, to what extent -- has from time to time caused as much controversy in European countries as it has in Canada. The International Fisheries' Commission, which has its headquarters at Copenhagen, has for some years been investigating the subject, but its conclusions have not been of a very definitive character.

Among those interested in the fisheries opinions are strongly held, but arguments are perhaps somewhat influenced by self-interest -- not certainly an unusual occurrence in this world. Owners of steam fishing craft generally hold that the use of the trawl has no adverse effect in the way of rendering the fishing grounds less prolific; in fact, some even contend that the action of the trawl upon the bottom is not unlike that of a harrow on a ploughed field -- cleaning it, and stirring it, so that it produces a greater quantity of vegetation and animalcules upon which fish feed. On the other hand owners of small boats hold that the use of the trawl is highly destructive, and that if not prohibited or strictly regulated will sooner or later destroy the fisheries and depopulate various sections of Europe....

One complaint against the use of the trawl is that it destroys the sea weeds on the bottom, among which fish deposit their eggs. Many naturalists, however, declare that the spawn of the vast majority of fishes does not attach itself to sea weed on the bottom, but hatches in suspension in the currents of the sea. The young fry are said to seek the bottoms of sand and mud mainly for shelter.

Another complaint is that the trawl averages blindly, taking immature and useless fish as well as fish suitable for food. No doubt there is something in that: whether the spawn and fry are on the bottom, or in a state of suspension there must be a considerable amount of destruction. But it should be noted that the steam craft which are mainly singled out for

---

[49]McKay refers to the general argument of Marx and Engels, *Manifesto of the Communist Party* : "...with the development of industry the proletariat not only increases in number; it becomes concentrated in greater masses, its strength grows, and it feels that strength more. The various interests and conditions of life within the ranks of the proletariat are more and more equalised, in proportion as machinery obliterates all distinctions of labour, and nearly everywhere reduces wages to the same low level." Karl Marx and Frederick Engels, *Manifesto of the Communist Party* (Moscow: Progress Publishers, 1971): 44.

[50]*Canadian Fisherman*, November 1918, 1082-1083.

condemnation use trawls, the meshes of which are considerably larger than the meshes of the drag nets used by small fishing boats, or the meshes of the drift or stationary nets used in the coast fisheries. The French official observes that the destruction of fry caused by the hand dip nets of the shrimp fishermen who wade into the sea to take their prey is quite appreciable, compared with the damage wrought by the large beam and other trawls used in combing the vast bottoms of the high seas.

The fact that in the North Sea, where intensive trawling has been practised for years, large specimens of the cod, haddock, soles, turbots, flat fish, etc., have become rare, no doubt gives support to the view that the trawl is a destructive engine of exploitation. At the same time it should be remembered that in Canadian waters, long before the steam trawler began to operate there, the depletion of certain areas was not an unknown phenomenon. These depletions have sometimes been attributed to over-fishing, and sometimes to migrations caused by the pursuit of predatory pests, like the dog fish. Certain kinds of fish like the mackerel will be very plentiful on certain parts of the Canadian coast for a season or many seasons, and then for a season or many seasons they will be mysteriously absent. Overfeeding certainly will not account for these disappearances. Some natural cause is at work. Man's wit is not yet able to discover it; but some day he may. Many rivers in Eastern Canada formerly teeming with trout and salmon, gaspereaux and smelts, have become nearly barren of any kind of game or food fish. This depletion has been ascribed to over-fishing, and the damage of dams and the debris from mills. Artificial culture has been invoked to restock such rivers -- not with conspicuous success. Old men have talked of climatic changes, marvelled at the spring freshets and summer droughts, when the river shrank into the swimming holes, they knew in their youth; and darkly hinted that Providence was wroth with the natives hereabouts. Then the scientific forester came along, and calmly asserted that not Providence but the improvidence of men who had carelessly let loose the element in which the arch enemy of Providence is supposed to have his being over the watershed of the river was mainly responsible for the incapacity of the river to bear fish as plentifully as it did in the old days. Careless sportsmen who haven't the wisdom of Indians have left camp fires burning in woods where the slashings of lumbermen made fine material for a blaze, and a conflagration swept a great forest. A river fed by a burnt-over watershed becomes a roaring freshet in the spring, when the snow melts, sweeping the spawn of trout and salmon to destruction, and shrinks to a shallow brook in summer, swollen at times by rains, because there is no subsoil to hold the moisture and seep it gradually to the river bed; because, too the greater the burnt area, the more it is like a desert, incapable of absorbing moisture from the air and precipitating rain like a forest land.

And so with greater knowledge it may be discovered that trawling and other methods of fishing -- though doubtless contributing causes-- are not the main causes of the depletion of certain fisheries, that the operation of natural laws over which man has no control affects the life of the sea in more potent and drastic ways than any artificial agency of man -- though it may be discovered, too, that the principal factor in this deterioration of the denizens of the deep has its origin in some at present unconsidered practice of man, just as the long continued process of dessication or drying up, which turned the cradle of the human race into bleak deserts of sand, no doubt had its origin in the careless use of fire by the nascent civilizations. Be that as it may, we no longer apostrophize the ocean in the manner of Byron: 'Man marks the earth with ruin -- his control,' for good or evil, does not necessarily stop at the borders of the sea.[51] No longer is it a generally accepted article of faith that the sea is inexhaustible; though it dies hard, that comfortable belief which by exonerating fishermen from any concern for their neighbours or future generations has rendered difficult the enforcement of government regulations designed to prevent the depletion of the fisheries. Nearly every Maritime government now assumes the right to regulate methods of fishing, and regards it as a duty so to do. Before the war there was in Europe an agitation to establish trawling zones in the North Sea under an international arrangement, giving to the various fishing grounds periodic opportunities of rest and recuperation, as a good farmer does with his fields. Since the outbreak of war there has been little or no trawling in some parts of the North Sea, but whether fish have increased in such regions remains to be seen. And until the zone system has been tried, no one can say whether it will prove advantageous to the fisheries. With the great fleets of trawlers now employed there is of course the possibility that intensive fishing in the zones open to fishermen might offset the recuperation of the zones temporarily closed. The value of a close season for lobsters, which have a limited habitat compared with herring or cod, is still a matter of dispute in some quarters.

One thing is certain: the steam trawlers cannot be ruled out of the reckoning, whatever may be their effect upon the fisheries. They are the mainstay of the fisheries of Great Britain, taking about 95 per cent of the

---

[51]McKay refers to Lord Byron's "Childe Harolde's Pilgrimage: A Romaunt," Canto IV, verse CLXXIX:
"Roll on, thou deep and dark blue Ocean -- roll!
Ten thousand fleets sweep over thee in vain:
Man marks the earth with ruin -- his control
Stops with the shore; upon the watery plain
The wrecks are all thy deed, nor doth remain
A shadow of a man's ravage, save his own,
When for a moment, like a drop of rain,
He sinks into they depths with bubbling groan,
Without a grave, unknell'd, uncoffin'd, and unknown."
Lord Byron, *The Complete Poetical Works*, ed. H. Frowde (London: Oxford University Press, 1909): 243.

catch of England and Wales. They have greatly increased the supplies of fish available for the food of the people. They are continually extending the sphere of their operations, exploiting fishing banks previously unknown or unworked, making profitable trips to regions where sailing vessels could not be employed to advantage. On the west coast of Africa the more powerful types of steam trawler are able to work their trawls on banks at a depth of 240 fathoms. This ability of the steam trawler to work at great depth, as well as its capacity to range far afield and still land its catches in a fresh condition seems to offer a means of meeting the complaints direct[ed] against its method of fishing; that is to say, under proper regulations extensive fishing may serve to mitigate, if not entirely overcome, the evils of intensive fishing.

61. The Knockabout Schooner[52]

The vogue of the large knockabout type of fishing schooner seems to be over. Shipyards in the Maritime Provinces which have for some years been busy building this type of craft are now idle or facing the prospect of idleness, as there is little demand for fishing vessels of any kind. W.C. McKay and Son of Shelburne[53] launched a knockabout schooner of 185 tons during the first week of September, and another of the same size and type, during the first week of October. These may be the last knockabout schooners to be built in Nova Scotia. At any rate the Nova Scotia fishermen are saying that this class of vessels have been a disappointment. Their principal fault is that they will not ride to anchor on the banks in a breeze of wind like the olden type of fishing vessels. A second fault is that they are slower than the older vessels in moderate winds. The experience of New England fishermen with the knockabout type has also been disappointing, and for the same reasons.

The knock-about type of schooners have an overhanging bow like a racing yacht, and no bowsprit. When at anchor the send of the sea lifting against the long overhang of the bow evidently hurls them backward, causing them to draw their anchors or part their hawsers. Some fishermen say that the reason that they drag their anchors or break adrift is that they have no bobstays like the older types, their idea being that the bobstay parts the sea. This explanation is hardly convincing. It is more easy to understand that a sea plunging against the bow of the knock-about takes a powerful grip on the whole forepart of her, especially as she has no fore-foot to help her lift on the on-coming sea. Then the knockabouts which have been built in Nova Scotia are larger, heavier vessels than the older types, and are in any case, less easy to hold. If they used heavier anchors and bigger hawsers they might ride out a breeze better, but the ordinary type of hawser is about the limit of size that can be conveniently handled and

---

[52]*Canadian Fisherman*, October 1920: 221-222.
[53]That is, the shipyard associated with McKay's family and operated by his father.

stowed in their narrow bows. They might possibly use chain cables, as the Frenchmen do, but the weight of a chain cable upon their overhanging bows might be a serious matter in a heavy sea. In any case Canadian fishermen do not believe in using chain cables on the banks, for reasons that experience has proven good.

The knockabouts fared badly in the great gale that swept the Grand Banks this summer. They were not, however, the only vessels that broke adrift. With few exceptions, all the vessels -- Canadian, French, and American -- lying in the sixty mile wide path of the gale, lost their ground tackle. Many also lost rails, and had their decks swept clear of boats and gear. Fortunately the gale came at the tail end of the season when most of the vessels had nearly completed their fares and were thinking of returning home. Had it occurred earlier the vessels would have lost a lot of time refitting, and missed the best weather for fishing. As it is, most of the Lunenburg Grand Bankers made good catches, but many lost gear worth $3,500, and that will take the profits off the summer's trip. After having such serious losses in the great gale, it may be imagined that the fishermen were not happy when they returned home to find that the bottom had apparently fallen out of the fish market.

To-day Lunenburg is rather down-hearted. There is now no talk of building fishing vessels. Nova Scotia yards have a few fishing vessels of the semi-knockabout type under construction which will be launched before winter sets in. There are also two or three fishing vessels, barques or schooners, under construction for the French government. When these contracts are [completed] the prospects are that the building of fishing vessels will offer little employment for some time. Newfoundland by all accounts is more down-hearted than Lunenburg, and not likely to order fishing vessels -- not more than a few anyway. Some hopes have been entertained of getting contracts for fishing vessels from South Africa, but one Nova Scotia builder turned out two very poor vessels for this market -- they were so badly put together that they cost a mint of money for repairs in Bermuda and St. Thomas -- and South Africa is evidently wary of coming to Canada for more fishing craft.

It would appear that Lunenburg, Riverport, and other fishing centres have been rather overdoing things. Having been making money for some years they have gone in for building fine big vessels -- a more expensive class of vessel than normal conditions in the fishing industry [warrant]. Some of the vessels launched in recent years have been too big for salt fishing. Of course, the vessels when not engaged in fishing are usually employed in the [coasting], West Indian or other trades, and during the war when there was plenty of employment for any kind of craft the larger they were the better. But while there will doubtless be in future some employment for small sailing vessels, when not engaged in fishing it is not likely to be so plentiful or so profitable as during the years of the war. The Canadian

Government Merchant Marine has established new services to the West Indies and South America; the Marine Navigation Company and the Houston Lines are running boats from Canada to Brazil, Uruguay and Argentina; probably we will have regular steamship sailings to the Mediterranean, calling at ports in Spain and Portugal. And with such services the small Nova Scotia sailing vessels are likely to experience difficulty in finding employment when the fishing season is over.

At the same time the cost of fishing vessels has increased so much that it is more important than it ever was that they be kept at work the year round. Before the war the average type of Grand Banker with equipment cost about $13,000 or $15,000. The latest knockabout schooners of 180 tons, with equipment are valued at $30,000 to $35,000. In some cases new companies have over-capitalized their vessel property. While the fishing vessels were making big profits it was not a difficult matter for promoters to sell shares to fishermen and others at prices that were somewhat above those demanded by the actual investment, but with the days of 80 or 90 per cent. dividends apparently over, there is now no eager demand for shares in fishing vessels. Now that the industry is getting down to rock bottom conditions again, this inflation of values may correct itself -- though it will continue to have the unfortunate effect of discouraging young fishermen from investing in vessel shares -- but there is no likelihood that the cost of vessels or equipment will fall to the pre-war level. Nova Scotia builders before the war were turning out fishing vessels at less than their economic value. Few of them were making a profit, and all were paying low wages, and some were working a ten-hour day. Now they are paying twice the wages they did some years ago, and working a shorter day; and material reduction of wages is out of the question with the cost of living what it is. Also the builders have to face greatly increased prices for all kinds of material. They make more use of machinery, but on the other hand pay heavy transportation charges on nearly everything they use. Little timber now comes down the river at the mouth of which the shipyards are located. Now timber is brought by rail long distances; sometimes pitch pine is brought from the southern states.

Lunenburg and other ports owing [owning] Grand Bank fishing vessels, will do well to consider the new conditions which have developed or are in the process of development -- to take stock of their position and work out a policy for the future. Their further progress, their present security, depends on their ability to provide an answer to the important questions which are pressing to the forefront. All these new steam ships services -- to what extent will they deprive fishing vessels of winter employment? Will it be possible to man the fishing fleet in summer if the men are no longer able to make trading voyages in winter? And supposing the steamers deprive the schooners of their occupation in winter, to what extent will it be profitable to use the schooners for fishing in winter?

That seems to be a question of some importance. And immediately it brings us broadside on to the great question which is worrying the Maritime fishing industry just now -- the question of markets. Lunenburg and other salt fishing ports have some times been accused of lack of enterprise in not going in for winter fishing. It has also been suggested that the fishermen sailing out of Lunenburg -- being usually shareholders as well as workers -- did so well in summer that nothing would induce them to try the winter fishing with its hardships and dangers. This might very well be a matter of pride for Lunenburg but the fact that Lunenburg vessels have never found it difficult to get fishermen to go on trading voyages in winter might argue the existence of other reasons why Lunenburg has never gone in for winter fishing to any extent. One very good reason was that Lunenburg, having a big stock of salt fish on hand, and pre-occupied with the problem of disposing of its summer's catch, was not likely to be interested in winter fishing. Any Lunenburg fishermen who had a hankering for winter fishing went to Boston or Gloucester, where he knew the winter fishermen could find a profitable market. If he had been asked to go winter fishing out of Lunenburg he would probably have observed that he did not believe in carrying coals to Newcastle. There is the rub. The greatest fishing port in Canada knows little or nothing of fresh fishing; it is little interested in the Canadian market. The greatest fishing port in Canada has no cold storage plant; Lunenburg fishing vessels have to go to other ports for frozen herring for bait. This is probably a poetic justice in this peculiar situation, but a discussion of the question, "Why Lunenburg hasn't a cold storage plant when Liverpool and [Lockeport] have," might bring out some information of importance as to Dominion Fisheries policy in the Maritime Provinces.

62. The Employment Question in the Fishing Industry[54]

Notwithstanding very notable developments in the fishing industry of Canada during the last quarter of a century, the number of persons engaged in production has declined by nearly one-third. In 1900 all persons engaged in catching and curing or canning fish numbered 99,269; in 1923, the persons so employed numbered 68,964. Between 1900 and 1913 the number of persons employed in this industry was usually over 90,000, though in 1907, a year of hard times, it dropped to 82,400. In 1915 the number rose to 102,182, the highest recorded; since when it has declined to 68,946 in 1923, the lowest figure for a generation.

The fact that the number of persons engaged in the fisheries has rapidly declined needs to be faced. If the rate of decline between 1913 [1923] and 1915 continued, there would be no fishermen in Canada fifteen years hence.

---

[54]Originally published as "The Employment Question," *Canadian Fisherman*, April 1925: 105.

Both the men catching fish and the persons employed in canning and curing establishments, were fewer in 1923 than at the beginning of the century. The number of fishermen declined from 81,064 in 1900 to 58,517 in 1923, and the number of fish factory employees from 18,205 in 1900 to 15,447 in 1923. Vessel fishermen declined from 9,205 in 1900 to 6,694 in 1923, and boat fishermen from 71,859 to 44,482.

On the other hand, the capital invested in the fishing industry on the productive side increased from $10,990,000 in 1900 to $47,672,000 in 1923. The value of the fish catch (marketed) increased from $21,557,000 in 1900 to $42,565,000 in 1923, according to Government statistics which are usually conservative.

The big increase in capital invested means, of course, a big improvement in the machines employed -- steam trawlers, larger and more expensive schooners, motor boats in lieu of sail or row boats. And an increase of 100 per cent in the value of the catch, divided among a number of persons engaged reduced by 32 per cent., means a certain improvement in the standard of living. Unfortunately it cannot be said that the improvement of the position of those engaged in the fishing industry has kept pace with the improvement of the position of those engaged in most other industries in Canada.

According to Canadian Government statistics, the cost of living has more than doubled since 1900, while the price of fish has shown a smaller increase. If the fisherman makes a better living today than he did in 1900, he owes nothing to the fact that fish prices have increased. Such gains in the economic or social scale as he has made are due solely to the fact that he is using more efficient machines or methods; a motor boat, for instance, provided by his own savings, or a steam trawler, provided by capitalists. Superior knowledge, representing accumulated experience, may also be a factor making for larger relative earnings; but sheer skill in seamanship and the practical operations of fishing is probably not as important as it was twenty-five years ago.

The fishing industry is not the only Canadian industry in which, in recent years, machines have played a more important role than men. Canadian manufacturing industries in 1922, despite the great developments in pulp and paper manufacturing, employed 26,000 fewer persons than they did in 1911, according to Government statistics, though the value of such industries increased by more than 150 per cent. The great agricultural industry only employed 6 per cent more persons in 1922 than it did in 1911 (including farmers' sons over 14 years of age), though its value [of] production increased nearly 170 per cent.

The major industries of Canada -- agriculture, mining, manufacturing, logging, and transportation -- in 1922 were only employing one per cent more persons than in 1911, according to Government statistics. Employees in these industries received more money wages. But since these industries did not materially increase the number of persons dependent upon them, they did not materially increase the market for the products of the fishing industry.

For a decade or more the evolution of Canadian industry has multiplied machines rather than men. And as of old the Canadian fishing industry has to find foreign markets for the greater part of its products. In 1923, the value of the catch exported to other countries was $27,800,000, more than half the total market value of $42,5465,000. What gains the industry has made in the Canadian market have been mainly due to its enterprise in pushing the sale of commercial fish in places where the only fish consumed before were of local origin or imported -- not to other major industries increasing the demand for fish.

63. The Machine Age and the Fisheries[55]

The ever-growing development of the machine process has caused resentment in the ancient and honourable craft of fishing, as well as in other crafts. Even where the machine has potently lightened labour, reduced the risks of life and limb, and augmented wealth production and thereby improved the standard of living, its invasion has always created resentment in the minds of older craftsmen. This is only to say that the general effect of the machine process has been to reduce or destroy the value of craft, skill and knowledge and thus strike at the individuality of the craftsman.

The shore fisherman in his own little boat is his own master, the regent of his actions, pursuing his calling according to his fancy on a sea that from infancy he has regarded as his own. His lot may be hard and dangerous but he is sustained by a sense of freedom and independence that flatters his personal importance. Though the material facts of his existence, wind and tide, the uncertain movement of fish, storm and fog, thwarts his will, all that he wrests from the sea he gains by virtue of his own skill, strength, courage and endurance. The mentality of the small boat fisherman has inevitably exhibited stronger spiritual qualities; it was not a fortuitous circumstance that Jesus chose his chief disciple from among fishermen, or that the statesmen of Queen Elizabeth associated the development of the fisheries with the problem of breaking the power of Spain. Along with marked individuality of character, the fisherman, however, has usually exhibited a conservative habit, a disposition to cling to the traditional methods and customs of his craft.

---

[55]*Canadian Fisherman*, October 1926: 301-303.

But every extension of the machine process, the use of the motor craft and steam trawler, railways and refrigerator cars, has been breaking up the old routine, and transforming the mentality of the fisherman, though not so rapidly as the transformation of the equipment with which his industry operates. This change often spells tragedy for the older fishermen, by sweeping away the environment in which their lives had been rooted by time-honoured customs and homely ties. This change, too, has spelt ruin for whole communities. For with the invasion of the fishing industry by the machine process the major operations tend to concentrate themselves in a few large ports where big fishing establishments have been [developed]. The fishermen, too, gravitate to the larger ports, where the cost of living is dearer than in the small fishing hamlets with their possibilities of farming when the fishing is not propitious. The younger adapt themselves to the new conditions without difficulty, but for the older folk the transition is rude and full of regrets for the old order.

Instead of being masters of craft, free on a little boat operated with the aid of a son or two, the fishermen are more and more being incorporated into the machine process, converted into cogs of a wheel, units of a process which is regulated by the ever-expanding series of requirements. With the development of the machine process the various factors in a given industry, those of both production and distribution, are obliged to accommodate themselves one to the other, and the more highly developed the industry happens to be, the more dependent it is for its successful conduct upon the correlation of those parts. The dislocation of the sub-processes in the scheme of machine production tends to interrupt the whole system and causes a general disturbance, not only within the particular industry itself, but in a variety of allied industries. In England where steam trawlers produce 95 per cent or more of the fish catch, the crew of these vessels are, as it were, harnessed by means of radio to railway time tables and market quotations at Billingsgate. This is all in accord with the scheme of everyday life growing out of the machine process, which requires that men shall ... adapt their needs and motions to the exigencies of an ever-increasing concatenation of economic forces, to an increasing standardization of industrial processes and communication services, to a growing regimentation of life. Schedules of time, place and circumstance more and more rule the activities of men, and the personal initiative and independence which were the birth-rights and prized privileges of generations of craftsmen tend to disappear into the limbo in which all-round skill and artistic spirit of such craftsmen have already largely vanished.

Even in the absence of intricate mechanical contrivances, the machine process may be said to have seized on an industry when its characteristic operations have been reduced to a procedure not requiring the craftsmanlike skill, individual reflection, elaboration and artistic perceptions which were essential to production in the handicrafts era. It is the character of the process rather than the complexity of the mechanical contrivances employed that produces the characteristic phenomena. When for instance, the railways put on refrigerator cars and quoted rates on fish, indicating a recognition of the possibilities of the industry, the way was paved for something like a revolution in the fish business, a change that at the outset had important consequences without calling for the employment of the steam trawler. The railways, mechanical contrivances of the first order, important factors in the general machine process, were however in existence for years before they had any notable reaction upon the fish industry in the way of increasing the transport of fresh fish far from tide water, no reaction at any rate comparable to that which followed the introduction of the refrigerator car.

Mechanical processes do not introduce themselves into the fishing industry so readily as into many other industries. But the influence of the mechanical process extends in all directions, calling into being new forms of business organization, new methods of technique setting up new aims and ideals. The machine process everywhere tends to standardization and in industries this tendency is promoted by mechanical contrivances and advertising. In the fishing industry the urge to standardization has also been in evidence; the public authority has been invoked to provide inspection, establish grades, to set up and secure standards through the aid of legal machinery -- departmental machinery of the state anyway.

The transition from the regime of craftsmanship to that of the machine process naturally does not follow a uniform procedure, the result being that here and there the new technique of the machine process does not develop rapidly enough to adequately meet the exigencies created by vitiation of the skill and knowledge of the older type of craftsman. Mr. H.B. Short and Mr. H.R. Silver recently pointed out that the methods of treating and curing salt dried fish do not always produce as satisfactory commodities as might be secured. And in this they voice the complaint that has been growing for some time, or at any rate a widely-held view that the salt fish industry is not making the best of its product. The treatment and curing of salt fish is a very ancient craft -- it might quite properly be called an ancient art -- an art that made the man who practised the drying part of it as keen an observer of sunrise and sunset as the painter of sky-scape, that lifted his eyes continuously to the heavens, and made him a courtier of sunrise and wind, linked his life to the varied phenomena of the weather, all the wonders of the universe, by the bonds of his hand work. This old art still survives, existing side by side with a newer technique more or less dependent upon the machine process. It was, and still is, in remote sections of the coast, a family art, and handed down for generations, man and wife and grown sons participating in some process of treating and curing. It was also to some extent a community art, different sections of the coast producing a distinctive product for a special market; the Gaspé coast turning out a product for Brazil,

Lunenburg for the West Indies. The fish merchants probably did not talk of standardization in the days when catching and curing fish were mere arts and crafts; but they knew where they could buy finished products of different types or grades and made their buying and marketing plans accordingly. There are those who claim that the finished salt fish product of an older day was superior to the product of some modern fish establishments which receive the green fish and put them through more or less mechanical processes under supervision of men supposed to be experts in the newer technique. There are those who claim that there are still sections of the coast, remote fishing hamlets, where the more primitive methods employed turn out salt-dried fish superior to the product of big fishing establishments in important ports. The validity of such claims in special cases of comparison could probably be proved; but that they would hold in a general comparison is open to question. For a long time there was a general belief that fish dried on stones were superior to fish dried on structures of wood. And there is still a belief that fish dried by the sun are superior to those dried by mechanical agencies. But these old beliefs raise questions science has probably not sufficiently explored to warrant a definite answer, though scientists are prepared to affirm that mechanical processes of curing fish present definite advantages over those of curing by the sun from the hygienic point of view....

The machine process which has extended its tentacles to practically all phases of the fresh fish business more and more also compels the salt fish business to organize itself around said process; that is to say, the salt fish business more and more pursues policies indicating its increasing need of adjusting its activities to the fact that modern life is so largely conditioned and governed by the machine process. Mr. Short and Mr. Silver, whose experience goes back to the day when the catching and salt-dried curing of cod was more of a craft or art than an industry in the modern sense, may have always had reason to complain that the finished salt fish product was inferior to what it ought and might be with more careful treatment at all stages of the finishing process. But evidently twenty-five or thirty year ago they were not greatly impressed by deficiencies of that character, or they would have fought a battle for remedial measures that might have carried the salt fish business to a higher latitude than the doldrum regions in which it now is, according to their own account. It is possible that the machine process, by decomposing the old craft of fishing, without anywhere developing mechanical agencies sufficiently advanced to fulfil adequately the functions formerly served by craft skill and knowledge, has resulted in the production at some points and places of salt-dried fish inferior to the production of 25 or 30 years ago. But it is not necessary to assume anything like a general deterioration of the finished production to account for the increasing insistence of the trade upon the need of greater attention to the finishing process. Changes in the organization of the industry and its marketing methods will explain that. Under the old regime the fish merchant usually sent his saltfish to foreign markets in brigantines and schooners. The fish were culled and graded by the vessel load. Fish were cheap, labour and everything else was cheap, and whether all the fish were treated and cured so as to grade as high as possible was relatively of little consequence. But, with the increasing costs of labour and everything else there has grown the need that the trade should obtain the maximum return possible for every fish handled. Another consideration is that the competition of fish producing countries has widened; and European countries have improved the quality and appearance of their salt fish products under the influence of markets more fastidious than those wherein a large part of the Canadian cure has usually been sold. Thus Norway has in some cases secured the cream of the trade in markets where Nova Scotia fish were once considered firmly entrenched. Another consideration is that now a large portion of the salt fish product is shipped to foreign markets by steamer, usually in small lots compared to the vessel loads shipped when the main reliance for transport was still on sail. This change in the methods of marketing has also brought with it an urge to standardization. The foreign buyer does not now usually pick and choose from a whole vessel load such supplies as he needs to meet the market requirements for an extended period. Owing to the increased facilities and celerity of steam transport he buys more or less from hand to mouth, and must place a consignment he receives upon the market within a short time. This makes it important in a new way that the consignment should be up to expectations in all particulars; otherwise the merchant's business is liable to be thrown out of gear in a way that it would not have been when he carried a large stock of various grades intended to meet requirements for a long period. Hence also it becomes desirable, and even essential to the satisfactory conduct of trade, that the grades should be few in number, and each of as nearly uniform appearance and quality as possible. Insofar, also, as advertising is used as a selling agent, there has developed the desirability that standard lines should be distinguished by brand names. California products of dried fruit have built up a large market by advertising named brands. By a co-operative arrangement the brand covers the products of numbers of producers, care being taken that the different users of the brand put up a product of uniform quality.

The ever-developing machine process, of which the modern system of communications, in all its ramifications (railways, steamships, telegraph, telephone, postal services, advertising) is a part, not only urges the producer towards standardization by penalizing him for irregularity in the quality of his products; it also tends to bring the purchasing power of the consumer under a certain standardized control. An extreme example of this effect is marketing by telephone. This implies a certain surrender of the right to pick and choose, the acceptance of a new dependence upon the judgment of others....

64. The Machine Age with its Trawler and Its Relation to Our Shore Fishermen[56]

For a good many years there has been a trek of population from the fishing communities of the Maritime Provinces and when the McLean[57] [MacLean] Commission is asked to recommend measures which will materially increase the opportunities of employment in the eastern Canadian fishing industry, it is expected to undertake a large order. There have been complaints in the past that the new methods of fishing, the more extensive or intensive use of some form of the machine, were reducing the opportunities of earning a living in the fishing industry. What makes the complaints especially bitter at the present time is that new avenues of employment are not so readily available today as they used to be. Time was when the Bluenose fisherman was pretty sure of a job at short notice if he went to New England, if not in a fishing vessel at least in a factory or some occupation. Now New England fisheries are also employing less men, and New England factory machinery is being moved to the southern states. Again, when the British Columbia and Pacific coast fisheries generally were in their earlier stages of development, offers for the services of experienced Bluenose skippers and men were very frequent and those who wished to go to the Pacific coast usually had their transportation paid. Further, the Canadian west was calling for young men from downeast in a way it is not doing today.

The problem which is now worrying the fishermen of the Maritimes and Quebec is part of the social problem of the age, the problem created by the rapid development of the machine which has the faculty of making possible big increases in production, but not itself being a consumer of many commodities it helps create or fashion for human needs, accentuates the difficulties of finding a market for the increased production....

Hon. A.K. MacLean's Fisheries Committee is investigating one of those tragic disturbances of the lives of hard working people which mark the path of what is called progress. What is happening to the Maritime fishing industry is a transformation such as has always followed the invasion by new powerful machines of callings that have been nearly stationary in their methods for generations. The advent of steam vessels, using the

---

[56]*Canadian Fisherman*, December 1927: 365-366; 394.

[57]McKay refers to the commission headed by Alexander Kenneth MacLean (1869-1942) to enquire into conditions in the fishing industry. MacLean practised law in Lunenburg, and ran for the Liberals in the federal election of 1900. He was elected to the provincial legislature in 1909 and 1911, and served as Nova Scotia's Attorney-General. He was also a federal politician, sitting for Halifax as a Liberal M.P. in 1911, a Unionist in 1917, and a Liberal in 1921. At the time of heading this commission he was president of the Exchequer Court of Canada.

beam or otter trawl, was followed by the practical depopulation of villages all around the coasts of England, Scotland and Ireland.

A special poignancy attaches to the menace which the steam trawlers have brought to the fishing ports of Nova Scotia, whose people for generations have studiously wrested a living from the sea. In the background is a great tradition of the days of sail and the pageant of four hundred years of stirring history; the grim chronicles of ports like Canso, Louisburg and Sydney, which were resorts of fishing vessels even before the fur traders began their adventures in the new world, or Cortes led his warriors through the mountains of Mexico. And in the foreground there still lingers a notable fleet of sailing craft, the only fleet of gainfully occupied [sailing] vessels in the world, whose graceful hulls and towering spread of canvas recall the famous clipper ships of a bygone day. This fleet of fishing schooners of which the *Bluenose* is the Queen has been dwindling for years, though the special conditions of its existence offer some hope that some survivals may grace Maritime ports quite awhile after the homely bald-headed schooners of the American Coast have disappeared from the seas.

Aside from the question whether the steam trawler represents a more efficient method of fishing and from the point of view of risk to life and limb a safer method, it is natural enough that not only fishermen, but many fish merchants and others, should resent its disturbing effects upon their lives and call for measures to preserve the old order of things. The ramifications of the fishing industry have long extended into many phases of the activities of the Maritimes. After the Bluenose sailor ships found themselves unable to make a living in the great ocean-trade routes, the only ship yards which survived were those which devoted themselves to the construction of fishing vessels and little brigantines, barks and tern schooners. The ship yards so employed afforded a market for timber much of which would otherwise have rotted in the woods; they furnished employment for carpenters, blacksmiths, sailmakers, riggers, sparmakers, boat builders -- a multitude of skilled craftsmen, who derived from their occupations a kind of satisfaction a mere machine tender never experiences -- the satisfaction of knowing that good workmanship not only contributed to the creation of a craft that was a delight to the eye, but also to the safety of friends and relatives, who trusted their lives in their handiwork, upon the stormy seas.

The little brigantines, barks and tern schooners turned out by these shipyards in the intervals of building fishing craft were familiar sights in most Nova Scotia ports. They carried fish and lumber to the West Indies, South America and the Mediterranean -- and sometimes to the ports of Atlantic states. Able, handy craft, they braved the tropical hurricanes and the bitter nor'westers that swept off the coasts of the Maritimes in winter. Small though they were, they were craft of which their home ports were proud, and among their captains and crews were men who not long before had sailed great clipper ships over the seven seas.

Steam ships have displaced the little sail vessels once engaged in the West Indian trade, as they have driven sail from all the other trade routes, in less than a generation. Some tern schooners are still owned in the Maritimes, but it is not easy for them to get outward or return cargoes. The West Indies dealer prefers to buy his fish in small lots delivered by steamer, instead of buying a vessel load. With steamers crowding the Caribbean, sailing vessels are in small demand to carry molasses, sugar or salt northward; even the Mosquito Coast of Central America does not want sailing craft to load coconuts for the soap factories of Saint John or Philadelphia. And as for carrying tropical fruit to American ports -- a trade that once gave considerable employment to the faster vessels and hard driving skippers of the Bluenose West Indian fleet -- that has long since been monopolized by fast steamers equipped with mechanical refrigerators.

Now the steam vessel with the otter trawl which has revolutionized the fishing industry of Europe has crossed the Atlantic to further upset the life of communities whose activities long based on the sailing vessel and its appropriate method of fishing no longer seem able to produce results adequate to their needs. These shore fishing communities are definitely menaced by the steam trawler machine. Even if they had the capital to employ an expensive machine like the steam trawler, that for many of them would be a bad venture because of the difficulty of marketing their catches. They have for quite a while been using a less expensive machine -- the power boat. In fact the employment of motor boats by shore fishermen has been one of the reasons why the shore fishing communities have been able until recently to maintain some measure of prosperity, instead of experiencing the fate which years ago overtook similar communities in England, Scotland and Ireland. There were other reasons, but of these more anon. The use of the power boat, however, did not bring about a change in the method of catching fish; the anchoring of long lines with baited hooks at intervals. The steam vessels dragging an otter trawl or huge bag-net with mouth extending over the bottom can catch many more fish than is possible by the older method.

The very efficiency of the machine creates the competition that worries Maritime fishermen, and also adds to the difficulties of the fishermen of Quebec.

But it is a very debatable question whether this efficient machine will be disposed of by suggestions made to the [MacLean] Commission that its use be prohibited from Canadian ports. The trawlers could make Boston or Gloucester their base of operations and sell their catches in Canada unless the Government placed a tariff on fish so high that it would be likely to lead to increases of prices of Canadian caught fish; that would greatly decrease the consumption of fish.

The Maritime fishing industry undoubtedly has great possibilities of development, but these will not be realized by following the plan of dark ages and killing inventors and smashing or prohibiting the use of efficient machinery. Some Maritime and Quebec communities are likely to suffer loss of population in the next decade or so, unless they can learn to produce a specialized fish product for the market. And unfortunately the loss in population will not be wholly due to migration to large towns or the U.S. Even though the fishing communities are populated by a hardy breed, there are people everywhere, especially old folks, who just hang on to existence, and a little shock such as may arise from a realization of an upset of their traditional environment, may shake them from the tree of life like ripe fruit. This is one of the tragedies of progress.

65. Too many fishermen[58]

In some parts of the Maritimes the chief trouble of the fishermen is a consciousness of a drift of things indicating a future in which they will not have automobiles to take their families to the nearest movies. But there are parts in which the fishermen even during the boom years were having hard times and have since sunk deeper into distress. Mostly the fishing opportunities in such parts are sub-marginal, because the nearer fishing grounds have been depleted and rail connections with the markets are lacking.

Clever propaganda has put the blame for the distress among the fishermen, partly upon the steam vessels using the otter trawl or dragnet, and partly upon control of the marketing facilities by big companies.

During the war Halifax and Saint John employed fourteen steam trawlers, but for some years the Dominion Government has only licensed three, all operating out of Halifax. The restriction of the use of these efficient instruments of fish production was imposed in order to lessen the competition the small boat fishermen had to meet. This policy did not reckon with the fact that other countries were building up fleets of otter trawlers and increasing their competition in the external markets which up to the end of the war had been taking about 85 per cent. of the Maritime catches. New England's diesel-engined otter trawler fleet has grown from less than twenty during the war to over seventy. And now the opportunities of the Maritimes to sell their fish, other than salmon, smelts, and lobsters, in New England are limited to the very rare intervals when demand exceeds supply at Boston sufficiently to set a price high enough to absorb the customs duty and leave a small profit.

---

[58]*Saturday Night*, 15 October 1938.

In Iceland, Norway, France and Germany large companies, employing otter trawlers, have become the main producers. They employ experts to process their fish for the world markets, and their salt-dried cod, haddock, hake and other ground fish have largely taken over the external markets once supplied by the Maritimes. Thus many fishermen who formerly produced for the external salt fish markets have been crowding their catches into the fresh fish markets, to the prejudice of prices.

Fortunately, the big companies have since the war, with government assistance in the matter of publicity, developed very important markets in interior Canada and also in Chicago and the American Middle West. The opening of these new markets has partly balanced the loss of foreign markets and saved many fishing communities from complete ruin. This change, however, has not met the need of an expanding market, and there are now more fishermen than are needed to supply the effective demand. Since the crisis of 1929 the exodus to the States and the West has eased, and for nine years, the fishing population has been increasing, though in the previous forty years it had been declining.

Some of the difficulties of the Maritime fishermen arise from technical, economic and social changes. Once good catches could be made near the shore and a sail boat sufficed; an instrument of production the fishermen often made themselves. The fishermen and their families cured the catches near their homes. Merchants in the harbour towns who were also builders and operators of fishing and trading vessels sent around little coasting craft to buy the cured fish and shipped the collections in their own seagoing vessels to foreign markets. Many fishermen found winter employment on these trading vessels.

Now large companies with cold storage plants have taken over the business of marketing and processing fish. Most of the fishermen have become dependent on the single operation of catching fish; usually they do not even clean the fish. Now also the fishermen have to go far offshore to make good catches and make long trips to and from the cold storage plants; so they have to employ motor boats, of which the first cost is considerable and the operation involves a constant cash outlay, unlike the sailboat.

Once the average fisherman was a small farmer, hunter and trapper -- or a sailor in winter. But with the destruction of the forests the game [have] largely vanished. Once the fishermen's equipment included a fowling boat. But on few parts of the coast now are the flocks of wild ducks and geese like vast dense clouds darkening the day, as they were less than thirty years ago.

Most of the varied forms of production for family use, which formerly contributed to a comfortable standard of living have been abandoned -- in some cases because the pioneer conditions which made them possible have vanished. The fisherman has also become a specialist, dependent on the cash sale of his catches; and a dollar is now the equivalent of 33 cents forty years ago.

Proposals for the solution of the fishermen's difficulties include complete prohibition of the use of steam trawlers. That would be to abandon any hope of recovering the foreign markets which have been lost to the otter trawler competition of other countries. And it would be followed by additions to the fleet of motor schooners using dories and long lines and a new return to the over-production which weighs down prices. Another proposal is a government subsidy to carrier boats to collect catches of the sub-marginal products in now isolated outports and transport them to the cold storage plants. The effect would be to pull down the fishing communities still enjoying some degree of prosperity to a common level of poverty.

Another proposal is that the government should guarantee a fixed price on the more common varieties of fish. This may become a political issue. It is not on all fours with a guaranteed price for wheat because the fishermen can increase their crop overnight. A limit would have to be set to the production entitled to the fixed price, as some European governments set a limit to production of farm crops on which they guarantee a price. The proposal at least has the merit of focusing attention upon the fact that unless some means of checking the constant tendency to overproduction is developed, the fishermen generally will be doomed to a further degradation of their living standards.

In some districts the fishing alone will not suffice for the decent maintenance of their present population. Sooner or later, the treatment being applied to the depressed areas in Britain will have to be tried, and the people moved out or industries brought in. Some communities could save themselves by developing summer resort attractions, as many communities in Britain did when their shore fisheries decayed before the competitions of superior technique.

The Educational Extension Work of St. Francis Xavier University, in encouraging co-operative enterprise and the revival of the handicrafts and cottage industry is having good results. But co-operative enterprise can do little to expand the fish markets, and the products of the handicrafts can only have a limited market, in competition with the products of machine industry.

If the Maritimes can rearrange their economy so as to provide new occupations for the surplus fishermen who are now wasting part of their labour on the production of unsalable fish, they will perhaps indicate the solution of the problem of assimilating immigration from the Mother Country.

66. The New Brunswick Farmer: How the Capitalist System levies tribute upon the product of his Labour[59]

"Grow, grow, grow, Saint John" is the frantic wail of a Kings County farmer writing to the Saint John Globe.

That farmer is dissatisfied with his condition, and he gives cogent reasons for his discontent. He declares that the farmers of his district are receiving less for their milk than they were thirty years ago, though the cost of production has greatly increased. He says he started in the spring of 1911 to raise hogs in the hope of getting 11 cents a pound -- a price which would only have given him a moderate profit -- and that in the fall he was only able to get 6 1/2 cents.

The farmers are beginning to realize that something is wrong. They find themselves unable to effect any considerable or permanent improvement in their position in the social scale, and they wonder why? They have never studied the nature of the economic forces which rule their working lives; they do not know that they are as hopelessly in the grip of the iron laws of capitalism as the city wage-earners. They only know that the march of progress brings them little or no benefits, and they eagerly grasp at the nostrums of political quacks in the [elusive] hope of [bettering] their condition. Our Kings County farmer's particular fetish is a larger market, and he calls upon Saint John to grow, grow, grow!

No doubt the farmers of the province would be able to sell more of their products if the population of Saint John and other cities increased rapidly. Probably too they would be able to get better prices for some of their products. But would they obtain any large or permanent benefits?

A little consideration enforces the conclusion that under capitalism the farmers as a class cannot hope for much more than a mere livelihood. The farmers of New England have access to markets of large cities; but are they better off than the farmers of New Brunswick? Tory politicians assured us last fall that the farmers of the United States were not as well off as our own farmers, and, as I shall show later on, they had some reasons for saying so, though probably none of the understood what the reason

---

[59]Colin McKay, *The New Brunswick Farmer: How the Capitalist System levies tribute upon the product of his Labor* (n.p. [Moncton?], n.d. [c.1913]. The SPC in general was interested in the plight of the farmers, and it is possible that McKay was influenced by Alf Budden's pamphlet, *The Slave of the Farm*, one of its most widely-read pamphlets. I thank Peter Campbell for this insight.

was. At present it is sufficient to point out that the lot of the New England farmer is far from enviable, for vacant farms even in fertile valleys are common enough there, and people do not leave the farm for factory towns unless their condition is rather undesirable.

Canada east and west has, it is said, enjoyed a prolonged period of progress and prosperity. But can it be said that the farmers as a class have obtained any adequate share of this prosperity? Certainly the New Brunswick farmers have not done so, and even the grain-growers of the West are anything but prosperous -- if we may judge from their clamorous complaints.

What is the reason the farmers as a class have not obtained anything like a fair share of the advantages accruing from the progress of science and invention? What is the reason the average farmer has not obtained more benefits from his increased powers of production made possible by the improvement of agricultural machinery, the growth of scientific knowledge of soil culture, the construction of railways, and the development of cold storage facilities and better commercial organization[?] Certain it is that the farmer's productive powers have been greatly increased. Mulhall,[60] the world-famous statistician, writing in the *North American Review* for February 1896 said: "When Malthus[61] wrote the labour of a peasant was sufficient to raise the food for ten persons; at present in the United States a male adult can raise food for one hundred and twenty persons." A.M. Simons[62] in the *American Farmer* declares: "It is safe to say that the productive power of the modern farmer, even if we do not include those who use the almost phenomenal machinery of some Western wheat farms, is at least ten times as great as that of the farmer of a few generations ago."

---

[60]McKay is referring to Michael George Mulhall (1836-1900), who in 1861 founded the English-language *Buenos Aires Standard* and published several books on Latin America. He also collected statistics and subsequently published three editions of them which went through several editions and enjoyed high status as reference works (although some data are not now considered as accurate as might be desired). See *The Progress of the World* (1880); *The History of Prices Since the Year 1850* (1885); *The Dictionary of Statistics*, 4th ed. ([1883] 1899).

[61]Thomas Malthus (1766-1834), the English academic, political economist, and clergyman, famous for his concept that population growth would outstrip the world's food supply, expounded in *An Essay on the Principle of Population* (1798).

[62]McKay is referring to Algie Martin Simons (1870-1950), the American journalist and socialist. He was editor of the *International Socialist Review*, 1900-1906; the *Chicago Daily Socialist*, 1906-1910; the *Coming Nation* (1910-1913); and member of the national executive of the Socialist Party of America (1905-1910). He became quite conservative in his political opinions. See his *Class Struggles in America* (1906), and *Social Forces in American History* (1911).

But how many farmers today are ten times better off than their forefathers of the first part of the last century? No doubt they have more luxuries, and their wives and daughters wear grander hats and dresses. Their labour is not so arduous because they have better implements. But relative to the improvements effected in the condition of other social groups they are probably in no better position than their forefathers were. Generations ago the farmers married when very young, raised large families, and were seldom worried by the cost of living. The average farmer today has not the same comforting sense of security of livelihood that his forefathers had. He handles more money, but it is doubtful if he sets a better table. His garments may be cut a little more [fashionably], but he has exchanged wool and homespun for cotton and shoddy.

One set of politicians declare that the farmers would be all right if they had reciprocity; another set affirms that they would be happy if they applied more intelligence and energy to the problem of production; and possibly both believe what they say, though if they do their beliefs are not very creditable to their intelligences. Anyone who understands the operation of the capitalistic system will not be inclined to believe that access to the American market is all that is needed to enable our farmers to attain to prosperity and happiness. The American farmers who have access to the American market are neither happy nor prosperous. In fact the average American farmer seems to be worse off than the average New Brunswick farmer. Prof. C.S. Walker[63] in a discussion before the American Economic Association in 1897 said:--

"By using all available statistics it becomes evident again and again that deducting rent and interest the American farmer receives less for his exertions than does the labourer in the factory or the hired man on his farm."...

Now compare the condition of the American farmer with the condition of the New Brunswick farmer. According to the census of 1901 there were 37,583 occupiers of farm lands in this province; the value of their lands, buildings, implements, etc., was $51,338,311; the value of the [product] was $12,894,076. Divide the value of the product by the number of farmers, and it gives you average yearly returns of $343. Like the average American, the New Brunswick farmer, if you allow him the moderate wage of $343, receives nothing for interest, or insurance, or depreciation on his large capital investment. But the New Brunswick farmer appears to be better off in that he receives a higher wage.

---

[63]Charles Swan Walker (1846-1933) was professor of mental and political science at the Massachusetts Agricultural College (now the University of Massachusetts). He was particularly interested in the connection between labour and agricultural issues. Among his works were "Massachusetts Farmers and Taxation," (1898).

Perhaps it may be said that a comparison of conditions in the United States in 1890 with conditions in New Brunswick in 1900 is not quite fair. Very probably the American farmers' earnings in 1900, expressed in money, were larger than ten years previous.... Other authorities say there was no important change in the condition of the farmer, which is not hard to believe as the city workers whose wages have advanced in recent years have not found their positions materially improved. Historically speaking the American farmers' condition in about the year 1880 ought to be compared with the New Brunswick farmers' condition in 1900, because the development of capitalism in the United States about 1880 corresponds with the development of capitalism in New Brunswick in 1900, in so far as the evolution of the exploiting agencies of capitalism are concerned, though perhaps not in respect to the application of the technical processes of capitalism to agriculture.

A consideration that will occur to many as affecting the force of the comparison is that the valuations of farm lands in the United States are higher than in Canada. But that is not hard to explain. The American farmer gets no return on his capital investment, and the only way he can realize on his capital is to hold out for high prices, which the great influx of immigrants sometimes enable him to obtain. Besides American farm lands are cumbered with mortgages amounting as far back as 1890 to over one billion dollars, and mortgages add to the valuation.

But whether the comparison we have made is strictly apt is of little importance. It has been made merely for the purpose of placing in juxtaposition facts and authorities, showing that in both countries the system of capitalism is able to absorb practically all the benefits of progress, and strip the farmers as a class of nearly all the fruits of their labour except a mere livelihood. One would infer that the farmers of New Brunswick today are somewhat better off than the average farmer in the United States, for the simple reason that capitalism is not so highly developed here, the exploiting agencies are not so well organized, and the process of exploitation is not so intense. But if they allow the system of capitalism to work its sweet will with them, they will doubtless soon enough be reduced to the condition of the American farmers, the great majority of whom do not now own the farms they operate.

A Rural Revolution

Very few people realize how capitalism in its later developments has affected agriculture and revolutionized the conditions of rural life. A few generations ago the farmers of this province lived in fairly self-contained communities, of which a village or small town was the center. Nearly all the essential industries were carried on within the community. The farmer himself was a Jack of All Trades, and his wife the mistress of many arts. The farmer went to the village and sold or exchanged his produce directly. He stood in a personal relation to his market, and received practically speaking, the use-value of the products of his labour. Sometimes he may have exported a few specialities to outside markets, but production for a general market was more or less incidental. His sons when not needed on the farm were able to secure employment in the local flour mills, spinning or carding mills, and the various handicrafts of the community; and when he needed labour he could draw on the supply which the small local industries kept in the community. The newcomer was welcomed to the community, for where products exchanged more or less approximately for their use values, more men meant more production and more production meant better conditions for all. A certain harmony pervaded their economic life, and was reflected in their social life which was marked by interesting manifestations of the spirit of co-operation, such as the harvest bees.

But today the New Brunswick farmer lives for the most part in a new set of conditions. Machine industries, centralized in the larger cities, have crowded out the village handicrafts, grist mills, etc., and the people who were once employed in them have been drawn to the larger cities. Many functions once performed by the farmer or his family on the farm or in the home have been incorporated in the factory system; such functions as butter making, spinning, weaving, sugar making, etc. Technically the farmer has become more or less of a specialist, leaving to others the task of working up some forms of his raw material into finished products, leaving to others all the work of delivering his produces to the consumer. He no longer products [produces] for a communal market. He sells practically all his product in an indefinite, impersonal general market, governed by forces of which he has little knowledge, and over which he has no control. He sells through commission merchants and middle men whom he may never have seen, and whose honesty he very often has good reason to doubt; a method of disposing of his products that few manufacturers would think of adopting.

Generations ago the farmers of this province were not worried by competition. Now, owing to the development of transportation facilities provided to a large extent by taxes, they find themselves in competition with the farmers of the whole of the Dominion: a competition so strong that they cannot profitably raise wheat and some other products.

Capitalism, it must be said, has carried the world forward to undreamed of heights of material achievement. But it has long since fulfilled its historic mission, and has become a vast system of oppression. In subdividing and specializing functions, it has, in agriculture as in other industries, made possible greater efficiency in production; the evil lies in the fact that the agencies it has created for the performance of these specialized functions are owned or controlled by the few. The farmer must utilize these agencies to dispose of his products, but instead of enabling him to improve his condition he finds that they are used to exploit him. The railway companies, which the farmer through taxation has so liberally subsidized, the cold storage companies, the commission merchants, and middlemen of all sorts, levy toll upon the farmers' product as it passes through their hands, taking all the traffic will bear, leaving the producers only enough to subsist, and reproduce more farmers to take their place when they have worked themselves to death. And right here it may be said that if the farmers of New Brunswick are not exploited to the same extent as those in the United States, it is probably because the cold storage system -- a powerful instrument of exploitation -- is not as yet very well developed here, and because too, the agencies of distribution are not, as the Hazen Agricultural Commission reported, as well organized as they might be.

Now there are those who say the farmer should receive the full value of the product of his labour; but that cannot mean the ultimate value -- the price paid by the consumer. The farmer cannot obtain, and is not entitled to, this ultimate value, because the distributive agencies are essential; they add value to the product and necessarily absorb a share of the ultimate value. But it is very evident that the farmer does not get anything like the full value which his labour gives the product; that is the consumer's price less the cost of, or legitimate charge for, distribution.

How can the farmers obtain the full social value of the product of their labour? Co-operation offers a means of escaping some forms of exploitation, but, short of the inauguration of the Co-operative Commonwealth, the farmers cannot escape every form of exploitation. Some years ago the fruit growers in a certain section of California established a co-operative society to market their fruit. In their first year of operation they increased their sales eleven times, but production increased rapidly, prices fell, the railways increased their toll, and in the course of a few years the fruit growers found that while they were doing more work they were little better off than they were before. About the only farmers who are obtaining any great benefits from co-operation are the farmers of Denmark. They are profiting because they have applied co-operation on an extensive scale. In the first place they have co-operated on the political field and have obtained a certain measure of control over the government and through the government of the railways and steamship lines which carry their products. They own cold storage plants, packing establishments, and practically every agency between the producer and consumer. But -- and this is an important point -- though they have eliminated the middlemen and other agencies of direct exploitation, these Danish farmers do not get the full social value of the product of their labour, and for this reason:

These co-operative farmers have to sell their produce to consumers, mostly city workers, who are exploited by capitalism to the top of their bent, and who are therefore unable to pay the social value of the products they consume, or to buy as much of the farmer's produce as they would if they received the full value of the product of their labour.

The Man of Galilee two thousand years ago said, "We are all members of one another", and his words are, if possible, truer today than they were when uttered.[64] As a class the farmers cannot obtain social justice -- the full social value of the product of their labour -- unless the working class in cities at the same time obtain social justice -- the full social value of the product of their labour. The farmer's title deed to his farm does not make him a member of the capitalist class. Some farmers may lift themselves into the capitalist class, just as some city workingmen do, but for the average farmer ownership of his farm is only a certificate to a steady job, a job at which he has to work long hours mainly for the benefit of persons he may have never seen. As a class the farmers receive no interest on their capital, which after all is only embalmed labour; and that being so, the farmers belong to the same economic category as the city workers, and have interests identical with those or other wage earners.

The whole fabric of capitalism, with its vast and complicated system of exploitation, rests upon the backs of the farmers, the city workers, the fishermen and others, who only receive subsistence wages. So comprehensive and co-ordinated are the processes of exploitation, it might be argued that when a society lady in New York buys a diamond collar for her pet monkey, the farmer in New Brunswick has to contribute a share of the cost. If the lady's husband is a banker he may be taking toll of the steel trust; the steel trust in turn takes toll of the automobile manufacturer through high prices of steel; the auto manufacturer takes toll of the Saint John landlord through high prices for his car; the landlord takes toll of the grower through high rents; the grocer, occupying a more or less strategic position in distribution, shifts the burden upon the whole-saler, who shifts it to the commission merchant, who shifts it to the farmer; but the farmer unable to shift the burden, has to grin and bear it -- with some help from his hired man, if he is better off than the average farmer. As every link in the chain which extends from the lady's pet monkey becomes heavier, owing to the fact that the owners of each link do a little exploiting on their own account, it is small wonder that the farmer complains of the weight of his shackles.

What are the farmers going to do about it? There is one thing they must do if they want to achieve social justice for themselves and their sons and daughters who rush into the cities. They must co-operate with their brethren in affliction -- the exploited city workers, to form a political party, capture the control of government from the exploiting class, and through the government to take the control of the instruments of

---

[64]McKay would have been on more solid ground had he attributed this insight to Paul rather than to Jesus; see *Romans* 12:5 and *Ephesians* 4:25.

capitalism out of the hands of the few and convert them into agencies of service, instead of agencies of exploitation. Co-operation for economic purposes will be valuable for the farmer, just as trade unions are for the city workers. But the only way for either class to achieve social salvation is for both to unite on the political field, conquer the political power, and use it to establish a Co-operative Commonwealth, in which production will be carried on, not for profits, but for use.

67. The Maritimes: Playground of a Happier Canada[65]

"A new economic order is necessary to bring real and lasting prosperity to the Maritimes or any other part of the world," said the editor of a leading Maritime daily paper. The personal views the editor expressed to me were very emphatic -- much more so than the views that find expression in the paper he edits. He recognizes the need of greatly increased wages, and a much larger amount of leisure -- of periods when workers may be free to plan the disposal of their time and free of worry for the future -- not the sorry leisure of the present when the worker wastes his time looking for the odd job and hope deferred makes his heart sick. But he does not see how high wages or proper leisure can be realized under competitive capitalism. Nor can anybody else of average intelligence. Even under the Roosevelt plan of industrial reconstruction great capitalists plan to protect the over-capitalization of great industries by asking that the government sanction wages as low as $10 and $11 per week.

A typical Maritime merchant said: "The established order is at the end of its tether; it has become a mere disorder. A very drastic change must come soon, or there will be a general collapse. Under the present system few investments are safe. Even investments in government bonds will lose their value if governments inflate money, as they may be forced to do. Thus we have come to a pass where we are obliged to face the need of establishing a system in which our children will at least have the security of assured employment at good salaries."

Take the case of Maritime communities mainly dependent on the building of vessels, yachts, boats, small-scale lumber operations, and the prosecution of the fisheries. Competitive capitalism offers them little or no hope of prosperity in the future. The present attempt to pump new life into the profit system by inflation can only benefit the strategically-placed profit-takers; small business will gain little or nothing; the middle classes generally will find the value of their remaining savings reduced; the wage and salaried workers, who have already borne the main burden of the depression, will be ground between rapidly mounting prices and slow and inadequate increases in pay. A few profiteers may be able to buy big

---

[65] *Canadian Unionist*, July 1933, 27-29.

steam yachts, but there will be diminished demand for the small yachts and boats for pleasure purposes, such as Maritime communities have specialized in. And further degradation of the standard of living of the wage and salaried workers generally can only have an adverse effect upon the fisheries, many branches of which are in a vassal position to great industry, in that they supply cheap food for the labour power of great industry.

But with the institution of the co-operative commonwealth, a planned economy, an equitable distribution of the products of industry, and planned leisure, these Maritime communities, which cannot look forward to any real prosperity under the profit system, could reasonably expect to enter a new era of progress, and share in the general prosperity.

Consider the effect of planned leisure. Backward Russia gives many of its workers a month's holiday at full pay; and all two weeks at full pay. Canada, with its much greater application of machinery, its highly skilled labour, and abundant natural resources, could give its workers much longer holidays. In boom years the average worker in manufacturing has rarely exceeded more than nine months' employment; over the period of the business cycle the average period of employment has been much less than that. Substituting planned production for the present anarchy of production, with its reckless waste of both labour and capital, would vastly increase the production of wealth, and permit all Canadian workers to have at least three months' recognized leisure, continuous leisure.

Than the Maritimes there is no better place for a summer vacation on the whole continent. They have all the requirements of pleasurable days; and the sea breezes assure cool and restful nights. In a co-operative Canadian economy the Maritimes would figure prominently in the planning of leisure. Now it is only the wealthy or the middle class that spend summer vacations in the Maritimes. But under a planned economy, with high production and equitable distribution, great numbers of workers and their families would be able to escape from the summer heat of the interior cities and enjoy the ozone of the Maritimes, to the great advantage of their health. There would be a big new demand for small yachts, co-operatively owned by several people, and for small boats for sport, pleasure, and amateur fishing. To meet this demand the Maritimes have a surplus of skilled workers trained in wooden-shipbuilding yards, whose occupation has practically vanished during the present depression. The construction of large wooden vessels, either for trading or fishing, is now largely out of the question; but an important revival of yacht and boat building would bring real prosperity to many Maritime communities -- and to a great variety of workers, from motor engine makers to the woodsmen for whom the supplying of vessel and boat timber has been more profitable than supplying lumber for export. Moreover, an extensive influx of summer visitors for a prolonged holiday would bring new

markets to the doors of the Maritime farmers, fishermen, fruit growers --
and of the handicraftsmen who still turn out products which ordinarily
cannot be marketed at a distance in competition with the products of
machine industry.

With an economic "system" which has no social purpose -- which has the
melancholy mission of perpetuating poverty and misery in the hope of
protecting privilege -- the Maritimes can never realize their possibilities as
a summer playground.

What will enable them to do so? Nothing less than a Canadian economy
organized on the principles of the All-Canadian Congress of Labour and
the National Labour Party -- planned production and equitable
distribution with provision for a long holiday for the masses of the
workers. Then Confederation, often denounced by the political spokesmen
of the Maritime bourgeoisie as a bad bargain, would appear in a new light.
If one wanted a special reason for bespeaking the support of Maritime
Labour for the Co-operative Commonwealth Federation, where it keeps to
the line of national Labour policy, it would be to point out that if the
Maritimes failed to realize the progress and prosperity promised by the
Fathers of Confederation, it was not because of the fact of Confederation
but because of the special development of capitalism that began at that
time; and that now capitalism, having entered another distinctly new stage,
in which devolution rather than evolution is found to be the order of the
day, the Maritimes have still less to hope from the continuance of the
established disorder of things.

About two years before Confederation was consumated, the capitalist
world gave birth to a prodigy -- the limited liability company. Adam
Smith had warned that the joint stock company, a new invention in his
day, would beget dangerous economic and social inequalities.[66] But the
joint stock company imposed on all stock holders the necessity of close
supervision of management, for failure meant that the stock holders had
to make good liabilities out of private resources or lose their standing as
business men. It did not admit of stock-jobbing.

With the legal authorization of the limited liability company, a sort of
Frankenstein monster was created -- the corporation without a soul, yet

---

[66]An interpretation of passages in Adam Smith, *An Inquiry into the Nature and Causes of
the Wealth of Nations*, Book V, Ch.1, Part III, Art.1, "Institutions for Particular Branches
of Commerce." Smith's critique of the joint-stock company was that it would tend to
break "that natural proportion which would otherwise establish itself between judicious
industry and profit." McKay was perhaps somewhat incautious in arguing that the joint-
stock company *as a form* was a novelty in Smith's time, for Smith's discussion itself
focuses especially on *seventeenth-century* companies. Adam Smith, *An Inquiry Into the
Nature and Causes of The Wealth of Nations*, ed. Edwin Cannon (London: Methuen and
Company, fourth edition, 1925): 232-248, quotation at 248.

endowed with legal immortality. It created in industry a new kind of ownership -- absentee proprietorship -- the thing that, as applied to land, the provinces of Quebec and Prince Edward Island had successfully rebelled against years before. With the limited liability company capitalism entered the era of stock-jobbing; of exploiting the savings of the middle class; of developing big business at the expense of little business, the family firm, and the truly individual enterprise; of the crudest chicanery.

This new instrument of capitalism played an important rôle in the decline of Maritime shipping and the disappearance of small Maritime industries. Britain, long the great generator of capital, was bent on developing her own shipping -- not investing in shipping enterprises in the Maritimes which competed for the ocean-carrying trade. In the transition from sail to steam, the Maritimes had neither the surplus capital nor the skilled workers to keep up their relative position in shipbuilding or ocean carrying; though the remarkable voyages of the Saint John built ship, *Marco Polo*, had been a great factor in stirring Britain to the effort that overcame the once formidable challenge of American shipping.

The limited liability company favoured the expansion of big industry; encouraged invention and increasing use of machinery. The bigger central provinces were in a better position to develop big industry than the Maritimes; and from the time Confederation abolished the customs tariff between the provinces any British capital available for industrial investment in Canada naturally preferred opportunities in the central, rather than the Maritime, provinces. The superiority of the industrial position of the central provinces, of course, increased with the development of the west. But that circumstance, due to geography, is not an adequate warrant for the pretension of those who still hold that Confederation was a bad bargain for the Maritimes.

There may be good reason for the oft-repeated claim of the proponents of Maritime Rights that the political policies have favoured the development of the central and western provinces, to the neglect of the Maritimes. But what are political policies? They represent the interests of the capitalist class in general. They change their aspects somewhat as this or that particular capitalist group acquires a special ascendancy as a result of log-rolling in Parliament and the changing fortunes of political parties. But political policies always reflect capitalist interests -- Liberal governments, elected on a free trade platform, have continued to protect the manufacturers. East and west, the capitalists shouted for land grants and subventions to railways until the other day; and now all they think of is making the workers pay for unwise railway building, the result of capitalist passion for bigness, or enlarged areas of exploitation.

The Maritimes can hold capitalism, not Confederation, responsible for the failure to realize their expectations of progress and prosperity -- as do, quite properly, the farmers and workers in all the provinces, who are rallying to the movement for a co-operative commonwealth....

The American plutocracy will be peculiar if, finding its privileges menaced by the demands of the workers and farmers, it does not seek a foreign diversion. True, a foreign war might give a president like Roosevelt the power he needs to put over his industrial program; but the lesser risk for the plutocracy would be to gamble on the chances of bending the administration to its will. It is easier to control governments than angry and disillusioned peoples.

Capitalism everywhere is a wild system -- not subject to intelligent control....The only sure salvation for Canada is that it speedily organize its economic life on the co-operative plan, and so present itself as an example to be emulated by the American workers and farmers, rather than a domain to be annexed in the interests of a new experiment in American economic organization "on a continental order of magnitude."

ii. The Workers of the Maritimes

68. The Awakening of Labour in Eastern Canada[67]

Something is evidently stirring in the Maritime Provinces. Every visitor says the East is waking up. Mostly the meaning of that expression is that the grafters are taking a new grip. But it is not only the exploiters of real estate values and business enterprises who are waking up. The workers are beginning to wake up. This at any rate is the case in Saint John.

There is something more than mere labour organization in the winter port. There is a real live labour movement. The workers are shaking off their lethargy. They are casting off the integument of an antiquated individualism that bound their minds in a narrow circle of thought, that made mental growth almost impossible, that hampered the progress of organized labour. One might I suppose draw with a certain amount of reason some analogies between the east of Canada and the east of Asia. A few years ago the Chinese were much attached to their queues; it is said that there was an old superstition that they would be drawn up to heaven by means of their hairy appendages. Workmen of eastern Canada have been much attached to the woolen appendages which the henchmen of capitalism pulled over their eyes; they have been expecting Providence or the government or another exalted agency to perform a miracle on their behalf, and shower the blessings of progress and prosperity upon them.

---

[67]*Eastern Labor News*, 12 October 1912.

But like the Chinese they are awakening to the needs of the time; they are beginning to realize the nature of the world in which they live. They are beginning to realize that God helps those who help themselves....

Probably one of the chief reasons why the workers of Eastern Canada have so little knowledge of the modern labour or socialist movements is the long work day. Physical exhaustion usually means mental inertia and that means apathy and hopelessness. A worker who has not studied history from the view point of the working class is bound to be a pessimist. He does not realize that capitalism like feudalism, like chattel slavery, like primitive communism, is a passing phase, a stage in the march of humanity. His mental operations are determined by his capitalistic environment. Like every other form of society, capitalism has created modes of thought which encourage loyalty to capitalistic institutions. The schools, the pulpits, the press, every agency of public education, and public opinion, inculcate ideas favorable to the maintenance of the capitalist system, and the workers unconsciously absorb capitalistic ideas. Thus he thinks that whatever helps the capitalist helps him, and votes for the political candidates put up by this or that group of his masters.

The worker must think for himself. He must realize his position in capitalist society; he must learn that while capitalism may at one time have represented a forward movement it has become a vast system of exploitation and now stands in the way of progress. When he thinks he will find out that he will have to put behind him most of his cherished beliefs and opinions ground into him by his capitalistic environment, and he will find the process of mental emancipation a rather painful one. For thought is always revolutionary and disturbing.

69. The Fear of Progress[68]

The other day a chap said to me: "Ugh. There's another labour agitator. He shouldn't be allowed to come here stirring up trouble."

"That man did not come here till he was sent for, as it happens," I said. "Some time ago the men of his trade here decided to move for more wages, and they sent for an International organizer to get leave to strike. The organizer is trying to get the men more wages and he is also trying hard to avoid trouble."

"But if it wasn't for those agitators there would never be any trouble. They stir up the men, and put big notions in their heads, so they begin to want more pay. The working class is getting too well paid, that's what's the matter with them. When they were getting a dollar a day and had to work 12 hours, they knew their place."

---

[68]*Eastern Labor News*, 2 November 1912.

The chap who uttered these original views was not a fossilized old money grabber; he was a young man -- a clerk working for a clerk's exalted wages. His remarks illustrate the peculiar twist in the minds of many people. We might say the clerk was jealous because most labourers get more pay than the clerk but that is not altogether the explanation. There are many others who have no reason to be jealous who are troubled with the same views. The matter with this class of persons is that they are slaves to custom, that they have never thought about the world in which they live. Some persons even take an austere pride in their ability to exist on low wages. Some persons are content with low wages for about the same reasons they are content to vote for the Liberal or Conservative party; they hold that what was good enough for their fathers or grandfathers ought to be good enough for them. Even workers sometimes say a day labourer isn't worth more than $2 a day, or whatever the wage of the locality may be.

As a matter of fact under present conditions many employers could not afford to pay their workers much higher wages. The larger capitalism, the greater corporations, absorb most of the advantages of the increased productivity of labour. Many small employers do not make as much in a year as their employees do. They are merely vassals of the larger capitalism.

I was talking to a master painter in Saint John a while ago. "There are some years," said he, "when my men make more than I do. That fact has given me cause to think [why] I don't call myself a Socialist. I can't say that I have studied Socialism. But I must say that what the Socialists say about the present system is right, and the only real salvation for the small employer and small business man as well as the wage earner lies in the direction of Socialism. My trade has not been much affected by machinery -- a painter today can do little more work than he could a generation ago, at least on the ordinary class of work. But most other industries have been revolutionized by machinery; it requires much less labour to produce a barrel of flour, a suit of clothes, and many other commodities today than it did a generation or so ago. But we haven't benefitted to any noticeable extent from the increase in the efficiency of labour generally. And why? As a master painter I compete with other master painters and have to figure on a job as close as I possibly can for fear I won't get the job. And because of this competition we cannot procure for ourselves or our employees a fair share of the fruits of progress in other industries. True, ever since I have been in business we have been increasing the cost of painting a house, but we have got little benefit, because the increase in charges has been absorbed by paint brush manufacturers and others."

Probably one of the reasons why the trade union movement is backward in the Maritime provinces is the persistence of the small employer.

Generally this class of employers has the most intimate personal relations with his workers, and he tries to give them steady employment. He is not making money. His workers know it and look askance upon the labour agitator who urges them to get together and demand more wages.

The organizer points out that the employers can ask more money on contracts and that it is up to men to unionize the whole trade and put the employers on an equal footing. But this view does not always appeal to the men who work for small employers. They figure out that if their boss does not have to pay the union scale, he can get more contracts than his rivals and gives them more steady employment, making it possible for them to earn more in the year than if they were getting the union scale.

Of course this view is shortsighted, not only from the standpoint of the trade, but from the standpoint of the individual. The workers who take this view are the greatest obstacle to the progress of the labour movement. They are the veriest creatures of circumstance. They live in a little rut, and are afraid to join a union, or assist in the emancipation of their class....

It seems to me that something more than the ordinary trade union propaganda is needed to arouse this class of workers. They should be shown how it is that neither their employers nor themselves are getting anything like a fair share of the benefits arising from the progress of industry generally. They should be shown that the small employer is nearly as much a victim of the larger capitalism as they are. If they considered the vast accumulation of wealth in a few hands through the robbery of the productive workers, they would not like the clerk to consider that they were getting all that they were worth. They would want to know why the workers as a class are not getting more out of life. And when they began to think about the matter they would soon see the iniquity of the capitalist system and instead of fearing the results of any change they would realize the virtue of Karl Marx's slogan addressed recently to the Trades Congress by Keir Hardie: Workers unite. You have nothing to loose [lose] but your chains and a world to gain.[69]

70. The Aristocracy of Labour and the Short-Sighted Workers[70]

"It's hard work getting the workers of this part of the world to realize their position," said a well known trade union official who was in Saint John a while ago. "So far from being class-conscious, many workers down East

---

[69]A reference to the closing words of the *Manifesto of the Communist Party* : "The proletarians have nothing to lose but their chains. They have a world to win. Working men of all countries, unite!" Karl Marx and Friedrich Engels, *Communist Manifesto*, trans. Samuel Moore (Chicago: Gateway, 1954), 82.

[70]Originally published as "Short-Sighted Workers," *Eastern Labor News*, 29 March 1913.

seem to be lacking in self-consciousness. If you propose a reduction of the hours of labour, they consider the question almost wholly from the viewpoint of the boss. They don't waste much time considering their own interests."

This self-effacing disposition of the workers is not the worst of it. In some cases their docility is accompanied by a shortsightedness, little short of foolish. Last year a union of certain skilled workers was organized in Saint John. Largely on a bluff the union officials, with the assistance of their International, secured an increase of wages for the members, and incidentally for many not in the union. The increases were not large but they represented dividends of several thousand per cent on the investment in union dues. The trade was and still is poorly paid; a similar increase every year for some time to come would not over-load the workers with wealth. The active spirits in the union made plans to strengthen its position by enlarging the membership and organizing allied trades. The programme was to go after another increase as soon as conditions were ripe.

A manager of a plant employing quite a number of men of this trade saw what was coming and understood a shrewd move. Voluntarily he gave the men a slight increase in pay. He understood the character of his men. Practically all of them dropped out of the union. Apparently they concluded that as their boss gave them a raise they had no further use for a union. Also they forgot that if it had not been for the activity of the union they would not have received either the first or the second raise. Many people cannot see the connection between cause and effect, even when it is glaringly obvious.

In the trade referred to one employer refused to have anything to do with the union; he "did not want any western ideas introduced here." A strike was declared against him. His shop is still on the unfair list, but he is paying much better wages than before the strike. The union benefitted even the strike breakers.

But the men who benefitted most think they have no further use for the union. Skilled workers are usually supposed to possess considerable intelligence. They must have brains, but intellectual power and intelligence are different things. It takes brains to put together or operate a complicated machine, but the men who can build an intricate machine may be without much intelligence -- that is, in the connection I am now using the word, a knowledge of the world he lives in and the forces which rule it. In this respect the longshoremen of Saint John have more intelligence than many other workers who consider themselves members of the aristocracy of labour. The longshoremen and coal handlers prove their possession of intelligence by getting more money than the members of many trades in which one must serve a long apprenticeship; also by their determination to use their union to secure further improvements in conditions. If the steamship companies were to voluntarily grant the longshoremen a raise would they conclude that their employers could be trusted to look out for their interests in future, and disband their union? They have sense enough to know that employers don't voluntarily raise wages except in the hope of checkmating a move on the part of the men for a bigger increase.

71. The Difficulties Faced by Socialists in the Maritimes[71]

In reply to your request for a letter on conditions in the Maritime Provinces from the Socialist point of view, I don't know what I can say that would be of any particular interest. The Socialist point of view has not yet gained much ground. These provinces occupy a peculiar position; the main streams of modern thought seem to have passed them by or at any rate have not disturbed to any extent the placid somnolence of their intellectual life. Outside of one or two cities, the small industry is the rule, and in a region of small industry, where the employer is obviously not getting rich, the ideas of Socialism do not meet with a ready reception. It is not easy to grasp the fact that the small employer is a mere vassal in many cases of the larger capitalism. And outside of the larger cities class lines are hardly apparent. The small town communities are often very democratic, employer and employee mingling freely in fraternal societies and social organizations of various kinds. Again there is a good deal of religious feeling and race -- or rather sectional -- prejudice.

Outside of the Saint John local, I believe the only Socialist organizations are in Cape Breton, the home of big industry. In Moncton, the railway town, there have been study clubs, taking up Socialism among other things, and a while ago Rev. Mr. Lawson of that place delivered a series of lectures, explaining the principles of Socialism in a very fair-minded manner. The *Eastern Labor News*, published at Moncton, opens its columns to articles of a socialistic character, though some years ago there were complaints because it did so. This paper has done and is doing good work for the working class, but it is not appreciated as it ought to be. Two of the daily papers in Saint John have frequently published reports of lectures by Socialists, and not long ago published a series of very good articles on Socialism.

The Socialist local in Saint John has been in existence over three years, and has held meetings weekly. Practically all the speaking has been done by F. Hyatt, A. Taylor and J.W.Eastwood, old countrymen. C.M.O'Brien addressed one meeting here, and Moses Baritz several.

---

[71]Originally published as "The Maritime," *Western Clarion*, 2 August 1913.

When the local was first formed here some of the comrades made the mistake of sneering at the trade unions in speeches and in letters to the *Labor News*, and this blunder has not been wholly forgotten yet. At any rate the trade unionists have held aloof. Often I have heard a trade unionist here remark, "The arguments of the Socialists are all right, but we don't want to have a bunch of foreigners coming over here telling us how to run things."

In the face of such conditions and such sentiments it is not an easy matter for organized Socialism to make progress in Saint John or any other part of the Maritime [Provinces], but I think there is a steady growing interest in Socialism, a lessening of the disposition to look upon it as a sort of foreign body. When I came here a little over three years ago I took steps, at the insistence of P.M. Draper, to revive the Trades and Labor Council, and at the first meeting Com. Eastwood aroused the ire of the delegates and had a narrow escape from physical violence. Com. Hyatt, who later became a delegate to the Trades Council, figured in some stormy sessions. But he has been doing good work for the trade union movement, and has evidently earned the confidence of the labour men, for recently they elected him Secretary of the Trades Council. My own impression is that he has done more to make converts to Socialism by his connection with the trade union movement than by any of his speeches in the Socialist Hall.

However, it is not so much the Socialist agitators as changing conditions that are responsible for the awakening of interest in Socialism. Saint John has been enjoying the long promised boom, and the workers have good cause to be dissatisfied with the results of the boom. Instead of bringing the anticipated blessings, the boom has brought high rents and high profits. A number of important construction jobs are in progress, and big construction companies have come in, introducing new methods, and a small army of labourers from other parts of the world. There never was so much discontent among the workers of Saint John. The changing conditions have aroused the workers. A large number of new organizations have been formed and the building trades secured the eight hour day this spring. Also the workers are showing signs of class consciousness, and talking of forming a political party. In the smaller towns throughout the Maritime Provinces there are also signs of an awakening. Mushroom organizations have sprung up at quite a number of points and forced advances in wages.

But in general the habits of thinking and feeling of the Maritime workers are those peculiar to small-scale industry, and it is not an easy matter to inoculate them with scientific Socialism. Still there is no doubt that Socialist ideas are germinating. The provinces are growing more and more industrial, and the new conditions produce new modes of thought. However, it is not always the fact of increasing exploitation that germinates Socialist ideas. Among the fishermen of Nova Scotia I have been surprised at the tendency to Socialist modes of thought and that in the districts where they are today more independent and prosperous than they have ever been. Probably the fact that the fishermen have long worked under a form of co-operation enables them to more readily grasp the possibilities of co-operation generally.

72. The Awakening of Labour in the Maritime Provinces[72]

Organized Labour in the Maritime Provinces has made considerable headway in the last few years. Also rents and the cost of necessities have made a substantial advance. Even unorganized agricultural labourers have secured increases of 50 per cent. or more in wages, but their remuneration is still very small.

Generally speaking, the workers are sunk in intellectual apathy. The main strain of intellectual progress has passed by; geographically and to a certain extent economically our position is in the nature of a back-eddy. Even in the few places where great modern industries have grown up there has been no general intellectual advance, partly because the native population finds it hard to abandon old methods of thinking, largely because of the influx of a class of labour ... not easily assimilated. Imagine, for instance, the proud highlander of Cape Breton, who traces his ancestry back for many generations, thrown into the industrial hopper with Polak and Slav! It is difficult to weld such discordant elements into a class conscious organization, united by common thoughts, and common purposes and needs. Taking the Maritime Provinces as a whole, a very large percentage of the workers still own their homes or other forms of property, and their ways of thinking and feeling are such as go with the possession of small properties. A labour movement seldom attains the dignity of a conscious struggle for the emancipation of the working class, until the great bulk of workers have been reduced to the ranks of the proletariat -- propertyless workers.

Even in a city like Saint John, alleged to be progressive, the ideas of the bourgeoisie still obsess the minds of the workers generally. For years the businessmen have been looking to the government, or Providence, or big capitalists to come along, and start Saint John upon the highway of progress and prosperity; while waiting for their Moses they sometimes make a half-hearted attempt to lift themselves by their boot straps. This peculiar mental attitude is reflected in the working class. They are generally looking for some outside power to come along and usher them into the house of prosperity. When the "boom" started Saint John working men were jubilant. What they expected to get out of it they didn't know themselves; but they expected some kind of a miracle. Saint John has

---

[72]*Industrial Banner*, 8 May 1914.

enjoyed a "boom," and about all the workers and small business men got out of it was increased rents and higher prices.

However, they are beginning to learn that God helps those who help themselves. They are beginning to realize that it is folly to put their trust in princes whether of church or state. If the working class wants anything of importance done, it has got to do it itself. Anything that capitalists or any of their henchmen do for the workers is generally in the nature of a boomerang, for the business of the capitalist class is to do the working class.

At the recent civic elections in Saint John the trade unionists ran "Jimmie" Sugrue as a candidate for the commission. He polled approximately 1,200 votes, about 60 per cent. more than the Labour candidate did two years before. This spells advance. If the workers organize on class lines only to play marbles, it is a good thing. Labour politics is experimental. One community profits very little by the experience of others. Hence it was perhaps natural that the campaign of the Labour Party did not exhibit any very clear appreciation of the purposes of a Labour Party. True, the Labour Party had a platform, but it was a mere reform platform. There was no frank acceptance of the fact that a real Labour candidate stands for a principle essentially revolutionary.

Against the Labour candidate the [principal] canvass was that business men were needed at City Hall.

The word business covers a multitude of sins, even from the eyes of the workingmen. Businessmen have no cause to boast; they have ruled us for a long time. And they have made a mess of it. They have had at their service all the wonderful powers of modern science, and could have made this world a paradise for all. But they have merely used the powers of science to exploit the masses. Although the productive powers of labour have been increased many times, what has it profited the labourer? The businessmen have controlled the wonderful forms and forces of modern industries, and failed to manage them intelligently. They have enslaved themselves as well as the workers. Yet they have the audacity to tell us we need business men in places of political power, and we haven't the sense or the courage to laugh at them.

In criticizing the conduct of the campaign of the Labour Party here, I am not condemning anybody; I merely wish to illustrate the stage of development which the Labour movement has attained. Toronto passed through the same stage some years ago. Two years hence I believe the Saint John Labour Party will be as class conscious as the Labour Party in Toronto is to-day. That is, the active spirits in the party will be more class conscious than they are to-day; it would be too much to hope that all those who will vote for a Labour candidate two years hence realized their position in society and understood the historic mission of the working class. As I said at the outset, we are still sunk in intellectual apathy; we are still shut out from the world of modern thought, and are expected for intellectual recreation to attend revivals or interest ourselves in the subtleties of medieval theology.

An apostle of Pastor Russell spoke in Saint John some time ago on the question, "Where are the dead?" A very large number of Saint John people evidently wanted to know where they were. President Watters of the Trades Congress discussed the question, "Do the workers know they are alive?" About twenty persons went to hear him....

PART IV

"The Mad Master of the Modern World"

Capitalism in Crisis
1919-1939

In this section are grouped together 37 of McKay's more interesting analyses of the interwar "Crisis of Capitalism." Although McKay had long been fascinated by the writings of political economists -- he had cited the writings of J.A. Hobson as early as 1899 -- it was in these years of crisis that he focussed generally on the structural dynamics of capitalism and on its endemic problems of underconsumption and disproportionate investment.

McKay was hardly unique in recognizing that the crisis of capitalism posed a fatal problem for conventional models of political economy that understood capitalism to be a system in which demand and production were in balance. According to mid-nineteenth century interpretations of Say's Law[1] against which McKay polemicized, no person produced "but with a view to consume, or sell, and ... never sells, but with an intention to purchase some other commodity, which may be immediately useful to him, or which may contribute to future production. By producing, then, he necessarily becomes either the consumer of his own goods, or the purchaser and consumer of the goods of some other person....Too much of a particular commodity may be produced, of which there may be such a glut in the market, as not to repay the capital expended on it; but this cannot be the case with respect to all commodities."[2]

This view had not always prevailed in political economy. Before Adam Smith, indeed as early as the 17th century, as T.W. Hutchison remarks, many writers had defended the idea that "economic activity in an exchange economy is in response to an effective or 'effectual' demand." Enlightened common sense took this as much for granted as it did the

---

[1]See W.J.Baumol, "Say's (at Least) Eight Laws, or What Say and James Mill May Really Have Meant," *Economica*, 44, 174 (May 1977): 145-61.

[2]Ricardo's paraphrase of Say, as cited in Vincent Bladen, *From Adam Smith to Maynard Keynes: the heritage of political economy* (Toronto: University of Toronto Press, 1974): 199-200.

productive benefits of the division of labour.[3] Writings of Quesnay and Mandeville espoused what could be broadly termed an underconsumptionist position, at least in the weak sense "of regarding a general deficiency of demand, or 'general over-production' (or under-consumption) as being at least a distinct possibility worthy of examination." Indeed, many of these political economists were also "'under-consumptionists' in the stronger sense of regarding deficiencies of effective demand as a regular and serious menace."[4] But the impossibility of general over-production had become an orthodoxy by the late nineteenth century. Little in the rise of marginalism from the 1870s on disrupted the liberal political economists' happy image of a capitalist economy which, disregarding minor local "gluts," could be relied upon to be self-balancing.

Some decisive challenges to this comfortable view came at the turn of the century. In the United States, Thorstein Veblen (*Theory of Business Enterprise*, 1904) presented a portrait of chronic capitalist crisis and stagnation; in Britain, J.A.Hobson (*The Problem of the Unemployed*, 1896) connected the problem of surplus production with the unequal distribution of income. It is suggestive of McKay's tilt toward British writers that it was Hobson, not Veblen, who provided the crucial theoretical guidelines for his writings on the interwar economy. Of course, Marxists could also cite the "tendency of the rate of profit to fall" in their work, although this element of Marx's theory was more often the distant starting-point of analyses not directly derived from it. M. Tugan-Baranovsky, for example, emphasized that the chaotic and unorganized nature of capitalist production, coupled with the drive to accumulate capital, and the resulting unequal distribution of income, led to the over-production of capital goods. This tendency was in turn aggravated by monetary factors: "In a monetary economy 'partial over-production' can, and does, develop into 'general over-production'. Economic fluctuations consist primarily in fluctuations in the production of capital goods."[5] Although there is no evidence that McKay ever read him, he nonetheless came close to adopting Tugan-Baranovsky's approach, by weaving together the quite distinct theoretical strands of (1)under-consumption and effective demand, (2)disproportionality and over-investment, and (3)politico-ethical uncertainty, all as integral aspects of the interwar crisis.

A hostile critic might charge McKay, not altogether unfairly, with unscrupulously combining explanations that contradicted each other; a more sympathetic view would discern a subtle and engaged intelligence concerned to give both economic and political elements their due. Thus,

---

[3]T.W.Hutchison, *A Review of Economic Doctrines 1870-1929* (Oxford: Oxford University Press, 1953): 346
[4]*Ibid.*, 346-7.
[5]*Ibid.*, 378.

following Hobson in emphasizing underconsumption as a kind of master-key to the crisis, McKay does not slight the importance of other elements: the postwar international monetary crisis; the impact of dramatically new patterns of demand and investment opportunities, as evidenced especially by the mass production of automobiles; a hypertrophic and speculative financial sector with an insatiable appetite for acquiring existing industries but unwilling to confront the risks of founding new ones; the related separation of ownership and control within industries; and, most interestingly perhaps, the cultural nihilism, confusion, aimlessness and obsolescence of a bourgeoisie which governed (but did not rule) through a disorganized and contradiction-ridden liberal state.

McKay never outlined the case for underconsumptionism in detail, but it was clearly an integral part of his interpretation of the crisis of capitalism from at least 1924 [§.75, "Over-Capitalization and Over-Production"]. He agreed with (and may very well have influenced) the economic argument outlined by A.R.Mosher in his influential pamphlet *The Way out of the Ditch*. Mosher had emphasized that "during the boom there had been a great over-production of capital goods -- newsprint mills, for example -- with a consequent diversion of purchasing power from where it was most needed, the market for consumptive goods. The inevitable result was that when it was belatedly realized that capital equipment had been created greatly in excess of requirements, the capital goods industries closed down, throwing many men out of employment and setting in motion the depressive forces which quickly ditched general business. Therefore, a fundamental requirement of orderly progress was the setting up by the state of a commission with authority to ration investment, to determine the proportion of the national income to be allotted to investment and the types and quantities of capital equipment needed for replacement and improvement and for the establishment of a balanced relationship between the various means of production needed to supply all the consumptive needs of the people" [§.106, "The Keynesian Prescription," originally published as "The Conversion of an Economist"]. Similar arguments were to surface in the political thought of J.S.Woodsworth, who announced his debt to J.A.Hobson in the budget debate of 1924.[6]

Why had capital gone on strike? McKay asked in 1935, and answered, in Hobsonian terms: "The real reason why capital is on strike is the failure of consuming ability to keep pace with productive capacity. There is everywhere a surplus of means of production and distribution -- surplus factories, ships, railway equipment."[7] McKay insisted that the vital nucleus of any explanation of the Depression was the labour theory of value. As he explained in 1933 to the readers of the *Canadian Unionist* in "The

---

[6]See Allen Mills, *Fool for Christ: The Political Thought of J.S. Woodsworth* (Toronto, Buffalo and London: University of Toronto Press, 1991): 174.

[7]C.M., untitled letter, *Labor World/Le Monde Ouvrier*, 25 May 1935.

Working of the Profit System." "To understand the capitalist economy," McKay explained, "we must have some knowledge of value, exchange value, and surplus value." An article produced for one's own use was not a commodity but simply a product. A commodity was produced as something which might satisfy a social need: it was a thing produced for sale, and as part of a social process. (It was a "crystallization of social labour.") The relative values of commodities was determined by the amount of average socially necessary labour embodied in them. As for socially necessary labour, its value was determined by the cost of the necessaries required to produce, develop, maintain and perpetuate labour power. Supply and demand exercise their influence only in the sphere of commodities: the labour power which determines value is applied in the sphere of production. Supply and demand only modify value, they do not determine it. As for surplus value, it was unpaid labour: labour power can in a few hours create the equivalent values of its own maintenance and reproduction, and then go on for more hours producing additional values, which are expropriated by the capitalist class.[8] There was nothing analytically startling in this straightforward exposition of Marx's theory, but the skill with which it was done suggested McKay had deeply internalized the Marxian value paradigm and knew it very well. He would put it more succinctly for the readers of the O.B.U. *Bulletin* in 1933: "Surplus values, the profits of capitalists, result from the circumstance that the system enables the capitalist to compel the worker to go on producing for several hours a day after he has worked long enough to produce the value equivalent to the wage he receives. Unpaid labour power is the source of surplus values."[9] He also drew the inference, which he saw confirmed in numerous statistical data, that while it was undoubtedly true workers generally received higher wages than they had a generation before, "relatively the position of labour has not improved as much as that of capital." An analysis of industrial development since Confederation showed, according to McKay, that capital had taken the lion's share of our "progress and prosperity." (In Ontario, while capital's share of the product of the manufacturing industries in 1871 was 24.3 per cent, in 1917 it was 28.1 per cent; labour's share of the product in 1871 was 18.7 per cent and in 1917 it was 18.0 per cent.)[10] It was obvious to McKay that the "crazy crises" that afflicted the world economy had been unknown before the development of the capitalist system based on machine production: "Hence, it requires no great leap of thought to arrive at the conclusion that the causes of the crises lie in the mechanism of the system itself. And then the question arises, why should the workers submit to the scourge of periodic crises if a better economic system can

---

[8]Colin McKay, "The Working of the Profit System," *Canadian Unionist*, May 1933, 201.

[9]Colin McKay, "Shibboleth of Individualism," *O.B.U. Bulletin*, 22 June 1933.

[10]Colin McKay, "The Workers Share Decreasing," *Canadian Railroad Employees Monthly*, June 1922

be established, in which such economic convulsions will be unknown?" [§.121, "A Philosophy for Labour Organization"].

McKay never fundamentally altered his position on the labour theory of value.[11] So far as he was concerned, the globalization of capital -- capitalist expansion on a world scale -- did not call for the revision of basic Marxist categories. In one remarkable piece, McKay anticipated with uncanny accuracy the extent to which capitalism's march to globalism would entail rising political nationalism, a debt bomb, experiments in state capitalism, and the crisis of the world monetary system: all features of our modern "globalized world" -- and none of which prompted him to think that the laws of capitalism had changed [§.84, "Capitalism's Fatal Defect"]. In important respects, McKay remained an SPCer to the end. He would not have accepted the tenets of dependency theory, nor any other formulation that distracted from the primacy of class struggle and relations of production.

Nonetheless, as a practical labour economist, and as a man who had read Vol.3 as well as Vol.1 of *Capital*, McKay was virtually driven to concede that the phenomenon of underconsumption in the Depression must have a variety of origins. In McKay's analysis of food production, for example, the "glutted markets, unprofitable prices, mortgages, and fear of foreclosure" were all vital reasons why agricultural production might not find a market. Behind such reasons was the ideal of personal liberty, which food producers had ardently pursued, which had been transformed into a "vampire of wretched servitude," dumping producers into socially unnecessary labour for which society would not reimburse them. "Thus notice is served upon the producers that a part of their labour was socially unnecessary. But the consequences do not end there. These producers who have wasted a part of their labour have less money to expend upon the goods of other producers, who in turn have less to spend on the goods of other producers, and so on" [§.85, "Under-consumption, A World Problem"]. Far, then, from being a simple "economic" phenomenon, underconsumption in this case turned out to be the complex result of an intricate matrix of economic and non-economic forces.

---

[11]And in this, as Peter Campbell suggests, McKay was unusual in the context of the socialist tradition as a whole, both major wings (the social democrats and the communists) having abandoned the use of the theory by the 1920s. "Right from the earliest days of the Communist Party of Canada," Campbell notes, "...discussion of the labour theory of value virtually disappeared from the party press. Discussing the labour theory of value became, for some Communists, one of those silly, sterile, educational debates engaged in by reformist Second International Marxists" (75). As a result, Communists came close to arguing from underconsumptionist positions, not inherently all that far removed from either Fabianism or Social Credit. Peter Campbell, "In Defence of the Labour Theory of Value: The Socialist Party of Canada and the Evolution of Marxist Thought," *Journal of History and Politics*, 10 (1992): 61-86.

This neo-Marxian reasoning led McKay to question the entire framework of economic analysis that had guided Canadian politicians and political economists for decades. The equilibrium belonged to the era of small individual enterprise producing for the parochial market. But the adjust of supply to demand ("the Manchester millennium of the economic harmonies") no longer worked. Since 1820, British workers had had but three years of prosperity in every ten; and elsewhere the "equilibrium" seem to ensure not balance but perpetual crisis.[12] Again there was little that was unusual theoretically about this position -- it could have been written by J.A.Hobson himself -- but in a Canadian context, it was an unusually clear-headed and frank analysis of the problem.[13]

As the night editor of a newspaper in Paris, as a staff correspondent on the International Labor News Service, and (after May 1930) an Ottawa-based journalist, McKay brought a wide-ranging outlook to his writings on the crisis. It is important to note that, for McKay, the crisis was merely sharpened -- and not initiated -- by the stock market collapse of 1929: he did not subscribe to the mythology of the "dirty thirties" succeeding the "roaring twenties". As Maritimers knew, the economic crisis began shortly after the Great War. An observer who had lived in Europe in the 1920s and attended to the British debates over rising unemployment was not likely to rhapsodize over the prosperity of the Twenties. McKay was deeply impressed by the severity of the 1920s slump in England, which he saw as a harbinger of drastic modifications in the capitalist system. With a million people out of work in Britain in 1923, even captains of industry realized that drastic modifications "must be made in the capitalistic system if grave disorders are to be avoided." Yet individually they could do nothing; and collectively they had no vision, however keen their appreciation of their immediate interests might be.[14] As for the "actually existing" alternatives to capitalist chaos, as an independent Marxist, McKay was neither dazzled by, nor dismissive of, the Soviet experiment, which he placed in the framework of a new economic form -- "state capitalism" -- whose nascent outlines could also be discerned in Europe and North America. He brought to his task of understanding the Depression a maturity, independence and internationalism that he did not check at the door of "working-class solidarity": the coal mines of the Gulag are not presented in glowing colours, as they were by the Webbs and, closer to home, by some Maritime Marxists.

---

[12]Colin McKay, "Blasting the Old Order, " *Canadian Unionist*, May 1935: 311-313.

[13]Note the very different analysis of Depression economics that emerged from the *autodidact* sociological tradition in French Canada: Jean-Claude Dupuis, "Reformisme et Catholicisme: La Pensée Sociale d'Arthur Saint-Pierre," *Bulletin*, Regroupement des chercheurs-chercheures en histoire des travailleurs et travailleuses du Québec, 49 (Hiver 1991): 25-61.

[14]Colin McKay, "England -- the Eternal Puzzle," *Canadian Railroad Employees Monthly* (January 1923): 185; 190.

He also brought to these writings an unusual theoretical depth. There are 204 specific references to authorities and publications in the located McKay articles of 1919-1939. Although some are to minor bureaucrats and functionaries, or to such mouthpieces as *Business Week*, many were to political economists and social theorists. At ten citations, Marx predictably was still the pivotal authority. Spencer was mentioned on five occasions, although in an increasingly critical vein. But J.M.Keynes (9 citations), Adam Smith (6), Proudhon (5), Kant (4), Ricardo (4), John Strachey (4), the Webbs (3), Stuart Chase (3), Kautsky (2), G.D.H.Cole (2), Rodbertus (2), John Gray (2), Andrew Ure (2), and Robert Owen (2) were also all in evidence. Among his contemporaries, McKay's reading extended to Hobson, R.H.Tawney, H.G.Wells, and Major Douglas. An attentive reader of McKay would have met through his writings many of the major intellectual figures of the interwar world. Although he did tend to argue from authority to a certain extent, McKay was (with a few exceptions) able to consider the merits of non-Marxist writers without automatically rejecting them as valueless because they were not part of the approved canon.

1. The General Sense of the Crisis: Economic Chaos and Cultural Bankruptcy

Much of McKay's work of the 1920s and 1930s was focussed on documenting the extent of economic disorder. He was especially impressed by the cultural limitations of a business class incapable of shaping any coherent response to its predicament.

Even before the crisis hit, the scope and seriousness of their system's economic problems were beyond the understanding of the bourgeoisie. "If the bourgeoisie were able to control the forces of production," McKay wrote in 1923, "there would be no depressions, for these phenomena strike terror to the heart of businessmen as well as workers. They ruin capitalists by the thousands. That is the proof that while the capitalists direct the productive processes they do not control them. They do not even understand why they cannot control them. They cannot admit that their system is at fault, or that they are incompetent." They were not far-sighted people guided by science, but pathetic wretches cowering in fear before mysterious agencies distributing rewards and punishments "like heathen deities." The typical bourgeois mind was fatalistic, prone to superstition and a mystical belief in chance.[§.52, "The Worker Must Learn to Think"]. Naturally, confronted with a world crisis like the Depression, the bourgeois mind had recourse to economic talismans and magic formulas. When they failed, it simply retreated into the memory of better days. McKay skewered the nostalgic reveries of Sir Arthur Salter,[15] a

---

[15]For J.S.Woodsworth's rather different views of Salter's economic analysis, see Allen Mills, *Fool For Christ*, 170.

former official of the League of Nations, who attempted to understand the newly disordered world in terms of an idealized portrait of the market as it had existed sometime before the Great War: Salter had praised the magnificence of the old balance of supply and demand; "the economic and financial structure" under which his generation had grown up was indeed, "at the moment of its greatest perfection, more like one of the marvelously intricate structures built by the instincts of beavers or ants than the deliberately designed and rational works of man." One can almost hear McKay snort with contempt when he reads this mellow evocation of capitalism's good old days (which reminds us of the market-worship of F.A.Hayek and his followers). All that was missing from Salter's idealization of the market, McKay argued, was any sense that this "moment of greatest perfection" had probably been "never more than an instant of time during the handicraft era, before the rise of machine industry." Salter did not understand that it had required "a cataclysm of the market about every ten years to enable supply and demand to find their adjustments" [§.98, "Blasting the Old Order."] Because neither the state nor the business class knew anything about the real science of capitalism, irrationality and anarchy prevailed. Those who profited from the workings of the capitalist order were too greedy and too short-sighted to devise a logical plan for the economy. For McKay, the railway system was a prime example of the profligacy and waste of the capitalist system, and public ownership of the C.N.R. was an example not of the pitfalls of state involvement in the economy, but of the ability of railway promoters to drive the state into a destructive over-expansion of the Canadian railway system.[16]

After 1929, even those McKay called the "jazz economists" -- those trendy modernists whose analytical abilities were often placed in the service of the capitalist order -- could no longer deny that the anarchy of capitalism had condemned millions to misery. This was not like any other business recession, McKay argued. It was significantly different from the major depressions of 1873 and 1893, as well as the minor recessions of 1885 and 1906. Recovery on these earlier occasions had been marked by heavy liquidation of the capital and credit positions built up during the preceding booms. In such "standard" crises, the individual and family firms went to the wall, and joint stock companies took their place; sometimes the little investors in the joint stock companies were obliterated to make room for the large corporations. All in all, capitalism was, in such "normal" crises, merely reviving itself through creative destruction. But in this Depression big business already reigned in virtually all important spheres: and now, instead of further squeezing small capital, big business was forced to turn to the state to protect itself

---

[16]C. McK., "Some Railway Comparisons," *Labor World/Le Monde Ouvrier*, 7 November 1925.

against workers and farmers.[17] Thus the state had become "the active partner of certain categories of capitalists, protecting them from risks, only by creating a Frankenstein monster to menace other capitalists." A specially protected form of property known as public debt was, throughout the western world, devouring other forms of capitalist property. Under both Hoover and Roosevelt, the American government had assumed direct and contingent liabilities on behalf of banks, railways, mortgage and insurance companies, and a great many other businesses, estimated at around twenty billion dollars. "In England, France, Germany, Italy," -- and in Canada -- "the chief business of governments during the depression has been to buttress industry by loans, subventions, subsidies; to put the power of public credit behind private enterprise."[18]

McKay noted other features that set this Depression apart. The previous two decades had witnessed an amazing development of automatic machinery, and this had displaced labour on a wholesale scale. The Depression also coincided with a drastic change in the possibilities open to workers: the end of mass migration from old to new countries had coincided with the end of the homesteaders' dream of independence on the land. Wage earning was no longer a "probationary state for great numbers of workers on their way to free homesteads." Technological unemployment and the decline of mass immigration were harbingers of the end of an epoch in Canada. To a significant degree, the Depression was the consequence of a structural imbalance within the system, triggered by drastic changes in productive capacity: "With the rapid advance of technology, productive capacity has developed so much faster than consumptive capacity that the necessity of establishing a balance between them has presented itself to the general consciousness as a problem of first importance demanding urgent attention."[18] Yet despite the intensity of the crisis and the combined social power of business and the state, no plausible solutions to the crisis had emerged. Most of the solutions proposed by business and the "jazz economists" who theorized its outlook -- such as centralized control under capitalist auspices -- evaded the system's need for a reserve army of the unemployed; none closed the gap between the productive and consuming roles of the worker. Invoking the aid of the state to protect the capital and credit structures built up during the previous boom could only mean devising policies "at the expense of the farmers and workers." Plans to buttress business by giving it huge

---

[17]C. McK., "Torch of Progress Must be Carried by Worker," *O.B.U. Bulletin*, 18 May 1933.

[18]Colin McKay, "The Disorderly Economic System,"*Coast Guard* 8 November 1934. It is interesting that this image of the "Frankenstein monster" is the very one which opens W.L.Mackenzie King's *Industry and Humanity,* although tellingly King's use of the metaphor is focused as much on the Great War as on the industrial system. See W.L.M.King, *Industry and Humanity: A Study in the Principles Underlying Industrial Reconstruction* (Toronto, 1973 [1918]), 14.

loans could only mean damaging tax increases for farmers and workers. Plans for currency inflation could be effected only by governments starting public works or wars, and would reduce the workers' purchasing power.[19] Piecemeal solutions thus only threatened to aggravate the more fundamental problems.

This was the overarching theme of McKay's first major analytical statement on the Depression, published in July, 1930, "The World's Dilemma" [§.79]. In it he suggested both the futility of Fordist prescriptions and the usefulness of theories of underconsumption. In "This Talk of Stabilizing" [§.80, "Can the Capitalist System Be Stabilized?"], McKay underlined the point that the Depression was not just a "passing circumstance in history," but a "crucial turning point in industrial civilization," which was forcing business to confront the fact that, despite the reams of statistics pumped out by "experts," they had been unable to predict at what point production had begun to exceed effective consuming power. Their "solutions" to the crisis were graphic illustrations of their intellectual bankruptcy. For if the maintenance of prosperity could have been guaranteed by the modest reforms they suggested, how could one explain their inability to prevent so massive a Depression, with all its human misery? Again and again, in these early assessments of the Depression, we hear echoes of McKay's earlier emphasis on cultural power, and on the need for the working class to develop both its own body of expert knowledge and a sense of confidence in its own prescriptions. Business could no longer present itself to the world as somehow more intellectually capable than the working class. The bourgeoisie had had the opportunity to build a "noble and stately civilization," but it had instead proved to be the most "aimless and incapable class that ever held the helm of society," spiritually exhausted, shorn of ideals, obsessed with sordid struggles for power, property and profits [§.81, "The Failure of Competition."] McKay here was integrating the cultural critique of his 1910-1913 writings with his largely post-war sophistication in economic theory.

He pursued his exploration of the cultural aspects of the business collapse in his brilliant article "A Problem for Canadians" [§.82, "The 'Ruling Class' Does Not Rule"]. He powerfully developed the image of capitalism as a Frankenstein: the creature had become the master of its creators, the capitalists who, however much they owned, could no longer claim in any meaningful sense to rule. The capitalist system could be seen as a Juggernaut, running out of control of the capitalists who owned but could not control it. The capitalists pretended they were the authors of progress and prosperity; in truth, they understood the economic machine very poorly. They merely had created a chaos of conflicting interests; and their "failure to use the materials and knowledge science has placed at

---

[19]"Alberta Sets the Pace," *Canadian Unionist* (June 1933): 7-9.

their disposal to create an economic organization and social order amenable to intelligent control" was "their great shame."[20] McKay drew a parallel between Canadian "captains of industry" and the sea-captains he had known, and sternly reminded his readers that a sea-captain who ran his ship on to the rocks would be speedily removed from command.[21] In sharp contrast to some academic interpreters of the Great Depression, who have tended to write as though Keynesian prescriptions presented themselves as rather obvious remedies, McKay viewed the crisis of the 1930s as something which placed the *entire* capitalist order (the politico-ethical hegemony of liberalism, liberal political economy *and* the respect due to captains of industry) in question. Possessive individualism -- what McKay called the "taboo of property rights" [§.83] -- was, for the first time since the mid-nineteenth century, fragmenting as a coherent framework of belief and of life.[21]

Because of this fundamental shift, McKay saw the early 1930s as a time of immense opportunity, a time when socialists could realistically commandeer the language of "commonsense" and articulate it to their collectivist project. Unlike businessmen and bourgeois politicians, socialists understood that the "crux of the problem of economic planning lies in the distribution of national income so as to permit consumption to balance production." The solution of this problem would require "limitation of private accumulation of wealth by wiser methods than those capitalistic governments are driven to adopt to keep capitalism functioning even badly -- high taxes and succession duties." In this special time, workers in general might begin to see through the vicious class prejudice which the capitalist press brought to bear upon individual working-class intellectuals.[22] Once they had awakened to the extent of bourgeois failure and the pathetic helplessness of those who owned (but did not truly rule) the capitalist machine, they would shake off "their

---

[20]Colin McKay, untitled letter, *Labor World/Le Monde Ouvrier,* 14 May 1932. Images of "Frankenstein" and "monsters" are common in left discourse of the 1930s, and close attention to them by historians would qualify the common assessment of a simplistic Marxian scientism wholly dominating the socialism of the day. For another example, and an analysis close to that of McKay, see G.D.H.Cole, *Economic Planning* [1935] (reprinted Port Washington and London: Kennikat Press, 1971): 8. Note, too, the parallels between his analysis and the work of William E. Stoneman, *A History of the Economic Analysis of the Great Depression in America* (New York and London: Garland Publishing, 1979).

[21]Colin McKay, "State Interference," *Canadian Unionist,* August 1936, 70-74.

[22]"Labour and the Technocrats," *Canadian Unionist,* Vol.6, No.9 (February 1933), 149; 156-157. "If a worker rises into the capitalist class, then that is proof that the capitalist system offers opportunities to all enterprising and industrious youths," McKay remarked of the way the newspapers treated labour critics. "If anybody criticizes the pretensions of capitalism, then he must be a low-brow or a member of the working class, in which there is not even potential intelligence." Perhaps McKay was speaking from personal experience.

present inferiority complexes" and take charge themselves.[23] As had been the case in 1913, in 1935 creating this effective alternative would require a new working-class culture.

Because this was a time when workers had an historic opportunity to remake society, McKay unremittingly critiqued the "false prophets" who threatened to drive these exciting possibilities into the blind alleys of Fordism, social credit, or a revived liberalism. Such palliatives fell drastically short. "Unless the system is drastically changed, unless the forces of production are brought under conscious control, and regulated in accordance with a predetermined plan, we cannot hope to get rid of the grim problem of technological unemployment," he argued in 1934. "The legal and property relations of the present social order have become fetters upon the forces of production..." While 25,000,000 workers in the western world stood idle, hundreds of millions lacked the ordinary means of decent living. Capitalism as a whole seemed insane.[24]

The forms and forces of production had outgrown the social, political and juridical relations -- or what was the same thing, the *property* relations -- in which they had hitherto functioned. These relations had turned into fetters, and further progress demanded their removal, whether by peaceful or violent revolution depending upon the attitude of the owning, but non-ruling, class. Closely following Marx's Preface to *A Contribution to the Critique of Political Economy*, McKay suggested that the very fact that the problem could be posed at all suggested that it might also be solved: "Man only takes up such problems as he can solve for the reason that he only becomes conscious of the existence of a problem when the material conditions for its solution have developed or are in progress of development." The problem of the 1930s, according to McKay, was to effect changes in the relations of production to prevent society, "already suffering from serious disorders, being carried deeper and deeper into chaos."[25]

2. McKay's Critique of Non-Socialist "False Prophets"

To an extent which may seem surprising to modern readers, McKay -- and much left-wing writing in Canada in the 1930s -- was preoccupied with turning back a powerful challenge from a host of non-socialist radicals, whose prescriptions for reform often superficially resembled those of the left. Although often remembered as a time when the Communist Party and the CCF built significant bases in the Canadian working class, the 1930s were also years in which a wide variety of left-liberal, populist, and

---

[23]Colin McKay, "Essentials of Economic Planning: A Critical Examination of the Swope Plan,"*Canadian Railway Employees' Monthly*, October 1931: 221-222.

[24]Colin McKay, "The Disorderly Economic System,"*Coast Guard* 8 November 1934.

[25]*Labor World/Le Monde Ouvrier*, 24 September 1932.

more specialized zealots won a greater percentage of the population (including many workers and farmers) to their non-socialist but seemingly redistributive programs. In the first half of the decade, before the On-to-Ottawa Trek and the rise of the Congress of Industrial Organizations, such bourgeois alternatives tended to crowd out those offered by socialists.

That McKay should pay such close attention to Social Credit may nonetheless seem surprising, given that Canadian scholars have described that movement largely as one of *petit-bourgeois* farmers. But the Social Credit movement did not in fact appeal only to farmers; it appealed to many workers, and was thereby able to disorganize and disarticulate a previous farmer-labour base, whose major intellectual figure had been William Irvine.[26] Canada thus won a place on the front pages of the world in this period not for electing any socialist government, but for providing the first laboratory in the world for the experiments of Social Credit -- and Social Credit, which effectively demolished a once-vibrant left movement in Alberta, was feared by socialists like McKay precisely because it managed to channel widespread discontent with the Depression into a very specific cross-class project, underpinned by a theory ultimately rooted in a curious attempt to revisit utopian socalism.

The diversity and appeal of false and superficial "solutions" to the crisis of capitalism drove McKay to write one critique after another. (In general, these were even-tempered and attempted to see the merit in the opponents' arguments, although under Depression conditions a heightened bitterness and urgency can also be noted). Three different and by no means narrowly exclusive sets of "false prophets" can be discerned in his writings, who can be roughly categorized as follows:

> *(a)Those offering solutions that preserved the fundamentals of liberal political economy, among them:*
> (1) a lowering of wages or a reduction of hours to restore the balance of capitalism;
> (2)a return to some form of *laissez-faire* or minimal state involvement in the economy;
> (3)a general currency inflation;
> (4)tinkering with the tariff.
>
> *(b)Those putting forward schemes of Social Credit and Monetary Reform, which were "liberal" insofar as they aimed at the preservation of individualism and private property, but somewhat*

---

[26]For cogent analyses of this phenomenon, see Larry Hannant, "The Calgary Working Class and the Social Credit Movement in Alberta, 1932-35," *Labour/Le Travail*, 16 (Fall 1985): 97-116, and Alvin Finkel, "The Rise and Fall of the Labour Party in Alberta, 1917-42," *Labour/Le Travail*, 16 (Fall 1985): 61-96.

"post-liberal" in their rhetoric of fairness and their ambiguous schemes of state-administered redistribution and planning;

(c)Post-liberal Comprehensive Schemes of State Capitalism, among them:
(1)Technocrats, New Dealers, and advocates of centralized state planning within a capitalist order;
(2)Fascists or proto-Fascists who linked corporatist economic planning with the suspension of the normal workings of parliamentary democracy.

McKay's rhetorical strategies varied according to the sorts of false prophets he was concerned to address. He reserved his most withering contempt for those liberals whose world-views had simply not taken into account the extent and seriousness of the Depression. To believe (as many political leaders in Ottawa seemed to still believe) that mild liberal palliatives such as tariff reform could accomplish very much in this situation was simply stupid. He took a much more careful, even gentle, approach to the "monetary utopians," whose many and various schemes he dissected with care. A typical McKay attack on "monetary utopianism" consisted of a claim that the scheme in question was doing nothing more than reviving a long-discredited nineteenth-century scheme of Proudhon, Owen or John Gray: clearly the dreamer in question had not realized that capitalism had changed since the days of handicrafts and competition. The CCFers and Progressives who dabbled in such matters were simply naïve souls, who had not read enough economic theory. He was willing to concede the merits of schemes for the corporatist reorganization of the state, but only on the Bellamyite grounds that such movements toward "state capitalism" might complete the process of consolidation and centralization, and thereby ease the pain and confusion of a transition to real socialism.

(a)Liberal Solutions which preserved the fundamentals of liberal political economy

Economic liberals who obstinately refused to acknowledge that the metaphor of equilibrium no longer captured (if indeed it ever had captured) the realities of the capitalist system were still thick on the ground both in the 1920s and in the 1930s; within their ranks were a number of Progressives, CCFers, and Conservatives as well as members of the Liberal Party. Some argued that by lowering wages, Canadian farmers (or the Canadian economy in general) would become competitive once again on world markets. Through the 1920s, McKay argued that the "cheap labour" panacea was a "mistake" motivated by class interests, and not by a serious attempt to grapple with the underlying causes of the crisis.[27] "Insidious propaganda for low wages" filled the pages of the newspapers, bolstered by selective readings from Canadian trade statistics. Trade unions apparently lacked the expertise or confidence to present their own readings of such statistics before the public.[28]

One of the most popular liberal fallacies was that of restoring economic balance by forcing down Canadian wages to an (ill-defined) world level. (The late-twentieth-century advocates of globalization are obviously not guilty of originality). One answer to Canadian employers and financiers who were advocating wage reductions to meet the challenge of global competition was that "this method of reviving prosperity" had almost everywhere proved a "flat failure" which had "aggravated the difficulties of business as well as of the workers." It had proved unsuccessful (argued McKay in 1931) in both Germany and Austria.[29] McKay suggested that such low-wage arguments might even find more supporters in Canada than in the United States, because of the dependence of Canadian capitalists on exports. Perhaps it was the salience of export trades in Canada that made businessmen here slow to see the case for high wages.[30] Anticipating, to some extent, the arguments of Keynes's *General Theory*, McKay warned business that, by pursuing narrow low-wage objectives, it was running the risk of pulling the house of capitalism down around itself. Those businessmen who demanded "rigorous economies" he likened to Samson: "the strong men with their singular passion for parsimony may pull the temple of finance down upon their heads." No more free high school education; slash provincial budgets; fire civil servants and reduce the pay of those who remain: all these right-wing prescriptions were not only wrong in themselves, but threatened the entire capitalist order with ruin.[31] And by creating a "debt panic" and acute fears about the fiscal strength of the Canadian state, businessmen ran the risk of provoking a run on the banks and an even more destructive economic crisis. Such an intensification of the crisis would hardly be in their interest -- but they were so incapable of thinking logically about capitalism that this simple fact had not occurred to them.

Some businessmen also argued for the general return of the ten-hour day. McKay, drawing on the labour theory of value outlined in the first volume of *Capital*, could see the selfish appeal of such an argument: lengthening

---

[27]See, for instance, Colin McKay, "Cheap Labour a Mistake," *Labor World/Le Monde Ouvrier*, 24 November 1923.

[28]Colin McKay, "The Crime of Low Wages," *Labor World/Le Monde Ouvrier,* 18 April 1925.

[29]"A Living Wage for Capital,"*Canadian Unionist*, May 1931, 287-288.

[30]Colin McKay, "Canadian Business Messiah Yet to be Found," *O.B.U. Bulletin*, 5 December 1929.

[31]Colin McKay, "Go Easy With the Axe! "*Canadian Unionist*, September 1932, 69.

the working day would give capitalists the ability to squeeze more surplus value out of their workers. However, "If the capitalists were well advised they would, in their own interests, move speedily to secure the adoption of the thirty-hour work-week by force of law. That would give society a chance to catch its breath, an opportunity to look around and note the forces that are hurrying capitalism towards anarchy." Those capitalists who prayed to discover ways of increasing profits seemed to be under the delusion that "the disease brought about by surplus profits could be cured by more profits." He estimated in 1929 that surplus values amounting to 78 per cent of the net value of the product remained in the control of industrial and merchant capital and of the landlords [§92, "The Labour Theory of Value and A Proposed Shorter Work-Day," originally published as "The Workers' Share"].

Unfortunately nostalgia for low wages and long hours was not confined to business circles. Farmers were in some respects "working people" facing the same enemies as workers, and in other ways "small businesspeople" who might be persuaded to see themselves as sharing a community of interest (and a common language) with the bourgeoisie. McKay paid special attention to dangerous and seductive arguments aimed at the United Farmers designed to persuade them that low wages for urban workers were in their interests. C.W. Peterson, editor of the Calgary *Farm and Ranch Review*, and operator of a large wheat ranch, thought that the farmers' fundamental difficulty was that while the prices for their products were fixed under free competition, the price of what the farmer had to buy was determined by wages paid in its production, wages which were "artificially established" rather than the results of free competition. Thus there was no real community of interest among farmers and workers, because the farmer was "the chief victim of a situation in which one class of labour is subsidized by wages maintained at an artificial level, while another class has its wages determined by free competition." Industrial wages absolutely controlled railway rates and affected "the cost of every commodity shipped from or to the farm." Hence the farmer paid tribute to urban labour on practically every dollar he spent, and thus helped "to maintain a scale of wages fantastically out of line with the earnings of himself and his hard-working family." In Peterson's argument -- and it was by no means an uncommon one -- it was the urban worker, not the businessman, who exploited the farmer.

The farmer/labour fissures Peterson was exploring (and hoping to widen) were by no means illusory. His analyses took dead aim at the farmer-labour alliance that had brought Irvine to the House of Commons and generated so many new ideas in Canadian political economy. He was in effect seeking to replace a "subject position" in which farmers saw themselves as producers and naturally allied with workers, with one in which farmers were "businessmen" in an antagonistic relationship with labour. McKay saw in Peterson's arguments -- "lawyer logic," he called them, using one of his most venomous insults -- a classic strategy of "divide and rule." Peterson's statistics were wrong: wages as a percentage of the net product was much lower than Peterson had argued. McKay also pointed out that the "monopolistic" urban workers had been unable to defend their wage levels.[32] As for the truly business-oriented farmers who were deaf to all such talk of solidarity with the workers, McKay urged them to look to their own economic interests. Curtailing the purchasing power of workers would not restore prosperity, and wheat farmers in particular were deluding themselves if they believed that cuts in the wages of flour mill workers would help them sell their wheat abroad. "Globalizing" arguments for cheapness would lead to poverty all around: farmers would confront a depressed market for their products, and workers would be forced to try to survive on shrinking pay packets. [33] As for the idea that western farmers should routinely destroy part of their crops to keep up prices -- McKay saw such a destructive proposal as conclusive evidence of the insanity of the capitalist world.[34]

McKay understood the hold of liberal ideas. He could even find compassion in his heart for the likes of Conservative Prime Minister R.B.Bennett, who was demonized by most of the left of his day (and by most historians since). Bennett was a victim of liberal ideology, incapable of thinking his way out of its categories. His efforts to do so -- in the 1935 "New Deal" Broadcasts that proclaimed the old order of the "open market place" defunct, "never to return" -- marked an important moment in bourgeois thought in Canada. But Bennett was someone struggling to understand a modern world without having the necessary conceptual tools to do so. Bennett's broadcast had not been particularly original, but it had bravely faced the dilemma. Bennett had admited that for four years his government had tinkered with the mechanism of the market, and achieved little; the automatic regulation of the market could not be relied on. At least Bennett had indicated the task which had to be undertaken by either capital or labour: the regulation of the economy. Whatever the pitfalls and difficulties of such regulation, "no planning authority at all concerned for the welfare of society could conceivably achieve such appalling mismanagement and waste of the nation's productive capacity as has been achieved by the automatic regulation of the mechanism in the market."[35] Although McKay expressed no confidence in the Conservative government's understanding of the challenge of comprehensive economic planning, he was prepared to admire Bennett's candour in breaking so completely with the market in his New Deal broadcasts. Where many historians have seen nothing but opportunism in

---

[32]Colin McKay, "Wheat and the Workers,"*Canadian Unionist*, December 1930, 171-172.

[33]C.M., untitled letter, *Labor World/Le Monde Ouvrier*, 1 August 1931.

[34]C.M., "Medicine Men and Their Nostrums," *O.B.U. Bulletin*, 3 November 1932.

[35]*Canadian Unionist*, May 1935, 311-313.

the Bennett New Deal, McKay more subtly and sympathetically tried to understand the cultural power of the old liberal capitalist order which had held Bennett captive.[36]

Yet understanding the dilemma of the Conservatives was not the same as overlooking the pathetic weakness of their response to the crisis. They had struggled to provide piecemeal relief, but the palliatives they had devised had lacked coherence or unity of purpose; indeed, in not a few instances, they aimed at contradictory purposes. And this was not surprising, either in Canada or elsewhere, McKay argued. The politicians, who were "for the most part believers in an economic theory the justification of which vanished some time ago with the disappearance of the *quasi-laissez-faire* conditions of the past," had thought the Depression was "but a recurrence of a periodic phenomenon which would be overcome in due course by the self-recuperative powers of the system." Now that the crisis was upon them, they understandably had no "understanding of the magnitude and complexity of the task with which the disaster of the depression confronted society." It would not be easy for people to undertake the "mental reorientation" demanded by the situation, and it would take time.[37]

A third species of liberal reformers critiqued by McKay were those who urged inflation as a possible cure for the Depression. Some of the Progressives fell into this category. McKay believed that Alberta had produced the most progressive farmers' movement in Canada, and indeed in North America, and greatly respected many of the Progressives: Robert Gardiner, Henry Spencer, E.J.Garland, and William Irvine in particular.[38] Yet he felt that the farmers in politics were far too apt to become "rainbow-chasers," far too tempted by any magical solution to the Depression, no matter what its provenance or implications. For George Coote, M.P., whom McKay regarded as the party's "chief

---

[36]McKay was equally unusual in declining to anathematize Ramsay MacDonald. "There can be no question of MacDonald's courage -- and little of his sincerity. But he has not been a serious student of capitalist economies or international finance, and has allowed himself to be persuaded that an unbalanced budget is a more serious matter than an unbalanced social system." C. McK., untitled letter, *Labor World/Le Monde Ouvrier,* 17 October 1931.

[37]Colin McKay, "State Interference,"*Canadian Unionist,* August 1936: 70-74.

[38]He explained the province's unusual reputation in terms of a curious reverse version of the frontier thesis: "Alberta set the limit of the last westward march of the farmers, the grain farmers at any rate. So it is not surprising that the Alberta farmers should have realized that they could not flee from the evils of the existing order of society, and there was no hope of continued progress and prosperity for them except by facing the necessity of a drastic reconstruction of society. Hence their progressive radicalism, and their leadership in the economic and political phases of the agrarian movement." "Alberta Sets the Pace," *Canadian Unionist,* Vol.7, No.1 (June 1933), 7-9. And then came Aberhart and Social Credit...

inflationist"[39] the magical solution was inflation. Once again, rather than instantly dismissing Coote, McKay struggled for balance, praising the M.P.'s "iconoclastic attacks" upon financial orthodoxy and the sincerity of his revolt against "the established order, or rather disorder, of things." But in his concrete analysis, Cootes was being both "utopian and reactionary," utopian in hoping that inflation would accomplish great things for the farmers, and reactionary in assuming that inflation would re-establish the conditions of a past age.[40]

McKay argued -- agreeing for once with Stephen Leacock -- that inflation could be regarded as providing only a temporary stimulus, and that "at the expense of the wage and salaried workers holding jobs when the inflation began, and other people having fixed incomes."[41] Although a quarter of a million indebted farmers stood to make some modest gains through a currency inflation, the policy hardly addressed the problems of insufficient demand for labour and for the commodities labour produced.

Other partial solutions were equally vulnerable to McKay's critique. Agnes Macphail was naïvely yielding to the "magic of money" in falling for J.M.Keynes's view that Britain's abandonment of the gold standard "has been charged with beneficent significance over a wide field."[42] William Green of the American Federation of Labor was no less naïve in arguing that a reduction of the working hours to thirty a week, without reduction of pay, would make it possible for 20 per cent more workers to secure jobs, for he reckoned without the inflationary impact of increased labour costs on the costs of commodities, and ignored the bankruptcies in marginal businesses that would almost certainly result from such a "reform."[43]

McKay also attacked tariff-centred reformism. For McKay, the tariff was essentially irrelevant to the crisis of capitalism. Echoing Marx, he wrote that "Our Labour economists tell us that free trade is as much interest to the workers as the manner of the dressing is to a roast goose" [§.82, "The 'Ruling Class' Does Not Rule"]. Tariffs, whether high or low, could not solve the problem of unemployment. The Progressives who thought otherwise, and who (for example) argued that rather than collect tariffs on imported automobiles, the Canadian state could have simply paid citizens the amounts received in such duties, were incorrect. It was reasoning like theirs that had allowed Mark Twain to make the prediction that in six hundred years the Mississippi River would stick out over the Gulf of

[39]C.M., "The Inflationists are Busy," *O.B.U.Bulletin*, 10 November 1932.
[40]Colin McKay, "Alberta Sets the Pace," *Canadian Unionist*, June 1933 : 7-9.
[41]Colin McKay, "Inflation Won't Help the Workers,"*Canadian Unionist*, December 1933: 106-109.
[42]Colin McKay, "The Magic of Money," *O.B.U.Bulletin*, 3 November 1932
[43]Colin McKay, "Shortening the Work-Week," *Canadian Unionist*, February 1937: 219-220.

Mexico like a fishing pole.[44] A society simply could not afford to neglect its productive base. Conversely, and contrary to the fond hopes of R.B. Bennett, Canada could not "blast its way to world markets," through a strategy of building tariff barriers or of somehow reinventing the British Empire. The real problems of the Canadian economy would not be solved by an expansion of the export trade. Real progress in solving such problems -- speaking in the specific case of the Atlantic fishery, but McKay's point applied equally to the entire Canadian economy -- required increasing domestic consumption, a very considerable improvement in the depressed living standards of the masses,[45] and a system of public economic planning to balance consumption and production.

McKay's general verdict on all these liberal responses to the Depression was that they revealed the tight grip ancient economic ideologies had on the bourgeois imagination. It seemed almost impossible for such people to accept that the days of *laissez-faire* liberalism had disappeared for good. Like R.B. Bennett, many were entranced by the notion of the "simple life" of the past. They were advocates of a kind of a Jeffersonian economic anti-modernism, with rugged individualism, agrarianism, and the Protestant Work Ethic combined to powerful ideological effect. But the Simple Life that they reverenced was largely imaginary. "The simple life of the pioneer was,... really a very complex life," McKay wrote discerningly, "it required for its environment forests and plenty of wild game and fish. The men were hunters, fishermen, tanners, trappers, meat and fish curers, mixed farmers, jacks-of-all-trades; the women had a greater knowledge of the manufacturing arts than a score of factory foremen today."[46]

McKay -- typically -- was not content merely to treat the back-to-the-landers with the sovereign contempt of a man in possession of correct theory. He quite freely conceded the attractiveness of their ideal. Drawing on his own childhood experiences, he respected the virtues of a more self-sufficient lifestyle than the one available to most urban workers. No more than fifty years before, he suggested, "a majority of the people were not at the mercy of the market," because almost every family "had a little farm; produced vegetables, grains, milk, eggs, meats; manufactured clothing, soap, candles, so on; could easily capture wild game and fish. The family was largely self-sustaining, self-employing. Its primary activities were regulated by its own requirements. It offered only its surplus products, or surplus labour time, on the market." In these pioneer Canadian communities, "it was usually the merchants who initiated the

[44]Colin McKay, untitled letter, *Labor World/Le Monde Ouvrier*, 16 May 1925.
[45]Colin McKay, "Consumption Fails to Meet Production in Fish," *Canadian Fisherman*, May 1936, 27-28.
[46]C. McK, "Depression -- Uncontrolled Production?" *O.B.U.Bulletin*, 25 January 1934.

modern industries as in medieval England -- but here mostly with borrowed capital." Gradually, with the emergence of a labour market, much of it supplied through immigration, the independent pioneer existence became possible only for "a limited number of people -- of Jacks-of-all-Trades and Jills-of-many-Arts -- in a given territory." Although the artisan, "owning his own tools of production and having easy access to his raw materials, continued to carry on for a while," power-machinery "more or less swiftly -- by underselling him -- 'freed' the artisan from his means of production; turned his ability to labour into a market commodity." Thus the economy of yeomen farmers and small producers within which *laissez-faire* might have seemed plausible had gone forever. Capitalism "established freedom of contract, and the free market," although this "freedom" left the worker free "to accept the terms offered, seek charity, or starve." Yet *laissez faire* somehow lived on as a grand ideal, even into the age of state-subsidized immigration and high tariff protection of the domestic market. Still "the beloved of the bourgeois economists, who say the world's troubles arise from interference with the mechanisms of the free market," the market mechanism was given almost magical powers to regulate production, to communicate the preferences of consumers, to raise and lower the prices of particular good, to regulate the volume of production, and so on.[47]

Adam Smith's vision of a "state of society in which...the producers for the market appeared free and equal; in which the enterprising and thrifty journeyman could easily become a master," had captivated many minds (including, McKay might have added, his own in an earlier day). But those who were able to live in the modern world with a certain degree of freedom -- the middle class -- had only "the illusion of perfect freedom. The owners of the means of production are free in a way the worker dependent on a job is not. But still they are dependent on the market." The quaint liberalism of the businessman stemmed from a systematic (if perhaps functional) misperception of his actual role in the social order: he had to think of himself as a "free and independent individual" and resist any "interference with his freedom to run his business in his own way -- even when demanding the favour of tariffs interfering with consumers." Yet in reality his success depended on the way his business fit into the "general scheme of social co-operation by which the wants of society are supplied." He was at the mercy of the consumer market, and also unwittingly had the power to influence it: "his products may play an important rôle affecting his interests and the interests of all other producers." Thus his freedom consisted of the freedom to get himself and everybody else into difficulties; it was "but the illusion of freedom." Businessmen hugged this illusion, but it had long stopped representing the predominant forms of enterprise, and this "cultural lag" had "a heavy responsibility for the tragic situation in which the world now finds

---

[47]§.98, "Blasting the Old Order"

itself."[48] More to be pitied than blamed, businessmen clung to a liberal individualism whose obituary had long ago been published.

(b)Schemes of Social Credit and Monetary Reform

Judging from the long line of polemical articles and letters he directed against the numerous proponents of schemes of social credit and monetary reform, McKay viewed them as pivotal figures in the ideological struggles of the 1930s. In many respects, he saw those captivated by such schemes as people who were not intrinsically reactionary, but who might be won over to a socialist position. In parts of Canada, Social Credit had swept all before it; it had done so because it had effectively organized and spoken to people -- not all of them *petit bourgeois* -- who had been devastated by the Depression. McKay viewed Social Credit as a formidable enemy and rather admired the fierceness (which he contrasted with the colder, more rationalistic Marxist approach) with which Social Crediters attacked the capitalist system [§.91, "A Critique of Social Credit"]. Just as it was wrong to see the Social Credit supporter as irremediably anti-working class, so too was it a mistake to view Social Credit doctrine as intrinsically right-wing or proto-Fascist.[49]

That said, McKay's purpose in his anti-Social-Credit writing was to undermine the doctrine and win its followers over to -- or back to -- a socialist perspective. Unlike William Irvine and others in the CCF, McKay was never seriously tempted by Social Credit solutions to the problems of the economy, even as stop-gap measures.[50] He viewed Social Creditors and currency reformers as dangerously naïve: they were reinventing the theories of the first utopian socialists, without taking into account the massive changes in the capitalist system over the past 150 years.

One of the principal illusions of Social Crediters was their assumption that bankers arbitrarily determined the volume of credit available at any time, and hence the amount of consumer purchasing power [§.93, "The

---

[48]*Ibid.*

[49]This was also the general line taken by J.A. Hobson, who wrote that he agreed with part of General Douglas's diagnosis of the problem -- that the depression arose from the failure of consumption, or effective demand, to keep pace with potential and actual production -- but noted that Douglas did not draw the conclusion that the disproportion between saving and spending originated in the unequal distribution of income. See Hobson, *The Economics of Unemployment* (London: Allen and Unwin, 1922): 119-124. See also Labour Party, *Socialism and 'Social Credit'* (London: The Labour Party, n.d. [1935]. For an overview of British responses to Social Credit, see H.I. Dutton and J.E. King, "'A private, perhaps, not a major...': the reception of C.E. Douglas's Social Credit ideas in Britain, 1919-1939," *History of Political Economy*, 18, 2 (1986): 259-327.

[50]Of course, McKay did not disregard the importance of building a more stable monetary framework, and underlined the significance of doing so in Europe [§S. 104, "Recasting the International Structure of Debt."]

Illusion of Credit Control."][51] Focussing on money and credit obscured the spread between productive capacity and consuming power that actually created the possibility of the economic crisis: "That business depressions, unemployment and poverty in the midst of plenty are due to the failure of Capital to pay Labour sufficient wages to buy back a proper share of the product or services is a fact not advertised by the economists either of the universities or the banks," McKay remarked [§.93, "The Illusion of Credit Control."] Although favourably disposed to the creation of a national banking system as a step in the right direction, McKay was under no illusion that this would solve the problem. Spokespersons for labour and farmer movements in Canada who proposed the public control of credit as a magic answer to capitalist economic crises were simply re-hashing the ideas of Rodbertus in Prussia, Proudhon in France, and John Gray and other economists in England. They were, in essence, calling for the latter's elaborate scheme whereby producers would exchange their commodities for an official receipt attesting to the labour time contained within them [§.94, "Blind Alleys of the Utopians"]. Nor were businessmen any more astute about the situation when they determined that the "fundamental cause of the breakdown" was the high cost of credit available to business [§. 96, "Rationing Investment: A Critique of Donald Marvin's Explanation of the Depression."] The reform of the business cycle was not a matter of regulating money supply, but of "articulating the production of consumptive goods to market capacity, of establishing and maintaining a balance between supply and demand" [§.94]. Focusing on just one aspect of the economic structure risked losing sight of the whole picture.

Such currency reformers as the "Equitists" he thought to be the almost literal reincarnations of the labour-value economists of a hundred years before. They were as oblivious as Robert Owen to the capitalists' ability to frustrate "any plan based on changes in the symbols of exchange values" [§86]. If, as McKay argued, the economic law of supply and demand must be reckoned with in any form of society, "then there is no escaping from the conclusion of our industrial unionists that a balanced economy can be achieved only by the conscious social planning by organs of society created for that purpose. It is precisely at this point that the philosophy of industrial unionism finds itself fundamentally at issue with Social Credit mysticism which does not recognize the need of economic planning for social ends, but merely, without knowing it, rings the changes on the monetary reform notions of the Utopian Socialism which arose in

---

[51]McKay's critique of Social Credit was more historically-rooted and subtler than many others on the left. Most others concentrate on dissecting the contradictions of the famous A+B Theorem. See, for example, H.T.. Gaitskell's discussion in G.D.H.Cole, ed., *What Everybody Wants to Know About Money: A Planned Outline of Monetary Problems.* (London: Victor Gollancz, 1933): 348ff.

England after the first great industrial depression in 1823 -- more than a century ago" [§.85, "Under-consumption: A World Problem"].

The Equitist plan[52] struck him as being "too Utopian to either commend or denounce. What I object to is that some of its advocates put it forward as a complete panacea, possessed of all sorts of magic virtues -- a means to an end, when it plainly enough predicates a Utopia" [§.87]. Following Marx, he also disputed that a socialist society would necessarily involve equality of payment: "Any kind of society which does not offer rewards to ability and energy would soon become stagnant." "'A dollar an hour for everybody, including the boss', may be a fine slogan," he remarked, "but it is as much of an abstraction as the Golden Rule and offers us as little light on the real social problem which confronts humanity." The present task was for man to become the "master of property," before he worried about "new measures of exchange."[53] Those who controlled the money and credit of a nation undoubtedly controlled a certain power over the nation's activities, "but the control of the symbol of wealth is not by any means the same thing as the control of the means of wealth production [§.88, "Monetary or Credit Reform Schemes Illusory."]

---

[52]As explained by "Spirea" [probably H.C. Ross, K.C., D.L.] in *Labour World/Le Monde Ouvrier*, 6 June 1925, the Equitist Plan was one in which society would be returned to a state of primitive equality. "I propose we substitute our present money based on results, for money based on time. By doing so, each would work an hour and get say $100. Then there would be no profit, rent or interest and land would be free.... we could begin over again with free land and each on an equal basis -- and this would be the method of doing so. Then in equality of opportunity and freedom, we will work out something else. For all that we do is work for each other, if we do anything at all. Doing nothing never creates anything -- not even a social problem." Hence under the Equitist plan people would exchange "work," i.e. notes representing work-time, and not commodities. This would provide "a measure that is common to both and time is the only measure yet found." *Labour World/Le Monde Ouvrier*, 18 July 1925 favoured Dr. Ross's ideas: "That Dr. Howard Ross's plan to end war known as the 'Equitist Plan' is bringing forward comments from thinking men is not to be wondered at: its sound logic cannot be denied. The proper application of Equity at all times must appeal to the rational mind." In a polemic with McKay, "Spirea" fully conceded that the plan was "Utopian" (*Labour World/Le Monde Ouvrier*, 1 August 1925). For an interesting discussion of the deep North American roots of such "equitist" thought, see James J. Martin, *Men Against the State: The Expositors of Individualist Anarchism in America, 1827-1908* (Colorado Springs: Ralph Myles, 1970). Of particular significance was the work of Josiah Warren, whose 1846 book *Equitable Commerce* (1846) "contained the now-familiar exposition of the labor note currency, with variations....Warren sought to solve the problem caused by the refusal of some members in his previous labor exchange to participate in accepting similar amounts of any member's time" (55). Much remains to be said about currency reform as a form of "middle-class socialism" in Canada.

[53]C. McK., "The Equitist Plan," *Labour World/Le Monde Ouvrier*, 3 October 1925.

Again and again, McKay warned against mistaking the "effects" of money supply and credit regulation for the "cause" of the gulf between labour's buying power and its ability to produce.[54] It was a matter of enduring disappointment to him that progressive people were repeatedly seduced by the easy logic of such superficial and utopian schemes: "It was disappointing to see the United Farmers in Parliament who started the session with a fair promise of constructive leadership turning aside to pursue the will-o'-the-wisp of monetary reform across the morass of capitalism."[55] Even the socialist parliamentarians in the "Ginger Group" would disappoint McKay by developing an excessive interest in reforming money.[56] The idea that "managed money" would manage prices assumed that money determined the exchange-value of commodities, and that therefore, if the value of money could be maintained in a constant relation to an index of the price of commodities, then "the commodities will assort themselves in the market in a balanced relation of supply and demand. In fine, that by managing money you arrive at a managed economy in which all products cease to be commodities and appear on the scene as products of socially necessary labour. Such an adventure is worthy of those whom the gods have afflicted. It is to arrive at the socially necessary division of labour, not by intelligent social action, but by magic."[57]

(c)Post-liberal Comprehensive Schemes of State Capitalism

If, for McKay, liberal and semi-liberal prescriptions were of little use in a post-liberal economic era, he had greater respect for (but also more fears of) ambitious plans to recast the capitalist order under the auspices of the state. "Socialization for the wealthy," "technocracy," the "New Deal": all suggested, to varying degrees, that at least some of the lessons of the Depression had been grasped. Suddenly everyone seemed to be talking about "economic planning" as a replacement for (or supplement to) the market mechanism: as McKay took delight in noting, even the august *Saturday Night* of Toronto had aired the question, "Does Canada need a five-year plan?"[58] McKay believed that even if economic planning produced only state capitalism -- in which production was not carried on by freely associated workers -- it would nonetheless serve "to dispel the

---

[54]Compare his discussion on these points with G.D.H.Cole, *Gold, Credit and Employment: Four Essays for Laymen* (New York: Macmillan, 1930).

[55]C.McKay, "No Use Monkeying With the Yardstick," *O.B.U.Bulletin*, 16 July 1931.

[56]Colin McKay, Untitled Letter, *Labor World/Le Monde Ouvrier*, 12 November 1932. See also Colin McKay, "The Illusion of Money," *O.B.U.Bulletin*, 29 September 1932, and "Intelligence or Gold? Capitalism's Money Dilemma is Complete," *O.B.U.Bulletin*, 21 December 1933.

[57]C.M., "War Will Not Save Capitalism," *O.B.U.Bulletin*, 8 February 1934.

[58]Colin McKay, "Essentials of Economic Planning: A Critical Examination of the Swope Plan,"*Canadian Railway Employees Monthly* October 1931: 221-222.

illusion that the inequitable economic and social relations men find themselves in are imposed by mysterious powers beyond human control. To undertake economic planning is to attempt to control economics, to effect the emancipation of men from the reign of blind economic laws [§.128, "The CCF and a Canadian Socialism"]. And although critical of Communists and of the Soviet Model, McKay noted that for many young workers, with brains, energy and industry to give, their dreams of a land of fair play and opportunity were now going under the name "Russia." He argued that, even though the attempts to realize the dream of a rational economic order were likely to fail in Russia, their failure would not cause the dream to die in the labour movement, for it had been "the theme of the prophets and seers of the Labour movement for over a century." What was new in the 1930s was "the harsh white light that has been swiftly cast upon the inadequacies of capitalism, a revealing illumination which has quickened understanding of the fact that only through the realization of the dream can the working class achieve social salvation."[59] Although McKay appreciated the courage and the conceptual innovation of many of those who had seemingly grasped the essence of Depression economics -- that the spread between productive capacity and the purchasing power of the workers' wage lay at the origin of the system's ever-worsening instability -- he was highly suspicious of most of the versions of "economic planning" that came on the intellectual market in the 1930s, including those from the Soviet Union. He suspected many of them of false advertising.

Economic planning, he warned in 1936, was an extremely vague phrase, ranging from any form of state intervention at one pole to the comprehensive socialization of economic functions at the other. In the United States, the Democrats praised Roosevelt's "economic planning," while the Republicans protested that it had undermined liberty: but the meaning of the phrase remained elusive. McKay felt it was important to try to narrow the concept of economic planning.[59] The imposition of tariffs upon imports, the payment of railways or shipping subsidies, factory acts, compensation laws, public utility commissions, all merely represented limited forms of *state intervention*. Even the seemingly innovative organizations of the Depression -- the United States National Resources Board and Civilian Conservation Corps, and the Canadian plans for the settlement of the idle city workers upon the land -- came under this heading. On the other hand, *comprehensive economic planning* would have a coherent and unifying purpose. "Genuine economic planning would have a general social purpose as its unifying principle. That purpose would be to supply all the legitimate wants of all the people. All economic activities would primarily be planned to serve

---

[59]For an interesting review of the concept of economic planning, and a discussion of the leading alternatives of the 1930s, see Cole, *Economic Planning*. Although McKay does not cite Cole, he probably had read him.

that purpose. The production of both capital and consumer goods would then be regulated in accordance with a pre-determined program for the improvement of the standard of living. Adjustments would be made to ensure the provision of the different categories of goods in their right relative proportions.... Economic planning means conscious control of both natural forces and economic processes, and therefore the freedom of the workers from the fear of unemployment, accident, illness, and a dependent old age."[60] Theoretically, economic planning -- at least that of any use to society -- would have to return to the theories of value of the earlier classical economists which had long been buried under the marginalist theories of their successors.[61]

When judged by these criteria, many popular schemes floated in the 1930s were found wanting. The plan brought forward by Gerard Swope, President of the General Electric Company, for example, was of some significance, but merely as a sign that the myth of rugged individualism had been transcended: it made no provision for the "effective participation of Labour in the management of industry, or what has come to be known as industrial democracy."[62] Neither, of course, did Fordism, narrowly defined. McKay saluted Ford for having disturbed the complacency of businessmen and having "flouted all the axioms of business," but he mainly drew on Ford for ironic criticisms of the capitalist order. [63]

McKay was somewhat more favourably disposed to the schemes of the "Technocrats," perhaps because the credentials of Howard Scott, the director-in-chief of their research organization, "a former Wobbly or member of the Industrial Workers of the World," had been satirized by the leading organs of capitalism. He was also influenced by the extent to which the Technocrats had drawn on the sociology of Ward: McKay singled out for praise the Technocrats' very Wardian "premise that the machinery of production is the result of the labours of generations of men whose names have mostly been forgotten; that, therefore, this machinery is a social heritage and should be socially owned and used for the common benefit, instead of being class-owned and used for private profit."[64] Ultimately, however, the Technocrats' solutions did not offer a way off the treadmill of capitalist accumulation.

---

[60]Colin McKay, "State Interference,"*Canadian Unionist*, August 1936, 70-74.

[61] C.McKay, "Thoughts on Economic Planning," *O.B.U.Bulletin*, 27 October 1932.

[62]Colin McKay, "Essentials of Economic Planning: A Critical Examination of the Swope Plan,"*Canadian Railway Employees' Monthly*, October 1931, 221-222.

[63]"Ford's Challenge to Modern Business," *Canadian Railroad Employees' Monthly*, (August 1924); 120; back cover.

[64]"Labour and the Technocrats," *Canadian Unionist*, February 1933: 149; 156-157.

But at least the Technocrats were ambitious, at least they conceived the order of the economic challenge! In Canada, state-level programs lagged far behind such schemes; they lagged far behind the state responses of most of the rest of the industrial world. Even the exceptional flashes of ambition and energy were insufficient. In British Columbia, for example, a version of the new deal entailed special tribunals to fix and enforce minimum wages for male workers; and this seemed to McKay an improvement on the American New Deal. And the province's marketing boards were an improvement on the existing model. But marketing boards in one province could hardly control competition in the external market. Intending to give the small businessman and producer a sense of economic security, British Columbia's New Deal might "give small business a little longer lease of life," but unless the social forces liquidating small business could be arrested, there would be no real reprieve.[65]

At the federal level, McKay discerned a tendency towards "socialization for the wealthy," a new pattern of a dense interweaving of state and corporate interests, through which banks (relieved of their legal obligations to redeem their promissory notes in gold), speculators (with the government becoming responsible for the chief hedging operations in the wheat market), and capitalists of all sorts (assured through amendments of the Winding Up Act that their concerns could carry on under economic pressure without having to liquidate and close up or go into bankruptcy) all found their place in the sun. Canada probably led the world, he wrote, in terms of such regressive "socialization."[66]

Even if Canada were in the forefront of state capitalism, McKay entertained few illusions about what this would mean for workers. "We are bound for State Capitalism, whether we like it or not, with the certainty that it will mean increased exploitation and degradation," he remarked in 1933. "[T]he mental inertia of vast numbers of workers still makes them accept the shibboleths of the defenders of private initiative and individualism." "For the mass of the people the exercise of these precious virtues has long been out of the question, but the illusion that they are sources of progress and means of development of personality still persists....[67] The American New Deal -- to take the most prominent North American example of state capitalism -- was at best mildly reformist, and at worst a farcical disaster.[68]

---

[65]Colin McKay, "British Columbia's New Deal," *Canadian Unionist*, January 1935: 196-199.

[66]C. McK., "Socialization is for the Wealthy," *O.B.U.Bulletin*, 27 April 1933.

[67]C. McK., "Shibboleth of Individualism," *O.B.U.Bulletin*, 22 June 1933.

[68]C. McK., "What Of The New Deal?", *O.B.U.Bulletin*, 7 September 1933; C.M., "N.R.A. Experiment Back To Where It Started," *O.B.U.Bulletin*, 22 March 1934.

Because such modest steps toward state capitalism failed to address the basic issues of the Depression, McKay feared that the middle classes, some farmers, perhaps even some workers might gravitate towards Fascism. He saw Fascism as both a cultural and an economic phenomenon, and saw no need to reduce it to one or the other. For middle-class and some working-class Canadians, Fascism represented a culture of militant antimodernism, born of the frustrations and dreams of the crisis of capitalism. A "movement of the emotions rather than of ideas," Fascism represented "a desire to retreat, to reproduce the simpler conditions of a past epoch." Incapable of taking "a rational view of evolution," Fascism wanted "the opportunities and equalities of the handicraft era without abandoning the advantages of machine production." In its frustration at its failure to attain this impossible goal, it found a scapegoat in racial, religious, or cultural minorities. In this way, McKay argued (striving as usual for analysis and balance rather than just denunciation) Fascism was "at once reactionary and utopian." [69]

Although McKay thought Canadians would probably *not* respond to the glaring irrationalities of Nazism (memorably characterized by McKay as a "mass movement in which millions of frustrated little men lost their minds, believing they were going to realize their hopes and dreams")[70] they *were* highly susceptible to the anti-modern allure of an older and better day, and might well respond to an authoritarian movement if it seemed capable of returning the country to the golden past. McKay identified the leading force behind the proto-Fascistic movements of the 1930s as finance capital, intent on increasing profits by lowering wages. The effect of this Fascist economic policy would be "a reduction of the purchasing power, of the effective demand, in the home market," which in turn would necessitate the fixing of prices at higher levels by state decrees, the subsidization of exports, and the restriction of imports by quotas, exchange controls and other devices. Under Fascism the political state, which in liberal countries had been covertly used to bolster capitalist privilege by such negative methods as tariffs, would be an open partner of finance capital, "using its powers in a direct and positive manner, to assist capital in intensifying the exploitation of the people" [§.100, "The Menace of Fascism."]

Canadian Fascism might dispense with the rabid scapegoating and coloured shirts of its European counterpart. It might indeed dispense with grassroots mobilization altogether: parliamentary democracy could be suspended, simply through an alliance of the old parties in a "National

[69]Colin McKay, "Canada's Fascist Rabble," *Canadian Unionist*, Vol.8, No.4 (September 1934), 81-83.
[70]C. McK., untitled letter, *Labor World/Le Monde Ouvrier*, 5 February 1938. See also Colin McKay, "Germany's Venture Into State Capitalism," *New Commonwealth*, 10 July 1937.

Government." "Behind the demand for a National Government is the essential Fascist purpose to strengthen the powers of the Federal Government and use them to buttress the position of finance capital by exercising some control over provincial finances," McKay remarked [§.100, "The Menace of Fascism."] "A union of the old parties from the top will suffice to set up the totalitarian State, that is, the State without the mask of political democracy, frankly using its power to repress the workers and farmers." Such a state would rally to its state-capitalist banners the (mainly middle-class) "muddle-heads" who could be terrorized by the specter of government deficits, and especially by the menace of the debts carried by the CNR. The National Government's actual objective would be to smash the CCF, to assist big business to expropriate little business, and to discipline the workers' movement [§.101, "'National' Government and Canadian Fascism."]

In his last year of life, when economic conditions suddenly worsened -- the index of employment on June 1, 1938, was 12.2 per cent below that of November 1, 1937, which suggested the emergence of an even more devastating crisis[71] -- McKay concluded that although Canadian society was "scarcely ripe for radical reconstruction," it was socially prepared for a Canadian form of Fascism [§.103, "The Middle Class and a National Government."] It was his most pessimistic estimate yet of the attractiveness of the "false prophets" who had misled Canadians -- and, perhaps, robbed workers and socialists of their best chance to create a truly counter-hegemonic historic bloc.

3. The Scope of Possible Remedies

If none of the ideas of the "false prophets" was really a plausible solution for the crisis, what economic policies should working-class Canadians support? McKay liked the answer given by one of his favourite economists, Rodbertus. Society "must step out of this vicious circle, in which she is driven about by prejudices and vested interests," and replace the so-called natural laws, insofar as they are harmful, by social laws. "For this she needs but clear vision and moral strength. It is the part of the politicians and economists to sharpen the first. Should the last be lacking for a free resolve, history will indeed have to swing the lash of revolution over her again."[72] Although it is part of the misleading academic folklore around Canadian socialism that old SPCers were hostile to all reforms of capitalism, in this case, the opposite is true. McKay was compassionately

---

[71]For an interesting analysis of the impact of the "recession within a depression" of 1937-38 and its theoretical significance, see Harry Magdoff and Paul M. Sweezy, "Listen, Keynesians!" *Monthly Review*, 34, 8 (January 1983): 1-11. This late-1930s reverse suggested that overaccumulation was more than a temporary phenomenon and in fact marked a decisive change in the functioning of the system.

[72]C.M., Untitled letter, *Labor World/Le Monde Ouvrier*, 8 August 1931.

well-disposed towards any reform which seemed likely to ease the pain of the workers, and he never nurtured the dangerous illusion that the worse things got, the better the prospects of socialism. He was consistently scanning the horizon for effective measures. However, he simply had too much experience and insight to mistake the mild ameliorative programs of the Canadian state for effective long-term solutions to capitalism's problems.

Skeptical, as we have seen, of most *general* schemes for "economic planning" under capitalism, McKay urged labour to support *specific* measures of planning which promised to bring great rationality to the system and more security to workers. A "rational business system" would be in the workers' interests, insofar as it allowed for the development of production. Bureaux of statistics, the Wheat Board, all the indications in the 1930s of a reorganization of economic thought would help workers. Workers could hasten the reorganization of the system simply by defending their own interests in the political field and (here was the inimitable McKay!) by presenting "logical arguments at all times."[73]

In the new social order, ruled by workers, the methods of the trust were to be applied with the object of providing employment and increasing wages. "Efficient production will be the first consideration; but provision will be made for the labour set free by closing down inefficient plants. In a regime ruled by labour the surplus labourers might be transferred to other industries, and of course conditions in essential industries would be made attractive, so as to assure a proper balance of production....A labour regime would see to it that essential needs were met before surplus labour was diverted to the construction of automobiles."[74] And a labour regime would so manage the relationship between railways and automobiles so that the country's massive investment in railways was not squandered: "Through co-operation it will be easier to protect the interests of railwaymen and motormen, as well as give the public the best possible service. Competition -- rate wars -- will only tend to press down the living standards of both groups of workers...."[75]

McKay could also imagine, in a state dominated by a historic bloc centered on the working class, a new emphasis on the leisure activities of workers and on maintaining a high level of consumption. The state could organize the leisure activities of workers, for example, and designate whole regions as suited to social tourism. "Substituting planned production for

---

[73]Colin McKay, "Co-ordination of Productive Forces Needed," *Canadian Railroad Employees Monthly*, February 1923: 204; 208.
[74]Colin McKay, "Modern Industrial System Limits Production," *Canadian Railroad Employees Monthly*, July 1923, 79;84.
[75]Colin McKay, "The Road-Rail Problem,"*Canadian Unionist*, December 1931, 126-127.

the present anarchy of production, with its reckless waste of both labour and capital, would vastly increase the production of wealth, and permit all Canadian workers to have at least three months' recognized leisure, continuous leisure" [§.67, "The Maritimes: Playground of a Happier Canada"]. Comprehensive state planning could also encompass estate duties and fairer taxation, in order to reduce the large size of public debt in Canada.[76]

What of the Keynesian models that would prove so influential (if also, in Canada, so partially implemented) after the Second World War? McKay was a well-informed observer of European economic developments, and he brought his labour readership word of such important developments as the success enjoyed by the government in Sweden in engineering a recovery (partly through stimulating the production of homes to meet the needs of low-paid workers.)[77] He clearly welcomed such "Keynesian" policies as partial, constructive responses to the crisis. To be sure, McKay was initially *extremely* hostile to Keynes himself, whom he identified as one of the most "unstable" of the "jazz economists." The darling of the "petty bourgeois socialists," a volatile and unstable man who got away with the "ballyhooing of a lot of bunk" and who had confessed his inability to understand Marx, Keynes was one of those "muddle-headed economists" who seemed to exercise such a strange power over the Progressives. Such types -- and McKay was clearly including Keynes in his indictment -- were just the "crafty 'medicine men' of capitalism," whose mumbo-jumbo was designed "to bewilder and awe the populace."[78]

It was a sign of Keynes's desperation that he felt driven to promote schemes of massive state expenditure, with government expenditures assuring the equilibrium of investments and savings. Increasing public debt in order to provide a means of investment of surplus profits which capitalists were disinclined to risk in private enterprise, struck McKay as an strategy unlikely to succeed in the struggle for stability. "Yet Keynes' view exposes the difficulty of capitalism," McKay conceded -- reluctantly, perhaps. "The system is congested by excess saving. As savings from wages are insignificant, we may say that surplus profits cause the congestion. If profits accumulate faster than opportunities of investment can be found, what then? Could not the other horn of the dilemma be avoided?" Yet Keynes, as a capitalist economist, could not see the obvious solution, which was to avoid the accumulation of surplus profits by the raising of wages or the lowering of prices.[79] In April, 1935, McKay

---

[76]C. McKay, "Public Debts and Capitalist Dilemma,"*Labor World/Le Monde Ouvrier*, 12 February 1938.

[77]Colin McKay, "The Workers Need Homes," *Canadian Unionist*, August 1935, 71-72.

[78]Colin McKay, "The Magic of Money," *O.B.U.Bulletin*, 3 November 1932.

[79]"Capitalism and the Railway Situation," *Canadian Railway Employees' Monthly*, November 1934: 232-233.

was still cheerfully dismissing the "half-baked theories of economists like J.M.Keynes," which had been decisively exposed by such Marxist theorists as John Stratchey.[80] The following June, 1935, he noted a recent study of the Brookings Institution, which had blown sky high "the wish-dreams of many reformers like J. Maynard Keynes, the wish-dream of a managed society through a managed currency, the false hope that by moving the bank rate of interest up or down, the rate of investment can be kept stabilized, and consuming capacity kept equal to production capacity."[81] By January, 1936, however, McKay's tone had abruptly changed: Keynes was now "the greatest of the liberal economists" who understood the connection between profit-making and war.[82]

The stage was being set for McKay's detailed and surprisingly favourable review of Keynes's *General Theory of Employment, Interest and Money* in April 1936. McKay was clearly impressed by Keynes's daring: "...Keynes now declares that the mechanism of the market no longer suffices as a regulator of production, and that state control and regulation of some important economic activities has become necessary to save the system from collapse....Keynes long pursued the idea that private banks, by raising or lowering the rate of interest, could regulate investment and control the price level, and thereby assure orderly business and full employment. Now, he has come to the conclusion that the intervention of the state is necessary to control both the amount and direction of investment, with the object of assuring a balanced development of the production of capital goods and of providing full employment" [§.106, "The Keynesian Prescription," originally published as "The Conversion of an Economist"]. McKay grasped that Keynes's program entailed a very different kind of state: "He makes that the king-pin of his program to save the system from collapse. He would have the state control the rate of interest and adjust the supply of money with the object of maintaining full employment. He proposes that the state start extensive public works in order to provide needed employment, and he would increase taxes to provide the wherewithal to pay for such works, defending this proposal as a means of redistributing the national income." Keynes was vague on certain points, and it remained unclear just how the production of capital goods was to be planned by the state organ responsible for investment planning.[83] But McKay took the measure of his book, and understood immediately the serious challenge it posed for the system it purported to be saving. In his very last article, McKay referred again to Keynes's emphasis on full employment, which he felt sometimes drew attention

---

[80]C.M., Untitled Letter, *Labor World/Le Monde Ouvrier,* 27 April 1935.

[81]C. McKay, "Mayor Evades Issue," *Labor World/Le Monde Ouvrier,* 15 June 1935.

[82]Colin McKay, "The Root Cause of War," *Canadian Unionist,* January 1936, 212-214.

[83]*Canadian Unionist,* April 1936, 302-304.

away from the more profound forces shaping economic development.[84] But the tone of the discussion was far different from those of the early 1930s.

It does not seem at all unlikely that, had he lived another twenty years, McKay would have recognized the importance of the work of those left Keynesians who saw in the works of Keynes not a series of minor recipes for how a capitalist society might get through a business recession, but rather as a profound (and so unanswered) challenge to the liberal capitalist order, and a culminating point of the underconsumptionist tradition that had held McKay's loyalty throughout his analysis of the crisis of capitalism.

i. The Marxian Framework

73. The False Doctrines of Political Economy[85]

[Editor's Note.--Political economy -- set on a pedestal particularly by European capitalists -- is described as a false doctrine by the writer, who is making a survey of European industrial conditions at first hand. Writing from Paris, France, Mr. McKay reviews the history of political economy, and points out that its principles as originally propounded were suited to the age of one-man industries when the proprietors were also the operators, but with present-day conditions it was useful only as a subterfuge by the capitalistic group in explaining the deficiencies of the general industrial structure.]

"Then damn political economy," said Delegate Brownlie, when in an impassioned speech before the British Trades Union Congress, he scouted the pretense of the politicians and economists that unemployment is due to unknown causes operating in the system of political economy under which we live, and therefore cannot be cured, but at best only alleviated. This impious utterance has greatly shocked the leader writers of the daily press and many profound explanations of political economy are being given the workers, along with the advice that it is their duty to endure as best they can the evils arising from the mysterious operations of economic laws. Incidentally it is suggested that if the workers would only labour longer hours for shorter pay the economic laws might take more mercy on them.

Adam Smith, who is not very popular with the modern counsellors of the workers, wrote the following:

---

[84]*Saturday Night*, 4 February 1939.

[85]Originally published as "Political Economy a Curse to Industry," *Canadian Railroad Employees' Monthly*, October 1922: 153; 155.

> Considered as a branch of the science of a statesman or a legislator, political economy proposes two distinct objects:--
> Firstly, to supply a plentiful subsistence for the people, or more properly to enable them to provide such a revenue or subsistence for themselves.
> Secondly, to supply the State or Commonwealth with a revenue sufficient for the public services.
> It proposes to enrich both the people and the sovereign....[86]

It seems hardly surprising that Mr. Brownlie should exhibit some impatience with a "science," the application of which for a century or more, has left 10,000,000 of his countrymen on the verge of starvation, has accentuated the problem of unemployment, and periodically brings the nation's industries to a state of paralysis.

A glance at the history of political economy will serve to show why its professors have no adequate answer to the questions the workers are asking with growing impatience. In the early stages of capitalist production the great mass of industries were carried on by private individuals or small firms, that is, the owners were performing useful functions. It was then possible for Adam Smith, Ricardo and others to make an impartial study of economic phenomena, and draw generalizations with respect to the laws of production without offending anybody. But steam power and the factory system brought in the impersonal corporation, with its numerous shareholders taking no active part in the conduct of their enterprises. A new class of absentee capitalists came into being, men who to some extent became parasites upon industry, and they did not want an impartial study of economic phenomena and candid conclusions drawn from properly classified facts. So the economists were soon contenting themselves with collecting statistics and facts, useful in the speculations of the stock exchange and commerce. They ceased to classify these facts and make generalizations from them, except for the purpose of proving to the capitalist class that their thrift, foresight, enterprise and ability were more important factors in the creation of wealth than the labours of the manual and intellectual workers, their hired men, and that they were justified in taking the means of a spacious life while leaving to their employees the lot of a beast of burden. Instead of developing a real science of political economy along the lines laid down by Adam Smith they began to devote

---

[86]McKay is citing, with minor modification, Adam Smith, *An Inquiry Into the Nature and Causes of The Wealth of Nations*, Vol.I: "Political oeconomy, considered as a branch of the science of a statesman or legislator, proposes two distinct objects: first, to provide a plentiful revenue or subsistence for the people, or more properly to enable them to provide such a revenue or subsistence for themselves; and secondly, to supply the state or commonwealth with a revenue sufficient for the public services. It proposes to enrich both the people and the sovereign." Adam Smith, *An Inquiry Into the Nature and Causes of The Wealth of Nations*, Vol.I, Book IV, ed. Edwin Cannan (London: Methuen and Company, 1925): 395.

their energies to discomfiture of their workers; they have to their own satisfaction overthrown Ricardo's theory of value, because in the hands of the socialists it offers an effective means of indicting the capitalist class for rapacity and incompetence.

True, the damning of political economy will not solve the problem of unemployment. But Mr. Brownlie's gesture has at least brought out an explanation of the problem of unemployment which ought to be highly edifying to the working class. A ponderous contributor to the London press cites the Malthusean theory, i.e., "the most obvious and least appreciated of natural laws, that a species tends to increase faster than its means of subsistence." In animal life, we are told, the balance is maintained by the massacre of the innocents; and, we are further informed that "humanity in all climes, since industry assumed its present form, has had its fringe of unemployment, the units of which suffer from atrophy and malnutrition, and become unemployment, and -- go out." One may gather from this that modern industry, which has greatly increased the productive power of labour, is not without its evils, since it has also increased the fecundity of the species. According to this view, progress can only hold out a direful prospect for the working class, since the greater the production, the more members of the class will be condemned to atrophy, and finally to "go out of existence." It is worth nothing, however, that the wise man says that humanity has been afflicted with this difficulty since industry assumed its present form.

Now let us cross the channel into France where wise men are busy urging the need of increasing the population. M. Gustave Terry of *L'Oeuvre* (not a labour paper) evidently considers himself the chief protagonist of the repopulation campaign. "Some syndicalists," he writes, "are saying that increasing the number of births will only increase the number of unemployed and the sum of human misery. They infer that the apostles of repopulation labour more or less consciously in the interests of capitalism, of reaction and militarism. They suggest that we want to increase the population to provide more cannon fodder and to promote strikes of the stomach which compel the labourers to take low wages."

Mr. Terry affirms that this reasoning involves a fatal sophistry. For him Malthus was plainly a fakir. "On the contrary," he says, "the peasantry attain prosperity by having large families to work on the farm, and to make the same thing true in the cities, it is only necessary to pass a law requiring adult sons and daughters to give their parents a portion of their salaries. Thus the workers or more properly the proletarians (since it is the propertyless workers who have the most children) will be assured of support in their old age in proportion to their contributions to the population.

"What is true of the individual is true for the nation. The rich nations are the most prolific, and they have the least to fear from war because they are the strongest. To labour for increased population is therefore a pacific enterprise."

M. Terry has probably forgotten that Germany and Russia were the most prolific nations in Europe, but it did not keep them out of the war. And he is not prepared to face the fact that the high cost of living, or rather low wages and uncertainty of employment, tend to prevent young people marrying and having families.

The arguments of the English Malthusean would justify a law making it a crime for workers to have children, while M. Terry's arguments would justify a law compelling them to have children. Both in their way are typical logicians of the bourgeois order, and neither sees that private ownership of the means of production having outlived its usefulness must give way to a better social order before the proletariat can develop any enthusiasm for increased population campaigns.

74. Marxism and Fatalism[87]

Sir-- According to a writer in the *Canadian Forum*, Marxism teaches:

"That historical events move in a pre-determined way....That history exhibits order, purpose, plan."[88]

This is news, if true. Do the Socialists see order, purpose, plan, in the present disorderly depression? Do they not rather say that capitalism is

---

[87]Originally published as an untitled letter to the editor, *Labor World/Le Monde Ouvrier*, 10 December 1932.

[88]McKay refers to Howe Martyn, "Marxism," *Canadian Forum*, 13 (December 1932): 92-94: "The nearest to a frank expression of Marx's philosophy is given in his doctrine of the Materialistic Interpretation of History, which is that historical events move in a predetermined and therefore predictable way, under the influence of natural laws such as that man requires food and clothing, that machines increase the amount of these man can produce, and so on....We can say that what has happened in the past is enough to refute the Materialistic Interpretation of History. History has not been as Marx said it was. History is not a record of evolution of classes and revolutionary struggle between them. It is not orderly and systematic at all, but a chaos of individual happenings, about the causes of which a generalization may perhaps be made here and there, but none so sweeping as Marx's. Even should some people choose to believe that history does exhibit order, purpose, plan, they are not bound to the Marxian theory because they can give other descriptions of the plan equally good or (as I think) equally bad." Martyn was a member of the League for Social Reconstruction and a participant in the planning sessions for *Social Planning for Canada*. See "Introduction," *Social Planning for Canada*, xx. His stance would not have been atypical of the LSR's somewhat superficial understanding of Marxism.

disorderly because it has no social purpose but only the individualistic purpose of private profit? For Marx the logical culmination of capitalism was a condition rendering necessary the submission of co-operation for competition in order to realize further progress. With the culmination of capitalism man completes his primary history -- the period in which he makes history unconsciously; thereafter society will take conscious control of the evolution of its affairs.

"No social order," said Marx, "ever disappears before all the productive forces, for which there is room in it, have been developed."[89] That is why Russia finds itself a long way from Socialism -- why the Bolshevists are developing the forces of production by typically capitalistic methods, with the only difference that instead of using the negative force of hunger to drive the workers they use the positive force of the State, and follow a general plan having a definite social purpose, which capitalism in other countries lacks.

The *Forum* writer asserts that "Marxism convinces the people that God is with them in a cause destined to victory.....Marxism is fatalistic."

But in society, struggle so far has been the law of progress. Feudalism had its good side and its bad side, and the evil side overcame the good. It has always been the evil side, from the point of the dominant class, that has constituted the struggle which makes the movement of history. No antagonism, no struggle, no progress. Said Marx:
"If at the epoch of the reign of feudalism, the economists, enthusiastic over the virtues of history, the delightful harmony between right and duties, the patriarchal life of the towns, the prosperous state of domestic industry in the country, of the development of industry organized in corporations, guilds and fellowships, in fine, of all which constitutes the beautiful side of feudalism, had proposed to themselves the problem of eliminating all which cast a shadow upon this lovely picture -- serfdom, privilege, anarchy -- what would have been the result? All the elements which constituted the struggle would have been annihilated, and the development of the bourgeoise would have been stifled in the germ. They would have set themselves the absurd problem of eliminating history."[90]

---

[89]McKay is citing without modification Karl Marx, *A Contribution to the Critique of Political Economy* (Chicago: Charles H. Kerr, 1911): 12.

[90]McKay is citing, with minor modifications, Karl Marx, *The Poverty of Philosophy*. See Marx, *The Poverty of Philosophy* (New York: International Publishers, 1969), 121-122: "If, during the epoch of the domination of feudalism, the economists, enthusiastic over knightly virtues, the beautiful harmony between rights and duties, the patriarchal life of the towns, the prosperous condition of domestic industry in the countryside, the development of industry organized into corporations, guilds and fraternities, in short, everything that constitutes the good side of feudalism, had set themselves the problem of eliminating everything that cast a shadow on this picture -- serfdom, privileges,

Until men acquire sufficient social [consciousness] to organize their social affairs on a co-operative basis and throw all their powers into the struggle against nature, social antagonisms, competition, will continue to be the more or less unconscious agent of progress.

ii. Causes and Dimensions of the Economic Crisis

75. Over-Capitalization and Over-Production[91]

Industry in Canada is too productive. That is the latest complaint. It will not offer much comfort to people out of work and in need of many of the products of industry. At their recent annual convention the shoe manufacturers adopted a resolution declaring that "the productive capacity" of the Canadian shoe manufacturing industry and the distributing facilities of the shoe trade of Canada "are much in excess of the requirements of the present Canadian population." To overcome this evil the manufacturers urged measures to increase the population by immigration, coupled with adequate protective tariffs. The retailers wanted curtailment of credit so as to make it difficult for new men to enter the trade, and also to bar from the trade persons not able to conform to certain financial, moral and commercial standards. Further, the retailers wanted a limitation of styles of shoes, a certain standardization of products after the dreadful plan the socialists are said to contemplate.

In other words the shoe manufacturing industry has reached a stage of development where its monopolistic features become apparent even to the manufacturers themselves, while the retail trade openly avows its desire to resurrect the restrictions of the ancient Guilds. They have no use for the "open shop" in their trade.

Now, for Canadian industries which have a productive capacity beyond their market, -- and it was said a great number of Canadian industries were in the same boat as the shoe factories -- immigration is desirable, if the immigrants have or can obtain money to buy shoes and other things. But immigration will not solve the industrial problem from the point of view of the working class, as the experience of the United States shows. That country is also troubled by the fact that its industries are able to produce more than its people can consume on their present wage standard, or foreign markets can absorb.

---

anarchy -- what would have happened? All the elements which called forth the struggle would have been destroyed, and the development of the bourgeoisie nipped in the bud. One would have set oneself the absurd problem of eliminating history."

[91]*Canadian Railroad Employees Monthly*, March 1924, 3-4.

If Canadian manufacturers are now confronted with a chronic condition of over-production, immigrants coming to Canadian cities will merely become competitors for jobs which are already insufficient for the present working population. That would mean wage reductions, with a consequent curtailment of the effective purchasing power of the home markets. In other words, the excess productive capacity of Canadian industries would be further emphasized. If the immigrants go on farms what then? Canadian farmers are already producing more than they can sell at a reasonable profit; they can only employ any considerable number of immigrants at wages which would mean a lowering of the standard of living.

Yet Canada, to support the inflated capitalization of her industries and railways, undoubtedly needs immigration -- also opportunities of employment and wage rates that would arrest the exodus of Canadians to the United States. Unfortunately the manufacturers have no definite policy calculated to create the conditions necessary for the satisfactory employment of an increased population.

The outstanding feature of Canadian development during the past two decades has been the rapid extension of the dominion of the financier over industry. The joint stock company has largely displaced the private employer in all the important industries; and mergers have united under one control numerous enterprises, once independent competing entities. Also, the leaders in the big industries have by means of agreement as to prices and market areas, largely abolished competition between the individual enterprises. In spite of the Anti-Combine Act it is common knowledge that such agreements exist. These mergers and agreements have vastly increased the powers of Canadian capitalism. The capitalists stand united against the buyers of their products and also against their workers. Commanding the home markets through protective tariffs, industrial managers have sought to increase the exploitation of the workers in order to sell their products in foreign markets. That the exploitation has been intensified is shown by Canadian statistics. Capital takes a larger share of the product. If the poor are not growing poorer, certainly the rich are growing richer. Improvements made in the housing of the working class during the last generation have not been noticeable; in fact there are everywhere complaints of inadequate housing. But the mansions of the wealthy today are infinitely more gorgeous than the dwellings of men counted wealthy 50 years ago. And for the pleasure and gratification of the capitalist class there are palatial hotels, city and country clubs innumerable, majestic steamers whose first class accommodations embody conceptions of luxury that were unknown in Royal yachts 50 years ago. But the quarters occupied by the crew of a great ocean liner was described by an English Admiral during the war as "gloomy kennels of a kind any decent man would be ashamed to keep mongrel dogs in." Again the capitalist class and their satellites have been able to acquire automobiles which represent a further levy upon productive labour. The workers' electric car has improved, but strap-hanging has increased.

Through mergers and combines and the general extension of the joint-stock system, Canada has become a country of large scale industries. In Montreal the capital invested in the average manufacturing establishment is $154,800; in Toronto, $128,200; in all Canada $84,229. Obviously the worker has little chance of starting a manufacturing enterprise of his own account, as his grandfather might have done with some hope of success. That means that those who control the profit making industries already in existence will also largely control the new industries which may be created in the future. They will sell shares to small investors, but they will know how to retain control.

If Canada is to develop, and opportunities of employment [are to be] provided, the monied interests must give more attention to the problems of utilizing the country's natural resources and creating new industries. Since finance began its campaign of domination over Canadian industry, capitalist enterprise has been less concerned about increasing and diversifying production than intensifying the exploitation of existing industries. In fact mergers frequently resulted in the closing down of plants here and there, and throwing workers out of jobs. In many cases the mergers were overcapitalized, and the people invited to exchange their savings for nicely engraved stock certificates. Then it was discovered that the merged enterprises could not pay dividends on the large capitalization, and the value of the stock certificates declined -- in too many cases, to zero.

That game is pretty well played out, so far as existing industries are concerned, although mergers and combines are still being made, with, however, the object of better regulating output and prices, rather than of attracting the savings of small investors. With existing industries now having an excess productive capacity, finance will have to turn to the creation of new industries based on natural resources. When that task is undertaken systematically, efforts to increase the population by immigration will not menace the position of the Canadian workers and drive them to the United States. But to assure any steady developments in the way of creating new industries Canadian financiers will have to show a more scrupulous regard for the interests of the small investor than they have in the recent past.

76. Over-capitalization and under-consumption[92]

...*The Financial Post* of Toronto, in a moment of illumination, summed up the situation, thusly:

"While the total income of the country is greater, the buying power is lower. If three men who used to earn $3,000 a piece, now earn $7,000, $1,000 and $1,000 the buying power has diminished, although the total income is the same. The man on the larger income buys very much the same amount of food and clothing, while the others are obliged to do with less. That is what has taken place in a large way."

Precisely. But the journal which recognizes this obvious circumstance, resolutely ignores its lesson -- that Canada is suffering from an orgy of involuntary economy, of enforced thrift on the part of the masses at any rate. It does not follow that an era of government extravagance would work a cure; in any case, that panacea is impossible. In Canada what is called government extravagance is mainly the consequence of the government's efforts to protect private enterprise from the consequence and blunders and worse of private enterprise. But insofar as the activity of business is dependent on buying power, prosperity depends not on private thrift, but on private extravagance. The difference between the United States and Canada may be explained; first, by the fact that the American worker has a higher wage to spend, and being surer of a job spends his wage as he goes along; second, by the fact that the interest- and dividend-receiving classes in the United States are wasteful and extravagant, spending a large portion of their current incomes in ways that give employment. The prodigality of the rich is the providence of the poor. Under the capitalist system that is the case. If the workers woke up, they would change that immoral condition -- but that is another story.

Canadian policy has been to exact huge dividends from business -- usually disguised by watered stock. So long as these dividends could be reinvested in new enterprises able to give markets for their products, there was something to be said for such a policy. But now production of goods can be rapidly increased; less than 200,000 Canadian grain growers in 1923 produced enough wheat to supply ten times the population of Canada, on the basis of wheat consumption in Canada. To promote good business, it is necessary to increase consumption, and that can only be done by increasing wages and restricting the portion of the national income annually turned into new capital demanding interest and dividends.

---

[92]Originally published as an untitled letter to the editor, *Labor World/Le Monde Ouvrier*, 17 December 1925.

77. Hysteria and the Business Cycle[93]

Capitalism develops more forms of hysteria in the course of a business cycle than the Labour movement has done in a century. It is continually running amuck among its own most cherished illusions.

Capitalism stands for unrestricted private enterprise and competition -- when it is on parade, with its brightest banners unfurled. But capitalist[s] parenthetically demand the protection of numerous forms of paternalism for themselves -- from high custom tariffs to low railway freight tariffs.

The latest capitalistic clamour about cutting out competitive railway services may have some justification. But it is mainly inspired by the desire to preserve low freight rates -- a laudable desire no doubt, from the business point of view. But it may be doubted that the economies which will be effected will materially improve the financial position of the railways, whose chief difficulty lies in the fact that they have not been able to obtain increases in rates commensurate with the advance in the prices of the things they carry and the advance in the cost of living generally. Some locomotives and passenger cars may be placed on the idle list, where they will deteriorate as rapidly, if not more rapidly, than they would in service. Some hundreds or thousands of workers may be thrown out of employment and incidentally help to throw more [grocers] and small merchants into difficulties or bankruptcy. The railway situation in Canada is more tragic from the point of view of the workers than from the financial point of view. In October, 1924, the railways employed 25,000 fewer persons than in October, 1923. These railways require an army corps of unemployed upon which they may draw at need. They could not function properly if they did not have a small army of men more or less trained to the railway service whom they can hire or fire at will - a host of men and their families living precariously, hanging on the ragged edge of existence.

Capitalism is callous towards this condition of so many workers. As Lord Milner[94] has pointed out, the gravest indictment of capitalism is precisely its indifference to the fact that it cares nothing about the fate of multitudes it needs one month, or one year; and throws out of work the next month or the next year.

---

[93]Originally published as an untitled letter to the editor, *Labor World/Le Monde Ouvrier*, 16 May 1925.

[94]McKay refers to the German-born British politician Lord Alfred Milner (1854-1925), who was an outspoken proponent of aggressive imperial adventures, but who also advocated advanced social reforms as a way of ensuring the quality, and therefore the leadership potential, of the British citizenry.

But while capitalism endures the interests of money and property will override the interests of mere men. The predominance of money or property is essential. If capitalism surrendered that principle it would surrender its very soul, its whole reason for being.

78. The Concentration of Industrial Capital[95]

The manufacturing industries of Canada employed 516,777 persons in 1924, only 974 more than in 1910, according to an industrial census for the year 1924, just issued. But the capital employed in 1924 was $3,380,000,000, compared with $1,247,000,000 in 1910, an increase of 183 per cent. Capital employed includes fixed capital of $2,310,000,000, representing lands, buildings, machinery and tools, and working capital of $1,228,000,000 representing materials and supplies in hand, finished products, stocks in process, cash, trading and operating accounts.

Gross production at factory prices was valued at $2,695,000,000 in 1924, compared with $1,165,000,000 in 1910, an increase of 132 per cent. Net production, the value added to raw materials, was $1,256,000,000 in 1924, compared with $564,000,000 in 1910, an increase of 123 per cent.

Allowing for price changes, the increase in net production in 1924 over 1910 would be about 50 per cent. To effect this increase, the number of employees required was only increased by one-tenth of 1 per cent. This indicates the increasing importance of the part played by machinery. But, as machines are poor consumers, productive capacity of Canadian manufacturing increased much faster than the consuming capacity of its markets. Thus, practically all these industries were practicing "ca'canny"[96] in 1924, and still are, though to a lesser extent.

A rapid concentration of manufacturing in a few years was indicated by the fact that the number of manufacturing establishments is given as 22,178 in 1924, as against 43,200, in 1920, a remarkable shrinkage for four years. Employees who numbered 685,349 in 1920 dropped to 516,777 in 1924, a shrinkage of 169,000, or about 25 per cent. Yet net production,

---

[95]Originally published as "Canada's Industrial Output Soars," *Labor World/Le Monde Ouvriere*, November 13, 1926.

[96]A Scottish mining term, meaning literally "to proceed warily" or "to be moderate," but in industrial working-class terms, to "go slow" -- to work at a slower pace than usual, in order to give the boss less surplus value for his investment. It was a strategy used to resist capitalist attempts to reduce wages or increase hours, and was effective because mine owners could not effectively supervise the day-to-day work of each independent coal miner. For its use in the coal mines of Cape Breton, see David Frank, "Class Conflict in the Coal Industry: Cape Breton, 1922," in Ian McKay, ed., *The Challenge of Modernity* (Toronto: McGraw-Hill Ryerson, 1992): 272, n. 19. A strategy it might be likened to under modern conditions of industrial legality is "work to rule."

allowing for price changes, was about the same in 1924 as in 1920. Capital employed showed a slight shrinkage, but of less than 2 per cent.

To reduce the number of manufacturing establishments by practically one-half in the four years following the post-war slump, lop off 25 per cent of the employees, and yet maintain or even increase the physical volume of production is an achievement of which capital is doubtless proud. It was made possible by the wholesale weeding out of less efficient plants by competition or mergers, and the concentration of production in the better equipped plants.

But in this immense reorganization, rendering 21,000 establishments superfluous, the capitalist class as such made little sacrifice, for the capital obligation resting upon industry was only reduced in an insignificant degree. Of course, by rendering one-fourth of their employees superfluous, the manufacturers helped to curtail consumption, and thereby no doubt found it harder to squeeze profits for capital. But the fact that while the machine helps to increase production, it is a small factor in consumption, that in order to keep machine-aided production functioning at capacity, consumption must be augmented -- through better wages and shorter work time permitting the employment of more workers and thereby increased effective demand -- will not become a serious concern of capitalists generally unless labour aggressively insists on consideration of its new wage philosophy as the starting point of a new industrial policy appropriate to present day conditions.

79. The World's Dilemma[97]

Several years ago the capitalist economists were saying that all that was necessary to bring about permanent prosperity was to increase production and practise economy. Now that capitalism is once again is [in] the ditch of a depression, the advice into [is to] decrease production and purchase more goods. The contradictions of capitalism which mark it as an unstable system -- nearing its dissolution -- must be becoming apparent even to the tired worker.

Capitalism certainly gave birth to a new conception of progress. Under the impulse of its technical requirements, the progress of the natural sciences and of the art of invention have become a triumphal march of the human mind. But as a method of promoting the general prosperity of the workers it fails lamentably to live up to its own cult of efficiency.

Consider the various remedies offered by the jazz economists for the present depression, with its wide-spread unemployment. The farmers, who a few years ago were being told that their lack of prosperity was due to

[97] *Canadian Unionist*, July 1930, 21-22.

backwardness of their industry, their general inefficiency and failure to adopt improved machinery, are now being told that their only salvation is to curtail their production -- by twenty per cent., is the official advice in the United States. All sorts of manufacturers, using as raw materials the products of farms, forests, mines and fisheries, are busy working out mergers or agreements to curtail production. Trading associations seek modifications of the anti-combine laws which will legalize agreements to restrict trade. None of these proposed remedies takes account of the plight of the unemployed; they can only have the effect of diminishing the available opportunities of employment.

Some of the jazz economists like Owen D. Young[98] propose another expedient which they claim will solve the farmers' problem as well as the crisis of industrial unemployment. They argue that the industrial nations which generate new capital faster than they can profitably reinvest it should export that capital and thus enable other nations to buy more of their products. Thus the farmers and everybody else will be able to increase production and sell their surplus in export markets, if they produce cheap enough. With all the industrial and agricultural countries having big surpluses to export, the "if" is rather formidable. In any case, this device for saving capitalism implies a competition in cheapening production which would increase the pressure on wage rates and the living standards of the workers the world over.

American or Canadian capitalism cannot hope to have a successful career of foreign investments. British capitalism did flourish on foreign investments for generations. British investments overseas were for a long time [direct] allies of British export trade. When British capital began its career of overseas investments, Britain was the workshop of the world, and there were vast areas of virgin land in the temperate zones awaiting railways and settlement. Often orders for British workshops were an express condition of the use of British capital abroad. The technical superiority of British workshops for a long time assured orders for railway equipment and all kinds of machinery required by new countries. And British exports did not then have to hurdle high tariffs.

Moreover, British capitalism developed a special economy, dependent largely on imported raw materials and imported food-stuffs. And, even though for generations it had no serious competitors, it had to export a steady stream of surplus population to new lands, and hold its workers to

---

[98]McKay refers to Owen D. Young (1874-1962), who was chairman of the board of General Electric from 1922-1939 and 1942-1944, deputy chair of the Federal Reserve Bank 1927-1938, and chair of the Federal Reserve Bank, 1938-1940. He was vice-president in charge of policy at General Electric, with a particular interest in employee relations. See *Selected Addresses of Owen D. Young and Gerard Swope* (1930).

a low scale of wages in order to generate capital to invest overseas as an ally of its export trade.

American and Canadian capitalists cannot expect foreign investments to serve their export trade to anything like the same degree. They do not need to import many raw materials or food for their workers. They are not eager to export population. Their workers not needed in industrial production cannot migrate to other countries where they can take up free land and make a living under pioneer conditions.

American investments in European industry have merely increased the competition which products of American factories have to face in the world markets, and even within the American home market. Ford tractors, made in Ireland, are now being shipped to the United States. Incidentally, these American foreign markets have created a new contradiction in American capitalism. Finance capital is clamouring for tariff reductions in order that European goods, made in factories in which American capital is invested, may be sold in the United States. A new conflict of interest arises between finance capital, on the one hand, and industrial capital and labour on the other.

There is small hope of capitalism being able to escape from its dilemma by using the surplus profits of human industry to aid or subsidize the export of surplus products. And there is quite as little hope that the expedient of curtailing production will eliminate unemployment and underemployment and spread prosperity among the masses. Under previous social systems, the deficiency of production was an obvious cause of the poverty of great masses of men: workers with hand tools could not produce as much wealth as workers with machines. But under capitalism we have the curious paradox of over-production being regarded as the cause of business depressions, unemployment, and poverty -- poverty in the midst of plenty.

It is true some of the jazz economists are now shifting the burden of responsibility from over-production to "under-consumption."[99] This is merely to state the obverse of the proposition but nonetheless it throws a sort of new light and offers a new starting point for an examination of phenomena of the business cycle. If under-consumption is the cause of

---

[99] By referring to underconsumption, McKay was referring to the influential writings of J.A.Hobson (1858-1940). Hobson was an iconoclast in economic theory and one of the major forces in British social thought in the twentieth century - although hardly a "jazz economist"! In such works as *The Social Problem* (1901), *Work and Wealth* (1914), *Free Thought in the Social Sciences* (1926), and *Wealth and Life* (1929), he questioned the attempt to separate economic and political analysis from ethics. Hobson is best known today for his theory of underconsumption (developed in *The Industrial System* (1909) and *The Problem of the Unemployed* (1896)), and for his analysis -- which significantly influenced Lenin -- of imperialism (*Imperialism*, 1902).

the depression and unemployment it seems a logical conclusion that normal progress and prosperity could be restored by increasing wages and thereby the consuming power of the masses.

But men like Ford who preach the doctrine of high wages and increased purchasing power are precisely the ones whose methods and policies tend to accentuate the evils of the business cycle. Mass production and rationalization have widened the spread between production and effective consumption because the profits of the rationalized industries have increased at a greater rate than wages. In the autocar industry, the rationalized industry par excellence, fluctuations of employment are more violent than in other industries. So far, mass production and rationalization of industry have only increased the tempo of the business cycle, and all the talk of ironing-out the business cycle has proved to be wrong.

Hundreds of well organized enterprises on this continent have for some time been operating on a five-day week basis, and paying high wages, as compared with the general run of wages. But according to a survey made by the U.S. Labour Department, nearly all of them are getting as high production per worker as ever they did and have maintained or increased profits. In other words their workers are not able to buy back any larger proportion of the products they help to create than they were before. The surplus still clogs the business machine.

For well-organized industries capital has nothing to lose and labour little to gain, except more leisure, from a five-day week. In such industries as railways the adoption of a five-day week would increase employment where operations have to be carried on almost continuously. Its general adoption would doubtless increase employment in relatively backward industries temporarily. But these industries would be impelled to utilize more improved machinery and increase their technical efficiency, and would soon be reducing the number of their employees again.

So far experience seems to indicate that labour on a five-day week basis is at its maximum efficiency, and if that is going to be the general rule the five-day week cannot be a permanent solution of unemployment; it is a belated demand, already.

When capitalist economists talk of ironing-out the business cycle, what they are thinking of getting rid of is merely the anarchy of business arising from competition between capitalist enterprises. If every industry was brought under centralized control -- and this objective is being pursued with vigour through the organization of holding companies, mergers and consolidations of all sorts -- such regulation of production to demand as it would then be possible for capitalists to make would not carry the assurance of steady employment for all workers. The constant factor in the business cycle would remain, the spread between the production of the workers and their consuming power in the form of wages. The swing of the business cycle would be less pronounced, and its tempo quicker, but the surplus products which the workers cannot buy back and consume or the capitalists dissipate would still clog the business machine.

Capitalism could not carry on without the existence of a reserve army of unemployed. If there were no such army from which labour may be easily recruited, the undertaking of new enterprises requiring many men would involve the enticing of men from existing enterprises and thereby tend to jack up wages generally. Even under socialism there may be need of a reserve of unemployed; but, if so, the rights of those who may be unemployed through the exigencies of large-scale enterprise to a decent living will be fully recognized and provided for.

This fact that the modern economic system requires, in order to start big enterprises, a reserve of readily available labour, is the fundamental justification of unemployment insurance. The employers ought to bear the whole cost because they profit by the existence of a reserve of unemployed.

Whether under capitalism the workers can materially improve their position remains to be seen. Broadly, we can only hope to overcome the disorderly phenomena of the business cycle, depressions, unemployment, etc., in proportion as labour acquires a larger share of the social product. Even in so-called periods of progress and prosperity that share is all too small, and relatively there is always poverty among the workers. It is probable that as industrial consolidations tend to become monopolies even the capitalists will favour the principle of public regulation which has already been applied to railways and various other public utilities. In some cases, though not all, the dividends a public utility may pay are limited by law, and when they have accumulated a certain surplus, the rates for their services are subject to revision downwards. If the railways want to make expansions they have to show the Railway Commission that their plans are justified by good business and public convenience or need, before they can go ahead. If such a requirement had been imposed years ago the railway promoters would have had difficulty in making fortunes at the expense of the people.....

It is estimated that fraudulent promotions in the United States involve a loss of one and a quarter billion dollars a year. Great sums are also lost in promotions and expansions which, while strictly legal, have no other good purpose than to siphon capital or credit into the control of get-rich-quick financiers. Stock-watering operations, as well as flagrantly fraudulent promotions, drain away the surplus social product which should go to labour in the form of increased wages.

If capitalists developed the devices for regulating the use of capital which are already being more or less effectively applied in the case of public utilities, and if they squeezed out watered stock and limited real capital investment to a fair return of five or six per cent., and turned over the balance of the social production to labour in increased wages, the capitalist machine, under the impulse of the increased purchasing power of the workers, would function with a vigour it has never before displayed, and the capitalists would probably be able to retain their control for a long time to come without fear of revolution. But since the capitalists regard their system as the ultimate goal of evolution, and consider they have an inalienable right to all the profits they can squeeze out of the product of social labour, it is probable that they will continue their present policy of trying to persuade the workers that permanent progress and prosperity will be found just around the corner of the next blind alley.

In any case, labour should shape its policies regardless of the promises of capitalists and their political henchmen to do anything for the workers except get off their backs, and build a Labour party with the express object of capturing control of capitalist domination and [establishing] a co-operative commonwealth.

80. Can the Capitalist System Be Stabilized?[100]

"This depression is more than a passing circumstance in our history; it is a crucial turning point in industrial civilization," says *The Business Week*. "It is not too much to say that the philosophy of individual and organized private initiative upon which our business system is founded and operated, under the leadership of businessmen, economists, and engineers who have replaced the kings and statesmen of the past, is definitely on trial today, more decisively than ever before."

Organs of big business admit that there is a direct [connection] between the depression and the curtailment of purchasing power. This shows that businessmen are looking at the depression from a new angle -- for them. But while they begin to see a new light they act in the same old way; they try to solve their immediate problem by reducing wages -- that is, by curtailing purchasing power. Thus they tighten the noose that is strangling business.

Businessmen have yet to face seriously the problem of a proper distribution of purchasing power. The bourgeois economists, who are supposed to be the guides, philosophers and friends of businessmen, usually dodge the issue. Some of them attribute the deficiency in

---

[100]Originally published as "This Talk of Stabilizing," *Canadian Unionist* (January 1931), 192-193.

purchasing power to deficiency in the supply of money and credit. That on the face of it looks like a trite explanation. The masses have had to curtail buying because their supplies of money and credit have been reduced. But, at the end of the business boom, big business had no lack of money or credit; corporations were loaning their reserve funds to brokers for speculative purposes.

In the first years of the boom a great many industries were undergoing rationalization; profits were ploughed back and productive machinery improved. During this period of technical progress, large numbers of men were employed constructing bigger buildings and better machines, and there was a wide distribution of wages. But in the later years of the boom the income of the masses who spend the great bulk of their earnings on consumptive goods failed to increase as fast as the ability to produce. The consequence was that there was a production of surplus goods which the ultimate consumers could not buy. ...

But there comes a time when it becomes obvious that the streams of goods flowing into the market are too great to be sold at a profit.

Then the crisis comes. The stock market collapses, as the wiser speculators offer for sale securities the prices of which have been bid up in the hope that the streams of goods crowding into the commodity markets would be sold at a profit and so permit the producing concerns to pay high dividends. The bankers who have advanced loans to producers and merchants refuse further credits, and ask repayment of their loans. The whole machinery of production slows down, and multitudes of workers are put on part time or thrown out of work altogether. The big reductions in pay-roll are not the full measure of the reduction in purchasing power; with uncertainty ahead even those who retain good jobs skimp their purchases and increase their savings in the banks against the chance of the depression annihilating their jobs.

In this situation some of the jazz economists, stock brokers, and bond dealers say that what is needed is to increase the supply of money in circulation. This is fairly obvious. But the problem is to get money in circulation where it will function as purchasing power and lead to the consumption of the surplus commodities that now glut the markets.

"Make money abundant and cheap," says a leading Canadian financier. "That will encourage corporations to borrow for construction work." But during the latter period of the boom many corporations were loaning surplus funds to brokers at 3 per cent. or less -- on call. If during the boom these corporations could not find constructive work on which to employ their surplus funds, what chance have they to do so now when business has dried up and commodity prices have in many instances fallen below the cost of production?

If the corporations could discover new processes of production and invent new industries which would not compete with existing industries suffering from inability to see their products, then they might want to borrow money for new construction work. In such cases, they would be able to get money pretty cheap. The financier admits that there is abundant money for call and short loans on the stock exchange. Why? Would the owners of the money be content with 3 per cent. if they could find opportunities for safe investment in productive industries?

The financier admits that the case of call money is ineffective to help the stock market because the speculators have lost confidence. With money already abundant and cheap, how will making it easier help the commodity market when established industries do not want money to expand, but purchasers for their surplus products? People who are interested in stocks and bonds hardly need to borrow money to enable them to purchase consumptive goods.

It is not proposed to make money cheap and abundant in order to furnish loans to the unemployed to enable them to become consumers. That would be the last idea of the financiers. Nor to make loans to the part-time employed to enable them to maintain their former standard of living.

What the financiers want is cheap money to enable them to finance the extension of their control over industries hard pressed by the depression and ready to surrender their independence for a song. That is the real reason of the ballyhoo to the effect that all that is necessary to restore prosperity is to cheapen money. Incidentally it diverts attention from the real cause of the depression -- the spread between productive capacity and the purchasing power of the workers' wages.

That men of light and leading among the bourgeois class talk about the possibility of stabilizing business, of making capitalism function smoothly, by stabilizing the value of money, or making it cheaper or more abundant, need not impress us. If the maintenance of prosperity is so simple a matter they ought to be ashamed for allowing the depression to break out and produce so much human misery. The capitalists who cannot understand that their system is a mass of contradictions and antagonisms, have a large capacity for self-deception; they are apt to think that anything which appears to them likely to serve their particular interests will also serve the general public interests; for them the "investing public" is the real public.

"We have no real science of society," laments Benjamin Kidd.[101] Certainly the bourgeoisie have not. The professors of sociology and political economy are expected to propound theories which harmonize with the way the millionaires who endow colleges get their wealth. The professors of political economy, in their efforts to avoid facing the truth, have exhibited an intellectual ingenuity that has made their so-called science a perpetual comedy.

The capitalists who bid the workers be patient because they will lead business into the promised land of stability and normality might as well cry for the moon. The only thing that never changes is the law of change.

The ancient gentile order of society had a certain stability: it existed for ages. It contained no private property, no class divisions, no unemployment problem. The capitalist system, which contains all these things and many others of a similar nature, has only existed a little more than a century, and already the antagonisms of its parts threaten[s] its early disintegration.

Certainly capitalism has the merit of having been an amazing adventure in technical progress. But while the development of the means of production has been remarkable, thanks to the scientists and inventors, the capitalist class has not learned to manage these means of production for the good of society as a whole. The bankruptcy of management invalidates the claim of the capitalists to continued ownership of the means of production.

Primitive communism, feudalism, capitalism have succeeded one another, as improvements in the means of production made new ways of living possible. And social evolution still proceeds at an accelerated pace. Feudalism developed within itself a trading class, which took power from the feudal lords and prepared the way for the rise of the modern capitalist class. Capitalism by its mode of wealth production and distribution has developed a class unknown in any previous social order -- the wage-receiving class. This class, a new creation, has an historic

---

[101]McKay refers to Benjamin Kidd, *Social Evolution* (London: Macmillan, 1894), 1: "Despite the great advances which science has made during the past century in almost every other direction, there is, it must be confessed, no science of society properly so called." Benjamin Kidd (1858-1916) was a largely self-educated intellectual whose *Social Evolution* argued that religion was required to compel individual selfishness to be subordinated to the common good, the fundamental trait of moral progress. This was one of the most influential and popular guides to "social evolution" in the late nineteenth century. Within a dozen years of its publication, the book had gone through three editions and seventeen reprints. It was still being used by the Workers' Educational Association as late as 1921. Kidd also wrote *The Principles of Western Civilization* (1902), *Individualism and After* (1908), and *The Science of Power* (1918).

mission, the creation of a new society. Arthur W. Pinero,[102] a British dramatist second only to Bernard Shaw, put in the mouth of one of his characters, *Agnes*, in reply to an aristocratic debauchée who had ridiculed her interest in the working class, the following:

"The toilers, the sufferers, the great crowd of old and young stamped by excessive labour,... those from whom a fair share of earth's space and sunshine are withheld,... who are bidden to stand with their feet in the gutter to watch gay processions in which you and your kind are borne high. Those who would strip the robes from a dummy aristocracy and cast the broken dolls into the limbo of a nation's discarded toys. Those who -- mark me -- are already on the highway, marching, marching: whose time is coming as surely as yours is going!"[103]

More and more the working class realizes that social ownership and control of the means of production offers the only way out of the morass of capitalism, with its disorderly business cycle, and poverty in the midst of abundance. More and more the working class begins to realize the greatness of its task. In all capitalist countries, and in face of great difficulties, it gathers strength for the achievement of its historic mission -- the abolition of class society, the emancipation of humanity.

That accomplished, man, as Engels remarked, will emerge from mere animal conditions of existence into really human ones. "The whole sphere of the conditions of life which environ man will come under the dominion and control of man, who for the first time will thus become the

---

[102]Sir Arthur Wing Pinero (1855-1934) was a British playwright who took as his special theme relationships between men and women of the middle and upper classes; he had twenty years of success, but his plays were considered dated by the postwar generation of theatre-goers and performers, and are rarely performed today. *The Notorious Mrs. Ebbsmith* opened in the Garrick Theatre on 13 March 1895. Note *The Social Plays of Arthur Wing Pinero*, 4 vols., ed. by Clayton Hamilton (1917-1922).

[103]McKay is quoting from Arthur W. Pinero, *The Notorious Mrs. Ebbsmith: A Drama in Four Acts* (Boston, 1895), 80-81: "AGNES. [*With changed manner, flashing eyes, harsh voice, and violent gestures.*] The sufferers, the toilers; that great crowd of old and young -- old and young stamped by excessive labour and privation all of one pattern -- whose backs bend under burdens, whose bones ache and grow awry, whose skins, in youth and age, are wrinkled and yellow; those from whom a fair share of the earth's space and of the light of day is withheld. [*Looking down upon him fiercely.*] The half-starved who are bidden to stand with their feet in the kennel to watch gay processions in which you and your kind are borne high. Those who would strip the robes from a dummy aristocracy and cast the broken dolls into the limbo of a nation's discarded toys. Those who -- mark me! -- are already upon the highway, marching, marching; whose time is coming as surely as yours is going!"

real, conscious lord of nature, because he has become master of his own social organization."[104]

81. The Failure of Competition[105]

The harshest indictment of the competitive system is not that it is productive of disorderly phenomena, such as unemployment and poverty in the midst of opulence. The present economic system is really no system at all, but a chaos of conflicting interests, a maze of disharmonies. Competitive private enterprise results in an enormous waste of many of the things it produces -- [a] waste of factories as well as of consumptive goods, even if society periodically suffers from "over-production." But that is not the worst of it. The gravest indictment of the commanding class of existing society is that it has failed lamentably to realize its opportunities. Consider the marvellous forms and forces of wealth-production science and invention have placed at the disposal of the owners of industry; then consider the uses they have made of them. They had the opportunity to build a noble and stately civilization, to provide the masses with a high standard of living, and leisure to cultivate the graces of life. But considering its opportunities the present commanding class has proved itself the most aimless and incapable class that ever held the helm of society. Their spiritual advisers have thundered from the pulpits, "Thou shalt not kill;" but they have drenched the earth with blood spilled in sordid struggles for power, property, and profits.

In the youth of their class they professed high ideals; but they have not realized one of them. They boast of the progress of society under that rule, but what progress there has been, especially in social amelioration, has been made in spite of them; they resisted factory laws, reductions in the hours of labour, pure food laws, every step in social advance.

It is frequently asserted, as a reason why workers should not expect increasing wages, that 50 per cent or more of business concerns do not pay dividends even in prosperous times. That is probably right. If the big fish do not always swallow the little fish, they at any rate swallow so much of the alimentary matter that the little fish do not get enough to grow fat. The multiplication of enterprises, needlessly competing with one another,

---

[104]McKay is citing and slightly modifying Frederick Engels, *Socialism: Utopian and Scientific*, Part III: "The whole sphere of the conditions of life which environ man, and which have hitherto ruled man, now comes under the dominion and control of man, who for the first time becomes the real, conscious lord of nature, because he has now become master of his own social organisation." See Engels, *Socialism: Utopian and Scientific* (New York: International Publishers, 1968 [1935]), 72. This was a very popular book for "scientific socialists," and was based on excerpts from Engels's *Anti-Duhring*.

[105]*Canadian Unionist*, April 1932, 192-193.

means tremendous waste, and it is not surprising that many business concerns, which still remain exposed to the rigours of competition, manage merely to keep afloat. Certain key industries come more and more to dominate all the rest, and are able to siphon the bulk of profits into their coffers....

During the Great War, when tens of millions of men were withdrawn from productive work, most of the nations maintained their workers on a better standard of living than ever before. Why? Because the state practically took over the direction of the major forces of production and assumed a large measure of control over distribution. It overruled private initiative at countless points, and, to a large extent, suspended the competitive struggle. The state allotted manpower where most needed, and prohibited the use of manpower in many unessential occupations....

Under competitive private enterprise increasing efficiency has produced a new phenomenon, labelled by the economists "technological unemployment." The workers therefore have no reason for enthusiasm for efficiency. It threatens their employment. And it results in the capitalists' restricting output -- adopting *ca'canny,* a high misdemeanour when practised by the workers.

But given a planned economy, with production for the use of the many instead of the profit of the few, increased efficiency would mean a greater share of good things for everybody, fewer hours of work and more leisure for intellectual and aesthetic pursuits -- now beyond the means and time of most workers.

82. The "Ruling Class" Does Not Rule[106]

The very serious situation which confronts us should be regarded as a challenge to human ingenuity and moral courage -- not a reason for counsels of defeatism. Progress will be served, but unless men in high places in politics and business show a better quality of leadership than they have in the past three years, the mounting volume of human misery, of thwarted hopes and ambitions, may result in a social explosion likely to be followed by a period of anarchy and confusion worse confounded. Our society is in a vicious circle driven about by prejudices. If it will not develop the vision and the moral courage to step out of it, and replace the so-called natural laws by rational laws -- if it will not call into play the intellectual abilities and moral qualities needed to substitute a planned economy for the present chaos of competitive enterprise -- then history is more than likely to swing the lash of revolution again. But society, without a plunge into worse disorders than now afflict many of its members,

---

[106]Originally published as "A Problem for Canadians," *Canadian Railway Employees' Monthly,* June 1933, 87.

should be able to make a new start along the avenue of progress and prosperity which science and invention has opened up.

Census returns show that, out of 2,564,879 salaried and wage workers in Canada on June 1, 1931, the number "not at work" was 471,668 or 18.6 per cent. The number classified as totally unemployed was 392,809. Making allowance for the changes in the employment index and in population, the number "not at work" in September, 1932, would be 883,000, and the number of "totally unemployed", 732,000....

The claim that Canada must wait upon progress in other countries to get rid of the evil of unemployment, is a shameless evasion. Let us admit that, to maintain a high standard of living, it will be necessary to exchange a large amount of Canadian products for foreign products that serve the requirements of the people. But in a country like Canada, with its varied resources and small population possessed of high technical knowledge and skill, getting rid of unemployment and providing everybody with an opportunity to earn a livelihood are surely tasks that can be accomplished, independently of what other countries may be doing....

In Canada, we have political freedom, but what does it amount to without economic freedom? And certainly our society is not one in which economic freedom prevails. In our society the system of production has the mastery over men instead of being controlled by them. Surely the capitalists did not will this depression. And if they could not prevent it, then they as well as the workers are but puppets of the forces of production -- slaves of the economic machine. Though the capitalists own the means of production, the economic machine, they are not its masters; they do not control it. Though the capitalists constitute an owning class, they are not a real ruling class.

There you have a fact, a condition, that is an affront to human dignity -- that ought to be regarded as a challenge to the capitalist class and every other class of men. Like Frankenstein, men have created a monster of which they are the victims; the creature is the master of the creators. It is an absurd situation. And in the face of the challenge of it, what are the leaders of the so-called ruling class doing? Some are talking about money reform and inflation, as if the printing of symbols of value adds to the sum total of real values in existence or changes the ownership of real values! Others are talking of the redeeming virtues, on the one hand, of free trade, and on the other, of protection. Our Labour economists tell us that free trade is as of much interest to the workers as the manner of the dressing is to a roast goose. There is and usually has been free trade between the nations in complementary products; nations do not impose tariffs on goods they cannot produce at home, except for revenue purposes, and then only on luxuries: a recognized mode of taxing the consumer which is not regarded as an undue interference with trade.

If all tariff barriers were cast down, what then? The free traders assume that it would lead to... a big interchange of goods. But most countries have now developed similar industries and are producing surpluses of similar kinds of goods. Most countries want to export similar surpluses. And there's the rub! Free trade might permit countries with low production costs and low wages to sell more goods at the expense of countries with higher wages. But world trade -- the sum total of both international and domestic trade -- would not be increased: and as all countries would have to reduce wages to the level of the successful competitor, world-purchasing power generally would be reduced, and the business world, and the workers, would soon be in a worse state than before.

Our Labour economists, therefore, recognize tariffs as a necessity, if only a necessary evil. Not only are they necessary as a means of providing some protection for standards of living. More recently they have become necessary as a means of protecting national currencies, of regulating the balance of trade so as to avoid a complete collapse of the foreign exchange value of a nation's currency. But while we are fated to maintain protective tariffs for some time yet, we know very well that tariffs, high or low, cannot solve the problem of unemployment.

The problem that confronts Canada can be solved only by Canadians. A shrinkage of about three billions in Canadian purchasing cannot be fully explained by a shrinkage of about half a billion in export trade. Domestic maladjustments are much bigger causes of our troubles than dislocation of international trade or international finance.

83. The Taboo of Property Rights[107]

Great are the taboos of Parliament Hill. If a matter comes up that involves even a slight questioning of the sanctity of the rights of private property, most of the M.P.'s begin to bristle like angry boars and the chamber becomes surcharged with feeling. Very few of the members elected by the old parties have risen above the ways of thinking and feeling of the peasant and the petit bourgeois. Even the leaders talk of the rights of property and the virtues of individualism in the language of a past era -- the era of individual ownership of property created by the labour of the proprietor. The persistence of the peasant and petit bourgeois attitude to property is a tribute to the power of taboos to retard the progress of culture among the so-called cultured classes.

It requires no great intelligence to perceive that the development of capitalism has produced a property form differing widely from individual private property. But the old line politicians mostly think and act as

[107]Originally published as "Most Canadian M.P.'s Bristle Like Porcupines When Property Rights Are Discussed," *O.B.U.Bulletin*, 13 April 1933.

though the property relations in which machine production is carried on were precisely the same as the property relations in which the individual hand-tool production was carried on. Yet it is plain enough that the important and powerful form of property today is capitalist-class property -- not private property.

Stocks and bonds are titles to revenues; their holders have no rights of private property in the enterprises on which the issues of stocks and bonds are based; they cannot put their hands on a brick or a cog and say, "this is my private property." And generally speaking, stock and bond holders have little or no control over "their property."

A recent investigation in the United States revealed that only 6 per cent of the corporate wealth was under the control of the owners; that is, persons owning more than one-half of the stocks outstanding. In the case of 58 per cent of corporate wealth the management was independent of the stockholders, by virtue of the wide dispersion of stocks. In the case of 22 per cent of the corporate wealth, legal devices -- non-voting stock and holding companies -- had removed control from the vast majority of owners. And 14 per cent of the corporate wealth was controlled by minority stock interests.

Capitalist property has largely replaced private property, and the ability of a few manipulators to control capitalist property has permitted wild abuses. In many enterprises the original investors, and often a series of investors, have had their titles to revenues robbed of all value....

Capitalist property has been the outcome of an historical process -- the expropriation of the individual producers of the handicrafts era from their means of production, and then the expropriation of many small capitalists by the big capitalists -- a process accompanied by the most outrageous forms of trickery, fraud, vandalism, and war. Yet for an institution having such ignoble origin, having the character of a ruthless plunderbund, old line politicians bespeak the tender solicitude once bestowed on private property founded on the individual labour of the proprietor. And why? If the politicians are really intelligent, the only explanation is that they are determined to serve their masters, the beneficiaries of privilege, to the best of their ability.

In that case, they are insincere and unscrupulous -- indifferent to the human interests of the people. It is, of course, possible that they are stupid and sincere; that they imagine that in defending capitalist property they are defending private property.....

84. Capitalism's Fatal Defect[108]

Marx conceded to capitalism the possibility of a long life through the export of capital to backward countries and their development under some form of imperialistic overlordship. Not so long ago China was regarded as a boundless field of investment for the surplus profits of the older capitalist countries.

But political and economic developments have greatly foreshortened the prospects of capitalism, drawing fresh strength and new leases of life from the exploitation of backward countries. Rising political nationalism in the backward countries is not friendly to money imperialism. The backward countries blithely default on interest payments and adopt forms of state capitalism that cramp the style of foreign-owned enterprises.

The greed of the investment bankers led them to overplay the game of investment in the backward countries. Confidence has been so shaken that it would be necessary to breed another generation of saps and suckers to enable the bankers to mobilize large sums for investment in the "backward countries."

Then all the nations are driven by their financial necessities to restrict imports; and, in proportion as they succeed in that, they also restrict exports. And, as all nations seek to get a stranglehold on more gold, they cannot export capital except in the form of a surplus of exports over imports. Capitalism is thus involved in a vicious circle; every move it makes to get out only increases its difficulties. Its hope of a long life through the export of capital to less developed countries has become a vain illusion.

For that, the world may thank, in large part, the amazing development of the role of money in the present day scheme. A commodity producing society cannot exist without a money commodity; and, thanks to the machine, the production of commodities in general proceeds much faster than the production of the money-commodity -- gold. The necessity of a money-commodity is the fatal defect of capitalism -- fatal in the sense that all the contradictions of the system of commodity production manifest themselves as monetary phenomena and thus impress themselves upon the consciousness of men. The fundamental contradiction of commodity production is that between the ever-expanding means of production and the ever-decreasing capacity of the workers, the constantly increasing proportion of the population, to buy back the goods they produce. This contradiction shows itself in a comparatively new form as an increasing disparity between money of

[108] *O.B.U.Bulletin*, 28 December 1933.

account and real money; and, men being money conscious, even the directors of the Bank of England are worried about it.

A few generations ago real money was used in practically all transactions. Not until the building of railways, the pioneer type of the modern corporation, made it necessary to collect scattered funds and concentrate them in banks, so they could be placed at the disposal of capitalists, did bank money begin to come in general use. Bank money, or money of account, consists of the banks' own resources and of the deposits of capitalists who make transfers to one another on the books of the banks by means of written orders or checks. It includes also the savings accounts of the workers, but they form a very small proportion of money of account.

The big development of money of account has been coeval with the rise of corporations, and it was not until about 1865 that England passed the Company Act limiting the liability of stockholders. At the time of Confederation bank money in Canada only amounted to $70,000,000. In 1929 it had increased to approximately 3 billions, on a base of about $123,000,000 of real money. During the present depression it has shrunk by over half a billion -- a portent for the next depression. And the government had to suspend the gold standard to save the banks from serious difficulties.

If capitalism gets out of the present depression, learning nothing more than it has up to the present, it will in a few years plunge into a worse convulsion. And the social faith in the solvency of the money system, so badly shaken in this depression, may be shattered in the next.

And how save the banking system from a persistent demand of depositors for their money? The government may empower the banks to pay their debts in "fiat" money. But printing something on scraps of paper and calling it "lawful money" could only delay bankruptcy a few months.

The state now issues token money, paper promises to pay in gold. But the amount of token money that can be put in circulation without promoting social insolvency is limited by the economic laws governing a society of commodity producers. The law governing the issue of paper money is that it must not exceed the amount of gold which would actually circulate if not replaced by symbols of gold.

Increasing the issue of paper money above that amount will not add one cent to the value of the current money in circulation. Issue of fiat money to pay the banks' debts to depositors would merely depreciate the value of money. Germany's experiences with inflation would be repeated. Prices would leap upward; what the producer gained as a seller he would lose as a buyer. The relations of debtors and creditors would be changed. Some new classes would gain control of real property; most people would be poorer.

Capitalism survived that experience in Germany because the other capitalist nations took measures to restore the financial system there. But in the next depression all capitalist nations will be in the same boat; none will be able to help save the other.

Moratoriums will be declared, but they can only provide a respite, not a solution. Nothing can stop paper money from becoming worthless. And the ownership of mills and factories will also become valueless; their owners cannot utilize them without money to pay wages. Real money, gold, will have gone into hiding, as a provision against pressing needs. The bankruptcy of capitalism will be complete.

Then it will be the mission of labour to organize society as a conscious economic organism and take over the control of the machinery of production in the general interest. Then the production and circulation of the means of sustaining life will become the function of a definite social organ -- the workers' economic union -- and production will be regulated in accordance with social needs. The stage of social consciousness will at last be reached and man will take conscious control of evolution -- become master of his fate. If the capitalists have the effrontery to ask compensation they will be paid in the money which their incompetence rendered worthless.

85. Under-consumption: A World Problem[109]

There should be no problem of malnutrition in Canada "except from the foolishness of man or the futility of administrators."

This statement was made by Lieut.-Col. J.H.Woods of Calgary, head of the recent Canadian delegation to the Assembly of the League of Nations. Mr. Woods was speaking in support of a proposal made by Stanley Bruce of Australia and backed by Great Britain, calling on the League to undertake an inquiry into the problem of why markets were glutted while many people were unable to procure sufficient food. This paradox has become an affront to whatever public conscience there may be the world over; and to throw light on its causes and recommend ways & means of removing them is an appropriate task for the League of Nations. The League has spiritual purposes -- the development of a world consciousness and a world conscience. But the realization of such purposes will be retarded until the world is assured a full belly. The maxim of the Salvation Army contains more truth than poetry. If there was an inherent contradiction between the spiritual and the material, the universe would

[109] *Canadian Unionist*, November 1935, 161-162.

be a house divided against itself. That idea is indeed acceptable to certain members of the ruling class who consider themselves superior to common folk, and lack the feeling of a common humanity which engenders the sense of social responsibility. These supermen who feel themselves above social obligations to their fellows which conflict with their personal interests accept that idea because it appears to justify the division of human society into classes. But if conscience is a spiritual force, it is also a social instinct which is usually dormant until some objective stimulus gives it occasion to assert its authority. This is certainly true of that complex of feelings, thoughts, and emotions which is called the public conscience. And what would be more calculated to arouse the public conscience than a world-wide inquiry into the problem of why, in the midst of markets glutted with foodstuffs, many people suffer from a deficiency of food?

In the discussion of this problem in the League of Nations Assembly, Mr. Woods brought out a point which seems fundamental, a pivotal point upon which any satisfactory solution of the problem must hinge. He spoke of the need, the importance of a balanced diet. He remarked that it was one of the ironies of the depression that in Canada many persons were now relatively better nourished than before. Men in construction camps had been provided with a balanced and complete diet, in consequence of which many had greatly improved their health. In Canadian cities the study of dietetics in connection with public relief had spread a knowledge of standard diets, the adoption of which by families on relief and other families on reduced budgets had, in many cases, resulted in improved health.

While these results may have offered some reason for gratification, Mr. Woods rightly considered them an ironic reflection upon our civilization. Unfortunately, there have been other results. Many families have lacked the knowledge or means -- in too many instances the latter -- to provide diets making for improvement in health. Even in Ottawa, which has probably suffered less from the depression than most other Canadian communities, an appalling number of cases of malnutrition have been reported among school children. And even the return of such prosperity as we have known in the past would not eliminate the whole problem of malnutrition, Mr. Woods observed.

If the much-desired edifice of a balanced economy is to be built, the starting point, the corner-stone, will need to be an estimate of the quantities of the different kinds of foodstuffs required to provide the people of a nation with a balanced diet. Without imposing a standard diet upon everybody, such estimates could be accurate within reasonable limits; the law of averages working over a large number of cases discounts the individual divergences.

Implicit in the proposal that the distribution of foodstuffs should be considered as a problem of achieving a balanced diet for the people is the question of the obligations of the food producers. Assume we have reliable estimates of the foods needed for a complete and balanced diet within the nation; also of the foodstuffs which can be profitably exported. Assume further that means have been found to provide all the people with all the purchasing power needed to procure a balanced diet. Can we then assume, as the Social Credit mystics do, that the problem of achieving a balanced economy would have been solved?

Suppose each food producer insists on his right to pursue his individual bent -- to produce what he likes, trusting to luck to sell it. That is the ideal of liberty which food producers have pursued in the past; it has always turned out to be a will-o'-the-wisp, leading them into a morass of glutted markets, unprofitable prices, mortgages, and fear of foreclosure. They have embraced an ideal of liberty which turned into a vampire of wretched servitude. And why? Because society will not pay for socially unnecessary labour. Produce supplies in excess of effective demand, and society, through its market mechanism, reduces the prices it pays to the producers. Thus notice is served upon the producers that a part of their labour was socially unnecessary. But the consequences do not end there. These producers who have wasted a part of their labour have less money to expend upon the goods of other producers, who in turn have less to spend on the goods of other producers, and so on.

Producers of food and other commodities whose production is greater than the effective demand set in motion the depressive forces which run in a vicious circle.

No doubt in existing society our difficulties arise less from over-production than under-consumption, from a lack of effective demand, that is of purchasing power, in the hands of the masses.... But in any form of society the economic law of supply and demand will continue to hold good. Even if everybody has purchasing power to satisfy his demand for particular goods, there might still be over-production of such goods; and such over-production would tend to general economic upset -- would become the starting point of forces of depression running in a vicious circle. Don't accept our word for it; think it over. For, if the economic law of supply and demand must be reckoned with in any form of society, then there is no escaping from the conclusion of our industrial unionists that a balanced economy can be achieved only by the conscious social planning by organs of society created for that purpose. It is precisely at this point that the philosophy of industrial unionism finds itself fundamentally at issue with Social Credit mysticism which does not recognize the need of economic planning for social ends, but merely, without knowing it, rings the changes on the monetary reform notions of the Utopian Socialism which arose in England after the first great industrial depression in 1823 -- more than a century ago.

iii. An Army of False Prophets

86. Equitist Plans and Bourgeois Speculations[110]

The so-called Equitist plan is one of those speculations which the bourgeois mind likes to play with. It predicates the existence of a Utopia, in which the master class will voluntarily surrender its control of the means of production, and the efficient worker be content with the same as the inefficient worker.

Utopia is a pleasant place,
But how shall I get there?
Straight across the corner,
And right around the square.

The Equitist doubtless will understand the logic of that jingle. It expresses the militant workers' view of magic carpet methods of reaching millennium. The power of capital, which rests on ownership of the means of production, cannot be exorcised by the geni of Alladin's lamp. The Equitist would first have to capture the government and construct a new order of society before they could put their plan in operation; and when the mass of the people develop intelligence and energy enough to do that, they will probably devise an even better plan of measuring services to society.

The Equitist plan may be the result of a reconstruction of the social order; it can never be a cause.

So long as the capitalists own the means of production and control the product they can beat any plan based on changes in the symbols of exchange values. And they are not going to be so foolish as to surrender their power of ownership until the working class is politically all powerful.

As for abolishing war by taking the profits out of it by conscripting wealth as well as men! That appears to have some merit; but, as those who propose it, only would put it in effect for the duration of the war, it is still a half-baked action. After the war Germany converted her internal war bonds into worthless paper; she conscripted wealth by wholesale. But the net result was the big capitalists vastly increased their power over wealth, and the German workers were reduced to a condition that could not very

---

[110]Originally published as an untitled letter, *Labor World/Le Monde Ouvrier*, 25 July 1925.

well be worse. You can't have capitalist ownership of the means of production, and abolish profits.

87. Illusions of the Equitists[111]

Having frequently enjoyed the interesting articles of Spirea, in your paper, I was interested in his observations on the Equitist Plan. But I suspect that anybody that can apply the pruning knife of good-humored satire to the tree of knowledge of this generation with his facile cleverness is accustomed to wandering with his head among the stars, and does not have his feet on the earth often enough.

As intimated before, the Equitist Plan seems to me too Utopian to either commend or denounce. What I object to is that some of its advocates put it forward as a complete panacea, possessed of all sorts of magic virtues -- a means to an end, when it plainly enough predicates a Utopia. Men have been imagining Utopias since the dawn of time. No doubt Utopias have an inspirational value; but their practical influence upon the evolution of human society is not very clear. The greatest Utopian, the greatest idealist, preached peace on earth and good will among men, but that did not prevent his "followers" staging the greatest war in history and invoking his blessing upon their efforts.

The Equitist Plan seems to me to be an individualist method of dealing with a problem of a collective character. It may be workable when society has entered the stage of anarchy which Prince Kropotkin[112] thought might be reached after mankind had been trained for generations in a socialist or collectivist order. And not until the stage of anarchy is reached will one hour of one man's time be considered as good as one hour of any other man's time. Wherein lies the equity in denying extra compensation for skill? The technician, or craftsman spends years to acquire skill, and is surely entitled to more pay than the unskilled labourer.

Society would have to be very purposefully organized to assure that equal payment for an hour's work would be equity. Supermen would be required to order the occupations of men. Inventors would have to give bonds that they would really invent something useful, after perhaps years of labour.

If men were equal in skill and energy and willingness to labour, equality of payment might spell equity. But men, being unequal in capacity and

---

[111]Originally published as an untitled letter, *Labor World/Le Monde Ouvrier*, 8 August 1925.

[112]Prince Peter Kropotkin was a renowned nineteenth-century Russian anarchist, author, and Spencerian.

inclination for service to society, equity requires payment proportionate to service rendered.

A collectivist regime would not be much of an improvement on capitalism, if it sought to establish equality of payment. Any kind of society which does not offer rewards to ability and energy would soon become stagnant. Under collectivism there will doubtless be differences in the rewards of managers and men, though not so great, as now. But on top of these different payments there would be a distribution of what is now more or less loosely called the surplus product -- that extra product -- which is guaranteed by associated labour, and which is now divided among the capitalists. Organization will doubtless greatly increase this generation of surplus product, and since it is the result of co-operative effort equity will require that it be divided equally among all workers.

That is the problem of the future; and I cannot see that making one man's labour for an hour equal to any other man's labour for an hour offers a solution.

88. Monetary or Credit Reform Schemes Illusory[113]

Of the making of Utopias through schemes to create new forms of money, or place money and credits under public control, there is no end. In periods of transition, when the control of economic power is passing from one class to another by processes generally little understood, proponents of schemes for reforming monetary systems and thereby eliminating the "root" of all social evils are always numerous. Doubtless it is a healthy sign that some people should endeavor to work out ideal monetary systems. Adventures in idealism are always interesting; but their practical value is problematical. Is the labour movement any stronger today, or the working class any nearer their emancipation from the wage system, because Bellamy[114] painted an ideal state of society in *Equality*, or Charles Sheldon[115] wrote *What Would Jesus Do?* [?]

Those who control the money and credit of a nation undoubtedly control a certain power over the nation's activities; *but the control of the symbol*

---

[113]*Canadian Railroad Employees' Monthly*, August 1925, 157-159.

[114]Edward Bellamy's (1850-1898) most famous work was *Looking Backward 2000-1887* ([1887] 1926), which he wrote after studying law and a career in journalism. His utopian novel inspired many imitators, and converted thousands in North America to socialist ideals.

[115]Charles Monroe Sheldon (1857-1946) was one of the most famous of the advocates of the Social Gospel in the United States, whose works had a marked impact in Canada. Among his titles are *In His Steps: 'What Would Jesus Do?'* ([1897]n.d.); *The Miracle of Markham: How Twelve Churches Became One* (Toronto, 1899); and *The Mere Man and His Problems* (1924).

of wealth is not by any means the same thing as the control of the means of wealth production. If public control of credits, or any scheme of currency reform, will produce the happy results predicted by those who exalt the importance of the symbol of wealth the labour movement is superfluous. Whatever form of property is most powerful will dominate monetary policy -- today it is stocks and bonds.

Suppose Canada nationalized its banking system to-morrow. That would place credit under "public control." But under capitalism the "public" is the possessing class. Nationalization of the banks might help the smaller bourgeoisie, although there is no guarantee that it would do so. It might possibly, if the government of the day was able to defy the great capitalists and grant ready credits to the small bourgeoisie, start one of those eras of "progress and prosperity", but relatively the position of the wage-earner, the worker without property, would not be improved. While the government is merely an executive committee of the capitalist class, public ownership or public control are only synonyms for state capitalism, and until the wage earners are in measurable distance of developing sufficient political power to control the government, it is largely a waste of energy on their part to work for the "public control" of the mere symbol of wealth -- money.

During the war Britain and Canada came as near "public control" of banks and credits, as it would be possible to do in any country where the government is controlled by the capitalist class. By government fiat, credits were created and made available to the "public." But it was not these credits that created the demand for goods; it was the insatiable maw of the war. During this period when bank credit was under government control, production was augmented and labour well employed. But did not prices advance faster than the rate of wages -- except perhaps in a few trades where labour was strongly organized, or where other exceptional circumstances gave labour an advantage? Generally, price increases kept well in advance of wages. The workers only benefitted, because they worked overtime, or had steady employment compared with employment in what is called normal times. But during the period of "public control" of credits the capitalist class made absolutely and relatively much greater gains than the working class....

In the realm of money there are possibilities, particularly in Canada, which should interest the wage workers; not because they offer panaceas for the workers' troubles, but because the sooner the capitalist system completes its natural evolution the sooner it will be ripe for conversion into the co-operative commonwealth. The amalgamation of industrial capital with money capital or high finance is one of the most conspicuous phenomenon of the times. And where the financial capitalist dominates industry, ousting from control the old type of industrial capitalist, we see a tendency to develop conditions such as exist in Cape Breton.

An industrial capitalist may be defined as the owner of an industry, or better still as the managing owner; he exploits workers and draws a profit, but he understands the industry he controls, takes a personal pride in the reputation of its products, knows a lot of his workers, regards many of them as persons, and is proud of the fact that many have served with him for years.

The money capitalist, on the other hand, is not interested directly or personally in industry; he draws his income from bonds or stocks in an enterprise of which he has no technical knowledge -- which possibly he has never seen. He is a new type of the ancient usurer. He lends money, not only to individuals, but to capitalist managers of industries, institutions and governments. The interests of these two types of capitalists are not identical; in fact there is an antagonism between them similar to that which exists between the industrialist and the landlord. The industrial capitalists' profits are reduced by the interest he often has to pay on borrowed capital; just as his profits are reduced by the rents he often has to pay the landlord, or by the additional wage necessary to enable his workers to pay the landlord for places to live.

Politically, also, the money capitalist and the industrial capitalist are often at variance. The great financiers favour a strong governmental power, independent of parliament and the people; they can control such a power either as bondholders or through personal and social influences. They generally support a forcible policy in external and domestic affairs and favour militarism; they are not afraid of war and public debts, because lending money to governments is good business, and they are always eager for government contracts which their influence enables them to obtain, and which they usually sub-let to industrial capitalists.

The industrial capitalist, on the other hand, has little use for militarism, war and public debts. They spell for him high taxes and increased cost of production. As we see in Canada to-day the industrialist is heavily taxed, while the money capitalist has huge investments in tax free war bonds; the industrial capitalist cannot control the government so easily as the money capitalist; hence he favors a strong parliament, rather than an all-powerful government.

When the financial capitalist is in the saddle we have suppressions of free speech, use of the military to over-awe strikers, legislative prohibition of the teaching of evolution, and an arbitrary attitude to any questioning of things as they are. The industrial capitalist, on the other hand, stands for temporizing policies; compromise by reforms and unemployment doles; the pacific methods of divide and rule, or of control by carefully camouflaged corruption....

...[W]hile the capitalist class control the means of production and thereby the products of associated labour, while the power of stocks and bonds and other property titles to wealth production is supported by the political, legal, and military arms of the state and by social custom, that class will be able to control in its own interest the most ingenious system of money or credit. *The only way in which labour can escape from the thraldom of capital is to conquer first the political power of the state;* the citadel of the economic power of capital. Once it has obtained political power and learned to use it; once it has taken possession of the means of production, money as a symbol of wealth will cease to have its apparent present importance, and the problem of devising a method or medium to assure an equitable distribution of wealth will not present serious difficulties.

89. The Insufficiency of Monetary Reform Plans[116]

...For the capitalists, and especially the small bourgeoisie, the economic world swarms with mysteries. The power of credit, the fact that a bank note holds within itself a social force far beyond its material consequences prepares the bourgeois mind for a belief in the existence of a mystical power operating without regard to realities.... It would be unreasonable to expect the capitalists to surrender their privileges; it would be stupid for the workers to rely on some act of grace to give them an equitable share of the world's wealth.

The theory that capitalism by a simple change in one of its organs could abolish all exploitation of labour is hardly tenable. The medium of exchange is not even a vital organ, as a dozen wars and the truck system have shown....

With the idealism of the Equitists I have no quarrel, any more than with the Golden Rule. Still Socrates, whose good intent was beyond question, developed a philosophy which eventually furnished the Grecian aristocratic reaction with its most potent intellectual weapon against the Athenian democracy, and helped destroy the most promising experiment in civilization of ancient times. The idealist dualism of the modern bourgeois world has the same metaphysical character; it is necessary to enable the ruling class to find some justification for their position in a social order where they are bewildered by the necessity of conducting their affairs in ways that clash with the current notions of justice and honesty, and to assign unknowable causes to economic and social phenomena which they do not wish to understand. And this idealist dualism dominates the minds of many workers, for whom the contradiction between the ethical professions and practices of their masters are equally bewildering and for whom the recurrences of

---

[116]*Canadian Railroad Employees Monthly*, November 1925, 223-225.

depressions appear as inexplicable events brought about by mysterious powers brutally indifferent to their hardships....

The Equitists have got hold of an important truth -- the truth that since men began to produce commodities for exchange in an impersonal market, instead of just for consumption in common among the tribe, they lost control of their products. With the advent of power machinery man has ceased to be master of his mode of production, and new forces have arisen out of social conditions more terrible than the forces of nature. The individual labourer is only one part in the whole process of social production. Even the powerful capitalists cannot always accomplish what they aim [for]; a mass of commodities invades their market and smashes their business. The capitalists propose, but a social power, stronger than them, disposes; this power is a blind force, the resultant of the labour of numerous producers without regard to the purchasing power of the market. The social co-operation which produces this potent social force is concealed behind the competitive struggle of individuals or corporations. Social and personal interests clash; the individual is at war with society....

Only labour can solve this social problem, and put this social terror in the limbo where science has sent the forces of nature that terrified primitive man. Only labour can do this, because its interests are finally the interests of society as a whole; because the self-preservation of the worker grows with the progress of society, and not with the prosperity of a limited class. It is not a question of labour possessing special virtues or greater humanity; it is a mere question of labour adapting itself to material necessity, although the conquering of the control of this social power, which vexes and alarms the capitalists will be accomplished by a spiritual revolution such as mankind has never experienced....

90. Is the Gold Standard to Blame?[117]

It is said that the gold standard has failed. Even a number of alleged statesmen are saying that. When statesmanship is confronted with national problems it is unable or unwilling to solve, it tries to divert attention by creating a bogey in the international field. In the past, governments, sorely beset by domestic troubles, have deliberately provoked foreign wars.

The old recipe of state-craft is not practical just now; but the quarrels about the gold standard may lead to a bigger and better war.

What has failed is, of course, capitalism. At times when the capitalist system worked more or less smoothly, nobody worried about the gold standard.

---

[117] *Canadian Railway Employees Monthly*, January 1932, 4.

Gold has been chosen as the commodity best suited as money. Bank notes, silver and copper coins are deputies of gold, in all gold standard countries.

It served in the following ways:
(1) As a measure of value -- a means of estimating the value of other commodities. It is a measure of value because it is recognized as the social incarnation of human labour.
(2) As a standard of price -- as a fixed weight of precious metal. The standard of prices measures quantities of gold by a unit quantity of gold. A ten-dollar gold piece always contains ten times the quantity of gold in a dollar gold piece.
(3) As a medium of exchange of commodities, services, bonds, stocks, etc.
(4) As a means of accumulation or hoarding, in bank accounts as well as in the miser's secret hiding place....

The collapse of capitalist prosperity cannot be ascribed to the gold standard, or the United States, with plenty of gold, would have continued to enjoy prosperity. The real cause lies in the bad planning and bad management of national industries -- above all, in the obvious impossibility of keeping industry operating to capacity when the masses of workers are not given sufficient wages to buy back a proper share of the goods they produce.

....As a measure of value, a standard of price, or a medium of exchange, gold has no magical powers. To assume that gold through these functions is responsible for the maldistribution of either capital or consumptive goods is absurd. One might so well argue that cotton-growing and manufacturing broke down because yardsticks failed to perform their functions.

The connection between gold and credits seems to leave room for a certain magic. But the effects of the apparent magic concern creditors and debtors; they only touch the wage-workers indirectly. Mismanagement of credit is an easy and partial explanation of some of the disorderly phenomena of capitalism. But there is no credit without a debt, and we might just as well blame the world's trouble upon the mismanagement of debts as upon the mismanagement of credits. In fact, the creditor who makes a loan, is less responsible than the borrower, the debtor, for the use made of the loan; it is the debtor who makes the first guess as to what he can do with a loan, and if he made a good guess he would not remain in debt.

The granting of a credit gives power to decide in what way a certain number of people shall be employed. For that reason, power to extend credits should not be left in the hands of concerns or individuals having no responsibility to the public. But that is only another way of saying that industry generally should be subject to public control and be conducted according to a plan designed to promote the general well-being.

The fact is that the public do place restrictions on the issue of credits. By law, the banks are required to hold a certain amount of gold against their note-issues. This limitation on the amount of loans is not so strict in Canada as it was before the War, the banks having been given new privileges. They were able to over-extend credits during the boom, a circumstance which doubtless helped to accentuate the severity of the present crisis.

But in a nation where all enterprises were fitted into a planned economy, and the proceeds of production were equitably shared, there would be no need to limit loans by a fixed relation to gold reserves. The creation of credit would be determined by the quantity and quality of labour which could be usefully employed.

Finally, in a nation where wealth was equitably distributed, and production properly managed, there would be no occasion for panics, -- no frightened capitalists with great stocks of securities to convert into gold to be moved from one country to another, and thus upset the financial machinery.

91. A Critique of Social Credit[118]

Advocates of Social Credit make a devastating critique of capitalism. They dramatize the problem of poverty in the midst of plenty. They give voluble expression to their emotional reactions to the evils of capitalism. They declaim their moral indignation at the brutal dilemmas in which the system involves the people. They urge revolt against the money power. They quote statistics with a facility which gives an apparent authority to their views.

Their undoubted sincerity, their earnest desire to rescue the mass of humanity from the indignities which an outgrown economic system imposes, their audacious assaults upon the citadel of capitalism, intrigue and impress their audiences. Socialists addicted to the cold-blooded Marxian analysis might learn something from them as to the tactical approach to an audience. The vigorous campaign of the advocates of Social Credit has no doubt served to arouse many people to a consciousness of the problems which must be solved, if progress is to continue in the future. But it has not helped to clear thinking about those problems. It has aroused hopes of a short cut to the solution of those problems, which is doomed to disappointment. For the major

---

[118]*Canadian Unionist*, June 1936, 9-11.

assumptions of the Social Credit theory are based on transparent fallacies.

The first chief assumption of the Social Creditors is that the troubles of capitalism are due, not to the inequitable distribution and use of purchasing power, but to a deficiency of total purchasing power. In other words, it is assumed that the purchasing power liberated in the process of production is never equal to the sum of the prices of the consumer goods produced. If that were so, business as a whole would always be bankrupt; there would have been no surplus profits to invest in new capital plants, or to expend on the palatial mansions and country clubs of the well-to-do.

....To say that there is a lack of purchasing power in the hands of *the consumer* is to make a general statement which is only a half truth. Many people certainly lack adequate purchasing power; on the other hand, Rockefeller and many others command a vast purchasing power over and above any possible need of expending it on consumer goods. But the Social Creditors are not concerned with the inequitable distribution of purchasing power or the use the possessors of great purchasing power make of it; they are concerned with the total purchasing power.

...The trouble of Canadian capitalism is not due to a lack of total purchasing power. Nor to the lack of a means of circulating purchasing power. Debits to individual accounts in Canadian banks last year totalled over $32 billion; a vast circulation of purchasing power by the currency of cheques. Yet the retail purchases of goods and services last year were probably under $3 billion. On the one hand, there was a circulation of purchasing power amounting to $33 billion; on the other, a circulation of goods and services having a retail value of $3 billion.

Obviously, the trouble of capitalism is connected with the ownership and use of purchasing power. And the ownership and use of purchasing power is determined by the property relations in which production and distribution are carried on. If the means of production and distribution were social property, the introduction of labour-saving machinery need not victimize the workers. The logical idea, then, would be that provision for the displaced workers should be a first charge upon the extra purchasing power generated by the machine until such workers found re-employment. And the extra production made possible by the machine need not glut the consumer market, because wages would be increased proportionately with the increase in production.

Now, with the machinery of production largely owned by one class and operated by another, the introduction of new machinery, while it may serve to increase the sum of purchasing power in the form of increased profits for the capitalist and lower prices to consumers, usually also serves to widen the gap between production of consumer goods and effective demand for them. The extra purchasing power goes to the owners of the machines, who may not see an opportunity to invest it in the production of capital goods, plant, and equipment. On the other hand, the loss of wages sustained by the displaced workers means a prompt reduction of purchasing power applied to consumer goods. And since, finally, the purpose of the production of new capital plants, or the operation of existing capital plants, is to sell goods in the consumer market, the displacement of men by machines increases the spread between the supply of consumer goods and the effective demand for them, and thus tends to defeat the purpose of the owners of the machine.

That tendency of production to outpace consumption, according to the Social Creditors, arises from a defect in the financial system. Make use of Social Credit and pay social dividends, and the problem of achieving a balanced relationship of production and credit will be solved. A century ago the Utopian Socialists proposed a similar solution. But they regarded their proposals as temporary devices to be used to facilitate the transformation of capitalism into a Socialist society. The Social Creditors say their proposals will regenerate capitalism, make the rich richer, the well-to-do better off, and abolish poverty among the masses. But if the object is merely to reform capitalism by increasing total purchasing power, why not raise wages? That would increase total purchasing power, and especially increase the purchasing power of those who spend nearly all their incomes on consumer goods. Increased wages would also mean a more equitable distribution of purchasing power, and lessened ability of the owning class to use surplus profits to construct surplus capital plant and equipment -- a waste of both capital and labour which is an important factor in curtailing the use of purchasing power in the consuming market and precipitating the periodic crises of capitalism.

Increased wages by increasing effective demand for consumer goods would undoubtedly stimulate the production of such goods. Social Creditors say the payment of social dividends would stimulate the production of consumer goods. Their critics say that since private parties own the goods in the market, they would take advantage of the artificial demand created by social dividends to inflate prices.

Of course, the Social Creditors claim that the special provisions for the "Just Price" and "Compensated Price" will prevent inflation. In his pre-election manual Mr. Aberhart wrote:

"Periodically a commission of our best experts from every sphere of life will be assembled for the purpose of deciding upon a fair and just price for all goods used in the province....This price must give the producer, importer or distributor a fair commission or turnover, and, at the same time, must not exploit the purchasing power of the consumer. Excessive profit will thus be eliminated. To help make consumption balance and control production a compensating price will be declared from time to time. This compensating price will be fixed according to the following formula:--

$$\text{Market Price} = \frac{\text{Total Consumption}}{\text{Total Production}} \text{X Just Price}$$

The difference between the Just Price and the Compensating Price will be made up to the retailer or consumer much in the same way basic dividends are issued and recovered."[119]

That apparently abstruse formula may impress the unwary wayfarers. But the mathematician who could arrive at the "Compensating Price" from that formula could work miracles. Yet Mr. Aberhart goes on to say how the difference between the Just Price and Compensating Price will be made up. "Money is only a ticket," say the Social Creditors. "Gold has no value; you cannot eat it."

The quality of being eatable is a pretty primitive measure of value. It is the test a baby applies to anything it can lift....

The chief function of money is to serve as a measure of value. And only the commodity form of money, gold or silver, or something having intrinsic value itself, can serve as a measure of the exchange value of other commodities. The next important function of money is that of a standard of price.

Both these functions of money are completely ignored by the Social Creditors. Money, they say, is only a means of circulating commodities -- goods or services. In this function of a medium of circulation, real money, gold, can be replaced by tokens of money, such as bank notes. The paper notes of the banks are promises to pay; they have no intrinsic value in themselves, but they represent value in possession of the bank, and are a first lien upon the assets of the bank....

Social Creditors have not taken the trouble to arrive at an elementary understanding of either the exchange of commodities or the rôle of money and its tokens. A simple freight car will serve to circulate many tons of freight in a week, a month or a year. A single dollar of money, or its tokens, may serve to circulate many dollars' worth of goods in one day. If a man sells a commodity for $1 and then uses $1 to buy another

---

[119]McKay is citing William Aberhart, *Social Credit Manual: Social Credit as Applied to the Province of Alberta* (Calgary, 1935): 8. However, he himself has introduced the ellipsis after the word "province", replacing original text which reads: "for the purpose of deciding upon a fair and just price for all goods and services used in the Province."

commodity, then the one dollar effects the exchange of $2 worth of goods.

The notion that a pile of commodities, on the one hand, should be balanced by a pile of money on the other is old. A century ago the Utopian Socialists of Britain developed a plan to "monetize" production. They organized a Society, established a central bank, opened labour exchange bazaars, or stores. A producer bringing a product to one of the stores was given certificates showing the value of the product as measured by the number of hours of labour devoted to its production. With these certificates he could buy from the stores, other products representing an equivalent amount of labour time....

In forming the society to "monetize" production, the Utopian Socialists were prompted by the theory of value of David Ricardo, London banker, and chief of the classical school of economists. Ricardo's theory was that labour was the substance [of] value, and labour time, the measure of value. But the British society found that it did not work. After a time its stores were overstocked with similar kinds of products, while it lacked products which holders of its certificates wanted to buy. The Utopians had not arrived at the understanding that exchange is determined, not by the actual amount of labour embodied in a product, but by the "average socially necessary labour" embodied in it....Had the Utopians understood that, they would have arranged commodities produced in the proportions required by their customers, and avoided the accumulation of surpluses of similar kinds of products which nobody needed or wanted to buy, while, at the same time, they lacked other commodities their clients wanted and had the purchasing power with which to buy. The Utopian experiment in the "monetization" of production failed because there was a failure to plan production. And, no other program for reforming the economic system will be successful unless it provides for social organs charged with planning production so as to assure the turning out of commodities in the proportions required to satisfy the wants of the people. Without intelligent planning of production the payment of social dividends would not assure that there would not be overproduction of wheat while there was a lack of utensils in the farmer-wife's kitchen.

Now, Social Creditors do not propose to plan and regulate production -- which would involve the socialization of the means of production; they can somehow socialize distribution by issuing tickets, based on Social Credit -- which is a meaningless abstraction unless the material wealth upon which the credit is to be based is first socially owned.

Social Creditors say the bankers create credit out of the blue by writing a ledger. But the bank's customer stands small chance of getting a loan unless he has first created a credit upon which to borrow. He must have assets as the base of his credit. As security, the banker may require collateral in the form of legal titles to property or revenue. The banker prefers to lend to a client who has goods in process of production. Such goods are the material base of the borrower's credit. The borrower creates the credit; the function of the bank is to make the borrower's credit liquid. The borrower hands the bank his I.O.U., which has limited acceptance, and the bank allows the borrower to use its I.O.U.s which are accepted wherever the bank has legal status, or is well known. The borrower's I.O.U., note, or lien on the goods he has in process of production becomes an asset of the bank; the drawing on deposit account which the bank opens in favour of the borrower becomes a liability of the bank. Social Creditors speak of the action of the banks in making an entry in its books signifying its assumption of a liability on behalf of the borrower as the creation of credit out of the blue. They speak of the liability of the bank as if it were an increase in the assets of the bank. True, the bank has acquired an asset in the form of borrower's note balancing the liability it has assumed. But that asset is temporarily non-active. And until the borrower redeems his note, the bank has lessened its capacity to lend, to some extent.

Credit is only another name for deferred payment, and, that being so, bank credit only circulates in the form of the bank's promise to pay, or I.O.U.; that is, in the form of a liability.

92. The Labour Theory of Value and A Proposed Shorter Work-Day[120]

If the capitalists were well advised they would, in their own interests, move speedily to secure the adoption of the thirty-hour work-week by force of law. That would give society a chance to catch its breath, an opportunity to look around and note the forces that are hurrying capitalism towards anarchy. But a story going the rounds of the capitalist press tells of the return of the ten-hour day as a sign of the restoration of prosperity.

One thing is certain: Capitalism cannot be made to function in an orderly manner by increasing the exploitation of the workers. It is in a dilemma now because it has wrung huge profits out of labour to put them into excessive productive plants, thereby starving consumption -- making it impossible for the masses with their small purchasing power to consume what they produce. But the capitalists pray for the discovery of ways to increase profits, as if the disease brought about by surplus profits could be cured by more profits. Thus Stanley Bruce of Australia calls upon the medicine men of finance to raise prices in order to assure good profits. The people, he said, simply "will not stand further pressure," and "to cut wages would provoke ugly resistance." But if prices were raised without raising wages the pressure on the workers would be increased; and a rise

---

[120]Originally published as "The Workers' Share," *Canadian Unionist*, April 1933, 183-184.

in prices without an advance in wages, instead of stimulating business, would mean a decrease of sales, a reduction of activity. Such is the wisdom of statesmen to whose mismanagement the workers submit.

Though far-sighted and humanitarian capitalists may favour reduction of the work-week, the vast majority of the capitalists will be opposed to it. As a class they have always opposed shortening of the working day, even when its length was such that the efficiency of the workers was seriously impaired.

The reason is plain. In labour time lies the secret of profits, the explanation of the mystery of surplus values.

In the existing system of commodity production, the simplest form of the circulation of commodities is commodity - money - commodity; the transformation of commodities into money, and the change of money back again into commodities; or selling in order to buy. But alongside this form there is another specifically different form: money - commodity - money: the transformation of money into commodities and the change of money back again into money; or buying in order to sell. The circuit M - C - M commences with money and ends with money, and would be purposeless if the money coming out at the end was only equal to that at the start. But money circulating in this manner becomes capital and produces a surplus value, profit. How it does so is still a mystery for many people.

It is clear that the ordinary commodity, a cabbage or sealing wax, cannot add to its own value. A capitalist cannot increase the value of a cabbage by buying it in order to sell; though he may make a profit by acting in conformity with old Ben Franklin's aphorism that "war is robbery, commerce cheating." How then does money beget more money? The possessor of money finds in the market one commodity, the consumption or use of which produces new values. The capitalist buys labour power, the capacity for labour, just as he buys any other commodity, at the market price which fluctuates around the cost of producing the labourer and reproducing his kind, a new supply of labour. Of all commodities labour power possesses the peculiar property of being a means, a source of more value than it has in itself. The application of labour power for part of the working day results in a product, the value of which is equal to the price the capitalist pays for labour power. But the capitalist does not then dismiss the worker. No. The worker continues to apply his labour power for the balance of the working day, and during that period when he works for nothing his labour power continues to produce value, surplus value, profits for the capitalist. That is the whole secret of profits -- that is the magic of the existing economic system, a contrivance to make workers toil without pay part of the day.....

93. The Illusion of Credit Control[121]

[*Editor's introduction*: "Many bourgeois economists, to divert attention from the real cause of the big spread between productive capacity and consuming power, seek to create the illusion that the troubles of Capital and Labour are due to some mysterious inability of money and credit to fulfil their supposed functions properly. Some Labour and Farmer members of Parliament have made statements which, as printed in the newspapers, divorced from their context, suggest that they share this illusion."]

That business depressions, unemployment and poverty in the midst of plenty are due to the failure of Capital to pay Labour sufficient wages to buy back a proper share of the product or services is a fact not advertised by the economists either of the universities or the banks. To admit that the surplus products which clog the machinery of business represent unpaid labour would be to admit that Capitalism is a "Rob Roy" system.

Whether or not there is a conscious desire to divert attention from the real cause of the business cycle and its disorderly phenomena, economists, bankers and businessmen generally express opinions chiefly remarkable for the way they confound cause with effect. Thus M.W. Wilson, General Manager of the Royal Bank of Canada, says: "The origin of the trouble (the present business depression) was the severe contraction in credit which followed the inflation of 1928 and 1929."

If it be true that the bankers have sufficient control over credit to be able to expand or contract it at will, then the bankers might be held responsible for the depression and its attendant evils. But Mr. Wilson takes a superficial view; his perspective does not extend beyond the financial aspects of the business cycle. He merely notes phenomena from his special point of view as a banker. A worker might as well say that the origin of the depression was the action of the boss in cutting him off the pay roll.

Broadly, the movement of business determines the volume of credit, not the volume of credit the movement of business. The movement of grain to Europe began to slow last June; business activity in other lines also began to decline. But the momentum acquired by speculation continued the expansion of credit until the stock exchange crash in October. During that period the expansion of credit, though it aided speculation, did not stimulate business proper.

In passing, it may be said that while the modes of production, the methods of business, determine the forms and methods of finance, it is

---

[121]*Canadian Railway Employees' Monthly*, October 1930, 237-239.

important not to under-rate the power possessed by bankers as custodians of credit. In the chain of cause and effect, the effect in its turn may become a cause. While, broadly, the state of business determines the state of credit, the state of credit may in turn affect business, though only in a minor way....

Some of the representatives of Canadian farmers in Parliament give the impression that they count easy credits and cheap money among their major goals of endeavour. Very evidently they do not mean to do so; they must know very well that monetary or credit reforms will not solve their difficulties.

That is not to say that the farmers should not seek monetary reform, any more than the industrial workers who realize that there is no real solution of the labour problem short of the transformation of Capitalism into Collectivism, should not in the meantime seek social reforms.

The farmers' demand for a national banking system should be supported by industrial workers -- that would be a step in the right direction. But it is probable that the advantages the farmers think they would obtain from a national banking system would not be realized -- or at most only temporarily. Naturally enough, the farmer feels aggrieved because he has to pay 8 per cent or more for bank loans, while there are times when the stockbroker can borrow money for as low as three per cent for speculative purposes.

But suppose the farmers were able to obtain cheaper money or easier credit. They could produce more cheaply; and they could compete more easily in the world-markets with the farmers of countries paying higher rates of interest. But the very fact of being able to take advantage of cheaper money or easier credit to increase production, would almost certainly lead to over-production, with an inevitable slump in prices....

94. Blind Alleys of the Utopians[122]

The League of Nations has ordered a world-wide investigation on scientific lines of the present business depression and its causes. It is not surprising that Miss Susan Lawrence, British Labour M.P., lamented that none of the leading economists, attached to the League, had undertaken to explain the causes of the business dilemma which has spread misery over the civilized world.

The economists of the schools have attempted many explanations of business depressions, unemployment and poverty in the midst of abundance, but they usually ignore the fact that the real cause lies in the

---

[122]*Canadian Unionist*, October 1930, 101-103.

relations of wages, rents and profits. Professor Jevons, despairing of finding the cause on earth, attempted to trace it to the spots on the sun, his theory being that the sun-spots affected the weather and the weather the crops. He was much disconcerted when the astronomers pointed out that his calculation that there was a periodicity of sun-spots corresponding to the appearance of depressions was all wrong.[123]

According to Conservatives in Canada, the present depression is due to Liberal policies. According to some of the Progressives, it is due to the contraction of credit, and the failure of bankers to permit the creation of sufficient purchasing power to enable consumption to balance production.

In Italy the Fascists attribute the depression to anti-Fascist agitation inspired by France. In Germany, the Nationalists blame it on the Treaty of Versailles and the Polish corridor to Danzig. In Japan the Conservatives put the blame on the decline of popular respect for ancestral spirits.

While the decision of the League of Nations to investigate the depression is of interest, it is to be feared that the nations will take such investigation as an excuse to ignore their responsibilities. The control and regulation of the process of production and distribution, carried on within a nation, is a nation's own affair; and if such control and regulation produces social justice and industrial peace at home, foreign trade need only be a matter of exchanging surplus products for other surplus products on a basis of fair dealing. It may be admitted that the League of Nations has some reasons for assuming a certain responsibility in the matter, since the economic forces which plunge nations into war are of the same nature as those which throw them into the ditch of a depression: but in the present stage of the game it is idle to expect that the proposed investigation will have any definite result of importance from the point of view of the workers. It may suggest some measures that might help the international financiers, just as the centralization of the control of national banks has made it [possible] to avoid the disastrous financial panics which formerly accompanied depressions.

If we are to have a real investigation of the depression, it is up to the industrial workers and farmers to make it; they are more interested in delving into the root causes than any class of businessmen; and they have the most to gain by removing the causes.

---

[123]This example obviously impressed McKay as an example of the obtuseness of bourgeois economics, although why metereological conditions would necessarily play *no* role in causing agricultural crises and hence economic crises, particularly in early nineteenth-century economies, is a point he did not fully develop. See Chapter Two, n.107.

Unfortunately, some spokesmen of the labour and farmer movements in Canada are proposing panaceas such as were proposed by bourgeois economists in England a hundred years ago, and by Rodbertus[124] in Prussia and Proudhon in France ninety years ago. The idea that public control of credit would make it possible to so increase purchasing power that consumption would balance production was advanced in England just a hundred years ago, as a cure-all for depressions, then a comparatively new phenomenon of business. The Equitist plan was developed at the same time. That was before Socialism had [any] claim to be scientific. But the Utopian Socialists of England at that period had a sufficient understanding of economics to perceive that these panaceas held only false hopes.

At the beginning of the factory system, commodities were produced to fill orders or to supply markets of which the capacity was pretty well known. The first factories were, in almost all cases, established by merchants, the first accumulators of capital -- mercantile capital, the profits of trade and sometimes of piracy. With the appearance of machine industry, which dates from about the end of the eighteenth century, the factory owner was impelled to speed up production; the capital invested in machines demanded that they be kept in operation 12 or more hours a day. Production no longer waited on orders, but began to outrun demand. The manufacturer began to try to force his goods upon the markets. And although manufacturing was far from efficient, production was greater than effective consumptive capacity, and a surplus of commodities piled up periodically. And over-production was followed by business depressions.

A hundred years ago depressions had already become a recognized feature of the economic life of England; economists advanced various theories as to their causes, and proposed remedies. John Gray,[125] in a book entitled *The Social System: Treatise on the Principle of Exchange*, published in Edinburgh in 1831, elaborated the theory of labour time as the unit-measure of value. His system called for a central national bank which, with the aid of its branches, would certify the time employed in the production of different commodities. In exchange for his commodity, the producer would receive an official certificate of its value -- that is to say, a receipt for the labour time contained in his commodity, and these notes

[124]Johann Karl Rodbertus (1805-1875) was a German socialist, politician, and writer, who rejected revolutionary change for gradualism through the parliamentary process. His writings include *Die Forderungen der Arbeitenden Klassen* (1839).
[125]McKay refers to John Gray (1799-1883), the radical political economist who developed a version of the labour theory of value in the 1820s. Among his works were *A Lecture on Human Happiness* (1824), *The Social System, A Treatise on the Principle of Exchange* (1831), and *Remedy for the Distress of Nations* (1842).

of an hour of labour, a day of labour, or a week of labour, would represent the equivalent which the holder could receive of any other commodities.

With this system, said Gray, "it would be as easy to sell for money as it is now to buy for money; production would be the uniform and inexhaustible source of the demand." The precious metals would lose the "privilege which they now have over other commodities and would take the place which belongs to them side by side with butter, eggs, cloth and calico; and their value would interest us no more than that of diamonds."

"Ought we to retain," Gray said, "our artificial measure of value, gold, and fetter thus the productive forces of the country, or ought we not rather make use of the natural measure of value, labour, and liberate the productive forces?"[126]

In order to solve this problem Gray found it necessary to propose the abolition of all the conditions of capitalist production. Under his system all capital was to become national capital and all land national land. And although he professed that he only wanted to reform money and liberate production, his system called for regulation of production, thus putting fetters on the production for individual exchange on the basis of labour time, which he proposed to free from fetters. Thus his bourgeois reform became a transparent absurdity.

Other bourgeois economists of that time argued that insufficiency of gold, money, and credit was responsible for depressions, unemployment and poverty. But ten years later economists of a new school were declaring that the troubles of business were due to the circulation of so much paper money not backed by gold that people had lost confidence in it. The pressure of this view led the British Parliament in 1844 to adopt the Peel Bank Act, by which the Bank of England was divided into a banking department and an issue department. The banking department could only get notes from the issue department by depositing an equal amount of gold with the latter. When the banking department was called upon for deposits, in order to get the gold to pay depositors, it had to return the notes to the issue department, the notes being thus withdrawn from circulation.

---

[126]John Gray, *The Social System: A Treatise on the Principle of Exchange* (Edinburgh: William Tait, Prince Street, 1831). The original reads: "And under the Social System it would really be so: as respects difficulty, there would be no difference whatever between buying and selling. Effectual demand would really depend upon production, because all production would cause effectual demand: the natural demand would be uniformly equal to the whole quantity produced...." (276). McKay captures the spirit, rather than the letter, of the text. It may well be that he relied on the extensive quotation of Gray in Karl Marx, *A Contribution to the Critique of Political Economy* (Chicago: Charles H. Kerr and Company, 1911), 104, which passage bears a close resemblance to his own version of Gray.

But, despite this device, three years later a financial panic occurred, and the Peel Act had to be suspended. During the panics of 1857 and 1866, the Act was also suspended.

Insufficiency of gold, speculation, the greed of trusts, and other factors undoubtedly accentuate the evils of business depression, but the fact that countries with a great diversity of monetary conditions have been troubled by depressions indicates that the real causes do not lie in currency or credit regulations or conditions. ...

After the Great War, there followed perhaps the greatest depression in the career of capitalism up to that time. The British, American, Canadian and other governments doubtless hastened the depression and aggravated its evils by authorizing measures to assure a speedy return to the gold standard. The deflation of currency which followed was perhaps unduly rapid; and it was detrimental to the interests of governments insofar as they represent the people, though not at all detrimental to the money-lenders. The position of creditors was vastly improved at the expense of the debtors. The Westminster Bank Review pointed out the other day that goods which in 1920 would have paid off £270 of the national debt, would last August have only paid off £100. During the war boom great numbers of farmers borrowed money to buy land and machinery, and insofar as they were debtors the postwar deflation of money hit them hard. The wage-workers were less affected because generally they are too closely exploited to be able to incur debts.

But whether governments had interfered or not, the cessation of the war demand for goods would very quickly have been followed by depression, falling prices, and currency deflation. Production had been speeded up by the war; it continued at a high rate of speed after the armistice; but when the governments stopped buying the stream of commodities piled up on the merchant's shelves or in the producers' warehouses. Business continued for a time to appear good; but commodities were not being absorbed by consumers.

The advance in commodity prices had been much greater than the increase in the rate of wages. The spread between producer and consumer prices was very great. The prosperity of the wage-workers was more an appearance than a reality; in 1919 strikes with the object of forcing up wages more in line with prices involved over 4,000,000 workers in the United States -- nearly half as many workers as were engaged in manufacturing.

Governments having ceased to be the big customers of the producers, commodities began to glut the market. Producers began to reduce prices in order to sell their goods, and competition for a place in the market forced all producers, not possessing a monopoly, to embark on a program of successive price reductions. Profits diminished, and though the spread between the commodity prices which determine the cost of living and wages was reduced, the increase in the workers' purchasing power thus resulting was more than counteracted by the curtailment of the distribution of wages through the relegation of millions to the unemployed or partly-employed lists.

But the post-war depression, like every other depression, originated in the conditions of capitalist production -- of competitive commodity production. While it may have been hastened by the fiats of governments persuaded that a return to the gold standard was necessary to enable business to adjust itself to the cessation of the war demand for goods, it was the outcome of the operations of the capitalist system as a whole, and not of any particular organ or agency of that system, such as the banks. Whatever control over issue of currency and credit bankers may possess, the exercise of that control is limited by factors over which they have no control. The only way bankers can issue credit is to make loans; and it [is] to their interest to increase loans. They do not contract credit because they want to, but because business cannot, in a competitive system, profitably employ it.

Some people apparently believe that it is possible to devise some method of public control of credit by which credit can be directly transformed into consumer purchasing power. But the big government credit placed at the disposal of the United States Farm Board did not create sufficient consumer purchasing to overcome the law of supply and demand. It enabled the Farm Board to take 70,000,000 bushels of wheat off the hands of the American farmers, but it did not make possible the marketing of surplus wheat at reasonable prices.

An issue of credit, such as the Canadian government's grant of $20,000,000 for unemployment, is only transformed into consumer purchasing power when distributed as wages, profits, or rents. The farmer's returns for his crops theoretically include wages, profit and rent, but in reality seldom represent a fair wage for his labour. The difference between the farmer and wage-worker consists mostly in the fact that the exploitation of the farmer is indirect, through capital invested in city industry and transportation.

A major cause of the deficiency of purchasing power, and therefore of depressions, unemployment and poverty, [is] that the industrial workers and farmers are not paid enough for their work to buy back a proper share of the production of wealth or services.

The capitalists spend only a portion of their profits on articles of current production; the rest is invested in new enterprises, life insurance, etc. If the new enterprises fail there is a loss of both capital and purchasing power. If they succeed only at the expense of established enterprises, there is no increase in purchasing power, but only a change in the source of the production of purchasing power.

The workers also curtail purchasing power by practising thrift. Their savings entrusted to banks, trusts, or insurance companies may be made the basis of credit to finance new enterprises; and in that case may become a source of new purchasing power -- if the new enterprises do not by competition reduce the business of the older enterprises, but insofar as the workers turn their wages into savings the general purchasing power of the market is to that extent curtailed; and new enterprises have less chance to succeed without the competition ruining old enterprises, precisely because there is less purchasing power to absorb their products. Again, where savings are used as the basis of loans to stock-brokers and traders, the amount of purchasing power is only increased by the profits which the bankers and traders may thereby make. In other ways, the effect of thrift in curtailing purchasing power is more pronounced than any consequence flowing from the conversion of savings into new capital undertakings.

Under a system of social production for use, there would still be need for a certain saving to provide for capital improvements, but that would be a social or public function -- not an individual need. Nobody would want to save to buy even a home, since one could use a publicly-owned home as long as he wanted to. Individual thrift would probably be rendered unnecessary by a generous use of the devices of old-age pensions, unemployment and sickness insurance, which capitalism itself is adopting to make thrift unnecessary -- probably because the capitalist machine functions with difficulty in proportion as the people practise thrift.

95. Commodities and Credits[127]

Who rules Canada? Mr. Bennett? or Mr. Banker? or Mr. Commodity? If the power to rule economic affairs rests with politicians or financiers, then the way economic affairs have been behaving is an insult to their intelligence and their pride. The truth is, as Engels pointed out long ago, that in a system of production of commodities for sale in an impersonal market, the commodities rule the producers.[128]

---

[127]*Canadian Unionist,* May 1932, 210-211.

[128]McKay is citing Engels, *Socialism: Utopian and Scientific,* 59-60: "...the production of commodities, like every other form of production, has its peculiar inherent laws inseparable from it; and these laws work, despite anarchy, in and through anarchy. They reveal themselves in the only persistent form of social inter-relations, *i.e.,* in exchange, and here they affect the individual producers as compulsory laws of competition....They work themselves out,... independently of the producers, and in antagonism to them, as

A while ago the Saskatchewan convention of the United Farmers of Canada declared that the present economic system must be replaced by a system of production for use, as under competitive production for profit the position of the farmers was as hopeless as that of the industrial wage workers. But in their amendment to the Rhodes budget [i.e., the budget presented by E.N. Rhodes, Minister of Finance in the federal Conservative government] the Farmers' group in Parliament were content to urge the nationalization of banking, which would be an important step towards the social control of credit. Organized labour should be as keen for the nationalization of banking as the farmers, but it is advisable not to have illusions about it. A step in the right direction will not solve all our problems.

The control of money and credits carries the power to decide how a considerable proportion of the population shall be employed. In the first instance, the decision is made by an entrepreneur, manufacturer, farmer, etc., who, believing he foresees a profitable market, borrows credit in order that he may employ machinery and labour to produce goods to supply that market. The banker's control of credit is limited to the acceptance or rejection of the entrepreneurs' proposition, and usually the banker is influenced more by security offered for a loan than by consideration of the business or social consequences of the particular enterprise for which credit is sought. With a number of banks competing for loans -- and they must make loans to pay interest on deposits as well as make profits -- this is inevitable. No one bank knows for what particular purposes all the other banks may be making loans and hence have to take a chance on the possibility that any particular loan will lead to production of an over-supply of any particular line of goods in relation to demand. With competitive production, producers are only apprised that supply has over-balanced demand by a fall in prices: a fall in prices is also the signal for bankers to be wary of new loans; and restriction of loans then may be as much in the interest of the producers as of the bankers.

One reason why a national banking monopoly is desirable is that it could exercise a better control over the use of credit and preserve a better balance between the production of different kinds of commodities than a dozen different banks (none of which knows precisely what the others are doing) can hope to do. It could, but there is no guarantee that it would, unless nationalization of the banks was accompanied by national economic planning.

Canada is suffering from an overextension of wheat-growing in relation, on the one hand, to the consuming power of overseas markets, and in

---

inexorable natural laws of their particular form of production. The product governs the producers."

relation, on the other, to the development of other Canadian industries. The farmers borrowed credit to buy land and machinery to increase the production of wheat in the hope of realizing profits. They made a bad guess as to their ability to make a profitable use of credit. The banks and the governments which organized farm loan schemes share the responsibility for the bad guess. But if a national banking monopoly had been in existence, would it have prevented the wheat growers' getting into debt? Not while governments and businessmen of all sorts believed that pumping in immigrants was the main thing necessary to assure the development and prosperity of Canada. There would probably have been political and business pressure upon a national banking system to make credit more easily available to farmers than it was; and more farmers in debt today. In the absence of national economic planning, a national banking system would hardly have followed a policy running counter to the general political and business policy of the country, and if it had been managed by men strong enough to do so, what would have been the result? Either immigration would have had to be curtailed, or the pressure upon the urban labour markets of this country would have forced down wages and reduced the demand for farm products. And if immigration had been stopped, European labour markets would have been more overcrowded, reducing wages and ability to buy farm products. In either case, the tendency would have been to bring on the depression sooner than it arrived.

The use made of credit is of first importance, and a national banking monopoly will not of itself guarantee the right use of credit. For that national economic planning is essential, and not only that, but a general nationalization of all the essential means of production and distribution. Economic planning, if it is to provide for the balancing of production and consumption, must involve a re-distribution of incomes. Social control of credit would accomplish something in that direction and make the disorders of the business cycle less pronounced, but social control of the physical means of production, as well as of credit, is necessary to the complete emancipation of farmers, as well as industrial workers, from exploitation.

While there must be a connection between the volume of credit and the volume of business, it is possible to exaggerate the importance of bank credit where corporations have piled up reserves available for working capital. According to Dr. Marvin, economist of the Royal Bank of Canada, the whole story of the depression may be written in terms of the relation of the volume of credit and the volume of production. In other words, he argues that contraction of the volume of credit is the fundamental cause of the depression. "The volume of credit," he says, "has fallen faster than the volume of production," and thus produced the fall in prices. This statement is at variance with the reports of the Dominion Bureau of Statistics on production, bank credits, etc.

During the recent boom industrial production in Canada reached its peak in January 1929 with an index of 209. It fell off to 203 in February 1929, and has dropped more or less gradually since then, going down to 128.7 in February of this year. Thus the decline in industrial production in three years was 38 per cent.

Now current bank loans in February 1929 totalled $1,249,000,000 and in February of this year they were $1,063,000,000, a decline of 15 per cent.

In the same period the physical volume of business declined 29.8 per cent and wholesale prices 27.3 per cent. Thus the main premise of Dr. Marvin's argument, so far as Canada is concerned, is wide of the mark. If credit was the only culprit, the current loans last February might have been reduced in proportion to prices, or down to about $837,000,000, and sufficed to maintain as much business activity as near the height of industrial production. In relation to prices, the volume of bank credit is now considerably greater than during the boom. This is due to freezing of loans, or slower circulation of bank credits. When it is argued that by increasing the volume of credit prosperity can be restored, the question of how new credit is to be put in circulation and kept circulating is ignored. Provision of credit to enable the paper-makers to build more paper mills or the farmers to increase wheat production would not help matters just now. In the end the volume and circulation of credit is largely determined by the circulation of commodities.

Suppose credit is applied to the production of capital goods, factories, railways, etc. If these capital goods can be utilized to turn out consumptive goods and services for which a market is available, the credit has been well used; if not, it is wastefully used. There has never been over-production of consumptive goods in relation to human wants; but there is frequent over-production of capital goods, and that is one cause of depressions, because it means that an unnecessarily large portion of the national income has been diverted from the service of consumption, which is the final end of all production. The regulation of the production of capital goods, a rationing of investment, is an important feature of the problem of establishing a balanced relation between the production of consumptive goods and the consuming capacity of the people. Failure to distinguish between the production of capital goods, which is not an end in itself, and the production of consumptive goods, is responsible for much loose thinking.

96. Rationing Investment: A Critique of Donald Marvin's Explanation of the Depression[129]

In an interesting diagnosis of the depression Dr. Donald Marvin, economist of the Royal Bank of Canada, says:

"When high prices for call loans cut off the supply of funds available for business and so increased the cost of what credit was obtainable that it could not be used profitably in business, it was inevitable that production should begin to fall off. That was the fundamental cause of the break down. When it is realized that this was the major reason for the depression, the remedy becomes self-evident. When credit is made plentiful, business will revive. Credit is neither cheap nor plentiful in gold countries at the present time."[130]

If this plausible explanation really goes to the heart of the matter, it is a serious indictment of the bankers. For banks are chartered by the public authorities and given important privileges in order that they may, among other functions, serve as reservoirs of stored purchasing power and supply business with needed credit. If industry and trade were denied legitimate credit at reasonable rates in order that loans might be made to facilitate speculation, then the bankers have a heavy responsibility for the depression and the great mass of human misery it has entailed.

But, however great their powers and responsibilities may be, the assumption that they, through the restriction of credit, are wholly or even mainly responsible for the depression will hardly bear examination. What Dr. Marvin regards as the fundamental cause was rather a defect in the gearing of the economic machine, which prevented the maintenance of a proper articulation of production and consumption, a balanced relation of supply and demand. While the ballyhoo of the speculative frenzy was at its height, bankers stated that there was no lack of credit for legitimate business. The trouble of business then was that the production of consumptive goods had already surpassed the capacity of the markets to absorb them, and most enterprises were not seeking additional credit because they could not see their way to employ it profitably. All sorts of corporations had accumulated large reserves but could find no better use for them than loaning them to brokers. Business was up against the fact that the supply of all kinds of goods and services exceeded the effective demand; and in such a situation it is of small consequence whether or not

---

[129]Originally published as "Rationing Investment," *Canadian Forum*, July 1932, 372-374.
[130]McKay is citing Donald Marvin, "Prospect of Recovery. When Credit is Made Plentiful, Business Will Revive -- Commodity Prices Controllable Through Credit Volume," *Saturday Night*, 27 February 1932, 26-27. The concluding word in the passage cited was actually "moment."

credit is available at any price. It is then a question of finding opportunities to employ credit profitably and, to the degree that such opportunities are lacking, the volume of credit in circulation is curtailed and the pressure of excess supply upon effective demand inevitably forces down prices.

Is it in the operations of credit that the fundamental cause of the depression is to be found? Or is it the operations of the economic system as a whole which, more by virtue of the ownership of the means of production than of the control of credit, distributes wages, salaries, interest, rent, and profits in such a way that an unnecessarily large proportion of the national income is diverted from consumption to the creation of capital goods, with the consequence that there develops periodically a wide gap between the production of consumptive goods and the capacity to consume them?

Dr. Marvin states that the following "three sentences constitute the whole story of what was wrong with the business engine and tell how distribution can again be made to function":--

> It is true that the price level depends upon the ratio of credit and production.
> When credit expands excessively, prices rise, and when credit is unduly contracted, prices fall.
> When the volume of credit is kept proportionate to the volume of production, prices remain stable.

That diagnosis apparently implies that those who control the issue of credit are able to determine the volume of production and the "price level." If that is the whole story credit must be a mystery even to the bankers, or they would in their own interest exercise a more intelligent control over it. There is certainly a direct connection between credit, production, and prices. But whether the volume of credit determines the volume of production, or vice-versa, is a question of not much greater practical importance than that as to whether the egg or the hen came first in the order of evolution. Since the purpose of production is to realize a profit from the sale of the products, credit, production, and prices must inevitably, in the final analysis, react to and be determined by the relations of supply and demand in the markets for consumptive goods. And in the consumer market the direct role played by credit is limited to the instalment plan. The producer or merchant may be using bank credit in order to loan his goods to the consumer but in the long run the instalment plan does not increase the market for goods. Whatever system of consumer credits might be devised, the law of supply and demand would continue to rule the consumer market. That law determines the prices of commodities and, if it causes prices to rise, either the circulation of commodities will be retarded or a larger volume of credit or money will be necessary to carry on business.

If there is a fundamental cause of the depression it is rooted in the operations of the economic system as a whole, and cannot be isolated from the factors behind the law of supply and demand. The business cycle is not merely the result of the anarchy of production -- the fact that no one producer knows what all the others are doing to supply the market demand, all are engaged in a wild scramble to get to the market first and dispose of their products. The boom and the depression have a common cause, a constant factor which trusts cannot regulate, and which cannot be abolished without a radical change in the relations of capital and labour. This constant factor is the dual position of the worker as a seller of his labour-power and a purchaser of the product of his labour-power; and the creation of a surplus product following therefrom which must result in an overproduction of commodities in relation to consuming power quite apart from the anarchy of production.

Those who control the surplus products use them to employ labour to produce capital goods, new factories, machines, ships, railway rolling stock, etc. In Canada during the recent boom years nearly one-half of the manufacturing effort was directed to the creation of what are classified as producers' goods. But the object of the production of capital goods being to produce consumer goods more cheaply and efficiently, the production of new means and facilities of production cannot go on indefinitely. If the new plants make it possible to increase the production of consumer goods at a rate faster than the increase in effective consumer demand, they can only be kept in operation by driving older plants out of business; and since the new plant employs fewer workers than the old to produce a given quantity of goods, the number of consumers in employment is reduced. For a time the new plants may flourish at the expense of the older plants, and the higher their rate of profit, the more promoters hustle to induce investors to put their money in competing enterprises. Before long there is an over-production of capital goods; that is first evidenced by a slowing up of the movement of goods at the producing end, then in weakening wholesale prices and later in retail prices. The boom is over. The production of capital goods begins to slow down when the movement of goods to the consumer market slackens, and large numbers of workers are thrown out of employment with a resultant weakening of consumer demand.

Some old enterprises occupying strategic positions, and some of the newer enterprises, may continue to make fair profits during a depression, as the dividend records for 1930 showed. But many of the older, less efficient, and less economical enterprises go to the wall -- a loss of capital and even a waste of capital if the enterprise is put out of business before it was really obsolescent from the point of view of a sound national economy.

The over-production of capital goods is a real evil; idle or partly employed factories, railways, ships, etc., mean waste of both capital and labour. Certainly improvements in the means and facilities of production leading to the creation of goods with less expenditure of capital and labour ought to be proper objects of endeavour; but the methods of business organization which accompany them tend to defeat the ends which make the saving of effort desirable. A scheme of things, policy, or practice, which results in the marvellous forms and forces of production only to keep them idle, or partly so, while armies of workers clamour for jobs, and multitudes lack proper food, clothing, housing, education, etc., is a tragically absurd reflection upon human intelligence.

It is not the disposition of credit that develops this dilemma, but the forms and powers of property which determine the distribution of incomes, along with the technical and social conditions which influence spending. Incomes are either spent on consumable goods or services, or upon capital goods which are created through the medium of credit based on people's savings in banks, in part at any rate. If the capital goods can be kept serving their purposes at capacity, they are the best form of saving; if not, then to the extent they are inactive they are a form of waste.

Obviously, if too large a share of incomes is expended on the production of new capital goods, the other portion of incomes will be insufficient to absorb the consumptive goods and services which the existing capital goods, utilized to full capacity, are able to produce. A part of the total capital goods becomes superfluous, and the object of producing new capital goods is negated, defeated. True, the object of the owners of the new capital goods may be realized if they capture the markets of the owners of older capital goods; but the general business economy finds itself up against the fact that productive capacity exceeds consumptive capacity, a situation which obliges industry to restrict operations, and reduce working staffs, thereby further curtailing consuming power, and making it increasingly impossible for demand to resist the tendency of surplus supply to force down prices.

The ironing-out of the business cycle -- the elimination of booms and depressions -- is a problem of articulating the production of consumptive goods to market capacity, of establishing and maintaining a balance between supply and demand. The typical method adopted by trusts to meet this problem is to curtail production, but that policy involves a waste of capital goods, and condemns the mass of the people to a low standard of living. To arrive at an adequate solution, one which will permit continuous progress and an improving standard of living, it will first be necessary to establish some form of control over the production of capital goods, a system of rationing investment. This is the logical starting point for economic planning. The task which challenges attention is difficult; it will not be accomplished without mistakes, but none of them [is] likely to entail such a heavy price as the present depression. Economic planning, even if only a process of trial and error, has become imperative, if revolution and possibly a period of anarchy are to be avoided.

There is probably no royal formula for the planning of the production of capital goods, the rationing of investment. Yet being largely a matter of the control of the issue of credit it should not present insurmountable difficulties to human ingenuity. Nationally considered, it is a matter of determining what proportion of the national income should be devoted to the creation of new means and new facilities of production. The major elements of the problem are the rate of depreciation of existing capital goods, and the measure of economy and efficiency realizable by the substitution of new capital goods of superior technique for older capital goods not completely obsolescent. In the process of what is called the "rationalization" of industry, scientific management has already acquired much experience in dealing with such technical questions.

National economic planning, however, while using the methods of "rationalization," will have to take account of factors that have not entered into the purview of the rationalizers of individual industries. Where the only or principal object of "rationalization" has been the economizing of human labour, it has to some extent defeated its purpose and aggravated the evils of the depression. The rationalization of the production of capital goods will need to take account of the effect of drastic changes upon the social conditions of the people. Of this an example and precedent has already been set in the Canadian fishing industry. The government has limited the use of steam trawlers because it deems their ability to increase the production of fish of less importance than the preservation of the means of existence of the shore fishing communities. In a planned national economy aiming at the most effective use of all workers, and improvement in general well being, efforts would be made to adapt the shore fishermen to other callings in order that the most effective instruments of fish production might be used to the fullest extent.

This example, however, serves to illustrate the need of social, as well as purely economic, considerations being taken into account in planning the production of capital goods. If a taboo was placed on science and invention, and the production of capital goods limited to the replacement of means and facilities of production, as they become obsolescent, a much greater share of the national income would be made available (through say higher wages) to people with unsatisfied consumptive wants; consumption would then tend to balance production, and business would become an orderly procedure, insofar, at any rate, as it is independent of natural calamities, such as crop failures. In such case, the most important social consideration, an improved standard of mass living, would be in line with [the] major requirement of an orderly system -- a balance of production and consumption. Of course there should be production of capital goods over and above what is needed to replace obsolescence, but there should be a limit determined on the one hand by gains accruing to the nation as a whole from technical improvements, and on the other hand, by the effects upon social conditions.

The regulation of the production of capital goods would involve a challenge to two of the greatest of human passions -- greed and fear. Unless a relatively small class were given an opportunity to monopolize the ownership of new capital goods, a limitation would have to be placed upon the amount of individual incomes which might be invested -- a curb upon the passion to acquire control of great wealth. A limitation would also need to be imposed upon the export of funds drawn from the national income for conversion into capital goods abroad. On the other hand, there would be nothing to do with the balance of income except to spend it on consumptive goods, and with consumption balancing production, the stability of business, the regularity of employment, would give everybody a new sense of security. Greed of great wealth and fear of want, the human fulcrums of the business cycle, would be exorcised; and the new sense of security, which would make saving mainly a matter of provision for old age, would permit a spiritual revolution in man's attitude to his work and to his fellowmen, and a real realization of the service-motive in business.

iv. The Death of Liberalism and the Emergence of "State Capitalism"

97. The Moral Suicide of Canada's Political Leaders[131]

Canadian statesmanship is distinguished by its superstitions. Messrs. Bennett and King[132] are restricted by vastly more taboos than a South

---

[131]Originally published as "Canadian Statesmanship Affected by Taboos," *O.B.U. Bulletin*, 1 March 1934.

[132]McKay is referring to the two leading Canadian politicians of the 1930s, R.B. Bennett of the Conservatives and W.L.M. King of the Liberals. R.B. Bennett (1870-1947) led the Conservative Party from 1927 to 1938. He championed traditional conservative views, and argued that the federal government could counter the Depression through tariff policies. In the eyes of many workers, he became the detested symbol of the old order, not least because of his violent repression of labour organizers and Communists. William Lyon Mackenzie King (1874-1950), besides being the longest-serving Canadian prime minster, claimed to be a progressive intellectual on the basis of his writings on the "labour question." See W.L.M. King, *The Canadian*

Sea savage. To their fetishes they bend the knee and bow the head in groveling servility. Ferri, co-founder with Lombroso of the scientific school of criminology, described servility as moral suicide.

Which is the worst form of servility or moral suicide -- that of the wage slaves, overawed by police, militia and now by tanks and gas bombs, or that of the statesmen paralyzed by their superstitious fears of what may be behind the crazy economic phenomena of capitalism run wild -- rendered impotent by their supine reverence of the dark gods that dwell in the financial sanctuary casting out spells to work upon human relations like furies?

There are political superstitions, too. If worthwhile legislation on behalf of labour is demanded, the politicians conjure up constitutional bogeys; but when it is a question of serving capital they always get round the constitution.

For any human purpose Canadian statesmanship is dead from the seat of appetite upward. And history, like nature, abhors a vacuum. Traditions weighing on the mind like a nightmare will not suffice for half a continent. To maintain the rule of traditions, which are ghosts of dead conditions, it would be necessary to arrest technical development, as Hitler, Mussolini and Roosevelt are trying to do, by forbidding the introduction of new machinery without permission. But if that is not a mere gesture for the edification of the ignorant who blame their troubles upon the machines, it is a kind of political consecration of the crisis, for capitalism can only get out of crisis by huge expenditures on new productive equipment -- or by war. And for politics to arrest technical advance is to handicap a country in the struggle for world markets....

98. Blasting the Old Order[133]

"The old order is gone -- never to return," said Mr. Bennett. "The open market place no longer exists." And since the mechanism of the market has broken down, the Prime Minister affirmed the necessity of government regulation and control of economic affairs.

Things do move, despite the pessimists -- in Canada with kaleidoscopic rapidity. In the more or less pioneer communities no longer than fifty years ago a majority of the people were not at the mercy of the market. Nearly every family had a little farm; produced vegetables, grains, milk,

---

Method of Preventing Strikes and Lockouts: An Address to the Railway Business Association (New York 1913); *Industrial Peace: An Address to the Industrial Peace Association* (Cincinnati 1913); and *Industry and Humanity* (Boston 1918), his *magnum opus.* He was -- at least in his writings -- a champion of a "new liberalism."

[133] *Canadian Unionist*, May 1935, 311-313.

eggs, meats; manufactured clothing, soap, candles, so on; could easily capture wild game and fish. The family was largely self-sustaining, self-employing. Its primary activities were regulated by its own requirements. It offered only its surplus products, or surplus labour time, on the market.

In such communities the forms of social co-operation were mainly confined to house-raisings, house-warmings, harvest bees, church festivals, neighbourly attendance on the sick, etc. -- free services without exchange of money.

In these pioneer Canadian communities it was usually the merchants who initiated the modern industries as in medieval England -- but here mostly with borrowed capital. Modern industry requires the social cooperation of many workers; and that in turn requires a labour market, the existence of a class of people who do not own land or other means of production enabling them to employ themselves. The independent pioneer existence is only possible for a limited number of people -- of Jacks-of-all-Trades and Jills-of-many-Arts -- in a given territory; and immigration produced a labour market.

The artisan, owning his own tools of production and having easy access to his raw materials, continued to carry on for a while. But power-machine industry, involving the social co-operation of many workers, more or less swiftly -- by underselling him -- "freed" the artisan from his means of production; turned his ability to labour into a market commodity.

Capitalism dissolved the neighbourly ties of pioneer Canadian society just as it dissolved the sense of duty which was the spirit of the feudal society of England. It established freedom of contract, and the free market. Or, at any rate, that was the theory. We know about how free the worker was in making a contract of employment with a large corporation; he is free to accept the terms offered, seek charity, or starve. We know that, while immigration was subsidized to increase supply in the labour market, high tariffs have been erected to raise prices in the goods market.

But we must take account of this theoretical free market which is still the beloved of the bourgeois economists, who say the world's troubles arise from interference with the mechanisms of the free market. This mechanism has worked well in the past, it is said. It is supposed to have enabled the preferences of consumers automatically to regulate production; the preferences of consumers for the goods competing in the market, raising or lowering prices of particular goods so that the producers can perceive what goods the consumers want, and regulate their production accordingly.

In the book *Recovery* by Sir Arthur Salter, formerly a high official of the League of Nations, we find the following beautiful picture of the market as it existed before the Great War:

"Over the whole range of human effort and human need, demand and supply found their adjustments without anyone estimating the one or planning the other...So supply and demand would circle round a central, though moving, point of equilibrium -- tethered to it by an elastic though limited attachment.... And what changing prices would do for commodities, changing rates of interest would do for capital....The economic and financial structure under which we have grown up was indeed, at the moment of its greatest perfection, more like one of the marvelously intricate structures built by the instincts of beavers or ants than the deliberately designed and rational works of man."[134]

Sir Arthur does not tell us when the moment of greatest perfection was. But it was probably never more than an instant of time during the handicraft era, before the rise of machine industry. Sir Arthur also neglects to point out that for over a century it has required a cataclysm of the market about every ten years to enable supply and demand to find their adjustments.

The famous equilibrium of the market, the adjustment of supply to demand -- the Manchester millennium of the economic harmonies -- the dream and desire of businessmen -- was only possible in the era of small individual enterprise producing for a parochial market. Once great industry appeared, impelled by its capital investment to produce on the chance of finding new far-away markets, production was thrown into the vicissitudes of the business cycle - crisis, depression, stagnation, recovery, boom ending in a new crisis, and so on. The mechanisms of the market [have] worked badly. Since 1820 the English workers have had but three years of prosperity in every ten. And most of that time Britain had a predominant position in the market; a near-monopoly position in respect to machinery and other things requiring technical skill to produce.

But until recently businessmen were enamoured of their capricious mistress, the market. Why? Rousseau or Adam Smith throw a light on that. They envisaged only small scale enterprises, competing on fairly equal terms. They envisaged a state of society in which, by contrast with feudalism, the producers for the market appeared free and equal; in which the enterprising and thrifty journeyman could easily become a master. But the advent of large-scale industry, while it increased the social co-operation for production, sharply divided society into two classes. The great French revolution promises Liberty, Equality, Fraternity: what it

---

[134]McKay is citing separate passages from Arthur Salter, *Recovery: The Second Effort* (London: G. Bell and Sons, 1932): 10, 11, 12, 13.

brought the worker was indeed freedom from legal compulsion to give a certain proportion of his time to the service of a feudal lord -- only, however, to be replaced by economic compulsion to serve a new set of masters.

Freedom is, of course, a relative condition. But the middle class having obtained freedom to buy and sell land, goods, and labour, had the illusion of perfect freedom. The owners of the means of production are free in a way the worker dependent on a job is not. But still they are dependent on the market. That dependence, however, is not clearly perceived.

The businessman thinks of himself as a free and independent individual and decries any interference with his freedom to run his business in his own way -- even when demanding the favour of tariffs interfering with consumers. But the success of his business depends on the way it fits into the general scheme of social co-operation by which the wants of society are supplied. But in capitalist society the producer does not accompany his products into the consuming market -- as was largely the case in the peasant economy -- so he does not usually know when the products pass out of the market and fall into consumption. He is at the mercy of the consumer market, with which he may have no direct personal relations, but in which his products may play an important rôle affecting his interests and the interests of all of the producers. His products may be the decisive item in forming a glut in the market, congesting circulation, driving prices to a ruinous level. What then is the freedom of which the businessman is so zealous? It is but freedom to get himself and everbody else into difficulties ; it is but the illusion of freedom.

Until recently the businessman has been unable to understand -- or has refused to understand -- that his enterprise is but a cog in the great scheme of co-operative social production and distribution; and that the proper gearing of his particular cog with all the other cogs is the condition of real freedom from cataclysms of the market, which ruin business and spread poverty and wretchedness among the people. Hence the businessman has hugged the illusion of independence and freedom; has preserved the ideas appropriate to the epoch of the individual enterprise and the family firm which long since have ceased to represent the predominant forms of enterprise. This cultural lag has a heavy responsibility for the tragic situation in which the world now finds itself. Business leaders might certainly be expected to have social ideas reflecting the realities of the social system in which they live.

Mr. Bennett has expressed some social ideas which, while far from new, are novel for a man of his position. But it is not the merit of the ideas which impresses; many leaders of business and culture see only the social dragons that stand in the way of their realization. They balk at the magnitude of the task of organizing a rationally-planned economy, of bringing the forces of production under the conscious control of appropriate social organs. They prefer to tinker with the mechanisms of the market, hoping that by some miracle it can be so improved that it will automatically realize the wish-dream of business -- a balanced relation of supply and demand and an orderly flow of goods into consumption at steady prices.....

In his radio speeches Mr. Bennett said that for four years his government had tinkered with the mechanism of the market with unsatisfactory results. The persistence of unemployment was the condemnation, final and complete, of the old system. Hence he concluded that the automatic regulation of the market could not be relied on to restore progress and prosperity. He, therefore, advocated government regulation and control and expressly stated that he did not mean fascism, which is government regulation and control in the interests of capital. If he meant more than that, he meant a planned economy in the interests of all the people. But unless he gets beyond the recommendations of the Price Spreads Commission he will make little progress in producing a rational organization of society upon the basis of economic planning motivated by the social purpose of providing everybody a standard of living in keeping with Canada's high productive capacity. But at least he has indicated the task which , if the capitalist will not undertake, Labour must undertake sooner or later if progress is to be the law of the future as it has been in the past. No planning authority at all concerned for the welfare of society could conceivably achieve such appalling mismanagement and waste of the nation's productive capacity as has been achieved by the automatic regulation of the mechanism in the market....

99. State Interference[135]

Spokesmen of special privilege warn Canadians against the perils of "economic planning." In the United States "economic planning" has become a political issue, with the Democrats vaunting the virtues of Roosevelt's "planning" and the Republicans protesting that it is undermining liberty. In most countries economic planning and its supposed threat to liberty have become a cause of warm controversy.

It is therefore important to try to visualize the question of economic planning in a proper perspective. Many forms of state intervention and control are commonly regarded as "economic planning." The imposition of tariffs upon imports, and the payment of railways or shipping subsidies, are forms of state intervention; and, in a sense, they constitute economic planning since they aim at results different from those which would be produced by the free play of economic forces. Such forms of state action

---

[135]*Canadian Unionist*, August 1936, 70-74.

are in high favour among those who are loudest in their denunciation of economic planning as a menace to liberty.

Evidently there is need to make a distinction between economic planning and mere state intervention. But such distinction cannot be easily made. The words "economic planning" have not yet acquired a precise meaning. When two persons are talking about economic planning it usually transpires that they have totally different problems and methods in mind. Study and analysis are needed to arrive at an understanding of the distinction between intervention and planning in the scientific meaning of the word.

Such study and analysis have been undertaken by economists working under the auspices of the International Labour Office of the League of Nations. Tentative conclusions based on a survey of measures taken by the governments of many countries to cope with the depression are now being published. The gist of these conclusions is:

"State intervention in the economic process...has been incoherent and heterogeneous to a degree....There was no thought-out policy or plan by which this intervention might be guided... The governments in the various countries acted for the most part on the principle of meeting difficulties as they arose...Of genuine economic planning there was practically none."

In the main, the government measures adopted during the depression may be appropriately described as "panic planning." They have been designed to provide piecemeal relief from the pressure of hard conditions; they have been palliatives -- not solutions. They have lacked coherence or unity of purpose; indeed, in not a few instances, they have aimed at contradictory purposes. This is not surprising. The politicians who determine public policy had little or no understanding of the causes of the depression. They were for the most part believers in an economic theory the justification of which vanished some time ago with the disappearance of the *quasi-laissez-faire* conditions of the past. They thought the depression was but a recurrence of a periodic phenomenon which would be overcome in due course by the self-recuperative powers of the system. They hopefully predicted that prosperity was just around the corner. They did not see that the completeness and suddenness of the collapse of the top-heavy structure of the fictitious prosperity of the boom period was a sign and portent that the foundations of the system had begun to disintegrate. They did not, therefore, realize the magnitude and complexity of the task with which the disaster of the depression confronted society. They have for the most part only recently begun to understand that something drastic happened in 1929, that there is something fundamentally wrong with the economic system. That, while not flattering to their intelligence, is still not surprising. The mental reorientation required to face frankly the fact that the system has become hopelessly incompetent to serve the needs of the people, and to realize that radical reconstruction is necessary, is not easy; it takes time.

Some naive beneficiaries of the system still believe that, if governments refrained from intervention, the free play of economic forces would automatically promote such harmonious readjustments of its creaking parts that it would function in a satisfactory manner. But, as for a hundred years the system -- save in war time -- has only given the workers three years of relative "prosperity" out of every ten, its functioning was never really satisfactory to them. On this point it is sufficient to quote the observation of League of Nations economists: "It is now generally realized in most countries that there can be no going back to the *laissez-faire* methods of the past."

State intervention in economic affairs is not a new thing. Protective tariffs, subsidies, factory acts, compensation laws, public utility commissions, represent methods of state action and interference with liberty. More recently extensions of national services have taken the form of organizations to protect and conserve natural resources. Typical examples are: the United States National Resources Board and Civilian Conservation Corps; the Canadian organizations for the settlement of the idle city workers upon the land. Such services have an economic purpose, though they also have a social motive insofar as they are designed to provide opportunities of work for the unemployed.

....State intervention in economic affairs, as will be manifest from the above summary of some of the various forms it has taken, has followed somewhat fortuitous and haphazard lines of development. It has lacked the coherency and unity of purpose which are implicit requirements of the concept of economic planning. Some types of state action have had overlapping purposes; each type aimed at special results in a particular sphere, and if it served other purposes in other spheres that was more an incidental consequence than the outcome of deliberate design.

Genuine economic planning would have a general social purpose as its unifying principle. That purpose would be to supply all the legitimate wants of all the people. All economic activities would primarily be planned to serve that purpose. The production of both capital and consumer goods would then be regulated in accordance with a pre-determined program for the improvement of the standard of living. Adjustments would be made to ensure the provision of the different categories of goods in their right relative proportions. It may then be found advisable to restrict the output of certain farm products. In that case, farmers who now partly waste their labour on sub-marginal land would be given more remunerative work producing articles of utility which many farm households now lack. It may be found necessary to compel monopoly industries to increase their output, as it is evident now some restrict production in order to hold up prices.

Genuine economic planning will come, despite the opposition of those who wish to preserve their liberty to exploit the workers. The taboos which privileged interests have established are losing their power over the minds of the plain people. Economic planning means conscious control of both natural forces and economic processes, and therefore the freedom of the workers from the fear of unemployment, accident, illness, and a dependent old age.

100. The Menace of Fascism[136]

Finance capital demands more profits.

To lower wages is the simplest way to increase profits. Nothing could be simpler. Still it is a short-sighted view overlooking the fact that the worker is a consumer as well as a producer. Many errors of economic thinking are due to failure to keep in mind this dual relationship to economic problems. The effect of Fascist economic policy, which is not thought of, is a reduction of the purchasing power, of the effective demand, in the home market.

The Fascists then seek to increase the profits of capital by fixing prices at higher levels by state decrees. But higher prices also reduce the purchasing power of wages; the absorbing capacity of the home market further declines.

So the Fascists subsidize exports in various ways, and restrict imports by quotas, exchange controls and other devices.

Whereas in "democratic" countries the political power is used to bolster capitalist privilege by such negative methods as tariffs, in Fascist countries the political state becomes the open partner of finance capital, using its powers in a direct and positive manner, to assist capital in intensifying the exploitation of the people.

As the home market shrinks, Fascism is impelled to pursue aggressive external politics....All the fine promises of Fascism are reduced to this: the people must be sacrificed to serve the need of capitalism for new markets and new fields of exploitation. It is the negation of all constructive policy, for it holds that recourse to war is the essential condition of a nation's survival. One successful war will not suffice, for the further development of the national capitalism made possible by new markets acquired by such

---

[136]Originally published as "What Fascism Exemplifies," *Labor World/Le Monde Ouvrier*, 27 March 1937.

war, would create a need for still more markets. The Fascist theory envisages a perpetual succession of wars, with head-on collisions between Fascist powers themselves...

Can Fascism deceive Canadians, as the Germans and Italians were deceived? The essential features of Fascism may very well be developed here, under another name. The coloured shirts and other theoretical trappings are not essentials. Behind the demand for a National Government is the essential Fascist purpose to strengthen the powers of the Federal Government and use them to buttress the position of finance capital by exercising some control over provincial finances. A national government would be apt to discover that the interests of finance capital require the suppression of free speech, the right of assembly, and the right to organize except in regimented unions.

101. "National" Government and Canadian Fascism[137]

The strength of the movement for a so-called "National" government should not be under-estimated. Behind it are powerful interests, for it is in line with Fascism. The big interests do not need to finance a Canadian Hitler to organize storm-troops. A union of the old parties from the top will suffice to set up the totalitarian State, that is, the State without the mask of political democracy, frankly using its power to repress the workers and farmers.

The organization of a "National" government is being advocated by the muddle-heads, as well as the troubled interests. There is an effort to create bogeys to frighten and stampede the unthinking voters. Able propagandists try to make one out of the railway debt. By misrepresentation they seek to create the impression that the railway debt is mounting at a rate that will soon bankrupt the country. But the public is not quite convinced. They wonder why, if the C.N.R. is such a white elephant, the C.P.R. should want to get control of it!

But arguments for a "National" government are plausible. Such a government, it is said, is needed to solve the railway problem. Both old parties are pledged to public operation of the C.N.R. Hence only a 'National' government, free and independent of old party promises, can solve the railway problem -- by handing the Canadian National lines over to the C.P.R. That is good lawyer logic....

The pundits harp on the failures and short-comings of political democracy. What they mean is that the game of party politics is ceasing to serve as camouflage for the antagonisms and contradictions in which society is entangled. In accordance with the theory of a sham democracy

---

[137]*Canadian Railway Employees' Monthly*, February 1935, 30-31.

we have been taught that the State is the organ of the popular will. But we begin to see that it is really an organ of the property interests -- and we see it having increasing difficulty in effecting compromises between the interests of the different classes of property owners.

So long as the chief direct activity of the State was the exercise of the police power, and the economic causes of class divisions were obscure, a political system under which the control of the State might pass from one party representing particular economic interests to another party representing somewhat dissimilar economic interests was permissible. "Turn about" in using the power of the State to advance the interests of the two groups was "fair play"; besides, it gave the mass of the people the illusion that they were masters of the State, controlling its policies and actions. Whatever party was in office, the State could be trusted to use its power to protect the general interests of the propertied classes. But now, with the masses becoming conscious of the real function of the State, with the difficulty of disguising the conflict between the interests of property and the welfare of the people, the continuous and complete control of the power of the State is desired by the big capitalists, and they seek to persuade the little fellow that a "National" government is necessary to protect the little fellow's interests, not only from the menace of the C.C.F. and other mass movements, but from the State itself, and its appetite for taxes. But we may be sure that a "National" government here, like the "National" governments of Mussolini and Hitler, would be a tool of the big interests. It would facilitate rather than retard the characteristic process of the evolution of property. As the first "National" government of France, that after the Great Revolution, sacrificed feudal property, so a "National" government in Canada would be impelled to assist big capitalist property to devour the remaining remnants of bourgeois property, to help big business expropriate little business....

In the circumstances, a "National" government, as an expression of Canadian Fascism, is on the cards. Mr. Stevens[138] is a symbol of the middle-class revolt against the financial overlords who have been mismanaging the economic system. A middle-class revolt is the first phase of Fascism. "The second stage," says *Harper's Magazine*, "is an intellectual fog in which the various wish-dreams of the different economic groups wander about looking for fulfillment. In the fog, the government adopts certain measures supposed to be necessary for the restoration of confidence and prosperity, and when the fog clears, the same old financial crowd is discovered running the works. The standard

---

[138]H.H.Stevens (1878-1973) was a controversial Conservative politician of the 1930s. In 1934 he headed the Royal Commission on Price Spreads, to investigate serious business abuses. Stevens called for drastic reform, founded the Reconstruction Party in 1935 to fight for the "little man" against the depression, and won nearly 10% of the popular vote (but only one seat, his own). He returned to the Conservatives in 1939.

of living is subjected to the needs of finance, every avenue of intelligent discussion is closed, and all safety valves are tied down."

A "National" government is desired by the interests precisely because it would permit such a strategy against the masses -- and the middle-class itself. Such a government could build a little boom on the quick sands of a sinking standard of living, but that boom would soon collapse in a deeper crisis. And then humanity, to save itself, would have to embark on the great adventure of achieving intelligent control of its economic affairs.

102. How A World War Would Transform The Government[139]

....How could Canada finance another major war? Today about 40 per cent of the assets of the chartered banks consists of government securities, compared with only about 2 per cent before the Great War. Now both the borrowing and taxing capacities of Canadian governments are pretty well strained. Resort to the issue of printing press money would be necessary to carry on the war after a few months. That, left to work its course, would mean a rapid rise of prices, and misery for those of fixed incomes; business would slow down because the future would be so uncertain that businessmen would contract their commitments.

But the government could not afford to allow inflation free rein. It would have to control prices, regulate wages, regiment labour. And, having thus left the profit motive little or no room to operate in it, would have to take over the planning and direction of nearly all economic activities. Another big war would compel Canada to resort to state capitalism or national [socialism].

Is it possible to believe that any sort of Canadian government or social system can sustain the effort of another great war without getting rid of the present burden of public debt? The government would be constrained to put the national finances through some process of bankruptcy, and that would inevitably topple the pillars of private financial capitalism. The value of existing government bonds, bank shares, insurance policies, would probably shrink -- probably to the vanishing point in a convulsion of social bankruptcy....

Whether sentimental loyalty to Britain should outweigh these cogent economic reasons against Canadian participation in another war is a matter for individual decision. But the idea that Canada owes any special obligation to the British ruling class may be offset by the immense tribute the Canadian workers have paid to British capitalists over generations

---

[139]Originally published as "Millionaire War Mongers," *Labour World/Le Monde Ouvrier,* 19 November 1938.

and by Canadian participation in the Great War. A pertinent question is: has the British ruling class made so good a use of the victory of the war to make the world safe for democracy as to justify Canadian participation in another war in the interests of that class?...

103. The Middle Class and a National Government[140]

...The index of employment on June 1, 1938, was 12.2 per cent below that of November 1, whereas between the like dates after the great panic of October 1929, the decline was 6.5 per cent. A doubling of the rate of decline of employment suggests that this depression may become more devastating than the last.

What is likely to be the outcome? Canadian society is scarcely ripe for radical reconstruction. Large sectors of the middle class, including the better circumstanced farmers, have a sense of particular wrongs which they attribute to particular causes; they are not conscious of a general wrong weighing upon them as a consequence of the chronic crisis of capitalist society, induced by the coming to a head of its inherent contradictions. They still regard the system as dynamic -- capable of further expansion. Accordingly, they see their difficulties as consequences of particular dislocations of the system, and believe that some adjustments will suffice to enable them to escape their frustrations and realize their ambitions. The import of the Spencerian theory that within a system evolution proceeds till it reaches a climax and that then a period of devolution follows has not come home to them.

Despite their frustrations of recent years, resulting from the narrowing of their economic base, the middle class still have a large measure of moral confidence, stout wills, and a conviction of political importance. The course of Canadian history may sometimes suggest to them that they have only had the illusion of political power. But that does not upset them. While an expanding economy opened up new economic opportunities, they were too busy taking advantage of them as individuals to perceive, except on rare occasions, the need of political action on behalf of the interests of their class as a whole. Because of the diversity and incompatibility of their economic interests they have not, and probably cannot develop, a full-fledged class consciousness, such as the upper class of capitalists has developed and the working class is acquiring. But the increasing instability of their economic basis has been making them aware of interests which are in conflict, on the one hand, with those of big business, and, on the other, with those of the workers. They are developing, however vaguely, a theory of middle-class interests, and a theory becomes a material force to the extent that it takes hold of a class.

---

[140]Originally published as an untitled letter, *Canadian Forum*, August 1938, 146-147.

The Canadian middle class is adept at organization when it has a purpose to serve. All things considered, it possesses more resolution and a greater potentiality of political power than the mass of the wage-earners or the small farmers. As the depression deepens the middle class will reach out for political power. Their essentially capitalist mentality will incline them to the idea of a National Government Party, parading its pretention to be the only possible instrument of national unity which will be described as the primary requirement for coping with the national emergency. By lavish promises the National Government party will attract the support of all the bewildered, the frustrate[d] and hopeless voters -- as well as the middle class. The government that it will set up will inaugurate a sham fight on big business for the edification of little business, while it proceeds to undermine the organizations of the workers and farmers. It will not need, at the outset at any rate, to adopt the ruthless methods employed by dictatorships founded on organized gangsterdoms. It will, on the plea of saving the country, be able to give capitalism a new lease of life, by intensifying the exploitation of the masses and making the masses believe that acceptance of a lower standard of living is a patriotic duty. The continuing necessity of ever-increasing exploitation will, however, force it to resort to ruthlessness sooner or later. And it will betray the middle class as unscrupulously as Hitler and Mussolini have done.

A national government in Canada will mean some form of Fascism, the final refuge of a capitalism too incompetent and corrupt to rule by the methods of political democracy. That may not be an unmitigated calamity. History will probably allow Fascism some merits. It speeds up the concentration of the control of industry: it eliminates superfluous enterprises. In Germany it has led towards a consciously planned economy -- though for the perverse, insensate purpose of preparation for war. Fascism strips the mystic veil from capitalism, which has concealed the harsh face of exploitation. During the bourgeois regime, mystery has shrouded the so-called economic laws, and the economic relations of men. Property has been represented as an [economic] category; its power to exploit labour has been understood by the worker, and the degree of exploitation has for him been an unknown quantity.

In the feudal regime the economic relations of men were fitted into a political framework. Serf, yeoman, baron, earl, etc., stood in relations to one another fixed by law or custom. Each knew what he owed in service and kind to his overlord, and -- before feudalism became corrupt -- what his overlord owed to him in the way of protection against enemies or misfortune. Each understood the degree of exploitation he had to submit to, and recognized that it depended upon degrees of political power.

Fascism is industrial feudalism. Under it, a political power, not a mysterious economic power, such as the law of supply and demand, determines the degree of exploitation, fixes wages and prices, regiments labour, tells the industrialist and farmer what to produce.

This political power, wielded by a government, is something tangible and concrete, making artificial laws against which people will know how to fight -- something different from the mysterious economic laws which have held the masses in thrall for generations.

v. The Scope of Possible Reforms

104. Recasting the International Structure of Debt[141]

[Editor's Note. -- The facts of the European economic situation as set forth in the following article are of inestimable value in forming a proper perspective, particularly because the writer is an economist and journalist of experience, and because he has written from a first-hand knowledge of the conditions described. He is at present in Paris, France.

In the course of his statements Mr. McKay takes the striking, but apparently logical view that the salvation of the present system does not lie in the cancellation of Inter-Allied War Debt but rather in the cancellation of internal indebtedness -- the sums which each nation borrowed from its own people. He declares that the only reason why this has not been advocated is because it would involve personal sacrifices among those who are nominally in control of finance. Mr. McKay points out that the cancellation of domestic loans would remove the greatest deterrent from European industry and would consequently be of inestimable benefit to labour because of the expansion that would be made possible. The article is probably the most valuable on the subject to appear in Canada and was written exclusively for the *Canadian Railroad Employees Monthly*.]

In the present struggle between Great Britain and France over the question of making Germany pay war reparations it is said that French policy is mainly influenced by political considerations, while that of England is dictated by economic considerations. France, it is claimed, wants to assure her political security and integrity, and to this end would impose on Germany burdens which will tend to prevent that country developing sufficient economic power to finance another war against France. Some British journals accuse France of imperialistic aims, including ambition to establish a political hegemony over the most of Europe. On the other hand, it is said that Britain is mainly concerned to assure the economic restoration of Europe, and thus, by reviving trade,

---

[141]Originally published as "Cancellation of Internal Debts Will Save Europe," *Canadian Railroad Employees Monthly*, September 1922, 116; 120.

enable her to employ her workpeople, many of whom are now receiving unemployment doles. Unfortunately Great Britain has no positive policy for the restoration of Europe; her proposal to relieve Germany for an indefinite period of the obligations to pay war reparations is a negative measure, and it is suggested in some quarters that this would enable Germany to attain a dominant position in the markets of the world. In other quarters it is pointed out that relieving Austria did not enable that country to effect a recovery or offer a market to the goods of Britain or any other country. But the implication has no great force. Germany is a country of varied technique and immense industrial vitality, and, though deprived of the iron mines of Alsace and Lorraine, has still large natural resources. On the other hand, Austria was deprived, by the Treaty of Versailles, of much of the territory containing the natural resources necessary for a successful industrial life. Austria herself is mainly an agricultural country, and, though she has valuable iron deposits, has no coal to work them.

France is in an unfortunate position financially. Although her government has incurred a floating debt of nearly ten billion dollars in order to provide money to restore her war ravaged departments, she still has 2,000,000 of her people living in huts or dug-outs. And she regards Earl Balfour's note, suggesting that unless the United States cancels her credits against Britain, Britain must collect the money owed her by France, as a demand to pay up, and also a notice that the settlement of the allied war debts must be considered apart from the question of German reparations. At the time the Balfour note was issued Lloyd George was urging France to forego her claims against Germany, though, unless she obtains money from Germany, France cannot meet the loans she has made for reparation work without imposing more huge taxes on her people, -- and her wage workers are now resisting the payment of income taxes.

Facing bankruptcy itself, the French Government finds it difficult to consider the possibility of the bankruptcy of Germany, and the disastrous consequences which would probably ensue to Europe as a whole and to France herself. But British policy envisages that possibility and fears it -- fears it would precipitate a world-wide financial panic which would stop the wheels of industry, fill the street with hoards of hungry workers, and plunge Europe into Bolshevism, and there are signs that even in France the financiers with international interests and an international outlook are beginning to fear that further pressure on Germany at the present time may lead to the complete collapse of her finances, and to an industrial debacle which may spread ruin over all Europe.

In the face of this possibility -- a bankrupt Germany tottering on the edge of Bolshevism -- French policy shows some signs of wavering. Poincaré is somewhat less intransigent than he was, but his difficulty is to find a way of retreat from his present position which will enable him to save his face.

Cross currents of economic interests which heretofore have been obscure are rising to the surface, and these may have an important effect upon the course of political affairs. Shortly after the breakdown of the London Conference it was announced that German Capitalists interested in German coal mines had acquired control of large iron deposits in Austria. Immediately important Paris papers put forward the suggestion that the great industrialists of France and Germany should endeavour to reach an agreement which would assure the effective exploitation of the iron mines of France and the coal fields of the Ruhr Valley. It was pointed out that Germany had the coal and France the iron, and that an understanding between the industrialists controlling these two materials was necessary for the efficient development of both industries. This proposal very evidently involved the hope that the great German industrialists would be able to obtain a control of the German government, and that the agreement between the industrialists of the two countries would soon be followed by an understanding between the two governments, an understanding that would protect the interests of the industrialists, though it probably would not be designed to promote the welfare of working people of either country. Hugo Stinnes, "The man for whom the war was made," as the Germans say, has vast interests in the Ruhr Valley, the district threatened by Poincaré's proposed occupation, and it is said his agents have been busy in French financial circles. Be that as it may, Premier Poincaré has shown no hurry to carry out his programme of seizing wages and guarantees in the form of mines and forests in the Ruhr Valley, and it is believed in some quarters that the delay is not unconnected with negotiations between the great industrialists looking to a scheme for mutual profit. The French industrialists who have iron to sell and need coal probably do not like the idea of German capitalists developing the iron mines of Austria. Moreover, if they can arrive at an economic understanding they would probably have more confidence in a German government controlled by the great German industrialists than in the present administration which is unduly subject to working class influence.

British newspapers are gravely discussing the possibility of Europe plunging into financial bankruptcy, industrial chaos and social anarchy. The *Westminster Gazette* "cannot understand the nonchalance with which the French contemplate the frightful possibilities of the future." Nor can it understand why the French apparently do not realize that "with the ruin of Germany will vanish the French hope of obtaining reparations." The *Daily News* says: "The causes which threaten to plunge Europe into anarchy are of two sorts: (1)The disorders, financial and commercial, which have caused the disturbing fall of the mark and the practical annihilation of the Austrian crown; (2)The menace of a French military intervention in Germany and the possibility of a military intervention in Austria. However, we believe that no nation is sufficiently foolish or wicked to precipitate Europe and the world in the frightful calamities which would result from military action by, it matters not what country."

Unfortunately, these alarmists are not without their *raison d'être*. The capitalist system in Europe may crack up in the near future, and, because the working class is nowhere sufficiently united and powerful to erect immediately a new order on the ruins of the old, a period of industrial stagnation and civil commotion would probably supervene. And if Europe takes the plunge, the reactions upon the American continent may be serious enough -- not all at once, perhaps, but in a very short time.

This danger, that the capitalist system may collapse, has recently become a nightmare of the capitalist class and has even developed a serious discussion of the necessity of cancelling the Inter-Allied war debts. The feeling is that the war debts hang like mill-stones around the necks of the capitalist nations, threatening to drag all of them into the abyss. Wm. J. Bryan, former candidate for the presidency of the United States, has declared that the crisis in Europe is so grave that the United States ought to undertake to cancel her war credits against the European nations as soon as they come together on terms satisfactory to themselves. A conference of American bankers at New York is reported to have adopted a resolution favoring a scheme of general cancellation of international war debts, and that is significant of the way the wind is beginning to blow. The United States would be the heaviest loser.

In capitalist Britain and America there is a growing annoyance with French capitalism because of its insistence on reparations from Germany. It is feared that French pressure on Germany will cause a convulsion there, which may generate an international financial panic and shake the whole fabric of capitalism to its foundations. But capitalist Britain and America are realizing that they cannot expect capitalist France to renounce its claims against Germany while they insist on collecting the money France owes them. Hence the proposal that the Inter-Allied war debts be cancelled or greatly reduced. This, it is assumed, would enable the nations to expand their industries and re-establish international trade on a great scale, but would it?

Suppose the United States Government cancelled its credits against European nations. That would not mean that the debts had ceased to be a burden upon the industrial economy of the world. The United States government would merely assume the obligation of meeting the claims of private money lenders. It would doubtless have to increase taxes, and thus impose new burdens upon American industry, and upon the American workingmen. But the result for the financial capitalists who loaned to the government the money that the government loaned to Europe would be satisfactory enough.

No doubt the United States government is in a better position to carry these obligations than the European governments, but this does not necessarily imply that their formal transfer to the shoulders of the American workers would solve the problem of the restoration of world trade. As a matter of fact the United States government is today paying interest on most of these obligations, because no European nation except Great Britain has made any budgetary provision for the payment of interest on their foreign war loans. It is, therefore, not the actual burden of debts owed to the United States that is to-day preventing the economic recovery of Europe, although, of course, the prospective burden may be discouraging enterprise; it is rather their internal war debts. The arguments for the cancellation of war debts as between nations apply with equal force to the question of cancelling war debts as between a government and its nationals -- that is, the internal war debts. But we do not find the financial capitalists advocating such treatment of internal debts, because that would involve personal sacrifices, which are not called for by the proposal to shift the burden of the international debts.

No plan of dealing with war debts, however, can be effective, unless it involves the cancellation of internal debts; that alone would relieve the burden upon the industry and labour of the world as a whole. The British Labour Party sees that more or less clearly. Its proposal for a capital levy amounts to writing off a large proportion of the internal war debt, or the cancellation of war bonds of large denominations, leaving the small holder of war bonds untouched. No doubt a proposal that the government should cancel its internal debts would be repugnant to the wage-worker having a few hundred dollars invested in war loans, but meantime this burden of debt is handicapping industry and causing unemployment, and a great percentage of workers -- who have not carelessly presented their war bonds to promoters of wild-cat schemes -- are selling them at reduced prices in order to live.

105. Unemployment as a National Responsibility[142]

During the war the great ones of the nations promised the workers a new world after the conflict, and the near-great talked of creating a new heaven and a new earth, as if it was an easy matter to improve upon the work of the Almighty. But it now appears that the promise was only intended for those who died and went -- let us hope -- to a new and better world. At any rate the great and the near-great no longer promise a new world for the workers who remain in the land of the living; on the contrary they are shouting from the house tops that the workers must go back to the old world, the old world of normalcy, the blessed world of profits for the few and low wages and long workdays for the mutable many.

---

[142]Originally published as "Unemployment a National Charge," *Canadian Railroad Employees Monthly*, January 1922, 18.

What is the import of this injunction -- back to normalcy? Does it not serve notice on the working class that so long as the capitalist system endures they must abandon hope of better things? Do not the capitalists realize that when they declare that the great need of business is a return to normal wages they are proclaiming their own incompetence, or justifying the contention that the capitalist system has outlived its usefulness and cannot carry civilization forward and spread its benefits over the masses of the people [?] What do they think the workers think of a system which can promise them nothing except a meagre livelihood -- and not even security of that meagre livelihood? Possibly they believe the workers don't think; at any rate after studying the election returns they might come to the conclusion that the workers are not consuming much gray matter in thinking about improving their condition. At the same time the election results indicate a widespread dissatisfaction with existing conditions, and turning out a government, while perhaps of no great importance from the worker's standpoint, is the most obvious way for expressing dissatisfaction. In any case the capitalists notice that their system can only be operated on a basis of low wages and long workdays must eventually make an impression upon the minds of the workers even in Canada, as it has in England where, as G.K. Chesterton points out, the breaking down of the capitalist system is evidenced by the fact that the workers are showing a growing disposition to refuse to work for it. Intellectual perception of the inability of the capitalist system to carry on satisfactorily is not, however, of itself sufficient to call a labour party into being, in opposition to the parties which uphold the present system of things. There must be the will to action, and at present the workers suffer from a lack of will power.

The capitalist class might have avoided the present criticism of their system and prolonged its existence indefinitely if at the conclusion of the war they had declared a general moratorium, and arranged for doles to those of their own class unable to earn anything by useful work, instead of doles to unemployed members of the working class. Relieved for four or five years of the immense mountain of war debts and profiteers' levies, an adjustment of international exchange might have been made, trade facilitated and industry kept going full blast. But the desire for interest and profits over-reached itself; production was allowed to slow down through lack of credits or badly balanced credits, and the process by which the individual capitalist sought to cope with his difficulties, reduction of employees and wages, only increased the difficulties of the business classes generally. It is a curious fact -- due to his individualistic outlook -- that the average businessman assumes that the only way to promote production is to reduce wages, though every reduction of wages must decrease the effective market demand for products, and thus further limit the possibilities of profitable production....

106. The Keynesian Prescription[143]

J.M.Keynes, the famous capitalist economist, has advanced abreast of, even ahead of, the position taken by the Right Hon. R.B. Bennett in the New Year of 1935 -- and held temporarily. Like Mr. Bennett in his [New Deal] radio addresses, Keynes now declares that the mechanism of the market no longer suffices as a regulator of production, and that state control and regulation of some important economic activities has become necessary to save the system from collapse. He sets forth his latest views in a new book entitled *The General Theory of Employment, Interest, and Money*.

Keynes long pursued the idea that private banks, by raising or lowering the rate of interest, could regulate investment and control the price level, and thereby assure orderly business and full employment. Now, he has come to the conclusion that the intervention of the state is necessary to control both the amount and direction of investment, with the object of assuring a balanced development of the production of capital goods and of providing full employment.

Readers of the *Canadian Unionist* may recall an article by A.R. Mosher,[144] entitled *The Way out of the Ditch*, which appeared several years ago when the depression was young. Mr. Mosher discussed the causes of the depression, and the measures necessary to get out of it and avoid a recurrence. In particular, he emphasized the fact that during the boom there had been a great over-production of capital goods -- newsprint mills, for example -- with a consequent diversion of purchasing power from where it was most needed, the market for consumptive goods. The inevitable result was that when it was belatedly realized that capital equipment had been created greatly in excess of requirements, the capital goods industries closed down, throwing many men out of employment and setting in motion the depressive forces which quickly ditched general business. Therefore, a fundamental requirement of orderly progress was the setting up by the state of a commission with authority to ration investment, to determine the proportion of the national income to be allotted to investment and the types and quantities of capital equipment needed for replacement and improvement and for the establishment of a balanced relationship between the various means of production needed to supply all the consumptive needs of the people.

---

[143]Originally published as "Conversion of an Economist," *Canadian Unionist*, April 1936, 302-304.

[144]Aaron Roland Mosher (1881-1959), a native of Nova Scotia, became the President of the All-Canadian Congress of Labour in 1927 after leading the Canadian Brotherhood of Railway Employees. He was president of the Canadian Congress of Labour, 1940-1951, and honourary president of the Canadian Labour Congress in 1956. Unlike many other labour leaders of the 1930s, Mosher was a strong supporter of the CCF.

Now Keynes has come round to the view expressed by Mr. Mosher and long held by labour that state action is necessary to control investment. He makes that the king-pin of his program to save the system from collapse. He would have the state control the rate of interest and adjust the supply of money with the object of maintaining full employment. He proposes that the state start extensive public works in order to provide needed employment, and he would increase taxes to provide the wherewithal to pay for such works, defending this proposal as a means of redistributing the national income.

Keynes denounces thrift. To discourage saving he would reduce interest, and even impose a stamp duty on idle money. He sees a time coming when the rate of interest will be reduced to a vanishing-point. Then the *rentier* (interest-receiving) class will disappear.

It will be noticed that in his program for the regeneration of the capitalist system -- which he himself calls epoch-making -- Keynes envisages ironical consequences. The professional duty of the orthodox economists for a long time has been to defend the interest-taker, the type of capitalist who takes little risk and enjoys a comfortable feeling of security; to defend also the promoter, the type of capitalist who has been looked upon as the maker of progress and who takes risks with other people's money -- to get rich quickly himself. Now Keynes proposes to save his chief clients by himself arranging their gradual -- though far from painless -- extinction.

It may, of course, be said that he proposes to save other classes of capitalists by sacrificing the two classes which are presently most unpopular. But how he could extinguish the value of interest-bearing property without at the same time wiping out the value of other forms of property is a point not explained.

Keynes is vague on other important points. State control of the amount and direction of investment implies the planning, by some collective organ, of the production of capital goods. His idea of discouraging saving by reducing interest and imposing stamp duties assumes that the rich will be induced to spend on consumptive goods all their incomes except the portion which the state may allow them to invest in capital goods. Then Keynes assumes that the whole production of consumer goods will be taken out of the market; that the production of consumer goods will just balance consumption.

But the production of some goods requires little labour compared with other goods -- wheat, for instance. It would be easy to increase the production of wheat beyond consumption needs; for if the incomes of the masses were increased they would eat less wheat and more of other foodstuffs. State planning of the production of capital goods will not assure that a surplus of wheat will not be produced, or that there will not be a shortage of other consumer goods upon which surplus incomes might be spent.

Evidently some form of collective planning of the production of consumer goods is also necessary. That, indeed, is implicit in Keynes's new program. A balanced development of the production of capital goods implies their use to produce consumer goods in the proportions required to supply the wants of consumers. But it is not clear that the Keynes program makes definite provision for a planned economy in this sense. Certainly his program, as far as developed, would make for much greater stability of business and much greater and regular employment. That it would assure the masses what they have a right to expect in an age of technological progress -- a steady advance in their standard of living -- is not certain.

Keynes [envisages] a much greater degree of collective enterprise. He believes that it is possible to "refashion private enterprise drastically" without destroying it. He sees collective enterprise and private enterprise living happily together. But here he hardly means private enterprise in the sense of that conception today. It is rather his "refashioned" private enterprise.

In any form of society taxi-driving, for instance, may well be a "refashioned" private enterprise. It is now recognized as a private enterprise, yet it is subject to various collective regulations -- fixing maximum fares, allotting taxi stands, prescribing the technical qualifications of the driver, prohibiting cruising on the off chance of picking up a passenger, etc. But this business by its very nature imposed a certain co-operation even when the individual cab drivers were usually the owners of the vehicles they operated -- co-operation to build and maintain a shelter on their stands and to provide telephones so that people might readily avail themselves of their services. It is probable that individual taxi-owners, by proper co-operation, could give the public as efficient service as big taxi companies do.

Since the taxi-drivers perform a special kind of public service and use the public streets, their right of private enterprise is more limited than the rights of many other forms of private enterprise. Their number is limited to the size and number of the stands the city authorities may choose to allot them. But they have sufficient right of private enterprise to permit of its abuse. There are usually too many taxis, the consequence being a waste of time, and small earnings relative to either the capital invested in the taxis or the hours on duty of the driver, or both. The exercise of the right of private enterprise to the extent of overcrowding an occupation defeats the object of private enterprise.

This is not necessarily a reason why collective enterprise should replace private enterprise in the provision of taxi service. It does suggest, however, that there should be some collective control in the way of regulating the number of taxis and drivers. Experience would soon determine the number required to give adequate service to the people, and then the taxi drivers would have fairly steady work and good earnings.

This need of some form of collective control to fit private enterprise into the social division of labour which would assure supplies of goods and services in the right proportions, and so obviate waste of effort and time, will have to be recognized by all producers of goods and services. Only socially necessary labour counts. And if the enterprise of the individual producing goods or services fits into the scheme of the division of labour which best serves society, then individual enterprise may carry on alongside collective enterprise.

This bringing in of the taxi business has been a way of following the implications of the Keynes program. From the Labour point of view there are defects in his program, flaws in his argument. But certainly his new program and the views supporting it will have merit in the sight of the labour economists. Advocacy of his new program constrained him to make a devastating criticism of the theory of the orthodox economists that low wages would increase employment and stimulate business. Incidentally, he has jettisoned most of the other dogmas of the economists whose melancholy duty it is to defend the perpetuation of poverty and misery in a world of potential plenty.

107. The New Deal as a Social Experiment[145]

Unquestionably Roosevelt's experiment is of immense importance to Canada -- and the world. History offers nothing to compare with it, except the Russian experiment. It is a colossal attempt at social revolution by collaboration of classes whose interests, if similar in the matter of production, are sharply divided in the matter of the distribution of the product. What the outcome may be cannot be foreseen as yet; but on it hang issues of tremendous importance. Sociologists looking on the United States as the greatest social laboratory in the world have expressed fear that the resolution of the problems presented by the amazing concentration of its wealth, and its polyglot population, would entail a series of class wars. But now we have the spectacle of the vast majority of the people enthusiastically welcoming a plan of economic reconstruction, which involves the apparent dethronement of the time-honored fetishes of rugged individualism and *laissez-faire*, and calls for a regimentation of capital and labour almost as complete, in some respects, as the

---

[145]Originally published as "Roosevelt's Plan -- So Far," *Canadian Unionist*, August 1933, 39-40.

regimentation that has been realized in Soviet Russia. An apparent revolution in sentiment and temperament, anyhow, but, since it was effected under the influence of a fear that troubled the plutocracy, as well as the middle class and the masses, it remains to be seen whether here has been a real and lasting conversion....

His program is full of contradictory policies, but action begets a kind of [dialectical] understanding capable of resolving contradictions in a higher synthesis. And though the great experiment at state-inspired economic recovery may presently have the appearance of preparing the conditions of a new depression, Roosevelt cannot afford to let it do that; he will be impelled to find a method of resolving the contradiction between his formula of progress, that "wages must advance faster than prices", and the fact that so far prices have advanced faster than wages. Having embarked on a great adventure in state capitalism -- which seems in line with evolution -- he cannot turn back without disaster to his reputation, and disillusionment and degradation for the people....But state capitalism, while it may provide employment at a living wage for everybody, is not the final goal of society; the Labour movement will not be absolved from its mission -- the capture of the political power of the state in order to establish a classless society, and open new vistas of progress and prosperity that the capitalists with their melancholy mission of perpetuating poverty and misery never dreamed of.

108. Economic Planning Under Capitalism[146]

....Since the crisis of 1929, economic planning has been the subject of a large number of books and many more articles, and good progress has been made towards the elaboration of a coherent theory of a planned economy. Theoretical research has produced the outlines of a systematically planned economy and indicated with reasonable clearness that it would be more capable of establishing an economic equilibrium than the unplanned individualistic economy, while possessing the advantage of providing greater well-being for the mass of the people.

Various types of collective economy have been proposed in the past; mostly they have postulated the abolition of private ownership of the means of production. Some recent explorers in this field have taken the view that a planned economy does not necessarily require the substitution of collective ownership for private ownership. They hold that if the National Planning Authority had sufficient power to exercise direction and control over the promotion and management of enterprises, the fact they might be privately owned would be of little consequence. This view accords with the course of business development; more and more the

---

entrepreneur becomes distinct from the capitalist, the person who supplies the capital....

A planned economy, of the rational and methodical organization of production, with the conscious intention of providing the fullest possible satisfaction of the wants of all the people is not, however, incompatible with the existence of various forms of private ownership, even of the means of production and distribution. In his argument for "The Functional Society," which is another name for a planned economy with a conscious social purpose, R.H. Tawney[147] says:

"If the creation of a functional society involved an extension of public ownership in certain spheres, it would in others foster an extension of private property. For it is not private ownership, but private ownership divorced from work, which is corrupting to the principle of industry; and the idea of some Socialists that private property in land or capital is necessarily mischievous is a piece of scholastic pedantry as absurd as that of those conservatives who would invest all property with some kind of mysterious sanctity. It all depends on what sort of property it is and for what purpose it is used. The State can retain its eminent domain and control alienation, as it does under the Homestead Laws of the Dominion, with sufficient stringency to prevent the creation of a class of functionless property-owners. In that case, there is no inconsistency between encouraging simultaneously a multiplication of small farmers who own their own land, or masters who own their shops, and urging the abolition of private ownership in those industries, unfortunately today the most conspicuous, in which the private owner is an absentee shareholder.

Indeed, the second reform would help the first. Insofar as the community tolerates functionless property, it makes difficult, if not impossible, the restoration of the small man in agriculture or industry, who cannot hold his own in a world dominated by great estates or capitalist finance. Insofar as the community abolishes those kinds of property which are merely parasitic, it facilitates the restoration of the small property owners in those kinds of industry for which small ownership is adapted."[148]

---

[147]McKay refers to Richard Henry Tawney (1800-1962), professor at the London School of Economics and president of the Workers' Educational Association (1928-1944). He was one of the most important economic historians in Britain during the first half of the twentieth century, whose academic works combined moral outrage and economic analysis. Among his important works were *The Agrarian Problem in the Sixteenth Century* (1912), *The Acquisitive Society* (1921), *Religion and the Rise of Capitalism* (1916), *Equality* (1931), and *Land and Labour in China* (1932).

[148]McKay is adapting R.H.Tawney, *The Acquisitive Society* (London: G. Bell, 1921; reprinted, Fontana Library, 1961). The relevant passage begins: "Thus, if in certain spheres it [the creation of a functional society] involved the extension of public ownership, it would in others foster an extension of private property...." (82)

In the planless, competitive society, the fact that a small business may be highly efficient and economical is no guarantee of its survival. Big business can drive a small business to the wall by cutting prices for a time; then it can recoup its losses by raising prices, because its control over the market increases as it crushes its small competitors. A planned economy may have room in it for many more small enterprises than exist today. That big business flourishes because it is always conducted more efficiently and economically than small business is not certain. The great growth of big business since prewar days has not, in any case, been accompanied, as might be expected, by declines in prices of goods mainly produced by big business.

In the capitalist system the objective of the magnates of finance is to set up a holding company controlling all the companies in a whole industry. If they achieved that, their next logical step would be to set up a super holding company controlling the holding companies of each and every industry. The super holding company would be the planning authority for all industries, the supreme Economic General Staff.

A planned economy would have a structure similar to that which would meet the big financiers' idea of a perfect system. But there would be a difference in purpose. In one case, the supreme general staff would be concerned with the promotion of the interests of a vast vertical private trust; in the other, it would be concerned with promoting the welfare of the general public....

109. The Possibilities of an Orderly Recovery[149]

The problem of keeping the Canadian economy expansive encompasses that of ending unemployment, that of assimilating immigrants, that of getting rid of railway deficits and lessening the burden of taxation.

Probably no country has a more elastic economy. The Canadian index of industrial production rose from 52 in March, 1921, to 147 in January, 1929; then fell to 63 in March, 1933; rose again to 133 in November, 1937; fell back to 109 in February, 1938, and then starting up again in June rose to 128 in November last. This dizzy career of industrial production may imply defects in the national economy, but it surely indicates a large capacity for expansion.

That is also inferable from the fact that there is no lack of the material conditions of expansion, undeveloped natural resources, surplus labour and potential loan capital.

---

[149]Originally published as "Orderly Expansion is Essence of Problem," *Saturday Night*, 4 February 1939.

Many people do not take the trouble to envisage the economic problem as primarily one of promotion of the conditions of orderly expansion -- or perhaps more properly adding new type industries.

They are apt to have their attention focussed upon the more glaring aspects of the problem such as the evil of unemployment, and while that is natural it inclines them to the illusion that remedial treatment of these glaring conditions, which essentially are effects of more obscure causes, will somehow work the needed solution.

Even J.M. Keynes in his *General Theory of Employment* assumes that if one condition of full employment is established all the other conditions will automatically take care of themselves.

Some think that a more or less satisfactory solution of the economic problem could be found through government assistance to back-to-the-land movements. But life on the farm cannot be self-sustained unless the numerous industries taken over by the factory system are returned to the farm and household; and that would mean the decay of the cities.

Perhaps all modern economic problems could be got rid of by scrapping the machines and returning to the use of the tools of the stone age. But then a great part of the human race would also have to be scrapped.

Some believe that shortening the work week would, by spreading employment, end or at least greatly alleviate the evil of unemployment. Some enterprises have indeed discovered that a 35-hour week gives the best and most economical operating results. But that cannot be true of all enterprises.

One thing shortening the work week would do, would be to lower living standards; it is therefore an irrational or defeatist proposal. With room for great improvement in the dietary, clothing and shelter standards of the multitudes a more rational aim would be two daily shifts of eight hours each. If there is a question of the right to, or desirability of, more leisure, it would be better served by extending the annual holiday than by shortening the work week. In any case, the length of the work week in any industry should be determined by technical and health considerations.

Some hold that raising real wages would solve all economic ills. In the boom period, 1924 to 1929, wages rose faster than retail prices. But the rise in real wages did not prevent the development of the conditions of a depression, any more than in previous booms.

It does not follow, moreover, that a rise in real wages would result in the absorption of the wheat surplus. The per capita consumption of wheat in the United States during the boom years of the twenties was about 20 per cent. less than before the war, a change attributed by a former Secretary of Agriculture to the rise in real wages. As the low income families consume more wheat than the higher income families, a rise in real wages might add to the difficulties of the wheat growers.

In any case, there would still be the problem of assuring the production of wheat in a proper proportion to the production of other commodities, so that by the process of exchange they would tend to cancel one another out of the market and into consumption.

Then there are those who believe that the "monetization of production" would prove the sovereign specific. This idea occurred to the English shopkeepers in the 17th century when as a consequence of trade (which had been largely a matter of local barter) rapidly expanding across parochial boundaries, money appeared to become omnipotent. It was later taken up by the French farmers.

It was tried out experimentally in Britain and various American communities over a century ago when the "monetization of production" was effected by stores and special banks -- over 170 of them in England -- issuing labour time notes in exchange for delivered products. Soon these stores were overstocked with articles for which there was no demand while they lacked supplies of the articles the labour note holders wanted to buy.

The experiments failed because the need of producing or assembling goods in the right proportions was lost sight of in the infatuation with the belief that labour time was the measure of the magnitude of value -- exchange value.

The "monetization of production idea" begat the notion of Social Dividends, or the issue of some sort of paper currency to every family. This project, if ever carried out, might prove a palliative, defensible as a form of charity; but it is a product of the sort of thinking which sees a perfect panacea in equality of wages, which even Marx ridiculed as "an insane wish, never to be realized."

Even absolute equality of all forms of income would not necessarily promote economic equilibrium on a level of full employment. It might begin to do so, if first, the buying habits of everybody were standardized on a uniform pattern. But that is out of the question. With equal incomes, there would still be inequality of expenditures on particular goods.

And there would still be the problem of assuring the production of the various commodities in such proportions that the supply of each would balance demand without a derangement of prices so severe as to produce a convulsion of the market before the needed readjustment could be effected.

The problem of orderly economic expansion, or of economic equilibrium on a level of full employment, can hardly be solved except by some degree of general economic planning designed to promote proportional production. "The realization of a proportional production is the entire aim of the science of social economy," said a classical economist. It is the aim of business enterprise too; willy nilly, the successively developed types of industrial and financial organization have extended the spheres of effective planning.

But the co-operation between industries which is a necessary condition of broad planning to promote general proportional production encounters the opposition of government policies and laws, which still seeks [seek] to preserve competition as the life of trade.

There is now a race between alternative voluntary co-operation of the organizations of producers for the social purpose of realizing, by democratic procedures, a well-rounded and balanced economy capable of providing for an increasing population and more fully utilizing the forces of professional and functional pride and the instincts of public service, and compulsory co-operation under the direction of a bloated bureaucracy with no better purpose than serving the lust of power of a totalitarian dictatorship.

If a democratic polity is to be maintained, current notions of freedom may have to be revised. The wheat growers' freedom, for instance, consists of the privilege of getting themselves into difficulties. True freedom is only realized by adaptation to the laws of nature and of economics.

PART V

The Struggle for a Better World

Industrial Unionism and the Struggle for Socialism 1919-1939

In this section are collected 26 of McKay's analyses of trade unionism and politics in the interwar period. McKay apparently never joined either of the two main parties of the Canadian left, the Co-operative Commonwealth Federation (CCF) or the Communist Party (CP). Instead, he stubbornly defended an independent left position on political questions and criticized both parties fairly sharply, the CCF for its alleged drift towards a vague populism and the CP for its apparent tendency to adventurism and its reliance on the Soviet model. These positions were broadly consistent with McKay's pre-war socialist writings. McKay's interwar writings on trade unionism, on the other hand, documented a sharp change in direction. The man who had once praised (and worked on behalf of) the American Federation of Labor now condemned international craft unionism as the bankrupt strategy of a "labour aristocracy," and argued instead for an all-Canadian industrial unionism. Industrial unionism came to mean much more to McKay than a technique for organizing labour; it came to represent, in his final writings, the best hope for Canadian socialism.

1. General Introduction

Immediately after the Great War, McKay's social and political writings were only tinged with socialist sentiment. His articles of this period are best categorized as mainstream new liberal in their idealist evocations of community interests and objectives, and in their avoidance of the tougher issues raised by class conflict and the labour theory of value. The War seems to have placed him in a centrist position very different from that of his writings on working-class culture (1910-1914): did his choice to fight in the war perhaps alienate him from his old radical colleagues, while at the same time poisoning his old attachment to the Empire? Whatever the case, McKay was curiously counter-cyclical: so far as one can tell, he was not drawn by the revolutionary ferment of the postwar years; on the other hand, in the depths of the 1920s, when the postwar labour insurgency was finished and many working-class radicals were moving to the right, his writings became more and more Marxist. (He was never more rigorously

Marxist than in the years from 1926 to 1939). Temperamentally the scientistic, evolutionary McKay was disinclined to chiliasm, and insofar as much of the postwar labour revolt was suffused with a sense of immediate and total revolution, on what was thought to be the Soviet model, he was unlikely to find much inspiration in it.

Certainly the tone of his writings from 1919 to 1922 is surprisingly moderate. In his discussion of collective bargaining and the "sanctity of contract" -- a doctrine whose authoritarian implications were just then being worked out in the coalfields of his native province -- McKay worked within a corporate, problematical language of "our civilization" and "society as a whole." There was little room for rank-and-file militancy and grassroots democracy in the vision of trade unionism he advanced immediately after the war: the trade unionist who violated the supposed sanctity of contract was placed under the same heading as the capitalist who had profiteered from war contracts. "Talk to any trade union official and you will find that he is alarmed by this growing spirit of revolt against the bond of obligation, this immorality of mistrust which begets recklessness and disregard of consequences. And it is significant that the trade union officials attribute the growth of this spirit of revolt and childish defiance to the fact that profiteering has dissolved the bonds of respect between master and man. Unless the primary virtue of fair dealing is given its proper place in the sun, the spirit of unrest and mistrust which is abroad in the land, may cause the dissolution of society as it exists today" [§.110, "The Sanctity of Contract in the Postwar World"]. Given his earlier writings, this was an elitist "labour aristocratic" way of viewing labour relations, characteristic of many powerful figures in the TLC. He predictably disparaged syndicalist tendencies within the French labour movement,[1] and, closer to home, criticized the philosophy of the One Big Union [§.111, "The Fallacies of the One Big Union"]. He also used the word "Bolshevism" to denote an uncontrollable and undesirable social crisis, thus suggesting a distanced skepticism about the Soviet experiment. Moreover, resolving the crisis of an "old system" of liberalism and possessive individualism "breaking down" seemed to McKay in his Labourist phase to be something that well-meaning and intelligent employers could carry out from above. The old system of production as an individual concern was evolving, as evidenced by working-class demands for involvement in decision-making in the workplace and the "minor voice" they had attained through Whitley Councils; soon private industry would be required to recognize the right of the workers to a voice in management. To refuse this reasonable request was "to encourage Bolshevism."[2] On this evidence, it is difficult to imagine McKay as an

---

[1]Colin McKay, "French Labor Discards 'Syndicalism,'" *Canadian Railroad Employees Monthly*, April 1924, 25-26.

[2]C. McKay, "Interdependence And Interrelation of Interests," *Labor World/Le Monde Ouvrier*, 26 June 1920.

enthusiastic admirer of the Winnipeg General Strike or the radicalism of District 26 in Nova Scotia. In the years immediately after the war, he was evidently much closer to the critique of the "ultra-radicaux" put forth by Gustav Francq in such works as *Syndicalisme ou bolchévisme, lequel?* (Montreal, 1919). It would be in Francq's bilingual newspaper *Le Monde Ouvrier/The Labor World* that many McKay writings would appear in the 1920s and 1930s.[3]

It seems that McKay had sincerely believed many of the promises of democratic social reform made in the course of the Great War. When the "Land Fit For Heroes" -- a unified society collectively pursuing the goals of egalitarianism and social justice -- failed to materialize, and perhaps in response to the British Labour Party's bleak performance in the 1920s, McKay's analyses rapidly became more radical. After about 1926 -- the year of the British General Strike, which may also have influenced him -- his writings, many of them published in the *One Big Union Bulletin*, the organ of the very union whose supposed utopian "fallacies" he had denounced in 1920, were once more explicitly Marxist in their mode of argument. Although welcoming reforms and concessions, McKay would never again idealize them to the extent he did the "sanctity of the contract" in 1920 and 1921. By 1936, McKay's position on "tripartite" arrangements had hardened. When he looked at minimum wage boards, for example -- which were key liberal concessions of the day -- he was toughly critical on technical grounds (they did not operate on the basis of realistic calculations of living standards) and suspicious that their import would be to undermine the accomplishments of organized labour.[4] Labour reform thought that did not recognize that the evils of "industrial autocracy, economic aristocracy or plutocracy" were all founded on "property and political office" was superficial, as witness the case of Mackenzie King [§.123, "Mackenzie King's Superficial 'Industrial Democracy"].

McKay's ideological development thus went curiously against the general interwar pattern. At a time when many Canadian leftists were softening an earlier "language of class" in order to build new political alliances, such as the CCF or the various front organizations influenced by the CP, McKay was even more convinced that it was vital to rest economic and political analysis on class, and that only the working class held long-term solutions to the crisis of capitalism. He argued for a "scientific socialism," predicated on the assumption that "the course of human evolution is in the general direction of the progressively increasing importance of the species over the individual, and therefore in the direction of progressive

---

[3]For Francq's position, see Geoffrey Ewen, "The Ideas of Gustave Francq on Trade Unionism and Social Reform as Expressed in Le Monde Ouvrier/The Labor World, 1916-1921," M.A. Thesis, University of Ottawa, 1982.

[4]C.McK., Untitled Letter, *Labor World/Le Monde Ouvrier*, 15 February 1936.

socialization of the economic life and with it of the political, juridical and moral life" [§.128, "The CCF and a Canadian Socialism"]. As the CCF turned towards the middle class as a source of support, McKay denounced the "illusion of small property," and urged the "average middle-class man" to reconsider the illusion "that his interests are identical with those of property. "Whatever the "vicarious self-importance" the middle-class man received "from identifying himself with the capitalist class," the middle-class man was still primarily a worker, and only his dignity or his snobbery stood in the way of his realizing his true class position: "So he remains hypnotized by his false hopes and illusions."[5]

2. The Transformation of Trade Unionism

Although McKay would be widely known in the 1930s as a leading theorist of the All-Canadian Congress of Labour, and argued forcefully for an independent Canadian labour movement, his outlook was always deeply informed by an internationalist, wide-ranging perspective. His sense of what trade unions should be and how they should function was very much affected by European and American models. In some respects, he was a pioneer of comparative labour history, attempting to find a Marxist explanation of world-wide patterns of class formation. A striking example is his analysis of the position of labour in North America in the 1920s, which draws on a wide range of comparisons, and relates working-class consciousness to such social phenomena as mass international migrations, rapid economic expansion, and the state of the labour market [§.125, "The Necessity of a Labour Party," originally published as "Some Reflections on Labor Policy"].

For McKay, trade unions were the cells of a new politico-ethical order, and consequently whether they assumed a "craft" or an "industrial" form was a matter of life or death, and not merely a question of organizing technique. On the structure and strategy of the trade union movement rested the hopes of the left.

Here again, his perspective changed through the interwar period. In 1920, he had critiqued the formula of the One Big Union as one which unrealistically centralized power, and therefore insulated leaders from the rank and file. The British trade-union formula, which preserved a greater degree of craft autonomy and focused workers on the achievement of political power through parliamentary means, was more realistic than the OBU model [§.111, "The Fallacies of the One Big Union"]. In 1923, he had come to the conclusion that even quite important trade union officials, who had done good service to their fellows, were still trapped in an old liberal way of thinking. They had, in essence, become individual "merchants of labour power. " Although they repudiated the suggestion

---

[5]"British Columbia's New Deal," *Canadian Unionist*, January 1935, 196-199.

that "labour is a commodity," they knew very well that if the union controlled the available supply of labour power, it could fix the price or wage at a comparatively high rate, in much the same manner as a merchant cornering the market for a given article. As merchants of labour power, traditional trade union leaders became increasingly trapped by a narrowness of vision: "The merchant cares nothing about what becomes of a commodity after he sold it; the labour leader is concerned about the conditions in which labour works, but not in the results of the application of labour power. But it is precisely in this result that labour is vastly concerned, and ought to be interested" [§.52, "The Worker Must Learn to Think"].

By 1926, he had become a critic of AFL unions, which stood convicted, by "students of sociology" among others, of having failed to work out a constructive philosophy for the new age. In the AFL, McKay now saw a movement whose psychology was still dominated by capitalist concepts. The typical craft unionist defined his craft as his capital, and saw his organization simply as a device to protect this small capital in the labour market. The archetypal craft unionist was no broader in outlook than the average small merchant, who was likewise interested in getting the best price for his commodities. The drab petit-bourgeois conformism shared by both was well-reflected in the dull and uninteresting pages of the craft-union publications, which eloquently testified to the inability of the leaders of AFL unionists to grasp the point that modern capitalism and its machine process had undermined the autonomy of craft "capital" [§. 112, "The Eclipse of Gompersism"]. Thus the philosophy of "trade unions" -- meaning "craft unions" in this context -- still rested "on assumptions which have long ceased to represent reality. More and more, the worker has found that his craft skill is a form of 'capital' for which opportunities for investment grow less. Unlike money capital, his form of 'capital' cannot be deposited in a bank to await a demand for it. If he ceases to exercise his craft skill, its value as 'capital' deteriorates; and he, as its proprietor, may also deteriorate. And finally, if he cannot find employment, he may be threatened with extinction along with his 'capital.'" Moreover, in the modern world, new inventions, industrial organizations, even fashions continually threatened to undermine the value of "craft capital." McKay was careful to note that this trend had not been a uniform or simple one -- "scientific development has in some cases increased the demand for skilled workers," as evidenced in the moulding trades -- but in general the skills upon which craft workers used to rely were threatened with obsolescence [§.118, "Machine Industry and the Erosion of Craft 'Capital'"].

McKay's moderate stance on the craft unions was mirrored by that of the Canadian Brotherhood of Railway Employees and Other Transport Workers (CBRE), the largest and most stable union with a headquarters in Canada. (The union claimed 17,600 members in 1928; 21,000 in 1943).

The Struggle for a Better World

Largely centred on the clerks, freight-handlers and various station service people employed by government railways in Canada, the CBRE had grown from modest beginnings in the Maritimes in 1908 to become the largest single labour organization on the railways by the 1930s (although the combined membership of the craft-oriented running trades was always larger). Although it had once made some effort to become an "international union" itself, the CBRE, which had been expelled from the Trades and Labour Congress in 1921 on grounds of "dual unionism," embraced nationalism in the mid-1920s and on both this ideological basis and on a program of supporting "industrial unionism," it sought to create a new labour central in 1926. In March, 1927, trade unionists representing a wide diversity of programs and positions -- among them the Amalgamated Carpenters of Canada, the Toronto Printing Pressmen's Union, the Communist-influenced Mine Workers Union of Canada, the One Big Union, the Canadian Federation of Labour, the National Union of Theatrical Employees, and above all the CBRE -- came together to form a new body called the All-Canadian Congress of Labour.[6]

Why, given his earlier advocacy of the AFL drive in Montreal and his explicit rejection of national unionism, did McKay now feel such an affinity for the ACCL and the CBRE? (The ironies were delicious: McKay had denounced the "fallacies" of the very OBU [§.111, "The Fallacies of the One Big Union"] which, now it was within the fold of the ACCL, even carried some of his articles in its own *Bulletin!*) Since he characteristically never explained himself, we are left to speculate. McKay's outlook had become markedly more Canada-centred after the War. Gompersism had proved disappointing in the 1920s. He could perhaps readily identify with a union headed by A.R.Mosher and M.M.MacLean, fellow Maritimers. At least initially, it seems (from the tone of the early ACCL journalism) that McKay might have seen the new labour central as much as a way of pressuring the TLC as anything: at first, he may not have made as complete a break with his old loyalties as his later writings suggest. But most of all, one might suggest, it was the combination of idealism and realism in the CBRE and the ACCL that appealed most to McKay. Ever since his Saint John days, McKay's Marxism had always been based on a tough-minded, realistic appraisal of the actual situation --not an exercise in the higher romanticism. His vision of a working-class culture was one of an organic fusion between the labour movement, the working class, and the working-class intellectual. In an imperfect world of difficult choices, the ACCL was probably the Canadian

---

[6]This synopsis of the CBRE and the ACCL is drawn from H.A.Logan, *Trade Unions in Canada: Their Development and Functioning* (Toronto: Macmillan of Canada, 1948), 135-143; 380-386. For a more "internal" version of the CBRE's history, see, *inter alia*, Canadian Brotherhood of Railway Employees, *The Canadian Brotherhood of Railway Employees and Other Transport Workers, 1908-1948: Forty Years of Progress* (Ottawa: Grand Division of the CBRE, 1948).

organization that most nearly approximated to the role of the "socialist intellectual" and "working-class culture" as McKay conceived it. (Our surprise at his choice may tell us more about the ways in which the ACCL has been misleadingly stereotyped as "right-wing" in the literature than it does about McKay's reasoning).[7] His contributions would make help make the *Canadian Unionist* one of the most sophisticated and interesting labour publications of the 1930s -- a major venue for Marxist, socialist and "Labourite" debate and discussion.

A major McKay argument -- and one he pushed further and faster than many in the ACCL would have liked -- was that the craft unions were finished. A critique of craft unionism worked out, in its fundamentals, in the mid-1920s, seemed all the more telling by the 1930s. Witness the pitiful perplexities of William Green of the AFL. He was placed in the difficult and futile rôle of the champion of Hoover's rugged individualism; and he was, in a way, no less forlorn in his fossilization than R.B. Bennett. His opposition to unemployment insurance was based on the liberal assumption that capitalists paid workers the proper social value of their labour -- "a fair day's wage for a fair day's work." He truly was nothing more than a merchant of labour-power, a craft union official whose vision of the labour movement did not rise "above the obtainment of a fair price for the commodity the worker has to sell, his labour power...." This was in no way a "tenable position from the point of view of those who have acquired a dialectical understanding of the relations of capital and

---

[7]Condemned (on the basis of leader A.R.Mosher's resentment of the CIO's emergence and his many run-ins with the CP) simply as an "anti-Communist" and even "right-wing" force, as wholly ineffectual, and as opportunistic, the All-Canadian Congress of Labour is now in serious need of a more nuanced and informed investigation. The influence of Marxist thought on the *Canadian Unionist*, and in McKay's extensive writings for both the ACCL and the CBRE in this period, makes the stock blanket characterizations of the ACCL's "anti-Marxism" seem rather unlikely. The ACCL's nationalism has also never been taken seriously as a form of labour thought -- Logan is not unusual in contentedly dismissing "the rantings of enthusiastic nationalists" (*Trade Unions in Canada*, 384) -- and yet, no less than the Group of Seven, the "broadcasting nationalists," and the United Church, many working-class people in Canada were clearly "imagining a new political community" in the interwar period. It seems curious that the old shibboleths against Canadian independent trade unionism have not been subjected to more scrutiny in this case. Finally, in the context of a literature very much taken with the foibles of the ACCL's leader, A.R.Mosher's seemingly quite acute economic analysis of the crisis of capitalism has also never been seriously examined. This indifference to the ACCL, often on the grounds of its "dated" focus on Canadian autonomy, its narrow emphasis on "industrial" unionism, and its vigorous defence of the public sector as an economic stabilizer is all the more curious, in that it would be precisely these characteristics that would eventually come to characterize the mainstream of the Canadian labour movement. In 1940, the ACCL was succeeded by the Canadian Congress of Labour, made up of the continuing ACCL unions and the Canadian sections of the CIO unions expelled from the Trades and Labour Congress at its Niagara Falls Convention in 1939.

labour -- and a proper conception of the mission of the Labour movement." Green's views were typical of someone whose ways of thinking had developed in the handicraft era. A compulsory system of unemployment insurance at least had the justification "of being an enforced funding of withheld wages -- a method of making a somewhat better distribution of the national income that [than] the capitalists willingly make."[8]

Green's position on unemployment insurance was of a piece with the craft unionists' failure to become "historically minded," their inability to acquire a "dialectical understanding" of their position, their refusal to take account of the transformed realities of capitalism -- "the constant improvement of machinery, the evolution of family firms into corporations, the linking up of many small enterprises into mergers and chains, the development of the holding company, combines, trusts, monopolies" -- and their clinging to their modest craft capital: all these placed the labour movement as a whole in a difficult position. Having been the "aristocrat of labour," a small property-owner whose "property" was his craft skill, the craft unionist was reluctant to identify himself with the class to which he in reality belonged, the working class [§.114, "The Labour Aristocracy and the Decline of the Craft Unions"]. Unless he did so, however, the trade union would remain ineffective and divided.

McKay was no fatalistic Marxist. Craft unionists who studied the course of history might be able to devise a different, more creative strategy. Doing so would have placed them in a dilemma -- "wholesale organization of unskilled workers would mean they would dominate the unions by weight of numbers, and the craftsmen would become an appendage of their own unions" -- but it did not necessarily follow that their dilemma was unresolvable [§.117, "The Failure of Craft Unions"]. In fact (and in a further demonstration of the adroitness with which he could manoeuvre within the seemingly deterministic world of evolutionary theory) McKay's interpretation actually emphasized not inevitability but choice. To an interesting extent, he interpreted the failure of the craft unions as a cultural failure, a failure of trade-union imagination. One could tell a lot about these unions from the tone of their journals: dull and uninteresting, McKay said, with a complacent tendency to echo bourgeois ideas [§.120, "Why Craft Unions are Backward"]. The problem of craft conservatism was compounded by the grip of an autocratic and unresponsive leadership in the craft unions. Such autocracy was no more surprising, in unions whose members considered themselves to be "aristocrats of Labour," than it was in the case of business corporations, which were likewise narrow in their objectives. Both craft unions and corporations were after the same thing: "how much each can get for its members."

---

[8]"Colin McKay, "Throwing the Load on the Workers," *Canadian Unionist*, July 1932, 27.

Autocratic control could be justified in terms of economic results, and hence one found in some craft unions bureaucrats who exercised a "radical dictatorship."[9] Returning to his Spencerian roots, McKay -- in his very last published article -- argued that craft unions had simply been overwhelmed by the laws of social evolution. "Labour organizations, like natural organisms, are subject to the law of evolution, or its obverse, devolution," he wrote. "The changes in their structure may be so slow as to be imperceptible to the ordinary observer, nevertheless changes take place under the impulse of forces engendered by changes in their external environment, and the influence of ideas." The craft unions were clearly declining; they only appeared to be organized on the nineteenth-century design of a "fair day's wage for a fair day's work," but were in fact far more preoccupied with competing with the jurisdictions of other craft unions. The implication of such jurisdictional disputes was that "the further development of given unions can take place only at the expense of others. At the same time, the ever-increasing number of such disputes and the vigour with which they are waged advertise the fact that the evolution of machine industry constantly narrows the basis of the craft form of organization."[10]

Industrial unionism was, on the other hand, fully in keeping with the trends of social evolution. Even employers had cause to approve of it: a contract with an industrial union gave greater assurance of uninterrupted operations than a contract with a craft union, because of the greater number of workers covered [§.119, "Industrial Unionism: The Workers' Answer to Mechanization"]. Twentieth-century North American labour movements were struggling with a transition analogous to that undergone by British labour movements decades before, although it was likely the transition on this continent would be faster and more dramatic. In Canada, the harbinger of the new unified labour order, at least in the transportation industry, was the Canadian Brotherhood of Railway Employees, for whose newspaper McKay so frequently wrote.[11] On a broader level, it was the All-Canadian Congress of Labour, of which McKay was (with M.M.MacLean and W.T.Burford) now a leading intellectual. McKay wanted to see the inclusiveness of the CBRE extended to a new national council of labour for Canada, paralleling the National Council of Labour in Britain, which wielded "no executive authority, but [exercised] functions which are of an analytical, advisory, consultative and conciliatory character only." A similar "advisory general staff" in Canada would comprise representatives of the labour unions, the National

---

[9]Colin McKay, "Progress Depends on Industrial Unionism," *Canadian Railway Employees Monthly*, October 1938, 283.

[10]Colin McKay, "The Broad Scope of Industrial Unionism," *Canadian Railway Employees Monthly*, March 1939, 66-67; 70.

[11]"Economic Progress Demands Industrial Unions," *Canadian Railway Employees Monthly*, October 1937, 245.

Council of the Co-operative Commonwealth Federation, and the CCF parliamentary caucus.[12]

3. Socialist Politics and the Crisis

McKay believed that any left response to the crisis of capitalism had to engage with the eclipse of individualist liberalism, both at the level of theory and in practice. His letters on Marxist theory in 1932 (one of which is reprinted in §.74 ["Marxism and Fatalism"]) sought to clear Marxism of the charge of a naive reliance on Ricardo's theory of value and of being crudely deterministic. The inference was that the Canadian left should, like Marx, base Socialist conclusions "on the general movement of capitalism, the tendency of competition to beget monopoly, and the growing necessity of men taking conscious control of the forces of production."[13] He was also impressed by Marx's finding in his 1859 *Preface* that "'No social order...ever disappears before all the productive forces, for which there is room in it, have been developed." Of course, by the 1930s he also could draw upon a long history as someone influenced by the works of Spencer, with all their evolutionary implications.

It was in light of this conclusion that McKay sharply distinguished himself from *both* the Communists and anti-Communists in their evaluations of the Soviet experiment. Having occurred in a backward country, the Soviet Revolution could not usher in socialism. The Bolsheviks were, on the contrary, developing the forces of production "by typically capitalistic methods, with the only difference that instead of using the negative force of hunger to drive the workers they use the positive force of the State, and follow a general plan having a definite social purpose, which capitalism in other countries lacks" [§.74, "Marxism and Fatalism"]. Observers who neglected the basic lessons of Marx were simply condemned to misinterpret the Soviet experiment. (There is no indication that McKay was familiar with Marx's writings on Russia, from which rather different conclusions could have been drawn). A true *socialist* revolution could only be a process, slow or rapid, by which the political and juridical superstructure of society changed as a result of transformations in its economic basis, the forces and social relations of

---

[12]Colin McKay, "A National Council of Labour for Canada," *Canadian Railway Employees Monthly*, Vol. 25, No.6 (June 1939), 157. The Communist Party was not to be included. Although there is little direct evidence, such positions likely reflect McKay's closeness to the ACCL, which was menaced by the rise of the CIO unions with their substantial Communist presence. It is suggestive that McKay's diagnosis of the need for a new labour central preceded so closely the negotiations that culminated in the formation of the Canadian Congress of Labour.

[13]C. McK., untitled letter, *Labor World/Le Monde Ouvrier*, 10 December 1932.

production. And those of Russia in 1917 did not favour a socialist transformation.

McKay outlined this politico-ethical framework explicitly in his writings in the labour press, and implicitly in his mainstream journalism. For a general (liberal) audience, McKay distilled the Marxist message to one that emphasized the point that, under the new conditions of social and economic life, the meaning of "freedom" had profoundly changed. The readers of *Saturday Night*, for example, were told in 1939 that the core problem facing Canadians was the problem of "orderly expansion." How could Canadians end unemployment, assimilate immigrants, rid themselves of railway deficits, and lessen the burden of taxation? The social and natural materials for an industrial expansion were at hand, but an indiscriminate expansion presented risks. Even J.M. Keynes in the *General Theory*, wrote McKay, had assumed "that if one condition of full employment is established all the other conditions will automatically take care of themselves." But it was by no means clear that this was the case. It could be that the whole notion of "equilibrium" had to be rethought, more radically than even Keynes had done. The example of Canadian wheat suggested that one of the underlying problems of the system was that of "assuring the production of wheat in a proper proportion to the production of other commodities, so that by the process of exchange they would tend to cancel one another out of the market and into consumption." Piecemeal efforts could not work. The problem of orderly expansion -- that is, realizing a proportional production -- required, rather, the imposition of conscious comprehensive planning. In 1939, McKay discerned a race between the voluntary and the totalitarian approaches to achieving such planning. If a democratic polity was to be maintained, "current notions of freedom" would like have to be revised. The wheat growers' freedom, for example, was now outdated, insofar as it allowed the producers to get into intractable difficulties. To him, a new definition of "true freedom" as a state made possible only by "adaptation to the laws of nature and of economics" was needed.[14]

McKay's overt political position moved from moderate Labourism in the early 1920s to what might be called "council " or "participatory leftism" in the 1930s. His initial post-war position was that of a moderate British Labour Party supporter. In 1923, McKay was certainly not very far to the left. In speaking of the crisis of unemployment in Britain, with more than a million British out of work, he thought it "fortunate that [Ramsay] MacDonald is a convinced pacifist, and a man of patience, anxious to keep the labour movement within the bounds of constitutional

---

[14]Colin McKay, "Orderly Expansion is Essence of Problem," *Saturday Night*, 4 February 1939.

methods."[15] In Britain, the left had discovered that organization of the workers on political lines had become imperative, "if labour [was] to maintain and advance its position in the social scale." Wage workers needed to learn from the bourgeoisie, which had "captured political power as a preliminary step to the establishment of their particular form of democracy.... Insofar as capitalism still represents the future of society, the workers have no particular reason to disdain the bourgeois plan and practice" [§.124, "The Two Arms of the Working-class Movement"]. McKay clearly placed a great deal of hope in the prospects of a Labour government. A true labour party, and one which was not merely an imitation of a liberal party, would have as its unifying ideal the "demand that society consciously undertake the organization of its economic powers with the object of providing, by means of the general duty of work, reasonable human needs." The Labour Party would not have to "destroy old institutions, uproot an old system of production and build a new system"; it would merely have to "establish a proper community control of the marvellous new forms and forces of production capitalism has called into being. They only have to democratize existing institutions" [§.132, "Labour Must Control Production"].

A true labour party would give form to that working-class culture McKay had dreamt of since 1913. In an article uncannily similar to the writings of Gramsci, McKay saw the new party as a force that would help "the worker to realize that his class has a mission in the world, much more important than wresting a few cents more an hour from a boss"; it would help restore that sense of human dignity that the modern industrial process tended to break down in the worker, it would, by bringing the worker into touch with new problems and personalities, stimulate the mind and strengthen the will; it would help the worker become part of the world and help workers to become strong without exploiting others [§.125, "The Necessity of a Labour Party"]. Measured against this high standard, the interwar versions of a "political arm of labour" were not impressive. McKay increasingly doubted the possibility of a strictly parliamentary path to socialism, and emphasized more and more the need for a very different kind of planning than that envisaged by the mainstream of the British Labour Party. He termed Ramsay MacDonald and other British Labour luminaries "foggy-minded, self-styled Socialists," and implicitly likened them to the nineteenth-century "sentimental Socialists" in Germany, who had had little direct contact with machine processes, and had been unable to rise above the Socialism of the *petite bourgeoisie* and the handicraftsman. McKay was reminded of Austin Lewis' *The Militant*

[15]Colin McKay, "England -- the Eternal Puzzle," *Canadian Railroad Employees Monthly* (January 1923), 185; 190.

Proletariat, published in 1910, which developed the contrast between "bourgeois Socialism" and "proletarian Socialism."[16]

McKay's coverage of Canadian social democracy in the 1930s was influenced by his understanding of the uninspiring and inconclusive record of the British Labour Party in the 1920s. In particular, he looked with a somewhat skeptical eye on the CCF. The CCF, initially very much a federation of various socialist and progressive groups, gradually became more centralized in its ideology and structure; it became the major expression of social democracy in Canada from the 1930s to the early 1960s. As a one-time SPCer, McKay was *relatively* open to the CCF. He defended, for example, its aim of a 'Canadian Road to Socialism,' implicitly contrasting this to the Communists' reliance on external models. It was true, he felt, that a "Canadian Socialist society must have a distinctive character reflecting its economic organization," and that the stage of political development attained in any country was of central importance to the strategy of socialists [§.128, "The CCF and a Canadian Socialism"]. He praised Angus MacInnis in particular (one of the stalwarts of the left of the party in British Columbia) for his independence and his grasp of economic issues.[17] He also had warm praise for William Irvine's *Co-operation or Catastrophe, an Interpretation of the Co-operative Commonwealth Federation and its Policy.* Irvine had had the insight that the various schemes of liberals and radicals, who believed "that intelligent planning is possible under private capitalism," were not the same as the plans of working-class socialists.[18] The dream sometimes professed by the CCFers -- that of uniting the oppressed in the countryside with those in the city in a common anti-capitalist struggle, aiming at the abolition of all classes -- was close to what McKay himself meant by a socialist movement.[19]

On the other hand, while appreciative of the ideal of farmer/worker alliance, McKay insisted this alliance be constructed on an articulating principle that was firmly working-class. (Here, of course, he was returning to arguments he had made in Saint John before the War). Voicing semi-officially the standpoint of the All-Canadian Congress of Labour, he warned that Labour had "to face the fact that the C.C.F. is attracting the support of elements which, if we may judge from the experience of other countries, may lead it to sacrifice the integrity of its principles in order to become the champion of policies more calculated to appeal to popular support than to assure the economic emancipation of workers and

---

[16]C.M., "Ramsay MacDonald, Norman Thomas and Marx," *O.B.U.Bulletin,* 12 April 1934.

[17]C.McK., Untitled letter, *Labor World/Le Monde Ouvrier,* 6 May 1933.

[18]C. McK., "Mr. Irvine on the Third Party," *Labour World/Le Monde Ouvrier,* 28 January 1933.

[19]Colin McKay, untitled letter, *Labor World/Le Monde Ouvrier,* 25 February 1933.

farmers." McKay even felt there was a possibility that the CCF might attract "so many disillusioned middle-class elements that there will be danger of its making compromises calculated to make it the medium of a fascist régime rather than the instrument of the economic emancipation of farmers and workers." He also feared that the CCF might come to exemplify a "pure and simple ballotism" that would be as limiting as the "pure and simple unionism" of the craft unions [§.127, "A Critique of the CCF"].[20]

McKay watched with mounting concern the party's progress in Ontario -- in which politically active workers who held positions close to those of McKay were removed from positions of influence -- and complained that the CCF was tending to become "a populist movement of farmers, small businessmen and professionals." Cash-strapped farmers had sought to modify the Regina Manifesto so that it was "little more than the expression of a desire to stem the tide of industrial concentration and financial brigandage. The delusions and illusions concerning money that have successively held sway over the farmers of England, France and America gain currency in Canada and appear as new discoveries. The cry is for cheap money, depreciated currency, as a means of reducing debt burdens; an inevitable demand, but not a solution; a temporary relief, after which the creditor class would drive harder bargains with the next body of debtors...."[21] The heterogeneous CCF provided a home for utopian socialists and monetary reformers: "These C.C.F. members who talk of debt as if it were the cause of all trouble fall into confusion because they imagine debts are somehow an effect of money and not a form of property," McKay observed in 1934. "That is why their 'socialism' is of the utopian kind."[22] Even William Irvine, praised in 1933 for his pamphlet, came in for criticism in 1934 for his starry-eyed pursuit of monetary reforms.[23]

---

[20]McKay's concerns about the CCF would have been sharpened by the CCF provisional committee's reluctance to redesign the organization's constitution so as to allow the continuous membership of the Canadian Brotherhood of Railway Employees and the All-Canadian Congress of Labour. A significant stumbling-block to the affiliation of these bodies was the provision that affiliation with the CCF was via provincial units. See Kenneth McNaught, *A Prophet in Politics: A Biography of J.S. Woodsworth* (Toronto, 1959): 260-261.

[21]C.M., "The C.C.F. Becoming a Populist Movement Amongst Farmers," *O.B.U.Bulletin*, 13 March 1934.

[22]C.M., "Woodsworth Protests Military Display at the Capital," *O.B.U.Bulletin*, 8 February 1934.

[23]C.M., "Money and Wm. Irvine, M.P.," *O.B.U.Bulletin*, 22 February 1934. William Irvine supported Social Credit motions in the House of Commons, down to the eve of the Aberhart victory in Alberta.

McKay did not in fact place much confidence at all in the CCF's founding document, the *Regina Manifesto*. The CCF was open to the criticism that its platform, "in some important particulars, looks more like an outline of state capitalism than of a Socialist society," and also to the charge that it had drawn to its ranks a gang of currency-reformers, utopians, a host of "mystic-minded persons who run bravely after illusions, imagining that economic planning is merely a matter of free credit and the elimination of money -- who, unable to understand the necessary relation between commodity and real money, would continue commodity production while dispensing with money" [§.128, "The CCF and a Canadian Socialism"]. Moreover, McKay observed in 1937, without strong organizations of the workers and farmers for economic purposes, a "labour-farmer" [i.e., CCF] government "could do little except to try to make the capitalist system function in a more orderly manner and provide more social relief for the victims of its disorders."[24] McKay never believed in a strictly parliamentary road to socialism; nor was he, in any conventional sense, a social democrat.

Communists, on the other hand, struck him as being victims of another version of magical thinking. They preached a willful disregard of the laws of social evolution. Communism was a test of Marxism only in a negative sense: the success of the Soviet Experiment would count *against* the plausibility of the Marxian theory, which argued that a country "must reach a high state of development before its transformation into social production becomes possible. That condition does not obtain in Russia and the Bolshevists are only proving the soundness of the Marxian theory when they recognize the need of encouraging the capitalist method of production" [§.129, "The Failure of Bolshevism"]. Although McKay acknowledged evidence of a rapid rate of Soviet economic growth in the 1930s, he saw this simply as an indication that planning under state capitalism could be more effective than passive resignation to the blind laws of economics.[25] McKay was willing to concede the attraction of an economy that seemed to provide jobs, and he was also persuaded that the Soviet Union had evolved a new and more egalitarian moral code for men and women that merited serious consideration in Canada.[26] But he found the Soviet experiment to be ill-conceived, a crash program of placing capital goods ahead of consumption goods that could only be problematic in the long term.[27] Planning in the state-capitalist Soviet Union had not resolved any of the fundamental problems of the capitalist

[24]Colin McKay, "The Genesis of Industrial Unionism," *Canadian Railway Employees Monthly*, June 1937.

[25]Old Bill', untitled letter to the *Labor World/Le Monde Ouvrier*, 18 July 1930

[26]Colin McKay, "Russia or Italy?" *Canadian Railway Employees Monthly*, June 1932, 134-135.

[27]Colin McKay, "The Real Danger from Russia," *Canadian Unionist*, March 1932, 174-175.

system. Most fundamentally, it had not resolved the problem of proportionality, of adjusting production and consumption. "Through mismanagement or technical incapacity of the workers, or both," McKay argued, "the new industrial enterprises are not functioning well -- are not turning out as many consumptive goods as expected... The net result is a shortage of consumptive goods in relation to a demand which is forcing up prices in defiance, it is said, of the will of state capitalism."[28] It was possible that the Communists in the Soviet Union were speeding up evolution, "but the course of historic development is not thereby changed. The processes of development are still essentially capitalistic; the main difference is that vested interests which retard the logical evolution of capitalism in other countries have been got rid of" [§.131, "Soviet Communism as State Capitalism."]

Communists in Canada were not even doing anything this positive. In McKay's view, one which perhaps had a significant impact within the All-Canadian Congress of Labour, Communists were simply adventurists. Their tactics within the labour movement were divisive,[29] and their approach to socialism smacked of religious fanaticism: the CP had no understanding that "organization and education are both necessary processes of social evolution, and since neither of these processes can be completed in a day -- any more than a youth can accomplish the biological evolution of becoming an adult in a day -- they call for the exercise of tact and patience -- qualities in which the hierarchy of the Communist Party of Canada is notably deficient." Communists seemed propelled by "a nebulous romanticism and fanatical fervour" to bestow on the idea of the social revolution "the narrow and incomplete character of an end in itself," and to be furthering the illusion "that the social organism can be radically changed in a day or so by a general strike, or a political upheaval of a fraction of the people" [§.130, "The Conceits of the Communists"]. Because neither their judgment nor their independence could be trusted, McKay would have excluded the Communists from his scheme for a new national council of labour.[30] So far as one can determine, McKay's verdict on the Communist Party was almost completely negative: he had no words of praise for Communist efforts to develop a "working-class culture" in theatre or history-writing, or for the Mackenzie-Papineau Battalion, or for the leadership of the On-to-Ottawa Trek of 1935 (perhaps the single most dramatic show-down between labour and the federal government in the years of the Depression). As much by his silences as by his denunciations, McKay declared himself emphatically to be an unorthodox, non-Communist

---

[28]Colin McKay, "You Cannot Dictate to Economists," *O.B.U. Bulletin*, 6 October 1932.

[29]Colin McKay, "Reds Doomed to Defeat," *Labor World/Le Monde Ouvrier*, 30 January 1926.

[30]Colin McKay, "A National Council of Labour for Canada," *Canadian Railway Employees Monthly*, June 1939, 157.

Marxist. At the same time, it is important to note the differences between McKay's critique of the Communists and those that were to come from more conservative labour writers (and from those which were to proliferate in the 1940s and 1950s). Negative as was McKay's critique, he never equated Communists with Fascists; nor did he imply that to be a Communist was to be disloyal to Canada. Because his critique was still situated within the horizon of a shared Marxist tradition, it did not develop any sense of a monstrous Communist "Other" in the style that the AFL unions had already refined and which would become commonplace, even within the CCF, during the Cold War .[31]

McKay's analysis of the problem of alliances is one that speaks directly to contemporary left-wing debates. This problem has recently been examined by Daniel Drache and Bryan Palmer (the first condemns Marxian dogmatism, and the second speaks of alliance-building as the road to defeat for radical labour in the 1920s to reformism in the CCF in 1933).[32] This question remains crucial to any conceivable "working-class culture" in Canada: since the industrial working class is now, and is likely to remain, a minority in Canada, one either builds alliances or rules other subaltern groups on their behalf.[33] Over most of the Canadian land mass, for example, the First Nations would find themselves excluded from a "purely proletarian movement." A "pure" working-class socialist revolution -- an event which, from the perspective of at least some writers within the OBU, CP, and Trotskyist traditions, was to be guided by a cadre of expert revolutionaries working within and for the industrial proletariat -- could only result in a dictatorship by a minority of the population, exerting power over natives, primary producers and other subaltern groups and classes: a recipe for bitter strife within the left. A difficulty, however, is that (if the past record of "post-capitalist experiments" is anything to go by) a Canadian socialism that fails to confront Canada's history as an imperial colonizer in the North and West will most likely

---

[31]See, for instance, "J'Accuse le parti communiste," *Labor World/Le Monde Ouvrier*, 1 June 1940.

[32]Daniel Drache, "The Formation and Fragmentation of the Canadian Working Class 1820-1920," 30; Bryan Palmer, "Listening to History Rather than Historians: Reflections on Working-Class History," in David J. Bercuson and David Bright, eds., *Canadian Labour History: Selected Readings* (Toronto: Copp Clark Longman, second edition, 1994), 59. A stimulating discussion in the international literature is Przeworski, *Capitalism and Social Democracy*, Chapter Three. A similar debate focuses on the question of alliance politics today, with Marxist-Leninists expressing misgivings about workers' parties (the "real" or "true" left) entering into arrangements with new social movements -- such as those of gays and lesbians, native peoples, feminists and so on -- for fear that such new social movements will dilute the oppositional anti-capitalist substance of proletarian politics. See Ellen Meiksins Wood, *The Retreat from Class: A New 'True' Socialism* (London, 1986), 173-179

[33]There are some pertinent comments on this issue in Reginald Whitaker's introduction to Irvine, *The Farmers in Politics*.xii.

simply perpetuate pre-existing patterns of domination. Lenin's brilliant and heroic perception of the perils of constructing a "dictatorship in the void," are pertinent here;[34] so, of course, is the entire twentieth-century record of "actually existing socialism." McKay offers us no ready solutions to this difficulty. However, what he stresses is that before entering any alliance with a subaltern group, the working-class movement must have a firm sense of the logic of its actions: it must have a "working-class principle of articulation," around which other subaltern groups, classes and movements may, exercising their own free agency, choose to group themselves. Any such position, in which the needs of all subaltern movements are articulated as part of a core socialist project defined in terms of the realm of freedom, would entail a transcendence of the mechanical and instrumental politics of "alliance" (such as it was practised in Farmer-Labour parties, for example) to the Gramscian politics of an *historic bloc*, unifying base and superstructure, theory and practice, intellectuals and subaltern classes and groups in a new philosophy of life, a new culture, a new post-imperial articulation of political life in northern North America.

4. Directions for the Future

In some respects, McKay articulated in the 1930s what would three decades later be called a "New Left" political agenda. He came more and more to emphasize the importance of grassroots democracy, the workers' direct involvement in planning, and the importance of such questions as peace. He had subtle insights into the problem of "uniting the fragments," of bringing the disparate forces on the left into harmonious, mutually respectful and powerful alliance.

In the past, and well into the 1930s, McKay had viewed parliamentary democracy simply as an illusion. He wrote in 1932 (echoing Rodbertus) that "civilization now is but the sham of political democracy. Only the workers by realizing industrial democracy can build a really decent civilization. If the workers lack the will and moral courage to remake the social order on a common sense basis, then history will swing the lash of revolution again."[35] The following year, he remarked that "...One dictionary definition of democracy is: political or social equality. In a world of economic inequalities, there is no social equality. And as politics mirror the economic interests of social groups, the theoretical democracy implied by one-person one-vote is hardly realized in practice" [§.133, "Real Democracy"].

By the mid 1930s, however, with two "would-be dictators" -- Premier Maurice Duplessis in Québec and Premier Mitch Hepburn in Ontario --

---

[34]See on this Moshe Lewin, *Lenin's Last Struggle* (London: Pluto 1975) Chapter One.

[35]C.M., Untitled Letter, *Labor World/Le Monde Ouvrier*, 31 December 1932.

threatening to "knock the national structure to pieces," McKay felt compelled to rethink this position and to defend at least some aspects of liberal democracy. Loose thinking, he argued, had led to the statement that "political democracy is a farce without economic democracy," and those who had used such slogans against Conservatives needed to reflect on the extent to which they were providing arguments for Fascists. In fact, political democracy and economic democracy were but different aspects of the "material basis of the life process of society," and the relative freedom enjoyed by Canadians in political life was a precious achievement, even if well-organized groups of capitalists had combined to dominate the system.[36] Since the Great War, McKay had rarely expressed an interest in elections or mainstream political parties in Canada, and these 1938 comments can be seen as something of a self-correction.

McKay was also coming to identify increasingly with Canada as something more than the merely geographical description of a part of the world's surface on which capitalist evolution and class struggle occurred, as they did everywhere else on the planet. This tendency to think in terms of a Canadian nation marked quite a departure for a worker-intellectual hitherto strictly internationalist in his overt labour politics (although also somewhat inclined to take the British Empire as his imagined community in his earlier writings).[37] As McKay came closer

---

[36]Colin McKay, "Nation Wide Interest in Trépanier's Fight," *Labour World/Le Monde Ouvrier,* 29 October 1938. McKay's support of Trépanier, a candidate backed by the Liberals and by *Le Monde Ouvrier,* should not be construed as an indication of a return to the Liberal fold on his part: Trépanier's election bid was widely seen as a challenge to the Duplessist Order. For an insightful discussion of this episode, and of the 1930s in Quebec, see Andrée Lévesque, *Virage à Gauche Interdit: Les communistes, les socialistes et leurs ennemis au Québec 1929-1939* (Montréal 1984).

[37]In "The Crews for A Canadian Navy," *The Globe* (Toronto), 24 July 1909, McKay discussed the problem of creating a viable navy at a time when fishermen, having largely abandoned the Banks fishery, were enjoying a standard of living and independence at work that would make them disinclined to accept naval discipline or naval wages. Writing for the mainstream press, his language was markedly "British imperial": "Whether or not Canada decides to create a navy it should take immediate measures to preserve its sea-going merchant marine and encourage its young men to follow the sea. That is a duty it owes to the empire, and to its own people. After all, a nation builds battleships mainly for the purpose of protecting its merchant shipping, and if we stopped to think that this mother country has really no reason to be afraid of the German navy for many years to come -- that the present clamor for more Dreadnoughts is due not so much to alarm at Germany's naval programme as to alarm caused by the growth of Germany's merchant marine and the menace to British control of the world's carrying trade which it involves, a menace brought home to the people by the fact that three of Britain's biggest shipping companies have obliged to come to an agreement with German firms, dividing certain trades between them -- if we recognized that the present clamor was really a manifestation of concern for what is doubtless the very life-blood of the empire, the supremacy of Britain's merchant shipping, then we might realize that we had duties to the empire as important as helping the mother country to

and closer to A.R. Mosher and his brand of Canadian industrial unionism, he started to see international unions as a declining force, and to argue that craft unionism and American unionism were closely intertwined in their narrowness of vision and their business assumptions. His opinion on the national question in Canada started to evolve.

In 1926, writing (with M.M. MacLean, the editor and publisher of the *Canadian Railroad Employees Monthly*) what was later to be seen as the first programmatic statement for the All-Canadian Congress of Labour Unions, McKay relied not so much on "nationalist" arguments as "pragmatic" considerations in his call for a new labour central. The Trades and Labor Congress, he argued, had become the largely moribund creature of craft unions and a well-oiled machine dominated by its leader Tom Moore. Outside the unions affiliated with it were some "very large bodies of organized workers in Canada, some national in scope, some sectional, others purely local, but all Canadian, in inception and purpose." These groups could be brought together in an "all-Canadian Federation or Congress," a central body that would wield a much greater influence than presently exercised by the TLC. Such a "real Canadian Federation or Congress of wage-earners" would be in a position to enlist the support of "the organizations of school-teachers, commercial travellers, farmers and other Canadian workers, who prefer to run their organizations as all-Canadian institutions, and who are not wanted in Mr. Moore's Congress...." This rival central organization might even draw into its orbit the United Farmers of Canada, "that powerful body" [§.113, "The Decline of 'International' Unions in Canada"]. McKay's new emphasis on Canada would generally have this rather down-to-earth quality. He was conscious of the rise of American Imperialism[38] and feared that Roosevelt might seek to rescue American capitalism through imperial expansion.[39] Without in any way subordinating the socialist movement to nationalism, or the working class to other social forces, a Canadian alliance of the left could be solidified by articulating a national-popular viewpoint under the hegemony of the working class.

---

strengthen her naval forces. It is not a mere coincidence that at the present there are hundreds of ships laid up in Britain, 600 sea-officers and thousands of seamen out of employment. But it is a sorry reflection upon our imperialism that while such a condition prevails in the mother country, Canada employs foreign ships to carry her coal, not in order to provide her people with cheaper coal, for prices of coal are higher, much higher, than before we admitted foreign vessels to our coasting trade, but to enable certain men already enjoying many public favors to increase their wealth: and, what is more, that we pay heavy subsidies to Canadian companies that employ foreign vessels." Thus were labour protectionism, the elevation of the fishermen, and the imperialism briefly united in McKay's analysis. To my knowledge, he never suggested any contradiction between British and Canadian patriotism.

[38]See Colin McKay, "American Imperialism," *O.B.U. Bulletin*, 1 June 1933.

[39]Colin McK., "American Imperialism," *Labor World/Le Monde Ouvrier*, 2 July 1938.

As someone who could read French and consulted *La Vie Ouvrière* to understand Québec politics, and as someone who had noted the decision of the United Farmers of Saskatchewan to make a close study of the subject of setting up an autonomous western state, McKay had a sharp awareness of the fragility of the Dominion of Canada.[40] It was, nonetheless, almost impossible for him to formulate questions about nationalism and nationhood in the context of the Spencerian Marxist paradigm within which his mind had developed. Despite deep familiarity with the streets and factories of Montreal and a long involvement with a bilingual newspaper, he never, apparently, explicitly wrote about the relationships between Francophones and Anglophones in Montreal or within the Canadian federation. To the extent that this theorist of the ACCL could be considered a nationalist, he was in essence a nationalist-by-default, who argued for national trade union forms that would bring together those excluded and marginalized by the craft-union and "internationalist" formula of the AFL.

McKay's deepest hopes for the future were placed in industrial unionism, considered not as a technique of organizing workers but as part of a much more inclusive vision of workers' struggle. Against those who maintained that labour unions merely represented a reaction to capitalism and would have no purpose to serve once capitalism passed, McKay argued that "labour unions will form the economic frame-work of Socialism; they will appoint the administrators of industry."[41]

He traced the intellectual origins of this ambitious conception of "industrial unionism" to early nineteenth century socialist thought in Britain and the works of such early twentieth century syndicalist writers as Tom Mann. Many of these British figures had been "keen students of economics, and therefore more clearly conscious of economic changes than the average worker. And what they observed in the later years of the last century was a rapid growth of corporations which supplanted the family firm and partnership, accompanied by a rapid extension of the machine process...."[42] The transformation of the workplace resulting from

---

[40]Colin McKay, "Canadian Fascism: Split in Ranks at Quebec," *O.B.U. Bulletin*, 6 July 1933; Colin McKay, "Nation Wide Interest in Trépanier's Fight," *Labour World/Le Monde Ouvrier*, 29 October 1938. McKay's fears with regard to the rise of right-wing populism in Québec were not unfounded: see Bernard Dionne, "Les 'Unions Internationales' et le conseil des Métiers et du Travail de Montréal, de 1938 à 1958," Ph.D.Thesis, Université du Québec à Montréal, 1990, Ch.2.

[41] "C.M.", untitled letter, *Labor World/ Le Monde Ouvrier*, 7 October 1933.

[42]Colin McKay, "The Genesis of Industrial Unionism (2)," *Canadian Railway Employees' Monthly*, July 1937, 165; 167. See also Colin McKay, "Industrial Unionism in Great Britain," *Canadian Unionist*, December 1936, 174-176, for further reflections on the historical background of industrial unionism. A skeptic might have noted that while McKay felt he had scored a fatal blow against utopian monetary schemes by tracing them to back to the Britain of the 1820s and 1830s, he evidently thought that

this corporate change had not only affected techniques of labour organization, but reshaped the very substance of working-class politics. Rather than a class divided by the "aristocratic aloofness of the craft union" into precisely demarcated groups -- the skilled and the unskilled -- the transformation of work established the preconditions of a very different kind of class struggle. The implications of machine production -- which had established a "democracy of technique, in the sense that all the workers engaged in the component subdivision of a single industry are equally necessary" -- meant that democracy of organization was now not just an ideal but a functional imperative. For the success of a union action under the new conditions, "the unskilled or semi-skilled worker is as necessary as the skilled worker." Skilled workers who clung to their prejudices did so at the cost of their own survival.[43] Once they understood the course of social evolution, they would realize that their place was in socialist industrial unions, fighting for direct workers' control, and playing their part in building the "transformed society of the future."

McKay entered any such discussion of the future with hesitation, for, like most Marxists, he was skeptical of elaborate blue-prints for the future: such intellectual constructions might come dangerously close to the daydreams of the utopians. But entering into such "realms of prophecy and speculation" could be justified as a way of placing industrial unionism in broader perspective, and defining more carefully its "message" and its "mission." That message, in a nutshell, was this: "the present economic system is a transitory phase of a process of evolution, ... destined to be succeeded by another system," one of collective planning of production to supply the wants of all the people. And the immediate mission was then "to organize the workers, so that when the control of political power passes from the privileged property-owning classes to the producing masses, that political power can be used in conjunction with [the] economic power of the organized producers to set up a new society in which economic democracy will be realized" [§.116, "The Future of Industrial Unionism"]. It was simply not enough for a left (or "labour-farmer") party -- such as the CCF, or even the CP -- to take control of the state. Without strong organization for economic purposes on the part of its key supporters, such a government would be able to do little more than "make the capitalist system function in a more orderly manner and provide more social relief for the victims of its disorders." And without effective organization at the base, the new order -- "an economic democracy" -- could not come into being. Utopianism was not the sole

tracing the ideals of industrial unionism back to the scheme of a grand national consolidated trade union in this period merely provided industrial unionists with a historical pedigree! The uses of history....

[43]Colin McKay, "Industrial Corporations Necessitate Industrial Unionism," *Canadian Unionist*, January 1937, 195-196.

prerogative of middle-class "muddle-heads." The true utopianism was to imagine socialism without workers' control. [44]

In these crucial writings, which he brought out near the end of his life, McKay returned to a core theme of his life and work: the articulation of a working-class culture in opposition to the values of liberalism and capitalism. The Spencerian organic metaphors he had so deeply internalized in his youth were once more put to good service. Industrial unions and farmers' organizations were the nuclei of the new social order: "an economic democracy ... implies control and management by economic organs instead of by political organs. The new organs of the control of the affairs of society will naturally be the industrial unions of the workers and the economic organizations of the farmers." The political parliament would likely be replaced by "periodical conventions of the representatives of industrial unions and farmers' organizations. These conventions, or industrial parliaments, will determine matters of policy on such questions as, for instance, whether more effort should be applied to the production of goods at the expense of provision of educational facilities, or vice versa; whether labour and materials should be added to the building of better homes for the many, or diverted to the building of aircraft for the use of the few, whether labour should be assigned to the reclamation of the drought areas of the West, or the construction of such projects as the St. Lawrence Seaway. McKay was realistic enough to realize that these Canadian workers' and farmers' parliaments would not be free of controversy or sectionalism. The socialist society of the future would still have hot political debates. But at least these debates would not be poisoned "by such a multitude of narrow, private interests as the questions which now agitate politics. The over-riding consideration would be -- what use of labour and materials will serve the greatest good of the greatest number?" As the contradictions of capitalism faded into memory, there would be no further need of a political state: the state, as the "organ of social consciousness," would become increasingly democratic, until the need of such a political institution separate from civil society would disappear altogether. This was a position that recalled Marx's own writings on politics.[45]

McKay did leave a certain space for "administrators" in the new society, who might be appointed, "from time to time," by the industrial parliament, or directly selected by the various national unions and farmer organizations. The administrators' place in the new society was a decidedly humble one: they were to be concerned with "economic

---

[44] Although, like apologists for the Soviet regime, McKay did not anticipate a complete equality of condition under socialism: he still thought there would be a discrepancy between the "rewards of managers and men," although not so great as in his day [see §.87, "Illusions of the Equitists"].

[45] C.McKay, "Thoughts on Economic Planning," *O.B.U.Bulletin*, 27 October 1932.

questions which will no longer have a political aspect....with the productive capacity of different industries, and the consumptive needs of people. Their task will be to regulate production so as to serve the social purpose, first, of supplying all the people with shelter, food and clothing; secondly, of improving the quality of these essentials of life; and, thirdly, of providing for luxuries"[§.116, "The Future of Industrial Unionism"]. Proportional planning was implicit in the socialist theory of value, and a new social order would achieve "the production of commodities in the right proportions. The realization of proportional production is the end and aim of the science of social economy...." [46] Although there was probably "no royal formula for the planning of the production of capital goods" (i.e., the rationing of investment), an intelligent response to the problem would probably not represent "insurmountable difficulties to human ingenuity." Since the greed for great wealth and the fear of want, "the human fulcrums of the business cycle," would be things of the past, planning would permit a "spiritual revolution in man's attitude to his work and to his fellow men, and a real realization of the service-motive in business" [§.96, "Rationing Investment: A Critique of Donald Marvin's Explanation of the Depression"].

McKay did not believe that the new economic order would extinguish all forms of private property. Both in terms of winning the support of small property-holders and farmers, and in the interests of rational economic planning, it was important not to confuse socialism with the abolition of all private property. "A planned economy, of the rational and methodical organization of production, with the conscious intention of providing the fullest possible satisfaction of the wants of all the people is not,...incompatible with the existence of various forms of private ownership, even of the means of production and distribution," McKay argued, revisiting Kautskyan arguments he had made before the War. (Excluded by definition from a socialist society, we should note, was private ownership of large corporations). He disputed the idea that big business flourished because it was always conducted more efficiently and economically than small business. Of course, the persistence of small ownership in the new socialist order would be accommodated by the "industrial parliament" only to the extent that it did not conflict with the overall planning of the economy by workers and farmers; and only for those who were not "absentee shareholders." Socialism, in McKay's vision was a new *order* in which society as a whole planned production for all; it would likely require a complex diversity of forms of property-holding.[47]

Planning and "real democracy" could be mutually reinforcing. With regard to capitalism, McKay underlined the extent to which the anarchy

[46]C. McK., untitled letter, *Labor World/Le Monde Ouvrier*, 17 September 1938.
[47]Colin McKay, "Economic Planning Under Capitalism," *Canadian Railway Employees' Monthly*, February 1938, 33-35.

of production and the chaos of capitalism precluded *anybody* from exercising power over the process, whether in a democratic or a non-democratic way. The transition to a new society would mean, for the first time, the possibility of *any kind* of effective supervision social evolution. The point was obvious when one looked at the Depression. "No ruler in Israel" would ever have permitted such an economic catastrophe. No one had wanted this crisis. In this sense, one could say, it was a symptom of modernity, of modern financial capitalism's unceasing and frantic pace of change [§.133, "Real Democracy"].

McKay visualized the path to the effective control of social evolution -- to a "real" or "social" democracy -- as a mainly peaceful one. There was nothing intrinsically revolutionary about a resort to violence, and under the new forms of political economy that had been established, "it is possible to carry on the revolutionary struggle at the ballot box." (Of course, it would never have been possible, for McKay, to consider merely winning an election to be sufficient for the achievement of the new society). Under conditions of political democracy, both the exploiters and the exploited were freer to develop their organizations, and the power of both was greater than ever before. It was possible that labour governments, "by carrying to their logical development the various devices and methods capitalism is already employing in an effort to prolong its life, may arrive at socialism." The creation of public holding companies might be an effective way of taking control of all industries "of which the private control permits the exploitation of Labour." Graduated income taxes and death duties would provide a means of reducing class privilege. Gradually, using a variety of devices, a working-class government "could eliminate private capital altogether, gradually or swiftly, as might be desired," without the need of a massive, perhaps violent, confiscation of private capital [§.126, "The Transformation of Capitalism"].

When McKay looked into the future at the end of the 1930s, he could see the outlines of the new world emerging from the ruins of the old. Like many of his contemporaries, he was also keenly aware of the imminence of an international catastrophe, likely to have an incalculable impact on the course of social evolution. As the Toronto *Globe and Mail* bayed for the blood of the Canadian working class in a new world conflict, McKay pondered the likely outcome of a new war for the Canadian state and the working class in general. How, he wondered, could Canada ever finance another major war? The result for a country in which "about 40 per cent of the assets of the chartered banks consists of government securities" would be a ruination of state finances, and enormous pressure on the already strained borrowing and taxing capacities of Canadian governments. Resorting to the printing press to make more money would mean a rapid inflation, misery for those in fixed incomes, and a slowing down in business. A war, McKay wrote in 1938, would force the state to "control prices, regulate wages, regiment labour. And, having thus left the profit motive little or no room to operate in it, would have to take over the planning and direction of nearly all economic activities." It would likely compel Canada to become either a land of fascism or of state capitalism. The long-term consequences for state finances would be extreme.[48]

McKay, who died seven months before the outbreak of the Second World War, never lived to see how close to the mark he had come in this and others of his predictions. Nor would he ever see the new social order the war actually did bring about -- an order which bore tragically little resemblance to that socialist society of free producers and workers' control in which, for over forty years, he had invested so many of his hopes and dreams.

i. Trade Unionism in the interwar period

110. The Sanctity of Contract in the Postwar World[49]

Just as the old feudal system rested on the sentiment of loyalty, the modern capitalist system reposes on public confidence in the integrity of the individual. In the beginning of the capitalist system the primary virtues were industry, thrift and honesty. Industry and thrift were necessary to the accumulation of capital; honesty -- the sanctity of contract -- [was] essential to carry trading beyond mere barter. Most modern businesses at some stage or another need credit, and credit depends upon public confidence.

The war like Pandora's box has let loose a whole breed of evils upon the world, and the most dangerous of the whole brood is the genii [genie] of dishonesty. This malign spirit undermines the foundations of public confidence, menaces the whole superstructure of our civilization. On the one hand is the profiteer who outrages the accepted ethics of decent business; on the other is the labour agitator who makes a mockery of the sanctity of contract. Both are traitors to their class, and both are a menace to society as a whole. Their actions are as acid dissolving the cement of confidence which holds men together in business and social relations.

And the worst offender is probably the profiteer, because he has more at stake, and because he betrays the class which for good or ill is the

---

[48]C. McK, "Millionaire War Mongers," *Labor World/Le Monde Ouvrier*, 19 November 1938.

[49]Originally published as "Cement of Confidence and Sanctity of Contract," *Labor World/Le Monde Ouvrier*, 25 October 1919.

managing class of society to-day -- the class which possesses the brains, the power and the responsibility.

The decent businessmen owe it, to themselves as well as to society, to rid their ranks of this pest. As the Dominion President of the Retail Merchants' Association said the other day, passing the buck is dangerous; it encourages the impression that all businessmen are tarred with the same stick, or lacking in courage to deal with the traitors to their class. Businessmen are under an implied obligation to be fair and square in their dealings with their clients, and the assumption is that under the normal operation of free competition they will have to be square and fair or lose clients. But during the war the operation of competition has not been normal; thousands of able and enterprising young men have been away fighting for their country who in peace time would have been starting businesses here and there -- keeping competition in operation as a force for fair dealing. The suspension of this form of competition during the war years has been the profiteer's opportunity, and it is not to his credit that he has taken advantage of it in the way he has done.

The profiteer has broken the bond which is implied in his position as a businessman, and his contempt for the ethics of business finds its reflex in the attitude of an increasing number of workingmen who disdain the authority of their duly elected representatives and flout the obligations of their union's contracts. Talk to any trade union official and you will find that he is alarmed by this growing spirit of revolt against the bond of obligation, this immorality of mistrust which begets recklessness and disregard of consequences. And it is significant that the trade union officials attribute the growth of this spirit of revolt and childish defiance to the fact that profiteering has dissolved the bonds of respect between master and man. Unless the primary virtue of fair dealing is given its proper place in the sun, the spirit of unrest and mistrust which is abroad in the land, may cause the dissolution of society as it exists today.

111. The Fallacies of the One Big Union[50]

The apathy of the average worker in this country to the question of independent political action is beginning to be disturbed. This is not surprising. The pressure of the high cost of living, combined with the spectacle of unexampled prosperity and extravagance on the part of the bourgeois class, has aroused him from his mental lethargy. The example of the farmers, the sudden appearance of a farmer-labour government in Ontario, have opened a vista of new possibilities....

---

[50]Originally published as "Trade Unionism vs. One Big Union," *Labor World/Le Monde Ouvrier*, 10 July 1920.

...The fundamental fallacy of the One Big Union is that it implies the concentration of power -- predicates the direction and control of supermen. And they are scarce even in the I.W.W. Were labour only interested in securing higher wages and shorter hours the One Big Union might serve as well and possibly better than craft unions. But the One Big Union is not competent to pass judgment upon the numerous questions relating to shop conditions which increase in importance with the increasing complexity of industry; each trade has its own particular problems which can only be satisfactorily dealt with by the craft union concerned.

It may, I think, be argued that the A.F. of L. is not wholly free from responsibility for the agitation for the One Big Union. The A.F. of L. has not in the past adequately recognized the importance of political power -- of securing political power for the workers. The O.B.U. proceeds on the assumption that political power is of little consequence, and political action not worth while. Its idea is that the power of capital lies almost wholly in the control of industry, and that direct action on the industrial field can achieve everything the workers want. Tests of their theory ought to have convinced O.B.U. advocates of its shortcomings. When they have resorted to direct action on a considerable scale they have had the tables turned on them. The political power has been evoked against them; the State has taken direct action on its side, and broken the industrial weapon of the direct actionists.

British labour, with greater experience and a better appreciation of the problem before it, has not coquetted with the idea of the O.B.U. It has formed powerful combinations and federations, but it preserves the distinctive features and essential autonomy of craft unions. It does not neglect the possibilities of action on the industrial field, but it has come to attach greater importance to the possibilities of action on the political field. Its major energies are now being devoted to the task of capturing political power. A One Big Union for political purposes might be a reasonable proposition. But British labour wastes no time talking about One Big Union even in politics; it utilizes every organization -- willing to advance on its objective -- ...political power.

112. The Eclipse of Gompersism[51]

Critical appraisals of the American labour movement, made by students of sociology, have begun to appear in the United States. They rather bear out recent criticisms of various British labour leaders that the official old-line American movement has not yet worked out the fundamentals of a constructive philosophy; that its psychology is still dominated by capitalist concepts....

---

[51]Originally published as "Capitalist Ideas Govern United States Labor Movement," *Canadian Railroad Employees Monthly*, June 1926, 81-82.

The argument of the typical trade unionist has been that his craft was his capital -- that his organization was simply a device to protect his craft, his property, and enable him to secure the best terms in the market for his craft-skill. And, insofar as he has remained true to type, the craft unionist has developed no broader outlook than the average small merchant who is interested in getting the highest price possible for the commodities he has to sell. Even where the development of the machine process has decomposed whole trades, enabling machine tenders to replace skilled craftsmen, the average trade unionist has been slow to realize how greatly the machine has revolutionized the relations of capital and labour -- how completely it has changed the character of the problem confronting the working class. Official organs of the craft unions are, for the most part, dull and uninteresting, occupied with side issues and obsolete points of view, as if those responsible for them were living in an older order, unable to rise above or beyond the conceptions of a time prior to the ruthless emasculation of craft "capital" by the machine process.

With all his gift of sympathy, his power of interpreting mass emotions, Gompers' intellectual outlook was essentially that of a merchant -- a merchant richly endowed with sentiment. Certainly he felt that the labour movement was an upsurge of great human forces inspired by loftier and more dignified aims than haggling for a few cents an hour; but he was unable to develop, in the sight of men, an adequate conception of the aims of the labour movement in its larger relations, or leave his followers the legacy of a programme looking beyond the higgling of the market place. Of course, he was necessarily preoccupied with the pursuit of small material ends, but, even so, his intellectual vision was not great enough to make him a cultural force of much importance, though his sterling character and deep humanitarianism made him a spiritual influence of real value.

But times change, and with them men's views and manners. The declaration that wages should advance as the productive power of industry increases, at least, constitutes a recognition that the machine process is the big factor in the economics of production. This certainly implies that the leaders of the craft unions have moved, or are moving, to a new point of view; the view that the modern labour question is primarily a social problem, largely created and conditioned by the machine process, and not merely a question of preserving property in craft. The logical development from this point of view should beget an understanding of the importance of the principles of industrial unionism, though officialdom will probably draw red herrings across the trail....

113. The Decline of "International" Unions in Canada[52]

International craft unions in Canada last year [1925] had 1,985 branches and 172,573 members, a loss from the previous year of 43 branches and 17,928 members, according to the annual report issued recently by the Federal Department of Labour. This shows a decline of more than one-tenth in one year. If that rate of loss continues there will be no "International" craft unions in Canada ten years from now.

The total membership of labour organizations in Canada last year is given as 271,064. This means that there were 98,491 organized workers not connected with the United States "Internationals."

The total membership of 271,064 for all groups last year was 10,421 more than in the previous year. Gains in membership of the non-American groups not only made up the loss of 17,928, sustained by the United States "Internationals," but an additional 10,421 -- or a total gain of 28,348 members. The purely Canadian unions, according to these figures, made a gain of 40 per cent, against a loss of 10 per cent sustained by the American unions in this country. And this loss would be increased if the C.B.R.E. membership figures were not, for the purposes of the Department's classification, included in the "International" group.

These are the figures, according to the Labour Department's classifications:

	Branches	Members
Internationals	1985	172,573
[the Department has included the C.B.R.E. membership figure in this group.]		
Non-Internationals	311	34,070
National and Catholic	99	25,000
O.B.U.	53	17,256
I.W.W.	6	10,000
Independent Units	40	12,165
TOTALS	2494	271,064

---

[52]*Canadian Railroad Employees Monthly*, June 1926, 86-87. This article was in many respects the "founding manifesto" of the All-Canadian Congress of Labour -- the new formation's declaration of war against the TLC and the international unions. (According to McKay's obituary in *The Canadian Unionist* (Montreal), February 1939, this piece was written jointly by M.M. MacLean, the editor and manager, and McKay.) H.A. Logan, *Trade Unions in Canada: Their Development and Functioning* (Toronto: Macmillan of Canada, 1948), 380, quotes extensively from it, without identifying "the writer" involved.

Outside of these groups, 73 other groups were listed, with a combined membership of 90,488, comprising school-teachers, commercial travellers, government employees, and other wage workers, not specifically identified with the Canadian labour movement, although they form an important part of the labour movement of more advanced countries. In addition, there are numerous farmers' organizations.

Thus, there are outside the unions affiliated with the Trades and Labor Congress, very large bodies of organized workers in Canada, some national in scope, some sectional, others purely local, but all Canadian, in inception and purpose. The unification of these groups, their bringing together in an all-Canadian Federation or Congress, presents a problem that challenges the attention of the best minds in the labour movement. A central body, uniting these varied groups for common action on broad lines of labour policy, would wield a much greater influence than that now exercised by the Trades and Labor Congress, whose membership is confined chiefly to delegates from the A.F.of L. Unions. A real Canadian Federation or Congress of wage-earners would doubtless enlist the support of the organizations of school-teachers, commercial travellers, farmers and other Canadian workers, who prefer to run their organizations as all-Canadian institutions, and who are not wanted in Mr. Moore's Congress.

The present Trades and Labor Congress has adopted the policy of refusing affiliation to Canadian labour organizations which are dual to branches of American unions. It may be doubted whether this policy is sanctioned by the considered opinion of the rank and file of the A.F. of L. unions in Canada. But it serves the purpose of Mr. Moore and the other masters of the game of union politics. Mr. Moore and the paid organizers of the A.F. of L., and its allied unions, have built up a machine which has dominated the Congress for years. And, while membership in the Congress is restricted to the A.F. of L. unions, a comparatively small number of men can continue to dominate it. The chief operators of the machine are highly skilled in union politics; but they are not big enough to face the prospect of having the power of the machine menaced by the influx of members from all-Canadian labour bodies, who might not be amenable to A.F. of L. discipline.

And, while Mr. Moore and his machine men are in control, they will be too much occupied with the everlasting game of union politics to give much attention to the major problems of better organization and more positive Labour policies.

Since 1919, the membership of labour unions in Canada has fallen off by 107,000. As the Train Service Brotherhoods, which are not connected with the A.F. of L., have held their own, and, as the all-Canadian unions have increased their membership, the A.F. of L. unions have lost considerably more than 100,000 members. In six years, under the inspired direction of

Mr. Moore, the A.F. of L. unions in Canada have declined nearly 40 per cent, and, for the last year covered by the report of the Labour Department, the rate of decline was considerably greater than the average for the five preceding years.

The time is ripe, it seems to us, for all labour bodies organized on Canadian lines to form a Central Federation or Congress, for the purpose of unifying and stimulating labour activities, and perhaps also of waking the A.F. of L. unions in Canada to the fact that they are without any real policy for the solution of labour questions in this country. The business of a Canadian labour movement is to come to grips with Canadian capitalism, to overthrow its political and economic power, and make Canada a country with working and living conditions the best attainable.

Mr. Moore's Congress has tied its own hands by limiting affiliation to branches of American unions. The unity of the Canadian labour movement, which the average worker desires, is thus being delayed by the intolerant assumption that Canadian workers organized in one form of union are superior to those organized in another form of union -- or rather by the assumption that all workers must submit to the same authority before they are qualified to co-operate for common purposes. Only through competition did capitalists learn the virtue of co-operation; it would seem that Canadian labour will have to go through the same experience. The numerous organized workers outside the present Trades and Labor Congress should get together and build up a rival Central Organization; build it up until it becomes big enough to absorb the present Congress, and effect the complete unification of the Canadian labour movement.

The possibility of a rival Central Organization to the Trades and Labor Congress becoming a power in the country is self-evident. As a fully autonomous Canadian organization, it would doubtless attract organizations of school-teachers, other workers, and probably the United Farmers of Canada, that powerful body whose leaders recognize that, in the struggle with capitalism, they and the industrial workers have certain very important common interests. An independent Canadian Federation or Congress, opening its doors to all unions in Canada, proclaiming its desire to effect the unification of all bona fide workers' organizations in the country, would probably soon be in a position to induce the A.F. of L. unions in Canada to change the attitude of their present leaders towards the question of promoting the unity of the Canadian labour movement.

114. The Labour Aristocracy and the Decline of the Craft Unions[53]

The inability of men to change their social institutions and their social ideals so as to keep them adapted to the development of technique, and the changes in business organization, has had tragic consequences at various stages of human history. At present our major social institutions are practically what they were in the handicraft era; but machinery has added greatly to men's powers of production. Now the social institutions based on legal and property relations appropriate to the handicraft era when in the main property was the result of the individual labour of the proprietor, act as fetters upon the new forces of production....

The craft unionists have not been historically minded. If they accepted the theory of evolution, they were blind to the fact that the constant improvement of machinery, the evolution of family firms into corporations, the linking up of many small enterprises into mergers and chains, the development of the holding company, combines trusts, monopolies -- they were blind to the fact that the evolution of all these new forms of capitalist organization, which accompanied the constant improvement in power-driven machinery was bound to make it increasingly difficult to utilize fully the marvellous new forces of production without drastic changes in the social institutions which were developed around individual private property and production mainly by hand tools....

It is well to remember that the craft unionists, in their [fundamental] attitude to social institutions, were in accord with so-called public opinion, and the dogmas of all the bourgeois economists. These oracles take a peculiar view of history. They, indeed, recognize that there have been feudal institutions, and that in these feudal institutions, the conditions of production were quite different from those of bourgeois society, the society in which things are mainly produced for exchange by the medium of money. But the bourgeois economists say the difference between feudal institutions and bourgeois institutions is a difference between artificial and natural institutions. In the feudal period of history, the institutions were artificial, and therefore changeable -- subject to the will of men. On the other hand, the institutions of the modern period are natural (or so the bourgeois economists held until recently, anyway). That is to say, the social institutions based on individual private property, and the social relations arising therefrom in which commodity production is carried on, developed in conformity with the laws of nature....

It is worthwhile trying to follow this singular manner of reasoning of the bourgeois economists, because it throws a certain light on the absurdities

[53]Originally published as "Craft Unions and Social Progress," *Canadian Railway Employees Monthly*, May 1935, 118-119.

and insanities of existing society. By such reasoning the economists cut the ground from under the bourgeois philosophers' doctrine of free will, and thereby absolved the bourgeoisie from responsibility for the consequences of their actions. At the same time, it gave sanction to the bourgeois to exercise a kind of freedom which feudal lords could not exercise except by an abuse of their right -- the modern freedom of pursuing private ends without responsibility for the social consequences, so long as one does not violate certain rules laid down by [the] political state, the chief purpose of which is to protect property rights in the means of production used by the few to exploit the many. Thus the economists having denied to humanity any power of free will over its own history, managed, nevertheless, to sanctify the free will of the individual exercised in the pursuit of private advantage, as a kindly force working so in harmony with natural laws as to promote always the greatest good of the greatest number; and to exalt rugged individualism as the highest virtue a member of society could possess.

This dualistic logic of the economists had another object. In existing society the processes of production have the mastery over men instead of being controlled by them. If the ruling class really ruled, controlled, the system, they would not have permitted the calamity of the present depression. Even many capitalists have been ruined. The bourgeois economists cannot ascertain the real cause of the bewildering come-and-go of fortune. The cause cannot be attributed to the stupidities and short-sighted policies of the "ruling" class. Nor can it be admitted that the cause resides in the contradictions of the system itself. So the bourgeois economists find the cause in natural laws. And, of course, men cannot control natural laws, though they may adapt themselves to such laws, and harness natural forces to their service.

Such was the ideology which expressed the interests of the bourgeois. It justified class exploitation of the masses, while absolving the exploiting class from the responsibility of being real rulers -- rulers of their system. It pervaded all the currents of "public opinion" impinging upon the mass of workers on this continent, influencing their ways of thinking and feeling, and that goes far to explain the tardiness of the mass of the workers in realizing the need of evolving industrial unions, to replace the outmoded craft unions.

...The important thing is to recognize that this depression has completely demonstrated the futility of craft unionism. The position of the United States craft unions today is an unhappy one. They have fumbled the opportunities offered them by the New Deal. And largely because they had no ideology, no policy even approximating the social philosophy possessed by Roosevelt at the inception of the New Deal. The craft unions accepted the bourgeois assumption that private property in the means of production was a natural and therefore eternal institution (even though private property has mostly been swallowed by corporate property). They never questioned the permanence or the righteousness of the social relations necessary to make property a means of exploitation. No industrial property can function as capital and produce profits unless there is a proletariat, that is, propertyless workers, who can be used to operate that property. For property to have value there must exist a social relation of master and servant, a class of owners and a class of dependent workers. The craft unionist thought of himself as a property owner -- his property being his craft skill. He was the "aristocrat of Labour." Hence his psychology was that of the small property-owner; and snobbishness being a characteristic of society divided into classes, he was loathe to identify himself with the class to which he really belonged -- the dependent worker class....

115. British Models of Industrial Unionism[54]

The labour movement in the United States is now struggling through a phase of development analogous to the experience of the British Labour movement some decades ago. That the outcome will be much the same need not be doubted, though the effort to emancipate United States workers from traditions which have become fetters may require greater energy. Trusts, combines, and company unions are more serious obstacles in the United States than they were in Britain, and what have often been an important source of strength to British workers in their struggles, the co-operative societies, are of little consequence in U.S. industrial centres. On the other hand, the harsher features of the capitalist system are more sharply developed in the United States, and during the depression the workers of that country have suffered a process of galling disillusionment. Hence, as they wake up to consciousness of their situation, the reactions of the U.S. workers are likely to be lively; having once achieved a clear recognition of the need of industrial unions and political action, they may be expected to try to make up for lost time.

Up to 1928 capitalism in the United States was in process of expansion, with more or less periodic interruptions in the form of depressions -- usually of short duration. Except during the depression periods the capitalists could afford to make concessions to the workers. Great numbers of immigrants from across the Atlantic -- over a million in some years -- flowed into the eastern labour markets. But this influx was more than offset by the continuous westward migration of people; in 1912 1,000,000 people entered the State of Texas alone. Except during the depressions, the relations of supply and demand in the labour markets, east and west, usually favoured the worker; jobs sought men. In this condition, the craft unions, representing the aristocrats of labour, were

---

[54]Originally published as "United States Labour Begins to Learn from Britain," *Canadian Unionist*, Vol.10, No.2 (July 1936), 36-37.

able to command high wage rates -- money rates -- though the real wages did not always justify the boasts of the great success of craft unionism. American costs of living were high, and craftsmen who, like the bricklayers, received $10 a day, were lucky if they got work for six months in the year.

However, many United States workers believed that the craft unions represented the ultimate in labour organization. They did not understand the implication of the fact that the craft union was only a special kind of business enterprise, engaged in selling the commodity labour power at the highest price obtainable, and, as a side-line, selling death benefits to its own members. The craft unionists had the small businessman's mentality and outlook. They were not only indifferent to -- they were instinctively opposed to -- the organization of workers operating machines, and unskilled and semi-skilled labour generally. They felt that if these other workers were organized their competition for high wages would lessen the chances of the craft unions securing and maintaining high wages. Moreover, they felt that their superior position as the aristocrats was measured in terms of the height of their wage rates above the rates of unskilled labour, having that snobbery which has been the peculiar social cement of competitive capitalism.

Like the small businessman, the craft unionists were slow to grasp the significance of the organization of big corporations, combines, and trusts. They regarded these business organizations as illegitimate interlopers which would be suppressed by the political authorities as soon as the latter woke up to the new dangers of democracy, which such organizations represented. They were slow to see that these big business organizations were the outcome of technological development -- that these new forms of business organization were made possible and inevitable by the extension of the machine process to all sorts of productions. They were slow to understand that the development of the machine process was decomposing crafts and trades, and destroying the value of craft skill. A generation ago it was still good advice for a man to say to his son: "Learn a trade; then if you want to try something else and fail, you can always fall back on your trade."

But such advice is of doubtful value today. A new machine invention may dispense with the need of an army of skilled men overnight.

Technical developments during the war and since rapidly extended the machine process and undermined the basis of the craft unions. Employment in U.S. factories began to decline after 1926, and, since the onslaught of the great depression, economic unemployment added to increasing technological unemployment has been most severely felt in those trades in which the craft unions had previously had their greatest strength. At the same time, United States capitalism, as a result of the depression, has been driven to a policy of harsh repression of free unions, wage-cutting and brutal suppression of strikes. And -- without a great war -- it is now doubtful that United States capitalism will ever recover sufficiently to permit it to resume anything like a generous policy towards labour.

In these changing conditions the United States craft unions have fared badly. A recent report shows the standing of various types of U.S. unions in 1935 as compared with 1920. Craft unions show a loss of 32 per cent in membership. Miscellaneous types of unions show a loss of 32 per cent. Industrial unions show a gain of 6 per cent. Semi-industrial unions which voted for the full industrial-union motion at the American Federation of Labor's convention in 1935, showed a gain of 5 per cent. But semi-industrial unions which did not vote for full industrial unions, show a loss of 60 per cent. These figures prove that craft unionism is failing, while industrial unionism is making progress -- if not at as fast a rate as might be desired. Acceleration of that rate is likely, however, in the near future.

A cursory review of the experience of the British Labour movement is of interest, because British experience sheds a certain light on the present situation of Labour in the United States and Canada. After the depression of 1873, British Labour for two decades or more obtained few advances in money wages. But real wages rose because the cost of living declined. Employment was fairly plentiful because large emigration overseas released the pressure on the labour market. The emigration of many enterprising workers tended to make the unions less aggressive than they might otherwise have been. Not until the depression of 1893 were there notable manifestations of militancy. In that year the Welsh miners staged an important strike, and four years later the engineering trades fought a hard battle.

But there was little general unrest in Britain until after 1905, when the cost of living began to rise. As real wages fell discontent grew, and this was accentuated by the introduction of "speeding up" practices, and a rapid increase in the use of machines. The unions became militant, and demanded wage increases. Export industries by then were being seriously challenged by the competition of Germany and the United States and were not disposed to make concessions to labour. Other industries hardened their hearts.

Some of the unions found themselves tied up by long-term contracts, fixing the money wages: contracts which in a period of rising living costs operated against the workers. Unions, free to strike for higher wages or shorter hours, found themselves handicapped by hitherto unsuspected weaknesses and shortcomings in their organization. Their very policy and outlook, which had been developed during decades when real wages had been increased by economic changes without special effort on the part of the workers, was an impediment to vigorous militant action. Their friendly benefit features weighted them with financial obligations, and greatly increased the difficulty of financing needed struggles on the industrial field. Bureaucracies, which had been developed in many of the older unions, naturally were inclined to use their power to make the protection of the benefit features a more important consideration than militant action to secure higher wages.

But what more especially the British workers learnt during the decade preceding the Great War was the inadequacy of organizations based on craft. The rise in the cost of living signalized a rapid development of the monopolist tendencies of British capitalism, the expansion of corporations, the advent of combines, gentlemen's agreements, and various other devices to limit competition. The control of industries was being concentrated in the hands of a few financial magnates. The business organizations which confronted labour became larger, more powerful. Employers were attaining a more or less united front.

In that situation, the division of the forces of Labour on craft lines was a weakness. Many struggles in the British Isles proved the need of organization on the basis of a whole industry. Not that the implied lesson has even yet been fully learnt by all British workers. But enough [learned] the lesson to permit broad modifications in union structures, and promote a wide understanding of the need of organization for political purposes as well as economic purposes. Once the narrow outlook of the craft union was abandoned, the workers began to envisage their special problems as part of the general problem of all workers. They perceived that control of the political power was an important element of the domination of the capitalist class, and that emancipation from the exploitation of that class could only be finally achieved by efforts on the part of the workers to acquire control of the political power and use it in the furtherance of the aims of their industrial unions. This new consciousness of the requirements of the workers' position in capitalist society has been reflected in British Labour policy, which, without ignoring workaday needs, keeps in mind and resolutely pursues the ideal of a society in which the workers will have the mastery over the processes of production instead of being the victims. Today the British Labour movement with all its imperfections leads the way [for] the Labour movements of the United States, and this country may follow. It is the stoutest bulwark of democracy in a capitalist world drifting to fascism; it is the movement which, above all, gives promise of a peaceful transition from the present economic disorder and social distress to economic order and social well-being.

116. The Future of Industrial Unionism[55]

"Write an article on the rôle of industrial unions in the transformed society of the future," said the Editor. That is not easy; it involves entrance, to some extent, into the realms of prophecy and speculation. Yet it may be worth attempting, because the broader the perspective in which industrial unionism is put, the more obvious its importance as a means of progress becomes. It must be taken for granted that, out of the disorderly, misery-creating society of the present, a transformed society will emerge. As Hegel said "Nothing is; everything is becoming... The present is the child of the past, but it is the parent of the future."[56] The present differs from the past; and the future will differ from the present.[57] The process of evolution still goes on in human society.

...The Third Estate, the bourgeoisie, had no blue-prints of the social system which was to develop after they acquired political power. They had only an ideal of liberty which they considered an end in itself; and their new liberty turned out to be only [an] "open market" for land, goods and labour. They did lip service to equality and fraternity. But they did not foresee that their revolution, made with the slogan, "liberty, equality and fraternity," would prepare the way for the disorders, inequalities and injustices of present-day society.

No more can the industrial unionist be expected to prepare detailed blue-prints of the future society. It is not a question of building a social edifice, using the word edifice in the architect's sense. Human society is a natural, living organism in which the only thing constant is change, even when the change is not perceptible to the senses. What can be foreseen is the general direction of the current of social evolution. Plainly the course of social evolution is in the direction foreseen and predicted by social scientists; that is to say, it is in the direction of subordinating the interests of the individual to the welfare of the public, and therefore in the direction of the socialization of economic life, and with, and in consequence of that, political, juridical and moral life. We can be certain that the executive guidance of the new society will not be as confused as the administration of national, provincial and municipal affairs now provided. We can be certain that the future society will not present the irrational and tragic aspects of existing society.

---

[55]*Canadian Railway Employees Monthly*, April 1937, 85-86.

[56]These quotations McKay is clearly borrowing from Enrico Ferri, *Socialism and Modern Science*, 94. McKay would have been on better ground had he identified the second part of the quotation with G.W. Leibniz, and not Hegel.

[57]Again a paraphrase of Ferri. The original in Ferri, *Socialism and Modern Science*, 94 reads: "...that the present differs from the past and that the future will certainly be different from the present."

Industrial unionism has both a message and a mission. In substance, its message is that the present economic system is a transitory phase of a process of evolution, and that it is destined to be succeeded by another system wherein men, by the collective planning of production to supply the wants of all the people, will become the conscious masters of economic forces instead of being their victims. The mission of industrial unionism is to organize the workers, so that when the control of political power passes from the privileged property-owning classes to the producing masses, that political power can be used in conjunction with economic power of the organized producers to set up a new society in which economic democracy will be realized.

A Labour-Farmer party in control of government is not enough. Without strong organizations of the workers and farmers for economic purposes, a Labour-Farmer government could do little except to try to make the capitalist system function in a more orderly manner and provide more social relief for the victims of its disorders. Workers for the Co-operative Commonwealth may be well advised to confine themselves to political activities while the economic organizations of the workers lack unity, and those of the farmers are mainly concerned with sectional interests. But the achievement of their objective depends upon the workers' and farmers' developing their economic organizations, and learning to make better use of them, not merely for the protection or promotion of their immediate economic interests, but to challenge the system by which they are exploited.

The industrial form of organization is needed not only for the every-day struggle; it is essential for the transformation of society, and it will continue to be necessary for the successful working of the transformed society. For the new society will be an economic democracy, and that implies control and management by economic organs instead of by political organs. The new organs of the control of the affairs of society will naturally be the industrial unions of the workers and the economic organizations of the farmers.

In the new society it is likely that the political parliament will be replaced by periodical conventions of the representatives of industrial unions and farmers' organizations. These conventions, or industrial parliaments, will determine matters of policy on such questions as, for instance, whether more effort should be applied to the production of goods at the expense of provision of educational facilities, or vice versa; whether labour and materials should be added to the building of better homes for the many, or diverted to the building of aircraft for the use of the few, whether labour should be assigned to the reclamation of the drought areas of the West, or the construction of such projects as the St. Lawrence Seaway.

There will be controversial questions to be settled: questions involving sectional interests. But they will not be complicated by such a multitude of narrow, private interests as the questions which now agitate politics. The over-riding consideration would be -- what use of labour and materials will serve the greatest good of the greatest number? With such a touchstone, questions of public policy will be easily determined.

The administrators of the new society may be appointed, from time to time, by the industrial parliament. But probably they will be selected directly by the various national industrial unions and farmer organizations. The administrators will be concerned with economic questions which will no longer have a political aspect. They will be concerned with the productive capacity of different industries, and the consumptive needs of people. Their task will be to regulate production so as to serve the social purpose, first, of supplying all the people with shelter, food and clothing; secondly, of improving the quality of these essentials of life; and, thirdly, of providing for luxuries. The problem is not simple, but already statistics are sufficiently developed to enable a fair estimate to be made of the quantity and nature of the goods which would be required to supply all the people during a year.

The planning of production to provide supplies in accordance with estimate requirements would be a matter of assigning labour and materials to the service of this or that industry; the problem of credit which vexes capitalist society would not arise.

The responsible administrators, representing the industrial unions and farmers' organizations, would, of course, be assisted by trained statisticians and other experts. There would, for instance, be scientists and research workers engaged in ascertaining the most efficient and economical types among the equipment in use, and in introducing and applying improvements in the means of production and distribution, in building construction, transportation, communication, and other industries.

117. The Failure of Craft Unions[58]

The C.I.O. has certainly demonstrated the superiority of the industrial form of unionism over the craft form. No observing person can fail to have been impressed by the fact, whatever he may think of the C.I.O. invasion of Canada. A clear recognition of that superiority undoubtedly explains much of the ire of Canadian organs of big interests, for they disclaim any opposition to the invasion of the A.F. of L. craft unions.

...Why...did the craft-union leaders fail?

---

[58]*Canadian Unionist*, June 1937, 8-10.

Well, they did not really try to make the best of their opportunities. They feared that the organization of the unskilled or non-craft workers would threaten the privileged position of the skilled workers. They did not want to give the unskilled workers a voice in union affairs, and they could not organize them without giving them a voice and vote. They were in a dilemma; wholesale organization of unskilled workers would mean they would dominate the unions by weight of numbers, and the craftsmen would become an appendage of their own unions. So there was no real attempt to organize the mass-production workers, except in limited numbers.

The fact is, the objects and functions of craft unions are incompatible with the organization of mass-production workers who cannot be placed in a standard, craft category. To take such workers into the craft unions in numbers would upset the entire structure of craft unionism. That, in the final analysis, is the reason for the impasse, the blind alley, the *cul de sac*, in which craft unionism finds itself.

...Of course, the old line craft-union leaders did their best to create the impression that the failure to organize the mass-production workers was the fault of the workers themselves. They said such workers were spineless material and that it was hopeless to try to organize them. They thought such workers were over-awed by the immense power of massed finance capital behind the mass-production industries, and were glad to be herded into company unions, as in a refuge. It was really the A.F.of L. leaders themselves who were overawed by the power wielded by the potentates of the mass-production industries, and who saw defeatism in the attitude of the workers because it was a reflection on [of] their own attitude. One need not suppose that they deliberately took the position that the mass-production workers were hopeless material from the standpoint of organization in order to cloak their own ineptitude. Conscious hypocrites are rare, for men have an innate casuistry which gives them a great capacity for self-deception. They probably did not understand that there was little or nothing in the craft union set-up, its objects and aims, its philosophy, which appealed to the mass of the workers outside the pale of the craft elect.

Consider the stand-point of these workers. They had "skills" of their own, developed by their parts in the machine process. As regards their effectiveness in keeping the machines going, they were highly skilled. But their skill was not of a type which they might regard as "property" as the craftsman had been wont to regard his skill. They knew that the craftsmen from their height as aristocrats of Labour looked down upon them as their inferiors, not only in social status, but in usefulness in the work of the world. They knew the traditional attitude of the craft unions was one of opposition to the organization of workers who were not recognized as craftsmen; an attitude which expressed the craftsman's intuition that his

position was somewhat precarious and depended upon the existence of a
mass of low-paid and therefore unorganized workers at a lower level to
keep the cost of living low; an attitude which served notice that any
organization dominated by craftsmen would not go out of its way to help
the mass of unskilled workers or semi-skilled workers to achieve any
material improvement of their lot.

If, from the standpoint of the A.F. of L. leaders, such workers appeared to
be hopeless material for organization, so, likewise, from the standpoint of
the workers, the A.F. of L. organizational plans and set-up appeared to be
equally hopeless. The A.F. of L. missed its opportunity because without
recognizing what its opportunity was, it attempted the impossible. Its fault
was its failure to recognize that its opportunity was one of organizing
industrial unions and of transforming craft unions where necessary. This
merit must be allowed to the leaders of the C.I.O. -- themselves in most
cases leaders of craft unions, -- that they recognized the nature of the
opportunity and took occasion by the hand. The funds liberally
contributed by various craft unions, as well as by the industrial union of
miners, made possible the industrial organization of the workers in mass-
production industries, where the workers themselves, unaided, might not
have been able to organize themselves for some time yet. But the most
notable thing has been the bold and enthusiastic response of the workers;
a response which must be attributed in great part to the fact that for the
first time they were offered a large-scale opportunity to get together in a
form of organization within which there is room for the widest possible
efforts to realize their deepest and most intimate needs....

The outstanding successes of the industrial union movement [have] lifted
the spirit of vast numbers of American workers from a plane of hopeless
resignation to a place of confident militancy. There is, of course, the
danger that its very successes may turn the heads of both leaders and
followers. The testing time of the new organizations is yet to come. But
unlike the craft-union movement, which has required as many apologies
from its adherents as any social movement of modern times, the
industrial union movement has a *character* at once stimulating and
steadying. It opens up a wide field of vision and gives a promise for the
future, which transforms it from a mere machine for raising wages and
reducing hours, into an engine of human liberation. The notion that the
great business of unionism is to protect the [worker's] property in his craft
is abandoned, and the problems of Labour are faced in terms of the
rights and duties of Man. The pettiness and cheapness inherent in the
craft union disappear in the splendour of the promise which the
programme of industrial unionism unfolds to the workers, -- a programme
whereby the Labour movement is transformed from a series of haphazard,
unco-ordinated struggles to maintain living standards above the
subsistence level, into a coherent, harmonious progress to the goal of
emancipation from the disorders of an outworn social system.

118. Machine Industry and the Erosion of Craft 'Capital'[59]

...All the arguments for trade unions assume that the possessor of craft skill is a possessor of a form of capital. That assumption was more or less well founded while the craftsman could readily find employment for his capital in the form of skill. The development of machine industry, however, has undermined the basis of such an assumption. But the evolution of ideas seldom keeps pace with the progress of technique. The philosophy of trade unions still rests on assumptions which have long ceased to represent reality. More and more, the worker has found that his craft skill is a form of "capital" for which opportunities for investment grow less. Unlike money capital, his form of "capital" cannot be deposited in a bank to await a demand for it. If he ceases to exercise his craft skill, its value as "capital" deteriorates; and he, as its proprietor, may also deteriorate. And finally, if he cannot find employment, he may be threatened with extinction along with his "capital".

Moreover, the craftsman's "capital" has frequently been rendered valueless by a new invention, a new combination of industrial forces, even by a change in fashions. It is true that scientific development has in some cases increased the demand for skilled workers. In the moulding trades, the increased use of machinery has actually called for higher degrees of skill than were formerly required, as a consequence in part of the moulding trades taking over forging work, and, in part, of the greater precision demanded by the increasing complexity and intricacies of machinery. But, in general, the effect of new developments of technique has been to render the skill upon which the craftsmen relied to provide them a livelihood more or less obsolete. Modern industry has tended to eliminate the need of personal individual skill of the kind which has been a proud possession of the craftsman, and to make production the result of the co-operating efforts of groups of workers. Mass production, or standardized production, which continuously extends its field because of its competing power in modern markets, reduces the need of skill to the production of models and moulds.

Skill, as a form of property, shares the impermanence of other forms of property. That forms of property have been a product of a process of evolution is frequently forgotten. But in the course of history there has been communal or clan property, family property, feudal property, private property, capitalist property. Different forms of property exist side by side. Today the capitalist form of property, the ownership of stocks and bonds, is the most desired. The individual owners of stock and bonds issued by a corporation cannot say that any part of the physical property of the corporation is their private property; their stocks and bonds give

---

[59]Originally published as "The Genesis of Industrial Unionism (4)," *Canadian Railway Employees' Monthly*, September 1937, 218-219.

them a legal title to revenues from the operations of the corporation. The capitalist form of ownership differs from private property which implies the personal possession and use by the owners.

Political systems are supposed to guarantee the inviolability of property rights, for such rights now rest upon the letter or spirit of the constitution of the country and the statutes ordained by the law-making authorities. "The rights of property," as a U.S. court declared, "rest not upon philosophic, moral, scientific or economic theories, nor yet upon the dictates of natural justice." But though the rights of property may transcend the dictates of natural justice or moral considerations, the political authorities which make the constitutions and laws establishing the rights of property, cannot guarantee the protection of those rights from the rude effects of the economic laws of competitive enterprise. Big business swallows small business; the growth of great property at the expense of little property is everywhere evident. The end and aim of the existing economic system is the accumulation of property, and since property is not unlimited, this means accumulation in few hands. The development of the economic system itself promotes the confiscation of little property by big property. Against this tendency the supposed guarantees of the law and the constitution are no bulwark. The rights of property resolve themselves into the right of the economically strong property to dispossess the economically weak property. The complaining cry of the dispossessed fills the land. But the courts give their benediction to the big expropriators of small property.

The possessor of small tangible property of the kind which yielded a revenue had a sense of superiority to the common run of propertyless persons. Similarly, the possessor of a craft flattered himself that he was superior to the unskilled worker. Though his property, his craft skill, was intangible, he felt it entitled him to regard himself as an aristocrat of labour. He had a sense of class interest which expressed itself in the way his union conducted its business. The object of his union was to control the opportunities for the employment of craft skill. To this end the union limited the number of apprentices and charged high initiation fees and high dues. Every precaution was taken by the union against the invasion of the craft; fights for jurisdiction were waged with even greater energy than fights for higher wages. The craftsman turned to his superior position and the power of his union to save himself and his family in the midst of the vicissitudes of the capitalist system.

But the craftsman's property has, like the more tangible property of the middle class, been undermined by economic development. Just as the evolution of big business has reduced the profitable opportunities of small business, so the technological developments which large-scale enterprise has made possible and necessary, have restricted the demand for craft skill. With the disappearance of opportunities for the employment of craft skill, the value of the craftsman's property has largely vanished. And with that, the craftsman has been increasingly stripped of all those material advantages which he possessed over the members of the working class who have no craft. He is no longer an "aristocrat of labour."

Insofar as the value of craft skill as a form of property has disappeared, the union formed for the protection of the craftsman in the possession of his craft property has become ineffective for its purpose. Such a union being based on the craft, the disappearance of the need of craft skill leaves the union without a foundation. The old reasons for an exclusive organization no longer hold. The strength of the craft union depended upon its ability to control the supply of craft skill. But the control of the supply of something for which the demand has shrunk -- in many industries to the vanishing point -- means nothing. The original and primary purpose of the craft union has thus ceased to be a practical purpose of any importance, to the extent that technical developments have rendered craft skill an anachronism.

The ineffectiveness of the craft form of organization, in the face of the great business organization which now dominates industry, is due to the narrowing of the economic basis of the craft -- to the practical disappearance in some cases of that economic basis. That is a fact which cannot be too strongly emphasized. A strong union structure cannot be sustained on a disintegrating foundation.

Many craft unionists have stubbornly refused to recognize how the position of their unions has been undermined by technical developments and new combinations of forces and processes in industry. Their mental outlook reflects the individualism of an older day. Like the small bourgeois, they look upon their problems as manifestations of a central property problem. Their social and political philosophy [is] essentially capitalistic, being pivoted on the property notion, but failing to take account of the fact that all property is transitory, and that property in craft skill is especially transitory and ineffectual. When the craft unionist is disturbed by the insecurity of his position, he attributes it to new inventions, to the competition of strangers coming into his town, or of cheap labour abroad. His reactions to the increasing pressure of corporations are practically the same as the reactions of the small businessman to the encroachment of big business. He blames his difficulties upon unscrupulous employers, and believes that if all employers were fair-minded his difficulties would be solved, just as the small businessman blames his troubles upon unscrupulous competitors, and believes that ethical sentiment in business is all that is needed to suspend the laws of competition to his advantage.

119. Industrial Unionism: The Workers' Answer to Mechanization[60]

In more senses than one, the machine has become the master of men. The great majority of wage-workers are now employed in machine process. The locomotive engineer may be said to be more directly engaged in the machine-process than the railway clerk. But the latter's labour, mental or manual, is an essential part of the process of adjusting the motions of machines and men to the railway's particular function, the transportation of passengers and goods.

The employment of a railway clerk depends on, and is determined and disciplined by, the machine-process. His mental reactions, his ways of thought, tend to reflect his relations to the complex organization he serves. A clerk in a store may think of himself as a future merchant proprietor, and plan accordingly. But the idea of becoming owner of a railway hardly occurs to the railway clerk. He may, indeed, aspire to the personal dignity of the presidency of a railway, but he knows his chances of realizing such an ambition are very much less than the chance of a clerk in a store to become a store manager or owner....

Who Shall Control the Machine?

The question of the right of any particular individual or group to control the use of the machine then comes to the forefront. Did capital, an abstraction, create the machine? How much of the labour, mental or manual, is embodied in the machine? Not much. The machine, completed last month, was only partially the product of the living workers who laboured on it. Not only James Watt, but the savage who discovered the art of smelting iron ore, shared in its production. By the natural rights doctrine, they have a right to share in the control of the use of the machine. But how shall they exercise that right? The legal fictions by which the dead hand of the past oppresses the living present are not so remote in their origins.

A distinctive psychological effect of the developed machine process is to raise in the minds of the workers the question of the validity of the natural rights doctrine, which the bourgeoisie during their struggle to overthrow feudalism invented as theoretical weapons to oppose the divine rights of the king and his delegated authority to the nobles, and which lies at the basis of the political and juridicial [juridical] structure of the bourgeois régime. The workers perceive that the natural rights doctrine, which served the bourgeoisie so well during their revolutionary struggles, are now used to oppose the aspirations of the workers to a share in the control of the machine and an equitable share in its products, and thus

---

[60]*Canadian Unionist*, September 1937, 95-96.

are obstacles blocking the only road which leads to progress and prosperity for the masses. They have not abandoned hope for the future. If the natural rights doctrine stands in the way of social ownership of the machine, and progress and prosperity for the masses, so much the worse for it. For most workers the perception that the natural rights theory had only a relative and temporary validity was perhaps more instinctive than conscious. In any case, they have adopted an increasingly iconoclastic attitude toward it.

The workers have more and more questioned and challenged the right of the employer to run his business in his own way. They have also been constrained to deny the right of individual freedom to contract on the part of the worker with the employer. Save for a few in whom the arrogant exercise of power has corrupted all the social instincts, even employers do not pretend that an individual worker and a corporation may bargain on the equal terms, which, even according to the natural rights doctrine, are supposed to be the condition of freedom of contract. In Britain, employers have recognized the advantage of collective bargaining to such an extent that it has been given legislative and judicial sanction. In a machine industry, employing many workers, a contract between the management and a union affords protection against strikes of special groups, which may dislocate or stop the smooth working of the correlated parts of the industry. If the attitude of employers on this continent towards the new industrial unions is less friendly than, say, the attitude of the Civic Federation of the United States to the A.F. of L. unions, that probably reflects a fear that the industrial unions will be less amicable than the craft unions have been. But, at least, an industrial union can, by contract, give the machine industry more assurance of uninterrupted operations than a contract with a craft union does, because the craft union represents only a section of the workers in the industry.

120. Why Craft Unions are Backward[61]

....The typical craft unionist's mind has been largely ruled by the ideas and prejudices of the *bourgeoisie*, and the *petite bourgeoisie* at that. Although he has built up great organizations, the trade unionist's conception of his opportunities and his purpose is narrow. As possessor of the commodity, craft skill, he was concerned to maintain or increase the price of that commodity by the control of the supply in the labour market, and that has been about the limit of his desires. His interests have been centered on the preservation of his craft, usually so intently that he did not see how technical development was undermining it.

The cultural achievements of the craft unions have been small. For the most part, the tone of official craft union journals is dull and

---

[61] *Canadian Railway Employees' Monthly*, November 1937, 281-282.

uninteresting. In part, they reflect the individualistic points of view of a past age; in part, they also echo the ideas which express the interest of the dominant ruling class of today, as complacently as if such ideas were products of Labour's thinking concerning the needs of its position in the world. They do not show an adequate realization of the implications of the fact that either evolution or devolution is bound to change the existing economic system, and that the future, if it is to be worthwhile, will call for important decisions and actions on the part of the organized workers.

Certainly, much credit is due to the craft unions for what they have done in the past to show the need, and prove the value, of organization. After machinery upset the handicraft economy, and, by reducing the opportunities of the journeymen to become master workmen, developed a class of permanently dependent wage-workers, it was natural that the skilled workers should begin the struggle against the bad conditions to which machine industry had reduced all wage-workers. Their skill gave them the important advantage that in event of a strike men to do their work could not readily be found. Their position resembled that of the senior apprentices of the handicraft era; their unions in some respects were natural descendents of the Guilds.

But if their inheritance of Guild traditions gave them certain advantages, it also inclined them to view their problems in terms of their own particular craft. That made for a variety of separate unions, each concerned only with the interests of its own members. Where better organizations, greater skill or fortuitous circumstances, enabled workers to achieve a superior position, they came to look upon themselves as aristocrats of labour. Naturally, they believed that their attainment of a superior position was due to their superior qualities. That they might have risen at the expense of their less fortunate fellow-workers was an idea that never occurred to anybody. On [the contrary,] for a long time there was reason to believe that every time the aristocrats of labour secured a rise in their wages, the less skilled workers were thereby enabled to secure increases also. That was apparently the case in the building trades during periods of expansion. In older England, the ability of the skilled trades to lift general wages by raising their own was not so apparent.

The idea that the aristocrats of labour by raising their own wages aided labour generally to secure wage increases is open to criticism on more than one point. Advances in money wages may be made without benefit to the workers, as they may be offset by increases in prices. Then, although Henry George may have exploded the old "wage-fund" theory, this is certain: If wages in the building trades are raised, either those people who have planned to build will hold up some of their projects to the prejudice of employment and aggregate wages in the building trades, or if they proceed with their building plans, they will have less money to spend in other directions to the prejudice of employment and wages in other occupations. Even on this continent the aristocracy of labour based on high wages has had a thin time since the World War.

The ever-increasing mechanization of industry and the standardization of the product, the multiplication of divisions of Labour through which the task of the worker is reduced to a simple but precise operation along an assembly line, -- in short, technological developments, spurred on by science and invention, have relegated whole crafts to the museum of history along with the stage coach and spinning wheel, and tumbled the craftsmen into the ranks of common labour. That act has disturbed even those craftsmen whose special skill is still in demand, and whose unions are still seemingly effective. It has led many of them to recognize that their own position is, in the long run, dependent upon the organized strength of the workers generally; that they cannot afford to be indifferent to the struggles of the other divisions of the working-class; that it is of vital concern to them whether the mass of the workers are rising or sinking in the social scale; that they cannot rise on the shoulders of the mass if it is sinking in the quicksands.

The aristocratic tendency has been breaking down. The locomotive engineers now join with other running trades to make common cause in efforts to improve conditions; representatives of a master-mariners' organization sit as delegates in the British Trades Union Congress; the "International" Typographical Union lends its aid to the organizations of the unskilled workers in mass-production industries. But unfortunately the aristocratic separationist tendency has not broken down completely or everywhere. It still has too much strength in sections of the craft union movement.

However, more and more craft unionists are taking stock of their position and considering the conditions and guarantees of their future security. More and more they perceive that being united in production, united under the yoke of the system which exploits them, they must be united in their struggles for an equitable division of production, and for emancipation from exploitation. More and more they realize that all members of the working class have common interests, that the promotion of these common interests is a condition in the long run of the improvement of the position of any division of the working class; that, therefore, it is a fundamental requirement that all Labour unions should unite their forces in the effort to achieve the common aims and purposes.

While the skilled workers have been thus arriving at a new conception of the requirements and possibilities of progressive Labour union action, one division after another of the unskilled workers has been rising out of its stupid lethargy, or mere servile acquiescence. The direct results of the awakening and the activities of the unskilled or semi-skilled are becoming of first importance, especially in the United States, where the upsurge of the workers in the mass-production industries has raised big and disturbing problems for the American Federation of Labor. The swiftness and sweep of this upsurge of a division of the working class, which until recently seemed to be lost in helpless apathy or purposeless and hopeless discontent, indicates a moral regeneration which may be highly significant for the near future.

121. A Philosophy for Labour Organization[62]

The struggle between industrial unionism and craft unionism has entered upon a phase which makes it of commanding interest. The spirit of partisanship on either side has been quickened; in discussions of the struggle it is difficult to avoid being dogmatic. The best we can hope to do is to aim at a dialectical view; to recognize that the struggle is the outcome of evolutionary processes which it is useless to oppose. With new inventions, new technological trends, continually producing new developments in industry, it would be a mistake to assume that the possibilities of the development of any form of Labour organization can be expressed by a rigid formula.

That was the idealistic enterprise the Industrial Workers of the World set for themselves some decades ago. They drew up a circular diagram, a "wheel of fortune," arbitrarily fixing the metes and bounds of each industrial union and the departments thereof.[63] They thus set themselves against the constant tendency of industry to develop new forms and forces, and their "perfect, fixed form of organization" being utopian, they naturally failed. Their diagram of Labour organization has been outmoded by the tremendous changes in industry and in business organizations which have taken place in recent decades. One may define the jurisdiction of an industrial union in order to obtain a temporary working rule; but in a changing industrial world it is not wise to assume that Labour organizations can be fitted into a rigid jurisdictional scheme. To what industrial union's jurisdiction would the passenger-trailer -- the house on wheels -- be assigned?

---

[62]*Canadian Unionist*, February 1939, 218-219.

[63]McKay refers to the organizational diagram known as "Father Haggerty's Wheel of Fortune," named after Father Thomas Haggerty, and publicized by the I.W.W. As David Bercuson explains, "In a scientific age this carefully divided wheel, with its spokes representing different groups and subgroups of industry and with a general administration at the hub, appealed to those who styled themselves scientifically minded." David Bercuson, *Fools and Wise Men: The Rise and Fall of the One Big Union* (Toronto: McGraw-Hill Ryerson, 1978): 124.

As with any living organism, the prime requisite of a Labour union is ability to adapt itself to changing conditions. The most serious criticism of the craft unions is that they have deliberately pursued the policy of making their jurisdictional claims an obstacle to needed adaptations to industrial changes. They have shut their eyes to the object lessons offered by businessmen.

Changes in business organizations represent conscious adjustments to technological trends. On the side of ownership and management, organization has expanded in direct ratio to the increasing importance of machinery. Combinations of capital have been developed in new and diverse forms. The co-operation of capitalists has developed to a point where ownership is shared by many capitalists. This development has produced a class of absentee owners whose enterprises are conducted by mangers, who are hired employees. The integration of business management is promoted by gentlemen's agreements, holding companies, combines, trusts, monopolies. Whether these business organizations are built vertically or horizontally, their bargaining power over supplies of materials or labour is vastly increased. A few financial magnates and industrial captains are able to exact tribute beyond the plundering capacity of ancient kings by divine right.

An analogous development to the integration of business management and business organization has taken place in the political world. The centralization of the control of campaign funds enables a few men to dominate their party. The central governments, by prodigally expanding the national debts, have become vast agencies for taking money out of the pockets of the people to pass over to the holders of government bonds. Centralization, integration, combination are manifest features of the processes by which the privileged interests strengthen their power.

The workers have been less responsive to the spirit of the times than businessmen. As a means of economic power, the craft unions are now like wooden ships against the iron-clad "dreadnoughts" of big business. Not only the extension of membership but the greater integration of Labour organization has become imperative. How to increase the power of Labour organizations through integration without building up too great a centralization of power is doubtless a delicate problem. It is a task which will demand eternal vigilance. It is, moreover, a task which the workers must perforce accomplish, or presently find themselves the victims of some form of Fascism. If they shirk the task because they are cowed by its difficulties, they and their children will pay a heavy price of oppression and misery. Providence helps only those who help themselves. Wishful thinking is not the driving force of progress; it is too often the refuge of apathy. Mankind solves problems only by tackling them. It makes progress by action based on critical observation of the actual facts of a situation. Struggle is the condition of any worthwhile achievement. The workers must go through years, perhaps decades, of hard struggle, not only in order to alter existing conditions, but even to make themselves fit to use the power which will be theirs in a world where progress will be a matter of intelligent adaptation of means to pre-conceived ends, and not a fortuitous consequence of the struggle of classes and nations, superimposed upon the anarchy of the blind forces of competitive private industry.

However, to build the integrated Labour organizations required to cope with the highly-integrated organizations of capital, and assure their democratic management, is a task which presents for the worker fewer difficulties than those which begin to confront the capitalists as a consequence of absentee-ownership. The capitalistic organization of industry turns increasing numbers of capitalists into parasites.

The titles to capitalist property -- stocks and bonds -- pass from hand to hand on the stock exchange without exerting any influence on production. The great financiers and speculators proclaim their conception of the parasitical role of capitalists by the practice of stripping them of their stocks and bonds by stock exchange manipulations, swindles, and other financial hanky-panky. A diminishing number of great capitalists siphon into their control an ever-increasing proportion of the profits of the great organizations of industry. The capitalist class is divided by divergent interests; between the different divisions thereof constant conflict rages; in the United States the capitalists have not been able to show a united front to organized Labour at -- for the capitalist class -- a critical juncture.

Now, it is true that there is still a deplorable lack of unity in the ranks of the workers. But the divisions are of a different nature from those of the capitalist class. The big capitalistic organization prospers by using competitive power to put the smaller capitalist organization out of business and take over its market. But even those workers who still have some reason to consider themselves "aristocrats of Labour" now know that the power of their craft union to maintain them in a favoured position is a diminishing power. Mechanical invention lessens the demand for craft skill. The very basis upon which the craft union can increase its strength by enlarging its membership is being undermined by technical progress.

The need which forces craft unions to hold on to some part of their shrinking basis, or to occupy new ground, helps to explain the vigour with which their jurisdictional disputes are waged. To maintain or increase their membership they have to extend their claims of jurisdiction to workers whose kind of work evidently does not fit into the original definitions of craft, since two or more unions may claim them.

This reaching out for new members has not increased the strength of the craft unions, but rather weakened them by wasting their energies in internecine strife, and making any kind of co-operation difficult. More and more craft unions have come to realize that this method of reaching out for members is outmoded. More and more craft unions are joining forces in industrial federations. More and more craft unions are lending aid to the organization of the unskilled and semi-skilled workers.

It is along such lines that progress will be made in building the integrated Labour movement which is necessary for the tasks of the future. Unlike the capitalists, the workers have common interests which can be served only by unity of purpose and action. The practical day-to-day struggle of their unions gives them a conscious understanding of the ways and means of realizing that purpose and steels their wills for the required action.

The economists, politicians, even the capitalists, can turn a blind, or at least a complacent, eye to the causes of the disease of the economic system which every so often bring on a paralysis, and confounds humanity with the crazy spectacle of idle machines, while the masses are ill-fed, ill-clothed and ill-housed. The manifold effects of this lunacy come home too closely to the workers for them to remain indifferent.

All the political phobias, social fetishes, and psychological bogies which are used to distract the workers' attention, will not suffice to keep them from thinking about the root causes of the insanities of the economic system. These crazy crises were unknown before the development of the capitalist system based on machine production. Hence, it requires no great leap of thought to arrive at the conclusion that the causes of the crises lie in the mechanism of the system itself. And then the question arises, why should the workers submit to the scourge of periodic crises if a better economic system can be established, in which such economic convulsions will be unknown?

Consciousness of the necessity of changing the system grows. With it grows the consciousness of the necessity of unions broadly based on a whole industry; also grows the awareness of the importance of unity in the whole Labour movement. As the reactionary interests seek to save the disease-ridden system by putting more burdens on the masses, more and more workers will be driven into ever-closer participation in the struggle. Such participation will ensure the democratic control of Labour organizations which is obviously essential if they are to function in the interest of the workers and the public in general.

ii. Labour Politics

122. Reconceptualizing the Private and the Public[64]

"It's surely a private matter," said the employer, referring to negotiations with representatives of a Union with respect to wages.

"Does the world nowadays recognize any question affecting industrial relations as a private affair?" asked the observer.

"I don't suppose it does," admitted E. "What with Government and trade union interference a man's private business is no longer his own affair. A man can't do what he likes with his own."

"Was there ever a time that a man could do what he liked with what he considered his private property?" asked O.

"Well, I think there was a time when the head of a family had the power of life and death over its members," said E....

"No doubt the progress of your business is largely due to your own enterprise, and hard work. But the progress of your business was made possible by the growth of the community, and by the extension of transportation facilities. Now when you have a dispute with your employees a large number of people are interested, because they are affected."

"You belong to an association. In spite of anti-combine legislation you are supposed to abide by certain regulations; there is a gentleman's agreement as to prices anyway. And every member of your association is interested in what wages you pay your workers. It is a question with them whether or not you have a competitive advantage. They do not appreciate the possibility of your plant being able to operate at lower wages; they will aid you to resist a demand for higher wages than they have to pay, because of their fear that they would soon be called upon to increase wages too...."

All this interdependence and interrelation of interests which is a necessary consequence of the transition from private to social production has inevitably modified the old conception of the rights of private property, and set up a tendency towards standardization. In England which is more advanced industrially than this country, standardization of wages has gone on at a great rate during the war. The tremendous wastage of the war, and the recognition that natural resources are not

---

[64]Originally published as "Interdependence And Interrelation of Interests," *Labor World/Le Monde Ouvrier*, 26 June 1920.

inexhaustible, have also set up a tendency towards standardization of products. A few years ago the idea that private enterprise should be obliged to standardize its products would have been considered even more intolerable than the idea that the State should step in and compel employers to recognize trade unionism and the right of collective bargaining.

In Britain the Whitley Councils,[65] which have a certain legal sanction, are the visible sign of the tendency towards the standardization of wages. Moreover they sound the death knell of the doctrine that a man's business is purely a private affair. Production is now a complicated social process -- not an individual concern. Some employers in Canada today do not recognize this. But the old attitude will not do. The old system is breaking down; the proof is that every where men are showing an increasing disinclination to work for a system in which they are supposed to have no control over the conditions of their employment. Through their unions men insist on a voice in determining their conditions of employment. Moreover, they are demanding a voice in the management of the industries in which they work. The Whitley councils give them a minor voice. Lloyd George has offered the workers representation in the management of Britain's railways; Premier Borden has made a similar offer to the workers on the Canadian National railways. Very soon, so-called private industry, must recognize the right of the workers to a voice in management. This is necessary to give the average worker what he now largely lacks -- a sense of responsibility. To refuse is to encourage Bolshevism.

---

[65]As James Naylor observes, the British-style Whitley Councils and American-style "company unionism" are not to be confused: "The Whitley Committee proposed a network of permanent bodies of employers' associations and unions at national, regional and plant levels in order to deal with a broad range of issues, including questions of production that had not before been considered legitimate areas of negotiation. While few real powers were given these committees (revolutionary shop stewards in Britain immediately recognized them as an attempt to contain precisely those 'disruptive tendencies' that promised to achieve real working-class gains), Alan Fox correctly notes that '[s]upport for Whitleyism could hardly be separated from support for strong and vigorous trade unionism.' Rockefeller councils, on the other hand, sought just the opposite. A creation of the ubiquitous Mackenzie King in the Colorado coal fields, the council there had sought specifically to exclude the United Mine Workers." James Naylor, "Workers and the State: Experiments in Corporatism after World War One," *Studies in Political Economy* 42 (Autumn 1993): 94. McKay's somewhat positive comments on Whitleyism are thus less surprising than they might seem at first sight.

123. Mackenzie King's Superficial "Industrial Democracy"[66]

...[William Lyon Mackenzie] King, indeed, said that all his life he has recognized that industrial democracy was a requirement of progress, but he has never really accepted the necessary implications of this view. With all his talk of the evils of industrial autocracy, economic aristocracy or plutocracy, he has not recognized that they are founded on property and political office. And as he has given no indication of a desire to abolish the privileges of property or blunt the power of the State as a tool of capitalist property, his proposal that labour and the community, as well as capital, should be represented on a common board to determine industrial policy would realize nothing more than a ghost of economic democracy.

124. The Two Arms of the Working-Class Movement[67]

It would doubtless be unfair to suggest that the policy of the American Federation of Labor with respect to independent political action by the workers has been responsible for preventing the rise in Canada of a Labour party proportionately as important as the Labour parties of Great Britain or Australia. Canada is a vast country, with a sparse population scattered mostly in small communities, while Australia has a close resemblance to Britain in that its population is mainly concentrated in a small number of communities. The difficulties of organizing a political party in Canada are obviously great -- [greater] certainly than those of organizing trade unions. But it is nonetheless true that the failure of the American Federation of Labor to realize the importance of independent political action has tended to retard the development of a political labour movement in this country, and that labour's lack of training in political method, as well as its lack of political power, is a source of weakness to the labour movement in all its phases, and a source of possible danger, too. For while the One Big Union may be dead or dying, the tendency of trade unions to drift into industrial combinations which resort naturally to the employment of One Big Union tactics becomes more marked. The "big idea" on which the One Big Union prided itself was that the struggle between capital and labour could be settled decisively by battle on the industrial field, providing the battle could be made sufficiently extensive. The craft union worked on that idea to some extent too, but it has become apparent that the craft union working independently sometimes advances its interests, at the expense of other crafts, as well as at the expense of capital. And because the labour problem is much bigger than any craft problem the power of the craft union acting independently to make and hold any substantial gains in the

---

[66]Originally published as "The Capitalist System," *Labor World/Le Monde Ouvrier*, 16 March 1935.
[67]*Canadian Railroad Employees Monthly*, April 1922, 19-20.

face of capital has very definite limits. This is shown by the fact that the Bricklayers' and Masons' Unions -- probably the most powerful of craft organizations -- are now in some parts of the country voluntarily reducing their wages, and in other parts making no serious opposition to wage reductions announced by employers. It is also shown by the fact that the United Miners and the Railroad Brotherhoods in the United States have entered into an alliance for mutual protection. The truth is that the craft unions tend to become, in so far as tactics are concerned, industrial unions; they are losing faith in the power of individual craft action and are seeking alliances outside their own immediate craft.

The effect of this programme must be a great extension of the area and character of the struggle. More and more strikes lose their individual or craft character; they affect such vast bodies of men that they become immediately matters of public concern. And because they at once affect the very life of the nation they invite the interference of the public authority, the political power of the state. That power naturally and inevitably, in the name of law and order, ranges itself largely on the side of capital, for it is the law and order of the capitalistic system that is at stake. The last railway strike in England at once became a political question; the government announced its intention of protecting the railway owners and breaking the strike at all costs. But the government there had to recognize the fact that labour was a power in politics; and it began negotiations, not with the strike leaders, but the leaders of the Labour Party....

In a similar situation in the United States or Canada, it may be doubted that an adjustment would be effected without serious disturbances. There is no powerful labour party, a state within the state able to act as a restraining influence upon the government or upon the employers and men immediately involved in the dispute. Strikes in the American coal fields in recent years have often been accompanied by bloodshed; in fact whole districts have been in a state of civil war for months. Usually there is conflict between the State and Federal authorities, which may have the virtue of preventing decisive action against the workers in small disputes until the crisis has passed; but which would be no safeguard against ill considered and reckless action in the case of a great dispute threatening the industrial life of the nation. Again, the political authority in this country and the United States is not confronted by a working class political democracy, standing as a sign and symbol that for political purposes the class divisions within the working class itself have been moderated, if not completely broken down; a weakness of the working class on this continent which is complicated by the existence of racial and colour divisions. A government could take drastic action against a body of foreign born workers without much fear of serious political consequences.

For these and other reasons organization of the workers on political lines
is imperative, if labour is to maintain and advance its position in the
social scale. The wage workers must take a lesson from the bourgeois, who
captured political power as a preliminary step to the establishment of
their particular form of democracy. The old guilds originally exercised
political functions, but except in the handful of free cities, were obliged to
surrender them as the feudal communities became co-ordinated into
feudal states. But they later became the starting point of the organizations
by which the bourgeoisie overthrew the feudal sate and established their
political democracy. The bourgeois political parties have appeared to be
divorce[d] from their organizations ostensibly for economic purposes; but
in reality employers' associations of all sorts are active in the control of
political machines and political policies. At the same time their political
parties are sufficiently democratic to attract all classes of people, who do
not penetrate below the surface of things.

Insofar as capitalism still represents the future of society, the workers have
no particular reason to disdain the bourgeois plan and practice. In
England the labour party has an existence distinct from the trade unions,
but it rests on the trade unions; it is a new arm of the working class
movement, tending to become the right arm. But there is little thought in
the minds of the real British working class leaders that the labour party
will ever render the trade unions superfluous. It is true some socialist
organizations have at various times assumed that trade unions have
outlived their usefulness and that every thing should be staked on political
action. The reaction from this idea has been advocacy in some quarters
of the general strike as the solution of the labour problem, but in general
these extreme views have been passing phases, and working class opinion
now is firmly convinced that the working class movement can only
proceed by using both arms -- political power and the power of trade
organization applied through collective bargaining or through strikes if
necessary.

125. The Necessity of a Labour Party[68]

There are signs that Labour on this continent is preparing for a new
advance. Leaders of trade unions are taking stock of the position in which
the postwar depression has left the movement; the rank and file are
showing an increasing impatience with old watchwords; only a handful of
ultra conservatives now advise labour to keep one of its arms -- its
political arm -- tied behind its back though there is still lack of unanimity
as to the best method of using that arm. But those who believe that labour
should use its political arm as a live member of its own body are growing
in influence. More and more, it is being realized that throwing labour's

---

[68]Originally published as "Some Reflections on Labor Policy," *Canadian Railroad
Employees' Monthly*, July 1925, 136-137; 145.

political arm into the scale of the old capitalist parties merely decides the issue between tweedledum and tweedledee -- so far as the solution of the labour question is concerned. Not that such gestures are futile; they serve to promote minor reforms; they have effected definite improvements in the position of the workers, but they have not prevented the capitalist class absorbing an increasingly larger share of the benefits arising from the evolution of new forms and forces of production. The opulence of the possessing classes has increased in a greater degree than the improvement in the standard of living of the working class. Mergers, combines, the growth of nation-wide employers' associations pursuing common policies and purposes, have vastly strengthened the power of the capitalist class. Against this power the industrial worker is much more helpless than he was a generation ago. If the worker loses his job now, he cannot secure a new one with the facility he was able to do on this continent a few decades ago.

...If the well organized employers' association today does not maintain a "black list," the average employer is class conscious in a way his prototype of a generation ago was not, and prone to refuse employment to a worker who has been active in the interests of his class. Unemployment is more chronic than it was, and more widespread, while the cost of living has enormously increased. There is everywhere less independence, or less security of livelihood, and the specter of unemployment haunts the ablest workers, imposing a strain that breaks many before their time.

Mergers and large scale production have vastly accentuated the need of strong labour organizations. But following the war the membership of the American Federation of Labor dropped from a little over 4,000,000 to 2,7000,000 in 1924. Important organizations, not affiliated with the A.F. of L. though working in harmony with it, also lost members. There has been a very serious decrease in the membership of the international unions located in Canada. The chief cause was the depression. But despite a much more serious depression in England, the unions there did not lose members to anything like the same degree.

Considering that the United States made a rapid and notable recovery from the depression while England has only made a very partial recovery, the relative stability of the British unions is interesting. The wide difference in the economic conditions of the two countries, in the composition of their workers, makes comparisons inconclusive. But it is a fair question whether the British labour movement by developing a political arm as part of its own body has not acquired a source of strength not yet possessed by the labour movement of this continent. It is [a fair] question whether a definite interest in politics, a political ideal and programme that looks beyond the passing issues of an election, is not a cohesive force of very considerable importance. It is significant, at any rate, that the British and other European labour movements, while reeling from staggering blows on the economic field, have displayed a splendid spirit of militancy and made unexampled progress on the political field. The labour movement on this continent since the war has not exhibited a general activity at all equal to that of the British movement. Yet retaining his membership by paying dues was only a temporary problem for the American worker, and should have been no problem at all, in view of the war time prosperity.

...It is a serious matter that the labour movement on this continent should not have been able to hold its membership better. The very substantial advances it made during the war boom, in the way of improving conditions, should have inspired greater faith in its further possibilities, a keener sense of the importance of united efforts, a stronger determination to extend the advantages gained. Was there failure of leadership? Blaming leadership, however, merely begs the question. No leader, of a democratic movement at any rate, can ever be ahead of the movement whereof he is chief. Anybody who steps in advance of a popular movement is usually regarded as a crank. Leading forlorn hopes is the function of lieutenants. Gompers certainly held some ideas which were well in advance of that aggregation of ideas which formed the front of what has sometimes been called Gompersism. It would be as quixotic for the general official head of a great labour organization to make himself the special champion of advanced ideas, as it would have been for Generalissimo Foch to have led a flight of war planes over the German lines. A man, to reach the headship of a democratic organization, must have special qualities of head or heart; he must have vision, keen if limited in range, and, since his position enables him to take a wider survey than the units of his organization, it may and often does become his duty to hold back his followers lest they fall into dangers not visible from lesser points of vantage.

When all is said, the question arises: are the leaders of the labour movement in Canada and the United States not ultra-conservative? It must be admitted that their attitude to political action in the past had some justification. If they sought to force the growth of a labour party they would probably have done more harm than good. The Federal system of government obtaining in Canada and the United States makes it more difficult to obtain results on the political field than is the case in Great Britain, the more especially as results beneficial to labour imply an invasion of property interests. Again, while the population of England is homogenous, compact and stable, on this continent population is scattered over vast areas, composed of many races, inchoate and accustomed to changes of occupation and residence in a way unknown in England. Moreover, the evolution of industry in England has been a relatively slow, or rather, a prolonged process, while on this continent the expansion of industry has been rapid, and the changes in the whole economic order almost apparent from day to day. Great industrial cities have grown up almost over night. Compared to the vast movements of peoples on this continent the migration of the Goths and Vandals who overthrew the Roman Empire were picayune pilgrimages. Over 1,000,000 people poured into the State of Texas in one year; 200,000 Canadians invade the U.S. in a year, and hardly cause a ripple.

Such being the features of life on this continent, it was inevitable that trade unions should concentrate their efforts upon the economic field. It would have been almost impossible to interest the average automobile mechanic in Detroit in the formation of a political party to send labour representatives to sit in a legislative body in Washington. Around him he saw industries growing like green bay trees, wealth production increasing as if by magic, and his interest was naturally in a union that would help him to obtain an immediate benefit from the general development -- an increased wage. Preoccupied with personal concerns, and usually indulging the hope of grasping an opportunity to lift himself out of the working class, the average worker on this continent has only been interested in joining with his fellows to obtain an obvious and more or less immediate benefit. His more generous environment, and natural optimism, have militated against the growth of class consciousness. Certainly this continent has always had its class distinctions; but they have not the obvious character of those of older countries.

...The reasons why labour in this country should set seriously about the task of developing its political arm for its own purposes are so obvious that they are often overlooked. A political party is necessary to the creation of distinctive labour ideals, and to the expression of the aspirations of the working class as a whole. The craft union is necessarily restricted in aims and outlook; important as its functions are, it cannot of itself fulfil the larger purpose of the labour movement, the obtaining for the worker of his proper share of the wealth created by social production. Comparatively successful as the craft unions have been in the U.S. they have fallen far short of possible attainment....

In this country there are prominent trade unionists, in a position to give a decided impetus to the development of a Labour party on the only lines it can proceed with hope of success, who are rather wary of exercising their influence because Communists are active in political labour movements. But the Communists cannot dominate a Labour party, if the trade unionists make up their minds to control it, and no Labour party will amount to anything until the trade unionists determine to put their shoulders to the wheel. In England years ago the heads of trade unions were likewise inclined [to] hold aloof from politics; now they are expected to take a first-class interest in the Labour party, as a matter of course....

...A Labour party is a means of preventing premature actions which might bring crushing defeat upon some important labour interest. On the other hand, a defeat at the polls is never a disaster, and involves no losses comparable to the sacrifices required by a strike of any magnitude and duration....

But, what is perhaps more important in the long run, a Labour party provides a rallying ground for all classes of workers, a means of common action, a school for training workers in public affairs, a means of breaking down the class prejudices which exist among different grades of workers. A Labour party helps the worker to realize that his class has a mission in the world, much more important than wresting a few cents more an hour from a boss; it helps restore that sense of human dignity which the modern industrial process by making him a cog in a machine tends to rob him of; it gives him vision, and a new hope and enthusiasm which make him a better union man. It brings him into touch with new problems, and new personalities; stimulates his mind and strengthens his will. It enables him to obtain a better perspective of the world he lives in and to feel himself a part of and at home in a great movement destined to abolish poverty and satiety, to give men full opportunity to be joyful and strong without drawing their strength from the bodies of the downtrodden, -- to establish upon earth that realm of justice and beauty whereof sages have dreamed and poets sung.

126. The Transformation of Capitalism[69]

How will the transformation of capitalism into a socialist society be effected?

In the past the evolution of human society has been marked by revolutionary periods -- periods of rapid transition in which violence and bloodshed were sometimes the means employed to release new forces of progress. The civil war in England in Cromwell's time, and the French Revolution were phases of the struggle to overthrow feudalism and open the way for the development of capitalism.

Mere resort to force is not necessarily revolutionary; every Act of Parliament or decree of a city council has behind it the police force, and militia bayonets, if the ruling class deems them necessary. The "Second Industrial Revolution" is now said to be proceeding, at a rapid rate, through the concentration of financial control and the swift introduction of automatic machinery. A social revolution is the process, slow or rapid, by which the political and juridical superstructure of society changes as a result of alterations in its economic basis, the means of production and distribution.

---

[69]*Canadian Railway Employees' Monthly*, February 1932, 29-30.

The coming revolution will probably not follow the model of past ones; it will not necessarily require violence or bloodshed. The forms of political economy have been established; it is possible to carry on the revolutionary struggle at the ballot box.

The modern working class is unlike any previous class which aspired to political power in order to achieve economic security. Capitalism has not only created this class by divorcing the worker from ownership of the tools of production; it has also developed conditions that teach the workers the value of organization and discipline and widen their intellectual horizons. And by the necessities of capitalist development, the working class constantly increases in number; even on the farms of Western Canada the machine process is reducing the number of landowners, and increasing the number of tenant farmers and hired labourers.

On the other hand, the capitalist class is better organized than any other exploiting class of the past, and controls greater resources....Governments, under political democracy, are no longer supreme in the way they once were. Not only is their authority limited by constitutional inhibitions, (which happen to be in the interests of the capitalist class); their exercise of authority is, to some extent, limited by their fear of the popular vote. Government resistance to the aspirations of the working class is now less harsh than the opposition of capitalists.

In a political democracy, both the exploiting class and the exploited class are freer to develop their organizations than either were under autocracy. The power of both is greater. Both organized Capital and organized Labour now frequently use their strength more recklessly and harshly than the government itself. Instead of standing above them, the government now rather stands below them; though it bows to Capital much more readily than to Labour. While too often unscrupulous minions of capitalists, governments have done much by Labour legislation to mitigate the harshness of the capitalist régime.

If the appearance of Labour governments in office in Britain and Australia is any prophecy of the future, Labour is on the road to the conquest of political power. Just how Labour governments, having attained real power, will accomplish the transformation of capitalism into a socialist order, nobody can say. Conditions are changing so rapidly that many of the problems that now appear as formidable obstacles may have completely disappeared by that time.

But this may be said: Labour governments, by carrying to their logical development the various devices and methods capitalism is already employing in an effort to prolong its life, may arrive at socialism. For instance, capitalists have created holding companies and investment trusts as a method of concentrating the control of numerous enterprises and stabilizing profits. A logical development would be the creation of national, provincial, municipal or co-operative holding companies, to take over the control of all industries of which the private control permits the exploitation of Labour. The holding companies mostly issue their stocks and bonds in exchange for paper titles to ownership in the enterprises, the control of which they desire to consolidate. The state could take over the control of all industry by the same process, exchanging public bonds for corporation securities.

How would this method of expropriating the exploiters benefit the workers? Would the result not merely be to guarantee the capitalists security of income? When the Meighen government expropriated the railways now comprised in the Canadian National system, it did a good stroke for the capitalists by guaranteeing interest on about $900,000,000 of paper securities which, through the bankruptcy of private management, had become practically worthless. But even supposing a Labour government permitted the same amount of profit to flow to capitalists as they had formerly received, Labour would stand to make definite gains. When new investments of capital were made in a new industry, there would be no opportunity for vast profits; such as Ford and other magnates have made out of the automobile industry. Equally there would be no further opportunities for private individuals to make fortunes through increases in rents. Every increase of social wealth from then on would redound to the public good.

Then a Labour government could resort to other devices adopted by capitalism to moderate the rigours of its oppression of the masses. Graduate income taxes and death duties offer a means of reducing the payments Labour would have to make to capitalists. Once all capitalist wealth has taken the form of bonds issued by states, municipalities and co-operative societies, progressive income, property and inheritance taxes can be raised to any height desired, and there could be no dodging such taxes. Through these devices which capitalism invented and uses for its own purposes, Labour governments could eliminate private capital altogether, gradually or swiftly, as might be desired.

It may be asked why private capital should not be confiscated at one stroke instead of first compensating it at full value and then taxing it out of existence. By the method of direct confiscation, it would be difficult to differentiate between great possessions and small, between titles to capital mostly representing fraud, and titles having some justification as representing capital which has been honestly employed in the essential work of the world. Direct confiscation would engender sharp opposition; perhaps provoke the capitalists to rebellion. But high and increasing taxes are something capitalists are already well accustomed to; they could not very well make larger doses of their own medicine an excuse for rebellion.

By drawing out the process of expropriating private capital over a decade or so, it would be less harsh and painful, as the new generation growing up would be educated away from the idea of acquiring control of capital as a means of exploiting the workers.

127. A Critique of the CCF[70]

From the standpoint of intellectual interest in social problems, Winnipeg is perhaps the intellectual centre of Canada. Its admixture of population, its geographical position which makes it not only a connecting link between east and west but the storm centre of the struggle between agriculture and the manufacturing industries, the battle-ground of political philosophies, the point of publication of papers in many languages, are reasons for Winnipeg's being in some respects the most important social laboratory in the Dominion.

Although old Quebec City claims a labour union that has had an uninterrupted existence for over one hundred years, and although the old Provincial Workmen's Association of Nova Scotia was probably the first in Canada to elect a union representative to a legislative body,[71] it was probably no accident that Winnipeg sent the first Labour man, A.W. Puttee, to the national Parliament, produced the nucleus of a parliamentary Labour party, and threw up the leader of the first alliance of industrial workers and farmers committed to a policy of industrial and social democracy. If Winnipeg had not sent Labour representatives to Parliament at the time the embattled farmers of the west first showed their consciousness of the need of political power to effect their economic emancipation, the ground for such an alliance would probably have remained untilled; and the Co-operative Commonwealth movement would not have yet been born. But, whatever credit belongs to Mr. Woodsworth for the launching of this movement, it is to the intelligence and energy of the Winnipeg workers that, in the last analysis, the main credit is due.

The President of the All-Canadian Congress of Labour having participated in the launching of the Co-operative Commonwealth Federation, it is fitting that in this edition of the *Canadian Unionist* there should be some discussion of the attitude of industrial unions and the National Labour Party to the new movement born of the recognition of farmers and industrial workers that they can only solve their problems by making political democracy -- heretofore, for them, a slippery by-way paved with illusions -- a highway to industrial and social democracy. On

---

[70]Originally published as "Labour-Farmer Co-operation: Winnipeg's Contribution," *Canadian Unionist*, March 1933, 173-175.

[71]McKay was not quite accurate here. He was presumably referring to the *appointment* of Robert Drummond, leader of the P.W.A., to the *non-elected* legislative council.

that road co-operation is enjoined; progress, as we know it, is a matter of the substitution of organization for chaos, order for disorder, co-operation for competition. Industrial unions are based on definite economic and social principles; the National Labour Party, an outgrowth of industrial unionism, represents the political reflex of the principles of industrial unionism. Complete implementation of the principles of industrial unionism would mean the realization of the Co-operative Commonwealth.

So it may be said that industrial unions, the National Labour Party, and the Co-operative Commonwealth Federation have the same ideal. As to the principles which should guide the every-day struggle, the C.C.F. is less explicit than its Labour affiliates; but in so far as the C.C.F. has formulated its principles of action they are near enough in line with the guiding principles of the national Labour organizations to permit, and invite, the fullest co-operation. It is necessary, however, to face the fact that the C.C.F. is attracting the support of elements which, if we may judge from the experience of other countries, may lead it to sacrifice the integrity of its principles in order to become the champion of policies more calculated to appeal to popular support than to assure the economic emancipation of workers and farmers.

The necessity of compromise must be recognized. The individual must make compromises in order to live; if one refused to compromise with a motor car at a street intersection, he would either complicate his problems or end them. A political party will never get anywhere if it waits until all its adherents are sufficiently educated to take a scientific view of every problem. Nothing is constant in this world. Truth, as a principle, may always be true; but truth looks different to different generations, viewing it from different material conditions. Thus a principle cannot be embodied in a dogma that will always give the principle intelligent expression. Still less can the policies designed to give effect to principles be regarded as permanent guides to action; policies may change with conditions without a real departure from the principle to which a policy aims to give effect.

But while full co-operation with the C.C.F. is the desire and the purpose of its national Labour affiliates and certain compromises may be accepted for the sake of presenting a united front and promoting mass education, the Labour affiliates will maintain the right of free criticism -- and of free action. No compromise will be made that is calculated to make them lose sight of the purpose -- the realization of industrial and social democracy. An organization that loses sight of its ideal is in danger of losing its soul. And what makes the national Labour unions important and significant is that they have an ideal worth striving for. The craft unions not having an ideal that rose above the competitive system -- every craft for itself and the devil take the hindmost -- never had a real soul to lose; but they have lost even the combatant spirit -- the courage -- that they possessed in the days when they had a *raison d'être*, the days when employers conducted small enterprises and were too individualistic to organize in nation-wide trade organizations.

While recognizing that there is a possibility that the C.C.F. movement may attract so many disillusioned middle-class elements that there will be danger of its making compromises calculated to make it the medium of a fascist régime rather than the instrument of the economic emancipation of farmers and workers, it must be admitted that the propaganda it has so far been responsible for has been of a nature calculated to enlighten the masses, and show them their servile position in the present social economy. Most of us are economic illiterates, and we cannot understand advanced Labour or farmer economics before we have learnt the ABC's of economics. Socialist organizations have not made progress in this country commensurate with its condition of highly developed and concentrated capitalism -- about 600 of 23,000 factories in Canada control about two-thirds of the total manufacturing output. And why? Probably because the socialists have tried to force the red meat of Marxian economics upon economic illiterates -- a people little removed from the pioneer stage.

With a Farmer-Labour political union, headed by a Winnipeg man, and having its centre of gravity west of Winnipeg for the time being, it is of first importance that national Labour organizations should take cognizance of the conditions of prairie agriculture and consider if, why, and how those conditions should influence national Labour policy, particularly in its political aspects. One may judge from such organs as *The Western Producer* and *U.F.A.* [*United Farmer of Alberta*] that the economic education of the prairie farmers is so advanced that a great many realize that there is no real economic salvation for them under the system of competitive commodity production. Nevertheless, even members of the Ginger Group admit that a restoration of boom-time prices of wheat would play hob with the western farmers' interest in the C.C.F. political movement....

Now consider Adam Smith's natural price, or David Ricardo's theory of value and prices. Modern economists have tried to bury the theories of the classical economists under a mountain of rubbish -- such as Rogers & Marshall's marginal utility theory of value. But this depression, like others, has shown the stark reality of the classical economists, the foresight of Adam Smith who predicted that the joint-stock company which appeared with the machine would produce intolerable social and economic inequalities, and who never dreamed of the limited liability company which only came into being in England in 1865 by virtue of a legal enactment which permitted an orgy of financing ending in a great financial crisis two years later, and which permitted the development of the giant corporation, "without a soul" -- that is, without the responsibility imposed upon the earlier joint-stock companies.

According to the classical economists the value of an article is its cost of production plus the average rate of profit. The cost of production according to Ricardo, chief of the classical school, was determined by the cost of living labour, and embalmed or dead labour, that is, capital.

But producers of commodities do not always realize the value of their products -- the cost of production plus the average rate of profit. If they did everybody would be happy, except the wage workers who would be exploited anyhow. Prices range above or below values, according to the relations of supply and demand. But prices always gravitate towards values - that is, to the cost of production plus the average rate of profit.

If then the costs of production of wheat and other farm products have been reduced, the farmers cannot expect a return to boom-time prices, unless they can overthrow Ricardo's law of values or unless a war or some other catastrophe occurs. Normally the farmer is not able to include the average rate of profits in the price of his products: he is lucky if the price yields him a fair wage for his labour.

The conclusion which seems inevitable is that -- failing a great war which will raise more problems than it solves -- the farmer has scant reason to hope for a return of boom-period prices. And neither have the industrial workers any reason to hope for a return of boom-period wages, because in a régime of competitive commodity production labour power is a commodity the wage or price of which is determined by the prices of the products of the farmers, who are evidently condemned to an era of low prices.

While farming is mostly carried on by individual producers, urban industry is largely controlled by corporations. The equality in the relations of producers which prevailed years ago when urban industries were also carried on by individuals or family firms has vanished. The manufacturing corporation is protected from the full rigours of competition by the high cost of establishing competing enterprises, by combines, gentlemen's agreements, spheres of trade. On the other hand, the farmer has to submit his products to a market in which competition still reigns in full vigour....

In the Co-operative Commonwealth, government will cease to be the organ of the supremacy of a privileged class, and hence what are now its main functions will vanish. Government will be concerned with the planning, regulation and control of production and distribution, and the organs from which government will derive its mandate will not be political parties, but the industrial organizations of the producers --

farmers and industrial workers. And the realization of the purposes of the government will be mainly effected through such industrial organizations.

This makes it necessary to face a fact that the C.C.F. movement has not adequately recognized, if indeed, it has given it even casual recognition. The Co-operative Commonwealth cannot be realized by political action alone. As a mere political party, the C.C.F., called upon to form a government, could not accomplish anything worth while, if the workers and farmers were not well enough organized on the economic field to enforce the decisions of the new political government. The capitalists, by declaring a lockout, could defeat the purpose of a Co-operative Commonwealth party government, if the farmers and workers lacked economic organizations strong enough to take over the business of carrying on production.

Therefore we say that every spokesman of the C.C.F. should also be a propagandist of industrial unionism and economic organization among farmers. To effect their emancipation from class rule, workers and farmers must develop economic as well as political organization. Neither political nor economic power, separately used, will effect the desired emancipation: the two must combine.

To quote Daniel DeLeon[72]:

> The fact of economic despotism by the ruling class raises, with some, the illusion that the economic organization and activity of the despotized working class is all-sufficient to remove the ills complained of.
> The fact of political despotism by the ruling class raises, with others, the illusion that the political organization and activity of the working class is all-sufficient to bring about redress.
> The one-legged conclusion regarding economic organization and activity fatedly abuts, in the end, in pure and simple direct action, the bombism as exemplified in the A.F. of L., despite its Civic Federation affiliation, as well as by the anarcho-syndicalist so-called Chicago I.W.W. -- the Bakouninism, in short, against which the genius of Marx struggled and warned.

---

[72]Daniel DeLeon (1852-1914) was leader of the Socialist Labor Party in the United States in the 1890s; he was also editor of *The People* in the 1890s and the *Daily People* in the early twentieth century. He campaigned, on strict Marxist grounds, for socialist unions to compete with AF of L unions, which position contributed to a split in the ranks of the Socialist Labor Party. That this article should cite the rigorous, not to say dogmatic, DeLeon at such length on the question of combining political and economic organization suggests the distance McKay had travelled since 1900, for DeLeon was conventionally hailed by the "hard leftists" and criticized by "gradualists."

The one-legged conclusion regarding political organization and activity as fatedly abuts, in the end, in pure and simple ballotism, as already numerously and lamentably exemplified in the U.S. socialist party, -- likewise struggled and warned against by Marx as 'parliamentary idiocy.'

128. The CCF and a Canadian Socialism[73]

There is some captious criticism of Mr. Woodsworth[74] because he talks of developing a distinctive type of Socialism in Canada and not adhering slavishly to the British, American or Russian models. A Canadian Socialist society must have a distinctive character reflecting its economic organization, which cannot be the same as that of a banana republic. The general strategy of political Socialism in regard to the main problem it has to solve is not a matter of making formulae independently of the stage of the political development of the country. Also, the tactics employed in dealing with special problems must take account of the special conditions in which the problems are set. In any case, political Socialism in no country as yet has been successful enough to prove its right to be taken as a complete model by Socialists in other countries.

Marx was scornful of those who proposed to make history by formula, after the manner of the Utopians.

The C.C.F. may be open to criticism on the ground that its platform, in some important particulars, looks more like an outline of state capitalism than of a Socialist society. But that is hardly a good reason for not voting for it when the alternative is either of the old parties. And there is no good excuse for the workers taking the C.C.F. less seriously than the capitalists whose political henchmen and newspaper organs are saying that it must be crushed at all costs.

The first item of the C.C.F. program is:

"The establishment of a planned, socialist economic order, to make possible the most efficient development of the national resources and the most equitable distribution of the national income."

Other items of the program seem to imply reservations as to the extent of the socialization to be undertaken.

---

[73]Originally published as "Pitfalls for C.C.F.," *O.B.U. Bulletin*, 1 February 1934.

[74]James Shaver Woodsworth (1874-1941) was the most prominent Canadian socialist parliamentarian of his day; serving as M.P. for Winnipeg North 1921 to 1940, he led the CCF from 1932 to 1940. His comments on the need for a distinctively Canadian approach to socialism can be found in *The First Ten Years* (1942).

But planning is the essence of a progressive program, the planning of economic activities for the social purpose of achieving the most equitable distribution of the national income. The planning of Mussolini and Hitler has not been directed to the regulation of the processes of production for a social purpose but, rather, to a regimentation of the people in the interests of capitalistic control of the processes of production.

Once economic planning is undertaken, the secret of those economic and social mysteries which now cast a paralyzing spell over many minds will begin to reveal itself. To quote Marx:

"The life-process of society, which is based on the process of material production, does not strip off its mystical veil until it is treated as production by freely associated men, and is consciously regulated by them in accordance with a social plan."[75]

Economic planning might produce state capitalism -- in which case production will not be carried on by freely associated men. But it would nonetheless serve to dispel the illusion that the inequitable economic and social relations men find themselves in are imposed by mysterious powers beyond human control. To undertake economic planning is to attempt to control economics, to effect the emancipation of men from the reign of blind economic laws. Now the capitalist world swarms with mysteries, is full of fetishes before which the minds of men bow down in hypnotic impotence, the reason being the self-evident fear that the capitalists themselves do not control economic affairs. But once collective economic planning is undertaken, once the idea is accepted that human intelligence can control economic affairs, if only in the interests of the capitalists, then the question will inevitably arise, Why not control economic affairs in the interests of the people?

It would be a Utopian enterprise to attempt to prepare a blueprint and detailed picture of a Socialist society in Canada or any other country.

Those who desire a political party with a magic wand capable of transforming society overnight are dreamers possessed of servile souls. There is the naive belief that history is made by great men. Without doing anything to assist in their own emancipation, they want to wake up some fine morning in an intelligently organized society from which oppression, poverty and misery have vanished.

---

[75]McKay is citing and slightly altering Karl Marx, *Capital: A Critique of Political Economy* : "The life-process of society, which is based on the process of material production, does not strip off its mystical veil until it is treated as production by freely associated men, and is consciously regulated by them in accordance with a settled plan." See Karl Marx, *Capital: A Critique of Political Economy*, trans. Samuel Moore and Edward Aveling, Vol. I (New York: International Publishers, 1967), 80.

The prophetic construction of Utopias which has been the pastime of generous natures are no better guides for the transformation of the society than are the chaotic mess of laws by which bourgeois legislators seek to reform humanity, with the result only of stifling it like the silkworm in the cocoon.

If before the French Revolution the nobility had said to the bourgeoisie: "But what sort of a world will this new world of yours be? Show us its exact contours, and after that we will decide" -- what answer could the bourgeois have made? Certainly they could not have foretold the consequences of their doctrines of Liberty, Equality, and Fraternity.

All that scientific socialism affirms is that the course of human evolution is in the general direction of the progressively increasing importance of the species over the individual, and therefore in the direction of progressive socialization of the economic life and with it of the political, juridical and moral life.

Certainly the C.C.F. will attract mystic-minded persons who run bravely after illusions, imagining that economic planning is merely a matter of free credit and the elimination of money -- who, unable to understand the necessary relation between commodity and real money, would continue commodity production while dispensing with money. But if the C.C.F. is not to fizzle out like the patrons of industry[76] or the populist movement in the United States as an adventure in futile reforms, those who understand the economic problem will need to rally to it and see that it is not diverted from the first project in its platform -- economic planning in the truly democratic manner. Achievement by mass action will, in any case, depend on the method of trial and error.

129. The Failure of Bolshevism[77]

Of course, the horrible example of Russia has disposed of any pretensions the workers may have had to political power or industrial control, that is, in the minds of many good people. And meantime, no doubt, the workers ought to be content with the wonderful "reconstruction" we have heard so much about in other countries, the reconstruction promised to those who fought to make the world safe for democracy and the full dinner pail.

But workers in other countries may pursue their political and other programmes without regard to the success or failure of Bolshevism. Time

---

[76]Notwithstanding the name of the group, the nineteenth-century Patrons of Industry -- which might loosely be categorized as populist -- mainly drew its support from the farmers. It enjoyed much support in southern Ontario.

[77]Originally published as "No Short Cut to New Era," *Canadian Railroad Employees Monthly*, June 1923, 51; 63.

has already pretty well proved the correctness of the view of those British labour leaders who went to Russia and decided that the Bolshevist adventure had no lessons of any particular importance for labour elsewhere. They recognized that Bolshevism was an inevitable outcome of the peculiar conditions in Russia where the persistence of feudalism under the aegis of Czardom had prevented the rise of a middle class powerful enough to carry Russia abreast of western civilization; they saw no reason to commend it, and they did not deem it their duty to attempt to read Russia out of the comity of nations. After all, Bolshevism is Russia's business.

Russia never had a real bourgeois revolution, like England and France and America....The Bolshevist revolution...smashed the feudal power in Russia, achieving what the Duma, representing the Russian business classes, had ineffectually attempted. That in the process it also swept away the incompetent Russian business classes is no doubt deplorable, and for this reason: Russia must complete her evolution along capitalist lines before she can hope to set up a higher order of society. Lenine and Trotski would have been powerless if the feudal regime of the Czar had not been rotten ripe for revolution, and the fact that they smashed the power of Russian feudalism with communist phrases on their lips, while annoying to the capitalist world, was not sufficient to set up a communist state.

Whether the Bolshevists were or are sincere is no great matter. Those who tell us that Lenine and Trotski have demonstrated the fallacy, foolishness and criminal recklessness of the Marxian theory have little or no knowledge of that theory. The success or failure of the Bolshevist adventure has this importance for the Marxian theory: its success would discredit the Marxian theory; its failure will prove the soundness of the Marxian theory. The materialistic conception of history excludes the possibility of establishing a communist or a collectivist regime in a country like Russia, a country where industry is poorly developed and where the great mass of the people are engaged in agricultural pursuits. The Marxian theory is that capitalist production must reach a high state of development before its transformation into social production becomes possible. That condition does not obtain in Russia and the Bolshevists are only proving the soundness of the Marxian theory when they recognize the need of encouraging the capitalist method of production. What they are trying to do today, apparently, is to establish a regime of state capitalism. Possibly, if they can retain control of the political power, their system of state capitalism may assure the worker more security of livelihood than the states, whose political authorities are nominally representative of the people but in practice usually the agents of the capitalist class. But that remains to be seen.

The important thing is that the world's labour movements have no reason to be daunted by the failure of the Bolshevist adventure, or to abate one jot of the determination to achieve political power, and use it to transform the capitalist regime into a system of production for use when in the fullness of time the technical developments in industry have made such a change possible, and desirable in the interests of the masses.

130. The Conceits of the Communists[78]

Adherents of the Communist Party in Canada are having a hard task persuading anybody that acceptance of Moscow's views as to what is required by the Canadian situation is compatible with acceptance of the materialist conception of history. In Russia the Communists have been opportunist to a degree -- now compromising with capitalism as in the [New Economic Policy], then swinging to a full-fledged collectivist policy, and at one and the same time pursuing reformist ideals and revolutionary ends. But the Canadian Communists have been committed to a policy and tactic which savours of religious fanaticism rather than of economic determinism. In any case, Communist tactics in this country are not easy to understand except on the assumption that the Communist leaders regard themselves as anointed prophets of a gospel which in itself possesses some abstract virtue, some miraculous power of effecting sudden conversions of the people. In methods and manner, Communist propaganda is hardly a reasonable system of education: rather it is a fanatical affirmation that those who are of the elect need no enlightenment and that those who are unbelievers are either hopelessly fat-headed ignoramuses or conscious hypocrites and traitors to the cause of labour.

In the up-to-date Canadian Communist view, the union official who does not attempt to play the rôle of a Charlemagne and rush his union into a fight for any or no reason is a faker and betrayer of the cause. It would seem to be a primitive conception of history from which springs the idea that the military tactics of the paladins, who led a few hundred tribesmen bound together by ties of common blood, and who if they did not win were usually slaughtered, are the appropriate tactics for modern struggles between great masses of men, often divided by race, language and creed. Human intelligence being what it is, and modern conditions what they are, the labour general's problem of preserving the unity of his forces, of getting them to undertake common action, is a vastly more complicated problem of leadership than that of the tribal chief who led his blood relatives to war. No union vests the power of life and death in its headman....

There is no magic in organization *per se*, any more than in the "manifestos" which the Communists issue so frequently, as if they were

---

[78]*Canadian Unionist,* August 1930, 53-54. Parallels might be drawn between McKay's critique of the CP and that of the OBU.

messages from heaven endowed with the power of suddenly converting the workers to a full understanding of the need of social revolution. That is to say, organization and education are both necessary processes of social evolution, and since neither of these processes can be completed in a day -- any more than a youth can accomplish the biological evolution of becoming an adult in a day -- they call for the exercise of tact and patience -- qualities in which the hierarchy of the Communist Party of Canada is notably deficient.

Whether in its theoretical expression as a scientific exposition of social development, or in its practical expression as a political party, socialism is a natural product which must pass through the phases of infancy and youth in order to attain a mature development. This is a necessary law of the evolution of anything in the natural or social world. But in other countries as well as Canada the enthusiasts of new movements have lost sight of that law. In the development of scientific, or fact-founded, socialism notably, enthusiasts in the early stages have affected a clannish exclusiveness, a superior virtue, as though they possessed a special vision and a monopoly of wisdom giving them the right to treat as heretics all who do not see eye to eye with them. This lofty conceit in the case of the Communists is joined with a nebulous romanticism and fanatical fervour which gives to the idea of the social revolution the narrow and incomplete character of an end in itself, and begets the illusion that the social organism can be radically changed in a day or so by a general strike, or a political upheaval of a fraction of the people.

This hope of transformation of capitalism into socialism by a sudden and violent strike has been fed by the swift rise of the Dictatorship of the Proletariat in Russia. But it is necessary to recognize that the seizure of political power by the Communist party in Russia was, owing to the peculiar conditions in that country, an adventure very different from the conquest of political power by organized workers in countries like Canada, possessing political democracy and a large, well-organized and intelligent bourgeois class.

In Russia capitalism was only a small island in an ancient feudal regime. An autocratic czar and landlords for the most part controlled the political power. Russia had not experienced a religious reformation or bourgeois political revolution. The mass of the people were illiterate and steeped in superstition.

When the corrupt czarist regime collapsed Kerensky, representing the bourgeois class, attempted to appropriate the political power. But neither capitalists proper, nor small businessmen and traders, had any real training in political method: quite unlike the capitalists and middle classes of, say, England, who since the business revolution under Cromwell have been exercising political power and who, if sometimes divided by divergent interests, have learned to unite their forces in opposition to efforts of the working masses to ameliorate their lot.

The Kerensky government was weak and incompetent because the Russian bourgeoisie lacked unity and political experience; because the middle class as such was an insignificant proportion of the total population. The small but well-organized and well-disciplined Communist party overthrew Kerensky and seized the political power. The special circumstances favoured the Communists. On the one hand, their slogan "The Land for the Peasants" had an appeal that it could not have in Canada where the farmers already own their lands -- nominally at any rate. On the other hand, the soldiers who with inadequate arms and food had opposed the well-equipped and well-fed legions of Germany, were ready to turn their anger against both feudal nobility and the bourgeoisie, believing both were responsible for the failure to provide proper army equipment and supplies. These were factors, favourable to the Communists, which were peculiar to Russia.

The Soviet conquest of political power constituted a social revolution in the proper sense of the word, since it was accompanied by a transformation of the economic base of society, the transfer of ownership of property from a ruling class to a previously subject class. But it did not establish socialism; it only prepared the way for the construction of the economic foundation of socialism.

In Russia a dictatorship has been necessary, and in the circumstances it would be idle to dispute that it has justification. It does not, however, follow that the Russian experience must inevitably be duplicated in other countries, in which political democracy has been long established and in which it is possible for the workers by organizing a party of their own to secure control of the political power.

The normal processes of social transformation are evolution and revolution. By evolution, we mean the transformation that takes place from day to day; almost imperceptible, but continuous and inevitable: by revolution we mean the concluding and critical phase of evolution, the culminating phase when the economic foundation, or property base, of society being changed, the whole political, juridical and ethical superstructure also undergoes a radical transformation. Rebellion and individual violence may also contribute to changes in the social cosmos, but they are not normal processes of social physiology, but rather, of social pathology -- disease.

Human society being a natural living organism, it is by no means certain that it will undergo sudden transformations, any more than any other living organism. It is true that De Vries and Burbank discovered that some species of plants "exploded suddenly" -- and produced new species. But in the course of their natural evolution they accumulated, over long periods, tendencies giving this power of sudden transformation. Society may have similar "explosions" as the result of accumulated tendencies held in restraint by its political envelope, but analogies between natural and social phenomena should be accepted only with caution.

Supposing the appearance in England of a Labour government having such a majority that it need have no fear of a Fascist movement, it would probably, nevertheless, find it expedient to proceed slowly with the task of using the political power to divorce the capitalist class from its control of economic power. Even the Communists in Russia have found it necessary to make compromises and adopt social reforms, the seeking of which by labour organizations within bourgeois society is denounced by some Communists as a means of prolonging the life of that society, and evidence of the fakery of labour leaders. Marx himself advocated reforms because they would "render less painful the birth of the new society."

Insofar as the Communists follow the tactics of revolutionary romanticism they act as if they believed there was some magic in their doctrines, capable of suddenly changing people's ideas and transforming society. A belief in magic is also implied by their penchant for making fetishes of their doctrines and insisting that anybody who does not subscribe to their doctrines is without any kind of understanding or any loyalty to the labour movement. A belief in magic also seems necessary to explain their fanatical passion for making converts, a passion which apparently blinds them to the elementary principle of pedagogy that education is necessarily a gradual process. Their propaganda certainly does not provide the sort of scientific education which the workers need and would appreciate.

Communist failure in organization work springs from a similar lack of practical understanding and scientific education. Here again belief in magic is apparent; it takes the form of acceptance of the idea that the hierarchy dwells on some Mount Sinai whence they hand down commandments of mystical authority that the rank and file must obey at peril of their souls. That the Communist Mount Sinai is in Moscow does not render this idea of red magic any more palatable to Canadian workers, whose experience is that Communist efforts at organization lead to disruption. And most of the Communist leaders do not even have the excuse of the generous impatience which marks some well-meaning men in whom the power of impulsive feeling is the dominant factor of their natures.

The exhortation of Marx, "Workers of all Countries, Unite," sharply in contrast with the modern policy of the Communists of sowing seeds of discord where they cannot divide and rule, does not envisage a social revolution effected by any magic formula of communism, but rather emphasizes the scientific view that socialism cannot be achieved until it becomes a vivid ideal in the minds of the workers by virtue of a clear perception of their class interest and the strength [that] organization for political action as well as for struggles on the economic field will give them. This is the task of education, aided by organization, and such education and organization must for a long time to come at any rate have a more practical purpose than the inculcation of a belief in a rigid doctrinaire philosophy.

131. Soviet Communism as State Capitalism[79]

The Moscow *Daily News* reflects the growing pains of Russia and at the same time a sense of adventurous achievement. The news items indicate that the Russian experiment is an adventure in State capitalism under pressure. The achievements in State capitalism are imposing as contrasted with the present retrogression of private capitalism, and it would seem that the major forms of Russian development will follow the lines of State capitalism for some time to come.

The Communists are speeding up evolution; but the course of historic development is not thereby changed. The processes of development are still essentially capitalistic; the main difference is that vested interests which retard the logical evolution of capitalism in other countries have been got rid of.

The organs of a Socialist society appear to be in process of development though they are weak and insignificant as compared with organs of State capitalism. Important industrial enterprises are developing their own co-operative farms to supply their workers with a percentage of food stuffs. The various extensions of co-operative enterprise from a community centre suggest the revival of the ancient communes of gentile society in a higher form and equipped with modern machinery. The membership of co-operatives and labour unions are large, but they are a long way from occupying the place they are destined to take in a Socialist society, for in a Socialist society the political State -- or most of its apparatus -- will disappear and the labour unions, the farmers' organizations and the co-operative societies will become the administrative organs.

---

[79]Originally published as an untitled letter in Labor *World/Le Monde Ouvrier*, 26 November 1932.

iii. The Struggle for Industrial Democracy

132. Labour Must Control Production[80]

A Labour Party, which is not merely a Liberal party under another label, has a platform of principles. And all these principles have a common denominator -- the demand that society consciously undertake the organization of its economic powers with the object of providing, by means of the general duty of work, reasonable human needs. This is the wish of all workers who do not nourish the hope that fortune will some day knock at their door, and lift them above the general duty of useful work.

Now the direction which society must proceed in order to affect the desired reconstruction is not a matter of speculation; the road is clearly indicated by the fundamental facts of the existing system of production and the social relations to which it has given rise. Every intelligent worker knows that production on a small scale is not as profitable as production on a large scale; and production on a large scale is one form of co-operation. Also the workers know very well that private ownership of the means of production has become an instrument for the exploitation of labour, and that it produces the paradox of poverty in the midst of plenty, of millions unable to get work because private ownership controls a surplus of products which the workers have created, but which owing to their small wages they are unable to consume. These facts present themselves to the every day experience of the working class; they are the corner posts of a situation from which labour must lift itself if the lives of millions are not to be bound forever in [sorrows] and misery. And from such facts Labour is led to two practical conclusions: that co-operation, which the capitalists know well how to employ for purposes of control and also for increasing production, is imperative for the working class, and that private ownership of the means of production must be replaced by some system of community control if the working class as a whole is to share adequately in the benefits of civilization....

The labour movement has...an advantage over the bourgeois movement of the past. Labour leaders know what they want in the sense that the bourgeoisie never did. They are not called upon to destroy old institutions, uproot an old system of production and build a new system; they only have to establish a proper community control of the marvellous new forms and forces of production capitalism has called into being. They only have to democratize existing institutions.

---

[80]*Canadian Railroad Employees Monthly*, February 1924, 207-208.

133. Real Democracy[81]

It is not capitalism but democracy that is on trial, says J.E. Lawson, M.P. for a Toronto riding. And being from the intellectual centre of Canada he leaves it to be inferred that capitalism is finished in the sense of being perfect, and not in the sense in which the unemployed think it is finished.

...One dictionary definition of democracy is: political or social equality. In a world of economic inequalities, there is no social equality. And as politics mirror the economic interests of social groups, the theoretical democracy implied by one-person one-vote is hardly realized in practice.

Another definition of democracy is: "government of the people by elected representatives." That is to say, the government of a lot of people by a few people. But what is on trial is not the government of some people by other people; but the government of the people's affairs, more especially their economic affairs.
No man, or group of men, really governs, controls, rules, our present economic system. No ruler in Israel would permit the economic affairs of the people to fall into the present disorder if he had the power to prevent it. Change, the condition of progress, was never speeded up, to such velocity, as under modern financial capitalism; and to assume that capitalism is finished in the sense of having reached perfection, is to assume that evolution has attained its peak, and that, in accordance with the pessimistic philosophy of Herbert Spencer, the changes occurring henceforth will be in the direction of devolution. It is neither capitalism nor political democracy that is on trial -- but the ordinary common sense of men, freed from childish prejudices. The question for the jury is whether men will take conscious control of the forces of production which they have called into being and which now have the mastery over them -- the capitalist as well as the worker. And that is a problem of establishing some rational form of industrial democracy, involving not the destruction of the wonder working machinery of production developed under capitalism, but its better utilization in the interests of the people as a whole.

134. Economic Democracy Must Come![82]

....The outstanding defect of political democracy is that those who possess economic power control the political power. In theory indeed, the right to vote gives the average citizen power of control over political affairs; practically, this power is of small use to the mass of people. The sense of personal importance and political liberty which derives from the right to

---

[81]*Labor World/Le Monde Ouvrier*, 8 April 1933.
[82]*Canadian Unionist*, March 1936, 266-267.

mark the symbol of the unknown quantity on a ballot paper is an illusion which permits the masses to be repeatedly betrayed by the governing classes.

Political democracy is not without merit in that it is, or ought to be, a training school for economic democracy. The appearance of dictatorships throws doubt on that. But it is to be noted that the peoples now under dictatorships had a limited experience of political democracy. In any case, men must somehow contrive to achieve economic democracy if the mass of the people are to regain anything like the liberty, the freedom from class exploitation, they enjoyed for ages when the clan was the economic and social unit.

Freedom is relative. The owner of property which yields rent or profit from the employment of labour is free to spend his winters in Florida. The pioneer had a kind of freedom not enjoyed by the modern wage worker in cities.

He was free to take up virgin land, to build a log cabin, to stock the family larder with wild game, fish, berries, maple sugar, etc., so long as he did not have to recognize legal titles to the private ownership of the land about him -- titles perhaps granted by a far-away legal authority. In these conditions a man made employment for himself. But now private ownership has invaded practically all the frontiers where there is a tolerable climate, and the natural conditions in which free game and fish were abundant have mostly vanished.

Technological development has produced new economic and social conditions, and a new kind of property, capitalistic property, the result of the labours of many men working with machines, as distinct from individual private property which was the result of the labour of the proprietor and perhaps an apprentice or two. In these changed conditions, a conception of freedom, different from that of a simpler day, is required. Most men are now producers of commodities. That is, they are dependent upon the market wherein they must sell something, in order to buy therein what they need.

Look back to the pioneers in this country, or the yeomen of England in the era of cottage industries. The members of a family, then, produced most of their requirements; the family was practically self-sustaining -- had a high degree of economic independence. That is, the working producers were independent of their fellow producers to an extent unknown today; they had a kind of freedom impossible today -- freedom from the necessity of co-operative (or social) effort.

Yet in pioneer conditions there were numerous forms of social co-operation. There was a social consciousness of needs that could be best served by co-operative effort. Such collective effort, however, was the voluntary co-operation of men and women living, for the most part, on a plane of social equality, and having nearly equal economic opportunities.....

The "rationalization" of industry, which has been undertaken by capitalists and their managers, is a form of economic planning. Its motive, however, is to increase profits; a motive which defeats itself because the usual result is a reduction of the purchasing power of the workers, a main factor in the market for consumer goods. Economic planning with a social purpose is something else again; something that only the socially-minded members of the privileged class recognize as a necessary condition of continued progress and enlarging prosperity. Members of that class are, for the most part, opposed to the rational organization of production and distribution. Their anti-social habits, begotten by their use of the power of property to appropriate the best fruits of the labour of the masses, have become so deeply ingrained as to have acquired the strength of instincts which seem to them as natural and right as the instinct of self-preservation. Indeed, they connect their right to retain their privileges, and their liberty so to mismanage things to get the world in such a mess as it is today. Therefore they oppose the rational organization of society in the name of liberty. But it is only their peculiar liberty they are thinking of -- liberty to exploit the masses. To a planned economy, they oppose the liberals' idea of a "free" economy, the nearest approach to which was during the handicraft era when the production of commodities was mainly carried on by the muscle power of a master worker and an apprentice or two; and the producers were approximately economic equals. This opposition to planned economy has its comic side. A "free" economy in the liberal's sense of the word, is impossible with great industry and near-monopolies and combines occupying strategic positions on the route of the product to the consumer. To approximate such a "free" economy it would be necessary to scrap the machines, to return to the hand tools of the pioneer -- and also to revive all the natural conditions of pioneer days.

iv. Optimism of the Will

135. The Shadows Fade[83]

Can the contradictions inherent in the capitalist system be reconciled by reforms? Or must those contradictions, coming to a head, doom it to dissolution?

---

[83] *Canadian Unionist*, December 1935, 196-198.

There is the contradiction between surplus supplies of goods and the unsatisfied wants of the people, between plenty and poverty.

There is the antagonism between the machine and man. To many the machine appears as a Frankenstein monster. Either science and invention are foes of the workers, or the system in which we live is irrational!

There is the contradiction between the general demand for peace and the constant increase in the supplies of implements of war.

There is the contradiction between the demand for foreign markets and the building up of barriers to international trade.

Wealth accumulates, but misery spreads. The few enjoy the fruits of the labour of many. A vicious competitive struggle of producers goes on, yet the labour of the individual is only a part of the whole process of social production, a co-operative process. The interests of the individual are at war with the welfare of society.

Such contradictions were unknown in primitive human societies. In the long ages of primitive communism man was master of his mode of production and thus master of his fate in so far as the superior forces of nature allowed. Only with the division of society into classes did there arise a conflict between individual and social interests.

The grim joke is that the present "ruling class" find themselves in the tragic predicament of not being able to rule their own system. The capitalists are caught in a web of contradictions. The great requirement of the business community is a big increase in mass purchasing power, and that means higher wages or lower prices. But business has been saddled with a top-heavy capital structure; and, to meet the claims of capital, high prices and low wages are the apparent requirement. The capitalist thinks in terms of profit, and therefore he tries to depress wages and raise prices.

As stated, the thing needed to keep the productive machine working is an increase of consuming power. But no capitalist is willing to follow a wage or price policy adapted to that general principle. The particular interest of the individual capitalist is at war with the general interest, not only of society but of his own class.

The contradictions of capitalist society are reflected in the sphere of morals. While mystery shrouded the social process of production, the origin of the social motives of men could not be discovered. General class interests appeared in the guise of superior moral motives. A ruling class could compel a subject mass to recognize the class interest of the rulers as a moral law. But the interests of the individual members of the ruling class are not always in accord with the general class interest. Hence the dualism of bourgeois morality: one code for Sunday and another for work days.

The great Kant was the philosopher *par excellence* of the bourgeois class in its infancy. Rising capitalism required freedom for the producers of commodities, freedom of competition, freedom of exploitation: incidentally, it required a free labour market, a mass of workers free to labour on dictated terms or starve. Thus "freedom" became the slogan of the young bourgeoisie in its struggle for political power; the French added the slogans "equality" and "fraternity."

Kant's philosophy was the expression of the conception of freedom answering the needs of the rising bourgeoisie; it shortly found an appropriate echo in the French Revolution.

Kant's ethics were based on his doctrine of the freedom of the will, but he held that this freedom was not absolute, that it must be subject to moral law. If the new bourgeois society followed logically the principle of free competition, it would soon work its own dissolution, like a convention of Kilkenny cats. So the welfare of the whole bourgeois class had to be paramount to the interests of the individual, and the codes of conduct which served the welfare of the whole class had to be recognized as moral laws.

In the "sublime" ethics of Kant, the categorical imperative, "the timeless moral law," was summed up in the sentence:

"Act so that you, as well in your own person as in the person of every other, at all times look on man as end and never simply as a means."[84]

This had led some of the admirers of Kant to claim that he was the founder of socialism. But this Kantian formula is nothing else than the Golden Rule, the central social principle of primitive Christianity, and even of gentile society while the maternal law still reigned.

In the classless societies of antiquity, a man did not use his fellow tribesmen as a means to an end. And in animal societies, the strong do not exploit the weak of the same species. Cold-blooded fish may use the young of the species as a means to an end -- the satisfaction of hunger. Otherwise it is only in human societies, where social inequalities have developed, that the famous Kantian moral law has itself an "end" to serve.

---

[84]Part of the categorical imperative, which in a more modern translation reads: "For all rational beings stand under the law that each of them should treat himself and all others never merely as a means but in every case also as an end in himself." Immanuel Kant, *Foundations of the Metaphysics of Morals*, trans. L.W. Beck (New York: Macmillan, 1969): 59.

It is man alone, in a class society, who uses his fellows as a tool, and in particular exploits the young of his species.

Kant's ethics attempted to provide an ideal reconciliation of the contradiction between individual interests and social welfare in bourgeois society. What he arrived at was an ambiguous excuse for the inability of the bourgeoisie to live up to its moral codes. Though society exists in time and space, the moral law, he said, stood outside of time and space, directing its commands to the individual, not to society. Hence the moral law could never be fulfilled. But when one's private interest led him to violate the moral code which expressed the general interest of his class, that should be attributed to the fact that man was half animal, as well as half angel. The individual must develop his better nature rather than seek to reform society. Such was the reactionary conclusion of the dualist philosophy of Kant. It is not surprising that, in spite of his categorical imperative and his admiration of the French Revolution, he advocated freedom only for the citizens of the state, and did not recognize workers or women as citizens.

In spite of private property and individual enterprise, capitalist production is essentially social production. The production of commodities for the satisfaction of society's wants takes place in what is called a system of the division of labour, but that is only another name for the co-operation of labour. The exchange of products is necessary to complete the process of production; without exchange there would be no economic society. A man who produces an article for his own use creates a product, not a commodity. In so far as he is a self-sustaining producer he has nothing to do with society. But if a producer of a commodity is to realize its value in exchange, he has to make an adaptation of his effort to the general division of labour within society. If commodities were always produced in the right proportions and always sold at the right prices, there would be a balanced relation between supply and demand. But isolated producers working on their own calculations cannot possibly achieve a [proportional] production. And until recently they resented any suggestion of social control, that is to say, any conscious attempt to adjust their operations to a general plan of production. They would not stand for any interference with their liberty of action, except such interference as tariffs, which gave them special privileges. But the individual's freedom and independence was only an illusion. He was free only to get into trouble. When he failed to adjust his production to the effective social demand, he could not get a proper price. Under private ownership it is almost impossible to avoid antagonism between the individual and the social character of production. This antagonism gives rise to the contradiction between the purposes of the producers and the results achieved; it engenders social forces which thwart the aims and plans of men and deliver them to misery and ruin.

Is anything like real freedom attainable? Man adapts natural laws to his ends only when he has learnt to understand them. But he does not attain freedom of natural laws in the sense of being independent of them. Human nature is part of universal nature. Man cannot kick the earth from under his feet. He cannot suspend the law of gravitation, though he may get around it.

So man must understand the social forces which his productive activities set in motion before he can control them. Already we understand the necessity of having the present haphazard, individual productive efforts related to, and regulated by, a conscious social purpose: Mr. Bennett has put the seal of approval on that.

The sun begins to shed light before it rises above the horizon; and just so, a new, impending system of production sheds its light upon the minds of men, before it has fully materialized. The new understanding does not fall from heaven. It grows out of the social-economic development. It dispels the mysteries which bewitched the mass mind and permitted the ruling class to get away with the sorry pretence that their privileged position was the outcome of superior abilities and virtues and not of a particular development of private property under the aegis of a class-dominated state.

The new understanding enables the workers to emancipate themselves from the traditional superstitions and ideas which expressed the interest or ignorance of the ruling classes. It enables them to overcome the capitalist philosophy, with its dualistic, metaphysical modes of thinking. It enables them to see that philosophy has completed its quest, found out that what it was seeking was not a mystical explanation of life, but an understanding of the nature of the human brainwork, of how the faculty of thought functions.

It is the triumph of proletarian thought that we are now able to dispense with philosophy, and put in its place the science of the human mind, as part of natural science.

And for that reason we can predict that with the economic change to which we are now hurrying -- the substitution of a consciously managed system of production for use in place of the haphazard un-co-ordinated production of commodities for profit -- there will be an equally fundamental spiritual revolution. There will be an end to class antagonism; the interests of the individual will no longer be at war with the welfare of society. The darkness shrouding the motives will be dissipated. With the social regulation of production man will become fully the master of his fate.

Socialist Vision and the Realm of Freedom:

An Open Letter to Colin McKay

Ian McKay

So then, putting away falsehood, let all of us speak the truth to our neighbours, for we are members of one another.[1]
--Paul

The realm of freedom really begins only where labour determined by necessity and external expediency ends; it lies by its very nature beyond the sphere of material production proper. Just as the savage must wrestle with nature to satisfy his needs, to maintain and reproduce his life, so must civilized man, and he must do so in all forms of society and under all possible modes of production. This realm of natural necessity expands with his development, because his needs do too; but the productive forces to satisfy these expand at the same time. Freedom, in this sphere, can consist only in this, that socialized man, the associated producers, govern the human metabolism with nature in a rational way, bringing it under their collective control instead of being dominated by it as a blind power; accomplishing it with the least expenditure of energy and in conditions most worthy and appropriate for their human nature. But this always remains a realm of necessity. The true realm of freedom, the development of human powers as an end in itself, begins beyond it, though it can only flourish with this realm of necessity as its basis.[2]
--Karl Marx

Kingston
March, 1996

Dear Colin,

Hello from the 1990s, near the 100th anniversary of your first appearance as a young radical journalist and labour organizer. You have no reason to know me -- we're not even related, as I have explained a hundred times to people who ask me about this book -- but over the past fifteen years I have come to feel that I know you. I first met you on the pages of the Moncton *Eastern Labor News* (1910 circulation: c. 750), during my first real experience of research in a labour paper. And what an experience it was! Serving up reprints from the working-class and socialist papers of other lands, printing hundreds of quotations from a star-studded international cast of celebrities (Thomas Carlyle, Jesus Christ, Abraham Lincoln, William Gladstone -- all these, and more, in the first two issues alone), and featuring articles on topics seemingly chosen at random (organized labour in Germany side by side with the marriage customs of New Guinea): the *News* was truly an educational, if confusing, guide to the pre-1914 local working class. Lost in this whirlwind of fact and rumour, I looked around for the sorts of local working-class intellectuals and activists such historians as E.P. Thompson, E.J. Hobsbawm, and Rolande Trempé had made so famous. This proved a bit discouraging. There *were* some Socialist Party of Canada activists, who seemed to live up to their advance billing as dogmatists;[3] but meanwhile, from the Moncton trainmen, came this earnest advice, straight from a Horatio Alger novel: "Don't stand around on the street corners expectorating tobacco juice on the sidewalk. Such habits never brought out of a man all the good there was in him and are filthy habits. Get a book, a slate and pencil, or a newspaper, and qualify yourself more thoroughly for the battle of life." One heard calls for a mass mobilization of workers on behalf of the Springhill miners' strike -- a virtual civil war lasting over 22 months -- but they were set beside pleas with capitalists to be nicer to their employees. A warm Maritime welcome was extended to the revolutionary Big Bill Haywood, the legendary radical of the Western Federation of Miners, but then there were those Moncton machinists who passed a resolution of sympathy in 1910 regarding the death of King Edward the Seventh: "It was fitting that they as the most aggressive and progressive union men in Moncton should take the initiative in this respect and show to the world that organized labor is not backward in its recognition of a greater sovereign nor in its loyalty to the powers that be."[4]

Out of all this confusion, in 1910 there emerged a different voice: yours. You seemed to be that rare bird, a homegrown Marxist who didn't just repeat the words of luminaries from other places, but put the theory to work on and in the world around you. At times, as in your call for a "working-class culture" and in your application of Marxian theory to the fishing industry, you seemed almost to reflect the theoretical atmosphere of the 1970s more than that of the 1910s. I left the *Eastern Labor News* for a long time, but the memory of those remarkable articles did not leave me. Over the following decade the "Colin McKay" file was never decisively closed -- although for a time I had one file for the "Colin McKay" who wrote the sea stories and the articles about the fishing industry, a second file for that other "Colin McKay," the labour activist in Montreal, and a third file for the "Colin McKay" who wrote on economics in the *O.B.U. Bulletin, Le Monde Ouvrier/The Labor World,* and *The Canadian Railway Employees Monthly.* It took time and much luck to connect those three McKays together.

What lessons do your writings teach? For historians of Canadian socialism, they teach us that, for far too long, we have been too content with simple-minded dichotomies ("democratic socialist"/Marxist, evolutionary/.revolutionary, "impossibilist"/pragmatist, above all left/right) and not enough concerned to explore the intellectual worlds of Canadian socialism at a subtler, less polemical level. Your work confirms what others are also finding: that there were not two but many traditions within Canadian socialism; and it dramatizes what has been said less often, that Spencer's evolutionary paradigm was so powerful an influence that one can hardly attempt to write the history of early Canadian socialism without taking it into account. That's not all: you have so much to teach us about the ambiguities of turn-of-the-century liberalism, the response to the Depression, the history of capitalism in resource economies, the reception of Keynes -- all subjects that are still remarkably little-studied in this country, and on which you wrote what were in many cases the first sustained Marxist analyses. Finally, you have a lot to teach us about us: about our present in the light of your past, about what can and can't be preserved from the tradition you represented, about how and why socialists can re-invent themselves, their "socialism," their history.

•

Pioneering, sometimes acerbic, independent-minded, and well-researched your writings may be, but they have been almost entirely forgotten.[5] In other countries, the writings of Marxist intellectuals like you receive scrupulous attention. Not in Canada, where, even on the left, it's been readily assumed that most Canadian radicals and socialists were no-nonsense pragmatists, unconcerned with religion, philosophy, science, history. No, our leftists were simple folk, with straightforward interests that can easily be "read off" more or less directly from their class position.[6] Often the implicit assumption in the historiography has been that ideas were just covers for underlying class interests.

I think much has been lost because of this narrow approach. Let me give you some examples. General intellectual histories of the Canadian response to Darwinism impoverish themselves by avoiding the extensive working-class polemics on the subject. The Keynesian welfare state rises in the historians' reconstructions of twentieth-century Canada, but it does so in magnificent but improbable isolation from the working-class movement and its intellectuals.[7] Philosophical Idealism, propounded at Queen's, is sometimes presented as a virtually hegemonic ideology in turn-of-the-century Canada -- it is one area of cultural and intellectual history on which we have a number of first-rate monographs -- but we are given no idea of Idealism's powerful Spencerian and Marxist enemies.[8] Secularism and social reform are analyzed in ways that misleadingly marginalize the role of Marx and the movements influenced by him.[9] Again and again in the writing of Canadian intellectual and cultural history, the implicit message has been that, while Stephen Leacock and Andrew MacPhail were "intellectuals" worthy of commemoration, their left-wing working-class critics were not. I think the labour papers, the Charles Kerr books, and the progressive campaigns in the daily press were as influential as anything written or proclaimed in the seminar rooms at Canadian universities in these years, and certainly far more significant when we come to explain Canadian working-class philosophy, sociology, and literature in all its diversity. The silence from intellectual and cultural historians on these issues has been deafening.

To the Canadian historians' general anti-intellectual bias and the intellectual historians' elitism we can add the left-historians' tendency to blind partisanship. We Marxists often like to pick sides when we write about the radical socialist tradition. Often the story is constructed as a melodrama, with the "Proletarian Pauline" poised on the brink of a succession of political perils. Each of these perils is given a name ending in "ism" to make it *sound* like an easily diagnosed disease or readily recognizable obstacle (e.g., adventurism, utopianism, opportunism, chauvinism, impossibilism, revisionism, mechanism, economism: I imagine that even in eternity, Colin, you don't have the time to listen to me rhyme off all the comminatory "isms" experienced left-wing polemicists have at their disposal!). Of course, each one of these diagnoses covers an immense amount of territory, and no rules seem to govern how such labels are used. No matter: our Proletarian Pauline may be menaced by them in turn, or even in deadly combinations. The "Perils-of-Pauline" style allows the left-historian the luxury of writing from a position of absolute certainty. He or she applies the labels without ever needing to explain why he or she is so *positive* about everything. History becomes a thinly-disguised polemic. Even today, in depressed post-Soviet times and in the quiet eddies of the liberal academy, some leftists still adopt the ultra-Leninist tone, propounding self-evident political truths, reading enemies out of the fold, conducting campaigns of political hygiene to remove the last traces of a bad "ism."

This may be fun and energizing for some people, and a psychological necessity for others, but I suspect I'm not alone in finding it all a bit much. It's surely time, now that the last after-shock of the Bolshevik Revolution has been registered, for a less dogmatic approach. I've long suspected there is an inverse relationship between the level of left vitriol and the usefulness (or even relevance) of left historical investigation. In the 1990s, alas, there are no massed audiences waiting to pelt the heretics. The anathemas are proclaimed to empty air. The old polemical style sits uneasily with the new social and cultural realities -- and it does so all the more when, as is so often the case today, it involves middle-aged, tenured academics posturing as the last true revolutionaries, working out their political and personal frustrations by savaging each other and defending what remains of the True Faith. Rather than indulging in self-righteous academic polemics, it would probably be more interesting and politically productive to take up aerobics -- and think of how many trees we'd save!

So -- to get back to the point -- why were you forgotten? I think the answer lies partly in this deeply engrained habit of treating the past as a politically edifying melodrama. You do not fit into either of the two main left historiographical camps: and your stories and your activism complicate the tidy narratives we have already evolved to "explain" Canadian socialism. We like stories about Communists battling Social Democrats for union members, but you don't fit: you represent a Marxist path *between* the social democracy of the Co-operative Commonwealth Federation and the Marxism-Leninism of the Communist Party.[10] (By your very existence, you make us uncomfortably aware that these categories are far less airtight than we had suspected.) You don't help answer the leading questions (e.g., "The Communists: Heirs or Gravediggers of the Revolution? The CCF: Movement or Party?") -- but then I'm not the only one who thinks that these leading questions have become pretty lame. You won't fit theoretically, until we ourselves have rethought our socialism and come to a more subtle and less dismissive attitude towards the holism, scientism, determinism, teleology -- in a word, the evolutionism -- of an earlier generation of socialists. You don't fit culturally, into a present world in which "intellectual" means "academic" and "workers" are stereotyped as "rednecks": you belong to a time very different than ours, when (at least in some places) socialists and workers were in close contact, when an autonomous working-class culture seemed about to flower, when there was no doubt that the privileged university and the society it represented was bankrupt, and when many of the brightest and most courageous minds were in the working-class movement. In short, you don't fit our tidy scripts for Canadian socialist history.

The field of Canadian socialist history is strange: we find many titles and only a few general ideas or debates. Many questions -- about Canadian exceptionalism, the relative weight of British and American influences, the extent to which rank-and-file members identified with the doctrinal and organizational divisions orchestrated by their leaders -- remain unexplored. And Canadian historians seem to find it hard to imagine that Canadian socialists may have taken themselves seriously as thinkers -- as people shaped by, and shaping in turn, the great socialist ideas of their age. The SPC's Spencerian Marxism, the CCF's Christian-Spencerian-Marxian Evolutionism, the CPC's Dialectical Materialism -- all remain relatively unexplored, as though ideas were somehow peripheral to the major socialist movements in Canada.[11] Judgements in this business are swift but often uninformed, and often incredibly harsh -- there is perhaps no more unforgiving or ungenerous animal on God's earth than the Canadian socialist historian dissecting the deficiencies of his or her left-wing adversaries, ancestors and colleagues.

But it's much easier to point out these historiographical failings than to break with them. We all write from a place and a time, on the basis of truths we take to be self-evident and within grand narrative structures (as is especially the case with post-structuralists, who have installed a "grand narrative" into their very collective name). Inevitably, as human beings, we are all "dated." The preoccupations of the 1990s are unlikely to be those of the 2040s, and in passing judgement on you, Colin, a man inescapably shaped by the Edwardian intellectual and social world in which you attained maturity, we should be aware of the (potentially) chastening gaze of posterity on us. At the same time I'm conscious of that opposite left-wing tradition, no less partisan, which involves the warm cozy uplifting celebration of the saintly souls who went before us. It has been very difficult for Canadian historians of socialism to work their way out of this disabling dichotomy: to appreciate and understand *difference* without necessarily either denouncing it as heresy or sentimentally patronizing it as a charming anachronism.

In your case, what I deeply admire I also find problematical: I concede the intoxicating power of the theory of social evolution, but disagree with the way you used it. Yet I don't feel in a position to be judgemental about this. As I've worked to understand your world and your assumptions, I have often thought that, surprisingly, there are major similarities between your left and ours. Your left knew it had to wrestle with a revolution in human thought, the defining Moment of Evolution, and if socialists did not do this, they would be forever obsolete. Twenty or thirty years after you died, leftists knew they had to wrestle with a revolution in human thought, the defining Moment of Culture, and if they did not do this, they would be forever obsolete. Twenty years after that, leftists (and critical theorists) knew they had to wrestle with a revolution in human thought, the defining Moment of Discourse, and if they did not do this, they would be forever obsolete. Every so many years, in other words, a new great "Master Word" seems to sweep all before it, and all the left intellectuals hasten to adapt to the new dispensation. Given these fluctuations, it would take a very arrogant person indeed to pour scorn on you for genuflecting before Messrs. Spencer and Kautsky, when present-day left intellectuals are bowing no less reverently before Messrs. Foucault, Derrida, and Deleuze. Every so often, it seems, new words of power -- evolution, culture, discourse -- *seem* to redefine the very reality about which they speak. Those whose present-day project is that of discerning in the history of hierarchy and oppression the real possibilities for a new order of equality and freedom -- today they are mostly "Marxists" and "neo-Marxists," although their names are many -- can neither avoid nor wholly embrace these words of power: they must somehow probe the social and cultural fault-lines of the present with *and* against them, they must somehow live not only in awareness of the cultural world around them (which for us is the fragmented, fragmenting world of postmodernity) but in continuity and connection with the tradition that explains why they are here. If the writing of socialist history has become more sensitive, discerning and generous by the year 2040, those who look back at the socialists of our late twentieth century will understand that, just as you had little choice about the matter of living in the "moment of evolution," we have had little choice about living in the "moment of discourse." The interesting question will perhaps be not *whether* we were influenced by such master-concepts, but *how* we were influenced and what we did with that influence: whether we were wholesale converts or debunkers, or critical and selective interpreters. It is a question of how complexly and wholly we live our historical moment: for which, of course, a balanced appreciation of past moments in the history of socialist thought is our best (perhaps our only) guide.

Who, I have sometimes wondered, will read *For a Working-Class Culture in Canada?* I'm doing you a rather odd favour, Colin, in reviving your work in the late 1990s. Twenty years ago there would have been quite an audience for you; twenty years from now there may be such an audience: but now? You are being published when the socialist ideal is in eclipse, and all good liberals rejoice in the supposed death of Marx. (Marx, like the novel, has been undergoing these periodic "deaths" since the 1890s.)[12] Marxism is over, we are told again and again. Judged a failure by history, even according to its own tough criteria, Marxism is finished, and "we are on our own." In Ronald Aronson's *After Marxism*, surely destined to become *The God That Failed* of its time, this is a message repeated over and over and over again.[13] However crude and fallacious it may be, the academy's current "Death of Marx" makes it unlikely your work will find a warm reception within its walls. And outside them, the cultural channels that once connected a Marxist like you to thousands of readers have been sealed -- the essentially decommodified spaces in which you interacted with your readers have been diminished since the 1930s by the hypertrophic growth of commercial media, which have progressively encroached on the non-market cultural spaces where effective intellectual resistance has traditionally taken shape. (That this book can appear at all is evidence that the re-commodification of culture still has a way to go: not every part of the state has been contracted out. On the other hand, that it will reach a tiny percentage of the Canadian population is an illustration of just how effectively liberal bourgeois hegemony has crowded out alternative cultural spaces since your death).

You have few friends today. You're too Marxist for people in the ever-more-liberal social democratic tradition, too "workerist" and grassroots for the remaining Marxist-Leninist vanguardists, too economically oriented and "top-down" for the anthropologically inclined labour historians, too gender-blind for the feminists, and *way* too Marxist for the post-Gramscian cultural-studies crowd. You come at the "left" intellectuals of the 1990s from an odd angle, challenging popular and comfortable "post-Marxist" narratives, unsettling traditional maps of ideology in Canada, and humbling academic leftists (including me) by your record of a half-century of unpaid intellectual work on behalf of the movement.

In *our* nineties, the project of "working-class culture" of which you spoke so eloquently in 1913 looks no nearer realization than it did in *your* nineties, and I suspect it today faces even more powerful obstacles. The most serious barrier is the public and private cultural apparatus, which every minute of every day works to normalize an official truth about liberalism. (Almost every television commercial is, in its own modest way, a mini-sermon on individualism). And if, as you argued and I believe, it's vital to undertake the construction of a historic bloc animated by a new working-class culture of resistance (redefined, I'd say in amendment to your original formula, to include all the insulted and the injured of the liberal order) then I'm afraid that twenty-first-century socialists are indeed right back at the beginning: more knowledgeable and experienced, but also far less energetic and coherent, and reeling from the onslaught of a second liberal revolution of the 1980s and 1990s that has upended the postwar new liberal compromise. You would grimly recognize what passes for advanced political thought today -- reverence for an implacable process of "globalization," deification of the market, reduction of "society" to a mere aggregation of self-interested individuals, insistence that this reduction must hold across vast reaches of time and space, as the one unilinear logic of our time -- as a vulgar rehash of the worst banalities of nineteenth-century social thought, the crassest and most reductionist reading of the *worst* of "Spencer." This is why so many of your turn-of-the-century critiques of liberalism have a real resonance today: we confront a similar ideological matrix, armed today with a totalitarian will to impose its definitions on the entire globe. What we lack, and what you had, was a sense that liberalism had run its course -- that it was soon to be confronted, and confounded, by a confident, dynamic working-class and socialist movement.

You breathed a different air than we do, and it shows in everything you wrote. Right down to the 1930s, you believed that the ideals of collectivism and socialism were in the vanguard of human history; few people think that now. Today's intellectual fashion, even on the "left", is high liberalism. (Even in so-called "Radical Democracy" one sees the re-invention, in mind-numbing neologisms and arabesques, of positions J.S. Mill developed with much more flair and cogency more than a century ago). Everyone now agrees that the individual, sovereign in his or her own seat of reason, has natural "rights" (particularly to property) that take precedence over civil society and the State. Spencer's most extreme *laissez-faire* ideas resound in every newspaper and on every talk show; the inherent evil of the state, the inherent goodness of entrepreneurial culture, have become the commonsenses of the day. As your inheritors, we feel beleaguered -- and who, in fact, are "we", anyway? Certainly no self-evident, self-confident "historical subject" about to embark on making history with a clear sense of direction and purpose, like the socialist working class you thought would inaugurate the new age and in your lifetime. No community are "we", but a thousand self-absorbed fractions, incapable of setting an agenda for a meeting, let alone carrying out a social revolution. You wrote hopefully of the decline of the old individualistic outlook; under postmodern conditions of hyper-commodification, we live with the baleful consequences of its development as the secular religion of our time, the *real* illusion of our epoch. Liberalism now dominates the left, and even in such tendentially oppositional movements as ecology, feminism, or gay liberation a liberal vision of personal empowerment and a liberal rhetoric of "rights" often take precedence over the counter-liberal, socialist imperatives of connection, belonging, community and duty.

What, for people today, is socialism? In the 1930's you would have said, socialism means socialization and democratization of the means of production, distribution, and exchange -- and, no less important, it also means direct working-class cultural and political power. We would say.... Well, perhaps the first thing we would say is "Any attempt to say 'We would say' assumes a privileged, gender-free, colour-blind, regionally indifferent vantage-point from which any 'we' can be conceptualized and counterposed to some 'Other' : the first task is to problematize this 'we' and deconstruct the concept of identity implied by it." (I'm not joking, Colin: in *our* nineties, some left academics really *do* talk like this!) Since this deconstructive "first task" is inevitably never finished -- even the most provisional, not to say linguistically contorted and paranoid, construction of a "we" inevitably falls short of the Kantian universalism that provides the unacknowledged underpinning of postmodern ethical thought -- a community of resistance never takes shape (at least not in academia). Today, political thought on the academic left generally requires that one (a)shows precisely how dismally all forms of social thought and *praxis* failed in the past, compared to *my* approach -- in this age of the "posts," one cultivates a sneering, dismissive approach to thinkers in the past; (b)demonstrates how much more *exciting* social thought is today, especially *my* own social thought -- it is important to be both *new* and *improved*; (c) establishes how completely separate and distinct the position *I* hold is from the position held by anyone else -- a *brand name* is absolutely essential in this business; and (d)proves everyone else is falsely appropriating a generic voice, by claiming to speak for a community rather than for an individual. Unable by definition to generate conceptions of a system-challenging social movement (for the obvious reason that it rejects as "essentialist" that most basic of Marxist postulates, the power and importance of something called the "capitalist system") most of this rarefied academic left-talk is really radical liberalism, pure and simple: liberalism in its blithe disregard of, or contempt for, all those who made history before us (except a very few carefully defined number of 'ours'), liberalism in its fetishized pursuit of difference and its precise demarcation of boundaries (always accompanied with lots of revolutionary rhetoric: but in effect merely a tidy process of drawing lines on the social surface, rather like measuring off private lots in a new subdivision) and liberalism in its strong sense of contributing to the free marketplace of books, broadcasts, and reviews (and not the counter-liberal realm of factory occupations, farmgate defences, shopping boycotts, popular parties, and direct action). When Marxist social thought is once again a major focal point of intellectual energy and struggle -- and the periodic "rebirths" of Marx are as cyclical and predictable as his repeated "deaths" -- it will be its task, not to deride those caught within this postmodern force-field, nor to diminish the real oppressions (of gender, sexual orientation, nationality, and so on) which give such radical-liberal options such superficial plausibility, but rather to show that radical-individualist "solutions" to social and cultural problems inevitably perpetuate many of the oppressions they purport to abolish.

But perhaps these are verdicts that should be left to those discerning and sensitive historians of the year 2040 with greater powers of sympathetic insight and historical distance than I can possibly have. The point is that now the "left" has generally collapsed into an overarching liberal hegemony that can, to a large extent, structure even the "public" and the "opposition" to which it responds. The term "left" itself has become a faded old tag on a piece of luggage, vaguely designating a direction long since forgotten and generally considered *passé*, like a quaint old seaside resort long past its prime. "Left" has become almost meaningless. For you, the working class and the working-class interest could be taken as obvious and real points of departure. For many people today, including those who are skeptical about capitalism and the liberal order, the very idea of any class-centred "we" seems ambiguous, question-begging, even an oppressive return to old teleologies and master narratives; and "class interest" is commonly written off as a dated fantasy, when it is not derided as masculinist, racist, speciesist, and so on. One rarely hears today of a "Canadian working class" -- there are, after all, many mutually exclusive definitions of Canada -- or even an "Ontario " or "Nova Scotia" working class. The very term "working class" has remained stubbornly and revealingly confined to the academy, in a way you would not have expected in 1911: the words "working class" never really became "true words" in Canada, designating an obvious and generally acknowledged social fact as, to some extent, they did in Britain and in much of Europe.

So, Colin, we're really back in the nineties again: your book comes into a cold, cold world. In *our* nineties we're inherently more skeptical (and with good reason) of some of the utopian energies that made *your* nineties such a time of radiant hope. From the 1890s to the 1990s, and contrary to all the confident socialist expectations, liberal individualism did not disappear: after a momentary setback (1940-1975) it has returned with a vengeance. Liberal individualism has even advanced in your absence: the very concept of interests above and beyond the individual is now frequently dismissed as a fiction. The formulations of postmodernism -- hyper-liberalism propagated in an academic hothouse via fax, modem and Internet -- develop a social imaginary that parallels in practice and theory the ultra-liberalism of Spencer (who, much more than Hayek, deserves credit as the unacknowledged master thinker of the late twentieth century: there is little in *The Road to Serfdom* that Herbert had not expressed, rather better, in *The Man Versus The State*). In communities of critical intellectuals, centered in but not confined to the universities, the entire "problem-set" of Marxism -- the system of production, the traditions of property-holding, the distribution of wealth, death and disease in the workplace, the law of value, the class-determined unequal chances in life -- has largely come to be seen as *passé* . I do not believe, as some late Marxists seem to believe, that identity politics is by definition divisive and counterproductive: it has arisen, in its pervasively powerful form, for very real and valid reasons. But the manner of its articulation under conditions of postmodern liberalism is such as to to relegate inherently *collective* issues (not just of class, but of ethnicity, gender, sexuality, nationality and so on) to the margins, in an essentially liberal assertion of the present-day centrality of *personal* identity.

So, if there isn't a sympathetic audience, and if the times are indeed so grim, why do the book? I've wondered, often, about that. There's the historical and scholarly interest of it, of course; all fifty people in Canada who are obsessed by the history of early Canadian socialism are in for a real treat! And then, undeniably, there's the personal pleasure of revisiting another day, and re-experiencing its hopes and dreams. But antiquarianism and nostalgia, understandable as they are in a bad conjuncture, can also be ethically problematical and politically disabling: as they say, nostalgia tells it like it wasn't. I think the only valid reason to bring out *For A Working Class Culture in Canada* and to begin to reclaim the forgotten history of the "Socialism of the Third Way" in Canada is in anticipation of a better day. Radical energies may revive, and should that happen, historians today can do much to ease the path of future socialists. If we are to re-invent Canadian socialism, we can only do so if we have an ecumenical sense of the theoretical and political riches of the great Canadian socialist tradition: all of them. In any such revival of the left, working-class and socialist historians will be able to teach no directly applicable lessons, but the memories they reconstruct may be useful in reshaping the underlying assumptions of radical strategy. By constructing and re-constructing the history of the socialist movement, we can try to preserve and strengthen the identity of a Canadian Socialism that is more than the sum of its constituencies and their separate grievances. We can also (on the model of your critique of Social Credit as a displaced utopian socialism) warn against paths that experience suggests contain pitfalls or lead nowhere. In other words, I think we need a better approach to the history of socialism not just because good history is better than bad, but also because it's going to be important, when moments of opportunity arrive, to have a clear sense of the entire socialist and radical tradition. Even within the walls of the academy there are glowing embers, memories of resistance to save for the future.

The opposed forces and interests characteristic of a capitalist system routinely create the social preconditions of movements aiming at post-capitalist alternatives, whose chances depend on their accurate understanding of those conditions and on their ability to act politically in order to anticipate the realm of freedom. That, in my view, is your central idea. It's still perfectly valid. We -- that is, the "we" who hate capitalism and long for its complete replacement by a different way of life based on Paul's truly revolutionary doctrine that "we are members of one another" and Christ's revolutionary *praxis* in his opposition to the moneylenders of the temple (and building of course and primarily on the great humanitarian legacy of Marx and Gramsci) -- *we* are the inheritors of an extraordinarily rich socialist tradition. It is certainly our prerogative to squander this legacy in the self-absorbed pursuit of sectarian difference, or throw it away in frustration and misunderstanding because it does not always tell us quite what we want to hear or answer quite the questions that today are thought to be the vital ones. Or we can chose to live in a more complex and humane relationship with the socialist past, to be careful of the dreams of the dead, to take up and transform this complex inheritance.

And for all that we are constantly being told that the future will look *nothing* like the past, and that all bets are off, I think much of this inheritance is going to be of use. No matter how many times the inmates of postmodern high schools and universities are informed that all the ideas of socialism are superseded and *passé*, and that their task is to remake their individual souls for a life of eternal insecurity and nervous exhaustion in the global marketplace, such students are unlikely to absorb this ideology with complete passivity or without noticing interesting anomalies. When they encounter the harsh realities of the labour market, in the meaningless and deadening McJobs that they have to settle for, such old socialist notions as class oppression, surplus value, the reserve army of the unemployed may all start to make a certain and surprising amount of sense. Notwithstanding the undoubted usefulness of the deficit as a disciplinary agent, when such subaltern postmoderns think about politics, they may also wonder about the extraordinary largesse government continues to show towards the corporations. (Not much "restraint" in evidence there!) And such people may well come back to socialist ideas, not as "optional extras" or "fashion statements," but as perceived necessities for their economic survival, because they will feel that they *need* to answer the hegemonic arguments that, today, are aimed at the destruction of their own medical care system, their own social security, their own country, *their own lives*, all in the name of an abstract totalitarian doctrine of market globalization. And with this rediscovery of much of "socialism" -- whose re-emergence is not surprising, given the social force-field associated with capitalist social relations -- may well come the need for "Marx," precisely to the extent that the conceptual took-kit associated with his name still contains some useful ways of probing the liberal capitalist order that continues to define many of our personal and collective experiences of life.

For a Working-Class Culture in Canada can only be justified as a way of thinking about the possibilities of a renaissance of socialist hope, as an element in a rethinking of the history of our great tradition that is also a way of adapting it for the future. Recovering your forgotten voice is then part of this labour of recovery that is also, then, a dream and an anticipation.

•

Even the casual reader of your work can sense that a radical of your day lived in a world enlivened by hope. You breathed a different air than we do. History was on your side. You were one of a special group of working-class men and women who constructed a formidable presence in the early twentieth century, and who were the incarnation, and also the proof, of the forward movement of "social evolution."

What gave particular strength and coherence to the cultural formation you helped build in the early twentieth century was the autodidact tradition. When you and other working-class intellectuals talked about workers transforming themselves and their world, you had a commonsense model right in front of you: yourselves.

"Autodidact" is a relative term.[14] In your case, much of what you needed you learned from school, from church, from other workers, from the editors of labour papers, from the Charles Kerr list, and from the socialist movement. Your "autodidacticism" emerged from the hours and hours you spent poring over Herbert Spencer, Karl Marx, and countless other intellectual figures, while you were on steamers, in the sailors' boarding-houses, at the library in Montreal. When it came to political economy and social theory, you mainly educated yourself -- and revelled in doing so. A vivid sense of debating the whole world, of being intellectually superior to Stephen Leacock and the comrade-in-struggle of the most famous intellectuals of the tradition, living and dead, permeates your work. Autodidacts were not, contrary to much of the discretely patronizing writing about them, simple-minded souls thirsting for certainty in a difficult world.[15] A profound sense of working-class self-respect and pride set you against the professors and clergymen and newspaper editors, against all the acknowledged and respectable intellectuals of your day. For you, many of these professional intellectuals were lapdogs of the establishment; and others were frivolous *poseurs*, those who could afford to treat ideas like playthings.[16] What you had so painstakingly acquired was, on the other hand, real knowledge -- knowledge as definite and as well-reasoned as that of any university intellectual. You did not write to please but to tell the truth.

In many respects, yours was an Enlightenment vision, in which the honest working-class investigator "dared to know" -- whatever the cost -- and then defied the powerful, speaking truth to power. You were marginalized, but you did not take it sitting down: you argued with the world, you mobilized counter-opinions, you treated with a scoffing irony the supposedly authoritative viewpoints of the bourgeoisie and its numerous intellectual allies. One reason perhaps you read so much of (and into) Spencer was that he too was in many respects a marginal man and an autodidact. Skeptical of tradition, disrespectful of intellectual authority, favouring the well-trained intelligence of the artisan over the useless erudition of the parasite, and envisaging a new ethical culture, Spencer (especially the young Spencer) was, contrary to his present image, very much a sympathetic figure for many working-class autodidacts like you.

Then and now, it would be a mistake to patronize you. Working-class intellectuals like you could zero in on the weaknesses of an opposing economic argument with something like an unholy joy. In my own biased opinion, I think your interpretation of currency reform as a displaced form of utopian socialism, your skeptical but respectful analysis of Keynes, and your clear-headed and internationalist articles on labour party-formation should be ranked among the best Marxian writings in Canada on those subjects: they are in my estimation more subtle and insightful than (say) C.B.Macpherson's more famous (but more class reductionist) analysis of Social Credit. Yet even among contemporary "working-class historians," there is a faint tone of condescension when discussing the "working-class autodidacts": one sometimes receives the impression of giddy proletarian neophytes loose in the shopping mall of ideas, stocking up on intellectual products that they neither understood nor could put to discerning use (and unlike contemporary Canadian shoppers, showing an inexplicable fascination for the dated product line of Marx and Spencer).

I think such an impression is inaccurate. You working-class autodidacts were far less eclectic than some descriptions suggest; your processes of intellectual self-formation were anything but haphazard. Often absorbed by the question of *who* workers were reading, or *why* workers were reading these people, working-class historians have too seldom asked the equally interesting question: *how* were workers reading? In your case, Colin, I am deeply impressed not by the extent to which Marxist quotations enter your work (after all, anybody can quote without comprehension), but by the *way* they are used: I'm even struck by the slight misquotations (rarely affecting the text's meaning, but confirming the extent to which the quotation had been committed to your memory). Your mobilization of anti-bourgeois counter-authorities sometimes may look like name-dropping, but for the most part it really wasn't. It was a matter of a deep internalization of the authorities you wrote about and your drive to enlist all the resources of western culture in your quest of a better world. You knew these people well. One sometimes wonders if they weren't your truest and best friends, as night after night you wrote against the darkness and silence all around you.

"The working class must develop a new philosophy of life": not many people in Canada, so far as I know, put it with your cogency, and went on to fight for the new working-class culture with such life-long determination. Antonio Gramsci, the greatest Marxist of the twentieth century, is the major international theorist you most closely resemble on this question (although there is no chance of your having been influenced by him); among the great Canadian socialists, perhaps W.A.Pritchard paralleled your thought most closely.[17] Gramsci's argument about working-class culture was that from a few working people, intelligently reflecting on the prevalence of harsh conditions, a more general revolutionary movement could emerge. Ultimately the masses would build a movement in which the immediate objectives of particular subaltern groups and classes would be both expressed in and transcended by a great revolutionary working-class party.[18] Both for you and for Gramsci, the "question of culture" was in reality nothing less than the "question of socialism." The cultural revolution you both envisaged was a massive phenomenon in which the transformation of property relations figured as only one part (albeit a decisive part) of a much bigger whole. This new culture would involve a new psychology, a new literature, a new moral code: not, of course, the liquidation of the achievements of bourgeois civilization but the overturning of its hierarchies and its outworn traditions.[19] Any attempt to juxtapose "cultural" with "political" work, with the implication that the latter was somehow more in touch with the serious issues of life, was therefore superficial and even dangerous: cultural and political struggles were indivisible. To borrow a phrase or two from Stuart Hall, for both you and Gramsci, challenging ruling ideas meant contesting the limits of "what will appear as rational, reasonable, credible, indeed sayable or thinkable, within the given vocabularies of motive and action." This meant in practice to use unconventional words and to attack bourgeois complacency in unexpected ways, to extend the limits of the "sayable or thinkable." (Your vicious attack on what sounds like a rather innocuous banquet in Saint John, which you transform into a virtual metaphor for the diseases of capitalism, is an example of a deft use of the trope of synecdoche [§.26, "Capitalism -- The Modern Frankenstein"]; your fable of capitalism on the desert island illustrates the potential -- to my eye not quite realized by your story -- of political fable [§.20, "The Wise Men. A Fable for the Otherwise"]). The power of the dominant ideas was their ability to become common sense. For this to happen, they did not have to achieve a sort of total brainwashing (though sometimes, influenced perhaps by the American social control theorists you read before 1914, you suggested as much); they simply had to have the power to confine to safely marginalized areas the wide range of alternative conceptions of the universe. Both for Gramsci and for you, the direct cultural power of institutions, ultimately secured through (but not reducible to) the private ownership of the means of production, was a central issue: "The monopoly of the 'means of mental production' -- or of the 'cultural apparatuses,' to use a more modern phrase -- is not, of course, irrelevant to this acquisition over time of symbolic dominance vis-a-vis other, less coherent and comprehensive accounts of the world."[20] So Hall carefully revamps a case for material determination that you yourself would have put more emphatically.

Your pivotal articles on culture -- "Working-Class Culture" and "Working-Class Morality" -- anticipated Gramsci's parallel analysis of "Socialism and Culture" by three years. Yet, the more one learns about your time, the less one wants to claim any absolute originality for you as the founder of a brand new conception of "working class culture." It becomes clear that the project of socialism as a whole philosophy of life was widely supported on the eve of the Great War, both in North America and Europe.[21] This dream was to be *partially* realized in Canadian history. In the One Big Union and Socialist Party of Canada, in District 26 of the United Mine Workers of America, at times in the Communist Party,[22] in some of the local units of the Co-operative Commonwealth Federation, in elements of the All-Canadian Congress of Labour, and certainly in much of the labour press, we see "a new philosophy of life, a new culture" taking shape. Yet it also seems this working-class culture early on reached a kind of threshold it could not cross. It seems to have been, throughout, a phenomenon that pertained to a minority (even if a large and significant minority) that found it difficult to transcend particularities of region and skill, gender and class, race and nationality. Not that many of these new cultural formations did not do their utmost to include a diversity of cultural forms and reach out to a wider range of the oppressed. Certainly in the movement as a whole, and perhaps in your own thought, there was no resistance to using many different strategies -- summer camps and song-poems,[23] boys' socialist brigades and graffiti on coal cars, fantasies and humour -- to convey the message of the culture, *provided however that such cultural expressions emanated from the unified and coherent politico-ethical critique of the liberal order developed by intellectuals attached to the free working-class movement and guided by socialist ideals.*

The italicized qualifying clause here is, of course, of decisive importance: the working-class culture to be constructed was to be a *socialist* and a *rationalist* culture. Clarity is important here, for not everyone who has spoken of "working-class culture" has had the same idea in mind. As an entrenched skeptic about all things Bolshevik, you would not have sympathized with Soviet proposals in the 1920s for a "Proletarian Culture" nor with Lysenko's quite different subsequent elaboration of a "Proletarian

Science" as a part of a Marxist-Leninist orthodoxy (especially not if you had realized the suspension of normal empirical and theoretical standards implied by this Stalinist adventure in plant genetics). Closer to home, I think you would have also resisted the "anthropological turn" among Canadian working-class historians in the 1970s and 1980s who, drawing in large part on such anthropologists as Claude Lévi-Strauss, Ruth Benedict, Clifford Geertz and Bronislaw Malinowski, and in even larger measure on the British and American historians who had been influenced by these anthropologists, put forward a new concept of a "working-class culture." The core argument of this anthropologically-influenced tradition was that "class struggle and culture, *not class itself*, as an analytical category, ... are the *primary concepts* upon which classes themselves arise and assume importance."[24] In reply, one imagines that you would have objected strongly to visualizing classes as rising on the basis of *concepts*, no matter how primary; but I also suspect you would have objected even more strenuously to the further development of the concept of working-class culture in the historiography. For governed by this central (basically Hegelian) theory of the *conceptual* foundations of class, these historians went on to set their goal as the illumination of those aspects of the past (baseball, fraternal orders, trade unions, rough entertainments, cruelty to animals, and heavy drinking, among other things) in which this *working-class concept* or *essence* could be seen at work, at least if viewed from a certain perspective. They tended studiously to avoid those aspects of the past (such as religion, ethnic and racial identities, temperance agitations, patronage networks, and working-class imperialism and militarism, to name but a few) which, although seemingly important to actual flesh-and-blood Canadian workers, did not correspond to this *a priori concept* and which consequently could not be seen as bearers of the working-class essence or idea

This is *not* the place to debate the success or failure of the important paradigm of culture which for over a quarter century has established a strategy whereby class is conceptualized as rising up and assuming importance in terms of primary cultural concepts and essences. But this *is* the place to emphasize that this modern line of enquiry is quite different from your own approach. Against the modern working-class historian's concept of working-class culture as expressing a pre-existing essence or identity, and of class as rising on the basis of *primary concepts*, your position was that working-class culture *had to be constructed by both socialists and workers*, that there was no pre-existing "class identity" upon which socialists could simply draw, but at most a potential identity which, if they properly understood the real forces of the world around them, they might be able to make a reality. Moreover, one task of the new working-class culture was precisely the obliteration of the old suspicions, habits, prejudices (one is tempted to say "folklore") of the past -- that is, many of those habits and traditions that were later often fondly included in "working-class culture." For you, working-class culture was something socialist intellectuals and workers had to build together. It did not already exist, it had to be created: "The working class must develop a *new* philosophy of life, a *new* culture" [§.49, "Working Class Culture", emphasis added]. On the one hand, then, we have a sense of "culture" as a "reflection" of a pre-existing "identity," which in a sense is always already inscribed in consciousness, awaiting its expression; on the other hand, in your work, we have a complex sense of a contingent labour of class construction, consolidation, and re-articulation. Your working-class culture was in essence to be a Proletarian Enlightenment, in which workers and socialists would act together to generalize the gift of scientific reason. This difference in the two approaches to the question of working-class culture is that, perhaps, between the unintentionally revealing phrase "history from the bottom-up," with its undertheorized implication of cultural hierarchy and its overtones of both patronage and "salvage anthropology," and "reconstruction in the light of reason," which is how one might distill your autodidact ideal of the new culture and the new philosophy.

Perhaps it is because of this distance between the two ways of thinking that we today find it hard to imagine a Canadian working-class newspaper running what amounted to commentaries on Kant and Hegel, and also why you might well be mystified by the suggestion that you would have been better advised to focus your cultural writing on baseball and bear-baiting. Perhaps it is this distance between the two radically different concepts of working-class culture which we feel when we read of the proudly materialist funeral of Tim Walker, that "old-timer" of the SPC, radicalized in Nova Scotia in the big strike of 1909-11 and later a trade-union stalwart of the Vancouver Island miners. Walker died in 1935, and his funeral oration included these words: "About that time [1909-10] he came under the influence of the works of Marx, which changed his whole psychology. He studied Marx, Engels, Dietzgen, Spencer, Darwin, Huxley and many other progressive scientists until his understanding of working class problems was second to none."[25] Walker, Pritchard, McLachlan, Buck, Wallace, Woodsworth, Macphail: above and beyond their political differences, did they not share this same ideal of a working class proudly appropriating and mobilizing the entire legacy of western civilization, to free humankind from its chains?

This widely-shared Enlightenment ideal of a "working-class culture," brought into unusually sharp theoretical focus in your writing, was the animating force behind your campaign to destabilize and unsettle the "horizon of the taken for granted." Much of your work took up the cause of the Enlightenment -- i.e., reason's confrontation with apathy, conservatism, and superstition -- probably because you considered workers were blinded by the many pre-Enlightenment traditions in their lives.[26] The Christian faith, which in some important respects harboured a pre-bourgeois traditional communitarianism in *both* its Protestant and

Catholic manifestations, was a decisive fact of Canadian social and intellectual life: you certainly must have thought so, for you focused on religion consistently in your early years. In my opinion, these writings went a long way beyond merely "expressing" in religious language an identity and a consciousness already worked out in the sphere of "class."[27] No, you seemed to sense that religious questions were of central significance to workers, that however we set the borders of "culture," concepts of the soul, of the meaning of death, of sin, and of the good life are certain to figure centrally in it. In your Enlightenment view, churches (but most of the time not Christianity *per se*) posed an obstacle to the construction of working-class reason. You spent much time trying to destabilize and discredit conventional religious understanding by comparing the sad record of "churchianity" with the teachings of Christ, and by implying -- on the basis of evidence that seems somewhat fragmentary and tendentious to me[28] -- that a mass working-class defection from the churches was just around the corner. Before 1913, I am not sure whether you hoped to accelerate secularization or to encourage the growth of a distinctive working-class theology. Only after 1913 -- I suspect the decisive influence here was Arthur M. Lewis's *Evolution Social and Organic* -- did your tone on religious questions become markedly more skeptical, more "Kautskyan."[29] Although your religious commentaries lacked theological depth and complexity, this does not mean that Christianity was not a core value in your early years; again and again, you would come back to Paul and his organic image of the ties among people, and you would often develop the image of Jesus-the-liberator, scourge of the comfortable, friend of the poor. Into your last years, you may well have quietly remained a kind of "cultural Christian," drawing your (largely implicit) ethical standards from the tradition, but there is no avoiding the overall decline of religious references in your arguments.[30]

The working-class Enlightenment also required a completely different approach to education. As with religion, here too you began with enthusiasm and openness, and concluded with skepticism. You first saw technical education as a tremendous breakthrough,[31] then later as a minor bourgeois palliative. In general, at least to my eye, your sense of education as a challenge and opportunity to the new philosophy of life is superficial (and markedly inferior to that of Gramsci) because in focusing so narrowly on *content*, it ignores the question of *process*: the pedagogy of the oppressed is nowhere described. How was the socialist party to create the disciplined and effective processes through which pernicious old cultural habits could be eliminated and the proletarian Enlightenment secured?[32] So you fired your volleys at Professors Stephen Leacock and Goldwin Smith, in frustrated resentment against their position of educational privilege: it was amusing, forceful, even fun -- but no substitute for theorizing an alternative to the established educational system.

Finally, no reader of yours in the 1990s can avoid what you so stubbornly avoided in almost all your cultural writings: the gendered dimensions of power. What most clashes with a modern left sensibility is your almost complete silence on gender issues: so far as I am aware, your collected works on this question are included in this book, and frankly they don't amount to very much. (And even the three readings dealing explicitly with women in this book convey, by their "off-hand" anecdotage and more specifically by the implied male subject-position they construct, a vivid sense of the low priority the women's question occupied in your mind). Women were peripheral in your conceptualization of the "new way of life" and if the reasons for this are to be found in your own particular experiences, the point can still be argued that without more attention to gender, any new "philosophy of life" was not nearly as new as it needed to be.[33] One could also remark that for someone who was so attached to Montreal, and wrote so much in that city's labour press, you seem to have spent almost no time on the "national question" in Québec: almost all of the writings in *Le Monde Ouvrier/The Labor World* might have appeared in any North American labour paper. You spent even less time on the "national questions" posed by Amerindians (who appear, when they appear, as abstractions glimpsed through the heavy anthropological lens of Morgan). From the perspective of the 1990s it is difficult to imagine a balanced, well-considered strategy for *Canadian* socialist cultural transformation that does not address these core questions.

These missing foci in your writings on the project of cultural revolution suggest to me that, for the most understandable of reasons, you weren't quite able to pull it off. Your analysis remains pitched at a high level of internationalist generality. We don't find here a coherent *strategy* of building this working-class culture in this place -- an actual strategy of *cultural revolution*. (And here -- to complicate the dichotomy earlier developed between the two concepts of "working-class culture" -- one might suggest that closer attention on your part to the diversity of the many cultures and idioms characteristic of the subaltern classes and groups you hoped to unify might have helped "ground" the project of Proletarian Enlightenment). In your immensely suggestive writings on the eve of the Great War, we find tantalizing fragments -- and, as is so often the case with fragments, one is tempted, at the risk of falsely idealizing the moment, to attribute to them a coherence they (possibly) did not actually have, to "read in" the missing "whole" to which (perhaps) these fragments once belonged. *Mea culpa*. On the other hand, there is also the risk of neglecting the fascinating richness and novelty of these writings in one's concern to establish one's critical distance from them. Against our list of failings and lacunae, some of them obviously quite serious, let us place your lively sense of a whole order around you -- churches, schools, political parties, factories -- interlaced and interconnected, no one part of which could be ignored. Your cultural writings remain, I think, brilliant anticipations of a dawn that did not come, and inspirational resources for Canadian socialists today.

When the next great army of Canadian radicals arises -- as it surely will -- it will find great resources of hope and struggle in your thought, and especially (I think) in your insight that there is no working-class "essence" or "concept" that a working-class culture can simply reflect. On the contrary, working-class culture, i.e. the People's Enlightenment, is a project requiring active construction (and not one of interpreting reality from the so-called "bottom up," but rather a common struggle mounted by intellectuals, workers, and those drawn from other allied subaltern classes and groups, united in a great horizontal alliance of radical equals in which there would be no top and no bottom). It is a vision of an expanding and dynamic realm of freedom steadily encroaching on the kingdom of necessity. A new philosophy of life. A new culture.

•

I deeply admire your visionary concept of "a new philosophy of life, a new culture." And I envy you the chance of living in that pre-1914 moment when the pillars of the liberal order could at times seem so slender and fissured and the army of redressers so powerful and confident. Yet when I turn to the actual *content* of the proposed Proletarian Enlightenment -- that is, the actual teachings of the "new philosophy of life" -- I have to register a much more complicated response. I might put this in three points:

(1) The evolutionary core of the new philosophy was immensely complicated -- far more complicated than the existing historiography (which is often just crudely *wrong*) suggests. Against this historiography, one wants to register a basic point, amply confirmed by your writings: there was no one obvious political reading of evolutionary theory.

(2) There were some obvious advantages to working within the Spencerian tradition, and historians who are prepared to admire the holism and self-confidence of the turn-of-the-century socialists should also open-mindedly investigate the philosophical underpinnings of these admirable qualities.

(3) However, in the long term, Spencerianism presented some serious problems, in that you were unable either to explain *particular* developments in capitalism or to distinguish your approach from that of non-Marxist new liberals. The "new philosophy" was internally flawed and, to some degree, its subsequent erosion can be accounted for by its internal contradictions.

As you can see, I 'm trying to walk a very fine line when I discuss your Spencerianism. I'm not all-knowing, and neither were you: but sometimes, when we sit down to write, we try to sound as if we are. I'm struck by the

real risk of unfairness here in taking you to task for not seeing abstract
dangers and deficiencies that could only appear glaring in hindsight. It
would obviously be unreasonable to ask you to transcend your own
context, and to work through implications of evolutionary thought in ways
nobody else was doing at the time. (After all, if someone digs up my
words after 60 years, how likely is it that they will say: "His issues are
exactly the same as our issues, and he puts them *exactly* the way we do!")
On the other hand, the risks are just as big the other way. They are the
risks of sentimentality and patronage. Leftists often create saints, pat the
heads of favourite sons and daughters, and in other ways behave more
like devotées of a secular religion than people on a tough-minded quest
for historical understanding. (One might call this the *Prophet in Politics*
syndrome.) There is the added complication that the tradition to which
you belonged all your socialist life, Evolutionary Marxism, is now in total
eclipse. Simplistic polemics (in which Evolutionary Marxism = "Socialism
of the Second International" = Revisionism = Liberal Social Democracy =
Liberalism) have made it difficult to develop a more complex and subtle
sense of how evolutionary theory interacted with socialism (including
revolutionary socialism) in the twentieth century. This is, in brief, a mine
field of complications and controversies.

Despite all these difficulties, I want to try to make my complicated case.
On the one hand, you were right in many respects about capitalism, about
how it could be resisted, and about the need for a non-authoritarian, open
"Marxism of the Third Way". On the other hand, much of the *intellectual*
apparatus of the proposed culture was simply not up to the job of
transforming a liberal order or sustaining an alternative culture. In other
words, although I wouldn't want to underestimate for a second the
effectiveness of various bourgeois hegemonic strategies, not to mention
the outright repression of enemies of the liberal order, I'd like to open
discussion on the *internal flaws* that probably helped seal the fate of the
"new philosophy of life."

Evolution: here is the key to your thought. Not so much a mere concept,
Evolution (capitalization *does* seem in order here!) was an incalculably
powerful cosmic force. Evolution cannot be denied, Evolution writes the
obituary of liberalism, Evolution dictates that the economy shall follow a
certain path, Evolution sets terms for the analysis of religion, "Evolution
Cannot be Discredited" [§.32] : *it cannot be discredited*, or the labour
movement itself will suffer a terrible reverse. Here you were nothing if not
a man of your times. As Mark Pittenger has recently shown, in a useful
account of turn-of-the-century American socialists, almost all these people
believed Evolution was on their side, and also that its natural scientific
interpreters must be captured for their cause.[34] There was more than a
whiff of incense when socialists wheeled out the word Evolution: one
rather loves the inimitable Arthur Lewis who, in arguing that Evolution

explained why classes came into being in one age, and disappeared in the next, went so far as to use the mystical phrase, "inscrutable power."[35]

Perhaps, when most late twentieth-century people think about the Theory of Evolution, they think of Darwin, biology, and perhaps of contemporary debates about teaching "creationism" in the schools. When you early-twentieth-century socialists thought about Evolution, you thought about something much, much bigger: a great, massive force, a universal principle, above all a *social and natural phenomenon* that was both the scientific *explanation* of change, the *process* of change, and the *politico-ethical practices* predicated on the awareness of this phenomenon of change. You thought above all of Spencer and of his new science of "sociology." The key idea was the inevitable adaptation, through processes of functional and structural differentiation and integration, of society as a social organism to its environment. Evolution was your master-concept, and Herbert Spencer for three decades the Master Thinker. At least in your case, down to the 1920s, I don't see any exaggeration in calling you a Spencerian Marxist: whenever you discuss evolution, the Master's voice -- Spencer's words, Spencer's mode of reasoning, Spencer's certainty -- really can't be missed.

As I was saying to you earlier on, Colin, your book is untimely in so many ways; but your Spencerianism just puts you over the top in terms of untimeliness. *Everybody* who has read this letter has complained about there being too much Spencer (and those who know they will always detest Spencer on sight and in principle should feel free to skip this section.) Spencer was one of the most Eminent of the Eminent Victorians; many of his books bear witness to the Victorian social scientist's belief that More was Better. I doubt that I could find a sincere admirer of Spencer today in a day's walk. Virtually *nobody* reads Spencer today. He is that rarest of rare birds: a major nineteenth-century philosopher who is almost completely without twentieth-century supporters.[36]

Which is why, Colin, I experienced a certain sinking in my stomach when I first began to realize just how Spencerian you were, particularly in the period of your most interesting writings on working-class culture. You're Spencerian even when you don't mention him explicitly: so much of your language, your underlying cast of thought, derives from him. And, initially, this seemed an indictment of you both for having been so dumb as to have immersed yourself in the Spencerian morass in the first place, and then for poor judgement for not having quickly extricated yourself after you discerned the Master's reactionary agenda. For me, the irony of this situation came home when I thought about you reading Spencer at sea (as you probably did). Bouncing on the waves of the Caribbean, in some state-subsidized (but probably defective) fruit ship, you were enthralled by the writings of a man who not only would have ended all such state subsidies, but (so you at any rate believed) would have done away even with the modest safety measures (such as compulsory safety inspections) on which your life depended.[37] Given this, your attraction to Spencer seemed ... quixotic, to put it mildly.

After a lot more reading and reflection, I think I have arrived at a better understanding of how an honest and intelligent working-class intellectual like you (and thousands like you) could find inspiration in Spencer. Working-class Spencerianism makes sense in the context of the cultural crisis sparked by the scientific materialism of the nineteenth century (a crisis identified with, but by no means confined to, Darwinism; it extended to liberal political economy, traditional vs. historical readings of the Bible, and so on). This cultural crisis was experienced by many workers no less than by the bourgeoisie. I think intellectuals like you found in Spencerianism something richer and more satisfying than Darwinism -- a way of handling the pervasive turmoil unleashed by modernity. Spencer gave you what Darwin could give you only intermittently and partially: a Philosophy of History. Not only that, but Spencerian socialism gave you a seemingly revolutionary way of grasping the entire Cosmos, breathing new life into politics and social action, and providing a *telos* for working-class self-activity. Left Spencerianism could explain why the struggles of a few garment workers in Montreal were of *cosmic* and not merely local significance. In other words, it not only offered a vocabulary for the discussion of those contemporary issues on the immediate agenda, but also a way of thinking about life's ultimate meaning.

The claim that working-class intellectuals and workers themselves were confronted by the cultural crisis unleashed by the scientific materialism of the nineteenth century will ring strangely in ears attuned exclusively to the world of elite opinion. Yet a "crisis" in Christianity was broadly experienced, among working people as well as theologians. There is, of course, no unanimity among scholars as to the extent and nature of this "crisis" : certainly the notion of a simple, unilinear movement of "secularization" has to be treated cautiously. And then there is danger as well in seeing the crisis as one of "Darwinism" *per se.* The point has been established that, had Darwin never written a line, the idea that the history of humankind is best understood in evolutionary terms (in an explanatory vocabulary from which the direct action of Providence was excluded) would nonetheless have been pervasive in social thought. For although Darwin was the name that came to be attached to this massive upheaval, it would have happened without him. Secular and materialist thought, much of it linked to the idea of evolution, was simply too widely distributed over too many fields. Marx, for example, was strongly influenced by at least six major evolutionary intellectuals -- and it is still debated today how much he ever actually drew from Darwin.[38]

And even without Marx and without Marxists, we know that many working-class intellectuals would have gravitated to materialist and evolutionary accounts of the social world. In their fascinating biography of Darwin, Adrian Desmond and James Moore document just how strong the association was between "materialism," evolution and scores of popular working-class agitators: Patrick Matthew who used "nature's law of progress" to denounce aristocracy in 1827, George Holyoake who used "transmutation" to critique Christianity in 1844, radical journalists who published shocking revelations on "the origin of man" to provoke reaction in 1854, and Alfred Russel Wallace (sometimes considered the codiscoverer of the principle of natural selection) who cut his intellectual teeth in the socialists' "Hall of Science."[39] (In his case, and he is not an isolated figure, the direction of influence went from working-class politics to science). Among some radical workers, there clearly was a longstanding fascination with the implications of materialism and evolution. When *The Clarion,* the leading socialist paper in early-twentieth-century England, took a vote of its readers as to whom they considered to be the greatest figure of the age, "the man who had contributed most to the progress of the race," its readers named Charles Darwin.[40] Two epochal books came out in 1859, one of which was Marx's *Zur Kritik der politischen Ökonomie* in June; but for many years, the name of Marx was eclipsed by that of Darwin, whose *Origin of Species,* brought out in November, won an instant mass readership.

You, too, coming from your Church of England home, and deeply imbued -- as we can clearly see from your early writings -- with an evangelical sense of the need to minister to a fallen world, confronted this body of Darwinian thought, which was by the 1890s a well-established if not "orthodox" way of thinking. Yet, for you, as for many of the newly proletarianized and urbanized, there was much in this and other "scientific" ways of thinking that seemed bewildering. Your visceral reaction to Goldwin Smith's political economy expressed something more than an objection to traditional liberal political economy: it was a shocked outburst of revulsion against such a cold-blooded, analytical, "scientific" way of construing relations between human beings. And it is interesting that your first response to the challenge of this bourgeois modernity was to turn to Christ, in what was effect a return to the Arius's conception of Jesus as a prophet, rather than as the incarnation of God. This Christology carried both idealist and materialist implications: it suggested a complete divorce between God and the social world of the late nineteenth century (which was no longer regarded as a reflection of His providential plan); but it also echoed a history of dissident Christian thought, extending at least as far back as the Bogomils, which stressed the entirely human nature of Christ, conceptualized as the prophet of the Kingdom of God, combatting the evil of an almost Satanic world. Obviously it would be over-interpreting your work to see it as a commentary on these theological issues, but they are clearly implied in all your responses to secular modernity, when, sensing acutely that politico-ethical ideals could not be derived from material facts, you sought your answers in a radical re-interpretation of the Christian message.

Some scholars like to imply that only people who were poorly educated -- working-class people like you, I guess -- were drawn to Spencer. According to Richard Hofstadter, the historian who was most responsible for a vastly expanded and unusable definition of "Social Darwinism," Spencer wrote "in language that tyros in philosophy could understand," and thus became "the metaphysician of the homemade intellectual, and the prophet of the cracker-barrel agnostic."[41] Translation: know-nothings and country bumpkins who did their thinking around cracker-barrels might fall for Spencer, whereas *real* duly-certified thinkers (no doubt like Professor Hofstadter) had the taste and discrimination to avoid him! Nonsense. Did John Stuart Mill, or Charles Darwin, or hundreds of other Eminent Victorians acquire their knowledge of and admiration for Spencer around the cracker-barrel?[42] (John Stuart Mill as a regular in the old corner store: the mind boggles!). Weren't agnostics to be found in nineteenth-century laboratories as well as around cracker-barrels? And weren't *many* intellectuals in these days before the full twentieth-century professionalization of scholarship self-trained?

So much for Hofstadter's snobbish dismissal of the Spencerians; but the same point, more subtly, comes through in Mark Pittenger's much better and more recent discussion of evolutionary socialism in the United States. He argues that "nervous middle-class readers who felt themselves buffeted by social and economic change" would find themselves comforted in "an all-encompassing explanatory schema, easily reducible to a few stock phrases and lending scientific sanction to a reasssuring faith in inevitable progress...."[43] Spencerian socialism seems, on this account, a byproduct of a strange kind of middle-class metaphysical neurasthenia. But how much sense does this make? Would nervous, marginal people, their frail little belief-structures under attack by capitalist modernity, really be inclined to adopt the most revolutionary and secular belief-structure available to them, in a wholesale rejection of their prior tradition? And, if we look at the evidence, does this label "middle-class" really get us anywhere, in understanding people like Jack London or the founders of the Socialist Party of Canada or W.U. Cotton or you? Curious: Hofstadter dumps on the Spencerians because they've (metaphorically) got dirt under their fingernails, and Pittenger is on their case because they're fidgety middle-class neurotics. The eye of history can be critical indeed.

(You' ll be glad to know, assuming that in eternity you're still somewhat sympathetic to Spencer, that there have been some exceptions to this Spencer-bashing. One recent discussion of Spencer's anticipation of systems-theory argues that his ideas are still useful and relevant,[44] and that he pioneered the functional analysis of general systems, wherein lies his lasting contribution. It was only by forgetting this "systems-theory" aspect of Spencer that his critics were able to misinterpret "survival of the fittest" as a prescription that fit individuals rather than whole societies.[45] Sociologists habitually cite Durkheim when they want to legitimate a structural-functional analysis, and blithely overlook Spencer's more complete, complex and earlier development of the framework.[46] Yet those sociologists who actually take the trouble to read Spencer often report a sense of surprise at the cogency of what they find).

If we elect to discard the "cracker-barrel" hypothesis, we might begin to explain the appeal of Spencerian philosophy to so many working-class people by looking a bit harder at the thought of Herbert Spencer himself. For one of the stranger ironies of the way this discussion has proceeded among left historians is that the same people who have been so emphatic in their claims that socialists misread Darwin in a simplistic and one-sided way, then give us a version of Spencer that is nothing but simplistic and one-sided. They are content to dismiss the entirety of Spencer's thought as straightforwardly reactionary -- it apparently reduces to the simplistic and dangerous application of biological analogies to social process and the most reactionary interpretation of "the survival of the fittest." An anti-feminist and Social Darwinist, Spencer was simply the unintelligent, right-wing vulgarizer of Darwin. Spencer was also the perverter of innocent Marxists, whom he turned off the founders' true path into the thickets of eugenics, evolutionary socialism, sexism, imperialism and racism. That so many working-class and socialist theorists gravitated to him in an earlier age tells us a lot about their lack of education, their anti-modern anxieties, their gullibility, their hostility to women, their shallow grasp of historical development, and (above all) the superficiality of their Marxism. Shallow people gravitated to a shallow thinker: serious socialist thought in North America only began when the "Vogue for Spencer" had ended.

Although, in some specific respects, this position is just plain inaccurate -- a outright misrepresentation of what was in fact the case -- my primary objection to it lies in its polemical *one-sidedness*. It is a desperately one-dimensional interpretation. It assumes that there was only "one true way" to appropriate Spencer, and thereby diminishes the creativity and resourcefulness of his many working-class disciples.

Now since, as I've said, everybody who has read this "open letter" has nicely (or otherwise) told me to cut down on the Spencer, I'll keep my refutation of the received view as brief as possible (and put a lid on my outraged indignation). After all, what matters for me is *not* the reputation of Spencer, but the reputation of working-class Spencerian Marxists like you. What we need to prove is *not* that Spencer has been cruelly misrepresented, but that his writings were susceptible to many divergent and plausible interpretations. After all, if the received view is correct, then you stand convicted of being as lame-brained as your "cracker-barrel"

Master. But if Spencer was more than the received wisdom allows, then you -- and many, many other Canadian socialists -- deserve a more favourable hearing. Perhaps you were even cleverly constructing a kind of "reverse discourse," appropriating concepts drawn from a very influential philosophy of your time and playing them against the very politico-economic framework which they were supposed to strengthen. That, in fact, is just what I am going to say that you did.

Briefly, the received wisdom about Spencer is that he was a "Social Darwinist," who perverted Darwin's theory of natural selection by applying it to society. The refutation of this notion can be put quite summarily:

• *It is a myth to say Spencer vulgarized Darwin or turned good Marxists off a well-marked Marxist path*. There was no scientifically established "Theory of Evolution" that scientists had worked out and which Spencer then "distorted" or "misapplied." Spencer's first evolutionary writings antedated the publication of *Origin of Species*; and Darwinian and Spencerian theories of evolution were not the same (Spencer's theory was much more Lamarckian than Darwinian -- he gave up with the greatest reluctance on the notion of the inheritance of acquired characteristics). Spencer, then, did not just "borrow" from Darwin or try to "Darwinize" social reality: he was an independent force in evolutionary theory. He did not want to "biologize" the study of society so much as he wanted to uncover the essential processes by which both nature and society evolved. It is therefore misleading and unfair to call Spencer a "Social Darwinist."

• *It is a myth to believe that Spencer's theory was clearly inferior to that of Darwin*. In fact, Spencer's was probably the most comprehensive and consistent body of evolutionary social theory available. In many respects, Spencer was more suited to the underlying project of Proletarian Enlightenment: Darwin gave you a rather diminished sense of human possibility in a cosmos characterized by contingency, whereas Spencer presented a teleological vision of humanity attaining a "social state," characterized by peace, order, and good (i.e. minimal) government. The socialist attraction to Spencer was thus perfectly logical. He gave socialists Evolution, but one which was more purposive and future-oriented than the process of natural selection emphasized by Darwin, with its unavoidable and disquieting emphasis on the sheer brute fact of survival.

• *It is a myth to believe that there was an obviously "correct" socialist response to evolutionary thought*. All the readers of Darwin's work, and *especially* his working-class and socialist readers, confronted the flexibility of his doctrine of evolution and the ambiguity of many of his explanations: what followed from Darwin's work was in no way obvious.[47] To emphasize only the reactionary implications (eugenics, intensified racism towards the First Nations, etc.) is one-sided. It is fair to say that

Darwinism opened up the prospect of separating the study of humankind from that of nature;[48] and that Spencer's systematic system was one of the greatest, most brilliant and most determined attempts to prevent the intellectual universe from shattering into fragments under the weight of the great new evolutionary insights. (There had to be one process, everywhere, at all times present: there simply *had* to be).[49] Marx and Engels are a good illustration of how leading intellectuals of the day felt they had to respond to the force of evolutionary arguments. But they were simply all over the map in their attempt to work out a convincing response to scientific evolutionary theory. There was (and is) no "Marxist tradition" to provide sure, "scientific" guidance on these matters.[50]

• *It is wrong to see Spencer as a philosopher for the simple-minded. Spencer -- even if not read today -- had a major influence on modern social thought.* Spencer was a well-regarded thinker of his time -- in the eyes not just of Hofstadter's cracker-barrel yokels, but in those of John Stuart Mill, Alfred Wallace, and countless others. He was well-regarded, in part, for good reasons. As you knew well, Colin, Spencer's *The Study of Sociology* is mainly a cautious and sensible book about how to conduct social investigation. Philip Abrams -- who describes the field of sociology in late-Victorian Britain as constituting itself largely in a reaction against Spencer -- nonetheless observes: "In many ways, ...the contemporaneity of Spencer, like his achievement, is astounding. *The Study of Sociology*, with its treatment of social institutions as ossified social forces, of history as a process of mutual aggression and defense among forces and institutions, its coordination of structure and function, its analysis of the nature of social facts, its masterly working out of the flow of unanticipated consequences, its conception of functional differentiation as the defining attribute of modernity, its elaborate account of the intellectual hazards of sociological inquiry, is perhaps the most successful textbook of general sociology yet produced in Britain."[51] It is quite true that Spencer sometimes used far-fetched biological analogies that, to a modern ear, are unintentionally comic.[52] On the other hand, so did everybody else, Marx included.[53] Other Spencerian metaphors (structure, function, differentiation) were to enjoy real staying power in social thought: we still use them today. Whether modern scholars like it or not, Spencer not only should be remembered as a founding figure in sociology, but also of social history, development studies, systems analysis, and other disciplines. Spencer's admittedly quite pronounced rightward drift in later years (and the shadow that Fascism cast over all political uses of evolutionary theory) have led historians to overlook his lasting contributions to the human sciences; but Spencer's ungrateful academic inheritors are everywhere.

• *It is a myth to believe that Spencerian socialists were necessarily of a reformist bent.* Although there was no mid-nineteenth-century "Marxist tradition" of analysis on the question of Evolution, there was a massive socialist conversion to the Darwinian perspective later in the century. Both *revolutionary* Marxists (e.g. Lenin) and *evolutionary* Marxists (Plekhanov) were *evolutionary* in stressing the possibility of a unified theory that could explain developments from the level of the cell to the level of the cosmos. The *theory of social evolution* was to be preserved virtually intact in Soviet Dialectical Materialism, which preserved many essentially Spencerian attributes. Historians who suggest that *evolutionary theory* automatically and necessarily led to *evolutionary politics* are simply in error.

• *It is a myth that Spencer was simply a reactionary.* In his youthful works, he was a radical libertarian whose sympathies were with the Chartists, the land reformers, and the democrats. The startling fact is that the very Spencer who attracted the working-class thinkers like Wallace (the co-discoverer of natural selection who went so far as to name his son Herbert Spencer Wallace)[54] Sam Gompers[55] and the anarchist Joseph Labadie and yourself *was in many respects a radical*: radical in his basic philosophy, radical in his method, radical in his findings, radical in his family background. Here the level of falsification has been high indeed. Educated "on the extreme wing of Dissent, in an austere Unitarianism, indissolubly welded to an iron individualism,"[56] Spencer carried with him all his life an acute distrust of the established church, the landlord class, and everything else associated with "Old Corruption." He came from a *radical* background -- *radical* both in the sense that this term has in European political history (this is, of *radical liberalism*) but also in a more general intellectual sense (i.e., of or pertaining to the doctrine that one must go to the very roots of a phenomenon one wants to change). Here was an inheritance of radicalism that would push the young Spencer into the debate over disestablishment of the Church of England and also into association with radical political economists at *The Economist*.[57] Spencer sympathized with the democratic demands of the Chartists, and spoke in the levelling, no-nonsense, practical tone of the more radical Mechanics' Institutes. Both Spencer and his friend Thomas Hodgskin, the Ricardian socialist whose *Labour Defended against the Claims of Capital* would later so deeply influence Marx, could consider themselves *radicals*, united in a common cause against privilege, corruption, and the established church.[58]

• *In fact, an examination of his earliest and (from a radical perspective) best book,* Social Statics*, reveals the young Spencer's deep affinities with anarchism.* This is not my own idiosyncratic judgment: many knowledgeable anarchists (Prince Kropotkin, among others) thought Spencer was an anarchist, too.[59] *Social Statics* outlines a vision of necessary progress staggering in its sweep and breathtaking in its moral absolutism.[60] For Martin Eden, Jack London's fictional seafaring hero,[61] and for you, a real-life seafaring socialist worker, books like *Social Statics* swept you up into a great vision of equality, fairness, and natural law. This astonishing cosmic vision of betterment was intellectually satisfying in a way more cautious and less progressive Darwinism never was: here was a truly *revolutionary* vision of *Evolution*. To a sense of Evolution as foreordained Progress was coupled a fierce moral absolutism, a divinely-sanctioned drive to ethical perfection that spurns all tradition, all argument from authority, all the compulsions of the state. For Spencer, the law of equal freedom -- which says that society should be so structured that the liberty of each is assured, limited only by the like liberty of all -- is a divinely-ordained ideal, and should not be qualified. Certain political conclusions followed: the withering-away, and perhaps the total disappearance, of the state, which was after all only incidental to human development;[62] the securing of the rights of all those subordinated by patriarchal authority, including women[63] and also children; the end of compulsory education;[64] the achievement of peace through anti-militarism and quasi-pacifism;[65] respect for peoples other than the British;[66] and so on. Granting that the young Spencer also expresses little compassion for the halt and the weak, and sees society as being pervaded by a stern discipline, "which is a little cruel that it may be very kind,"[67] the consequences of his position could be surprising, especially given his "right-wing" reputation. Spencer even applies the right of equal freedom to the ownership of land, and concluded that private property in land should be abolished.[68] It is therefore a grave oversimplification simply to see Spencer as a reactionary -- unless one can conceive of mid-Victorian "reactionaries" who wanted to nationalize land and to bring in equal rights for women! It is in Spencer that we see how liberal assumptions, taken to their conclusions, can undermine a liberal framework altogether: *Social Statics* was quite logically taken up as a bible by elements on the extreme left.

• *It is then a myth to believe that workers who adopted Spencer as a radical inspiration were simply "misinterpreting" him.* There were substantial pro-working-class elements in Spencer's early thought. Working-class Spencerians were simply highlighting the radical parts which really were in the text, and quietly marginalizing the other elements. Here the charge of gross oversimplification falls, not on those workers who found radical arguments in *Social Statics*, but on those scholars who have depicted it as just another argument for *laissez-faire*.[69] If *Social Statics* may have led some middle-class Victorians to harsh policies towards the poor (they were going that way anyway), many more travelled from Spencer to utopian socialism, Marxism, anarchism, and the Single Tax of Henry George.

Let's sum up. We could analyze the impact of Spencer on working-class intellectuals like you under the somewhat awkward heading of the "four radicalisms":

• *Epistemological and Ontological Radicalism*: Spencer teaches that underlying the apparent solidity and stability of tangible things and perceptible events is an unceasing, powerful, universal, logical, comprehensible, and forward-moving process called Evolution. The existence of such a global process meant that the "things" we can know and our way of knowing them are subject to constant (but not random) change. Evolution is understood as a massive, universal, omnipresent, inescapable process shaping all things and all living beings at all times.[70] We are dealing here with both *realism* and *materialism*: a belief in the existence of an objective, law-governed material world independent of human perception, and a belief in society as a real entity, with definite properties, generating real social facts that are best explained in terms of other social facts. Spencer was not intent on "biologizing society": his project was the much more daring one of penetrating to the *essential logic of development* of both nature and society.[71] *One evolution going on everywhere in the same manner* -- here is a slogan that encompasses much of Spencer.[72]

• *Methodological radicalism*: the key thesis is that scientific answers to politico-ethical questions can be derived from the analysis of social facts without the necessity of invoking a Divine plan, a "human nature," or "Great Men." (In deliciously ironic fact, Spencer and not Marx is the original critic of what Marxists have traditionally called (without knowing they were citing Spencer) the "Great Man Theory of History.") Sociology, the value-free and scientific analysis of social evolution over time and across space provides an exclusively secular way of comprehending social life: it is based on the construction of rational frameworks of analysis which precedes the collection of individual facts, and the use of the comparative method across societies. Although it could never attain the exactitude of the physical sciences, Sociology could still be a science, for human beings had at least some capacity to predict social development.[73] This world of Sociology was a value-free, and consequently wholly secular, world. The Deism of *Social Statics* yielded to agnosticism and secularism in the later Spencer, whose works became notorious as abrasive critiques of religious hypocrisy.[74] Insofar as your "new philosophy of life" required a more secular approach to society, Spencer's sociology was the clear and obvious resource upon which to draw. Spencerian-Marxism was Dialectical Materialism *avant la lettre*: sweeping, cosmic, scientistic, capable of absorbing any and all factual or interpretive challenges, a profoundly contradictory but alluring body of theories providing knowledge of the past and a sense of certainty about the future.[75]

• *Economic and Social Radicalism*: the key thesis here is that individualism and self-sufficiency in economic life are the most appropriate conditions for the social organism. Most of Spencer's views were simply those of the mid-Victorian Cobdenite liberal universe, including opposition to state intervention in banking, support for a free labour market and free trade, and opposition to state reforms such as public health through improved sanitation, poor laws, state education, and so on. However, once one had followed Spencer and jettisoned the notion of an unchanging essential core, a "human nature," in human beings, and accepted that humans varied extraordinarily "in instincts, in morals, in opinions, in tastes, in rationality, in everything,"[76] it also became much harder to reify liberal-capitalist social relations as the *only* possible decent arrangements that human beings could come up with: why shouldn't human political institutions be as variegated as human natures? Insofar as skepticism towards party politics, representative government, and corruption are "radical," then one could say Spencer, well into his career, was a radical influence in that specific sense. And he is also a "radical" insofar as the Spencerian utopia, like the Marxian realm of freedom, is a place of the utmost spontaneity and freedom.[77] Contrary to legend, Spencer did not admire the methods of big business, nor did he sympathize with militarism: neither of these so-called "Social Darwinist" traits can be accurately attributed to him.[78] The point is this: the socialists and working-class intellectuals who drew from evolutionary theory conclusions totally opposed by the increasingly reactionary Spencer were not "misreading" Spencer so much as they were reconstructing him, and (many scholars would say) thereby making their conclusions more consistent with his premises.

• *Political Radicalism*: the key Spencerian political thesis is that the state serves virtually no useful function and in most cases acts as an illegitimate barrier to the expression of the rights of the individual. We cannot predict the consequences of any political act or any piece of legislation: the results anticipated from any law are greatly exceeded by the results not anticipated. Today's right-wingers may quite justifiably base themselves on *The Man Versus the State*, with its long lists of ill-fated government interventions and failures. (Its standard of rhetoric is much higher than those normally attained in their work, and it might set these neo-liberal philistines a good example). However, a left-wing socialist like you could also find some things here of interest. You could draw from Spencer the additional insight that any explanation of the social order had to start not with an examination of high politics but with an understanding of political economy. It was foolish for dreamers and idealists to try to change the world without studying economic realities. The opponents of the political economists needed to calm down and realize that society, like nature, could be understood scientifically; that "out of the properties of men, intellectual and emotional, there inevitably arise certain laws of social processes, including, among others, those through which mutual aid in satisfying wants is made possible."[79] The Spencerian message to socialists, then, could be quite similar to the message they also picked up from Marx: to change capitalism, one had to understand its laws; without social science, there could be no effective social revolution; without a genuine social revolution, no legislature in the world could "enact" socialism. Moreover (and this must have made intuitive sense to many working-class people) there was no point in idealizing the state as the "voice of the community" as so many new liberals were apt to do. For many workers, the state was most directly experienced at the end of a policeman's truncheon and in front of an electrified barbed-wire fence around a strike-bound coal mine. Workers who had been round the block with Mackenzie King and his new liberal labour legislation might well look with considerable caution at schemes for a greatly expanded state, rightly suspecting in many instances that workers might be further ahead with a smaller state and a fighting chance against the capitalist enemy.[80] And they might read *The Man Versus The State* with the respect one accords a tough-minded analysis prepared by a man who has become one's enemy.

You just can't read *Social Statics* without noticing that Spencer wrote biting, lively attacks on the social world around him, that he was an apostle of an unflinching moral extremism, and that he was fearless in applying his principles. If that is so, then what becomes of all the things contemporary historians write that (gently or otherwise) make fun of workers for being influenced by Spencer? I think they tell us more about the ways in which scholars travel in packs, lazily repeating academic folk wisdom -- and never going back to the original sources! Everybody seems quite willing to pontificate about the bad influence of Spencer without ever reading a word of Spencer himself. Or they just make simplistic readings of the later Spencer --*The Man Versus The State* -- and treat that as *the* Spencerian statement. But if this body of writing was much more complicated and ambiguous, is it not possible that, rather than being duped by Spencer, workers were reading *intelligently, adapting* (shall we say) this massive intellectual *organism* to their own proletarian *struggle for existence?* What if you were exercising the same qualities of skepticism and independence in your relationship with the Master that characterized your work in general?

There is no claim here that Spencer would have agreed with the radical interpretations made in his name; indeed, we know that he went out of his way to denounce the working-class autodidacts who were making use of his framework.[81] This does not prove that the workers were "misreading" him. *There is no necessary, automatic identity between what an author writes, the readers receive, and posterity remembers.* For many interpreters, those who concluded from Spencer's doctrine of Evolution that a greater degree of state planning and social cohesion was necessary, in view of the much higher levels of functional and structural integration and differentiation demanded by the new "social state," were more logical than those who tried to cobble together traditional Victorian liberalism with what would appear to have been a decidedly post-individualist framework of social and economic thought. Certainly the "Spencer" socialists constructed (over the outraged protests of the actual Spencer) enjoyed an intellectual influence that long outlasted that of the man himself. We are just starting to realize how massive and long-lasting the impact of Spencer was on the Canadian and American left.[82]

So much for the stereotype of Spencer. So completely has the philosopher-sociologist's reputation collapsed, however, that anything that looks remotely like a *defence* of Spencer encounters entrenched skepticism, even hostility. Nothing I can say will convince those who have, all their adult lives, demonized the poor man. So persisting skeptics should put this letter down, go to the library, and check out *Social Statics.* (Avoid the massive, unread pile of the "synthetic philosophy," unless you want a melancholy reminder of the tragicomic results of encyclopaedic obsession. At Queen's, some of these heavy volumes had not been checked out since 1910! And there's a good reason for that!) Then, once you've spent three or four hours with *Social Statics,* I think you'll see what I mean -- and why a succession of British and North American radicals found Spencer the key intellectual to argue with and against as they thought about property and power in a fast-changing society.

Now we need to go further to get the true measure of the complexity with which you responded to Spencerian ideas. It's really important to watch *how* you turn-of-the-century working-class intellectuals were using Spencer, and in particular which books of Spencer were emphasized above others. It's very useful for people looking at Spencerian socialists to get a handle on *which texts* of Spencer were the most influential.

It is of the utmost significance to me, Colin, that *Social Statics* was *the* book for you, the one from which you quoted at length.[83] In doing this, you were turning not just to the Spencer of Evolution, but to the Spencer of transcendental ethical critique. Spencer's stands on particular issues, his personal nonconformity, his belief in a sense of right or wrong that had survived the eviction of the Almighty from most systems of social explanation, his vision of an urgent need to understand social evolution and thereby help society adjust to it: this is a politico-ethical thread that cannot simply be reduced to a cosmic philosophy for the poorly educated and the gullible. Subsequent scholars who missed (or underestimated) this moral strand in working-class Spencerianism were missing something very, very important. You read Spencer intelligently, non-fatalistically, selectively, even skeptically. Certainly, in your work, "social evolution" has an imperative, moral dimension, and it does so right down to 1939. However, when Spencer's subsequent writings conflicted with the ethical position of *Social Statics,* you (along with Henry George) objected. You were not a passive recipient of the thoughts of others, but the active shaper of your own theoretical sensibility. The "Spencer" you constructed in your mind was thus infinitely more interesting and complicated than the "Spencer" routinely denounced in the strange stories historians of socialism have woven about these times.

Any suggestion that there was something like a necessary connection between "evolutionism" in philosophy and "evolutionism" in politics seems to overlook the very complicated and various ways in which theory is received, not to mention a huge volume of empirical evidence.[84]

I know, when I write this, that I'm being somewhat biased. I'm looking in your work for an intelligent, two-sided relationship with theory, and there is much evidence of it. But let's be honest: if I were intently compiling a "brief for the prosecution," and searching for reductionism, vulgar determinism, scientism, etc.etc., I'd find lots of those things, too. It would be fair enough, for example, to say that you often go from a theory in natural science directly to an observation about society (a very Spencerian habit). Yet even in such cases, which have been amply denounced in the Western Marxist literature for over forty years (to the point of monotony: *Telos* take note) we find some interesting complications. Often you wanted to find in natural science ways of restoring to the "inscrutable" world of Evolution a measure of human purpose and agency. A prime example is the way you cite the biologist De Vries [§.30, "Socialism as the Science of Evolution"]. Sure, we can legitimately cite this as yet another awful example of "Second International Marxism," plundering science as usual. Personally, however, I find it more interesting to notice that what you were looking for from De Vries was a scientific argument *against* fatalism. As Spencer himself almost said, when one person looks at the work of another, pre-existing desires and theoretical frameworks will have much to do with what is seen and what is overlooked.[85]

You working-class intellectuals were not "seduced" or "misled" or "beguiled" by Spencer. You used him, and quite consciously. You deliberately reconstructed his thought, and cited him as a cultural authority for opinions he himself would not have held. On issues that directly touched the well-being of Canadian working people, such as the relief of poverty or the health and safety of people at work, you never followed Spencer's anti-statist line. At the very time you were ingesting the laissez-faire verities of Spencer, you were also fighting for improved factory inspection in Quebec!

I'm arguing that working-class intellectuals like you exercised creativity and discretion in how you "constructed" and "reconstructed" the European theorists you studied so zealously.[86] And we see this most clearly, Colin, in your own radical theory of working-class culture. By shifting the responsibility for directing social evolution on to the shoulders of the working class, you in effect used a Spencerian social language of organicism to provide "scientific" justification for the traditional Marxist exaltation of the proletariat as the universal class in waiting. (In such bodies as the Socialist Party of Canada and the Industrial Workers of the World, the resulting ideology sounded a bit like Spencer, a bit like Marx, and most of all like a daring attempt to appropriate, reconstruct, and hence completely subvert the discourse of evolution.)[87] The "Spencer" you reconstituted as an authority for the left was, one might almost say, the new version of Paul, preaching a gospel of connection and solidarity. And if (as the beleaguered Master kept complaining) this militant (r)evolutionary prophet bore little resemblance to the actual Spencer of the 1890s, he nonetheless did bear a strong resemblance to the young Spencer, that firebrand who hammered out, for all places and all time, an inflexible standard of morality in *Social Statics*. Again and again, you, Phillips Thompson,[88] William Irvine,[89] and many other Canadian radicals came back to these powerful, "scientific" metaphors of connection and belonging. Spencerian evolution, this supposed source of callous "survival-of-the-fittest" rhetoric, was on the extreme left key to the development of a scientific (and hence respectable) counter-liberal socialist discourse of community, solidarity, and progress.

There was quite simply no automatic connection between the theory of Evolution and a specific political trajectory, whether on the left or on the right. (Evolutionary theory, Pittenger notes, could even be called on to justify the assassination of Czar Alexander II, who could be considered a diseased organ requiring excision.)[90] There was no *necessary* correspondence between an element in evolutionary theory and a political idea: no necessary class-affiliation or political identity came stamped on the back of such evolutionary ideas as "function" or "structure" or "organ," and no necessarily conservative or reactionary "charge" necessarily accompanied the language of organicism. Most early twentieth-century political *revolutionaries* were *evolutionary* in their underlying conception of the social and natural world.

To conclude this section on Spencer: working-class Spencerians like you were not dupes. You were able to borrow, adapt and re-configure the Spencerian legacy according to your own sense of constructing a "unified field of human knowledge." This was not a *misreading* but in many respects a logical and consistent reading of the social implications of Spencerianism.[91] Rather than stupidly misinterpreting Spencer, Colin, it seems you were in good company in trying to make him more consistent. As David Wiltshire puts it, "Spencerian evolution, developed to account scientifically for the postulates of individualism, entails social and ethical conclusions which contradict it, and leads to a vision of society in which individualism has no place."[92] The only weak defence Spencer could offer against T.H. Huxley's critique -- that if the resemblances between the body politic and the body physiological are any indication, "the real force of the analogy is totally opposed to the negative view of State function" -- was to concede a cardinal difference between the individual and the social organism, a concession so substantial that some felt it represented the abandonment of the core of his entire program.[93]

It is thus grossly one-sided simply to present the rise of Spencerian Marxism as a morality tale in which socialists "fall prey to the Spencerian cosmic evolutionism and teleological optimism," without considering the extent to which these socialists also *reconstructed and selectively applied* the Spencerian tradition in their own work.[94] Working-class socialists like you were more than just prey, and this Perils-of-Pauline narrative is patronizing and *passé.*

•

Now it gets tricky, because, having said all that, I want to add that I just can't think the way you thought. This inability on my part is obviously a reflection of how a Marxist late in the century looks at life differently than a Marxist of the early twentieth century. Still, I really don't think your framework can ever be revived in its original form, and it is interesting to explore why this might be so. From a position late in the century, I look at your confidence in Evolution, Science, and Progress, and your program for the Proletarian Enlightenment, with a certain amount of sadness. It will be a very long time before the traumatized survivors of the twentieth century will ever share your necessitarian optimism. I am as sure that your holistic evolutionary outlook can no longer guide politico-ethical life, as you were absolutely positive that it must. In this respect, I confess I cannot without a certain sense of irony enter into the hopes and ideals you summed up in that grand phrase "social evolution." Tragically, a human being has no choice about being "afterwards."

You saw one great Evolution and one scientific logic: politics and scientific discovery were closely aligned. (The One Big Union, one might say, could draw upon the truths of the One Big Science). Unfortunately or otherwise, not many philosophers of science and not many natural scientists believe that there is in fact only one "scientific logic" in the natural sciences, nor much likelihood of a universal integration of scientific knowledge. And when we move outside the hard sciences, I am even less sure about what the One Big Science would look like. The "disciplining" of knowledge, the explosion of information, the incommensurability of paradigms: all of these place a question mark over your implicit goal of a unified evolutionary theory covering all of natural and social life. We live differently nowadays. We breathe a different air. "I have written the definitive, final version of the History of Canada, based upon the scientific method and a thorough examination of *all* the facts:" the historian who wrote that sentence today would not be commended for her industry but scorned for her positivism and her arrogance. Implicitly historians (even those who, like me, are drawn to a realist epistemology) long ago accepted the fact that they can at best write contingent, conditional and qualified versions of the "truth." Whatever we historians *say* about truth, especially in polemics with post-structuralist nominalists, we *act* as if the historical truth, like Marx's realm of freedom, is simultaneously real and not-real, something that cannot ever be fully attained, yet which we can continually use as a transcendent measure of what our own work should, but cannot, be. And this is, I think, a local example of a more general phenomenon. Across many fields of endeavour and enquiry today, there is an unbridgeable chasm between the certainties of evolutionary socialists like you and the world of the left in the 1990s. Respectfully exploring your side of the chasm does not mean, in the end, that I can ever cross over and join you there.

And make no mistake: on your side of the great divide, I find much that I admire. You Spencerian Marxists had a tremendous sense of holism, a sense of being part of a massive process of evolution, one process, pushing onwards, everywhere and in all times, on the street corner and in the stars. You were certain that this process of evolution -- Natural Selection and Social Adaptation -- was a proven scientific fact. And this certainty would be, if anything, strengthened in the Marxist-Leninist tradition which succeeded you and which also (if more discretely) took out massive loans from Spencer, even as it denounced his life and work. Dialectical materialism no less than Spencerian Marxism was filled with this cosmic certainty. In its name epistemological positions and hypotheses about historical development were hypostatized into quasi-religious doctrines and placed beyond any realistic strategy of empirical validation.[95] At the same time, this sense of a cosmos driven by Evolution (or by the Dialectic) to an ever higher order of complexity enriched individual lives and endowed fragmented experiences with a sense of meaning. The necessity of progress, the possibility of knowing the destination of History-with-a-capital-H: these are powerful ideas to have on one's side. I'd even go so far as to say that our incredulity towards such master-narratives is a poor politico-ethical substitute for putting something meaningful in their place.

But I also find, on your side of the divide, much that I would criticize. Viewed from a neo-Marxist perspective of the 1990s (and I concede that this perspective is one that will some day also seem full of paradoxes and curiosities) there were substantial costs entailed with so whole-hearted an adoption of evolutionism. Class and class struggle, central to any Marxian approach that could be effective in the modern era, *are not dignified with any causal importance in the Spencerian universe.* In your work, and in much early CP and CCF thought, there is a rather abstract quality to the discussion of class and class conflict. I used to be puzzled by this: why was it that, when we look back over (say) the great class war in the Nova Scotia coalfields of 1909-11, we find not one sustained, serious analysis from the large Marxist left? Now I think I at last can understand why: this disregard for the specificity and complexity of the local and particular stemmed from your confidence in evolutionary theory. Why bother with an exacting analysis of the empirical details, if the general pattern is always already known with certainty? In this way, although you were hardly the prisoner of Spencer, you unknowingly did incorporate into your own reconstruction of him elements that in the long term could only be highly problematical for the "new philosophy of life."

More fundamentally, I'm struck by the limited explanatory value of the theory. I don't mean that I think a social science should work with the same precision and emphasis on prediction as natural science; I mean, rather, that so general and sweeping a concept of social evolution did not readily lend itself to historically specific investigations. "Adaptation" is really too vague and all-embracing a notion to work in this capacity.[96] "Organicism" is equally vague and/or misleading as a model of society, however powerful it may have been as a source of politico-ethical metaphors.[97] Likewise with the efflorescence of "culture" as a way of explaining social evolution and even the particularities of personalities: such concepts as "culture" and "personality," handled in this Spencerian way, become generic abstractions about things in general, not determinate abstractions about concrete realities in particular. Like all the abstractions shaped by Evolution, the method began with what all epochs have in common, and came only later to their differences: thus the specifics or particulars were always subordinated to the general and generic.[98] Spencerian *Naturphilosophie* first convinced converts they held the key to the universe, and it then let them down when they tried to use that key to open up the more proximate mysteries of the social world around them. Evolution was a fertile and powerful source of metaphors and politico-ethical critique; but only to the extent that socialists were able to develop more powerful and focused abstractions were they able to grasp the specifics of the liberal capitalist order.

•

How am I doing, walking that fine line between passing judgment and warm-hearted-sentimentality? I'm trying to say that I can really see Spencer's huge drawing power for you, and I can see how Spencerianism contributed to the intoxicating, brilliant vision you had of a working-class culture that itself could master Evolution and shape it for a revolutionary, emancipatory purpose. To some extent, I think that vision is one which still lives on, and which is, even yet, one I and others should try to recapture. But it will have to be recaptured in another, non-deterministic, way. We don't -- forgive us, but we really *just can't* -- believe any more in an inevitable progress of history, in a process of Social Evolution that is leading humanity ineluctably forward and to which human beings must adapt. We breathe a different air. (When we postmoderns read Darwin, the first thing we notice is the sheer contingency, the sheer *meaninglessness* in conventional terms, of natural selection.)[99] If we have regretfully stopped thinking that One Big Union can change everything in the world, we -- or at least, I suspect, most of those who continue to see ourselves as continuing the socialist project -- have also stopped believing in the One Big Science that can explain it.[100]

Certainly in the early years of this century, your belief in this "One Big Science" was evident in virtually everything socialist you wrote. Even when you are discussing other authorities, there is a Spencerian undertone. Spencerian biological metaphors and "scientism" were echoed in your enthusiasm for the criminologist Ferri, the least admirable of the many European intellectuals you promoted in Canada.[101] Spencerian materialism could also be found in your depiction of Dietzgen (right down to the mid-1930s!) as *the* socialist philosopher of cognition, who had finally solved the mysteries of the mind. Darwinian necessitarianism was advanced when you promoted Kautsky as the leading authority on party organization and class alliance. And a very Spencerian spin was put on Engels, whose amazingly popular *Socialism: Utopian and Scientific* proposed a very un-Marxian, very Spencerian equation of freedom and necessity.[102] In brief, we find ourselves in many of your first writings on socialism imprisoned in a universe whose entire history -- "from the cell to socialism," as Colletti acidly remarks[103] -- can be explained by a comprehensive theory of evolution.

The "new philosophy of life", the "new culture" meant, concretely, some specific philosophical positions. First of all, a "hard" materialism: Matter first, ideas second. Look first to the base, then to the superstructure. Humans must eat before they organize political parties. These formulae used to dazzle the converted, but after a century of debate, I suspect that many people realize they solve precisely nothing. (Now if only more late twentieth-century minds would show the same skepticism about claims regarding the omnipresence and *inscrutable* power of language!) In my view, such materialist monism abolished vital distinctions necessary for the project (even the very concept) of human emancipation. Marxian Evolutionism confused, in the most reckless manner, realism and materialism (this is probably Engels's least beneficial contribution to socialist thought).[104] And it's interesting, don't you think, that nobody has ever really managed to follow such hard-core materialism consistently in actual political analysis? No matter how hard-boiled they tried to be, Marxists kept bringing up wispy things like values and ideas and emotions when they finally got down to talking politics. I wish, Colin (and I admit that it is ahistorical to wish this) that before you'd bought so heavily into this so-called "materialism," you had read all the fine print ("Well, of course, I only meant....in the *final analysis, a tendency working itself out over the millennia, ideas themselves become material forces* [which obviously undermines the entire position, if it is to mean anything at all], *the primacy of class as an ultimate precondition of capitalism, not as something people talk about or think about every day...*".) Even today, many believe that the true Marxist *has* to have a total theory of the universe, in which "matter" is primary: that such a theory is as unprovable and mystical as anything to be found in religion bothers them not at all. (How could anyone ever possibly *know* in advance that in all places and at all times in this or in all other universes, "ideas" and "matter" interact in a predetermined way?) This way of thinking about Marxism takes it to be a total and totalizing theory: there is (or should be) a "Marxist" position on the nature of the molecule, the future of Christianity, the question of Québec independence, and every other topic under the sun. I'm not sure if this is an Absolute Materialism or an Absolute Idealism.[105] I am convinced that it's Absolute Dogmatism, and (I'm sorry, Colin) for most purposes, Absolute Futility. I mean no offence, but Marxists who pretended to have solved all the philosophical issues that have confronted people for at least thirty centuries made themselves look more than a little ridiculous. A Marxist who adheres to the Trotskyist line on radioactivity or the Stalinist position on language or -- closer to your heart -- the Dietzgenian position on brain chemistry, was most often behaving like a dilettante: taking a position on radioactivity and linguistics and brain chemistry that he or she really had not researched or intensively thought through. And how today, under conditions of the knowledge explosion, could even the most formidable team ever attempt such breath-taking feats of intellectual synthesis as would be required for a serious, non-superficial, totalizing Science?

Taken as a guide to the study of actual history, Spencerian evolutionism (and its unacknowledged and world-historic offspring, via Plekhanov: Soviet Dialectical Materialism) meant that the activist or the scholar knew most of the answers in advance of any concrete research or *praxis*. As Lucio Colletti remarks (with specific reference to Kautsky but I think his words can be applied to your whole tradition): in such work history and nature are simply "seen as two particular moments of the genus 'evolution.' There is no grasp in his work of the displacement or reversal by which in history what was once fundamental or specific becomes secondary or generic, and, on the contrary, what was once particular or generic develops into an essential or specific characteristic." Social life -- for Kautsky and Ferri certainly -- comes to be considered a specification of the instinct of self-preservation; "it is never characterized by the *exclusion* of the characteristics of this struggle at other levels, and their replacement by basically new or historical-human characteristics which subordinate the older characteristics to them. Instead, the new elements are *added* to the original ones, which thus remain fundamental."[106] In Kautsky, Colletti argues, "production and social relations, material and ideological relations, are... disposed in a chronological series, as *before* and *after*. Nature and history are reseparated; the necessary reference to the present moment is lost and consequently we are left with nothing but a *philosophy of history*."[107]

Evolution as a historical abstraction generated such vacuous generalities as "adaptation" and "the struggle for existence" and "societal instinct" and "functional integration," none of which could possibly be of sustained use for workers struggling to understand and overthrow the liberal capitalist order. (After all, what in human experience couldn't be considered as "an adaptation"?) What your new philosophy of life, your new culture really required were the *determinate abstractions* of Marx, generated through a process of logico-empirical investigation into the necessary and sufficient conditions of possibility of specific social phenomena. It was precisely these determinate abstractions -- social formation, social labour, surplus value, class, class conflict, the realm of freedom -- that "cosmic socialism " (to borrow Rée's useful phrase) tended to obscure.[108] I am struck by the extent to which, working through an imposing galaxy of socialist writers and thinkers,[109] you came by the 1930s to emphasize the history of political economy, which gave you very different conceptual resources for your quite astonishing writings on Social Credit as a displaced form of socialist utopianism. The new emphasis on the critique of political economy (which one might suggest is the proper focus for a Marxist) in your 1930s work, and your imaginative, detailed use of the history of political economy, are signs both of your ability to grow intellectually even as you entered the final decade of your life, but also of an erosion of the seamless universe of "cosmic socialism."

However, for all these indications of a change in your intellectual direction in the 1930s, anticipated by your detailed investigations before then, would you think me unfair to suggest that even in the later works you never really internalized the logico-historical principle of determinate abstraction that is the principal methodological innovation of Marx? As I read them, your specific investigations of places and events are often somewhat vague and general in their description of massive, all-embracing trends, and then disarmingly anecdotal and relaxed in their treatment of specific historical evidence: a mixture of high abstraction and naive empiricism that many have found characteristic of cosmic evolutionary schemes and philosophies of history in general. (Thus, in your article on New Brunswick agriculture [§.66, "The New Brunswick Farmer"] we get Capitalism, Evolution, and the Labour Theory of Value on the one hand, and on the other, vague and casual comments about the social composition of the New Brunswick countryside). It often seems that this new philosophy of life did not really appreciate the need to explore the concrete historico-social conditions under which a given working class defined itself and, in a complicated, tentative, contradictory and open manner, began to articulate "interests" opposed to those of other people. Rather, class and class interests were essences, which could be discerned everywhere. Similarly, your "working-class culture" lacks a dynamic articulating principle which would allow us to grasp the relationship between its directly reflective role (as an expression of obvious and direct economic interests) and its dynamic role (as a world-view transcending such immediate interests in a philosophy of the whole of life anticipating socialism and, beyond that, the realm of freedom).

Outside the realm of class, these lacunae, even in the 1930s, are striking: you wrote often in *Le Monde Ouvrier* and Montreal was, I suspect, the city about which you dreamt at night: but where, in all your work, is there an acknowledgement of the French-Canadian fact? You lived in a federal state with many constitutional debates, but where is the constitution?[110] Even in the writings devoted to the working class and primary producers, *a priori* assumptions predominate to the extent of crowding out factual consideration of the empirical world.[111] Given such weaknesses, the "new philosophy of life" cannot be said to have been powerfully equipped to interpret Canadians' particular and increasingly complicated experience of twentieth-century modernity.

The most telling indication of weakness came in the 1930s, which should have sounded the death-knell of capitalism. Instead the decade signalled the demise of your "new philosophy of life." The project of the working-class Enlightenment rested on a gamble: the gamble that the Owl of Minerva could be forced to take flight sometime *before* dusk: that some definite patterns, grasped in theory, could then be changed through political struggle. Unfortunately, the new philosophy was unable to explain the Depression in a convincing way. It failed to connect very generalized Spencerian figures of the "dissolution" of functionally integrated systems, and the only somewhat less abstract Marxist discussions of the labour theory of value, to this *specific case* of economic collapse. This should have been the Finest Hour of the Marxist. It was, instead, the Day of the New Liberal.[112]

Make no mistake, you were brilliant at diagnosing the irrationalities of capitalism and original and incisive in your command of the history of socialist economic thought. But what I don't find in your Depression writings is a plausible, socialist economic alternative to the collapsing liberal capitalist order. Instead, there was a turn to new liberalism and Keynes. For years, Marxists like you had run up a massive account with the new liberals, borrowing freely from the works of Hobson in Britain or Ward in the United States. One might say that, in the 1930s, those debts came due with a vengeance. Keynesianism, dovetailing neatly with some traditional concerns of the left, and with a long left tradition of "underconsumptionist" analysis, effectively displaced Marxist approaches based on the labour theory of value.[113]

Of course, I'm running the risk of committing the "theoreticist fallacy" here. Many things besides problems in Marxist theory contributed to the triumph of the new liberalism. Realistically, we have to remember that, whatever impression is sometimes conveyed by our labour historiography, the Liberal Party has historically been the party most supported by Canadian workers: the roots of working-class liberalism in Canada run very deep, and time and again it is to the Liberal Party that many Canadian workers have looked when they felt endangered. (It is a measure of our wishful thinking that there is not one good monograph on working-class liberalism in Canada!) And beyond widespread allegiance to the Liberal Party is the subtle, pervasive, and powerful influence of the liberal order to which most Canadians owe their allegiance. The triumph of new liberalism on the left, in the CCF for example, was hardly surprising given the liberal assumptions prevalent even in the seemingly radical *Regina Manifesto.*[114] Even much of the Communist Party's cultural work, after the turn to the "united front" in 1935, tended to emphasize the "democratic struggles" of the "Canadian people" as much as the traditions specific to the working-class and socialist movement. (It is ironic, given your own transition to a pragmatic labour nationalism in the 1920s, that the CP itself moved in this same direction in the 1930s and 1940s: it showed immense creativity in developing a "reverse discourse" on the Canadian state, appropriating certain elements of the Canadian myth-symbol complex and using them for its own, radical purpose).[115] It is hardly surprising that Canadian radicals and socialists have generally succumbed to the enormous pressures of the liberal order that surrounds them. At the same time, it is telling that even at a time when the capitalist system was obviously in crisis, and even in intellectual contexts wide open to radical political economy, we see an open door to underconsumptionism and to Keynesianism.

Why? I see in this transition an underlying indication of weakness in the new working-class "philosophy of life." Once it emerged that Marxist approaches (as interpreted in your Spencerian tradition) did not address the *specific* logic of the depression, the new liberal theories of Keynes could be seen as plausible alternatives. Moreover, there was a curious fit between a Spencerian Marxism (which by virtue of its organicism was already halfway to new liberalism) and the new economics (emerging as it did from an underconsumptionism that had always seemed rather attractive to the left, especially in the British Labour Party).[116] Putting it baldly: in the depths of the worst economic catastrophe they had ever known, people needed both abstract explanations and real alternatives. However well your generation of Marxists worked out as editors, agitators, and union organizers (working in effect to force the liberal order to change -- to transform the very formulas of exploitation and surplus extraction by requiring a much higher level of state investment in health, education and welfare), you did not successfully generate convincing explanations of, or remedies for, the economic catastrophe. The new liberals seemed able to do so and ultimately carried the day, with the ruinous results that are all around us in the post-Keynesian 1990s.

The bitter irony is that the very postwar culture of consumption -- mass advertising, mass entertainment, mass meaninglessness -- that perhaps more than anything has undercut older proletarian traditions of resistance and the prospects of your "new philosophy of life," was in some measure aided and abetted by leftists who assented to the new liberal economics. Fixation on the economic sphere, on aggregate demand, and on *consumption*, meant that socialists had few defences against a new liberal economics and politics that simply promised more consumer goods and more efficient economic management. In embracing forms of economic analysis that privileged consumption over production, wealth over equity, and in saying yes to Keynes, the left to some extent signed its own death warrant.

Of course, I can't *prove* this. Perhaps it's not the sort of thing one ever could "prove." But I strongly suspect that the collapse of the prospects of the "new philosophy" had as much to do with intellectual failure as state repression. (Those who feel inclined to emphasize the role of state repression in containing the left might reflect that the severity of state violence in the 1930s did not match that of the previous two decades: think of the civil wars in the coalfields). Quite apart from the obvious deficiencies of Dialectical Materialism -- that mish-mash of contradictory evolutionary ideas that many in the 1930s would have taken to be *the* authoritative version of Marxism -- I am also thinking about a general sense of a widening gulf between Marxist intellectuals and their working-class audience.[117] I am thinking about a waning sense that the philosophical stance cherished by your generation of autodidacts was useful any more. Some of those who had so confidently written their obituaries of the liberal tradition lived to read their own obituaries as written by the new liberals, whose ideas became a pervasive commonsense of the postwar world.

Colin, I am not passing judgement on you, so much as trying to reflect on certain disabling habits of thought on the left. I personally think you were an exemplary figure in the 1930s. You struggled hard against "obvious" and trite responses to the Depression, and demanded of your readers that they think hard about the underlying economic pattern. Your response to Keynes's *General Theory of Employment, Interest, and Money* was measured and intelligent; you readily discerned the *radical* implications of a position that argued that economic equilibrium might exist at very low levels of activity.[118] (Would that the economists coming after you had been so discerning!) In cautiously welcoming Keynes, you were atypical on the left only in that you *generally* maintained your critical distance from him. In some ways, a more common figure on the non-Communist Party left of the 1930s was the Marxian intellectual who, often *via* underconsumption and institutionalism, gradually came to argue in terms not easily distinguished from those of the reformist institutionalist mainstream of the economics profession. G.D.H. Cole, Harold Laski, and John Strachey could all be understood in this way. Your case, I think, is much more ambivalent: you remained warily interested.

No, rather than pressing for a cheap "conviction" on the charge that you weakened or "betrayed" the socialist tradition, I'd say you yourself paid a price for the Spencerian inheritance: that there were ultimately things in it that *did* prejudice the chances of building a successful new culture. A Marxist intellectual tradition that relied on methodologies derived from evolution and from Spencer could not readily generate the abstractions characteristic of a genuine social science, and therefore proved incapable of providing useful or concrete general answers to burning issues in the Depression. And yet Marxist intellectuals -- those who wished to continue the general politico-ethical legacy of Marx and of socialism -- had no choice but to try and produce convincing explanations of the social crisis all around them.[119] They found that new liberal ideas focused on consumption, more than the classical categories of socialist political economy, fit together only too comfortably with their old evolutionary habits of thought.[120]

It would be a gross error to suggest you tamely went along with the new style of economic reasoning, with its short-term projections and stunted historical sensibility: in writing historical essays on the labour theory of value, you were hardly in step with the Deweyite pragmatism of the 1930s. Still, I think it is valid to say that the "new philosophy of life" failed at the decisive moment when it was asked to inspire "new strategies of struggle." The generic abstractions characteristic of both Evolutionary Marxism and its Dialectical Marxist offspring were incapable of providing a determinate analysis of a specific situation. Evolution explained everything, but, alas, when brought to bear upon a concrete politico-ethical problem like the Depression, it also explained nothing.

And this was not merely a failure of "economic analysis": it was also a failure of the paradigm to meet the persistent human need for politico-ethical standards. For me, the most damaging part of this Spencerian-Marxist inheritance is the inability to discuss ethics coherently. Look at the way you have to smuggle in any vocabulary of morality, rather than giving us a clear, emphatic position! If the "philosophy of the whole way of life" was going to emphasize Dietzgen, Kautsky, Engels and Ferri, then it was likely to view the whole sphere of ethics as something inherently "un-materialist" and "utopian." (And this was no simple economistic distortion of the original Marx and Engels: they too were notoriously slippery whenever it came time to articulate a clear ethical position.) Ethics, one is so often told in "the tradition," is the stuff of the silly utopians, flabby professors and the "new true socialists" -- not for the likes of (self-defined) real revolutionary Marxists! But then unexamined ethical terms and descriptions come right back in, taking up squatters' rights in the books of Marxists great and small.....[121]

You yourself adopted Ferri's strategy of using biological figures that discretely conveyed an unmistakable ethical message.[122] As a result of this scientistic subterfuge, the person who wanted to know what socialists like you meant by progress, freedom, liberation and justice just had to guess.

This materialistic eviction of the language of ethics simply meant that the language of good and evil, ejected from the front door, promptly re-entered through the back. Marxist debates are crowded with such binaries as traitors and heroes, faithfulness and betrayal, higher and lower, undeveloped and developed, none of which have any precise scientific or "materialist" meaning, and all of which are most often simply left unexamined. In the absence of any detailed guidance, many Marxists turned to the crassest forms of utilitarian consequentialism -- Trotsky's *Their Morals and Ours* is a chilling example -- and came to consider questions of right or wrong strictly in terms of the *consequences* of actions. These abstract ethical positions had real-world implications. What R.H.Tawney once memorably called the "radiant ambiguity of the word 'Socialism'" is a lot less dazzling after the word (and the consequentialist ethic) has been repeatedly soiled through its use as an alibi for mass murder.[123] Is it really so remarkable that your project of a new philosophy of life failed to dislodge many people from their traditional attachment to family, church, and traditional political party, if it also failed to address problems of human values choices -- all those everyday questions of politico-ethical life?

Maybe we have already come close to tracing the *internal* reasons why, in the decade after your death, we discern a precipitous decline in the vision of a "new philosophy of life, a new culture," both in the labour press and more generally in the working-class movement, in Britain, the United States, and Canada.[124] I suspect this massive decline was underway even before you died. As I read the League for Social Reconstruction's *Social Planning for Canada* and its pathetic paragraphs on "capitalist culture," for example, I'm struck by just how little the discussion in this most Fabian of the classic texts of Canadian socialism relates to the insights you working-class intellectuals had painstakingly developed years earlier. The luminaries of the LSR held workers to be culturally undeveloped by virtue of their long hours of labour: the "leisured classes" are supposedly the "cultural classes," whereas workers are "barred from participation in cultural activities," as are those whose "spiritual horizon is ever clouded by the haunting fear of economic necessity." These banal bromides could only emerge from minds free of any conception of the significance of culture *or* class in the struggle for socialism.[125] "Working-class culture" was entirely marginalized in this document.[126] It is apparent that trade unions, over time, also became less and less interested in developing a "new philosophy for a whole way of life," at the ultimate cost, perhaps, of entering a period of extreme pressure and fragmentation without a coherent defence of the conceptual framework underlying such ideals as the "general welfare state."[127]

For you the project of constructing a working-class culture was still the key to your life; even after you died, the articles were still appearing, establishing connections between the present and the traditions of the socialist past. You believed in a working-class culture until the day you died, but it would only be a slight exaggeration to say of your core idea -- that the working class in real life could and should build "their own philosophy of life, a new culture" -- that it died with you. I think that was a tragic loss. If ever we see a mass movement on the Canadian left again, it will need to recapture your vision and learn from your errors and achievements. The Proletarian Enlightenment conveyed a sense of the wonder of the world, and the boundless freedom that would soon be the workers to enjoy.[128] No doubt sometimes this breadth and openness makes for unintentional humour today -- I think you must be the only person on the planet who analyzed *both* "The Artificial Propagation of Fish and Lobsters" and the supposed pitfalls of Kantian dualism! -- and sometimes it sounds like, and probably was, sheer dilettantism. But I am also struck by the grandeur of your vision: that the working class, in developing a new "philosophy of life," would be able to absorb and integrate within itself all the new knowledge of the modern world. In critiquing the specifics of that philosophy of life, I also mean to remember and pay homage to the nobility of the general project.

•

As I wrote that last sentence the radio carried yet another item on the death of socialism and the newspaper beside my desk is full of enthusiastic burble over downsizing the state. If anyone was ever skeptical about the power and pervasiveness of hegemonic representations of the social world, the world of 1990s politics -- Herbert Spencer's revenge! -- should be enough to put all doubts to rest. With amazing thoroughness and speed, views once associated only with the lunatic right have become standard editorial fare in the *Globe and Mail* (the Canadian newspaper which serves as the *Izvestia* of the new totalitarian liberalism, wherein the bleakest and most inhuman elements of nineteenth-century social thought are trumpeted as though they were breathtaking twentieth-century advances in human understanding, and wherein "Whack 'Em and Stack 'Em" has become the inspirational neo-liberal call to battle against proletarian demonstrators). Where is the Marxist tradition in the midst of this classical liberal onslaught?

A further reason for reviving the memory of your work is to help us gain a deeper understanding of, or at least a better sense of historical perspective on, what the phrase "the Marxist tradition" might mean in this context. Unless we are to revive the popular but futile essentialist game of establishing "true" and "false" Marxisms, prophetic paths and tragic detours, saints and heretics, we need to face up to the inescapable reality that there are many voices within Marx, Marxism, and any possible Marxist tradition. Ever since Marx (who himself was reported to have said he was not a "Marxist") there have always been a multiplicity of "Marxisms" -- that is, a wide variety of ways of weaving into a politico-ethical framework the many and varied insights associated with the name of "Marx." "The adjective... [Marxist] is like money that has been worn out from passing through too many hands," remarks Dante Germino, who goes on to cite Gramsci's remark that such questions as "Are we Marxists?" and "Do Marxists exist?" occasion rivers of ink and stupidity to flow, "since raving and Byzantinism are the imprescriptible heritage of human beings."[129] The point of the comment is obvious: the whole "litmus test" approach to determining Marxist credentials should be left to fools, sectarians, ideologues and obscurantists. We have simply been through too many "totalizations" of the Marxist tradition, from the Darwinian Marx of the 1890s to the Spinozist Structuralist Marx of the 1970s, each one of which was presented as the last and most authoritative version, and each of which was duly superseded by something else. Some Marxists today still agree with you: the core of "the tradition" is the labour theory of value; for others, this theory is peripheral to the project of historical materialism (more Marxists write as though it were peripheral, mind you, than actually come out and say so); finally, others just quietly ask, "Which of the four labour theories of value in Marx did you have in mind?"[130] And so it goes, through all the fundamental philosophical issues. Ethics? Marx is, or is not, concerned with transcendent values. The dialectic? No Marxism without dialectic, say some; the dialectic is an irrational holdover from Hegel's Absolute Idealism, say others. Apart from the absymal record of Soviet Marxism, few things have discredited Marxism quite so much as the endless proliferation of seamlessly independent Marxisms.

Is "Marxism" dead? "Marxism" cannot die because "Marxism" was never alive. It was never a single entity endowed with life. (One of the most telltale fallacies of the "Death of Marx" industry is the *fallacy of personification* -- treating "Marxism" as a homogeneous, clearly demarcated historical personality, rather than a complex and internally heterogeneous set of social and intellectual relationships). Are today's intellectuals betraying "Marxism"? The question only makes sense if "Marxism" was like a religion (with its own internal criteria of truth, proceeding ultimately from faith) or like a person (one imagines "Marxism" waiting tearfully by the phone for a call from a faithless lover). "Marxism," as a clearly-defined unitary and cohesive tradition, *never existed*. There never was "a" Marxist ontology, "a" Marxist epistemology, "a" Marxist ethics. What did exist were Marx's writings and the many Marxisms organized by people inspired, in innumerable ways, by those writings, and often claiming sole access to the one true interpretation of Marx.[131] In attempting to construct a usable definition of Marxism today, one might say at most that "Marxism" denotes not adherence to a certain philosophy nor devotion to a method; it does not entail loyalty to a political practice, nor membership in a particular type of party. It is simply a way of crafting a political and cultural *praxis* in the present by mobilizing certain key determinate abstractions to establish a *relationship* between the ideal of the future -- the *realm of socialist freedom* -- and the reality of the past -- *the realm of necessity*. As a relationship rather than a thing, Marxism cannot then be defined in terms of mastery of certain theories or adherence to certain positions. It was neither conclusively encapsulated in final form in Russian Dialectical Materialism, nor is it conclusively buried with the waning of that particular school. Even the greatest of the twentieth-century Marxists, Antonio Gramsci, never claimed to have interpreted Marx "correctly," that is, literally, "because he held the creative core of Marxism to be a quality of openness to the flux and change of history rather than a set of doctrines extracted from Marx's texts."[132]

"Marxism" cannot be buried once and for all because it never existed, not in the reified or personified sense in which it would make sense to lament (or celebrate) its alleged passing or to contemplate covering it with earth.[133] Every generation of radicals and socialists, confronting the legacy of Marx along with that of so many other socialist writers, weaves elements of that legacy into a new pattern. Every left generation has had to mourn (as well as celebrate) its past and reconstitute its present. Our own generation is no exception. Reports of the "Death of Marx" are not only greatly exaggerated, but wholly misconceived: if Marx had some true and useful things to say about the capitalist system and the ways in which it could be transcended, his words might well be as useful (or at least as interesting) now as they were in 1900 or 1867, capitalism having proved itself to be rather more durable than either Marx or you anticipated. What we are witnessing is not the death of Marx but the disintegration of parties and states which, by violently decontextualizing and hypostatizing certain elements of the various nineteenth-century Marxist traditions, attempted to legitimize their claims to state power.[134] What *is* eroding is not the influence of particular Marxist ideas and ideals, but the possibility of thinking of Marxism as a comprehensive theory with its own doctrine of the universal laws of social evolution, traceable to Marx via Spencer (in the case of much of the Second International) and Plekhanov (in the case of the Third), and ultimately sustained as a form of thought through repetition as an official ideology. I think we would both agree, Colin, that the disappearance of these authoritarian states and the secular religion they encouraged is no great loss for those oriented to the realm of freedom.

Agnes Heller has an interesting (although perhaps overly dichotomized) way of putting this sense of a distinction between two takes on Marx. She distinguishes between Marxism as a philosophy of history and Marxism as a theory of history. Marxism construed as a philosophy of history attempted to explain the origin and destiny of the universe. (Both Spencerian Marxism and Dialectical Materialism fit this pattern). Guided by this cosmic vision of natural and human history, Marxists would argue that freedom was the recognition of necessity. Whether it proclaimed its adherence to the violent overthrow of the capitalist state or not (a declaration frequently made in a slippery, "last-instance" manner), the politics emerging from this Dialectical Materialism was *evolutionary* in the sense that it held that there was a uniform and objectively determined process of evolution, uniting humankind with nature and which humankind might *hasten* but not structure. Figures in the development of this Dialectical Materialism obviously include Engels, Plekhanov, Stalin, Trotsky, Lukács, and Althusser, each of whom (for all their differences) embodied a very powerful will to totalize, from the cell to socialism.

Post-orthodox Marxism (or more commonly, but much less exactly, "neo-Marxism"), derived largely from Marx and Gramsci, entails a wholly different approach to the construction of theory, centred on discovering the concrete necessary preconditions for historical transformations, and it is formally silent about many issues, such as the nature of death or the future of the universe, the underlying structure of matter or the existence of God, about which it has *nothing* important to say. In a post-orthodox Marxist world of discourse, there would be no drive to create a single "Marxist philosophy," based on Hegel, Kant, Aristotle, Spinoza, Derrida (or the next philosopher who happens to rise to the top of the charts in the philosophy departments.) Naturally, such Marxists will be interested in connecting Marxist questions and theories (the "Marxist problematic") with philosophical traditions that ask the same sorts of questions about the critique of political economy. (For example, to sustain a sense of the logical possibility of the critique of political economy, against the many poststructuralists who would deny the very possibility of such an exercise, one might well start re-reading Kant and the Kantian Marxists to establish (critically) what it is to establish the limits of knowledge. But such recourse to philosophy should not be undertaken with the delusive notion of a unified field theory, but as contingent and specific defences of the logical possibility of doing political economy.)[135] Marxists should avoid the temptation of arguing as though a once-and-for-all resolution of the big philosophical issues has taken place, and as though Marxists have patented a formula for unlocking most of the mysteries of human existence. Nobody with half a brain believes this story any more. The quest for such philosophical finality is a nineteenth-century will-o'-the-wisp. It's time to give it up.

Post-orthodox Marxists take up the position that Marx is most usefully interpreted as providing a theory of history focused specifically on the logico-historical preconditions of the capitalist system. There may well be no overall dialectical pattern to history, so far as we know: actually, questions about "history in general" and "the universe in general" seem rather unaswerable and pointless. (As human beings, we may well be bound to ask them, but we should not do so *as Marxists* -- and with the tragic understanding that definitive answers are likely always to elude us). Much about the past and future of humanity is unknown and likely ever to remain so. Large parts of human experience, including many things that are very important to people, lie outside the Marxist perspective (which is therefore not the only valid and useful perspective on the past or the present). Post-orthodox Marxists strive for a sense of the whole and to see the system within the detail: but they retain a much greater degree of skepticism about the finality with which "the whole" can ever be represented, about the extent to which they have performed that famous "last analysis."

If the Marxist-Leninist Philosophy of History -- History-with-a-capital H -- can be seen as the faithful reflection of the *Communist Manifesto* and of Engels's *Anti-Duhring*, the post-orthodox Marxist theory of history -- history-with-a-lower-case-h -- is inspired by the magnificent third volume of *Capital* and by the 1857 introduction to the *Grundrisse*. In this counter-evolutionary approach, there is no such thing as "history" in the singular, and consequently "History" will neither absolve, convict or even say "how's the weather?" to us. Nor can large groups of people -- nations, ethnic groups, classes, or genders -- be said to carry "historic missions" (or suffer from "historic collective guilt.") There is no logic *inherent* in the *totality* of history (although there are some very interesting and important logico-historical patterns that we can understand in particular historical circumstances). There is no single or necessary pattern of historical development from the primitive to the civilized, or from the lower to the higher: *there may not even be a cosmic force of Evolution which merges our history with that of an evolving nature*. (As to whether it is useful to postulate a process of "evolution" governing biological adaptation to the environment, a post-orthodox Marxist might feel that this is a question best left for evolutionary theorists and biologists: and he or she will not put off making other, more specific kinds of analysis while waiting for their inevitably complex and qualified answers). There is no Reason-in-History (with a capital-R and a capital-H), but there can be reasoning about history (with a lower-case r and a lower-case h): there are things we can know about the past, and these things can be useful as we construct, under conditions not of our choosing, the possibility of a more humane and generous future. Marxists using logico-historical analysis may learn much about the past and develop interesting and helpful general explanations of specific historical developments and events, often by "working backwards" toward the preconditions (including discursive preconditions: why not?) of particular phenomena.[136] The knowledge thus generated may be helpful, even indispensable, in specific political and social struggles.

And because there is simply no way of knowing if there will ever be a final totalization of history, i.e. an "end of history" from which we can confidently assess which forces are "progressive" and which "regressive," there can be little confidence in consequentialism as an ethics -- that is, in saying "the ends justify the means " -- because we lack sure knowledge that there ever will be an "actually existing" realm of freedom in whose name we can confidently treat people merely as means. (What our normative judgments *are* based on is another question, to which Kant has contributed important insights). Because neo-Marxists do not know how history ends, and even doubt whether the phrase "how history ends" has any non-contradictory meaning, we cannot apply swift-and-sure judgements about the correctness and incorrectness of various positions: we humans live (and will for the conceivable future will always live) in doubt. In this line of thought, which no less than "cosmic evolutionism" can also be traced directly to Marx, a theory of history does not have to pretend to explain the origins and destiny of the entire universe, nor does it hold out the possibility (even the *ultimate* possibility) of a unification of all knowledge on the basis of something called the "materialist dialectic." On such major questions as the nature of matter, the existence of God, the origin of species, or even the chances this year of the Montreal Canadiens, Marxists *qua* Marxists really have nothing important to say. (Unlike Trotsky, then, we make no claim that anything in the Marxian tradition provides guidance for students of radioactivity, and unlike Stalin we have no *Marxist* opinions about plant genetics). Post-orthodox Marxists do not have any certainty about the future, and do not view socialism as an inevitability. We view freedom as something achieved by each generation in the face of necessity, and not, as in the Dialectical Materialist tradition, in terms of the domination of nature or the acceptance of natural or historical necessities that are prior to and outside humanity. (We make no claim to an understanding of laws of history applicable to the entire history of the human species: to our eye, such overarching "laws" that have been thus far proposed are so general as to be tendentious). Post-orthodox Marxists as I have defined them here would argue that Dialectical Materialism compounded the teleology inherent in Spencerian Marxism by replacing its implicitly Lamarckian mechanism of change with a mystified, triadic version of the dialectic of Hegel. This move permitted the most naive empiricism to coexist with the most mystical essentialism.[137] It had the political advantage, of course, of calming uncertainty and doubt. One recalls that *de omnibus dubitandum* was Marx's favourite motto.

This post-orthodox argument that the legitimate province of Marxist theory is the critique of political economy may sound, to your Spencerian ears, like a Marxism suited to an age of reduced expectations. Fair enough. As I said, Colin, you and I are of different times. We breathe a different air. Still, be careful before you reach for your arsenal of (generally good-natured) epithets. (Ramsay MacDonald sentimentalists! The new true socialists! *Jazz* social thinkers!) For example, superficial resemblances to the contrary, this post-orthodox Marxism is not just relativism. Because politico-ethical values can be derived from Marx's transcendental concept of the realm of freedom, post-orthodox Marxists can bring a consistent non-relativist transcendental ethical standard (and not a view of ends justifying the means) to our work. Nor is this all. The various ideas which this post-orthodox position retains from Marx -- and they are numerous indeed, because (as so many scholars have now shown) Marx much of the time was working in this mode and *not* as a philosopher of nature or history -- are susceptible to exactly the kinds of empirical validation normally used in human inquiries, because they are *focused and determinate abstractions*, and not the pre-ordained fulfillments of a teleological philosophy. Marxism is construed by post-orthodox Marxists as a limited but powerful this-worldly vocabulary with some useful things to say to people living in capitalist societies about the ways in which "freedom" could be made into a "real ideal." That is the time-bound extent of its usefulness. It seems enough to be getting on with.

But now I've set up this tidy dichotomy -- and obviously I incline to the post-orthodox Marxist end of this imagined polar opposition[138] -- I want to complicate it. Take you, Colin. There can be no doubt that for most of your life, you were under the influence of Marxism as a Philosophy of History, and hence on the Other Side, so to speak. If we follow left convention, we will now attempt to resolve the issue by launching a "polemic", whose very structure (as Michel Foucault rightly remarked) insofar as it is modeled on war, seems a foreshadowing of oppression.[139] Many studies of your generation, even a relatively sophisticated book like Pittenger's study of evolutionary Marxists in the United States, as well as numerous feminist critiques of turn-of-the-century socialism, fall into this time-honoured form of the war-of-words. At a time when Marxist intellectuals are really feeling the heat (and the frustration of living at a time of heightened political irrationality), they also are tempted to release their frustrations by firing on each other, or on easily-identified villains from their complicated past.

Apart from the unattractive and ahistorical *hubris* involved in all such exercises in self-righteousness, one is even more impressed by their uncreative tedium. In your case, Colin, hunting for "bad ideas" has all the challenge of shooting fish in a barrel.[140] The more creative challenge is to retain a sense of balance and community: to retain the real analytical and empirical insights in the texts, and the notion that, over and above the differences I have mentioned, we and countless others share a common identification with the socialist realm of freedom. Why, if you were able to read Spencer creatively (and, in a real sense, "construct" your own Spencer for your own purposes) should we be so narrow and polemical in our own response to the Marxism of an earlier generation? Those tensions I have described in dichotomous terms -- philosophy of history/critique of political economy, orthodox/post-orthodox, etc. etc. -- might then be better captured as points on a continuum of Marxist ethico-political positions. Rather than hoping to resolve such differences through polemical warfare, we might come to see them as constructive tensions within a socialist community, to be resolved through dialogue and in the common experience of people's struggle.

And, I suspect, it may be in precisely this kind of historiographical exercise, this attempt to recover for the future both the strengths and limitations of our many past "Marxisms," that the new post-orthodox dispensation has the most to offer. It would allow socialists of all types to appreciate more clearly and sympathetically that even within seemingly holistic, even "totalitarian," theoretical universes, there was often a much greater degree of internal heterogeneity than might have initially been suspected. For example, not many leftists today would argue with the fact that Stalin did terrible things to the Marxist legacy (not to mention millions of his fellow Soviets). Yet it is also a fascinating fact that, prompted by the writings of both Lenin and Stalin, the Communist Party of Canada carried out pioneering and important work in cultural life and in the writing of Canadian history -- especially with regard to the "national question." (One thinks of the pathbreaking and impressive work of Stanley Ryerson). Turning to your work, one finds that even given the limitations of the framework you used (or which used you?), there are original and powerful new insights into culture, post-competitive capitalism, and trade unionism. Going back even further, and looking at the case of the much-demonized Engels, we could set against the truly awful *Dialectics of Nature* the great humanitarianism and socio-historical specificity of *The Condition of the Working Class in England.*

In other words, recognizing the specificity of each of the "Marxisms" and "socialisms" of the past would not mean that everything achieved within that framework would be reduced either to its Grand Assumptions or to its place in an overly teleological sense of ideological development. We need to evolve a post-polemical way of addressing shared weaknesses and strengths -- not just because this is the "nice thing to do," but because otherwise we risk squandering all that earlier generations of socialists achieved. In Canada especially, each generation of leftists seems condemned to reinvent the wheel, having forgotten (or mercilessly trashed) the achievements of its predecessors. Post-orthodox Marxists, surveying what are undoubtedly the ruins of past paradigms, are in exactly this position, and incur the risk of too readily distinguishing themselves from "the tradition" by oversimplifying and distorting its history. (We too need to beware the "Death of Marx" game). Here, I think, you and your generation have much to teach us. The selective appropriation you carried out in the case of Spencer can serve as a model for the work of selective critique, appropriation and conservation we need to carry out in the case of orthodox (and so-called "Western" or "culturalist") Marxism. In the works of those influenced by the great speculative cosmic evolutionary system erected by Spencer and refined by the Soviets, post-orthodox Marxists might often find fascinating insights and important metaphors not simply reducible to the context in which they occur. We can appropriate such insights while reserving the right to question the necessitarian optimism and evolutionary certainty that contemporaries believed were their logical preconditions.

We should also work on fashioning a new way of talking about contradictions and heterogeneous elements within the transcended frameworks. In your case, for example, one could certainly, working from the "model of war," ruthlessly drive home the contradiction between the evolutionary-determinist premises of your political economy and the voluntaristic, even utopian, program you laid out for cultural struggle. (To an extent, perhaps, I have already done this). The polemicist could have great fun bringing out the inconsistencies and contradictions of a "scientific" and "value-free" paradigm that is transparently shot through with non-scientific assumptions and human values. You believed, for example, that the regulation of the production of capital goods could exorcise greed of wealth and the fear of want, and effect a "spiritual revolution" in attitudes to work and economic life.[141] You even spoke of the new union movement as an "engine of liberation" that opened up a prospect on a realm of freedom.[142] Easy targets. But, instead of firing on them, would it not be more constructive to retain these human values, by distancing them from your determinist-evolutionary paradigm, and re-inserting them into the counter-evolutionary framework of post-orthodox Marxism? [143] (And would it also not be more honest to say that is very probable that all conceptual frameworks constructed to interpret and solve human problems must always confront a similar tension?) Why should our skepticism about overly constraining narratives and metaphysical schemas require us to do without your wise, penetrating, strangely contemporary analyses of the cultural contradictions of capitalism, which you brought to such a pitch of intensity in the 1930s? Certainly a post-orthodox Marxism that takes Marx's motto *de omnibus dubitandum* seriously will resist any sense that it has spoken the last, concluding word on the problem of subjectivity in socio-historical analysis. All our frameworks are contingent, historical constructions. They do not shed light on eternity. And they are not well designed as instruments of war.

Colin, I suppose these notions of the inevitability of uncertainty and of the proper province of post-orthodox Marxism as lying strictly in the critique of political economy might sound like a terrible diminution of the dream. Some, less generous than you, will doubtless mutter about "apostasy" (now there's a charming and unselfconsciously revealing word abroad in the discourse of the "secular" Marxists of the 1990s!) I can imagine what you *might* say (using your wonderfully idiosyncratic rhetoric) in rebuttal: here is a fine example (here you might reach for your most damning adjectives) of vapid, pessimistic, *Jazz* middle-class eclecticism![144]

Actually, I think it's a much more hopeful perspective than one based on a view of Marxism as a single integrated system, totally unified by its own distinctive philosophy, at loggerheads with every other philosophical tradition in a war of all against all. And I'd say in response that post-orthodox Marxism as I have attempted (very tentatively) to describe it here does not in fact have *anything* to do with vapid eclecticism, *anything* to do with post-Marxism as it is rapidly mutating in cultural studies, *anything* to do with postmodern intellectual fashions. It has to do with facing reality, and preserving those aspects of Marxian thought that are of continuing worth to the socialist movement. Those aspects are numerous indeed.

Post-orthodox Marxism is not eclectic at all. This is because there is within it a dynamic integrating categorical imperative -- precisely the principle which underlies the entire edifice of *Capital*, from start to finish: *the realm of freedom*; and an integrating methodology, *determinate abstraction*; and many widely shared and empirically solid hypotheses that have been shown to be useful to anybody who wants to understand the liberal capitalist world: *the labour theory of value, the theory of class formation and class conflict, the theory of commodity fetishism*, to name but three. Post-orthodox Marxists would modestly claim to inherit all the useful tools of political economy that have allowed Marxists to develop a good general understanding of local events in particular times; they would less modestly place all such findings of political economy under the sign of the realm of freedom, with its inescapable corollary that the means justify the ends. This post-orthodox Marxism would hold that many determinate abstractions drawn from the Marxist tradition have been shown to be *relatively* effective as testable and interesting hypotheses and generalizations within carefully defined conditions.[145] And although it's obvious that the resources of the Marxist traditions are available for many uses and abuses, and are at least relatively autonomous from any politico-ethical intention -- consider academic Marxism, in which the tools of class analysis often have had so little to do with any actual political *praxis* -- post-orthodox Marxists would nonetheless hold that many of these analytical tools are (even and perhaps especially under conditions of postmodernity) actually indispensable for the resistance movements of subaltern classes and groups, who will succeed only to the extent that they develop a vision that goes beyond their particular constituency. And it is "pragmatic" not in epistemology -- for within these conditions it is held that contingent and time-bound but nonetheless *actual truths*, i.e., something much more than the pragmatists' widely-shared hunches, may be known -- but only in the sense that it views the point of theory as providing us with conceptual tools enabling us to illuminate the specific historical problems characteristic of a capitalist order. Philosophy is no longer seen as imparting deep truths, in the manner of a religion; rather, it just helps us refine our arguments and be a little bit clearer about the way we define the historical problems that are the principal focus of post-orthodox Marxism. We cannot predict beforehand which of the many ideas of Marx, or of the many Marxist traditions, will figure prominently in resistance movements of the future, although those methods and insights that have, over time, been found useful are likely candidates to be considered by such movements. How theory is activated politically (that is, how it becomes "real" in any full historical sense) cannot be determined in advance.

I think for all but a few people, Dialectical Materialism is finished as a great unifying system, primarily as a result of its own internal contradictions and partly because of its own patent inability to bring humanity nearer to the realm of freedom. Your own Spencerian version of Marxism -- in many ways the *Beta*-version of Soviet Marxism -- is an even more distant memory. But many important ideas of Marx are still extremely powerful. People united in solidarity against the corrosive nihilism of the neo-liberal order will keep coming back to them, not because pontificating academics or hectoring militants tell them to, but because these just are powerful tools for understanding the present order. (That they need to be combined with many others should go without saying). As long as there are people working for other people, there are going to be interesting questions: who gets to be comfortable and who gets to be poor? who gives the order and who has to take it? who gets a job and who gets to be jobless? why do the banks make record profits while people are freezing to death on the streets in a Canadian winter? And to these Marx-type questions, Marx-type answers are going to be pertinent, with or without some overarching vision of something called social evolution.[146]

For all the rhetoric that surrounds totalitarian liberalism today, in many ways as thoughtlessly triumphalist and idiotic as the talk you ruthlessly satirized in 1912, it is *still* the case that there are no compelling *liberal* arguments to legitimize the disproportionate power wielded by large corporations. And no matter how disparate and divided the new social movements may be, most of them cannot avoid the shared realities of life in a liberal capitalist order. It is difficult to see how anyone who wants to analyze this fascinating anomaly of disproportionate corporate power within an ostensibly egalitarian liberal order, whether a gay activist tracking the corporate profits derived from the AIDS crisis, or the feminist wondering why single mothers can't find affordable housing, or the environmentalist investigating why no corporations or governments seem to be very motivated to do anything about global warming (which poses some direct challenges to our continued existence as a species),[147] or just anybody wondering why so many Canadians are freezing to death on the streets in winter in one of the wealthiest societies the planet has ever seen -- can avoid asking Marx-type questions and wrestling with Marx-type answers, even if in ways more inclusive and less economistic than was the case with your class-centered generation. This does not mean that such movements and activists should dissolve the identities and the specific traditions they have developed since the 1960s; it merely means they may have more in common than they realize. Unless Marx was totally wrong, and social and political inequality vanishes under capitalism, the kinds of analysis he undertook of class power will always be of interest to people who want to explain and change the capitalist world around them.[148] Marxist hypotheses are probably going to be of continuing interest to radical movements of all kinds because Marx was likely right in thinking that there are intractable conflicting forces and tendencies in capitalism, and new liberals wrong in thinking that such forces could be permanently overcome by massive state spending.

What is surprising, in a way, is just how limited the liberal capitalist order has been in winning friends and influencing people. The system quite routinely generates armies of people who long to live in a better, more humane, more integrated way. That their visions of how to do so come in a million shapes and sizes is today a given (and in my opinion even an achievement). But what is less commonly said is that in the context of a continuing capitalist order this diversity can often be focused on particular, unifying projects. Whether or not socialist parties of a new type, or organizational forms we can barely guess at, will be there to provide continuity and leadership is an open question. But what seems certain is that, for any group seriously engaged in contesting relations of power and property in the modern world, many of Marx's ideas, blasted out of their dated philosophical context and reappropriated and put to work in a thousand new ways, will continue to make a lot of sense. The Marxist analysis of the capitalist system will recommend itself to social movements, both "new," "old" and "middle-aged," not because it provides the secret to all things, but because it gives us powerful insights into some quite important puzzles -- like why present-day liberal governments feel they must to demolish the welfare state and retract the "social wage" achieved in the 1940s, with serious implications for virtually everyone and every movement in our society. Rising against this neo-liberal politics of class hatred, the people-in-struggle may well find, years after the supposed Death of Marx, that it is perennially necessary to reinvent him.

What then can be retained from your "new philosophy of life" in this post-orthodox, problem-centered Marxism? In my view, much more than one might have initially supposed. Once it is no longer expected to explain the origins of the universe and the destiny of humanity, Marx's specific method of investigation -- a counter-evolutionary, backwards-working, Kantian method of exploring socio-economic phenomena by examining their conditions of possibility, with the aim of forming "determinate abstractions" to capture *both* a phenomenon's historical uniqueness *and* its socio-historical typicality -- emerges not just as a method for exploring the capitalist system but as one of the most powerful conceptual tools ever evolved in social science.[149] Once the theory of value is understood in its specific historic context (that of the period of manufacture and the first period of the industrial revolution), it becomes possible to develop a more holistic understanding of late capitalism (and retain the labour theory of value as an irreplaceable resource for the ethical critique of this system). Once the Marxist concept of the working class is no longer given an unconvincing and ethically dubious "functional" reading (i.e., "we should support the working class because only the working class can overthrow the system"), it re-emerges as an entirely valid emphasis: no longer bearing some abstract, ahistorical and unprovable "mission," the working class (along with other subaltern classes) still has a powerful claim to the attention of all radicals, because class realities are overwhelmingly important for most human beings and loom as large as other sources of identification (such as race, ethnicity, nationality, gender, religion, region or sexual orientation); moreover, no realm of freedom worthy of the name could possibly be based on the generalized class exploitation and oppression typical of capitalism.[150] Once such concepts as social labour, social formation, and mode of production are freed from having to disclose the social universe's "innermost secrets," they can all be "de-essentialized" without robbing them of their analytical force.[151] Once Marxists are released from the burden of having to pretend to have a scientific explanation for the universe, once socialists in general have shaken off the weight of cosmic evolutionism, they are also liberated from the necessity of atheism: Marxists *as Marxists* would have no need to take any position on religious issues, because such issues lie far outside the real competence of the Marxist tradition. In fact (and this has already occurred in Liberation Theology, to date one of the western hemisphere's most powerful and sophisticated Marxist movements of the twentieth century) the methods and insights of Marx may work most commendably when integrated into a religious anti-capitalist ethic.[152] The collapse of Dialectical Materialism and the general project of Marxism as a total philosophy of social evolution is really only a "catastrophe" for us if we, having failed to outgrow the Spencerian thirst for a grand system to explain everything, allow ourselves to be persuaded that what was valuable about the ideas of Marx was that they once provided a total philosophy of life. But if we do not buy this Spencerian (and later Stalinist) view, the picture suddenly looks different. What has happened can be interpreted as the end of ways of thinking that are no longer useful or plausible -- and therefore a new opening up of new possibilities for struggle and community, of our own chance to imagine "a new philosophy of life, a new culture."

Finally. The greatest of all the concepts in the Marxist tradition is of course its precise, rigorous and yet visionary idea of the realm of freedom. You upheld this tradition yourself. (I expect however you might follow the mainstream of the Dialectical Materialist tradition in suspecting that there is something inherently idealist in the way Marx in *Capital* holds up a transcendent ideal of freedom, which "really begins only where labour determined by necessity and external expediency ends.") This realm of freedom lies beyond material production, beyond the "wrestle with nature" which will forever and always, under all possible modes of production, characterize the life of humanity. If a Marxist Philosophy of History (and the practice of Dialectical Materialism) suggested that the realm of freedom could be actually realized, perhaps even within the near future, for the post-orthodox Marxist the picture looks different: it is evident from Marx's own words that *we never get there*. Yet even though this is the case, even though freedom can then only consist in the associated producers governing the human interaction with nature in a rational way, "bringing it under their collective control instead of being dominated by it as a blind power," there is still a point -- in fact it is *the* point of everything a Marxist does or says in theory and politics -- in holding up a higher ideal of freedom, a *true realm of freedom,* which begins beyond anything which could ever feasibly be achieved by humanity on earth.[153]

Both connected to the earth (for the realm of necessity is both its logical precondition and its material basis) and removed from the earth (for it could *never* characterize any mode of production on earth), the realm of freedom is a way of historicizing and making specific the concept of an ethics suited to human beings. Marx here presents us with a vista of human beings struggling toward an infinite horizon of freedom as a manifestation of their humanity: he affirms a deontological ethic of freedom, even a freedom which, although it cannot be realized on earth, is nonetheless held before us as a regulatory ideal. *And it is this ideal, in fact, which emerges not just as the great conclusion to his analysis of capitalism, but is also the precondition of every word of all three volumes of his masterpiece.* The realm of freedom exists as "an anticipation that is embodied in a kind of human activity that prevails over the blind power of the realm of necessity. " In contrast to his semi-finished position in the preface to *A Contribution to the Critique of Political Economy* in 1859, Marx in his *magnum opus* is saying that humankind does -- and must -- set goals beyond that which it can attain, and which remain beyond any of its possible embodiments on this earth. Socialist society would be "a society heading toward, and approaching the realm of, freedom -- that is, an association of free human beings. But such a society is not and will not be this realm of freedom." We glimpse this realm of freedom in concrete projects -- when we struggle together in communities of solidarity against capitalism and the liberal order -- but we only approximate the transcendental project which remains *both* our reality *and* something forever beyond our experience.[154] Marx's transcendent concept holds out the realm of freedom as one of the free play of physical and spiritual powers, of the spontaneous activity of freely co-operating individuals, of the right to be lazy and eat well and play music. It is a politico-ethical concept, dialectical in the best sense, which can then be used to explore what human relationships in capitalist society are not and what socialist relationships might some day be. A vision of "a full experience of this real life without its negative aspects," the realm of freedom is present throughout Marx's entire work, and most especially his lacerating, brilliant analysis of commodity fetishism. It is both real and ideal: real, because it is a reflection of real life itself, without its negative aspects; and ideal, because it takes the form of a transcendental projection. The vision of an ever-receding realm of freedom does not give us the satisfaction of a "happy ending" to the human narrative, but it does leave us with a vista of openness, a sense of a (perhaps) never-ending struggle to make an ideal real, to explore the limits of "freedom" in the full Marxist sense of an intelligently managed relationship with nature and the free, generous play of a liberated human creativity. Colin, you might well find these passages from Marx high-flown nonsense (and they're admittedly not drawn from Volume I, which you would have been taught to revere above all others); or perhaps Marx's deeply utopian vision would strike a chord in you.[155] Personally, I think the latter is far more likely, because throughout your work, and especially in the articles of the 1930s, I find in you as well a quest for what *might be* and *should be* and *is not yet*.

What finally impresses me most about your work, Colin, is not so much any specific ideas of yours and not so much the concrete deeds on behalf of workers: I am more impressed by the fact of the work itself. I am moved by the actual real-life demonstration you provided of the possibility of "a new philosophy of life, a new culture." From my own point of view, not all of your intellectual enthusiasms were wise, Colin: I guess I've made that clear. But I find all of them, in another sense, inspirational. They were all assertions of your freedom to think, in the face of the indignities of a brutal order that systematically drives that freedom out of working people. They all testified to your will to master the thought of the ages -- and not just as an individual intellectual, but as a working-class thinker writing both to and for the working-class movement. I think of you, night after night, your head buried in Rodbertus or some report on railway finances or Social Credit, mining for insights into your present, our past: night after night trying to connect with the past generations of socialists who had come before you, and with the workers of your own day, and with the generations yet to come: night after night, after the demands of your day job were met, and you could live a few hours in your own realm of freedom.

Best wishes, And In Solidarity
Ian

Endnotes

[1] *Ephesians*, 4: 25.

[2] Karl Marx, *Capital*, trans. David Fernbach, Vol. 3 (New York: Vintage Books, 1981): 959.

[3]See Nicholas Fillmore, *Maritime Radical: The Life and Times of Roscoe Fillmore* (Toronto: Between the Lines, 1992) for a biography of the most famous of these Maritime SPCers.

[4]*Eastern Labor News*, 14 May 1910.

[5]It's not quite true that your work has been entirely overlooked in modern Canada. In addition to receiving some attention from regional historians such as David Frank and Nolan Reilly in their important study of Maritime socialism -- who drew attention to your analysis of fisheries in particular -- you are cited directly in John C. Bacher, *Keeping to the Marketplace: The Evolution of Canadian Housing Policy* (McGill-Queen's Press, 1993) -- my thanks to Sean Purdy for this reference. And an extensive quotation from your article in the *Industrial Banner* championing craft over industrial unionism can be found in Bryan D. Palmer, *A Culture in Conflict: Skilled Workers and Industrial Capitalism in Hamilton, Ontario, 1860-1914* (Montreal and Kingston: McGill-Queen's University Press, 1979), 200-201, where it is somewhat enigmatically interpreted as capturing "much of the new unionism's meaning in southern Ontario...." (200) From a very different ideological quarter: H.A. Logan paid you the compliment, in *Trade Unions in Canada: Their Development and Functioning* (Toronto: Macmillan, 1948), 380, of quoting at length from the article you co-authored with M.M.Maclean in 1926 [§.113., "The Decline of 'International' Unions in Canada"] but -- characteristically -- you do not even make it into his index.

[6]Russell Hann's evocation of the intellectual and cultural world of Phillips Thompson stands as an exemplary exception to a general pattern of anti-intellectualism in Canadian labour historiography. See Russell Hann, "Brainworkers and the Knights of Labor: E.E. Sheppard, Phillips Thompson, and the Toronto News, 1883-1887," in Gregory S. Kealey and Peter Warrian, eds., *Essays in Canadian Working Class History* (Toronto: McClelland and Stewart, 1976): 35-57.

[7]Doug Owram, *The Government Generation: The Intellectual and the State in Canada, 1900-1945* (Toronto: University of Toronto Press, 1986): xi; 104.

[8]See, for example, Leslie Armour and Elizabeth Trott, *The Faces of Reason: An Essay on Philosophy and Culture in English-Canada, 1850-1950* (Waterloo, 1981). Of course, it's rather unfair to take potshots at so heroic and pioneering a book in so under-researched a field as the history of philosophy in Canada. And the authors explicitly did define their focus as *professional philosophy*. Yet, even so -- professional philosophers were clearly not working in a vacuum, and greater appreciation of the extent to which Spencerian ideas were influencing many working-class Canadians would have significantly affected the tone of this invaluable investigation.

[9]The labour press (and labour articles in the daily press, such as the ones you wrote for the Montreal *Herald*) undoubtedly reached more people than the six thousand odd students in universities in Edwardian Canada. For a stimulating discussion of secularization and philosophy, although one which underestimates the extent to which Marx and Spencer were intensively read in

Canada, see Ramsay Cook, *The Regenerators: Social Criticism in Late Victorian Canada* (Toronto, Buffalo and London: University of Toronto Press, 1985).

[10]Located as you were far from its Western Canadian epicentre, you never became particularly prominent in the Socialist Party of Canada; and as you were a sharp-tongued critic of both the Communist Party and the Co-operative Commonwealth Federation, you denied yourself the camp followers of the sort who later burnished the memories of Tim Buck or J.S. Woodsworth, A.E. Smith or Frank Underhill (who were really no more significant or intelligent than you were, but who can be presented as founding fathers of one or the other of the "main" socialist traditions in Canada).

[11]It is noteworthy that even in his fascinating introduction to William Irvine, *The Farmers in Politics* (Toronto: McClelland and Stewart, 1976 [1920]): xii, Reginald Whitaker refers the reader to the distant legacy of Hobbes. However, the much more powerful influence in *The Farmers in Politics*, and one much more directly connected to the strategy of co-operatives, was obviously Spencer.

[12]In "The Many Deaths of Mr. Marx," a talk I delivered to the Underhill Colloquium at Carleton in March, 1996, and which I will some day try to get into print, I took a comparative look at these "Deaths of Marx" -- the contemporary, postmodern "Death" is the fifth, and has thusfar fallen far short of its antecedents in its theoretical and literary quality. I argue that the "Death of Marx" is an invented tradition of the late-nineteenth century.

[13]Ronald Aronson, *After Marxism* (New York and London: Guilford Press, 1995).

[14]MacIntyre, *Proletarian Science* 94.

[15]As Peter Campbell (author of a fine study on the Marxism of the Third Way in Canada) has remarked of the Socialist Party of Canada and the One Big Union, many working-class intellectuals had received better educations than most workers of their day. Campbell, "'Stalwarts," 18 .

[16]The bourgeois writer toys with ideas, dances with words, and abhors the earnestness and the zeal and the "laboured prose" of the autodidact: the autodidact for his part distrusts the bourgeois writer as a poseur, a mere writer of words when words are not enough, a light-weight. (In Jack London's work, this perception is joined to a powerful sense of the crisis of masculinity, in a way that I don't see working in yours: even your stories of the sea have a very different bearing towards gender than that). You opposed Stephen Leacock, partly because he was a mainstream economist, but also, I suspect, because of his easy, bourgeois manner. He was exactly what you wanted to avoid in intellectual life.

[17]It would of course be fatuous to suggest you are the "Canadian Gramsci," especially given the latter's whole-hearted opposition to the kinds of Spencerian holism that were attractive to you. Nonetheless, there are some fascinating parallels when it comes to considering how both of you saw the

intellectual tasks of the working-class movement. Gramsci's important "sociological" move was to consider not just the class origins of intellectuals, but also their "functional" role. For Gramsci, whose education at the University of Turin did not efface his substantial sense of being a marginalized autodidact, the significant lesson was that an insurgent working class required its own organic intellectuals -- tied intimately to the movement and to the processes transforming working-class life -- in order to undertake the intense labour of criticism that preceded any authentic social revolution. This would appear to be only a slightly more abstract version of the position you presented in your classic articles of 1912 and 1913. I think the key here is that you both never stopped being aware of the ideas actually held by the majority of working people around you; that you both came from, and remained connected to, social contexts that impelled you to question the autonomy of intellectual life and the value of studying ideas "for their own sake." In other words, you appropriated elements from traditions that were not wholly conducive to the working-class struggle, and were able to integrate them effectively in new frameworks precisely because of your involvement in the concrete *praxis* of the workers' movement.

[18]Forgacs, *Antonio Gramsci Reader* 58.

[19]Forgacs, *Antonio Gramsci Reader* 74.

[20]Stuart Hall, "The Toad in the Garden: Thatcherism Among the Theorists," in Cary Nelson and Lawrence Grossberg, eds., *Marxism and the Interpretation of Culture* (Urbana and Chicago: University of Illinois Press, 1988): 44-45.

[21]The *International Socialist Review* in 1901 proclaimed its role to be the articulation of a "a philosophy of the whole of life." Pittenger, *American Socialists* 117.

[22]I think you rather unfairly dismissed the Communist Party's cultural work in your zeal to tag the Communists with the label of "religious zealotry." Not only did the Communists create a vibrant sub-culture, with a rich institutional matrix, but they also made lasting contributions to the Marxist discussion of Canadian political economy and history. The pathbreaking work of Stanley Ryerson was only the most well-known of these contributions. Of course, the Communists returned your compliment and ignored your work, since an important part of *their* party mythology was that they alone were the only *serious* Canadian Marxists.

[23]See Halker, *For Democracy, Workers, and God* 23; 79.

[24]Palmer, *A Culture in Conflict* xvi, emphasis added.

[25]Obituary for Tim Walker, *Western Socialist*, 19 June 1935 [my thanks to Peter Campbell for this reference].

[26] To an extent historians of the working class and of socialism have not always realized, early twentieth-century Canada was *not* in any profound cultural sense a uniformly capitalist country, and what Paul Buhle terms the "bourgeois revolution of the mind" can hardly be taken as a settled fact of the Canadian cultural reality c.1900. Paul Buhle, *Marxism in the United States:*

Remapping the History of the American Left. (London: Verso, 1987): 94. Buhle has suggested that if "much of European Socialist theory had adapted itself to the task of finishing the bourgeois revolution of the mind, Americans did not need or desire Socialist assistance. Socialist activists sought the certainty of evolutionary science but felt no need for extended theoretical discourse over the details." Whatever the merits of this argument in the American case, it's hard to see it in Canada. In Canada, most of the land-mass was populated by peoples for whom an endogenous bourgeois revolution had not really started; and even in the thinly-settled south, rural areas can be termed "bourgeois" only after registering some important qualifications. And why, if Buhle is right, did the most Enlightenment-oriented social theorists -- like Spencer and his innumerable socialist followers -- develop such a mass following in the United States, to the extent that Spencer is generally considered *the* most widely-read philosopher in the mid-to-late nineteenth century? And what of religion? Unless we are to go along with a reductionist equation of Protestantism with the spirit of capitalism, it is far from evident that North American religion in the nineteenth century was uniformly "bourgeois" in any straightforward sense -- i.e., encouraging an individualistic orientation to society and accepting profit-making and the acquisition of property as good and worthy enterprises for Christians.

[27] Heron, "Labourism," 62-64, asks some good questions about the emphasis Canadian historians have conventionally attached to religion, and remarks, "The crucial question remains whether working-class leaders got their politics from Christianity, or turned to a common cultural reservoir to express their politics. After all, religious metaphors were the common coin of public discourse in Canada" (64). I am not sure this question can be answered in this form. The intensity with which you, Colin, pursued theological issues -- and you were not alone by any means among working-class intellectuals -- suggests to me that, for you, this was something more than using religious metaphors to express basically secular insights. In order to advance the discussion, perhaps closer attention could be paid to exactly *how* Christian working-class intellectuals distinguished themselves from their opponents by the particular way they drew upon the Christian tradition. How unusual, for example, was your relentless working and re-working of the organic passages from Paul? Were there changing patterns of Biblical citation over time? I cannot agree with interpretations of this problem (e.g., Spencer, "Alternate Vision," 95) which treat it primarily as a matter of the labour movement objecting to the extent to which the dominant culture exploited or limited the Church. It goes far, far beyond that.

[28] Not that much has actually been accomplished in exploring the extent to which Canada in general really was a "Christian nation" c. 1900. However, for an interesting discussion, see John Webster Grant, *A Profusion of Spires: Religion in Nineteenth-Century Ontario* (Toronto: University of Toronto Press for the Ontario Historical Studies Series, Government of Ontario, 1988), who points out that whereas in 1790 "not more than 10 per cent of the American people were church members" -- with obvious implications for the religiosity

of the numerous American immigrants to Upper Canada in the first third of the nineteenth century(33) -- by the 1870s virtually everyone in Ontario claimed some attachment to a church. At the end of the nineteenth century, there was no evidence of church decline: the numbers of church buildings continued to rise rapidly, and two surveys of church attendance undertaken by the Toronto *Globe*, one in 1882 and the other in 1896, showed that on a given Sunday roughly 45 per cent of the total population attended church at least once (197).

[29] For Lewis, the apex of all modern thought was the insight that the universe was a unity, inter-related in its parts. All talk of dualism, all metaphysical philosophy, all theology was henceforth *passé*: there was now simply one theory of social and organic evolution. (Lewis never seems to have pondered the real possibilities of a pantheistic religious interpretation going in precisely the same direction). Echoing Feuerbach and (in a muffled and distorted fashion) Marx, Lewis proclaimed: "It is no longer God and Man, nor even Man and God, but Man only, with God an anthropomorphic shadow, related to man not as his creator, but as created by him. God and Man are not 'two', but in reality 'one.'" Lewis, *Evolution* 133. In this interpretation, then, one could not simultaneously be a *real* materialist and a Christian, for the materialist conception of history explained "the origin, functions, and changes of religion," just as it did those of law. So how (asked Lewis) could any man who boasted "of his concurrence in this epoch-making theory, using one lobe of his brain," go on to use another lobe and maintain that Socialist philosophy had nothing to do with religion? Workers were not hungering for the milk-and-water comforts of "Christian socialism," but for the strong red-blooded wine of real materialism. And those who combined a private Christianity with a public Socialism -- one kind of knowledge for themselves and another for their audience -- were following "the fundamental principle of priestcraft, and the working class has had far too much of it already." Lewis, *Evolution* 4,5,6. I believe that this argument had a real, although not permanent, impact on you, Colin.

[30]Stein, "The Religious Roots of the Canadian Labour Movement," 69-101. His tentative exploration succeeds in breathing fresh energy into an old issue by giving working-class intellectuals, heretofore represented as the curiously passive recipients of a Social Gospel worked out by others, some credit for being intelligent shapers of their own theological views, and perhaps taking to the discussion of socialism much of the premillennialist emphasis of their religious upbringing. As Richard Allen perceptively remarks, "the core conviction" of both labour and socialist papers from 1872 to 1914 "was that God, however understood, was working to assure a future of justice and brotherhood in history...." Richard Allen, "Providence to Progress: The Migration of an Idea in English Canadian Thought," *Canadian Issues/Thèmes Canadiens*, 7 (1985): 45, n. 21.

[31]In the general fascination with technical education we have a very good barometer of "Enlightenment" enthusiasm within the early Canadian working class. For James Simpson, who combined sabbatarianism, prohibition,

Methodism, socialism, *and* an enthusiasm for technical education, see Homel, "Simpson," 164-165. There would be rich material in this topic area for a much fuller study of the image and ideal of the Working-Class Enlightenment.

[32]Harold Entwhistle pointed out some time ago in *Antonio Gramsci: Conservative schooling for radical politics* (London, Boston and Henley: Routledge and Kegan Paul, 1979) that Gramscian cultural analysis led to educational conclusions diametrically opposed to those of the New Leftists who often appropriated his name: "A striking feature of Gramsci's writing is its positive valuation of traditional, mainstream, humanistic culture. Throughout his own work his debt to this is immense; his erudition, especially in the fields of history and literature (including foreign literature), is impressive. There is no dismissal of this mainstream culture, its source in Graeco-Roman civilization, as 'bourgeois' in any pejorative sense." (18-19) Rather than elevating pre-existing working-class customs and ideas to the status of a "culture" in which one could see the anticipation of a new world, Gramsci tended to write critically of "folklore" and argued that a radical teacher would have a necessarily quite adversarial relationship with the folk-cultural views of his or her students (23-27, 73).

[33]Although a "gender reading" of your work in terms of its "exclusive masculine thinking" suggests just how oblivious you could be to women's struggles, one might also recommend your writings be examined with a view to changing attitudes towards masculinity. Working as you so often did in homosocial environments, in which traditional masculine physicality was emphasized, you responded in your fiction with depictions of men, some of whom were broken on the wheel of "masculinity," and others of whom discretely rebelled against the code. Perhaps it is far-fetched to read your sea stories with this late-1990s gender agenda in mind (at least one critic has found it ridiculous): yet I still find your story "The Mate from Maine" in which our hero, a delicate and well-dressed man, saves the day while the more conventional "masculine" captain proves a coward, raises some very interesting questions about gender elasticity. Perhaps once it is conceded that the early socialists were not as "universalist" as their rhetoric suggested, but rather saw the world in ways influenced by class, gender and ethnicity, we can then go on respectfully to reconstruct the masculine worlds of meaning and belonging that many such socialists did inhabit. Jackson and McKay, eds., *Windjammers and Bluenose Sailors.* For a feminist critique of the masculine bias of the movement, see Janice Newton, such as "From Wage Slave to White Slave: The Prostitution Controversy and the Early Canadian Left," in Linda Kealey and Joan Sangster, eds., *Beyond the Vote: Canadian Women and Politics* (Toronto: University of Toronto Press, 1989): 217-236.

[34]Mark Pittenger, *American Socialists and Evolutionary Thought, 1870-1920* (Madison, Wisconsin: University of Wisconsin Press, 1993).

[35]Lewis, *Evolution* 22

[36]All the more ironic, then, that Spencer's combination of evolutionary determinism and *laissez-faire* individualism should read so much like an eerie preview of the worst of contemporary neo-conservative thought.

[37]See Chapter 2, Note 50 for my sense that Spencer's views weren't as unsympathetic (at least in the 1870s) to working seamen as the ones you attribute to him. But the point is that you *thought* he was against safety-at-sea measures.

[38]Lawrence Krader, "Theory of Evolution, Revolution and the State: The Critical Relation of Marx to his Contemporaries Darwin, Carlyle, Morgan, Maine and Kovalevsky," Eric J. Hobsbawm, ed., *The History of Marxism.* Vol. 1, *Marxism in Marx's Day* (Bloomington: Indiana University Press, 1982): 203. On the myth of Marx writing for permission to dedicate the English translation of the second volume of *Capital* to him, see Ralph Colp, Jr., "The myth of the Darwin-Marx Letter," *History of Political Economy*, 15, 4 (1983): 461-482.

[39]Desmond and Moore, *Darwin* 40-41, 315, 412-413, 467, 508.

[40]Lewis, *Evolution* 38. Edward P. Johanningsmeier, in his interesting biography *Forging American Communism: The Life of William Z. Foster* (Princeton, N.J.: Princeton University Press, 1994), captures some of the flavour of turn-of-the-century "working-class Darwinism" in this description of Hermon Franklin Titus, editor of the *Seattle Socialist* (who sounds remarkably like his counterparts in Vancouver): "Titus was a full-fledged scientific socialist. 'The attitude of the Revolutionary Socialist is the scientific attitude, the modern scientific attitude in contrast with the ancient superstitious attitude,' he wrote. There was no room for 'dreams,' 'schemes,' or 'utopias.' In addition, he proclaimed, 'there are probably not ten thousand people in the United States who thoroughly understand the simple Principles of Revolutionary Socialism.' The process of the education of the working class must begin with the 'facts.' The concept of a strictly inductive, evolutionary socialism as opposed to normative socialisms based on 'dreams' recurs in Titus's writings. 'To the scientific man, facts are everything, theories nothing,' he explained. How can a socialist, or revolutionary, look to the future, given the necessity of focusing simply on the 'facts'? A prominent feature of Titus's political writing was his belief in Darwinism and the inevitable evolution of society according to the laws of natural history. 'Karl Marx,' after all, 'scientifically investigated the facts of human society and formulated its laws of development, as Charles Darwin did in the life history of animals other than man.' Thus, 'Marxism, like Darwinism, must be accepted and believed, if its facts are well established'" (33-34). On the immense cultural power of Darwinism, see also Valentino Gerratana, "Marx and Darwin," *New Left Review* 82 (November-December 1973): 60-82, although in my opinion Gerratana misses the crucial significance of Spencer in providing the nineteenth century with an interpretation of evolution that was more popular (because more teleological and hence "progressive") than that of Darwin. Gerratana, not so incidentally, still placed faith in the now-discredited

"Marx/Darwin" legend (which had Marx asking Darwin for permission to dedicate a volume of *Capital* to him).

[41]Hofstatder, *Social Darwinism* 31-32.

[42]"Herbert Spencer was a very remarkable man and at one time widely recognized as such. J.S. Mill expressed the view that he was 'one of the most vigorous as well as boldest thinkers that English speculation has yet produced, full of the true scientific spirit'; and across the Atlantic Mr. Justice Holmes wrote that he doubted 'if any writer of English except Darwin' had 'done so much to affect our whole way of thinking about the universe'." Greenleaf, *Ideological Heritage* 48.

[43]Pittenger *American Socialists* 19-20.

[44]Turner, *Herbert Spencer* 7.

[45] As Turner notes: "....many of the functional statements are, in reality, a shorthand way to phrase a more extensive 'group selection' scenario. Spencer's famous phrase 'survival of the fittest,' for which he has been so resoundedly condemned, is actually a way to summarize conflict and war among *societies*. That is, those structural or institutional features that promote the survival of a population in conflict with other populations are likely to be retained, as they are likely to prevail in a conflict. Contrary to William Graham Sumner's misrepresentation of Spencer, and many commentators since, Spencer's use of this phrase in his sociological works typically concerns the selective pressures that war and conflict between societies generate for certain kinds of structural arrangements within a society. Evolution proceeds by conflict, conquest, and retention of those structural features that facilitated a society's survival. Selection is not so much at the *individual* level, but at the societal level...." Turner, *Herbert Spencer* 107. Because in Spencer, the mechanism of social adaptation is generally seen as Lamarckian -- entailing an entire population's inheritance of acquired social characteristics -- there is no *logical* necessity for competition between individuals, for in principle all might improve themselves. Only at the lower stages of evolution will adaptation by some entail the deaths of others. See Peel, *Herbert Spencer* 23.

[46]Thorstein Veblen sagely remarked that Spencer's critics "stand on his shoulders and beat him about the ears" (cited in Bannister, *Social Darwinism* 66).

[47]For very interesting Canadian documentation for this observation, see R.J. Taylor, "Darwin's Theory of Evolution: Four Canadian Responses," Ph.D. Thesis, McMaster University, 1976.

[48]Roger Bannister, in a revisionist study successfully undermining the myth of a hegemonic turn-of-the-century "Social Darwinism," argues that there was "... no way of determining conclusively the inherent social logic of Darwinism, if there was one." Whatever the uses to which racists and eugenicists put *The Descent of Man*, "there seems little ground for assuming that Darwinism logically and immediately gave support to unbridled individualism, unregulated competition, and *laissez faire* or in other ways championed

brutality and force in social affairs. Instead, the more one stressed natural selection through struggle in nature, the more it appeared that human society operated on different principles." The true Darwinist, according to Bannister, realized that a gap had opened between society and nature. Bannister, *Social Darwinism* 33.

[49]Over-reliance on a stark "sacred/secular" dichotomy should not discourage us from seeing the parallels between the "secular" Spencerians and the "religious" theosophists (such as Phillips Thompson), the latter developing in religious idiom a vision of an indwelling evolutionary spirit parallel in many respects to Spencerian uniformitarianism.

[50]Marx and Engels said many things about evolution, some of them remarkable, and some of them silly: on occasion Marx expressed enthusiasm for evolutionary ideas that were far cruder than anything in Spencer. Contrary to the Myth of the Marxist Tradition, there was no one "founders' path" that honest socialists could follow on questions of evolutionary theory. Marx was searching as well for an "evolutionary logic," and although he never did attempt to dedicate a volume of *Capital* to Darwin (as Marxian folklore so long and so revealingly maintained), he did turn to other major evolutionary intellectuals. The most revealing episode in his search for confirmation of his historical theories in natural-scientific evolutionary thought came in August, 1866. Marx wrote to Engels to sing the praises of *Origine et transformations de l'homme et des autres êtres* by Pierre Trémaux, a French autodidact with a taste for geology. Trémaux's core argument was that the perfection of human beings varies according to the "degree of elaboration" of the soil upon which they live. Marx thought the book an advance over Darwin; Engels thought it nonsense; Marx disagreed, although ultimately (and revealingly) he chose not integrate it into his theory. Dominique Lecourt is right, surely, in seeing this as a moment that can tell us much about considerably more than a momentary lapse in judgement on the part of Marx: it tells us about underlying intellectual currents and forces. Marx, having accepted Trémaux, went on to spell out how useful his work might be in evolving a theory of forms of transition, a theory of degeneration, and a definition of evolution as "necessary progress." *Necessary progress* : that phrase sums up succinctly what a radical Philosophy of History was looking for from natural science. Marx, it seems abundantly clear from this, wasn't trying -- *pace* Krader -- to evict teleology from nature so much as evict non-Hegelian teleology from nature: he thus fell in with other scholars for whom "evolution" would in this sense be reducible to a simple theory of human descent, and even of a unilinear human perfectionism. An ideal of human progress would be strengthened by the natural sciences. And, according to Lecourt, because of this "necessitarian optimism," neither Marx nor Engels ever understood the theory of natural selection, because they could not accommodate the central place occupied in it by contingency. See Lecourt, "Marx ," 15-26.

[51]Philip Abrams, *The Origins of British Sociology: 1834-1914* (Chicago and London: University of Chicago Press, 1968): 72-73.

[52]As J.D.Y. Peel dryly notes in his wonderful study of Spencer's thought, "The point of comparing the ruling class, the trading or distributive classes, and the masses, to the mucous, vascular and serous systems of the liver-fluke" is a little less than clear. Peel, *Herbert Spencer* 178.

[53]Marx described force as the "midwife" of progress, delivering the old society pregnant with the new; similar imagery recurs in Kautsky, Lenin and Trotsky. (Of course, the "midwife" metaphor also implies -- or at least should imply -- rather more conscious volition and agency than normally conveyed by organicist imagery). See MacIntyre, *Proletarian Science* 108-113. "Marx himself had described force as the midwife of progress, delivering the old society pregnant with the new, an analogy followed by Kautsky in *The Class Struggle* (1892) and Trotsky in *Where is Britain Going?* (1926) and used frequently by British Marxists. But the organicist implications of this evolutionary tradition were more difficult to refute, and by the end of the 1920s Marxists were much more wary about drawing such close comparisons" (113). On the popular level, as you yourself observed, there were frequent references in Marxian work to the diseases and parasites infesting the system and afflicting the people. The images of Frankenstein and vampires and monstrosity could be said to be ingenious attempts to combine organic and mechanical interpretations of the social order (as well as to smuggle in an ethical critique in naturalistic clothes).

[54]Desmond and Moore, *Darwin* 534-535. I wonder if historians have not fallen victim, in their discussion of evolution, to something parallel to the "sacred circle" syndrome in discussions of Marxism, in which all the errors are attributed to Engels (Marx's evil twin, one supposes) leaving Marx completely unsullied by the charges of reductionism, scientism, etc. In the case of the history of evolution, all the good science and reservations about applying biological axioms to society belong to Darwin, whereas the role of distorter, simplifier and vulgarizer falls to poor old Spencer. Curious, then, that *Darwin* borrowed from *Spencer* the phrase "survival of the fittest," which he felt left *less* room in his theory for anthropomorphism and vulgar teleology!

[55]George B. Cotkin, "The Spencerian and Comtian Nexus in Gompers' Labor Philosophy: The Impact of Non-Marxian Evolutionary Thought," *Labor History* 20, 4 (Fall 1979): 510-511. Gompers was presented with volumes of Spencer's works after he was defeated as AFL president in 1894. Gompers *claimed* to have read Spencer with great care and interest -- and, after all, because of his compulsory vacation from office thanks to his socialist enemies, he did have the leisure time to do so.

[56]Wiltshire, *Social and Political Thought* 15 .

[57]I draw all the information in this paragraph from Peel, *Herbert Spencer*, 38-78.

[58]Note E.K. Hunt, "Value Theory in the Writings of the Classical Economists, Thomas Hodgskin and Karl Marx," *History of Political Economy* 9, 3 (1977): 322-345.

[59]As observed by Greenleaf, *Ideological Heritage* 70.

[60]Herbert Spencer, *Social Statics* 322-323.

[61]Peel, *Herbert Spencer* 2. The novelist Abraham Cahan described his hero in *The Rise of David Levinsky* as being converted to scientific socialism after an experience of intellectual intoxication: the "intoxicant" in question was Spencer's *Social Statics*. Pittenger, *American Socialists* 107.

[62]Spencer, *Social Statics* 24.

[63]We have it on the good authority of one Canadian scholar who has looked at W.D. LeSueur that Herbert Spencer was "certainly not a feminist." Clifford G. Holland, *William Dawson LeSueur (1840-1917): A Canadian Man of Letters* (San Francisco: Mellon Research University Press, 1993): 290. It's not nearly so cut-and-dried. In *Social Statics*, Spencer daringly applied the criterion of the law of equal rights to the question of women. In a chapter devoted to "The Rights of Women," he argued: "Equity knows no difference of sex. In its vocabulary the word *man* must be understood in a generic, and not in a specific sense. The law of equal freedom manifestly applies to the whole race -- female as well as male. The same *a priori* reasoning which establishes that law for men...may be used with equal cogency on behalf of women. The Moral Sense, by virtue of which the masculine mind responds to that law, exists in the feminine mind as well. Hence the several rights deducible from that law must appertain equally to both sexes." Spencer, *Social Statics* 173. Spencer later sought to suppress all memory of his early feminism, by erasing most of the chapter on 'The Rights of Women,' rewriting many other passages about women in reprints of *Social Statics*, and removing feminist statements from his *Synthetic Philosophy*. Yet his earlier position on the rights of women was not so easily cancelled, not in the memory of many socialists and feminists. In the monthly journal *Socialist Woman*, Spencerian-Marxist assumptions prevailed, and evolution was used to emphasize the historical specificity of women's experiences and therefore the need for an independent feminist perspective. For all his later back-pedalling, Herbert Spencer therefore cannot be overlooked in any meaningful reconstruction of the history of socialist feminism. For another discussion of gender ideology and Herbert Spencer, see Nancy L. Paxton, *George Eliot and Herbert Spencer: Feminism, Evolutionism, and the Reconstruction of Gender* (Princeton, N.J.: Princeton University Press, 1991). I wonder if her reading of Spencer might not tend too much to insist upon Eliot as the source of his feminism: Eliot met Spencer in 1851, but *Social Statics* was written in the 1840s and published in 1850. Is it then plausible to argue that Spencer depended on Eliot for his ideas, or that his later back-tracking on feminist issues was largely the product of his "anxiety of influence"?

[64]Spencer, *Social Statics*, Chapter Seventeen.

[65]Spencer, *Social Statics* 126. Spencer was at pains to show that "militant" and warlike societies evolved into modern and peaceful ones. History has not been kind to his hypothesis that "a long peace" would be accompanied by so vast an increase of manufacturing and commercial activity, "with

accompanying growth of the appropriate political structures within each nation, a strengthening of those ties between nations which mutual dependence generates, that hostilities will be more and more resisted and the organization adapted for the carrying them on will decay." Herbert Spencer, *The Principles of Sociology,* Vol. 2 (New York: D. Appleton and Company, 1909): 648.

[66]Spencer was not a "racist" in the nineteenth-century sense (although judged by a contemporary left tribunal, almost all western intellectuals of the last century, including Marx and Engels, might be condemned as "racists," since they generally talked quite easily in terms of the supposedly inherent characteristics of national and racial groups). Although never quite able to decide between environmentalist and hereditarian ways of conceptualizing racial differences, Spencer, as a gut Lamarckian, mainly held that the environment could prompt adaptations in one generation that might be passed on to the next. Environment and training could thus affect differences between races, peoples, and nations. And for someone often tagged with the label "imperialist," Spencer did odd things: he was an adviser to Asian governments, which he urged to a path of self-reliance. Spencer also later took pains to deny that "the social man" was in all respects "emotionally superior to the pre-social man." He hence likely would not have endorsed such Canadian strategies of directed cultural change as residential schools for Native children, because he would have believed them ill-advised attempts to change evolutionary patterns whose consequences could not be readily predicted, and also because they involved extensions of state authority, often in an unholy alliance with the church. As usual, the anti-Spencerian polemics distort and oversimplify. See Herbert Spencer, *The Principles of Sociology* 239.

[67]Spencer, *Social Statics* 352-353.

[68]Spencer, *Social Statics* 131-2.

[69]E.g., Turner, *Herbert Spencer* 10.

[70]For an excellent discussion, see Robert G. Perrin, "Herbert Spencer's Four Theories of Social Evolution," *American Journal of Sociology,* 86 (1980): 1339-1359. Perrin notes that attributing any single doctrine of evolution to Spencer may oversimplify because he in fact advanced four notions of evolution. The first, optimistic theory depicts social evolution as progress towards an ideal "social state" in which society is based upon amity, individual altruism, an elaborate specialization of functions, criteria which recognize only achieved qualities, and voluntary cooperation among highly disciplined individuals: this is of course the vision of *Social Statics.* Evolution in this sense is morally progressive change, both necessary and inevitable. The second sense of social evolution entails, first, the assumption of functional requirements for a society's continued existence and, second, the general proposition that whole societies tend to differentiate into 'societal subsystems,' the functions of which correspond to these requirements. "Social requirements" are dictated by conditions which are logically more primitive and which are temporally prior.

In this case, evolution is movement towards a first stage of "functional equilibrium," the emergence of structures in response to functional requirements. A third sense of "evolution" is that of an "increasing division of labour." A final sense of "evolution" is that of a tendency of the Earth to support a vast aggregate of societies, an aggregate that has become more and more various in its forms, and which is becoming still more diverse. There is a progressive trend toward economic integration, as the population grows ever more heterogeneous with regard to the separate functions assumed by separate nations. (Here Spencer anticipates much of the so-called theory of globalization). In this view, evolution is a force operating globally and differentiating the separate countries of the earth from each other in terms of their function within a world-system. Of course, this entails some tidying up of Spencer himself, who thought all four theories emerged from the same fundamental first principles, and used "social evolution" to apply to each and every one of them.

[71]See Turner, *Herbert Spencer* 43 for a discussion. Scott Meikle, *Essentialism in the Thought of Karl Marx* (London: Duckworth, 1985): 16 rebuts a similar charge of "biologizing" in much the same way in the case of Marx.

[72]Whether or not any non-contradictory definition could ever encompass so incalculably vast a force as "evolution" conceived in this way is completely open to question. It may have been a term for which no synonym could ever be supplied. Note on this subject Peter J. Bowler, "The Changing Meaning of 'Evolution,'" *Journal of the History of Ideas* 36, 1 (January-March 1975): 95-114.

[73]"Scientific previsions, both qualitative and quantitative, have various degrees of definiteness; and because among certain classes of phenomena the previsions are approximate only, it is not, therefore, to be stated that there is no science of those phenomena: if there is *some* prevision, there is *some* science." Spencer, *The Study of Sociology* 39.

[74]See Spencer, *The Principles of Sociology* Vol.2, 642, for acid commentary on missionaries. Late twentieth-century minds might not readily see just how abrasive those words would have sounded to many readers, who like many thousands of Canadians had rallied to the cause of Missionary Societies (which with temperance was one of the largest and most powerful crusades in nineteenth-century Canada). Spencer was also the scourge of religious hypocrisy, mocking those who preached the nobility of self-sacrifice on Sunday and practised the gospel of gouging other people the remaining six days of the week. These sallies against religious authority may seem somewhat tame in the 1990s, but they were not a century ago. Spencer, *The Study of Sociology* 179, 180. He wrote off many clergymen as people who had not understood their own religion. When viewed from the perspective of Social Science, religious creeds were obviously captives of their own assumptions. "Clearly," he writes disarmingly, "a creed which makes smoking one of the blackest crimes, and has only mild reprobation for the worst acts committed by man against man, negatives anything like Social Science." Spencer, *Social*

Statics 295. Pittenger calls Spencer's a "weak-kneed materialism, which left room for an ultimate 'unknowable,'" and implies that socialists who found it politically expedient could make religion a part of the Spencerian system (154). Here he surely fails to discriminate between religion as a source of explanation -- the Deity of *Social Statics* ultimately explains why one course of conduct is better than another -- and religious faith as addressing issues and concerns that are distinguishable from those normally addressed by social science. Is a full-blooded materialism necessarily a monism? Or, in fact, an atheism? There is no philosophical agreement on these questions, but Pittenger writes as though there were.

[75]See Wetter, *Dialectical Materialism* 280-561. For a lucid and informative commentary on Lenin's scientific and philosophical thought, see Anton Pannekoek, *Lenin as Philosopher: A Critical Examination of the Philosophical Basis of Leninism* (London: Merlin, 1975). This famous Dutch "council communist" is especially good on the connections between Dietzgen and Lenin.

[76]Peel, ed., *Herbert Spencer on Social Evolution* 7.

[77]Yes, Spencer was a drab writer and a bore: but, poignantly enough, he too dreamt of a "realm of freedom" not unlike that of the socialist tradition, in which "ways of living are no longer dictated; dress ceases to be prescribed; the rules of class-subordination lose their peremptoriness; religious beliefs and observances are not insisted upon; modes of cultivating the land and carrying on manufactures are no longer fixed by law; and the exchange of commodities, both within the community and with other communities, becomes gradually unshackled." Spencer, *The Principles of Sociology*, Vol.2, 659.

[78]His desired future is by no means an idealized version of Victorian Britain, where (according to him) trade is essentially corrupt, businessmen feed cannibalistically upon each other, and the motto is: cheat or be cheated. Spencer was not the "philosopher of big business," contrary to legend (and the fond hopes of his not-very-knowledgeable disciple, Andrew Carnegie). For a good discussion, see Peel, *Herbert Spencer* 214-8.

[79]Herbert Spencer, *The Principles of Sociology* 152.

[80]One reason why the Myth of the Simply Reactionary Spencer proved so successful was because late twentieth-century socialists came, for their own myopic reasons, to think of a large intrusive state as a sign of social progress. New liberals, deeply influenced by the organic metaphor, would see welfare legislation as a force that would simply increase the chances that adaptation to the social state would be successful; and any effective liberal theory should henceforth take as its unit of analysis the functional group, not the isolated individual. Spencerian new liberalism would ultimately come to fruition in Canada with the Co-operative Commonwealth Federation and the Liberal Party in the 1940s (whose adoption of such new premises should not be narrowly interpreted as the victory of bureaucrats and intellectuals, but of a more broadly based social tendency).

[81]For a parallel argument, see Martin's description of the anarchist appropriation of Spencer in his study *Men Against the State*, 234: "The writings of Herbert Spencer began to acquire the pliability of the scriptures during the last two decades of nineteenth century United States, in that their scope afforded the opportunity for diverse elements to dip in, extract, and manipulate, for various purposes, portions which might buttress some particular stand. For instance, the exponents of laissez-faire found therein the sanction for the maintenance of the economic and social status-quo. At the same time they found comfort and support for even greater expansion of monopoly enterprise in their Darwinistic content, which seemed to justify all this as part of a program of cosmic evolution of civilization....The American anarchists, on the other hand, hardly the friends of monopoly interests, appropriated these arguments of Spencer which appeared to substantiate their attack upon the state, the earlier output of the English sociologist furnishing especially welcome ammunition. Spencer's name acquired status among the anarchists for other reasons than as a champion of freedom and attacker of government. The ethical concept of equal rights and the evolutionary approach to societal growth were both incorporated within the structure of anarchist propaganda as corollaries to the... individual sovereignty principle and the anarchist concept of cultural change. No blanket acceptance of Spencer was implied by favorable mention when they found his ideas compatible; some of his views indeed received stringent treatment at their hands. Only a portion of the anarchist ranks accepted him in any capacity, and a swinging away from him as a potential prophet took place eventually when the man and his work began to be studied as a whole." (234) One has the impression that this "swinging away" occurred rather later in Canadian socialist circles -- but this is a matter still to be thoroughly investigated.

[82]Roger Bannister notes the massive international outpouring of books of "Socialist Darwinism" from 1890 to 1914. Bannister, *Social Darwinism* 136. He singles out in particular Arthur M. Lewis's *Evolution Positive and Negative* (1902); Michael A. Lane's *The Level of Social Motion* (1902); Walter T. Mill's *The Struggle for Existence* (1904); Ernest Untermann's *Science and Revolution* (1905); Karl Kautsky's *Ethics* (1907); Anton Pannekoek's *Marxism and Darwinism* (1912); and Henry Jager's *Social Evolution, or Socialism Made Easy* (1916). For further discussion of evolution and left-wing thinking, marred to some extent by Cold War rhetoric, see Conway Zirkle, *Evolution, Marxian Biology, and the Social Scene* (Philadelphia: University of Pennsylvania Press, 1959). For a modern assessment of attempts to integrate Marxian political economy with evolutionary theory, see Charles Woolfson, *The labour theory of culture: a re-examination of Engels's theory of human origins* (London, Boston and Henley: Routledge and Kegan Paul, 1982). Peter Campbell underlines the fascinating fact that, as late as 1914, the "Marxist" Socialist Party of Canada listed as many titles on its literature list by Spencer as by Marx. Campbell, "Stalwarts," 30. The Spencer/Woodsworth link remains to be systematically explored (we know Woodsworth read Spencer at university, but the more important question is: how much did Spencer's necessitarian optimism shape

Woodsworth's vision of the co-operative commonwealth?) On this point, Alan Mills remarks that "co-operative" and "co-operation" as concepts involve in Woodsworth a certain social ontology: "The particular ontology of society that underlay his main theory of cooperation asserted that, because of technological innovations associated with steam and electricity, industrialism engendered ever-greater economic specialization, centralization, interdependence, amalgamation, and integration. Society had become an 'organism,' 'a spider-web,' a 'system'; it was an 'association' of parts rather than a 'heterogeneous aggregation' made up of 'isolated atoms' of 'unrelated phenomena,' with 'little coherency' or 'active unifying principle'" (*Fool for Christ*, 69). These are very Spencerian-Marxist ways of looking at the social order. Mills further argues: "This conception of cooperation was fundamental to Woodsworth. From it he deduced his belief in public regulation, planning, and social ownership as well as his hope of the egalitarian distribution of wealth. In this primordial sense, cooperation was a technological and technocratic notion emphasizing the unimaginable efficiency and productivity of the contemporary industrial firm and the blessings of centralized procedures for making managerial decisions. We may call this sense of cooperation the 'technological' one." (69-70). Yet the earlier and more direct quotation is replete with organic, not mechanical, metaphors: a discrepancy that must surely be somewhat damaging to Mills's "technocratic" interpretation of Woodsworth. Mark Pittenger claims there was only *one* major American socialist intellectual in the period 1900-1908 who proclaimed an absolute disinterest in Spencer. Pittenger, *American Socialists*, 146. It would be fascinating to have more comparative work on francophone and anglophone sociology in Canada in which the intellectual influences involved in each respective camp were evaluated. For the francophone sociological scene in turn-of-the-century Montreal, see Pierre Trépanier, "La Société canadienne d'économie sociale de Montréal, 1888-1911: sa fondation, ses buts et ses activités," *Canadian Historical Review*, 67, 3 (1986): 343-367.

[83] *Social Statics* was also the major theoretical influence on Henry George, which made the battle between George and Spencer all the more bitter. See Raymond Geiger, *The Philosophy of Henry George* (New York: The Macmillan Company, 1933). Spencer reconsidered his earlier position on the public administration of land in 1883. After that, as Geiger remarks, "The fate of *Social Statics* was as inevitable as it was tragic. It was not murdered; it was mutilated, and for any self-respecting book that is by far the more deplorable calamity. In 1892, Spencer 'abridged and revised' the earlier edition and published it together with *The Man Versus the State*. He wrote in the preface to this edition that he had 'relinquished some of the conclusions drawn from the first principle laid down,' and also that he had been unable to 'prevent misinterpretation of my later beliefs'" (303).

[84] It's true that Pittenger concedes the multifaceted nature of Spencer's appeal: besides evolution, he writes, "Spencer was also respected for his affinity with materialism, evolutionary theory of ethics, anti-imperialism, moral repugnance at the conditions of modern labor, distaste for aristocracy, personal

nonconformity, and apparent ability to discover the imprint of scientific laws amid natural and social chaos" (Pittenger, *American Socialists*, 116). The trouble is that he then loses track of this complexity. It is apparent that many hard leftists were Spencerian-Marxists. Take for example Daniel DeLeon and the Socialist Labor Party, who were not exactly the blandest social democrats around: with them Spencer was a primary influence. In his articles on Spencer in 1891, DeLeon interestingly singled out Spencer's politico-ethical stature for praise along with Spencerian evolutionary theory; and Spencer (along with Marx, Morgan and Darwin) would remain, even to the 1940s, an intellectual influence in the SLP. There would simply seem to be no necessary connection, then, between admiration for Spencerian evolutionary theory and advocacy of the "parliamentary road to socialism."

[85] As Spencer expressed it in *Social Statics*: "Pull to pieces a man's Theory of Things, and you fill find it based upon facts collected at the suggestion of his desires. A fiery passion consumes all evidences opposed to its gratification, and fusing together those that serve its purpose, casts them into weapons by which to achieve its end" (177). Spencer himself was often a prime example of this.

[86] For Antonio Gramsci, who (like so many) denounced Spencer and the Spencerians while at the same time discretely adopting some of their ideas, it was possible to distinguish "organic movements" within a structure -- those which were relatively permanent -- from "conjunctural movements" -- those which were "immediate" and "almost accidental." Forgacs, *Antonio Gramsci Reader* 202.

[87] The legacy of the SPC stands in particular need of re-examination. I agree with Campbell's astute analysis of the dynamic quality of the SPC's Marxism, with its interplay between leaders and led. He emphasizes well the extent to which SPCers were guided by Marx's ideas even in their daily activities, and the emphasis in the SPC on the education and empowerment of workers themselves. All this in a party whose literature list featured Spencer's works as prominently as those of Marx!

[88] Russell Hann, "Brainworkers and the Knights of Labor," 49 notes that "Thompson had been deeply influenced by Spencer's notion of gradual social evolution and it formed a crucial aspect of his thought....The idea that the struggle for labour reform would have its outcome in some distant epoch was an important contribution to the creation of a new political and cultural strategy." This admiration for Spencer's evolutionism did not prevent Thompson from fiercely attacking the philosopher's *The Man Versus the State* for its views on *laissez faire* and state interference.

[89] As Irvine explains, "Society is like the human body. Once it was a social plasm, the simple form. As it evolved, it developed many parts and functions, in the performance of which groups of people act as units. It would be insane, if it were possible, to throw a man into a chemical solution that would reduce hm into his original protoplasm for the sake of sameness and primitive unity. For surely the unity of parts acting in harmony is higher and more admirable

than the original bit of jelly." Irvine, *Farmers in Politics* 184. Incidentally, this is a fine example of the "smuggling in" of ethics under the cover of a "neutral" scientific description.

90Pittenger, *American Socialists* 105-106. (Yet he then perplexingly then returns to the standard view: socialists faced the "inherent difficulty" of "trying to build a revolutionary tradition from the distinctly non-revolutionary materials of Spencerian social organicism and teleological universalistic evolutionism -- materials that stressed the natural and inevitable development of simpler social bodies into more complex and interdependent ones." I do not think the "essentialism" of this interpretation does Pittenger's useful account any good.) The more pacific R.H. Tawney would use something of the same argument for the "excision" of extraneous, non-functional parts in *The Acquisitive Society*, when he condemned those who drew royalties from coal seams on the one hand as "functionless," and urged recognition and rights for working people who performed invaluable "functions." R.H.Tawney, *The Acquisitive Society* (New York, 1948), Chapter 2. The notion of "function" had been changed in Tawney's work, however, in line with the neo-Hegelian idealism of the new liberals. For the most colourful and exciting use of a socialist language of medical cleansing -- complete with bloody wounds, white blood cells, and even torrential inundations of puss -- see Ferri, *Socialism and Modern Science* 17-18.

91According to Wiltshire, no major thinker after Spencer ever attempted to tie the organic analogy and individualism together. Wiltshire, *Social and Political Thought* 241-242. A sociologist like Frank Ward would powerfully polemicize against Spencer by skimming off Spencer's more colourful passages -- defending private control of sewage companies, for instance, on the grounds that recalcitrant householders could simply have their drainage facilities turned off! -- and by pointing to an obvious contradiction: "If the state, the supreme organ of integration, is to have practically no function.... what becomes of Spencer's increasing integration as a criterion of progress? The logical outcome of the social organism is not extreme individualism but extreme centralization." Cited, Hofstatder, *Social Darwinism* 80. The same contradiction may ultimately come to haunt neo-conservatism, which has to date characteristically combined the most "cosmic" and "sublime" vistas of globalization with the most "individualistic" and "atomistic" notions of domestic politics. Could one not logically argue that, if Canada is entering into a new era of globalization, we should have a much stronger, more aggressive, more integral state, all the more capable of integrating us smoothly into this new world order?

92Wiltshire, *Social and Political Thought* 2. J.A.Hobson and Leonard Hobhouse also worked from "Spencerian" organic premises to new liberal, statist conclusions. For a discussion of Spencer's influence on New Liberalism, see Hobson, *Confessions* 23; Greenleaf, *Ideological Heritage*, 168.; Michael Freeden, "Introduction" to J.A.Hobson, *Confessions of an Economic Heretic: The Autobiography of J.A. Hobson* [1938] (Brighton: Harvester Press, 1976).

viii; Kloppenberg, *Uncertain Victory* 5-7; Abrams, *The Origins of British Sociology* 87-92; Hobhouse, *Liberalism* 5-6. For Hobson's continuing and powerful legacy, see John Pheby, ed., *J.A.Hobson After Fifty Years: Freethinker of the Social Sciences* (London, 1993).

93See Simon, "Spencer and the 'Social Organism,'" 296, 298. For a discussion of Spencer's influence on New Liberalism, see Hobson, *Confessions* 23; Greenleaf, *Ideological Heritage* 168.; Michael Freeden, "Introduction" to J.A.Hobson, *Confessions of an Economic Heretic: The Autobiography of J.A. Hobson* [1938] (Brighton: Harvester Press, 1976). viii; Kloppenberg, *Uncertain Victory* 5-7; Abrams, *The Origins of British Sociology* 87-92; Hobhouse, *Liberalism* 5-6. For Hobson's continuing and powerful legacy, see John Pheby, ed., *J.A.Hobson After Fifty Years: Freethinker of the Social Sciences* (London, 1993).

94Pittenger, *American Socialists* 6-7; 11; 248. One might add that the metaphor of "falling prey" rather minimizes working-class intelligence and agency.

95Anyone who thinks this is unfair just needs to spend an hour or so -- more could be hazardous to mental health -- with a book like *Fundamentals of Marxism-Leninism. Manual* (Moscow: Foreign Languages Publishing House, 1963). It proceeds majestically, from the philosophical base ("Dialectical and Historical Materialism -- the Highest Stage in the Development of Philosophical Thought") -- through the eminently Spencerian proposition that "The development of society as a whole takes an ascending line, represents progress, a forward movement from lower to higher forms" (193) -- and reaches a climax with Academician V.A. Obruchev's ecstatic view of what human beings in the future will demand of science: "...to produce in factories all the substances known on earth, up to most complex -- protein -- and also substances unknown in nature: harder than diamonds, more heat-resistant than firebrick, more refractory than tungsten and osmium, more flexible than silk and more elastic than rubber..." (716). Of such durable elements were the dreams of commissars made.

96It's never clear whether the "adaptation" is of all of humanity to its position in the cosmos, or of one society to its position among other societies, or one individual to life with other individuals. Unless one is specific about how a particular change in society helps individuals adapt to some specific circumstance, the concept of adaptation quickly becomes tautological and vacuous. Anything may -- perhaps everything must -- be viewed as an adaptation to something or other. For a discussion, see Peel, *Herbert Spencer* 155

97Marxists can point to Marx's typically down-to-earth comment in his *Critique of Hegel's Philosophy of Right*: "There is no bridge by which one can pass from the universal idea of the organism (whether it be vegetable, animal, social, etc.), to the particular idea of the organism of the State or the constitution of the State, nor will there ever be." Karl Marx, *Critique of Hegel's Philosophy of Right* (Cambridge: Cambridge University Press, 1970):

14. There is an excellent discussion in Lucio Colletti, *From Rousseau to Lenin: Studies in Ideology and Society* (London: New Left Books, 1972): 24. For his part, Gramsci characteristically explored the common usages of the organic metaphor to highlight their contradictions. Economic determinists -- generally Spencerian-Marxists, who were thick on the ground in Italy -- had argued that the economy and the bourgeois state were analogous to the skeleton -- the true reality -- whereas other peripheral matters were conceptualized as "skin" or "appearances." But, Gramsci said, taking the metaphor at face value, it was not the case that skin and appearances were "illusions" and the skeleton the only reality. The whole attempt to depict history as a natural organism passing through fixed and predictable stages struck Gramsci as a philistine attempt to seek salvation in pathetic, pre-determined schemas, incapable of grasping human creativity. Societies were not organisms because their patterns of development were simply not so predictable. Germino, *Antonio Gramsci* 237. Peel adds further cogent criticisms of the organic metaphor. Societies do not really resemble organisms at all: they have no external forms, the units of society are not contiguous with one another in a mass, these units are moreover spatially mobile, and unlike an organism which has one center of consciousness, each unit of society is so endowed. Peel, *Herbert Spencer* 155. Wiltshire sees this discrepancy as a stumbling-block for Spencer's entire view of society: "If society can 'feel' only through the perception of its units, then only through the perception of its units has it any existence. For Spencer, by contrast, society was a real entity, existing independently of the perception of its constituent members. Only if thus conceived can its development be considered subject to the immutable laws of nature. The absence, in society, of a collective consciousness thus neatly incorporates three related problems: first, it sets up an insuperable barrier to literal acceptance of the 'social organism'; second, it confounds Spencer's realist view of society; and third, it raises the questionable status of the individual in evolutionary philosophy." Wiltshire, *Social and Political Thought* 234-235. When Spencer was resurrected to become a key inspiration of twentieth-century systems theory, which in essence took up the mission of the *Synthetic Philosophy*, many of these same dilemmas were apparent: a theory of *all* systems ran the risk of becoming so general as to be vacuous. It should be noted that this criticism -- that generic abstractions ultimately fail to produce anything more interesting than generalities and tautologies -- is true not only of organic/biological analogies, but also of many generic metaphors extracted from the natural sciences: from chemistry and physics (homeostasis and equilibrium, which have generated such circular and true-by-definition arguments from economists and economic historians); from mechanics (function and dysfunction as mechanical terms -- now enjoying a spectacular vogue in such circular and question-begging notions as the "dysfunctional family" or "dysfunctional behaviour"); from engineering (base and superstructure, *träger* as ways of describing policies and relationships); and from pseudo-cybernetics (feedback, learning curve, system overload). The best test of whether such analogies are still serving some useful social purpose would seem to be that of experience:

after the passage of years, does the analogy still seem to help us see something new about the past and present? Are there criteria according to which the implications of the analogy can be disconfirmed? Does it lead us to new or to entirely predictable results? These same questions will some day be asked, of course, of the many spatial and language-specific metaphors associated with the Moment of Discourse.

[98]Colletti, *From Rousseau to Lenin* 25.

[99]It is also striking that many of the major conceptual debates found among evolutionary thinkers c. 1910 -- for socialists, the most crucial of these was that dividing those who argued that evolution might encompass rapid, "revolutionary" change from those who derived gradualist conclusions from Darwinian theory -- are far from settled among contemporary evolutionary thinkers. On this theme, see in particular Ernst Mayr, *One Long Argument: Charles Darwin and the Genesis of Modern Evolutionary Thought* (Harmondsworth: Penguin, 1991).

[100]That the goal of a totally unified set of principles, able to explain all the forces known in the universe, is still actively envisaged by some formidable scientists is suggested by Steven Weinberg, *Dreams of a Final Theory* (London, 1992). A sharp distinction between intellectual life in the 1990s and intellectual life in the 1910s and 1920s is that socio-historical thought is almost completely insulated from such audacious scientific reasoning.

[101]As Pittenger acidly remarks, Ferri's "scientific" credentials as a criminologist "gave added weight to his pronouncements on the inferiority of blacks, women, criminals, and social outsiders of all sorts." Pittenger, *American Socialists* 126. One might also mention Ferri's views on "sexual degenerates." For the background, see Daniel Pick, "The Faces of Anarchy: Lombroso and the Politics of Criminal Science in Post-Unification Italy," *History Workshop* 21 (Spring 1986): 60-86. Canadian historians will be interested to know that Lombroso -- the Italian criminologist whose work underpinned that of Ferri -- used the visage of Louis Riel as one of twenty portraits in a page devoted to "Revolutionaries and Political Criminals -- the Semi-Insane and the Morally Insane" (69).

[102]This book-length excerpt from *Anti-Duhring* became the most popular introduction to Marxism apart from the *Communist Manifesto*. Gareth Stedman Jones, "Engels and the History of Marxism," in Eric J. Hobsbawm, ed., *The History of Marxism* Vol.1. *Marxism in Marx's Day* (Bloomington: Indiana University Press, 1982) 290-326. I can attest personally to the high regard in which this book was held by many Canadian left-wingers: A copy of it was pressed into my hands in the late 1960s by the ardently pro-Soviet General Secretary of the extremely idiosyncratic hard-left local of the New Democratic Party in Sarnia as the *only* book in socialist theory I would ever really need to read in my lifetime.

[103]Colletti, *From Rousseau to Lenin* 26.

[104]See Wetter, *Dialectical Materialism* 281-286; and Andrew Collier, "Materialism and Explanation in the Human Sciences," in John Mepham and

D-H. Ruben, eds., *Issues in Marxist Philosophy*, Vol.2, *Materialism* (Brighton: Harvester, 1979) 39-42, a discussion I found rather retrograde and pre-Gramscian in its Aristotelianism, but useful in distinguishing various meanings of the word "materialism." I think historians of socialism should consider calling a moratorium on the use of the "materialism/idealism" dichotomy, especially as a short-hand way of allocating people to the good side or the bad side of a tidy binary opposition.

[105]Colletti argues that monist materialism, especially one powered by a Hegelian dialectic conceived as a scientific description of matter rather than of a process of thought, entailed in fact an absolute idealism, a consistent anti-materialism. Colletti, *Marxism and Hegel*, passim. For example, the reductionist ultra-materialist ontology of Dietzgen -- which argued that the existence of physical and social objects was secondary to the ontologically primary level of matter, the fundamental building block of the universe -- cannot easily be reconciled with a realist posture that accepts that societies, human individuals, philosophies, mentalities and social relations of production all do actually exist, and are best analyzed in ways that do not attempt to see them only in terms of the atomic particles of the material universe. Realism requires a sense of duality: it requires there to be a reality outside the perceiving subject, a distinction between perceiving subject and that which is perceived. Post-structuralist thought has not, to my admittedly "realist" eye, resolved this problem.

[106]Colletti, *From Rousseau to Lenin*, 25.

[107]Ibid., 19.

[108]Ibid., 14.

[109]I cannot agree at all with Rée's suggestion that most socialist *autodidacts* were reading books by non-socialists, and were almost completely without access to the Marxist tradition. Rée, *Proletarian Philosophers* 9-13. This may have been true of a somewhat earlier period in Britain, although even then it sounds unlikely. It was not true of Canada.

[110]It is true that in one place you acknowledge the peculiarities of Canada's geography as an element in socialist strategy (§.124., "The Two Arms of the Working-Class Movement"). But such acknowledgements of a specific politico-economic context surface only occasionally in your work.

[111]Although there is much to dislike in Aileen S. Kraditor, *The Radical Persuasion, 1890-1917: Aspects of the Intellectual History and the Historiography of Three American Radical Organizations* (Baton Rouge and London: Louisiana State University Press, 1981) -- not least her irritating and question-begging habit of talking about "John Q. Worker" -- she may have something of a legitimate point when she discusses the tendency of radical historians to be too inclined to validate only those cultural patterns in the working class that conform to socialist expectations. Of the socialist movements, she remarks: "...none of the movements converted anything near the number of workers they needed. These considerations suggested the possibility that the radicals' perception of the worker was erroneous in the

same way that later radical historians' perception of him has been, and for the same reasons: their System-thinking made them see him only with reference to the System, its rulers and gravediggers, and the doctrinal needs of the radicals' own movements." (4) More pointedly, with regard to radical historians: "One is... not startled to discover, in this type of history, that the motives attributed to John Q. Worker are sorted into two categories: when he fights his boss he is acting autonomously and starting to wake up, but when he goes to church, dominates his wife, joins an ethnic choral society, refuses to work alongside a black, and votes for Bryan, he is not only responding to the influence of the capitalists and their agents but doing so discretely in each instance" (48). Of course, any adequate response to this challenge would need to transcend the tenacious liberal individualist atomism that structures Kraditor's discussion.

112 In power, as Adam Przeworski has noted, socialist parties of the day were caught without their own economic policy, and so simply borrowed from other sources. Adam Przeworski, *Capitalism and Social Democracy* (Cambridge: Cambridge University Press, 1985), 35. Out of power, socialist intellectuals were in a no more enviable position.

113For a general analysis, see Przeworski, *Capitalism and Social Democracy* 37.

114J.S. Woodsworth himself, as Alan Mills remarks, never ceased to be a kind of liberal, although his early thought was oriented to an ideal of co-operation. His views on overproduction and imperialism were eminently Hobsonian. Mills, *Fool for Christ* 71: "Raised on frontier liberalism, he would never cease to be a liberal of sorts. What his early account of cooperation did make evident, however, was the inordinate unliberal tilt in his thinking towards a definition of cooperation as unity, centralization, homogeneity and, if one is critical, conformity. And it was both a sociological and a normative unity that his theory presupposed. There had to be a rough identity of socio-economic characteristics on the part of Canadians as well as a shared moral purpose in order to realize the cooperative commonwealth." Yet Mills never draws what would seem to be the obvious connection to Spencerian-Marxism! And why an "inordinate unliberal tilt"? If Woodsworth identified with the British new liberal tradition, this would explain why traces of Manchester liberalism can be detected in his thought (167). On his underconsumptionism, see ibid., 165. I have to wonder why these views are identified with a "classical liberal" position, when they are so clearly traceable back to Hobson and the *new* liberal trajectory. It is suggestive that the "collective subject" of the foundational text *Social Planning for Canada* was "the Canadian people," and not the "working class." League for Social Reconstruction, *Social Planning for Canada* [1935]. Toronto: University of Toronto Press, 1975. xviii. That Frank Underhill's primary attachment was to the liberal tradition emerges from R. Douglas Francis, *Frank H. Underhill: Intellectual Provocateur* (Toronto: University of Toronto Press, 1986).

[115]This at any rate would be my reading of Margaret Fairley, one of the party's leading cultural figures. See David Kimmel, "The Spirit of Canadian Democracy: Margaret Fairley and the Communist Worker Worker's Responsibility to the People," *Left History* 1,1 (Spring 1993): 34-55. It would seem from this article that Fairley was more comfortable with the subject-positions "Canadian" and "the people" than she was with a vocabulary of class struggle (although admittedly the burden of the evidence is drawn from the 1950s, a rather different period). For Margaret Fairley's activities as a pioneering oral historian, who collected workers' autobiographies, see David Kimmel and Gregory S. Kealey, eds., "With Our Own Hands: Margaret Fairley and the 'Real Makers' of Canada," *Labour/Le Travail* 31 (Spring 1993): 253-85. This project would appear to have had much in common with liberal cultural experiments associated with the New Deal in the United States. It would be interesting to see some explorations of the different ways Canadian left intellectuals construed the notion of "working-class culture."

[116]James Mill, David Ricardo and W.S. Jevons had held that no meaning, other than an "evidently absurd and self-contradictory one," could be given to the concept of general over-production, a situation in which "industry would be stopped, employment fail, and all but the rich would be starved by the superfluity of commodities" (Hutchison, *Economic Doctrines* 40). J.A. Hobson in particular paid dearly for his often expressed conviction that the basis of all mainstream economic teaching since Adam Smith -- that "the quantity annually produced is determined by the aggregates of Natural Agents, Capital, and Labour available" -- was in error. On the contrary, "the quantity produced while it can never exceed the limits imposed by these aggregates, may be, and actually is, reduced far below this minimum by the check that undue saving and the consequent accumulation of over-supply exerts on production" (Ibid., 119-120). A full history of the triumph of underconsumption over Marxism as an economic theory on the left would also need to consider such popular economists as Stuart Chase in the United States, and the whole "institutionalist" school of economics in that country.

[117]Paul Buhle also notes a falling-off of working-class interest in "the classics" in the late 1930s: "A society where they expressed their class politics mostly within the factory, made any extra forum an overload. No amount of literature sales (purchases of the 'classics' fell off sharply after 1938), or sporadic study sessions or attempted popularizations of the *Communist's* format could change a fundamental attitude. Communism in America, unlike France, Italy, or pre-Hitler Germany, was a culture essentially for the intellectuals, the foreign born, and the exceptional autodidact." Buhle, *Marxism in the United States* 188. I am not sure if this generalization entirely applies to Canada.

[118]Stoneman, *Economic Analysis* 100. As Magdoff and Sweezy have commented, what marked this Keynesian landmark as a significant moment in economic theory was that, for the first time, "the possibility was frankly faced, indeed placed at the very center of the analysis, that breakdowns of the

accumulation process, the heart and soul of economic growth, might be built
into the system and non-self-correcting. The stage was thus set for a sweeping
reconsideration of the whole theory of investment." Magdoff and Sweezy,
"Listen, Keynesians!" 5.

[119]According to MacIntyre, *Proletarian Science* 158-159, British Communists
in the face of such difficulties turned increasingly to Rosa Luxemburg's
disproportionality thesis. I am unaware of any studies of Canadian Communists
which would allow us to compare their theoretical response to the Depression
with the Communists in Britain.

[120]As Colletti remarks, both old Marxists and new liberals were apt to
conceptualize "the economic factor" as a detachable if determinant part of the
social system. A feature of what he too generally calls the "Marxism of the
Second International" involved an oversimplification of what was meant by
the "economy," so that theories of crisis produced either an
"underconsumptionist" approach, which considered consumption *only* insofar
as it was external to production, or an alternative approach, associated with
Tugan-Baranowsky, "based on the opposite hypothesis of production alone *in
itself* understood as a *purely* economic base." Colletti, *From Rousseau to
Lenin* 19.

[121]See Steven Lukes, *Marxism and Morality* (Oxford: Oxford University
Press, 1987), chapter two, for a good discussion.

[122] For example, this passage: "..Socialism will assure to all individuals --
instead of as at present only to a privileged few or to society's heroes --
freedom to assert and develop their own individualities. Then in truth the result
of the struggle for existence will be the survival of the best and this for the
very reason that in a wholesome environment the victory is won by the
healthiest individuals. Social Darwinism, then, as a continuation and
complement of natural (biological) Darwinism, will result in a selection of the
best" (Ferri, *Socialism and Modern Science* : 56). The "best" is clearly not a
biological term -- in any truly Darwinian sense it merely signifies "the most
successful at surviving and reproducing"-- but a politico-ethical one: and Ferri
revealingly leaves it undefined. (Later, as a convert to Fascism, he
presumably had more direct means of determining whether a person was one
of the "best" or not.) In Trotsky's analysis of the problem of ethics, much the
same slight of hand occurs: here the words "strong" and "weak" stand in for
"good" and "evil." See Deutscher, ed., *Permanent Revolution* 340.

[123]Cited, Greenleaf, *Ideological Heritage* 349.

[124]The emergence of the Communist Parties had a paradoxical effect on the
strategy of "working-class culture": there was certainly no necessary and
remarkable rift between Spencerian-Marxists and Communists, and on many
fundamental questions of materialism, Dietzgen and Lenin marched hand in
hand. Communists in Britain left Marxist education in the hands of the Plebs
Leaguers, for example, who brought a largely Spencerian-Marxist cultural and
theoretical agenda to their educational work for the Movement. Labour
colleges, often deeply Dietzgenite, were strenuously attempting to build a

working-class culture through the 1920s and 1930s, but they ran into difficulties in the late 1930s (not the least of which was opposition from an increasingly unsympathetic CP, which had to attend to the latest philosophical breakthroughs in Moscow). In the United States, *pace* Pittenger, who would see the First World War as a decisive turning point against Spencerian Marxism, and who seems even to emphasize the decline of Charles H. Kerr after 1908 as significant, it would seem that the final demise of your particular dream of "working-class culture" came after the 1930s. There is some interesting corroboration in Peterson, "IWW," who notes that the collection he studied suggests a shift from a broad-ranging scientific materialism, embracing the critique of religion, Marxist theory, and political and industrial activism, to a mid-1930s emphasis on general current events; few of these later books were published by workers' organizations and they suggest a "kind of generic pro-New Deal popular frontism that mentioned socialist revolution less often, made less of a distinction between social reform and socialism, and blurred the gap between Communism and liberalism in a vague antifascism that made it difficult for radical workers to formulate strategies for postwar reconstruction or confront the emerging cold war of the late 1940s" (170). This transition was directly related to the decline of such radical organizations as the IWW. A sense of the decline of the autodidact tradition is also conveyed by Stuart MacIntyre, *A Proletarian Science: Marxism in Britain 1917-1933* (Cambridge: Cambridge University Press, 1980).

[125]LSR, *Social Planning for Canada* 36.

[126]As James Naylor astutely remarks, it is very important to remember that the CCF was (at least initially, and at least to some extent) a genuine federation, in which Marxists and even Marxist organizations were active, with SPCers and others simply reactivating the organizations and ideologies with which they were familiar and "reflecting perceptions of class and politics they had inherited from past endeavors." Nonetheless, as the CCF coalesced, it "reflected a fundamental transition in the nature of Canadian radicalism. This has been analyzed in terms of the conservatization or bureaucratization of the CCF, but a deep shift in the discourse about the social order is also apparent." Naylor, "Politics and Class," 3.

[127]For an argument along these lines, see Carroll and Ratner, "Social Democracy," 35. According to the authors, it is possible that the historic absence of a national work-class culture in Canada actively at odds with bourgeois hegemony, and the resulting weakness of the social-democratic settlement, now means that the attack on the Keynesian Welfare Sate can occur without any fundamental and visible reconstruction of official ideology, such as happened in the United Kingdom under Thatcher; they go on to note that under the Canadian state system, hegemonic crisis can be displaced in varying degree onto provincial state apparatuses. This is an interesting argument, although I think its implicit centralism could be countered with evidence demonstrating the vitality of working-class movements in particular provinces. A hegemonic crisis of liberalism might be played out quite

dramatically in provincial capitals, up to and including the violent occupation of legislatures (as was recently the case in Nova Scotia). Nor should one underestimate the extent to which the very self-definition and integrity of the Canadian state has relied since the 1940s on its ability to provide superior welfare-state programs. This does not negate their point, however, that such working-class struggles would be infinitely more significant if they were connected to a global strategy of resistance to the liberal order.

[128] As MacIntyre writes: "...even in its most dogmatic moments this Marxist intellectual culture possessed a sense of wonder and intellectual curiosity. The best working-class Marxists always retained their interest in a wide range of subjects and displayed a genuine humility. This sense of continuing wonderment can be illustrated in the following declaration from a student at the Central Labour College: 'Having set out upon an educational mission we are given an insight into the abstract conception 'Knowledge'. What appeared before to be something small and limited, and which could be easily overcome, now appears as something which has no limits. Indeed it is the contrary. It is man's power to understand the understandable that is limited.'" MacIntyre, *Proletarian Science* 96. And Rée remarks, in a wonderfully moving passage: "The socialist philosophies of Jackson, the Dietzgenites, and the Victorian autodidacts are over and done with. Professional philosophers, wary of undisciplined pulpitry, may find little to lament in that; and modern Marxists, intellectual arsenals crammed with a century's acquisitions of sectarian derision, may feel quite satisfied too -- for surely these philosophies were just various mixtures of economism, mechanism, evolutionism, idealism, humanism, and revisionism, and probably of 'Stalinism', too. But this vocabulary of comminatory '-isms' may not be a good instrument for measuring what has been lost. The main point about these philosophies is that they answered a need, not for a particular theoretical orientation within philosophy, but for the cultivation of unconfined and unrelenting reflection, for an opportunity to try and sort out your most fundamental values and beliefs, your sense of how your own initiatives and inertias may fit in with the larger rhythms of life, human society, and the universe as a whole." Rée, *Proletarian Philosophers* 131-132.

[129] Germino, *Antonio Gramsci,* 56; 65-66.

[130] "There is no such thing as *the* labor theory of value. Rather, a number of distinct theories, logically independent and of unequal importance, can be imputed to Marx. The main varieties interpret the theory as explaining: first, the condition of possibility of exchange and profit; second, relative equilibrium prices under capitalism; third, labor's right to the whole product; and fourth, the rational allocation of goods under communism." Jon Elster, "The Labor Theory of Value: A Reinterpretation of Marxist Economics," *Marxist Perspectives* 1, 2 (Fall 1978): 70.

[131] This is why it is relatively meaningless to speak of someone being, or not being, a Marxist: the criteria for membership in the club are vague, contested, ever-shifting, and often seemingly arbitrary. (Would *you* want to be

a member of a club that admitted Pol Pot?) Attempts to distill an essence of Marxism have not been very successful, because they so often they attempt to reify that which is always more subtle and difficult to capture: a relationship between past, present, and future.

132Germino, *Antonio Gramsci* 74.

133Those post-structuralists and post-Marxists who write of the "Death of Marxism" are buying into precisely the sort of essentialist master narratives they, in other contexts, contest.

134This is to construe tradition not as an inherently conservative concept -- a "morality of settled habits" -- but as a framework retaining conservative and explosive elements, allowing for an experimental attitude towards the future through criticism of the missed opportunities of the past. See Bronner, *Socialism Unbound* xiv.

135I find myself that a lot of the conventional Marxist literature on the new critical theory is weakened because it takes for granted -- and at the highest pitch of outraged righteous indignation -- precisely those assumptions about reality that post-structuralism and postmodernism have "problematized," without ever really engaging in the arguments of the other side. To my eye, the best rejoinders to postmodernism -- and it should be critiqued, on both ethical and epistemological grounds -- can be found in the Kantian tradition. See in particular Christopher Norris, *The Truth about Postmodernism* (Oxford: Blackwell, 1993), and *What's Wrong With Postmodernism* (Baltimore: Johns Hopkins University Press, 1990).

136This discussion owes much to Walter L. Adamson, *Marx and the Disillusionment of Marxism* (Berkeley: University of California Press, 1985), ch.1. However, instead of his typology of "four histories" -- which to my eye is not constructed according to consistently defined criteria -- I have combined his "pragmatological" and "counter-evolutionary" histories into one pole, and his "anthropological" and his "nomological" histories into another. This would appear to fit more accurately the actual *uses* of history among Marxists.

137For an interesting discussion, see Galvano della Volpe, *Logic as a Positive Science*, trans. Jon Rothschild (London, 1980), Chapter Two, and Fraser, *An Introduction to the thought of Galvano della Volpe* (London: Lawrence and Wishart, 1977): 21.

138I would agree substantially with Paul Buhle when he remarks, "...the entire transition from supposedly utopian to supposedly scientific socialism had been made too easily, too carelessly. Lack of self-consciousness in this enterprise betrayed an eagerness to avoid the reality of the self, to escape into comforting abstractions. Marxist claims, Marxist texts, neither guaranteed political understanding nor political continuity. They validated class concepts and class expectations for specific sectors, and permitted an interpretation of the recurrent economic crises. They failed worst in the precise area where they seemed to succeed best, inducing self-confidence in the activists to know omnisciently the next development ahead." Buhle, *Marxism in the United States* 120.

[139]Michael Foucault, *Remarks on Marx* (New York: Semiotext(e), 1991): 181, where he notes: "I find this 'model of war' not only a bit ridiculous but also rather dangerous. Because by virtue of saying or thinking 'I'm fighting against the enemy,' if one day you find yourself in a position of strength, and in a situation of real war, in front of this blasted 'enemy,' wouldn't you actually treat him as one? Taking that route leads directly to oppression, no matter who takes it: that's the real danger. I understand how pleasing it can be for some intellectuals to try to be taken seriously by a party or a society by acting out a 'war' against an ideological adversary: but that is disturbing above all because of what it could provoke. Wouldn't it be much better instead to think that those with whom you disagree are perhaps mistaken; or perhaps that you haven't understood what they intended to say?"

[140]On the "model of war," your life and work could be discredited, first by treating the texts which "deviate" from Marxism (e.g., Port Sunlight, the Dominion Coal Company, etc. etc.) as "essential" and reducing all the others to so much "window-dressing," second by undermining any claim to originality by suggesting how much you borrowed from others, and third by the conventional *ad hominem* method of reducing your analysis to your biography. I have left all the materials for such a reductionist attack in the texts. My only questions are: why bother? who benefits from such polemic? are such tactics in accordance with the ideal of the realm of freedom? what would anybody learn from the exercise?

[141]§.95, "Commodities and Credits."

[142]§117,"The Failure of Craft Unions."

[143]I call it a "framework" rather than a "philosophy" because I accept Rée's point that it is far from evident that Marxism requires its own philosophy (or that it ever could "be" a philosophy). Rée, *Proletarian Philosophers* 3. As Rée goes on to note, philosophers in the new Soviet Union were initially blocked from entry into the Academy of Sciences on the grounds that philosophy was an enemy of Dialectical Materialism (63). Lenin held, on the other hand, that philosophy was a critically important weapon in the hands of the proletarian revolution, and that the struggle between idealism and materialism was in a sense one between proletarian and bourgeois positions. The entire debate smacked of the iconoclast/iconodule wars in Byzantium -- in this case, as in so many others, the prototype of so much of what passed for "Marxism" and "Marxist debate" in the Soviet Union. A similar point (albeit from a very different perspective) is made by Frederic Jameson, "Actually Existing Marxism," in Saree Makdisi, Cesare Casarino, and Rebecca E. Karl, eds., *Marxism Beyond Marxism* (New York and London: Routledge, 1996).

[144]That "jazz" should have been the very epitome of the unstable, trendy, and insubstantial suggests the extent to which antimodernism had influenced even the socialist left in the 1920s and 1930s. There is much interesting work in cultural history that could be done on this pattern.

[145]But, if logico-historical analysis starts to point to internal contradictions and empirical disconfirmation, there is no reason to remain wedded to any

determinate abstractions, even the ones commonly seen as central to "Marxism," simply because we find it in Marx. None of the determinate abstractions is sacrosanct. The only exception to this rule is the Marxian categorical imperative, the "realm of freedom," whose removal would mean the total collapse of any coherent Marxism, post-orthodox or not. Attempts to make the tendency of the rate of profit to fall the keystone of social analysis are, in my opinion, good examples of theoretical constructs which are vulnerable to exactly this kind of logical and empirical testing: we need to ask if this supposed tendency satisfies the basic criterion of a determinate abstraction, or if it was constructed and now operates according to a very different logic (viz., logical atomism) -- one which perhaps predisposes it to function as a generic rather than as a determinate abstraction.

[146]Of the many "balance-sheets" being drawn up today of what is living and dead in the Marxist tradition, I have found that of Antonio Negri, "Twenty Theses on Marx: Interpretation of the Class Situation Today," in Saree Makdisi, Cesare Casarino and Rebecca E. Karl, *Marxism Beyond Marxism* (London and New York: Routledge, 1996), 149-180 to be particularly helpful and close to the "post-orthodox Marxist" line of argument I am developing here. Of particular interest is his attempt to periodize the "historical limits" of the law of value and the close links between his "ontology of living labor" and the realm of freedom. Such work is a striking indication that much of what has been described as the "Death of Marx" should also be seen as "Marx's Rebirth."

[147]And note that in the quotation from Marx, *Capital*, Vol.3 which heads this letter that "Freedom" is conceived as the governance by the associated producers of "the human metabolism with nature in a rational way": a far cry from the brain-dead, Victorian productivism so often attributed to Marx!

[148]As Stephen Bronner has observed, the erosion of socialism as the envisaged end-point of social evolution -- what he terms the "collapse of teleology" -- does not mean that many of the determinate abstractions of the Marxist tradition are in any sense invalidated. It "does not necessarily imply that Marx's 'labor theory of value' is simply worthless, that the rate of profit cannot fall, that capitalism has resolved its crisis character, that a simple integration or 'embourgeoisement' of the working class has taken place, or even that a society has been ushered into existence which makes the question of class irrelevant." Bronner, *Socialism Unbound* 147-148.

[149]As Lucio Colletti has explained, this involves "..an approach which can encompass the *differences* presented by one object or *species* with respect to all the others -- for example, bourgeois society as against feudal society -- and which does not, therefore, arrive at the *generic*, idealist notion of society 'in general,' but rather hangs on to this determinate society, this particular object in question. (The need for a method which does not give us abstractions, but facts). On the other hand, however, the individual fact, in its unique, absolute singularity, is as generic as the abstract genus. Hence the need for a non-empiricist method which is also -- as well as fact -- abstraction, and does not

preclude the specific *identity*, the *species*, and hence that typicality by which each object is what it is precisely because it is an expression of its 'class.' On one side, therefore, the need for observation-induction; in this respect an object or process is inconceivable if it is not this particular process, this particular *nature*. Yet on the other side, the need for hypothesis-deduction, i.e. a particular process or phenomenon is inconceivable for us if it is not itself a *model* or typical phenomenon." Colletti, *From Rousseau to Lenin* 8.

150The utilitarian-functional argument (viz., socialists must concentrate on the working class because only the working class can overthrow the system) treats the working class "externally", as though "it" were truly an object in the mechanism; if carried into practice, this theorization of workers as means rather than as ends violates the categorical imperative of the realm of freedom. So does so much Marxist philosophizing about working-class consciousness and "mission," which, in knowing in advance what "real" working-class consciousness should be, and in regarding living beings as important primarily because collectively they embody Reason or some other abstraction rather than because they are ends in themselves, seriously violates the ethical requirements of a theory of history. (It also leads to a style of history-writing impervious to normal tests of evidence: there is no way a claim that the "working class" bears a historical mission can be confirmed or disconfirmed). It's interesting, Colin, that so far as I can see, you rarely made this utilitarian/teleological argument for the centrality of class -- and I wonder if it wasn't more often made by socialists who had no personal contact with workers. Working-class history in general has been heavily burdened with the implicit assumption that the working class has a mission, which explains why, after a quarter of a century of intense Marxist labour historiography in Canada, we have had so many studies of the heroic moments of class warfare and radicalism, and so few of the more typical and unheroic cases of class accommodation and liberalism.

151I would be overburdening an already long letter if I tried to explore the similarities and differences between this sense of a continuous Marxist tradition, traceable as a theory of history to Marx and Gramsci, and salvageable within a post-orthodox, non-teleological framework, and the superficially similar post-Marxist accounts. So I'll just say that the differences -- clearly outlined in the entire foregoing discussion -- seem much more glaring to me than any similarities. See Ernesto Laclau, *New Reflections on the Revolutions of Our Time* (London: Verso, 1990).

152That is to say, since the realm of freedom in Marx is so clearly a transcendental concept, it is apparent that the differences between Marxist and radical Christian thought, both of which are inspired by timeless and universal ideals, the realm of freedom in the one case and Christ's kingdom to come in the other, is not as wide a gap as that, say, between Marxist and utilitarian/positivist/neo-liberal thought (with its vulgar denial of any possible world other than this one, and its brutal contempt for the realm of the spirit). Both serious Marxist analysis and serious Christian critiques of the horrible

cultural effects of the liberal order and capitalism will arrive at the same
position of unremitting criticism. From both perspectives, the contemporary
neo-liberal conflation of freedom and necessity will be seen as an undermining
of hope: indeed as a nihilistic, market-driven, world-destroying cultural
program of totalitarian dimensions. The rather superficial comments of the
young Marx on the subject of religion are one thing, but one learns more about
his mature viewpoint of the realm of the spirit from the pages of his *magnum
opus* in which this youthful analysis is simultaneously preserved, cancelled
and decisively superseded. One could even say that his analysis of commodity
fetishism, which requires the realm of freedom as its premise, undermines at
one stroke virtually all the unnecessary and counterproductive arguments
Marxists used to feel they had to make on behalf of atheism. It could well be
that the people in struggle require the resources of both traditions.

[153]Marx, *Capital* Vol.3 (1981 edition), 959.

[154]Franz J. Hinkelammert, *The Ideological Weapons of Death: A Theological
Critique of Capitalism,* trans. Phillip Berryman (Maryknoll, N.Y.: Orbis Books,
1986): 52-57. On this point there was a clear divergence between Marx and
Engels. It was -- as Gareth Stedman Jones reminds us -- one of Engels's major
"achievements" to posit "the ascent of man from the kingdom of necessity to
the kingdom of freedom," which kingdom was theorized in terms of *domination*
over the laws of nature and history. Gareth Stedman Jones, "Engels," 324.

[155]You wrote unabashedly, in §.125, "The Necessity of a Labour Party," of a
"realm of justice and beauty whereof sages have dreamed and poets sung."
Long may you be a fixture in that realm, Colin -- supplied, I hope, with the
things that gave you the greatest pleasure in life: your hunting rifle, your pipe
and tobacco, and most of all an infinite supply of books from the heavenly
branch office of the Charles Kerr company (many of them proving, no doubt,
that your presence in the hereafter is merely a bourgeois illusion.)

SELECTED BIBLIOGRAPHY

Manuscripts

Chapel Hill, North Carolina Davis Library
 Samuel Gompers Era: Papers of the President (Microfilm).
 The AFL and the Unions: National and International Records from the
 Samuel Gompers Era (Microfilm).
 Samuel Gompers Letterbooks (Microfilm; originals in the Manuscript
 Division of the Library of Congress, Washington).
Halifax, Nova Scotia
 Dalhousie University Archives.
 Andrew Merkel Papers.
Kingston, Ontario
 Undated family scrapbook, in the possession of Dr. Colin MacKay,
 Family Medicine, Queen's University.
Ottawa, Ontario
 National Archives of Canada.
 Board of Trade Records.
 Mackenzie King Papers.
 Wilfrid Laurier Papers.

Government Documents

*Report to the Honourable the Postmaster General of the Methods
 Adopted in Canada in the Carrying Out of Government Clothing
 Contracts.* Ottawa: Government Printing Bureau, 1899.
*Report of the Royal Commission on the Relations of Capital and Labour
 in Canada,* Evidence--Quebec, Part I. Ottawa, Government Printing
 Bureau, 1889.
Report upon the Sweating System in Canada. Canada, *Sessional Papers,*
 1896, Vol.11, Sessional Paper No.61.

Newspapers and Magazines

Adventure, 1907-1918.
American Federationist 1898-1905.
Amherst Daily News 1890-1900.
The Argus, 1904-5.
The Busy East [Amherst] 1911-1914.
Canadian Railway Employees Monthly, 1921-39.
Canadian Fisherman, 1917-39.
Canadian Forum, 1932-9.
Canadian Unionist, 1930-9.
Le Canard [Montreal], 1899-1900.
Citizen and Country, 1899-1901.
Coast Guard [Shelburne], 1936-9.
Cotton's Weekly 1909-13.
Eastern Labor News, 1909-13.
The Globe [Toronto], 1909.
Halifax Herald, 1901-21.
Industrial Banner, 1908-1914.

International Socialist Review, 1909-1914.
Labor Leader, 1935.
Labor Review, 1939.
Labor World/Le Monde Ouvrier, 1927-39.
Montreal Gazette, 1899-1900.
Montreal Herald, 1896-1906.
Morning Chronicle [Halifax], 1901-10.
Ottawa Journal, 1939.
La Presse [Montreal], 1899-1900.
O.B.U.Bulletin, 1930-5.
Saturday Night, 1935-9.
Shelburne Budget, 1890-1902.
Shelburne Gazette, 1903-1911.
Shelburne Gazette and Coast Guard, 1913-35.
Saint John *Standard*, 1910-15.
The Times [Yarmouth], 1908-09
Western Clarion, 1913.
Yarmouth *Telegram*, 1903.

Books, Articles, and Unpublished Secondary Sources

Abella, Irving. *Nationalism, Communism, and Canadian Labour*. Toronto: University of Toronto Press, 1973.

Aberhart, William. *Social Credit Manual: Social Credit as Applied to the Province of Alberta*. Calgary, 1935.

Abrams, Philip. *The Origins of British Sociology: 1834-1914*. Chicago and London: University of Chicago Press, 1968.

Adamson, Walter L. *Marx and the Disillusionment of Marxism*. Berkeley: University of California Press, 1985.

Allen, Richard. "Providence to Progress: The Migration of an Idea in English Canadian Thought." *Canadian Issues/Thèmes Canadiens*, 7 (1985): 33-46.

Andreucci, Franco. "The Diffusion of Marxism in Italy during the Late Nineteenth Century." In Raphael Samuel and Gareth Stedman Jones, eds., *Culture, Ideology and Politics*, 214-227. London: Routledge and Kegan Paul, 1983.

Armour, Leslie and Trott, Leslie. *The Faces of Reason: An Essay on Philosophy and Culture in English-Canada, 1850-1950*. Waterloo: Wilfrid Laurier University Press, 1981.

Aronson, Ronald. *After Marxism*. New York and London: The Guilford Press, 1995.

Atherton, Jay. "Introduction" to T. Phillips Thompson, *The Politics of Labor* [1887]. Toronto and Buffalo: University of Toronto Press, 1975.

Axelrod, Paul. *Making a Middle Class: Student Life in English Canada during the Thirties*. Montreal and Kingston: McGill-Queen's University Press, 1990.

Babcock, Robert H. *Gompers in Canada: A Study in American Continentalism Before the First World War*. Toronto: University of Toronto Press, 1974.

_____. "Saint John Longshoremen During the Rise of Canada's Winter Port, 1895-1922." *Labour/Le Travail* 25 (Spring 1990): 15-46.

Bacher, John C. *Keeping to the Marketplace: The Evolution of Canadian Housing Policy*. Montreal and Kingston: McGill-Queen's Press, 1993.

Bannister, Robert C. *Social Darwinism: Science and Myth in Anglo-American Social Thought*. Philadelphia: Temple University Press, 1979.

Bannister, Robert C. *Sociology and Scientism: The American Quest for Objectivity, 1880-1940* Chapel Hill and London: The University of North Carolina Press, 1987.

Barman, Jean. "'Knowledge is Essential for Universal Progress but Fatal to Class Privilege': Working People and the Schools in Vancouver During the 1920s." *Labour/Le Travail* 22 (Fall 1988): 9-66,

Barrett, L. Gene. "Underdevelopment and Social Movements in the Nova Scotia Fishing Industry to 1938." In Robert Brym and R. James Sacouman, eds., *Underdevelopment and Social Movements in Atlantic Canada*, 127-60. Toronto: New Hogtown, 1979.

Baumol, W.J. "Say's (at Least) Eight Laws, or What Say and James Mill May Really Have Meant." *Economica*, 44, 174 (May 1977): 145-61.

Beeson, E.W. *Port Sunlight: The Model Village of England*. New York: The Architectural Book Publishing Company, 1911.

Benjamin, Walter. "On Some Motifs in Baudelaire." In *Illuminations*, ed Hannah Arendt, 155-200. New York: Schocken Books, 1969.

Bercuson, David J. *Fools and Wise Men: The Rise and Fall of the One Big Union*. Toronto: McGraw-Hill Ryerson,1978.

Berle, Adolph A. and Means, Gardner. *The Modern Corporation and Private Property*. New York: Macmillan and Company, 1932.

Bernstein, Michael A. *The Great Depression: Delayed Recovery and Economic Change in America, 1929-1939*. Cambridge: Cambridge University Press, 1987; reprinted 1989.

Bierstedt, Robert. *American Sociological Theory: A Critical History*. Toronto: Academic Press, 1981.

Bischoff, Peter. "La formation des traditions syndicales chez les mouleurs de Montréal, Hamilton et Toronto, 1850-1893." *Bulletin*, Regroupement des chercheurs-chercheures en histoire des travailleurs et travailleuses du Québec 16, 1 (hiver 1990): 19-61.

Bittermann, Rusty "Escheat!: Rural Protest on Prince Edward Island, 1832-1842," Ph.D. Thesis, University of New Brunswick, 1991.

Bladen, Vincent. *From Adam Smith to Maynard Keynes: the heritage of political economy*. Toronto: University of Toronto Press, 1974.

Booth, Alan. "The 'Keynesian Revolution' in Economic Policy-Making." *Economic History Review*, Second Series 36, 1 (February 1983): 103-123.

_____. "Defining a 'Keynesian Revolution.'" *Economic History Review*, Second Series 37, 2 (May 1984): 263-267.

Boudreau, Émile, ed. *L'Histoire de la FTQ: Des tout débuts jusqu'en 1965* (Montréal: FTQ, 1988).

Bowler, Peter J. "The Changing Meaning of 'Evolution.'" *Journal of the History of Ideas* 36, 1 (January-March 1975): 95-114.

Bronner, Stephen Eric. *Socialism Unbound*. New York and London: Routledge, 1990.

Buhle, Paul. *Marxism in the United States: Remapping the History of the American Left*. London: Verso, 1987.

Campbell, J. Peter "'Stalwarts of the Struggle': Canadian Marxists of the Third Way, 1879-1939." PhD Thesis, Queen's University, 1991.

_____. "Making Socialists": Bill Pritchard, the Socialist Party of Canada, and the Third International." *Labour/Le Travail* 30 (Fall 1992): 45-63.

_____. "In Defence of the Labour Theory of Value: The Socialist Party of Canada and the Evolution of Marxist Thought." *Journal of History and Politics* 10 (1992): 61-86.

Canadian Brotherhood of Railway Employees and Other Transport Workers, *Forty Years of Progress, 1908-1948*. Ottawa: Grand Division of the Canadian Brotherhood of Railway Employees and Other Transport Workers, 1948.

The Canadian Newspaper Directory. Montreal: A. McKim and Co, 1901.

The Canadian Newspaper Directory. Montreal: A. McKim and Co., 1911.

Carroll, William and R.Ratner. "Social Democracy, Neo-Conservatism and Hegemonic Crisis in British Columbia." *Critical Sociology* 16,1 (1989): 29-53.

Carroll, William K., Linda Christiansen-Ruffman, Raymond F. Currie, and Deborah Harrison, eds. *Fragile Truths: 25 Years of Sociology and Anthropology in Canada*. Ottawa: Carleton University Press, 1992.

Chadwick, Henry. *The Early Church*. Harmondsworth: Penguin, 1967.

Childers, Marjorie Sue. "Social Change in American Sociology: The First Generation." Ph.D.Thesis, New School for Social Research, 1973.

Cole, G.D.H. *Economic Planning*. Port Washington and London: Kennikat Press, 1971 [First printed 1935].

_____. *Gold, Credit and Employment: Four Essays for Laymen*. New York: Macmillan, 1930.

_____, ed. *What Everybody Wants to Know About Money: A Planned Outline of Monetary Problems*. London: Victor Gollancz, 1933.

Colletti, Lucio. *Marxism and Hegel*. London: Verso, 1979.

_____. *From Rousseau to Lenin: Studies in Ideology and Society*. London: New Left Books, 1972.

Collier, Andrew. "Materialism and Explanation in the Human Sciences." In John Mepham and D.-H. Ruben, eds., *Issues in Marxist Philosophy*, Vol.2, *Materialism*. Brighton: Harvester, 1979.

Colp, Jr., Ralph. "The myth of the Darwin-Marx Letter." *History of Political Economy*, 15, 4 (1983): 461-482.

Conseil des travailleuses et travailleurs du Montréal métropolitain. *Cent ans de solidarité: Histoire du CTM 1886-1986*. Montréal: VLB éditeur, 1987.

Cook, Ramsay. *The Regenerators: Social Criticism in Late Victorian Canada*. Toronto, Buffalo and London: University of Toronto Press, 1985.

Cotkin, George B. "The Spencerian and Comtian Nexus in Gompers' Labor Philosophy: The Impact of Non-Marxian Evolutionary Thought." *Labor History* 20, 4 (Fall 1979): 510-23.

Creese, Gillian. "The Sociology of British Columbia." *BC Studies*, 100 (Winter 1993-94): 21-42.

De Bonville, Jean. *Jean-Baptiste Gagnepetit: les travailleurs montréalais à la fin du XIXe siècle*. Montréal: Les Éditions de l'Aurore, 1975.

de Lottinville, Peter. "Joe Beef of Montreal: Working Class Culture and the Tavern, 1869-1889. " *Labour/Le Travail*, 8/9 (1981-82): 9-40.

della Volpe, Galvano. *Logic as a Positive Science*, trans. Jon Rothschild. London: New Left Books, 1980.

Desmond, Adrian and James Moore. *Darwin*. New York: Warner Books, 1991.

Deutscher, Isaac, ed. *The Age of Permanent Revolution: A Trotsky Anthology*. New York: Dell, 1970.

Dickinson, John A. "La législation et les travailleurs québécois 1894-1914." *Relations Industrielles* 41, 2 (1986): 357-381.

Dietzgen, Josef. *The Positive Outcome of Philosophy*, trans. by W.W. Craik. Chicago: Charles H. Kerr, 1928. [First printed 1906].

_____. *Some of the Philosophical Essays on Socialism and Science, Religion, Ethics, Critique-of-Reason and the World-at-large*. Chicago: Charles H. Kerr and Company, 1917.

Dionne, Bernard. "Les 'Unions Internationales' et le Conseil des Métiers et du Travail de Montréal, de 1938 à 1958." Ph.D. Thesis, Université du Québec à Montréal, 1990.

_____. *Le Syndicalisme au Québec*. Montréal: Boréal, 1991.

Drache, Daniel. "The Formation and Fragmentation of the Canadian Working Class 1820-1920." In David J. Bercuson and David Bright, eds., *Canadian Labour History: Selected Readings*, 6-46. Toronto: Copp Clark Longman, second edition, 1994.

Dupuis, Jean-Claude. "Reformisme et catholicisme: la pensée sociale d'Arthur Saint-Pierre." *Bulletin*, Regroupement des chercheurs-chercheures en histoire des travailleurs et travailleuses du Québec, 49 (hiver 1991): 25-61.

Dutton, H.I. and King, J.E. "'A private, perhaps, not a major...': the reception of C.E. Douglas's Social Credit ideas in Britain, 1919-1939." *History of Political Economy*, 18, 2 (1986): 259-327.

Elster, Jon. "The Labor Theory of Value: A Reinterpretation of Marxist Economics." *Marxist Perspectives* 1, 2 (Fall 1978): 70 -101.

Engels, Friedrich. *Socialism: Utopian and Scientific*. New York: International Publishers, 1968.

Ewen, Geoffrey . "The Ideas of Gustave Francq on Trade Unionism and Social Reform as Expressed in *Le Monde Ouvrier/The Labor World*, 1916-1921." M.A. Thesis, University of Ottawa, 1982.

Entwhistle, Harold. *Antonio Gramsci: Conservative schooling for radical politics.* London, Boston and Henley: Routledge and Kegan Paul, 1979.

Ferri, Enrico. *The Positive School of Criminology.* Chicago: Charles H. Kerr, 1913; reprinted, Pittsburgh: University of Pittsburgh Press, 1968.

_____. *Socialism and Modern Science (Darwin-Spencer-Marx).* Chicago: Charles H. Kerr, 1909.

Fingard, Judith. "The 1880s: Paradoxes of Progress." In E.R.Forbes and D.A. Muise, eds., *The Atlantic Provinces in Confederation,* 82-116. Toronto: University of Toronto Press and Fredericton: Acadiensis Press.

Finkel, Alvin. "The Rise and Fall of the Labour Party in Alberta, 1917-42." *Labour/Le Travail,* 16 (Fall 1985): 61-96.

Forgacs, D., ed. *An Antonio Gramsci Reader: Selected Writings 1916-1935.* New York: Schocken Books, 1988.

Foucault, Michel. *Remarks on Marx.* New York: Semiotext(e), 1991.

Francis, R. Douglas. *Frank H. Underhill: Intellectual Provocateur.* Toronto: University of Toronto Press, 1986.

Frank, David. "Class Conflict in the Coal Industry: Cape Breton, 1922." In Ian McKay, ed., *The Challenge of Modernity,* 258-286. Toronto: McGraw-Hill Ryerson, 1992.

Frank, David and Nolan Reilly. "The Emergence of the Socialist Movement in the Maritimes, 1899-1916." *Labour/Le Travailleur,* 4 (1979): 85-113.

Fraser, John. *An Introduction to the Thought of Galvano della Volpe.* London: Lawrence and Wishart, 1977.

Freeden, Michael. "Introduction" to J.A.Hobson, *Confessions of an Economic Heretic: The Autobiography of J.A. Hobson.* Brighton: Harvester Press, 1976.

Friesen, Gerald. "'Yours in Revolt: The Socialist Party of Canada and the Western Canadian Labour Movement." *Labour/Le Travailleur* 1 (1976): 139-157.

Fundamentals of Marxism-Leninism. Manual. Moscow: Foreign Languages Publishing House, 1963.

Garraty, John A. *Unemployment in History: Economic Thought and Public Policy.* New York: Harper & Row, 1978.

Gauvreau, Michael. *The Evangelical Century: College and Creed in English Canada from the Great Revival to the Great Depression.* Montreal and Kingston: McGill-Queen's University Press, 1991.

Geiger, George Raymond. *The Philosophy of Henry George.* New York: The Macmillan Company, 1933.

Germino, Dante. *Antonio Gramsci: Architect of a New Politics.* Baton Rouge and London: Louisiana State University Press, 1990.

George, Henry. *The Science of Political Economy.* London: Kegan Paul, Trench, Trubner & Co., 1898.

Gerratana, Valentino. "Marx and Darwin." *New Left Review* 82 (November-December 1973): 60-82.

Gramsci, Antonio *Selections from the Prison Notebooks*, trans. and ed. Quintin Hoare and Geoffrey Nowell-Smith. London: Lawrence and Wishart, 1971.

Grant, John Webster. *A Profusion of Spires: Religion in Nineteenth-Century Ontario*. Toronto: University of Toronto Press for the Ontario Historical Studies Series, Goverment of Ontario, 1988.

Gray, John. *The Social System: A Treatise on the Principle of Exchange*. Edinburgh: William Tait, 1831.

Greenleaf, W.H. *The British Political Tradition*, Vol. 2, *The Ideological Heritage*. London and New York: Methuen, 1983.

Halker, Clark D. *For Democracy, Workers, and God: Labor Song-Poems and Labor Protest, 1865-95*. Urbana and Chicago: University of Illinois Press, 1991.

Hall, Stuart. "The Toad in the Garden: Thatcherism Among the Theorists." In Cary Nelson and Lawrence Grossberg, eds., *Marxism and the Interpretation of Culture*, 35-73. Urbana and Chicago: University of Illinois Press, 1988.

Hann, Russell. "Brainworkers and the Knights of Labor: E.E.Sheppard, Phillips Thompson, and the *Toronto News*, 1883-1887." In Gregory S. Kealey and Peter Warrian, eds., *Essays in Canadian Working Class History*, 35-57. Toronto: McClelland and Stewart, 1976:

Hannant, Larry. "The Calgary Working Class and the Social Credit Movement in Alberta, 1932-35. " *Labour/Le Travail*, 16 (Fall 1985): 97-116.

Heller, Agnes. *A Theory of History*. London: Routledge & Kegan Paul, 1982.

Heron, Craig. "Labourism and the Canadian Working Class." *Labour/Le Travail* 13 (Spring 1984): 45-76.

_____. "Towards Synthesis in Canadian Working-Class History: Reflections on Bryan Palmer's Rethinking." *Left History* 1,1 (Spring 1993): 109-121.

Hinkelammert, Franz J. *The Ideological Weapons of Death: A Theological Critique of Capitalism,* trans. Phillip Berryman. Maryknoll, N.Y.: Orbis Books, 1986.

Hinton, James. *Labour and Socialism: A History of the British Labour Movement, 1867-1974*. Amherst, Mass.: University of Massachusetts Press, 1983.

Hobhouse, L.T. *Liberalism*. New York: Oxford University Press, 1964. [First published 1911].

Hobson, J.A. *The Economics of Unemployment*. London: George Allen and Unwin, 1922.

Holland, Clifford G. *William Dawson LeSueur (1840-1917): A Canadian Man of Letters*. San Francisco: Mellon Research University Press, 1993.

Homel, Gene. "James Simpson and the Origins of Canadian Social Democracy." Ph.D Thesis, University of Toronto, 1978.

Hoskins, Ralph F.H. "An Analysis of the Payrolls of the Point St. Charles Shops of the Grand Trunk Railway." *Cahiers de Géographie du Québec* 33, 90 (décembre 1989): 323-344.

Hunt, E.K. "Value Theory in the Writings of the Classical Economists, Thomas Hodgskin and Karl Marx." *History of Political Economy* 9, 3 (1977): 322-345.

Hutchison, T.W. *A Review of Economic Doctrines 1870-1929.* London: Oxford University Press, 1953.

Irvine, William. *The Farmers in Politics.* Toronto: McClelland and Stewart, 1976. [First published 1920].

Jackson, Lewis and Ian McKay, eds., *Windjammers and Bluenose Sailors: Stories of the Sea by Colin McKay.* Lockeport, N.S.: Roseway Publishing, 1993.

Jameson, Fredric. "Actually Existing Marxism." In Saree Makdisi, Cesare Casarino, and Rebecca E. Karl, eds., *Marxism Beyond Marxism,* 14-54. New York and London: Routledge, 1996.

Jhally, Sut. *The Codes of Advertising: Fetishism and the Political Economy of Meaning in the Consumer Society.* New York and London: Routledge, 1990.

Johanningsmeier, Edward P. *Forging American Communism: The Life of William Z. Foster.* Princeton, N.J.: Princeton University Press, 1994.

Jones, Frank E. "The Evolution of the CSAA." In William K. Carroll, Linda Christiansen-Ruffman, Raymond F. Currie, and Deborah Harrison, eds., *Fragile Truths: 25 Years of Sociology and Anthropology in Canada,* 21-41. Ottawa: Carleton University Press, 1992.

Kant, Immanuel. *Foundations of the Metaphysics of Morals,* trans. L.W. Beck. New York: Macmillan, 1969.

Kautsky, Karl. *The Social Revolution.* Chicago: Charles H. Kerr and Company, 1908.

Kealey, G.S., ed., *Canada Investigates Industrialism: The Royal Commission on the Relations of Labor and Capital, 1889 (Abridged).* Toronto: University of Toronto Press, 1973.

Kealey, Linda. "Canadian Socialism and the Woman Question, 1900-1914." *Labour/Le Travail* 13 (Spring 1984): 77-100.

Kidd, Benjamin. *Social Evolution.* London: Macmillan, 1894.

Kimmel, David. "The Spirit of Canadian Democracy: Margaret Fairley and the Communist Cultural Worker's Responsibility to the People." *Left History* 1,1 (Spring 1993): 34-55.

Kimmel, David and Gregory S. Kealey, eds. "With Our Own Hands: Margaret Fairley and the 'Real Makers' of Canada." *Labour/Le Travail* 31 (Spring 1993): 253-85.

King. W.L.M. *Industry and Humanity: A Study in the Principles Underlying Industrial Reconstruction.* Toronto: University of Toronto Press, 1982 [1918].

Klee, Marcus. "The Communication of Class: CBC *National Labour Forum* and the Struggle for Working-Class Control of Radio Broadcasts During the Second World War." M.A. Thesis, Queen's University, 1992.

Kloppenberg, James T. *Uncertain Victory: Social Democracy and Progressivism in European and American Thought, 1870-1920.* New York and Oxford: Oxford University Press, 1986.

Krader, Lawrence. "Theory of Evolution, Revolution and the State: The Critical Relation of Marx to his Contemporaries Darwin, Carlyle, Morgan, Maine and Kovalevsky." In Eric J. Hobsbawm, ed., *The History of Marxism*. Vol. 1. *Marxism in Marx's Day*, 192-226. Bloomington: Indiana University Press, 1982.

Kraditor, Aileen S. *The Radical Persuasion, 1890-1917: Aspects of the Intellectual History and the Historiography of Three American Radical Organizations*. Baton Rouge and London: Louisiana State University Press, 1981.

Labour Party. *Socialism and 'Social Credit'*. London: The Labour Party, n.d. [1935].

Labriola, Antonio. *Socialism and Philosophy*. St. Louis: Telos Press, 1980.

Laclau, Ernesto. *New Reflections on the Revolutions of Our Time*. London: Verso, 1990.

Lafargue, Paul. *The Evolution of Property From Savagery to Civilization*. New York: Charles Scribner, 1905.

Larivière, Claude. *Albert Saint-Martin, militant d'avant-garde (1865-1947)*. Laval: Éditions coopératives Albert Saint-Martin, 1979.

League for Social Reconstruction. *Social Planning for Canada* Toronto: University of Toronto Press, 1975. [First published 1935]

Leblanc, André E. "Le Monde Ouvrier/The Labor World (1916-1926): an Analysis of Thought and a Detailed Index." D.E.S. Thesis (History), University of Montreal, 1971.

Lecourt, Dominique. "Marx in the Sieve of Darwin." *Rethinking Marxism* 5,4 (Winter 1992): 6-28.

_____. *Proletarian Science? The Case of Lysenko*. London: New Left Books, 1976.

Leier, Mark. "Kipling Gets a Red Card." *Labour/Le Travail* 31 (Spring 1993): 163-8.

_____. "Workers and Intellectuals: The Theory of the New Class and Early Canadian Socialism." *Journal of History and Politics*, 10 (1992): 87-108.

Lemaire, Christine. "Les femmes dans *Le Monde Ouvrier*, 1929-1937." *Cahiers d'Histoire* 6,1 (Autumn 1985): 63-81.

Lever Brothers, Limited. *The Story of Port Sunlight*. London: Lever Brothers, 1953.

Lévesque, Andrée. *Virage à gauche interdit: Les communistes, les socialistes et leurs ennemis au Québec 1929-1939*. Montréal: Boréal, 1984.

Levine, Gregory J. "Class, ethnicity and property transfers in Montreal, 1907-1909." *Journal of Historical Geography* 14, 4 (1988): 360-380.

Lewis, Arthur M. *Evolution Social and Organic*. Sixth Edition. Chicago: Charles Kerr and Company, n.d. [1910]).

Lewis, Robert. "The Segregated City: Class Residential Patterns and the Development of Industrial Districts in Montreal, 1861 and 1901." *Journal of Urban History* 17, 2 (February 1991): 123-152.

Linteau, Paul-André. *Histoire de Montréal depuis la Confédération*. Montreal: Boréal, 1992.

Logan, H.A. *Trade Unions in Canada: Their Development and Functioning*. Toronto: Macmillan of Canada, 1948.

Löwy, Michael. *The Politics of Combined and Uneven Development: The Theory of Permanent Revolution*. London: Verso, 1981.

Lukes, Steven. *Marxism and Morality*. Oxford: Oxford University Press, 1987.

Lustig, R. Jeffrey. *Corporate Liberalism: The Origins of Modern American Political Theory, 1890-1920*. Berkeley, Los Angeles and London: University of California Press, 1982.

McCormack, A. Ross. *Reformers, Rebels, and Revolutionaries: The Western Canadian Radical Movement, 1899-1919* Toronto: University of Toronto Press, 1977.

Maciejko, Bill. "The Working Mind: The Radical Workers' Response to Public Education, Winnipeg, 1912-1921." M.A. Thesis, University of Manitoba, 1985.

_____. "Public Schools and the Workers' Struggle: Winnipeg, 1914-1921." In Nancy M. Sheehan, J. Donald Wilson and David C. Jones, eds., *Schools in the West: Essays in Canadian Educational History*, 213-37. Calgary : University of Calgary, 1986.

McIntosh, Robert. "Sweated Labour: Female Needleworkers in Industrializing Canada." *Labour/Le Travail* 32 (Fall 1993): 105-138.

Magdoff, Harry and Paul M. Sweezy. "Listen, Keynesians!" *Monthly Review*, 34, 8 (January 1983): 1-11.

_____. "The Deepening Crisis of U.S. Capitalism." *Monthly Review*, 33, 5 (October 1981): 1-16.

Martin, James J. *Men Against the State: The Expositors of Individualist Anarchism in America, 1827-1908*. Colorado Springs: Ralph Myles, 1970.

Marx, Karl. *Capital: A Critique of Political Economy*, trans. by Edward Aveling and Samuel Moore. Vol. 1. New York: Modern Library, n.d.

_____. *Capital: A Critique of Political Economy*, trans. Samuel Moore and Edward Aveling, Vol. 1. New York: International Publishers, 1967.

_____. *Capital: A Critique of Political Economy*, trans. David Fernbach, Vol.3. New York: Vintage Books, 1981.

_____. *A Contribution to the Critique of Political Economy*. Chicago: Charles H. Kerr, 1911.

_____. *Critique of Hegel's Philosophy of Right*. Cambridge: Cambridge University Press, 1970.

_____. *The Poverty of Philosophy*. New York: International Publishers, 1969.

Marx, Karl and Friedrich Engels. *Collected Works*, Vol.5, *Marx and Engels: 1845-1847*. New York: International Publishers, 1975.

_____. *The Communist Manifesto*, trans. Samuel Moore. Chicago: Gateway, 1954.

_____. *Manifesto of the Communist Party*. Moscow: Progress Publishers, 1971.

MacIntyre, Stuart *A Proletarian Science: Marxism in Britain 1917-1933.* Cambridge: Cambridge University Press, 1980.

Mayr, Ernst. *One Long Argument: Charles Darwin and the genesis of modern evolutionary thought.* Harmondsworth: Penguin, 1991.

McKay, Colin. *The New Brunswick Farmer: How the Capitalist System levies tribute upon the product of his Labor.* N.p. [Moncton?]: n.d. [c.1913].

_____. "The Province of New Brunswick," in Fred Cook, ed., *Commercial Canada: Its Progress and Opportunities*: 142-145. Leeds: Redman Book Co., Ltd., 1913.

McKay, Ian. "Strikes in the Maritimes, 1901-1914." In David J. Bercuson, ed., *Canadian Labour History: Selected Readings*, 121-62. Toronto: Copp Clark, 1994.

McNaught, Kenneth. *A Prophet in Politics: A Biography of J.S. Woodsworth.* Toronto: University of Toronto Press, 1959.

McRobbie, Angela. "Post-Marxism and Cultural Studies: A Post-Script." In Lawrence Grossberg, Cary Nelson and Paula Treichler, eds., *Cultural Studies* 719-730. New York and London: Routledge, 1992.

Meikle, Scott. *Essentialism in the Thought of Karl Marx.* London: Duckworth, 1985.

Mercier, L.S. *Néologie, Ou Vocabulaire De Mots Nouveaux, A Renouveler, Ou Pris Dans Des Acceptions Nouvelles,* t. 1. Paris, 1801.

Mill, J.S. *Utilitarianism. On Liberty, and Considerations on Representative Government.* London: Everyman's Library, 1984.

Mills, Allen. *Fool for Christ: The Political Thought of J.S. Woodsworth.* Toronto, Buffalo and London: University of Toronto Press, 1991.

Morgan, Henry James, ed. *The Canadian Men and Women of the Time: A Hand-book of Canadian Biography of Living Characters.* Toronto: William Briggs, 1912.

Morgan, Lewis H. *League of the Ho-De-No-Sau-Nee, or Iroquois.* Rochester, N.Y.: Sage & Brother, 1851.

_____. *Ancient Society, Or Researches in the Lines of Human Progress from Savagery through Barbarism to Civilization.* Calcutta: Bharati Library, 1958.

Morris, Jenny. "The Characteristics of Sweating: The Late Nineteenth-Century London and Leeds Tailoring Trade." In Angela V. John, *Unequal Opportunities: Women's Employment in England 1800-1918,* 95-121. Oxford: Oxford University Press, 1986.

Morton, Desmond. "Aid to the Civil Power: The Stratford Strike of 1933." In Irving Abella, ed., *On Strike: Key Labour Struggles in Canada, 1919-1949,* 79-91. Toronto: McClelland and Stewart, 1974.

Naylor, James. *The New Democracy: Challenging the Social Order in Industrial Ontario.* Toronto: University of Toronto Press, 1991.

_____. "Politics and Class: The Character of 1930s Socialism in Canada." Unpublished paper, Canadian Historical Association, June 1993.

_____. "Workers and the State: Experiments in Corporatism after World War One," *Studies in Political Economy* 42 (Autumn 1993): 81-111.

Negri, Antonio. "Twenty Theses on Marx: Interpretation of the Class Situation Today." In Saree Makdisi, Cesare Casarino and Rebecca E. Karl, *Marxism Beyond Marxism* 149-180. London and New York: Routledge, 1996.

Newman, Michael. *John Strachey*. Manchester: Manchester University Press, 1989.

Newton, Janice. "From Wage Slave to White Slave: The Prostitution Controversy and the Early Canadian Left." In Linda Kealey and Joan Sangster, eds., *Beyond the Vote: Canadian Women and Politics*, 217-236. Toronto: University of Toronto Press, 1989.

_____. *The Feminist Challenge to the Canadian Left, 1900-1918* Montreal and Kingston: McGill-Queen's University Press, 1995.

Norris, Chrisopher. *The Truth About Postmodernism*. Oxford: Blackwell, 1993.

_____. *What's Wrong With Postmodernism: Critical Theory and the Ends of Philosophy*. Baltimore: Johns Hopkins University Press, 1990.

Oser, Jacob. *The Evolution of Economic Thought*, 2nd. ed. New York: Harcourt, Brace and World, 1970.

Owram, Doug. *The Government Generation: The Intellectual and the State in Canada, 1900-1945*. Toronto: University of Toronto Press, 1986.

Palmer, Bryan D. *A Culture in Conflict: Skilled Workers and Industrial Capitalism in Hamilton, Ontario, 1860-1914*. Montreal and Kingston: McGill-Queen's University Press, 1979.

_____. "Listening to History Rather than Historians: Reflections on Working-Class History." In David J. Bercuson and David Bright, eds., *Canadian Labour History: Selected Readings*, 47-75. Toronto: Copp Clark Longman, second edition, 1994.

Pannekoek, Anton. *Lenin as Philosopher: A Critical Examination of the Philosophical Basis of Leninism*. London: Merlin, 1975.

Paxton, Nancy L. *George Eliot and Herbert Spencer: Feminism, Evolutionism, and the Reconstruction of Gender*. Princeton, N.J.: Princeton University Press, 1991.

Peel, J.D.Y. *Herbert Spencer: The Evolution of a Sociologist*. New York: Basic Books, 1971.

_____., ed. *Herbert Spencer on Social Evolution. Selected Writings*. Chicago and London: The University of Chicago Press, 1972.

Penton, Edward M. "The Ideas of William Cotton: A Marxist View of Canadian Society (1908-1914)." M.A. Thesis, University of Ottawa, 1978.

Perrin, Robert G. "Herbert Spencer's Four Theories of Social Evolution." *American Journal of Sociology*, 86 (1980): 1339-1359.

Peterson, Larry. "The Intellectual World of the IWW: An American Worker's Library in the First Half of the 20th Century." *History Workshop* 22 (Autumn 1986): 153-172.

Pheby, John, ed. *J.A.Hobson after Fifty Years: Freethinker of the Social Sciences*. London: Macmillan, 1993.

Pick, Daniel. "The Faces of Anarchy: Lombroso and the Politics of Criminal Science in Post-Unification Italy." *History Workshop* 21 (Spring 1986): 60-86.

Pierson, Stanley. *British Socialists: The Journey from Fantasy to Politics.* Cambridge, Mass. and London: Harvard University Press, 1979.

Pinero, Arthur W. *The Notorious Mrs. Ebbsmith: A Drama in Four Acts* (Boston, 1895).

Pittenger, Mark. *American Socialists and Evolutionary Thought, 1870-1920.* Madison, Wis.: University of Wisconsin Press, 1993.

Przeworski, Adam. *Capitalism and Social Democracy.* Cambridge: Cambridge University Press, 1985.

Radforth, Ian and Joan Sangster. "'A Link Between Labour and Learning': The Workers' Educational Association in Ontario, 1917-1951." *Labour/Le Travailleur,* 8/9 (Autumn/Spring 1981-1982): 41-78.

Rée, Jonathan. *Proletarian Philosophers: Problems in Socialist Culture in Britain, 1900-1940.* Oxford: Clarendon Press, 1984.

Reimer, H.J. "Darwinism in Canadian Literature," Ph.D. Thesis, McMaster University, 1975.

Robertson, Marion. *King's Bounty: A History of Early Shelburne, Nova Scotia.* Halifax: Nova Scotia Museum, 1983.

Rouillard, Jacques. *Histoire du Syndicalisme Québécois. Des origines à nos jours.* Montréal: Boréal, 1989.

Rouillard, Jacques. "L'action politique ouvrière, 1899-1915." In Fernand Dumond, et al., eds., *Idéologies au Canada français 1900-1929,* 267-312. Québec: Les Presses de l'Université Laval, 1974.

Salter, Arthur. *Recovery: The Second Effort.* London: G. Bell and Sons, 1932.

Salvadori, Massimo. *Karl Kautsky and the Socialist Revolution 1880-1938.* London: New Left Books, 1979.

Samson, Daniel, ed. *Contested Countryside: Rural Workers and Modern Society in Atlantic Canada, 1800-1850.* Fredericton: Acadiensis Press, 1994.

Sangster, Joan. *Dreams of Equality: Women on the Canadian Left, 1920-1950.* Toronto: McClelland and Stewart, 1989.

Schmiechen, James A. *Sweated Industries and Sweated Labor: The London Clothing Trades, 1860-1914.* Urbana and Chicago: University of Illinois Press, 1984.

Shore, Marlene. *The Science of Social Redemption: McGill, the Chicago School, and the Origins of Social Research in Canada.* Toronto: University of Toronto Press, 1987.

Simon, Walter M. "Herbert Spencer and the 'Social Organism.'" *Journal of the History of Ideas* 21, 2 (April-June 1960): 294-299.

Sivachev, Nikolai. "The Rise of Statism in 1930s America: A Soviet View of the Social and Political Effects of the New Deal." *Labor History,* 24, 4 (Fall 1983): 500-525.

Skelton, O.D. *Socialism: A Critical Analysis.* Boston and New York: Houghton Mifflin, 1911.

Small, Albion. *General Sociology: An Exposition of the Main Development in Sociological Theory From Spencer to Ratzenhofer.* Chicago: University of Chicago Press, 1905.

Smith, Adam. *An Inquiry Into the Nature and Causes of The Wealth of Nations,* ed. Edwin Cannon. London: Methuen and Company, fourth edition, 1925.

Smith, Goldwin. "Genesis and the Outlook of Religion." *The Contemporary Review,* 78 (July-December 1900): 898-908.

Spencer, David. "An Alternate Vision: Main Themes in Moral Education in Canada's English-Language Working-Class Press 1870-1910." Ph.D. Thesis, University of Toronto, 1990.

Spencer, Herbert. *The Man Versus The State.* London: Watts & Co., 1909.

_____. *The Principles of Sociology.* Vol. 1. New York: D. Appleton and Company, 1893 [Third Edition, Revised and Enlarged].

_____. *The Principles of Sociology.* Vol. 2. New York: D. Appleton and Company, 1909. [Third Edition, Revised and Enlarged].

_____. *The Principles of Sociology,* Vol. 3. New York: D. Appleton and Company, 1897.

_____. *Social Statics; Or, The Conditions Essential to Human Happiness Specified, and the First of Them Developed.* New York: D. Appleton and Company, 1875 [Reprint of 1850 edition].

_____. *The Study of Sociology.* New York: D. Appleton and Company, 1875.

Stedman Jones, Gareth. "Engels and the History of Marxism." In Eric J. Hobsbawm, ed., *The History of Marxism.* Vol. 1. *Marxism in Marx's Day* 290-326. Bloomington: Indiana University Press, 1982.

Stein, James Frederick. "The Religious Roots of the Canadian Labour Movement: The Canadian Labour Press from 1873 to 1900." M.A. Thesis, University of Winnipeg/University of Manitoba, 1986.

Stetson, Charlotte Perkins. *In This Our World.* Boston: Small, Maynard and Company, 1893.

Stoneman, William E. *A History of the Economic Analysis of the Great Depression in America.* New York and London: Garland Publishing, 1979.

Sweezy, Paul M. "The Crisis of American Capitalism." *Monthly Review* 32, 5 (October 1980): 1-13.

Tawney, R.H. *The Acquisitive Society.* London: G. Bell, 1921; reprinted, Fontana Library, 1961.

Taylor, R.J. "Darwin's Theory of Evolution: Four Canadian Responses." Ph.D. Thesis, McMaster University, 1976.

Thompson, T. Phillips. *The Politics of Labor.* Toronto and Buffalo: University of Toronto Press, 1975 [First Published 1887].

Trépanier, Pierre. "La Société canadienne d'économie sociale de Montréal, 1888-1911: sa fondation, ses buts et ses activités." *Canadian Historical Review,* 67, 3 (1986): 343-367.

Turner, Jonathan H. *Herbert Spencer: A Renewed Appreciation.* Beverly Hills, London and New Delhi: Sage Publications, 1985.

Valverde, Mariana. "'When the Mother of the Race is Free': Race, Reproduction, and Sexuality in First-Wave Feminism." In Franca Iacovetta and Mariana Valverde, eds. *Gender Conflicts: New Essays in Women's History,* 3-26. Toronto: University of Toronto Press, 1992.

Verzuh, Ron. *Radical Rag: The Pioneer Labour Press in Canada.* Ottawa: Steel Rail, 1988.

Ward, Lester F. *Applied Sociology: A Treatise on the Conscious Improvement of Society By Society.* Boston: Ginn & Company, 1906.

_____. *Pure Sociology: A Treatise on the Origin and Spontaneous Development of Society.* New York: Macmillan, 1925.

Weinberg, Steven. *Dreams of a Final Theory.* London: Hutchinson, 1992.

Wetter, Gustav A. *Dialectical Materialism: A History and Systematic Survey of Philosophy in the Soviet Union.* New York: Praeger, 1958 .

Whitaker, Reginald. "Introduction" to William Irvine, *The Farmers in Politics.* Toronto: McClelland and Stewart, 1976.

Wiltshire, David. *The Social and Political Thought of Herbert Spencer.* Oxford: Oxford University Press, 1978.

Wood, Ellen Meiksins. *The Retreat from Class: A New 'True' Socialism.* London, 1986.

Woodsworth, J.S. *The First Ten Years.* Ottawa: n.p., 1942.

Woolfson, Charles. *The labour theory of culture: a re-examination of Engels's theory of human origins.* London, Boston and Henley: Routledge and Kegan Paul, 1982.

Wrigley, G. Weston. "Socialism in Canada." *International Socialist Review* 1, 11 (May 1901): 685-689.

Zirkle, Conway. *Evolution, Marxian Biology, and the Social Scene.* Philadelphia: University of Pennsylvania Press, 1959.

INDEX OF PROPER NAMES

*indicates biographical sketch

*indicates biographical sketch

*indicates biographical sketch

*indicates biographical sketch

*indicates biographical sketch

*indicates biographical sketch

*indicates biographical sketch

*indicates biographical sketch

*indicates biographical sketch

Unionism
Leisure: in the socialist co-operative commonwealth, 264, 307; on the socialist "right to be lazy," 100-1n *See also* Mass culture, Temperance, Working-Class Culture
Liberalism, 1-83; and capitalistic individualism, 5; 16; and capitalistic *laissez-faire* 47-50; cultural impact of, 495; and so-called Free Trade, 76-9, 88-90, 151-2; and defence of free speech 28; influence of on Canadian Socialist League, xxix; hardening opposition of McKay towards, 98-9; new liberalism 20n, 402, 533, 565n80, 574n114; new liberalism and Depression, 290-8, 293-4, 372-3, 375-6, 377; postmodernism as ultra-liberalism, 498-9; in Spencerian thought, 520. *See also* Capitalism, Fascism
Liberal Party xvi; xxxii-xxxiv; critique of Conservative Party as interchangeable with Liberals xxxix; disarray in New Brunswick 95, 152; disillusionment with Liberal Party xxxvii-xxxix. *See also* Liberalism

M-N
Marxism: challenge of Depression and, 532-7; determinate abstraction as decisive breakthrough in social science, 531, 581-2n149; many voices within great Marxist tradition, 537; McKay's experimental, pragmatic attitude towards, xl, 493; post-orthodox viewpoint on, 537-8, 540-3; post-orthodox definitions of, 537-8, 546; and present-day supposed crisis of 495, 539-40; 548. *See also* Freedom, Marxist Hypotheses,
Marxist hypotheses, 499-500, 546-7; base-and-superstructure, 464; capitalism as a system of crises, 136-44; capitalist property vs. private property, 89-90, 93, 96-7, 148-51; class as primary aspect of the social order, 98, 179, 549; expropriation of the peasantry, xvii-xviii, 2, 136-44, 187-8; forces and relations of production, 117-8, 288; historical determinism, 313-5, 329, 411-2, 474-6; labour theory of value, 85-6, 118-9, 137, 279-81, 281n, 291-2, 336-8, 354-5, 470, 548-9, 578n130; primacy of

matter over mind, 105; realm of freedom, 29, 55, 100n, 491, 549-51, 581n147; tendency of the rate of profit to fall, 278, 580-1n145; unemployment and the reserve army of labour, 285, 319, 325
Maritimes, xv; xlv, 214-76; and *Bluenose* phenomenon, 216-7; conservatism of, 227; social progress in, 228-9; and Confederation, 265; trade unionism in, 267-8, 490; growth of socialism in, 273
Mass Culture, commodification of daily life, 495-7; impact of 131n; and Keynesianism, 533-4
Materialism, *see* Philosophy
Mechanization, *see* Technology
"Middle Class": political efficacy of, 385-6; appeal of CCF for, 469. *See also* Professionals, Small Business
Monetary Reforms: critique of Depression-era panaceas, 290, 301, 327-8, 347-8, 400; Equitist Plan explained and critiqued, 299-301, 300n; 341-3, 346; Progressives as naïve supporters of, 294, 364; special appeal of for small businessmen, 346. *See also* Social Credit
Monopoly Capitalism, *see* Capitalism
Nationalism, Canadian: McKay's support for, 420-1; need for a distinctive Canadian socialism, 472-3; peculiarities of Canadian situation, 462. *See also* Trade Unionism (ACCL)
Neo-conservatism/liberalism of 1990s, 537, 547-8, 583n152
New Social Movements, 547-8
Nationalization: of banking system, 344, 357; economic recovery and, 365; in New Zealand, 49-50

O-P
Petite Bourgeoisie: *see* Small Business; Farmers; Fishermen; Handicrafts; Professionals
Philanthropy: and poverty, 36; Carnegie and Rockefeller as practitioners of, 74-6; critique of Spencerian approach to, 157-61; futility of bourgeois forms of, 101-2
Philosophy: class struggle in, 172, 578n128; dialectical materialism, 115, 518, 527, 529-30, 547, 570n95, 573n105; Kantian epistemology, 537,

540, 579n135; Kantian ethics, 486-7; materialist epistemology and ontology of Dietzgen, 113-4, 172, 172n, 572-3n104; "new philosophy of life," 529-30; as outmoded by Marxist science of cognition, 105, 179-80, 488; problem of Hegelian idealism, 114; perspectival epistemology of McKay, 68, 468; post-orthodox Marxist approach to, 580n143. *See also* Working-Class Culture

Poetry and Fiction: political fable, 136-44; poems in praise of Laurier, xxxiii-xxxiv; poems on "socialism," xxviii-xxix; on war of 1914-1918, xliv; Robert Louis Stevenson as requiem for the homeless McKay, li-lii; on workingmen of Montreal, 55-6

Poverty: causes of, 34-8, 153; in England, 77, 147; increasing, relative to wealth of capitalists, 316-7; Spencerian analysis of, 157-61

Progressives: propensity to favour monetary reforms, 294; *see also* Farmers; Labour Politics

Prisons and Jails: McKay critique of conditions of in Montreal, 10n

Professionals: as members of an "uneasy class," 90-5; and Socialist Party of Canada, xviin

Property: craft skills as property, 434-5, 446-7; distinction between capitalist and private forms of, 89-90, 93, 148-9, 170-2, 188, 334-5; in pre-capitalist societies, 187; "rights" of, 185-6, 287, 334-5, 446-7; and separation of legal title from real power, 150-1, 335, 454; variegated relations of in a socialist society, 96-7, 397-8, 425. *See also* Marxist Theories

Progressivism: defined, 19-20; Glasgow as a model, 23-4

Protectionism, *see* Tariff Policy

Q-R

Québécois ("French Canadians"), 508, 532; American Federation of Labor in relation to, 25-26; in Montreal, 24-7, 422; as trade unionists, 68-70

Race and Ethnicity: Asian immigration, xxxiv; Jewish immigrants in the Montreal sweatshops, 30-1; in Spencerian thought, 563n66

Railways: shrinking employment in, 319

Religion, xiii-xiv, 102-3, 549; capitalism and bourgeois Christian approach to poverty, 37-8,100; capitalism and Protestantism, 17-19; capitalism and Puritanism 166-167, 198; capitalism and working-class alienation from Christian churches, 56-7, 60-2; 99-103; 506-7, 556n30; secularization and evolutionary theory, 513-4, 556n29; secularization and historical criticism of the Bible, 63n; secularization and Spencerianism, 520; secularization and Sunday Schools' impact on working-class alienation, 129-30, 200-1; secularization and working-class alienation from churches, 56-7, 506-7, 556n30; sectarianism in Maritimes, 228; Social Gospel and Christ as apostle of Free Speech, 44-5; Social Gospel and Christ as workingman and socialist xxxv, 17, 28, 53-5, 103, 196-7, 262, 506-7, 555n27, 555-6n28; Social Gospel and Christianization of industry, 54; Social Gospel, early adherence to; xvi; 5-7; Social Gospel, preferred to atheism, 57; Social Gospel, McKay's rejection of,101-2; women's question and Christianity, 190-1. *See also* Sabbatarianism, Temperance, Working-Class Culture

Rural Life: critique of the myth of the "simple life," 296-7; Highland Clearances as archetype of transformation of, 187-8; impact of capitalism in New Brunswick, 256-63; memories of rural self-sufficiency, 1-2, 260, 373-4; rural workers and Cape Breton coalfields, 82; rural workers and Montreal sweatshops, 33; speculative conditions of wheat farming, 364-5; technological change in countryside, 146. *See also* Farmers, Fishermen

S-T

Sabbatarianism: McKay's critique of, 19, 166-7. *See also* Religion

Seafaring: as a factor in the life of McKay xii-xv; schooner *Bluenose* and McKay, xlvi

Shipbuilding, xvi, 240-3, 263-4. *See also* fishing industry, Maritime Provinces

Single Tax, 209-11

Skilled Workers: intelligence of, 129;